Lecture Notes in Computer Sc

T0230198

Commenced Publication in 1973
Founding and Former Series Editors:
Gerhard Goos, Juris Hartmanis, and Jan van Leeuwen

Vladimir Gorodetsky   Igor Kotenko
Victor Skormin (Eds.)

Computer Network Security

Third International Workshop on Mathematical
Methods, Models, and Architectures for
Computer Network Security, MMM-ACNS 2005
St. Petersburg, Russia, September 25-27, 2005
Proceedings

 Springer

Volume Editors

Vladimir Gorodetsky
Igor Kotenko
St. Petersburg Institute for Informatics and Automation
39, 14-th Liniya, St. Petersburg, 199178, Russia
E-mail: {gor, ivkote}@mail.iias.spb.su

Victor Skormin
Binghamton University (SUNY), Watson School of Engineering
Binghamton, NY 13902, USA
E-mail: vskormin@binghamton.edu

Library of Congress Control Number: 2005932314

CR Subject Classification (1998): C.2, D.4.6, E.3, K.6.5, K.4.1, K.4.4, J.1

ISSN   0302-9743
ISBN-10   3-540-29113-X Springer Berlin Heidelberg New York
ISBN-13   978-3-540-29113-8 Springer Berlin Heidelberg New York

Springer is a part of Springer Science+Business Media

springeronline.com

© Springer-Verlag Berlin Heidelberg 2005
Printed in Germany

Typesetting: Camera-ready by author, data conversion by Scientific Publishing Services, Chennai, India
Printed on acid-free paper   SPIN: 11560326   06/3142   5 4 3 2 1 0

Preface

This volume contains papers presented at the 3rd International Workshop on Mathematical Methods, Models and Architectures for Computer Network Security (MMM-ACNS 2005) held in St. Petersburg, Russia, during September 25–27, 2005. The workshop was organized by the St. Petersburg Institute for Informatics and Automation of the Russian Academy of Sciences (SPIIRAS) in cooperation with Binghamton University (SUNY, USA).

The 1st and the 2nd International Workshops on Mathematical Methods, Models and Architectures for Computer Network Security (MMM-ACNS 2001 and MMM-ACNS 2003), hosted by the St. Petersburg Institute for Informatics and Automation, demonstrated the keen interest of the international research community in the subject area. It was recognized that conducting a biannual series of such workshops in St. Petersburg stimulates fruitful exchanges between the different schools of thought, facilitates the dissemination of new ideas and promotes the spirit of cooperation between researchers on the international scale.

MMM-ACNS 2005 provided an international forum for sharing original research results and application experiences among specialists in fundamental and applied problems of computer network security. An important distinction of the workshop was its focus on mathematical aspects of information and computer network security addressing the ever-increasing demands for secure computing and highly dependable computer networks.

A total of 85 papers from 20 countries related to significant aspects of both theory and applications of computer network and information security were submitted to MMM-ACNS 2005. Twenty-five papers were selected for regular and 12 for short presentations. Six technical sessions were organized, namely: Mathematical Models, Architectures and Protocols for Security; Authentication, Authorization and Access Control; Information Flow Analysis, Covert Channels and Trust Management; Security Policy and Operating System Security; Threat Modeling, Vulnerability Assessment and Network Forensics; and Intrusion Detection. The panel discussions were devoted to the challenging problems in vulnerability assessment, intrusion detection and security policy management. The MMM-ACNS 2005 program was enriched by five distinguished invited speakers: Naranker Dulay, Ming-Yuh Huang, Sushil Jajodia, David Nicol, and Douglas Summerville.

The success of the workshop was assured by team efforts of sponsors, organizers, reviewers, and participants. We would like to acknowledge the contribution of the individual Program Committee members and thank the paper reviewers. Our sincere gratitude goes to the participants of the workshop and all authors of the submitted papers. We are grateful to our sponsors: European Office of Aerospace Research and Development (EOARD) of the US Air Force, US Office of Naval Research Global (ONRGlobal) and US Army Research Laboratory-

European Research Office (AFL-ERO) for their generous support. We wish to express our gratitude to the Springer LNCS team managed by Alfred Hofmann for their help and cooperation.

September 2005   Vladimir Gorodetsky
                                                                          Igor Kotenko
                                                                          Victor Skormin

Workshop Chairmen

General Chairmen

Rafael M. Yusupov	St. Petersburg Institute for Informatics and Automation of the Russian Academy of Sciences (SPIIRAS), Russia
Igor G. Plonisch	Air Force Research Laboratory (AFRL), USA

Program Committee Co-chairmen

Vladimir Gorodetsky	St. Petersburg Institute for Informatics and Automation of the Russian Academy of Sciences (SPIIRAS), Russia
Igor Kotenko	St. Petersburg Institute for Informatics and Automation of the Russian Academy of Sciences (SPIIRAS), Russia
Victor Skormin	Binghamton University, State University of New York, USA

Program Committee

Kurt Bauknecht	University of Zurich, Department of Information Technology, Switzerland
David Bonyuet	Delta Search Labs, USA
Shiu-Kai Chin	Syracuse University, USA
Marc Dacier	Eurecom, France
Dipankar Dasgupta	University of Memphis, USA
Dimitris Gritzalis	Athens University of Economics and Business, Greece
Alexander Grusho	Russian State University for Humanity, Russia
Ming-Yuh Huang	The Boeing Company, USA
Sushil Jajodia	George Mason University, USA
Victor Korneev	Research Institute "Kvant", Russia
Klaus-Peter Kossakowski	Presecure Consulting GmbH, Germany
Antonio Lioy	Politecnico di Torino, Italy
Fabio Martinelli	CNR/IIT, Italy
Fabio Massacci	University of Trento, Italy
Catherine Meadows	Naval Research Laboratory, USA
Nasir Memon	Polytechnic University Brooklyn, USA
Bret Michael	Naval Postgraduate School, USA
Ann Miller	University of Missouri-Rolla, USA

Nikolay Moldovyan   Specialized Center of Program Systems "SPECTR",
                           Russia
Andrei Sabelfeld   Chalmers University of Technology, Sweden
Ravi Sandhu   George Mason University and NSD Security, USA
Antonio Gomez Skarmeta   University of Murcia, Spain
Anatol Slissenko   University of Paris 12, France; St. Petersburg Institute
                           for Informatics and Automation, Russia
Michael Smirnov   Fraunhofer-Gesellschaft Institute FOKUS, Germany
Douglas Summerville   Binghamton University, USA
Shambhu Upadhyaya   University at Buffalo, USA
Alfonso Valdes   SRI International, USA
Vijay Varadharajaran   Macquarie University, Australia
Valery Vasenin   Moscow State University, Russia
Peter Zegzhda   St. Petersburg Polytechnical University, Russia

Reviewers

Venkatesan Balakrishnan   Macquarie University, Australia
Daniele Beauquier   University of Paris 12, France
Juan Blaya   University of Murcia, Spain
Mikhain Bolshakov   Moscow State University, Russia
David Bonyuet   Delta Search Labs, USA
Madhusudhanan Chandrasekaran University at Buffalo, USA
Shiu-Kai Chin   Syracuse University, USA
Ramkumar Chinchani   University at Buffalo, USA
Michael Clarkson   Cornell University, USA
Marc Dacier   Eurecom, France
Dipankar Dasgupta   University of Memphis, USA
Catalin Dima   University of Paris 12, France
Marie Duflot   University of Paris 12, France
Dimitris Gritzalis   Athens University of Economics
                                    and Business, Greece
Alexander Grusho   Russian State University for Humanity,
                                    Russia
Ming-Yuh Huang   The Boeing Company, USA
John Iliadis   Athens University of Economics and
                                    Business, Greece
Sushil Jajodia   George Mason University, USA
Maxim Kalinin   St. Petersburg Polytechnical University,
                                    Russia
Spyros Kokolakis   Athens University of Economics
                                    and Business, Greece
Victor Korneev   Research Institute "Kvant", Russia
Klaus-Peter Kossakowski   Presecure Consulting GmbH, Germany
Igor Kotenko   St. Petersburg Institute for Informatics and
                                    Automation, Russia

Table of Contents

Authentication, Authorization and Access Control

Information Flow Analysis, Covert Channels and Trust Management

Security Policy and Operating System Security

Threat Modeling, Vulnerability Assessment and Network Forensics

Intrusion Detection

Short Papers

Self-managed Cells for Ubiquitous Systems

Naranker Dulay[1], Emil Lupu[1], Morris Sloman[1],
Joe Sventek[2], Nagwa Badr[2], and Stephen Heeps[2]

[1] Department of Computing, Imperial College London,
180 Queen's Gate, London SW7 2AZ, United Kingdom
{n.dulay, e.c.lupu, m.sloman}@imperial.ac.uk
[2] Department of Computing Science, University of Glasgow,
17 Lilybank Gardens, Glasgow G12 8RZ, United Kingdom
{joe, nagwa, heeps}@dcs.gla.ac.uk

Abstract. Amongst the challenges of ubiquitous computing is the need to provide management support for personal wireless devices and sensors. In this extended abstract we introduce a policy-based architecture that supports management at varying levels based on the concept of a self-managed cell. Cells include policy-driven agents that support context-based and trust-based access control and system adaptation. Cells can also organize themselves through federation and nesting.

1 Introduction

Advances in ubiquitous computing infrastructures have the potential to dramatically broaden the role of computing in the everyday lives of people with a greater proliferation of personal wireless devices, and more significantly with wireless computing devices starting to be embedded in the environment: in buildings, in roads, in vehicles, in the landscape, in home appliances, in clothing, on packaging of consumer goods in shops; even as implants in plants, animals and humans. The challenges of ubiquitous computing will not only be about building such ubiquitous environments, they will also be about managing the resources and omnipresent information which ubiquitous systems will need to discover, capture, process and publish behind the scenes. This information will be ephemeral, mobile, fragmented and voluminous with no predictable flows between producers or users of the information.

1.1 Ubiquitous Systems Management

Existing architectures for network and systems management are aimed at large-scale corporate environments, telecommunications networks and Internet service providers and do not cater for ubiquitous environments, although specific techniques for monitoring, event correlation, service discovery, quality of service and policy-based management can be used to some degree. For ubiquitous systems, architectures are needed that can scale down to small devices with local decision-making. The limitations of small devices, e.g. memory size, CPU speed, battery life, screen size, network range and changing connectivity; require new techniques for optimizing resource usage and tailoring information within tight deadlines. Management will also need to be per-

V. Gorodetsky, I. Kotenko, and V. Skormin (Eds.): MMM-ACNS 2005, LNCS 3685, pp. 1–6, 2005.

formed according to measures of context and trust and tailored to the individual preferences and circumstances of users. Flexible techniques will be needed to filter information and perform access control, as well as defining and enforcing privacy. Users will expect management functions to be invisible and carried out automatically.

We are developing a policy-based architecture that supports management at varying levels of granularity, using the concept of a self-managed cell (or simply a cell). A cell consists of a set of hardware and software components that represent an administrative domain. Cells are able to function autonomously and thus capable of self-management. A cell could represent the resources available in a PDA, a body area network of physiological sensors and controllers. At the enterprise level, a cell could represent the resources and application components relating to a set of collaborating partners forming a virtual organisation spanning multiple countries. In each case, cells include and evolve the required management services, appropriate to the scale and environment of the cell. These management services interact with each other through asynchronous events exchanged over an event bus. In essence, a cell is a "closed-loop" system where changes of state in the managed objects and resources trigger adaptation that in turn affects the state of the system. In ubiquitous environments, the cells would also typically include management components that provide service discovery and contextual management.

A cell includes a policy-driven agent that supports context-based and trust-based access control and system adaptation for one or more ubiquitous devices. Cells can load additional management functions and organise themselves into larger management cells through federation and nesting. Potentially, each ubiquitous device that a user carries, and each device situated in the environment, is capable of being a self-managed cell and running a management agent that carries out management functions and policies. In practice, we envisage that some devices (e.g. sensors) will be too primitive to run their own management agent, but will be capable of being managed by an external cell, such as a mobile phone, over a wireless link, such as bluetooth. This extended abstract introduces the architecture of self-managed cells.

2 Self-managed Cells

Each self-managed cell consists of a number of core management components: the cell watchdog, the event service, the discovery service, the policy service, and the domain service. Cells can also load components for context and trust management as well as monitoring and intrusion detection. Proxies are required to interact with the various communication interfaces of devices and managed components, for example to enable cell policies to perform actions on device-specific management interfaces, and to convert low-level signals to cell events. The following outlines the core services of each self-managed cell.

2.1 Cell Watchdog

When a cell is first instantiated, it starts up the cell watchdog. This is a special service that is responsible for loading and instantiating the core components of the cell, typically from local storage (e.g. a memory card), or from a remote cell. The cell watchdog is also responsible for cleanly removing and restarting core components when a core component fails, or if a core component needs to be updated. Essentially the cell watchdog has the responsibility to ensure the survivability of the core management components, and ideally should be in firmware and always alive.

2.2 Event Service

Management systems are essentially event-driven, as changes of states need to be notified to several, potentially unknown management services. Examples of events include: the discovery of a new device, a change in context (e.g. battery level low), an intrusion alert. The event service provides at-most-once, persistent publish/subscribe delivery and is used for both intra-cell and inter-cell management. The event service supports event correlation for flexibility.

2.3 Discovery Service

The discovery service is responsible for detecting the presence of devices that come into wireless range. These may be primitive devices that are managed by the cell, devices that are managed by others cells, or devices that are not currently managed by any cell. Once a device is discovered, the discovery service communicates with the device to get further attributes (e.g. type, profile, services provided) and generates a "new-device" event for other management components. The discovery service needs to distinguish between transient failures, which are common in wireless communications, and when some device is really no longer available (e.g. out of range or switched off).

2.4 Policy Service

The policy service is responsible for the execution of policies. Policies are rules that govern the choices in behaviour of the cell. Two kinds of policy are currently supported. Obligation policies (event-condition-action rules), which define what actions to carry out when specific events occur, and authorisation policies which define what actions are permitted or not permitted, for what or for whom, and under what conditions. Policies can be added, removed, enabled or disabled to change the behaviour of a cell. See cell policy language (section 3).

2.5 Domain Service

The domain service provides a means of hierarchically grouping references to objects (c.f a filesystem). Objects include devices, services (including core services), policies, neighbouring cells. For example, when a new device is discovered, a reference to it, is normally added to the domain /dev as well as to application-specific domains, for example, /music/headset/bluetooth. Domains are also used to define authorisation policies in the cell policy language, e.g. objects within the subject domain /players/mp3 are permitted to perform the action play on objects in the target domain /headsets.

2.6 Context Service and Trust Service

In addition to the core components, cells can also load a context service and a trust service. These allow context and trust information to be defined, gathered and combined, and used in evaluating policy constraints. Changes in context and trust can raise events that trigger obligation policies that cause adaptation.

3 Cell Policy Language

Central to the management of cells is the Cell policy language and interpreter. The language is loosely based on the Ponder policy language developed at Imperial College London. All primitive policies are encapsulated into one composite type called the *relationship*. There are no roles, groups, or management structures. There are no domain scope expressions. Subjects can be based on credential verification as well as domain membership. The language includes explicit support for domain creation/removal as well as enabling/disabling of policies. Composite event can be defined. There are explicit rules for authorisation conflict resolution based on explicit relationship ordering rules. The syntax is also cleaner and less cluttered than Ponder and is suitable for interactive execution.

3.1 Relationships

Relationships encapsulate one or more policies. Currently obligation (event-condition-action) policies and authorisation policies are supported. Relationships can also encapsulate other relationships. Relationships are created, enabled, disabled, removing as a whole, e.g. policies cannot be added to a running relationship, other than by disabling and removing the relationship, and replacing it with a new relationship with the additional policy. The policies act as an atomic unit, for example, disabling an individual authorisation may lead to unexpected results. The policy service includes a multi-threaded interpreter for concurrently executing obligation policies. The following examples illustrate the Cell policy language.

Example 1. Authorisation policy. Members of the family domain are allowed to play games on the pda but only at home or in the car.

```
context home_car: location=home or location=car

auth+ /family -> home_car ? /pda/games.play
```

Example 2. Authorisation policy. Doctors who can present a credential issued by the British Medical Association (BMA) can issue commands to the cell's medical devices in an emergency in the UK.

```
credential medic:role=Doctor and issuer=BMA and issueyear>2005
context UK_emergency: location=UK and condition=wounded

auth+ -> medic and UK_emergency ? /medical/devices.commands
```

Example 3. Obligation policy.   On discovering a new bluetooth headset add it to the sound/output/bluetooth domain.

```
on HeadsetDetect (X) -> X.type=bluetooth ?
                    /sound/output/bluetooth.add(X)
```

Example 4. Obligation policy. After 20 failures to enter a PIN, disable the Mobile Phone policy and enable the Stolen mobile phone policy

```
event Stolen: count (PIN_failure, 20)

on Stolen () -> /policy/mobile/normal.disable (),
                /policy/mobile/stolen.enable ()
```

4   Inter-cell Interactions and Self-organisation

Although self-managed cells provide the management capability for supporting configuration and adaptation within a device, there is a need to support management across multiple cells. The cell architecture supports two forms of inter-cell organisation:

- *Federated* to support peer-to-peer interactions between cells in order to collaborate and share resources, for example police, ambulance and fire workers collaborating and sharing resources at car-accident. Management relationships between federated cells are often transient, but can be longer-lived.
- *Nested,* where several cell nest within an enclosing cell and nested cells are not visible to cells external to the enclosing cell i.e. any management interaction is via the enclosing cell. Cells can move and out of enclosing cells, for example, the cell of a patient returning home, may nest in the home cell, and be governed by the policies of the home cell.

We model cell-cell interactions through relationships. Each cell defines its own relationships with respect to other cells. When a new cell is discovered it is subject to a similar procedure as devices. However for cells, additional actions and protocols are supported including exchange of policies, event registrations, and domain membership details. These protocols allow cells to share management information and resources and self-organise through federation and nesting.

5   Current Status and Future Work

We are currently developing Java-based implementations of the cell architecture to run on Series 60 Nokia phones, HP iPaq PDAs and laptops over bluetooth, wi-fi, and GPRS. We are also experimenting with body sensor nodes with Zigbee wireless capability that communicate by low-power radio with the iPaq. A simulator to test larger cells and more easily simulate repetitive events or devices coming into and out of range is being developed.

There are many issues still to be resolved, such as making sure the protocols optimise the use of battery power; how to make sure a device is 'owned' by the appropriate cell and not taken over; how to present management information and policies to end-users and elicit policy settings; investigating the best design patterns for inter-cell management; how to specify and implement privacy policies that allow users to control access to personal information, and what mechanisms to use to anonymise personal information and prevent tracking.

Acknowledgments

The authors wish to thank the UK Engineering and Physical Sciences Research Council for their support of this research through grants GR/S68040/01 and GR/S68033/01.

Critical Information Assurance Challenges for Modern Large-Scale Infrastructures

Ming-Yuh Huang

The Boeing Company,
P.O. Box 3707, MC 7L-49,
Seattle, WA 98124-2207
ming-yuh.huang@boeing.com

Abstract. Today's information assurance (IA) is no longer about keeping people out. It's about letting people in — the right people, securely, to the right place. In modern military and commercial systems, partners, suppliers, and customers are all constantly accessing the infrastructure through the network. Once there, each needs to be taken directly to the appropriate data and resources. Secure and efficient access control in this context lays the foundation of next-generation business paradigm shift. Such new paradigms create new revenues and increase operation efficiency. Those who fail to make the transition are bound to face daunting challenges in competition. IA is a business enabler. It is vital piece that allows the paradigm shift to take place. This is the new but realistic way to look at security. This paper examines a broad range of critical issues in today's closely knitted environment and discusses potential architectural and technological directions from the perspective of large and distributed infrastructures. To fully illustrate the significant issues, this paper also uses a major cyber crime case that went through the US Federal Court in 2001 for analysis purpose.

1 Background

First international connection to the ARPANET was made by University College of London (England) via NORSAR (Norway) in 1973. In the same year, Bob Metcalfe's Harvard Ph.D. thesis outlines idea for Ethernet. The concept was tested on Xerox PARC's Alto computers, and the first Ethernet network was implemented. In 1978, TCP split into TCP and IP and, in 1980, ARPANET suffered the first significant network security failure due to an accidentally-propagated status-message virus. The network was grinded to a complete halt on October 27th.

It was not until later part of 1980's that a major cut-over to TCP/IP was made and Internet became truly available. IETF was established and ARPANET creased to exist in 1990. Nevertheless, prevalent usage of Internet will not come until mid 1990's when WWW (World Wide Web) became greatly accessible. Since then, computing and Internet have fundamentally changed human society.

1.1 Castles and Moats

In process of computing technology evolutionary, information assurance (IA) usually comes along as after-fact patch-up measures. IA is often treated as the necessary evil

V. Gorodetsky, I. Kotenko, and V. Skormin (Eds.): MMM-ACNS 2005, LNCS 3685, pp. 7–22, 2005.

that creates inconveniences and performance downgrades. It is there because it's mandated.

In the 1980's and 1990's, the security concerns brought upon by the network connectivity forced us to became very good at building castles and moats. DEC (Digital Equipment Corporation) was a relatively progressive company at that time and its SERVNET effort at the end of 1980's served as a good example. The concept of SERVNET was to connect all of DEC's customers together so that DEC could deliver new paradigm of field services such as on-line service delivery (instead of a man with a van), remote system patches and distributed preventive maintenance remotely. Such thinking was innovative at that time and clearly had its business advantages. So new business paradigm led to new IA requirements:

1. Businesses were living within the castles and DEC saw a business opportunity by connecting them together.
2. Security implication was paramount and DEC was planning to deploy a large number (multiples of hundreds) of VMS machines as gateways/firewalls for these connections.

In reality, DEC could not possibly hire enough system administrators to man these gateway machines 7x24. Nevertheless, the risk was high due to potential intrusions to DEC as well as liability from possible intrusions amongst the customers. Consequently, DEC's Artificial Intelligence Technology Center located in Marlborough, Massachusetts developed a real-time expert system in Knowledge Craft to analyze VMS syslog files as security monitoring. The code name was ESSENSE (Expert System for SERVNET Security). ESSENSE led to one of world's earliest host-based intrusion detection system (IDS) product in the early 1990's — PLOYCENTER Security ID.

1. New business paradigm led to new IA requirements.
2. New IA requirements led to new IA technology development.

The beginning of IDS technology illustrated that the focus of IA then was to protect the perimeters. This is often described as the French-bread model — crunchy crust and soft inside. The focus of the protection is on the boundary. Thus, following that strategy, we became very good at building tall, thick walls and deep moats for these medieval castles. On top of that, in order to facilitate connection to the outside, we also became very proficient in putting in draw-bridges and drilling holes on the castle wall to accommodate various protocols. The assumption was such that if the wall was thick and tall enough, the number of the holes was controlled and the activities around the wall were well monitored, everything would be safe. It was not until after year 2000, this castles-and-moats model started to fall apart. The evolution has accelerated into a revolution, and the world is moving rapidly away from the castles and the moats.

2 Fundamental Changes to the Sociological Computing Game

2.1 The Slippery Definition of "Computing"

21st century computing is that of a revolution, not an evolution.

"Computers" were first invented to calculate the trajectory of the artillery shells. However, the very definition of "computing" has been changing even since.

1. While mainframes dominated the landscape in the 60's and 70's, computing was very much limited to the scope of "calculations" such as payroll, accounting, number crunching or engineering calculations.
2. When mini-computers became available in the 70's and 80's, computing took a broader jump into areas such as graphics, messaging (email/notes), real-time data acquisition/monitoring, education, software development and business operation, while the heavy lifting such as weather prediction were still left to the mainframes.
3. In the 1990's, when PC/workstation and network connectivity became widely available, the definition of computing took on another meaning. Computing was about word processing, spread sheet, email, chat, graphics, WWW and e-commerce. At this point, much of the daily number crunching needed was buried between the CPU, memory and registers.
4. In the 21st century, coupled with increased CPU & memory power, network connectivity became the major player and has produced more intrinsic impacts to the very definition of computing than anything else. At this point, computing is far from number crunch. Computing is about MP3, VOIP, personal assistance, video teleconferencing, virtual holiday, online auctions, virtual enterprise, pervasive information access, e-government and network centric operation. People are just figuring out what to do with all the increased computing power and connectivity.
5. For the future, one may extrapolate that given the connectivity and the bandwidth, connectivity becomes storage, connectivity becomes CPU, connectivity becomes application, connectivity becomes knowledge, and connectivity becomes part of human daily life. Computing will be much more sociologically oriented — arts, human interactions and health. Further, upon the rendezvous with bio-technology, computing will be a much bigger part of human life.

New computing technology encourages new business paradigms. Recursively, new business paradigms accelerate the development of new computing paradigm. How we use, or intend to use, computing today is very different from the past. Connectivity and computing power brought a fundamental change in today's business model. IA needs to address the requirements coming from the new paradigms, not the old paradigms. Protecting 90's computing/business paradigms adds very little to where we need to go in the future.

2.2 The Ever-Changing "Value"

Historically, human use rare commodities such as gold or silver for "value" manifestations. As civilization progresses, so are the manifestations of values — coins, money, deed, bond, credit, etc. Today's IA protects the value of the past. It fails to recognize the new values brought along by the new business paradigm shift.

In the past, protecting the server itself was important because that's where the action was. However, in today's context, protecting the transactions and the data across multiple distributed servers is even more important. In this new business paradigms where data and transactions are distributed everywhere and shared by many international partners, different sets of requirement such as export control or federated authentication and authorization need to be enforced. Protecting just the server itself becomes insufficient. One can even venture to say that if the transactions and data are protected, the server itself can be sacrificed. On the networking side, dutiful IP packets inspection to protect castle walls and moats aides little in detecting and preventing hackers from executing fake transactions from within to steal millions. The value is at transaction and data, not castle and moats. We have become the ever-chasing security Don Quixote — good in protecting the walls, not the values.

2.3 The Concept of "Collaborative Sharing"

The concept of ownership is no longer based on that of owning the data physically. Instead, it is based on the accessibility to the data. Given the web and the encryption technology, data can be everywhere — just like encrypted satellite downlink. As such, the ownership is being defined as the "entitlement" to read, write and make use of the data. Business transactions go beyond the delivery of business artifacts such as a piece of singed paper or even its digitally signed electronics copy. It will be based on direct information access and manipulation owned by the other party. For example, in a virtual Just-In-Time (JIT) environment, customers ordering parts will not be just sending digitally signed Purchase Orders to the suppliers. They actually manipulate the supplier's computing infrastructure and interact with the ordering system. This updates the production data corresponding to the parts needed. As a result, the order is automatically incorporated into the supplier's production process, as well as supplier's partner network for any inventory supply support. Conversely, when the parts are delivered, there will be no digitally signed paper-equivalence to "document" the delivery information. The supplier actually modifies the customer's system to reflect the delivery. This results in virtual JIT updates of accounting business process and even the manufacturing inventory system across the entire virtual enterprise with multiple distributed business partners around the globe. It is a much tighter integration at the business and computing level.

2.4 "Business Objects" vs. "System Objects"

Business information residing on the computing infrastructure takes two forms of existence — the data itself (business objects), and their electronic manifestations — files, databases or electronic communications (system objects). Traditional IA implementations treat business objects as system objects and protect them as such. However, the line of distinction between business object and system objects has always been blurry and the level of implementation has been coarse.

1. Business objects (e.g. an engineering design) do not necessarily map to system objects (e.g. a file). They are many one-to-many, many-to-one or even many-to-many mappings. Protecting business objects does not equate to protect system objects.
2. While business objects tend to have more level of abstraction to faithfully reflect the business needs, system objects are bounded by the system environment (e.g. file system). Consequently, not all the level of granularity can be appropriately implemented in system objects. Since IA has been designed to protect system objects, this level of protection is coarse.

blocked. Increased variety of protocol adds to the complexity of the problem. It is quite common for products to wrap a risky protocol inside a less risky one to increase the possibility of passing through a firewall. Since inbound HTTP is so common these days, this is often the protocol of choice. Furthermore, the information used to identify the protocol type can also be altered. For example, port 23 is the standard "well known port" for e-mail. Since it's usually taken for granted that other machines use this port for such purpose, if an application uses port 23 without prior arrangement then firewall machine will risk either blocking a benign convenient access or allowing a malicious attempt in disguise. An insider could easily configure an email server to a different port and bypass firewall block as long as the correspondent knows about the port change. Under the same token, it is also possible to modify the TCP header and even forge the TCP header checksum. There is no sure way for the firewall or router to know how the packet is being used without detail analysis. The previously mentioned volume issue coupled with the protocol variety makes this an infeasible option.

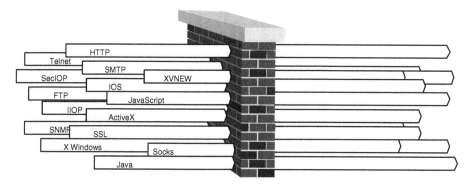

Fig. 2. Protocol varieties create holes on firewall

3.3 Visibility

Increasing usage of encryption technology also provides another obstacle that prevents firewall and router machines from examining the packets in detail. Application level encryption obscures the data while leaving the packet information alone. When monitoring, the network devices must trust the packet header information without being able to look inside. It has no way to tell that what looks like an normal web page being sent out from the company's public web server is really an email or a telnet access.

The usage of application level encryption such as PGP and S/MINE encrypted email is gaining ground. Packet level protection is being provided by protocols such as SSL, and its successor — TLS. This provides TCP level network connection protection. For levels above IP, IPSec is coming into play today. IPSec is designed not only to protect data at the packet level, but also to protect the network infrastructure itself. Thus, IPSec encrypts and digitally signs all of the header information in the protocols that it wraps. This includes all TCP headers along with the associated checksum, packet type and TCP port number.

The only solution is to decrypt the packets at each network access point, read, copy and analyze header information and then re-encrypt the packets before sending it on. In addition to the added computation expense, this defeats the purpose of the trusted relations between the communicating parties and exposes them to immense risks. Instead of providing security by increasing visibility on the encrypted packets, this solution actually created new points of failure from the information security's perspective.

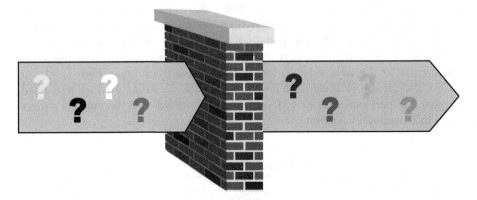

Fig. 3. Encrypted traffic visibility problem for firewall audit

4   Intrusion Detection Systems (IDS)

Large-scale heterogeneous networks generate tremendous amounts of temporal event data in very diverse formats. In reality, much of these data has very little to do with security at all. Most of them are related to system/network faults as a result of wrong configuration. When doing analysis, only careful analysis can distinguish between security and non-security data. This is an extremely noisy environment. When IDS attempts to analyze and correlate these events, correct interpretation of the event semantics becomes very important to minimize false positives (false alarms).

1. Intrusion detection architecture. Today's IDS products depend heavily on centralized event processing — a traditional passive and one-way information-processing architecture. IDS sensors are placed at many locations in the network. The sensors' role is to collect data and perform simple analysis. Bulk of analysis, discovering and correlation are done at the centralized monitoring engine. This architecture faces considerable challenge when scaling up to meet the demand of today's large and complex networks. Too much burden is being placed on the central machine to perform the analysis. Also, in a centralized event-processing architecture, by the time huge amount of data arrives at the centralized location the contextual information needed to properly analyze the event has already been lost. That information existed only in the original environments where data were generated. Without the right information for interpretation, it is difficult to perform adequate correlation. Worse even, the time latency might have made it impossible

to go back and collect critical environmental information to confirm or exonerate the suspicions.

2. Host-based and network-based IDS. Host-based IDS works by monitoring system generated events, correlating them with other information such as user or application profiles, to detect intrusions. Network based IDS works by examining network traffic, most often IP packets, to recognized known attack patterns such as spoofing or flooding. One major problem is the separation of network IDS and host-based IDS. When today's attack happens, it cuts across multiple platforms — network and host devices. There is no limitation as to what the intruder can do. In fact, many hacking tools available for download from the web actually offer the combined network and host attacks. When attacks happen across network and hosts, it is necessary to detect by analyze network and host events together. Failing to do so implies many missed opportunities. Realizing this, today's network and host IDS products are adding each other's functionality and coming together slowly. However, at this stage, IDS lack the capability for effective coordinated protection.

3. Network-based IDS. There is a difficult for network based IDS to scale up dealing with network traffic volume. The variety of protocols adds to the burden of performance. Encryption creates opaque tunnels that cannot be analyzed. The encryption problem is particular serious because when coupled with traffic volume, it creates large and opaque pipes that are almost impossible to audit. Also, as the infrastructures move toward switched environment. Visibility in this environment presents yet another challenge to network based IDS. In a switched environment, if two machines are connected via a switch at two different ports, their communication will never go higher than the switch itself. With a hierarchical switch architecture, local traffic will never be visible for network IDS to monitor. One solution is to deploy IDS on each switch all the way down to the lowest level. This is an extremely expensive solution with serious performance consequences. Switched environment does not implied no attacks, it simply means the fundamental working principles of network based IDS is facing a real challenge.

4. Static Data collection. Today's IDS' static data collection method contributes to high false positive (false alarm) rate. Traditionally, IDS are setup to monitor a fix set of events. This fix set is adjust only when the operator change the auditing parameters. The model works well as long as there is a knowledgeable operator sitting in front of the console around the clock to respond the attacks in real time and to adjust the parameters to trace the progression of the attack. Without this, the traces of the attack can be easily lost and the system ended up with a large set of irrelevant data — more false alarms. Today's IDS has very little audit tuning taking place to ensure right set of data is being collected. The issue of high false positives will remain and it is a critical real-life operation problem.

5 A Real-Life Awakening

Examining the real-life failures of today's on-line transaction systems provides useful insights into how the traditional IA is failing by just protecting the castles and moats.

Criminal activities in the "U.S. vs. Gorshkov" case took place during 1999 and 2000. Several complaints were filed with the F.B.I. in multiple jurisdictions including computer intrusion, system outage and attempted extortion. The coordinated effort of several offices and investigating agents ultimately resulted in an undercover operation that took place during November 2000. Two suspects were arrested in Seattle as a result of the FBI undercover operation that involved fictitious international job advertisements and interview offerings. They were subsequently charged with numerous offences.

The internet-connected computers at the undercover operation were fitted with keystroke recorders. One of the suspects logged in to their "home system" and the keystroke recorder obtained the system name, username and login password. FBI subsequently reconnected to the remote system and downloaded approximately 2.3GB of compressed data. The downloaded data was analyzed in conjunction with data obtained from victims' systems. This revealed the true nature and the extent of the criminal activities that had been conducted. Seized evidence and victim data revealed that the following types of incidents took place during the 1999–2000 timeframe:

- Numerous computer intrusions including the subversion of systems and networks, for example ATM connected systems at a school district in Michigan
- Computer outage, for example at an internet service provider in Bellevue, Washington
- Credit card fraud, for example at online retailers and internet payment systems
- Attempted extortion, for example at a bank in Southern California
- Large-scale identity theft

Compromised systems were frequently used as web relays/proxies. If the compromised system had "business value" then it was also used for other purposes. In one instance a system connected to a high-bandwidth ATM network was employed as a Domain Name Server (DNS) and Internet Relay Chat (IRC) server. In another instance the web site of an online bank had undergone creative enhancements that bypassed the normal user log-on procedure.

The evidence also contained numerous Perl programming language software scripts and temporary file residuals resulting from their execution. The Perl scripts implemented a virtual web browser and were customized for email, auction and payment functions. The Perl scripts appeared in numerous forms of developmental evolution ranging from simple connection test scripts, SSL connection test scripts with embedded links to X.509 certificates through to connectivity to a fully integrated backend database. Thousands of email addresses were mined from the seized evidence. These addresses were correlated to activity at a web email service provider.

The Ebay auction scripts represented a full-function user account creation/management and auction creation/bid/close capability. The auction management capability also included a feature that limited transactions to below the $500 PayPal threshold. Support for the automated generation of Ebay buyer and seller feedback was also incorporated. The $500 threshold check and automated feedback represent a deliberate "fly below the radar" strategy.

The PayPal scripts demonstrated the capability of being able to create and manipulate PayPal accounts. The PayPal accounts were associated with stolen credit card information. The ingenuity of the Perl scripts also provided a clear evidence of suspects' in-depth understanding of the operation of the email, PayPal and Ebay web servers. All of these systems had been carefully analyzed and effectively reverse engineered by the suspects. Not only were the systems understood in terms of implementation technology but also in terms of business level transactions and the relation between these systems and others with which they had interaction.

The nature of the computer intrusion attack methodology is also noteworthy. We frequently hear that attacks follow an intelligence and reconnaissance phase. Intrusion Detection Systems typically report sensor events during reconnaissance probes (e.g., port scans). The intelligence phase of these attacks consisted of assembling a long list of potential target systems. There was no need to initiate reconnaissance probes. One-click "attack/compromise/subvert" scripts were developed. These scripts targeted known and "as-yet unknown" (i.e., unpublished) vulnerabilities and fully automated the installation of trojan-horse software, root kits, web proxies/relays as well as the search, gathering and retrieval of information contained on the compromised system and the network to which it was attached to. The targeting of the "as-yet unknown" vulnerabilities highlights the limitations of today's IDS and anti-virus systems which primarily based on the "20-20 hindsight" band-aid approach and working at the wrong level of abstraction. It also highlights the fallacy that there is benefit in keeping unpublished security vulnerabilities secret until patches are available.

The case was prosecuted in Seattle US Federal Court in 2001. The Federal Prosecutors successfully presented the cased by showing the reconstructing the fraud transaction scenario. The effort eventually led to multiple criminal convictions.

5.1 Check-List Mentality

Modern day system development has become increasingly complex and this has led to the common approach of relying heavily on the integration of "off-the-shelf" components. When systems are constructed in this manner, security functionalities, if addressed at all, also frequently end up being simply "off-the-shelf", component-based castles-and-moats solutions. This "checklist-mentality" is incapable to address the distributed collaborative nature of the new online business paradigm. It treats security as a second-class citizen and defines IA merely as the sum of security functionalities of all products to be integrated into the system. However, is the sum of parts equal to the total? Protecting the castles (firewall, IDS, encryption, security file system, virus checking, user authentication, PKI, etc.) offers little protection to the true values (the inter-castle transactions) in this new business paradigm.

5.2 IA System Engineering Process

For the purpose of expediency and convenience, security is usually not tightly integrated into overall system architecture from the start. One critical question must be asked — Can IA be simply treated as a last minute add-on or should it be part of the entire solution and thus be integrated into the system engineering process from the very beginning? Software development utilizes software engineering process. In contrast, there is no IA engineering process where the security requirement is defined, analyzed, architected and then finally implemented, tested and maintained in the target environments. If such an IA engineering process exists, specific requirements of the new business paradigm should have been able to be captures along the way.

5.3 Trusts and Assumptions

When the business paradigm shifts from trading within the castle to trading between amongst the castles, trusts become a critical issue. What are the assumptions being made here? Can assumptions, and the trusts that come along with it, be inherited from the old paradigm?

1. Virtual web browser and virtual web server. Beneath the reality of on-line business transactions, all tangible communication protocols, including HTTP and HTTPS, represent nothing more than a stream of bits formatted according to a specification. Most protocols, including HTTP and HTTPS, were specifically designed to permit interoperability between the different components that implement the same protocols. Anything that communicates like a web server is most likely a web server. Likewise, anything that communicates like a web browser is likely a web browser. These assumptions carry a significant implication on how a system is assembled in the first place.
2. Transaction states. Both web servers and browsers incorporate means of implementing "states" to support the concept of "web sessions" in support of higher level "business transaction sessions". "Web sessions", for example, can be achieved through the use of cookies or by identifiers that are generated on the fly and embedded in script code for a given session. A common assumption here is that anything that maintains a correct, consistent, & logical state-based transaction is assumed to be truthful and legitimate transaction partner.
3. Virtual users. Web proxies and relays have been developed as a means of bridging between routable and un-routable IP address spaces as well as providing firewall capability. Web proxies and relays can both be constructed to mask the true origin of the web traffic. The web server's view of the web client is thus further obscured. These intermediate, "apparent traffic" origins can also be used by criminal elements to mask routes tracing back to sources of undesirable activity. The usage of web proxies and relays can further amplify the deployment and effectiveness of "virtual web browsers", permitting a single virtual browser backend to mimic the behavior of a large number of "human" users.
4. Virtual messaging. Numerous "free" web-based email services exist. These include for example, Yahoo!, Gmail and Hotmail to name a few. A feature-rich messaging system can be constructed using the virtual web browser and "free" email services. Such a messaging system can create and manipulate web-mail accounts, send, receive, parse and process messages and utilize a database system to maintain user context, as well as message context, message content and web session, business transaction states. Use of proxies/relays allows the messaging system to appear as multiple "human" users. Traffic and user-activity resulting from the synthetic users goes easily undetected by the email service provider. One fatal assumption is being made here — a logical sequence of email messages validates the legality and trustworthiness of an on-line transaction.
5. Virtual payment and virtual payment trigger. There are numerous web-payment services in existence today. These services frequently associate a bank account or

credit card to an internet identity. Their intent is to facilitate the transfer of funds between parties conducting business online. The "PayPal" online payment system is an example. The virtual browser can be used to create an automated payment system. With an appropriately constructed virtual browser, traffic generated by these synthetic users is again indistinguishable from human users. The virtual browser, combined with proxy/relay intermediates that give the appearance of multiple, legitimate, synthetic users, can literally create, manage and pay for items that do not even need to exist.

6. Visibility and scopes. Sensors are limited in their visibility. Businesses that provide web services such as email, payment and auction have severely limited abilities to detect their users' participation in such illegal activities because their ability to observe is well constricted within their own domains. This constraint holds true in both computing and business contexts. Not having the sensors in the right place or not sampling data at the right time within an on-line business transaction system guarantees that unusual behavior will go undetected. In fact, improper placement of sensors can convey the false impression that everything is normal and "safe".

7. Wrong sensors. Sensors and security applications are at the wrong level of abstraction. As the case clearly illustrated, neither today's neither network-based IDS nor today's host-based IDS can be of much value in this kind of real-life transaction-level intrusion. Sensors suitable for the platforms (network and host-based IDS) are not necessarily appropriate for detection at the application and transaction levels. What is not observed can never be seen.

6   The Future Beyond the IA Corner Stones

21st century business paradigm shift presents additional and unique challenge beyond traditional security areas. This complexity rises due to the increasingly frequent, dynamic and finer-granularity level of interactions between collaboration partner users and often distributed, and diversely owner, data. Such intensive interaction is a vital function for the modern virtual enterprise. Legacy IA comes out short addressing this critical issue.

6.1   Multiple Authorization Requirement Sets

Take a large multi-national virtual enterprise for example, in order to effectively perform collaborative engineering, design, manufacturing or even coalition warfare operations; partners need to access and share value assets on a very frequent basis. The business logic of who can access what, at what time, under what conditions, is a very complex one. The logic could contain export control regulations from multiple countries. It could also contain business contracts between any partnership arrangements within this virtual enterprise. Moreover, each partner likely also has internal operation process and standards that dictates additional protections and disclosures. For all of them to be enforced appropriately, the security mechanisms (e.g. access control list, user group setting, and access matrix) buried deep within the end environments (e.g. file-system, database) must be correctly configured. This is no

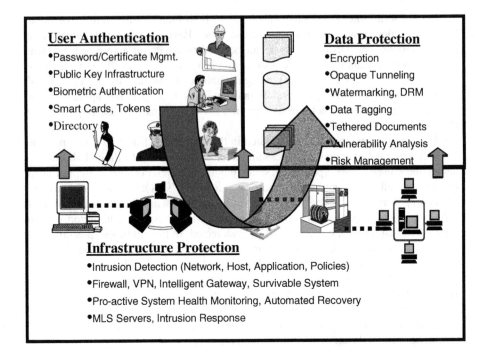

Fig. 4. Challenges in providing the right mapping from the user to the data

small task considering the complexity of authorization logic within this diverse context and the difficulties of configuring the cumbersome, inflexible, low level system security mechanisms.

6.2 Consistency, Correctness and Completeness

Consider the following set of hypothetical access control requirements:

- Mechanical engineers who are citizens have access to privileged engineering information
- Interns have no access to any information
- Any one with access to secret information has access to both privileged and confidential information
- Technicians have access to privileged information only if they have clearance
- CEO cannot be auditor, and vice versa

It is not difficult to see that access control policies are in reality a formal logic model.

- $(\forall X)\,(\forall \tau)\,(M(X) \wedge C(X) \wedge \Pi(\tau) \Rightarrow A(X, \tau))$
- $(\forall X)\,(\forall \tau)\,(I(X) \wedge (\Pi(\tau) \vee \Gamma(\tau) \vee \Sigma(\tau)) \Rightarrow \neg A(X, \tau))$
- $(\forall X)\,(\forall \tau)\,(S(X) \wedge \Sigma(\tau) \Rightarrow A(X, \tau))$
- $(\forall X)\,(\forall \tau)\,(\forall Z)\,(\Sigma(\tau) \wedge A(X, \tau) \Rightarrow (\Pi(Z) \vee \Gamma(Z)) \Rightarrow A(X, Z))$

(1)

- $(\forall X) (\forall \tau) (T(X) \wedge \Pi(\tau) \wedge A(X, \tau) \Rightarrow CL(X))$
- $(\forall X) (CEO(X) \Rightarrow \neg ACT(X))$
- $(\forall X) (ACT(X) \Rightarrow \neg CEO(X))$

Where the first axiom reads as "for all X, for all τ, if X is a mechanical engineer, X is a citizen, τ is a privileged engineering information, then access is allowed for X to τ". The last two read as "for all X, if X is CEO, then X cannot be an accountant" and "for all X, if X is accountant, X cannot be a CEO."

As one can see, it is quite possible for the requirements sets to be in conflict with each other without carefully examination particularly when the logic are implemented in the low-level, trivial, system-level security mechanisms. It is also possible that the authorization requirement sets do not cover the entire access control space needed from both logical and business perspectives. In a one-castle scenario, this issue is less pronounced due to the lower complexity level. However, the complexity multiplies when the number of partners, data and data ownership increases. The issue is both a logical one as well as a business one. Thus, mathematical modeling of the formal access control policies is essential before the complex logic is implemented into the target system environments. Legacy IA does not address these challenges, especially considering the fact that there has never been IA engineering process to follow to capture the requirements.

6.3 Dynamism

Access control requirements in virtual enterprise change all the time. There are contract expiration, updates as well as suspensions. There are also people, organization and data updates. Whenever there is a change, all systems need to be updated. Legacy IA treats authorization as a matrix conceptually with users on one side and data objects on the other side. This matrix is sparsely populated and the cells represent allowable access of a user to an object. The cells are eventually implemented into the end systems. In the old business model where activities only take place within a castle, this matrix is relatively small and updates are also straight forward. In the modern virtual enterprise, the scale and complexity make the matrix very large. When authorization requirements changes occur, it becomes also extremely difficult to these cumbersome, inflexible, low level system security mechanisms. Without an explicit policy representation and a management framework, legacy IA is incapable to catch up with the rate of change in today's virtual enterprise.

6.4 Coherent Implementation

For a large virtual enterprise with many systems, business mandates that same set of authorization requirements needs to be enforced across multiple environments for the same set of data objects. For example, export control regulation on the same set of design data regardless whether it's accessed through CAD/CAM system, file system or databases should be consistent with each other. Legacy IA focuses on islands of enforcement. Such coherent implementation is unattainable by today's IA.

7 Conclusion

Security without being cognizant of the underlying business paradigm it needs to protect is a risky business. This paper presents many critical modern IA shortfalls. These failures largely come from inheritance the old IA paradigm and the inability to recognize the revolutionary security requirements. Having all the tools, lumbers and materials does not equate a house built. It is the blueprint that put the house together. Ad-hoc application of materials and tools builds only leaky house. IA also needs to be more than the last minute patch-up. It needs to be a business-enabler — the technology that leads the creation the next generation of business paradigm. Playing the IA catch-up game and gambling on the shaky security assumptions are major roadblocks to the security of modern large-scale infrastructures.

Rule-Based Topological Vulnerability Analysis*

Vipin Swarup[1], Sushil Jajodia[2], and Joseph Pamula[2]

[1] The MITRE Corporation, 7515 Colshire Drive, McLean, VA 22102
[2] Center for Secure Information Systems, George Mason University,
Fairfax, VA 22030-4444
{jajodia, jpamula}@gmu.edu
swarup@mitre.org

Abstract. Attack graphs represent known attack sequences that attackers can use to penetrate computer networks. Recently, many researchers have proposed techniques for automatically generating attack graphs for a given computer network. These techniques either use model checkers to generate attack graphs and suffer from scalability problems, or they are based on an assumption of monotonicity and are unable to represent real-world situations.

In this paper, we present a vulnerability analysis technique that is more scalable than model-checker-based solutions and more expressive than monotonicity-based solutions. We represent individual attacks as the transition rules of a rule-based system. We define noninterfering rulesets and present efficient, scalable algorithms for those sets. We then consider arbitrary nonmonotonic rulesets and present a series of optimizations which permit us to perform vulnerability assessment efficiently in most practical cases. We motivate the issues and illustrate our techniques using a substantial example.

1 Introduction

An attacker typically penetrates a computer network by probing and modifying the network configuration and by exploiting vulnerabilities. For instance, an attacker might execute a sequence of actions that first probe a network for vulnerable systems, then exploit a detected vulnerability to gain user-level privileges on a remote host, then exploit another vulnerability to gain root-level privileges, and finally use the privileges to compromise the system. As another example, consider a network with firewall rules that prevent external packets from reaching a critical server directly. An attacker might launch an attack on port 80 of some internal machine (thus bypassing the firewall) and then use that intermediate host to attack the critical server.

---

* The work of Pamula and Jajodia was partially supported by the National Science Foundation under grants IIS-0430402 and IIS-0242237, Air Force Research Laboratory, Rome under the grant F30602-00-2-0512, and the Army Research Office under the grant DAAD19-03-1-0257.

V. Gorodetsky, I. Kotenko, and V. Skormin (Eds.): MMM-ACNS 2005, LNCS 3685, pp. 23–37, 2005.

Several graph-based vulnerability analysis techniques have been proposed to analyze the vulnerability of networked systems to composite attacks. These techniques model a computer network as a state transition system. A state represents a computer network configuration (e.g., network topology, software versions) as well as attacker capabilities (e.g., sniffed passwords, access to user or root-level shells). State transitions represent actions that modify network configurations and attacker capabilities. Analysis techniques determine, for instance, whether an attacker can reach a compromised state from an initial state; the likelihood of him doing so; a minimal set of actions that, if thwarted, would prevent an attacker from reaching any compromised state; a representation of all attack paths available to an attacker; etc.

One approach [14,7,15,6] to vulnerability analysis is to use model checking to find attack paths that compromise a stated system security goal. While this approach is very general and takes advantage of the substantial body of work on model checking, its complexity grows exponentially in the size of the state space and hence it does not scale to the enormous state space of real-world computer networks. This problem has been addressed in an alternate approach [12,1] that makes the assumption that an attacker's capabilities and the exploits available to him are never reduced by any action. With this assumption (called monotonicity), the complexity of vulnerability analysis grows linearly in the state space size and it results in efficient and scalable algorithms. However, this is not a realistic assumption. For instance, buffer overflow attacks typically result in the termination of the attacked service, thereby preventing other uses of that service. In some cases, the exploit may cause the host to crash and even to halt, or may not provide the attacker with sufficient privileges to restart the service.

In this paper, we present a rule-based approach to vulnerability analysis. We use a state transition model as in prior work, but we express state transitions as a set of rules. Rules may reduce the capabilities of attackers (e.g., as in the buffer overflow case), and may depend on the absence of certain capabilities or configuration attributes (e.g., a rule may depend on the absence of a service). We examine common rule cases that represent typical attacks and we present efficient and scalable vulnerability analysis algorithms for them. We motivate the issues and illustrate our techniques using a substantial example.

The remainder of this paper is organized as follows. Section 2 presents a formal model for graph-based vulnerability analysis. In Section 3, we define and analyze the notion of noninterfering rules and we present efficient algorithms for testing the security of systems under such rules. In Section 4, we consider rules of arbitrary form and we show that, under a reasonable assumption, we can still test system security efficiently. Section 5 presents related work and Section 6 concludes this paper.

2   Topological Vulnerability Analysis

We model the topological vulnerability analysis problem using the state transition system approach. A state represents a computer network configuration (e.g., network topology, software versions, etc.) as well as attacker capabilities (e.g., sniffed passwords, access to user or root-level shells, etc.). State transitions represent actions that modify computer network configurations (e.g., changing firewall rules) and attacker capabilities (e.g., exploits of vulnerabilities). The initial state of the transition system represents the capabilities of a specific adversary, e.g., an adversary with root access on a networked computer that is external to the networked system under consideration. The goal states of the transition system represent compromised states, e.g., states where the adversary has root privileges on critical servers.

2.1   Model

Formally, a *state transition system* is a tuple $T = (S, \tau, s_0, S_G)$ where S is a set of states, $\tau \subseteq S \times S$ is a state transition relation, $s_0 \in S$ is a start state, and $S_G \subseteq S$ is a set of goal states. A system $T' = (S', \tau', s_0', S_G')$ is a *subsystem* of system $T = (S, \tau, s_0, S_G)$ if $S' \subseteq S$, $\tau' \subseteq \tau$, $s_0' = s_0$, and $S_G' \subseteq S_G$. We write $T' \leq T$ to denote that T' is a subsystem of T.

A state $s_n \in S$ is *reachable* from state $s_0 \in S$ if there exist states $s_1, \ldots, s_{n-1} \in S$ such that $(s_i, s_{i+1}) \in \tau$ for $0 \leq i \leq n - 1$. A *vulnerable state* is a state from which some goal state is reachable. A *successful attack path* is a sequence of state transitions that takes a transition system from its initial state to a goal state. We are interested in attack graphs which represent all the successful attack paths in a system.

Definition 1. *Let $T = \langle S, \tau, s_0, S_G \rangle$ and $T' = \langle S', \tau', s_0', S_G' \rangle$ be state transition systems. Then, T' is called an* attack graph *of T if $T' \leq T$ and if all states in S' are both vulnerable and reachable from s_0' in T'.*

Definition 2. *G is called the* greatest attack graph *of a state transition system $T = (S, \tau, s_0, S_G)$ if G is an attack graph of T and if for all attack graphs G' of T, $G' \leq G$.*

Proposition 1. *Every state transition system has a greatest attack graph.*

We define topological vulnerability analysis to be the construction and analysis of greatest attack graphs. In this paper, we focus on the construction of the graphs and present efficient algorithms that map state transition systems to their greatest attack graphs.

2.2   States

A state represents a computer network configuration and attacker capabilities. A state is defined to be a set of ground predicates (called *attributes*). Let $\mathcal{K}$ be a finite set of individual constants and $\mathcal{P}$ be a finite set of predicate symbols. Each predicate has an assigned arity ≥ 1. Then the (finite) set of all atoms, $\mathcal{G}$, is defined as follows: all constants in $\mathcal{K}$ are in $\mathcal{G}$; further, if $p \in \mathcal{P}$ has arity n and if $k_1, \ldots, k_n \in \mathcal{K}$ then $p(k_1, \ldots, k_n) \in \mathcal{G}$. Finally, the set of all attributes is $\mathcal{A} \subseteq \mathcal{G}$ and the set of all states is $S = 2^{\mathcal{A}}$.

For instance, we use the attribute $reachable(s, d, p)$ (where s, d, and p are constant strings) to denote that network packets that match pattern p can traverse the network from source IP address s to destination IP address d. In this paper, we restrict p to be a port number. As another example, we use the attribute $sh(a, u, h)$ to denote that the attacker a has an executable shell on host h with privilege level u. Finally, we use $service(f, p, u, h)$ to denote that the service f is running on port p of host h with privilege level u.

2.3   State Transition Rules

Let $A, B, C, D \subseteq \mathcal{A}$ be sets of attributes with $A = \{a_1, \ldots, a_m\}$, $B = \{b_1, \ldots, b_n\}$, $C = \{c_1, \ldots, c_j\}$, and $D = \{d_1, \ldots, d_k\}$, and consider the transition relation $\delta(A, B, C, D) \in S \times S$ given by:

$$\delta(A, B, C, D) = \{(s, s') \mid (s, s' \in S) \wedge (A \subseteq s) \wedge (B \cap s = \emptyset) \wedge (s' = (s \cup C) - D)\}$$

Informally, the transition rule $\delta(A, B, C, D)$ applies to states that contain the attributes in A and do not contain the attributes in B; the rule transforms a state by adding the attributes in C and deleting the attributes in D. We represent $\delta(A, B, C, D)$ by the transition rule:

$$a_1, \ldots, a_m; b_1, \ldots, b_n \vdash_\delta c_1, \ldots, c_j; d_1, \ldots, d_k$$

The transition relation of a set of transition rules is given by the union of the transition relations of the individual rules. Note that we only consider ground rules in this paper; in our examples, a rule with variables should be interpreted as the set of ground instances of the rule.

Proposition 2. *Let $S = 2^{\mathcal{A}}$ for finite $\mathcal{A}$. Then, any transition relation $\tau : S \times S$ can be expressed as a finite set of transition rules over $\mathcal{A}$.*

Definition 3. *A state transition rule system is a tuple $T = (\mathcal{A}, \Delta, s_0, S_G)$ where $\mathcal{A}$ is a set of attributes, Δ is a set of transition rules over $\mathcal{A}$, $s_0 \in 2^{\mathcal{A}}$ is a start state, and $S_G \subseteq 2^{\mathcal{A}}$ is a set of goal states.*

2.4   Goal States

We consider attackers whose goal is to acquire some set of attributes (i.e., capabilities). A *goal state* is defined as a state that contains the desired attributes. We require that if state s is a goal state, then every superset of s is also a goal state. For instance, a goal state can be defined as any state which contains the attribute $sh(Charlie, root, DBMS)$.

We call s a *minimal goal state* if s is a goal state but no proper subset of s is a goal state. Let $\Psi(s) = \{s' \mid s' \subseteq s, s' \text{ is a minimal goal state}\}$ be the set of all minimal goal states that are subsets of s. We say that goal state s_1 *dominates* goal state s_2 (written $s_1 \geq s_2$) if $\Psi(s_1) \supseteq \Psi(s_2)$.

2.5   Example 1

We now consider an example consisting of four distinct exploits. Each exploit is represented as a state transition rule. An attacker can chain these together in various ways (see Figure 1), some of which let him penetrate a protected network. We will use this example in the remainder of this paper to illustrate and motivate our algorithms and contributions.

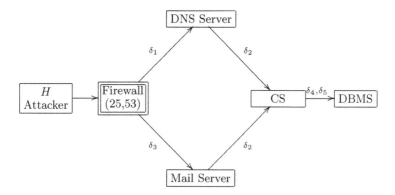

Fig. 1. An example of exploit chaining

Exploits *BIND NXT Remote Root Exploit*

The incorrect processing of DNS NXT records by a BIND name server may allow an attacker to gain a *root* level privilege on a remote vulnerable name server [3,19]. Let P be the primary name server which is authoritative for some domain, say "foo.com". The attacker A first establishes his machine H as the authoritative name server for some subdomain of "foo.com", say "bar.foo.com". The victim name server V is then interactively queried for some host in that subdomain. V then queries P which redirects the query to H. H returns a NXT record containing exploit code, overflowing V's buffer, and spawning a shell for the attacker. The shell has the same process level that the DNS process had. Note that the exploit requires that H is not running DNS on port 53. We model the exploit as a rule δ_1.

$$a_1, a_2, a_3, a_4, a_5, a_6, a_7, a_8, a_9; b_1 \vdash_{\delta_1} c_1; d_1$$

where: $a_1 = sh(A, root, P)$, $a_2 = sh(A, root, H)$, $a_3 = reachable(H, V, 53)$, $a_4 = reachable(V, P, 53)$, $a_5 = reachable(P, H, 53)$, $a_6 = service(DNS, 53, l_1, P)$, $a_7 = service(vul\text{-}DNS, 53, l_2, V)$, $a_8 = DNS\text{-}authority(P, \text{"foo.com"})$, $a_9 = DNS\text{-}subdomain(P, \text{"bar.foo.com"}, H)$, $b_1 = service(DNS, 53, l_3, H)$, $c_1 = sh(A, l_2, V)$, and $d_1 = service(vul\text{-}DNS, 53, l_2, V)$.

Generic SSHd Remote Buffer Overflow Exploit

The remote SSHd buffer overflow exploit allows an attacker to get a shell on a remote host with root privileges. We model this exploit by a transition rule δ_2

where an attacker A on host H launches a remote SSHd attack against a victim host V.

$$a_1, a_2, a_3 \vdash_{\delta_2} c_1; d_1$$

where: $a_1 = reachable(H, V, 22)$, $a_2 = service(vul\text{-}SSHd, 22, root, V)$, $a_3 = sh(A, l_1, H)$, $c_1 = sh(A, root, V)$, and $d_1 = service(vul\text{-}SSHd, 22, root, V)$.

Remote Buffer Overflow Exploit in Sendmail

A popular message transfer agent, Sendmail, can be remotely compromised allowing an attacker to gain a *root* level privilege on a remote victim's host [2]. A malicious custom e-mail message is sent to the victim's machine V, which overflows the victim mail server's buffer. We model this exploit as a rule δ_3. An attacker A launches the exploit from his machine H.

$$a_1, a_2, a_3 \vdash_{\delta_3} c_1$$

where: $a_1 = reachable(H, V, 25)$, $a_2 = service(vul\text{-}Sendmail, 25, l_1, V)$, $a_3 = sh(A, l_2, H)$, and $c_1 = sh(A, l_1, V)$.

Anonymous FTP .rhosts Remote Login Exploit

The purpose of the *FTP .rhosts* file attack is to obtain a trust relationship between two hosts, say H and V, as described in [15,6]. The FTP vulnerability allows an attacker A to write/overwrite any files in the home directory of an FTP user F. This permits an attacker to create/modify a .rhosts file in the FTP home directory on host V, and thus to masquerade as a legitimate user of the system without the need for a password. We model the FTP .rhosts attack as a transition rule δ_4.

$$a_1, a_2, a_3, a_4 \vdash_{\delta_4} c_1$$

where: $a_1 = sh(A, l_1, H)$, $a_2 = service(vul\text{-}FTP, 21, l_2, V)$, $a_3 = reachable(H, V, 21)$, $a_4 = writable\text{-}ftp\text{-}home\text{-}dir(F, l_3, V)$, and $c_1 = rshTrust(H, l_3, V)$.

And finally, we model the remote login trust exploit as a transition rule δ_5.

$$a_1, a_2, a_3 \vdash_{\delta_5} c_1$$

where: $a_1 = sh(A, l_1, H)$, $a_2 = rshTrust(H, l_3, V)$, $a_3 = reachable(H, V, .rlogin)$, and $c_1 = sh(A, l_3, V)$.

Chaining of Exploits. Let $\Delta = \{\delta_1, \delta_2, \delta_3, \delta_4, \delta_5\}$ where the rules δ's are as described above. These exploits can be chained together as illustrated in Figure 1 depicting two simple attack paths. A firewall with only two ports in an open state, ports 25 and 53, isolates the internal hosts from the external (Internet) hosts. That is, the firewall only allows DNS and mail network packets into the network. Also, note that the critical server (CS) and DBMS host are not directly accessible from outside the network. This can be represented by the following reachability predicates:

reachable(H, DNS, 53), reachable(H, Mail, 25),
reachable(DNS, CS, all), reachable(Mail, CS, all), and
reachable(CS, DBMS, all).

The attacker's goal is to gain root level privilege on server CS, and a user level privilege on host DBMS. Figure 1 depicts two different attack paths that achieve the attacker's goals in this system. In one attack path, the attacker first gains root level privilege on the DNS server. Once inside the network, the attacker gains appropriate privileges on hosts CS and DBMS. In the second attack path, the attacker first gains root level privilege on the Sendmail server instead of the DNS server.

3   Noninterfering Rules

We first consider a class of rules (which we call noninterfering rules) that can never interfere with an attacker's goal of performing a successful attack. While these rules can provide the attacker with new capabilities that assist him in his goal, they can never restrict the set of goal states that he can reach. This means that an attacker can invoke such rules freely (whenever they are applicable) without worrying about the order in which he invokes them, and he never needs to backtrack in order to reach his goal.

Definition 4. *Let $T = (\mathcal{A}, \Delta, s_0, S_G)$ be a state transition rule system. We say that a rule $\delta(A, B, C, D) \in \Delta$ is a noninterfering rule in T if:*

- *For all $c \in C$ and for all rules $\delta(A', B', C', D') \neq \delta(A, B, C, D) \in \Delta$, $c \notin B'$.*
- *For all $d \in D$ and for all rules $\delta(A', B', C', D') \neq \delta(A, B, C, D) \in \Delta$, $d \notin A'$.*
- *For all $d \in D$, d is not a member of any minimal goal state in S_G.*

We call a set of noninterfering rules a *noninterfering ruleset*.

Proposition 3. *Let $\delta \in \Delta$ be a noninterfering rule in system T and let s, t be states such that $(s, t) \in \delta$. Then, for every goal state s_g that is reachable from s, there exists a dominating goal state $t_g \geq s_g$ that is reachable from t.*

Figure 2 presents an algorithm for constructing the set of noninterfering rules of a state transition rule-system. The complexity of *computeNRS()* is $O(|\mathcal{A}|^2.|\Delta| + |\mathcal{A}|.|S_M|)$. Figure 3 presents an algorithm for extending a state transition sequence using only noninterfering rules. *findMaximal()* takes as arguments a partial attack path *seq* (in reverse order, so s_0 is the last element of the state sequence *seq*), and a noninterfering ruleset Δ. It uses the rules in Δ to extend *seq* until the path cannot be extended further, and it returns the resulting path (again in reverse order). The complexity of *findMaximal()* is $O(|\Delta|^2.|\mathcal{A}|^2)$.

Proposition 4. *If $T = (\mathcal{A}, \Delta, s_0, S_G)$ has a goal state that is reachable from s_0, and if Δ is a noninterfering ruleset in T, then findMaximal($\langle s_0 \rangle, \Delta$) is a successful attack path in T.*

In particular, if the first state in *findMaximal($\langle s_0 \rangle, \Delta$)* is not a goal state, then T is secure, i.e., no goal state is reachable from s_0.

Input:
    Δ – set of rules.
    S_M – set of minimal goal states, $S_M \subseteq S_G$.
Output:
    Δ' – set of noninterfering rules.
Algorithm:
$computeNRS(\Delta,\ S_M)$
    $P = Q = R = \emptyset$
    for each $\delta(A, B, C, D) \in \Delta$ **do**
        $P = P \cup A$
        $Q = Q \cup B$
    for each $s_m \in S_M$ **do**
        $R = R \cup s_m$
    $\Delta' = \emptyset$
    for each $\delta(A, B, C, D) \in \Delta$ **do**
        if $C \cap Q = \emptyset$ and $D \cap P = \emptyset$ and $(D \cap R = \emptyset)$ **then**
            $\Delta' = \Delta' \cup \{\delta\}$
    return Δ'

Fig. 2. Computing the noninterfering rule subset of a ruleset

Input:
    seq – a reverse attack path, $seq \in S^*$.
    Δ – set of noninterfering rules.
Output:
    A maximal state transition sequence
Algorithm:
$findMaximal(seq,\ \Delta)$
    $s = head(seq)$
    if $A \subseteq s$ and $B \cap s = \emptyset$ for some rule $\delta(A, B, C, D) \in \Delta$ **then**
        $s' = ((s \cup C) - D)$
        return $findMaximal(s'.seq,\ \Delta - \{\delta\})$
    else
        return seq

Fig. 3. Computing a maximal state transition sequence using a noninterfering ruleset

3.1 Monotonicity

A ruleset Δ is called *monotonic* if for all rules $\delta(A, B, C, D) \in \Delta$, B and D are empty. Clearly, if $T = (\mathcal{A}, \Delta, s_0, S_G)$ is a *state transition rule-system* with monotonic ruleset Δ, then all rules in Δ are noninterfering rules in T. Hence, from Propositions 3 and 4, monotonic rules may be applied in any order and *findMaximal* yields a successful attack path if one exists.

4 Nonmonotonic Rules

We now consider transition rules $\delta(A, B, C, D)$ where A, B, C, D can be arbitrary sets of attributes. Such rules (called *nonmonotonic rules*) can represent actions

an algorithm ($TVA()$) that returns a successful attack path if one exists. TVA takes a partial reverse attack path σ as an argument, together with Δ and Δ'. It also takes a fourth argument as which is the set of attributes that were deleted by the last rule that was applied thus far. TVA first applies $findMaximal$ to extend the attack path since noninterfering rules can be applied in any order as shown earlier. If the path is successful, it returns the path. Otherwise it tries to recover the attributes in as. We have not included the pseudo-code for $recoverAttributes$. However, when an attribute is first acquired, we mark the attribute with the attack path that causes it to be acquired. Then, to recover an attribute, $recoverAttributes$ reapplies the rules in the stored attack path. Having done this, TVA then tries completing the attack path. If it fails, it backtracks and then tries each rule in $\Delta - \Delta'$ in turn; after applying each rule, it recurses to repeat the above process.

We observe that in practice, most attributes that are lost due to some exploit (e.g., as in the buffer overflow examples) can be immediately recovered without impacting the attacker's ability to reach a goal state. In this case, the algorithm does not backtrack and remains efficient. Thus, the algorithm backtracks only in the unusual event that the lost attributes must be recovered in a delayed manner. Figure 6 shows a graphical representation of $TVA()$ algorithm.

4.3 Example 3

The BIND and SSHd buffer overflow exploits described in Example 1 exhibit the property of privilege loss: they provide an attacker with a root shell on the target machine but terminate the BIND or SSHd service. Since the attacker has root level privilege in the shell, the attacker is able to restart the previously crashed BIND or SSHd service.

We can represent the transition rules for restarting the BIND and SSHd daemons on host V for an attacker A as follows. Let δ_6 be the transition rule for restarting the SSHd daemon. Then,

$$a_1 \vdash_{\delta_6} c_1$$

where: $a_1 = sh(A, \ root, \ V)$ and $c_1 = service(SSHd, \ 22, \ l_1, \ V)$. Similarly, we can write the transition rule for restarting the BIND daemon.

5   Related Work

Dacier et al. [4,5] and Ortalo et al. [8] represent the vulnerabilities in a system by means of a privilege graph where nodes are sets of privileges owned by users and edges represent vulnerabilities. Our attack graph representation is motivated by their work. However, while they focus on security metrics that are based on privilege graphs, we focus on the efficient construction of greatest attack graphs.

Templeton and Levitt [18] proposed a "requires/provides" model that models attacks in terms of their preconditions and postconditions (expressed as predicates over capabilities). The models presented in [1,7,14,13,15,6] all model at-

Input:
    σ – a reverse attack path, $\sigma \in S^*$.
    Δ – set of rules.
    Δ' – noninterfering ruleset of Δ.
    as – attributes to be reacquired.
Output:
    A successful attack path, if one exists; else $\langle\rangle$.
Algorithm:
$TVA(\sigma, \Delta, \Delta', as)$
    $\sigma' = findMaximal(\sigma, \Delta')$
    $s = head(\sigma')$
    if $s \in S_G$ **then**
        return σ'
    else
        if $as \neq \emptyset$ **then**
            $\sigma'' = recoverAttributes(\sigma', as)$
            $\sigma''' = TVA(\sigma'', \Delta, \Delta', \emptyset)$
            if $\sigma''' \neq \langle\rangle$ **then**
                return σ'''
        for each $\delta(A, B, C, D) \in \Delta - \Delta'$ **do**
            if $A \subseteq s$ and $B \cap s = \emptyset$ **then**
                $s' = (s \cup C) - D$
                if $s' \neq s$ **then**
                    $\sigma'' = TVA(s'.\sigma', \Delta, \Delta', s - s')$
                    if $\sigma'' \neq \langle\rangle$ **then**
                        return σ''
        return $\langle\rangle$

Fig. 5. $TVA()$ algorithm

tacks using a similar approach. Our model is also based on this representation of attacks.

Phillips and Swiler [9] present a model which uses "attack templates" and a "physical network topology" description to generate attack graphs. Swiler et al. [17] describe a tool that implements this model but they do not present or analyze the algorithms used to generate attack graphs. We present several scalable algorithms for our formal model of vulnerability analysis.

Ritchey and Ammann [14] propose the use of model checking to automatically generate attack paths, while Sheyner et al. [15,16] propose the use of model checking to automatically generate attack graphs. Jha et al. [7,6] present two analyses of attack graphs. Ramakrishnan and Sekar [10,11] use a model checker to discover individual vulnerabilities on single hosts. Ritchey *et al.* [13] present improvements to Ritchey and Ammann's model [14] by presenting a more expressive model for the connectivity of networks. This body of work provides a model checker with a model of a specific system and of known attacks, and a safety property; the model checker determines whether the given safety property is satisfied in the model. When the safety property is not satisfied, the model checker generates a counterexample in the form of an attack path. While

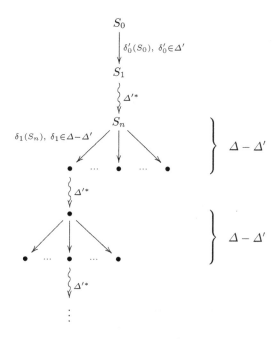

Fig. 6. Graphical representation of *TVA()* algorithm

the model checking techniques appear promising for automatic attack graph generation, these techniques break down when handling non-trivial, real world examples. The model checker's complexity grows exponentially in the size of the state space and hence it does not scale to the enormous state space of non-trivial, real world computer networks. In this paper, we present scalable algorithms for common real-world situations.

To compensate for the state explosion problem inherent in the model checking approach, Ammann *et al.* [1] propose "a more compact and scalable graph-based approach to network vulnerability analysis". Their approach relies heavily on the assumption of monotonicity: (i) an attacker can gain capabilities, but never lose them; and (ii) gaining additional capabilities does not reduce the exploits available to an attacker. The problem with this approach is that it does not allow for non-monotonic rules in a system. In this paper, we present efficient algorithms for vulnerability analysis of a system containing monotonic and non-monotonic rules, thus reflecting a model for real world examples.

6   Conclusion

In this paper, we have presented a formal model and a set of scalable algorithms for performing topological vulnerability analysis. Our approach is more scalable than model-checker-based solutions and more expressive than monotonicity-based solutions. We represent individual attacks as the transition rules of a rule-based system. For noninterfering rulesets, our algorithms are similar to monotonicity-based solutions. For arbitrary nonmonotonic rulesets, our algorithms remain efficient in the most common case where if an attacker loses a previously acquired capability, then the attacker can reacquire it when desired. The algorithms only backtrack in the event that this does not hold. Our approach permits the modelling of real-world situations where exploits have the side-effect of temporarily reducing an attacker's capabilities.

References

1. Ammann, P., Wijesekera, D., Kaushik, S.: Scalable, Graph-Based Network Vulnerability Analysis. Proceedings of the 9th ACM conference on Computer and Communications Security. (2002) 217–224 ACM Press
2. CERT: CERT Advisory CA-2003-07, Remote Buffer Overflow in Sendmail. http://www.cert.org/advisories/CA-2003-07.html
3. ADM   Crew: BIND   NXT   Remote   Root   Exploit. http://adm.freelsd.net/ADM/exploits/t666.c
4. Dacier, M., Deswarte, Y.: Privilege Graph: An Extension to the Typed Access Matrix Model. In: Gollman, D. (ed.): Proc. Third European Symposium on Research in Computer Security (ESORICS'94). Lecture Notes in Computer Science 875, Springer-Verlag (1994) 317–334
5. Dacier, M., Deswarte, Y., Kaniche, M.: Models and tools for quantitative assessment of operational security. Proceedings IFIP SEC (1996) 177–186
6. Jha, S., Sheyner, O., Wing, J.M.: Minimization and Reliability Analyses of Attack Graphs. Technical Report CMU-CS-02-109, School of Computer Science, Carnegie Mellon University. (February 2002)
7. Jha, S., Sheyner, O., Wing, J.M.: Two Formal Analyses of Attack Graphs. In Proceedings of the 2002 Computer Security Foundations Workshop, Nova Scotia, Canada (June 2002) 45–59
8. Ortalo, R., Deswarte, Y., Kaaniche, M.: Experimenting with Quantitative Evaluation Tools for Monitoring Operational Security. IEEE Transactions on Software Engineering, Vol. 25(5) (September/October 1999) 633–650
9. Phillips, C., L. Painton Swiler: A Graph-Based System for Network-Vulnerability Analysis. Proceedings of the 1998 workshop on New Security Paradigms. ACM Press, Charlottesville, VA, USA (1998) 71–79
10. Ramakrishnan, C.R., Sekar, R.: Model-based Vulnerability Analysis of Computer Systems. Proceedings of the 2nd International Workshop on Verification, Model Checking and Abstract Interpretation (September 1998)
11. Ramakrishnan, C.R., Sekar, R.: Model-Based Analysis of Configuration Vulnerabilities. Journal of Computer Security. Vol. 10 (1–2) IOS Press (2002) 189–209
12. Ramsdell, J.: Penetration Analysis Application. The MITRE Corporation. (April 2001)
13. Ritchey, R., O'Berry, B., Noel, S.: Representing TCP/IP Connectivity for Topological Analysis of Network Security. 18th Annual Computer Security Applications Conference. (December 2002)
14. Ritchey, R.W., Ammann, P.: Using Model Checking to Analyze Network Vulnerabilities. Proceedings of the IEEE Symposium on Security and Privacy. (2000) 156–165

15. Sheyner, O., Haines, J., Jha, S., Lippmann, R., Wing, J.M.: Automated Generation and Analysis of Attack Graphs. Proceedings of the IEEE Symposium on Security and Privacy. IEEE Computer Society (2002) 254–265
16. Sheyner, O., Wing, J.: Tools for Generating and Analyzing Attack Graphs. Proceedings of International Symposium on Formal Methods for Components and Objects, LNCS 3188 (2004) 344–371
17. Swiler, L.P., Phillips, C., Ellis, D., Chakerian, S.: Computer-Attack Graph Generation Tool. Proceedings DISCEX '01: DARPA Information Survivability Conference and Exposition II. (June 2001) 307–321
18. Templeton, S.J., Levitt, K.: A Requires/Provides Model for Computer Attacks. Proceedings of the New Security Paradigms Workshop. Ballycotton, County Cork, Ireland. ACM Press (2000) 31–38
19. US-CERT: Vulnerability Note Number: 16532—BIND NXT record processing may cause buffer overflow. http://www.kb.cert.org/vuls/id/16532

Models and Analysis of Active Worm Defense

David M. Nicol and Michael Liljenstam

University of Illinois, Urbana, IL 61801
dmnicol@uiuc.edu
http://www.project-moses.net

Abstract. The recent proliferation of Internet worms has raised questions about defensive measures. To date most techniques proposed are *passive*, in-so-far as they attempt to block or slow a worm, or detect and filter it. *Active* defenses take the battle to the worm—trying to eliminate or isolate infected hosts, and/or automatically and actively patch susceptible but as-yet-uninfected hosts, without the knowledge of the host's owner. The concept of active defenses raises important legal and ethical questions that may have inhibited consideration for general use in the Internet. However, active defense may have immediate application when confined to dedicated networks owned by an enterprise or government agency. In this paper we model the behavior and effectiveness of different active worm defenses. Using a discrete stochastic model we prove that these approaches can be strongly ordered in terms of their worm-fighting capability. Using a continuous model we consider effectiveness in terms of the number of hosts that are protected from infection, the total network bandwidth consumed by the worms and the defenses, and the *peak* scanning rate the network endures while the worms and defenses battle. We develop optimality results, and quantitative bounds on defense performance. Our work lays a mathematical foundation for further work in analysis of active worm defense.

1 Introduction

A computer worm is so called because it has a life of its own. Once burrowed into a susceptible system, it attempts to propagate through the network. The usual means is through "scans", it attempts to connect to and infiltrate other hosts throughout the network. Worms interfere with normal use of computers, and exact an economic cost of eradicating them and repairing systems infected by them. Worms have the potential to wreak havoc on the systems they infect, and on the networks they traverse. This potential has been realized already, several times.

The large-scale worm infestations in recent years have triggered several efforts to model worm spread in order to understand how the low-level factors in the propagation mechanism translate into macroscopic behavior, assess threat levels of different worms, and evaluate the effectiveness of detection methods and proposed counter-measures. Staniford appears to have been the first to recognize that the macroscopic propagation of the Code Red v2 worm could be

V. Gorodetsky, I. Kotenko, and V. Skormin (Eds.): MMM-ACNS 2005, LNCS 3685, pp. 38–53, 2005.

well modeled through the logistic equation [10]. This model and the equivalent *simple epidemic model* from the epidemic modeling literature (see e.g. [3]) have since been used in several studies [11,6,7,5,13,14]. [12] proposed a model to take removals into account (based on the *general epidemic model*) and [1] proposed a discrete time model.

Our work is unique in considering a wide space of defensive capabilities, and in sample path comparison of them. It is most similar in spirit to [7,1,14] as we use epidemic models to evaluate proposed worm counter-measures. We extend simple epidemic models to consider the interaction of worms and counter-worms and other "active" counter-measures.

For the purpose of illustration the experimental portion of our paper uses parameters reflective of the Code Red v2 worm, released in July 2001. It is important to remember that as far as the mathematics goes, time-scale is irrelevant. Having said that, it is true that very fast worms have had their propagation shaped by the impact they have on the network infrastructure, and the simple mathematical models we develop would not apply.

We focus on worms that spread *autonomously* by probing other systems for vulnerabilities that can be exploited to propagate from one machine to another. This class of worms captures the essence of the rapidly spreading large-scale infestations seen to date, such as Code Red v2, Code Red II, and Nimda in 2001, and Slammer, Blaster, and Welchia in 2003. Thus, we deliberately exclude most typical email born viruses that require a user action to enable infection. In contrast, worms such as Slammer have proven that the time-scales involved for fast moving autonomously propagating worms can be so short that human intervention to stop them is impossible. Consequently, this class of worms poses a substantial threat and a trigger for development of automated defensive mechanisms, such as those we consider in this paper.

In the wake of one worm attack (Blaster), a counter-worm (Welchia) was launched that sought hosts infected by Blaster, attempted to patch them, and use them to find other infected hosts. Whatever the intentions of the authors might have been, Welchia had consequences as bad or worse than Blaster—it was harder to get rid of, and effectively created a denial-of-service attack on patch servers, so that people trying manually to protect their systems had a harder time doing so. The question is raised therefore of the effectiveness and impact that an "active defense" might have. We examine this question agnostically and without overt consideration of the legal and ethical issues raised by wide-spread active defense. It is enough for us that an organization as large as the United States Department of Defense could mandate such measures on its own gargantuan networks; we seek to understand the power and the limitations of active defense deployment, should they be deployed. Our approach is analytic. We consider four aspects of active defense—patching uninfected hosts, increasing the active defense population by using uninfected hosts that are susceptible to the worm, suppression of infected hosts discovered through scans, and suppression of infected hosts discovered through scans *and* traffic analysis. Using a very general discrete stochastic model, we show that adding each capability (in that order) to the active defense assumptions results in a stochastically stronger increase in worm-fighting power. Using a continuous model we quantify some aspects of active defense behavior, and prove some results about it.

2   Active Defense

Imagine a network where there are N hosts with a particular set of vulnerabilities, and then a worm is released that is able to exploit one or more of these. We suppose that a host infected by this worm scans the network looking for vulnerable hosts it may infect. We assume that a scan consists of a random selection of an IP address— if that host is susceptible and uninfected it immediately becomes infected. In our discrete model we assume that the address selection is oblivious to the state of the network. This means that non-uniform random scanning can be accommodated in the model, so long as the sampling is not affected by any knowledge of other hosts, infected or not. This does not preclude the sort of stratified sampling seen in some worms (where hosts "closer" to the infected one are sampled with higher probability), but it does preclude a dynamic partitioning of the search space based on coordination among infected hosts. We assume a random delay of time between successive scans from a host, once again assuming that the sampling is independent of network state.

Under these assumptions we can picture the behavior of a worm on a time-line populated with scan events. Each scan event has a source and destination identity. Each of the susceptible hosts has a state of uninfected, or infected. A scan event that has an uninfected host as destination changes that host's state, and thereafter it contributes to the scanning. (It is straightforward to augment the model to account for latency between when a scan is sent and when it is received, we have not done so for simplicity of exposition).

2.1   Defense Capabilities

At time 0 the worm is launched from w_0 of the N susceptible hosts. Each infected host scans the network using a randomized strategy that is oblivious to the network state. We assume that the worm immediately inhibits further penetration through the same vulnerability, but that a counter-worm scanning it can recognize the presence of the worm, (e.g. through observation of banner information that the host's software returns, revealing a version and build that admits penetration through the known vulnerability).

We envision a model of *active defense* as follows. At time $T_0 > 0$, some I_0 hosts begin executing an active defense. Each of those hosts scans, using a strategy (probably, but not necessarily random) that is oblivious to the network state. Whenever one of these scans targets a susceptible but uninfected host, that host becomes (instantly!) patched to prevent infection from the worm. We call this a **simple patch** defense. This defense (and all the others we consider) presumes that the defensive mechanism was prepared before the worm was launched. So-called 0-day attacks, ones that exploit previously unknown exploits, are fairly rare. The vulnerabilities that worms exploit are more typically announced when discovered, often with patches available. More often than not the patch code reveals details worm writers use to target as-yet unpatched systems. It is not unreasonable to suppose then that patching defense code could be crafted along with the patch. A reason for not releasing the patching defense in anticipation of a worm is that the release would contain the code to exploit the vulnerability, with no work or further cleverness needed by a worm-writer. A patching defense must be coupled with a worm-detection mechanism, such as those proposed in [5,13].

One could increase the presence of the active defense by increasing the number of hosts running the patching logic. So we define a **spreading patch** defense as one where, when an uninfected susceptible host is scanned, it is endowed with a counter-worm that both patches, and scans. While the number of patching hosts remains constant in a simple patching defense, it grows in a spreading patch defense. Such a mechanism has been seen in the wild [4].

A third presumed defensive capability is worm suppression. Suppose that when a patching host scans an infected host it is able to identify the host as infected, and to suppress the infecting scans from being seen elsewhere, thereafter—it is able to *nullify* the infected host. For example, the spreading-patch worm might have an ability to cause the infection traffic to be filtered by a nearby router; another way might be if every machine in an organization had a "lock", such that when the proper "key" is applied, some or all of that machine's external communication is inhibited—an organization's active defense posture would include selective suppression of machines thought to be infected. For our purposes, the important thing is that the infected host be discovered by a scan, and that thereafter it is no longer a source of infection. We call this a **nullifying** defense.

A fourth presumed defensive capability takes advantage of the fact that some attacks are complex enough to require that the attacking host use its legitimate IP address as source in its packets (and we may anticipate that in the future the ability to spoof source addresses will become much diminished, through more active router verification procedures). Because of this, a patching host that *receives* a scan from an infected host could turn around and nullify the infection. In this **sniper** defense one expects that infected hosts diminish in number faster than when they are discovered merely by scans.

2.2 Metrics

There are different ways of assessing an active defense. When host integrity is paramount, then an appropriate metric is the number of hosts infected by the worm. We define $I(D, t)$ to be the cumulative number of hosts infected by time t under defense D. This metric is a random variables; we will say that D_i is more *powerful* than D_j if for all $t > 0$ and $n > 0$,

$$\Pr\{I(D_i, t) > n\} \leq \Pr\{I(D_j, t) > n\}.$$

When this relationship holds we say that the distribution (with respect to randomness due to sampling) of $I(D_j, t)$ is *stochastically larger* than $I(D_i, t)$[9], denoted $I(D_j, t) \geq_{st} I(D_i, t)$. D_i is more powerful in the sense that it does a better job at preventing susceptible hosts from becoming infected. This stochastic ordering is strong in its implications. It is known that if $X \geq_{st} Y$ and f is any increasing function, then $E[f(X)] \geq E[f(Y)]$. This has bearing then for any system metric that depends monotonically on infection counts, e.g., the probability of system failure would likely be monotone increasing in the number of infected hosts.

An active defense may increase the overall scanning activity on the network, and there is evidence that intense scanning can harm the network [2]. When network health is the principle concern, then measures of scanning history, and/or scanning intensity are appropriate. If $\lambda(D, t)$ denotes the scanning rate due to both worm and defense D, then we assess a defense in terms of its peak scanning rates over some interval $[0, t]$:

$$\max_{0 < s < t} \{\lambda(D, s)\}$$

We might also assess it through its aggregate scanning rates (the space-time product) over some interval $[0, t]$:

$$\int_0^t \lambda(D, s) \, ds.$$

3   Ordering of Defenses

Intuition suggests that the four active defensives (five, if we include the empty defense) we've outlined might be ordered in terms of power. We now show that this is exactly the case. In the comparisons made, we use the *Common Sample Path* assumption, that once a host is infected (or takes on the counter-worm), its scanning behavior is completely determined by a random number stream that is independent of any other. When we compare two defenses, we assume that a host uses that same stream in both systems, which allows us to compare the two systems on commonly constructed sample paths. The implication is that once a host is infected (or starts to run a counter-worm), its sequence of inter-scan delays are the same in both systems, and the pattern of hosts scanned are the same in both systems. Thus, if the two systems cause a host to be infected at the same instant, on the sample paths being compared that host will scan exactly the hosts at exactly the same time, in both systems.

The results to follow are based on a construction we call the Sample Path Graph (SPG). For every susceptible host h_i let $\mathcal{I}_i$ be a sequence of pairs (t_i, dst_i) identifying the time since the host started infection scanning, and a destination dst_i of a scan. $\mathcal{I}_i$ is ordered by increasing values of t_i. We define C_i similarly, describing the scanning pattern once a host starts running a counter-worm. We construct a graph whose nodes represent hosts that are assumed to be infected already at time 0 (and which have scanning sequences), nodes representing hosts that eventually start counter-worm scans (with their own scanning sequences), and susceptible hosts. The graph contains a directed edge for every potential scan described in the sets $\{\mathcal{I}_i\}$ and $\{\mathcal{C}_i\}$ whose target was susceptible at time 0. The edge is directed from the source of the scan to the target; an edge will be called an *infection edge* or *countering edge*, depending on whether it comes from an infection or counter-worm sequence, respectively. The node for host h_i will have values $S(h_i)$ recording the earliest time it was scanned by an infected host, and $C(h_i)$ recording the earliest time it was scanned by a host running a counter-worm. Some of the edges are labeled with the time of the scan—these edges are particularly important in our analysis. The values of $S(h_i)$ and $C(h_i)$, the edges labeled and the values of those labels all depend on the particular defense. However, common to those defenses are the following rules:

- All hosts assumed to be already infected at time 0 label each of their edges with the corresponding scan time;
- all hosts that are used to start the counter-worm label each of their edges with T_0 plus the corresponding scan time offset contained in the scan sequence.

The differences between different defense's SPGs are characterized as follows:

Empty Defense (D_0)

1. The node for host h_i defines $S(h_i)$ to be the smallest label among all labeled infection edges directed to it; $S(h_i) = \infty$ if no such edge exists.
2. A host h_i labels the infection edge corresponding to the jth element of $\mathcal{I}_i$ (say, (s_j, dst_j)) with value $S(h_i) + s_j$, $j = 1, 2, \cdots$.

The difference between the simple patch defense and the empty defense is that susceptible hosts are protected from infection if they are touched by a countering scan before being touched by an infection scan.

Simple Patch (D_1)

1. Item (1) from the Empty Defense rules.
2. The node for host h_i defines $C(h_i)$ to be the smallest label among all labeled countering edges directed to it; $C(h_i) = \infty$ if no such edge exists.
3. If $S(h_i) < C(h_i)$ the node labels the infection edge corresponding to the jth element of $\mathcal{I}_i$ (say, (s_j, dst_j)) with value $S(h_i) + s_j$, $j = 1, 2, \cdots$.
4. If $C(h_i) < S(h_i)$ the node does not label any of its edges.

The difference between a spreading patch defense and a simple patch one is that a host that receives a countering scan before any infection scan becomes host to counter-worm software, and generates its own countering scans.

Spreading Patch (D_2)

1. Items (1) from the Empty Defense rules, (2), and (3) from the Simple Patch rules.
2. If $C(h_i) < S(h_i)$ the node labels the countering edge corresponding to the jth element of $\mathcal{C}_i$ (say, (s_j, dst_j)) with value $C(h_i) + s_j$, $j = 1, 2, \cdots$.

The difference between a nullifying defense and a spreading patch defense is that when a countering scan reaches a host that is already sending infection scans, the infection scans stop.

Nullifying Defense (D_3)

1. Item (1) from the Empty Defense rules, item (2) from the Simple Patch rules, and item (2) from the spreading patch rules.
2. If $S(h_i) < C(h_i)$ the node labels the infection edge corresponding to the jth element of C_i (say, (s_j, dst_j)) with value $C(h_i) + s_j$, for all j such that $S(h_i) + s_j \leq C(h_i)$.

And finally, the difference between a sniper defense and a nullifying defense is that infection scans that encounter hosts running countering scans cause the host sending the infection scan to cease. This may occur before the host is itself scanned by a countering scan (which has the same nullifying effect).

Sniper Defense (D_4)

1. Item (1) from Empty Defense rules, item (2) from the Simple Patch rules, item (2) from the Spreading Patch rules.
2. If $S(h_i) < C(h_i)$, let k be the smallest index for $(s_k, dst_k) \in \mathcal{I}_i$ such that $S(h_i) + s_k > C(dst_k)$, and define $K_i = S(h_i) + s_k$. The node for h_i labels the infection edge corresponding to the jth element of C_i (say, (s_j, dst_j)) with value $C(h_i) + s_j$, for all j such that $S(h_i) + s_j \leq \min\{C(h_i), K_i\}$.

The construction above make the conditions under which a given infection edge is labeled increasingly restrictive, as we move through sequence of defenses. This implies that if we choose a host h_i and defenses D_a and D_b with $a < b$, then the set of labeled incoming infection edges it has in the SPG for D_b is a subset of the labeled incoming infection edges it has in the SPG for D_a. This fact enables us to prove the central results comparing different defenses.

Lemma 1. *Consider two defenses D_a and D_b, $a < b$, under identical boundary conditions. Let G_a and G_b be corresponding Sample Path Graphs constructed under the Common Sample Path assumption, and let $S^{(y)}(h)$ and $C^{(y)}(h)$ denote the $S(h)$ and $C(h)$ variables for host h under defense $y \in \{a, b\}$. Then for every host h, $S^{(a)}(h) \leq S^{(b)}(h)$ and $C^{(b)}(h) \leq C^{(a)}(h)$.*

Proof. Without loss of generality renumber the hosts by increasing value of $S^{(b)}(h)$, we induct on this order. Consider the base case of h_0. Both $S^{(a)}(h_0)$ and $S^{(b)}(h_0)$ are defined by edges from hosts assumed to be infected at time 0, and are thus identical. In both G_a and G_b host h_0 gets the same set of labeled countering edges from the initial set of hosts running the defense, and $C(h_0)$ in both graphs is no larger than the smallest of these labels. However, in G_b there may be more countering edges labeled, and hence the possibility of a shorter path to h_0 through those edges, whence $C^{(b)}(h_0) \leq C^{(a)}(h_0)$ and the induction base is established. For the induction hypothesis we assume that the assertion is true for all hosts $h_0, h_1, \ldots, h_{n-1}$ for some n, and consider host h_n. Let e be the labeled infection edge coming into h_n whose label defines $S^{(b)}(h_n)$, and consider its manifestation e' in G_a. By the construction of SPG's, an infection edge may appear labeled in the SPG of one defense D_u and not another D_v if its target h_y has a smaller value $C(h_y)$ in G_v than in G_u, or if G_v is nullifying and scans a countering host. In all cases the only way a labeled edge appears in G_u and not G_v is when $u < v$. Consequently e' appears labeled in G_a. This in turn implies that the node h_m from which e' is directed satisfies $m < n$, as it is directed from the same node in both G_a and G_b. By the induction hypothesis $S^{(a)}(h_m) \leq S^{(b)}(h_m)$, which implies that the label on e' is no larger than the label on e, and thus, that $S^{(a)}(h_n) \leq S^{(b)}(h_n)$. A similar argument shows that the labeled countering edge g which defines $C^{(a)}(h_n)$ (when this exists) has a labeled counter-part g' in $C^{(b)}(h_n)$, whose label is no larger in G_b than it is in G_a, and thus that $C^{(b)}(h_n) \leq C^{(a)}(h_n)$. This completes the induction.   □

From this result comes the main result.

Theorem 1. *For defense D_i and every time t, let $I(D_i, t)$ denote the number of hosts infected by time t (including those that later become nullified). Then for $a < b$, $I(D_a, t) \geq_{st} I(D_b, t)$ for every $t \geq 0$.*

Proof. Lemma 1 shows that for any sample path of scans and every time t, the number of hosts h with $S^{(a)}(h) \leq t$ is greater than or equal to the number of hosts h with $S^{(b)}(h) \leq t$. For any sample path these counts define the random variables $I(D_a, t)$ and $I(D_b, t)$. Coupling results in [9] establish the result.   □

These results show that the difference between defenses is structural, and strong. The results are very general, free of distributional assumptions other than independent of sampling from network state. However, they don't give much insight into how well these defenses perform.

There is one exception, in the special case where the counter-worm has the same scanning characteristics as the worm. Then we may assume that whenever a host is entered either by a worm, or a counter-worm, its pattern of scans (inter-scan delays, sequence of targets scanned) is the same under any defense. From the point of view of the same path analysis we've done, it means that whenever a node is triggered to scan we may assume it does so with exactly the same pattern regardless of if that is an infection or countering scan. This means that any host that scans in an empty defense also does so in a spreading patch defense, only possibly earlier (if the scan is a countering scan).

These observations establish the theorem.

Theorem 2. *Suppose that the scanning structure of the counter-worm is identical to the worm. For every time t let $\lambda(D_0, t)$ and $\lambda(D_2, t)$ denote the instantaneous number of hosts scanning under the empty defense and spreading patch defense, respectively. Then for every t, $\lambda(D_2, t) \geq_{st} \lambda(D_0, t)$.*

This theorem is a strong statement about a condition when adding defense is worse, from the point of view of the network. Increasing functions of $\lambda(D, t)$ include the peak number of hosts scanning over an interval, the space-time product of the bandwidth devoted to scanning, the probability of network partition, and so on. The stochastic ordering asserts that the expectation of each of these is larger when we use a spreading patch defense than when we use no defense at all.

4   Epidemic Models

We use a style of modeling based on well known models from the epidemic modeling literature. In typical simple epidemic models we consider a fixed population of N, where each individual is susceptible to infection, and each individual will, at any given time, be in one of a small set of predefined states. For instance, in the *simple epidemic model* [3] (aka the SI model and equivalent to the logistic equation) an individual is either in state S (susceptible to infection) or I (infected). We denote by $s(t)$ and $i(t)$ the number of individuals in state S and I respectively at time t, and thus $\forall t, s(t) + i(t) = N$. For large enough populations, the mean rate of state changes $S \to I$ can be modeled as:

$$\frac{ds(t)}{dt} = -\beta s(t) i(t)$$

$$\frac{di(t)}{dt} = \beta s(t) i(t)$$

where the constant β is the *infection parameter*, i.e. the pairwise rate of infection. β reflects the aggregate scanning rate of an infected host, as well as the mean probability of selecting a given address for an individual probe attempt. The system boundary conditions are given by the number of initially susceptible hosts $s(0)$ and initially infected hosts $i(0)$. This model rests on assumptions of *homogeneous mixing*, which correspond well to a uniformly random scanning worm spreading freely through a network, so in the following we will refer to this the **Random Scanning Worm Model**.

Other scanning strategies are possible. For instance, worms such as Code Red II, Nimda, Blaster, and Welchia utilized preferential (rather than uniform) scanning techniques where addresses close in the address space to the scanning host's would be probed with higher probability. Other suggested possibilities include a "Divide-and-Conquer" approach to probing the address space (see "partitioned permutation scan" in [11]). Here each worm is assigned a disjoint fraction of the address space to probe.

Other simple tricks for speeding up the propagation have been suggested, such as the use of pre-compiled hit-lists or using inter-domain routing tables to only scan routed space [14]. We can incorporate these into our framework; hit-listed hosts can be made to be infected as a boundary condition, and use of routing tables just increases β to reflect that the scanning is over a smaller address space.

The early stage of infection is the most critical time for any counter-measures to be effective. Since the worms behave similarly in the early stages we will, in the following, focus on random scanning worms as this is the type of worm that has been observed in the wild to date.

In [7], Moore *et al.* note that when considering the effectiveness of defensive measures, it is preferable to consider the quantiles of infection rather than the mean number of infections due to the variability inherent in the early stages of infection growth. However, we prefer to use these mean-value based models, because they lend themselves to analysis in a way that stochastic simulations do not. Moreover, we are mainly concerned with the relative performance of different defenses as we compare them, and we believe that the relative performance can be credibly determined in terms of the mean, even though the predicted mean absolute performance should be viewed with caution.

The simple epidemic model we study is suitable only in contexts where the worm scanning is unaffected by the network topology. This assumption is fine for worms whose mass and scan rates aren't constrained by bandwidth (as was the case with Code Red, and others), but is not acceptable when network constraints hinder worm growth. In related work we are exploring how to incorporate network constraints into efficient simulation of worm dynamics [8].

4.1   Spreading Patch Counter-Worm

Consider the spreading patch counter-worm model discussed earlier, and assume that it uses the same vulnerability and propagation strategy as the original worm. Under these assumptions the second worm will spread at (approximately) the same rate as the original worm, seeking the same susceptible population of hosts. A simple model is:

$$\frac{ds(t)}{dt} = -\beta s(t)(i_{\mathrm{b}}(t) + i_{\mathrm{g}}(t))$$

$$\frac{di_{\mathrm{b}}(t)}{dt} = \beta s(t) i_{\mathrm{b}}(t)$$

$$\frac{di_{\mathrm{g}}(t)}{dt} = \beta s(t) i_{\mathrm{g}}(t)$$

where i_b refers to infections by the malicious (bad) worm and i_g refers to infections by the spreading-patch (good) worm. Given β and $i_b(0)$, system behavior is governed by the time T_0 at which spreading-patch worms are released, and the number of worms I_0 released then. We assume that the spreading-patch worms are launched on "friendly" machines that are not part of the susceptible or infected set.

Spreading-patch worm effectiveness as a function of response time and initial population is shown in Figure 1. An effective response requires a combination of low response time and a sufficiently large initial population. Launching a single counter-worm has little effect, and the window of opportunity for launching even a thousand spreading-patch worms disappears after a couple of hours.

At T_0, $i_b(T_0)$ hosts have succumbed to the original worm and there are $s(T_0)$ remaining susceptibles. How many spreading-patch worms must be launched to protect a given fraction fraction p of those remaining susceptibles? If we consider the fraction of infection growth due to the spreading-patch worm

$$\frac{di_{\mathrm{g}}(t)/dt}{di_{\mathrm{g}}(t)/dt + di_{\mathrm{b}}(t)/dt} = \frac{i_{\mathrm{g}}(t)}{i_{\mathrm{g}}(t) + i_{\mathrm{b}}(t)}$$

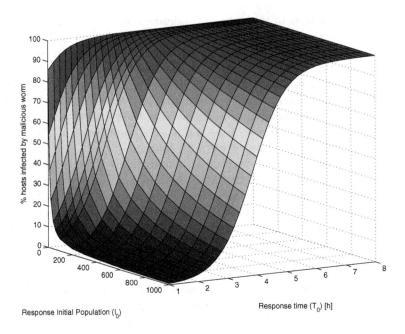

Fig. 1. Effectiveness of spreading-patch worm as a function of response time and initial counter-worm population

we see that since the propagation rates are the same, the proportions of the susceptible population consumed by each worm from T_0 onwards simply correspond to their proportion of the population at T_0. Thus, ultimately the fraction of hosts which were susceptible at T_0, but eventually are patched is

$$p = \frac{I_0}{I_0 + i_b(T_0)}.$$

Solving for I_0 we get

$$I_0 = \left(\frac{p}{1-p}\right) \cdot i_b(T_0) \tag{1}$$

Thus, the fraction of all susceptibles $s(0)$ that will be protected is

$$\tilde{p} = \frac{p \cdot s(T_0)}{s(0)} = \frac{p[s(0) - i_b(T_0)]}{s(0)} = p\left(1 - \frac{i_b(T_0)}{s(0)}\right)$$

If the infection is caught early on, then $i_b(T_0) \ll s(0)$, and the protected fraction $\tilde{p} \approx p$. Thus, equation (1) can be used as a guideline for selecting I_0 given only an estimate of how many hosts have been infected at the time of response ($i_b(T_0)$), assuming that the response occurs early. Such an estimate can reasonably be obtained by analysis of observed scanning behavior.

The spreading-patch worm model considered here assumes only that it scans at the same rate as the original worm. It does not assume any information about the malicious worm and its behavior. As worms to date have exploited vulnerabilities that were previously known, it is not unreasonable to suppose that a patching worm might be developed when the vulnerability is identified (but before it is announced), against the possibility of needing to use it. Such a worm would not be launched before needed, because it could be captured and analyzed for the means to exploit the vulnerability. However, the fact that the spreading-patch worm has higher impact on the network (Theorem 2) than no defense at all encourages us to explore counter-worms that have stronger capabilities in worm identification and suppression, with smaller impact on the network.

4.2   Nullifying Defense

Next we develop a continuous model of the nullifying defense. Using notation similar to that for the spreading patch defense, we develop state equations

$$\frac{ds(t)}{dt} = -\beta s(t)(i_b(t) + i_g(t))$$

$$\frac{di_b(t)}{dt} = \beta s(t)i_b(t) - \beta i_b(t)i_g(t)$$

$$\frac{di_g(t)}{dt} = \beta s(t)i_g(t)$$

Here we see a new component to $(di_b(t)/dt)$, the subtraction of hosts due to being scanned by the counter-worm.

Under our assumptions, in the limit of increasing time t, the aggregate scan rate under the spreading patch defense is proportional to the number of "outside" spreading-patch hosts I_0 plus the initial susceptible population size $s(0)$— eventually every susceptible host is running either the worm, or the counter-worm. However, in the case of nullifying worms, the aggregate *peak* scan rate may be smaller than the aggregate peak scan rate of the unfettered worm.

Theorem 3. *Suppose that I_0 initial nullifying worms are released at time T_0. If $I_0 \leq i_b(T_0)$, then the aggregate peak scan rate using the nullifying worm is less than the peak scan rate of the unfettered worm.*

Proof. Let $i_n(t)$ be the aggregate number of infected hosts that a nullifying defense has identified and contained by time t, and let $e(t)$ be the number of formerly susceptible hosts that have been "enlisted" to run the nullifying worm. At any time t the aggregate scan rate of a defense is proportional to $i_b(t)+i_g(t) = i_b(t) + I_0 + e(t)$. From the invariant $s(0) = s(t) + i_b(t) + i_n(t) + e(t)$ we replace $e(t)$ in the scan rate expression to see that the scan rate at t is proportional to $I_0 + s(0) - s(t) - i_n(t)$. The maximum value of this term will always be less than $s(0)$ if $I_0 < s(t)+i_n(t)$ for all t. Examination of derivatives shows that $s(t)+i_n(t)$ is monotone decreasing, hence its lowest value is the asymptotic value of $i_n(t)$, say, $\mathcal{N} = \lim_{t\to\infty} i_n(t)$. By assumption $I_0 \leq i_b(T_0)$, and clearly $i_b(T_0) < \mathcal{N}$. The conclusion follows immediately.   □

It is interesting to compare this result—which says if one *limits* the initial infection of the counter-worm you can bound the peak scan rate from above, with the spreading-patch defense results which turn these inequalities around. With the spreading-patch defense a minimum size of the release needs to be $I_0 > i_b(T_0)$ to give it enough mass to overtake the original worm. But because the nullifying worm fights by decreasing the number of scanning worms, it gets by with a smaller initial counter-worm population.

Another capability a nullifying defense could have is that it stop all defensive scanning, upon centralized command. This would help mitigate against over-whelming the network with scans from the defenses (a characteristic reported of the counter-worms seen in the wild). Denote the defensive worm stopping time by t_s. The modified state equations after time t_s are

$$\frac{ds(t)}{dt} = -\beta s(t) i_b(t) \tag{2}$$

$$\frac{di_b(t)}{dt} = \beta s(t) i_b(t) \tag{3}$$

$$\frac{di_g(t)}{dt} = 0 \tag{4}$$

Figure 2 illustrates the evolution of system state where the nullifying defense is propagating without stopping. Also shown, is the resulting peak total population (directly related to peak bandwidth in our model) as a function of stopping time t_s. Taking the time at which the defensive worms are stopped as a control parameter, we see that the minimized peak scan rate obtained by optimally selecting the stopping time is no larger than the peak scan rate if the defenses are never turned off. This capability can only improve the peak scan rate over that of the earlier nullifying defense we considered.

For $t < t_s$ the scan rate is proportional to $i_b(t) + i_g(t)$; the peak scan rate achieved after t_s is proportional to $i_b(t_s) + s(t_s)$, for the original worm will eventually infect all hosts left unprotected once we stop the defensive scans. Examination of derivatives shows that

$$\frac{d(i_b(t) + i_g(t))}{dt} = \beta \left(i_b(t)(s(t) - i_g(t)) + s(t)i_g(t) \right)$$

which we observe is positive at least as long as $s(t) \geq i_g(t)$. Likewise, derivatives show that $i_b(t) + s(t)$ is a decreasing function :

$$\frac{d(i_b(t) + s(t))}{dt} = -\beta i_g(t)(i_b(t) + s(t)).$$

If the nullifying defense scans are stopped at t_s with $s(t_s) \geq i_g(t_s)$ we are assured that the peak scanning rate of the system is

$$\max\{i_b(t_s) + i_g(t_s), i_b(t_s) + s(t_s)\}.$$

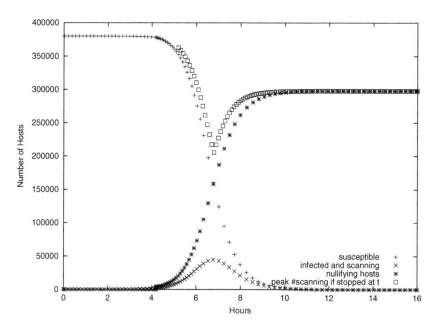

Fig. 2. Peak bandwidth used by the nullifying defense (and original worm) as a function of when it is switched off

So long as the first argument is increasing and the second argument is decreasing, the stopping time that minimizes the maximum occurs when the arguments are equal, e.g., when $i_g(t) = s(t)$; since $i_b(t) + i_g(t)$ is still monotone at this point, t_s minimizing the peak aggregate scanning rate satisfies $i_g(t_s) = s(t_s)$.

We are in a position now to quantify the performance of a defensive worm. We can show that the minimal peak number of hosts scanning is at least $(1/3)(s(0) + I_0)$, provided that $I_0 \geq i_b(T_0)$, a result which we state formally.

Theorem 4. *Consider a nullifying defense that is launched at time T_0 with $I_0 \geq i_b(T_0)$ initial instances, and whose scans can be stopped on command. The stopping time t_s which minimizes peak scanning is the unique solution to $i_g(t_s) = s(t_s)$. A lower bound on the peak number of hosts scanning is $(1/3)(s(0) + I_0)$.*

Proof. We first note that under the assumption $I_0 = i_g(T_0) > i_b(T_0)$, that $i_g(t) \geq i_b(t)$ for all $t \geq T_0$. This is a result of both the worm and the counter-worm competing for exactly the same pool of susceptible hosts—at the same rate (per host)—with the counter-worm starting with at least as many hosts as are in the infection at the time the counter-worm is released. A consequence is that the time t_s when $s(t_s) = i_g(t_s)$ occurs before the time t_b that $s(t_b) = i_b(t_b)$. This fact turns out to be important as we ask for conditions under which $i_g(t) \geq i_n(t)$, where $i_n(t)$ is the number of infected hosts that have been nullified. We know that $i_g(T_0) > i_n(T_0)$; analysis of the derivative of $i_g(t) - i_n(t)$ shows that this difference grows so long as $s(t) \geq i_b(t)$—a condition which can only occur after the stopping time t_s. Finally, we note the invariant

$$i_b(t) + i_g(t) + i_n(t) + s(t) = s(0) + I_0.$$

At the stopping time, $s(t_s) = i_g(t_s)$, and $i_g(t_s) > i_n(t_s)$, whence

$$i_b(t_s) + 3i_g(t_s) > s(0) + I_0.$$

It follows that $i_b(t_s) + i_g(t_s) > (1/3)(s(0) + I_0)$. □

We see that under the theorem's assumptions, the capabilities nullifying defensives have over spreading-patch defenses (suppress an infected host's scans, stop the "good worm" scanning) serve to give it greater power, but the peak number of hosts scanning (both worm and counter-worm) is still at least one third of the initial susceptible population. It should be noted that this result depends signficantly on an assumption that the counter-worm's scan rate is identical to the worm's. We are exploring the consequences of relaxing this assumption, as well as pushing on looking for ways of countering worms with increasing power, while reducing the impact on the network.

5   Conclusions

This paper studies active defenses against Internet worms. We use discrete and continuous mathematical models to study a hierarchy of worm fighting capabilities. We are able to prove a number of results about these models, including

- strong stochastic ordering of infection counts in a hierarchy of five defense types;
- that a simple counter-worm defense has a stochastically larger aggregate scanning intensity than does the unfettered worm;
- that by starting a defense with enough outside hosts scanning to implant counter-worms, any desired fraction of the remaining susceptible hosts can be protected from a worm;
- that by starting a nullifying defense with few enough outside hosts, the peak scanning intensity is less than the unfettered worm;
- even when peak scanning time is minimized under the nullifying defense, it is still the case that the peak number of hosts scanning is at least 1/3 of the total number of susceptibles;

There is much work yet to be done. This paper does not address the very significant problem of quickly and automatically *detecting* when a worm attack has been launched—we have looked only at the relative effectiveness of measures put into place after the detection. Our experiments of effectiveness of defense *as a function of response time* (Figure 1) show that rapid detection is absolutely critical.

Acknowledgements

This research was supported under Award number 2000-DT-CX-K001 from the U.S. Department of Homeland Security, Science and Technology Directorate.

Points of view in this document are those of the author(s) and do not necessarily represent the official position of the U.S. Department of Homeland Security or the Science and Technology Directorate. In addition this research was supported by SPAWAR contract N66001-04-C-6013. Accordingly, the U.S. Government retains a non-exclusive, royalty-free license to publish or reproduce the published form of this contribution, or allow others to do so, for U.S. Government purposes.

References

1. Chen, Z., Gao, L., Kwiat, K.: Modeling the spread of active worms. In *INFOCOM 2003* (2003)
2. Cisco. Dealing with mallocfail and high cpu utilization resulting from the "code red" worm. http://www.cisco.com/warp/public/-63/ts_codred_worm.shtml (October 2001)
3. Daley, D.J., Gani, J.: *Epidemic Modelling: An Introduction.* Cambridge University Press, Cambridge, UK (1999)
4. Ferrie, P., Perriot, F., Sz or, P.: Worm wars. *Virus Bulletin* (www.virusbtn.com), Oct 2003. http://www.peterszor.com/welchia.pdf [Last accessed Oct 01, 2003
5. Liljenstam, M., Nicol, D., Berk, V., Gray, B.: Simulating realistic network worm traffic for worm warning system design and testing. In *in Proc. of the First ACM Workshop on Rapid Malcode (WORM'03)* (Oct 2003)
6. Moore, D., Shannon, C., Claffy, K.: Code-red: a case study on the spread and victims of an internet worm. In *in Proc. of the Internet Measurement Workshop (IMW)*, Marseille, France, Nov 2002. ACM Press
7. Moore, D., Shannon, C., Voelker, G., Savage, S.: Internet quarantine: Requirements for containing self-propagating code. In *Proceedings of the 22nd Annual Joint Conference of the IEEE Computer and Communications Societies (INFOCOM 2003)* (April 2003)
8. Nicol, D. M., Yan, G.: Simulation of network traffic at coarse time-scales. In *Proceedings of the 2005 Conference on Principles of Advanced and Distributed Simulation* (2005)
9. Ross, H.S.: *Stochastic Processes.* Wiley, New York (1983)
10. Staniford, S.:   Code Red Analysis Pages: July infestation analysis. http://www.silicondefense.com/cr/july.html (2001)
11. Staniford, S., Paxson, V., Weaver, N.:   How to Own the Internet in Your Spare Time. In *in Proc. of the USENIX Security Symposium* (2002) http://www.icir.org/vern/papers/cdc-usenix-sec02/index.html.
12. Zou, C., Gao, L., Gong, W., Towsley, D.: Code red worm propagation modeling and analysis. In *9th ACM Conference on Computer and Communication Security (CCS)*, Washington DC (Nov 2002)
13. Zou, C., Gao, L., Gong, W., Towsley, D.: Monitoring and early warning for internet worms. In *Proceedings of 10th ACM Conference on Computer and Communication Security (CCS'03)* (2003)
14. Zou, C., Gong, W., Towsley, D.: Worm propagation modeling and analysis. In *Proceedings of the First ACM Workshop on Rapid Malcode (WORM)* (2003)

Prevention of Information Attacks by Run-Time Detection of Self-replication in Computer Codes

Douglas Summerville, Victor Skormin, Alexander Volynkin,
and James Moronski

Binghamton University, Binghamton NY 13902, USA
{dsummer, vskormin}@binghamton.edu,
alex@volynkin.com, jim@moronski.com

Abstract. This paper describes a novel approach for preventative protection from both known and previously unknown malicious executable codes. It does not rely on screening the code for signatures of known viruses, but instead it detects attempts of the executable code in question to self-replicate during run time. Self-replication is the common feather of most malicious codes, allowing them to maximize their impact. This approach is an extension of the earlier developed method for detecting previously unknown viruses in script based computer codes. The paper presents a software tool implementing this technique for behavior-based run-time detection and suspension of self-replicating functionality in executable codes for Microsoft Windows operating systems.

1 Introduction

Due to its high interconnectivity, global dimensions and very large number of entry points, the Internet is increasingly vulnerable to information attacks of escalating sophistication. Any biological system, being gigantic in terms of complexity, interconnectivity and number of entry points, is also vulnerable to sabotage by foreign microorganisms, which are, in many ways, similar to information attacks. The proliferation of biological systems in spite of these attacks can be explained by their very effective defense mechanisms capable of the detection, identification, and destruction of most foreign entities that could have an adverse effect on the system. The ability of immune mechanisms to reliably differentiate between "self" and "non-self" at the protein level inspired the authors to utilize the concepts of genetic composition and genetically-programmed behavior as the basis for the development of a novel approach to the detection of malicious software [1].

Most information attacks are carried out via Internet transmission of files that contain the code of a computer virus or worm. Upon receipt, the target computer executes the malicious code resulting in the reproduction of the virus or worm and the delivery of its potentially destructive payload. Self-replication, which is uncommon in legitimate programs, is vital to the spread of computer viruses and worms allowing them to create computer epidemics thus maximizing the effectiveness of the attack. As with any function, self-replication is programmed; the sequence of operations resulting in the self-replication is present in the computer code of the virus. The

V. Gorodetsky, I. Kotenko, and V. Skormin (Eds.): MMM-ACNS 2005, LNCS 3685, pp. 54–75, 2005.

implementation of the function of self-replication is not unique; there is more than one sequence of operations that can perform this task. Moreover, it is expected that these sequences are dispersed throughout the entire body of the code and cannot be detected as an explicit pattern. While self-replication can be achieved in a number of different ways, this number is definitely finite. Consequently, developers of new malicious codes are destined to utilize the same self-replication techniques again and again.

Previously we developed the computer virus detection system based on these principles [2], [3]. This system is able to detect the *gene of self-replication* (*GSR*) in most script viruses written in Visual Basic, Java and other high-level script languages. However, there was still a large family of viruses that could not be successfully detected by this technique, as it was unable to deal with regular and, especially, encrypted compiled executable code. While the same principle could still be instrumental, its different implementation had to be developed for extracting self-replication sequences from such viruses. The technology presented herein is applicable to the most common and difficult, in terms of detection, computer viruses and worms which are represented by an already compiled, often encrypted, executable code; the detection is conducted at run-time during normal code execution under regular conditions by monitoring the behavior of every process with regards to the operating system's system calls, their input and output arguments and the result of their execution. Unlike existing antivirus software, this methodology facilitates preventative protection from both known and previously unknown attacks.

The authors do realize that a very sophisticated attacker can further modify the self-replication mechanism and are prepared to face the next step in the ever-escalating "arms race".

2 Background

Modern computers are designed for a wide variety of purposes, frequently to be accommodated by a single machine. Allowing for such unification and scalability requires an increasingly complex computer software and hardware infrastructure. Currently, this infrastructure is facilitated by a computer operating system, which abstracts details of the hardware from application software. Applications (programs) interface with the operating system through the Kernel Application Programming Interface, or *system calls*. Therefore, system calls do play a major role in the interaction between the software and the operating system characterizing the behavior of both malicious and legitimate computer programs.

Unlike legitimate programs, malicious software performs operations that adversely affect various hardware/software system components. There are a vast number of operations that can be considered malicious and generally speaking, could be detected within the sequence of system calls. However, the sequence of system calls produced by an application can be huge and the malicious operation can be dispersed throughout the sequence, making run-time detection a non-trivial task. Self-replication is a function common to the most insidious malicious programs, including all viruses and worms that cause computer epidemics maximizing the impact of an information attack. Thus, the search for malicious programs can be narrowed to the search for self-replication activity in the sequences of system calls.

The concept of detecting the *GSR* is generic in its nature; therefore it can be applied to any computer system without necessarily binding it to a specific operating system. The remainder of this paper deals specifically with the Microsoft Windows® operating system, but the basic principles can be applied to any operating system on any computer hardware platform.

When dealing with system calls in Windows® kernel, it is important to realize that a system call by itself is a rather complicated entity. Apart from the call to a specific interface there are also many important parameters passed, such as the origin of the system call (process and thread identifiers), control flags, input arguments, data structures, output parameters and the result of call execution. All of these parameters must be taken into consideration for the detection of self-replication activity.

3   Definition of the Gene of Self-replication

The *GSR* is viewed as a specific sequence of commands passed to the computer operating system by certain program code that causes this code to replicate itself through the system or multiple systems. Replication can be accomplished in several ways depending on a particular computer system as well as the software the system is running. For example, computer viruses designed for the Microsoft DOS® operating system utilized direct access to hardware for this purpose. With the widespread introduction of microprocessors that allowed for different privilege level accesses, and operating systems supporting and enforcing these access levels facilitated new methods of self-replication. Computer viruses began employing different software APIs, from hijacking a simple email client API to interfacing very complex OS. Nevertheless, the most sophisticated and versatile viruses are still implemented in assembly language (ASM) and assembled into executable files. Since computer viruses are expected to self-replicate and this task cannot be accomplished without interfacing the operating system, monitoring and analyzing system calls to certain OS APIs provides the means for the detection of this common feature of malicious software.

3.1 GSR Structure

Virtually every process running in the system produces system calls; however they are not mixed and can easily be differentiated for every process and thread. In all cases, system calls, generated at run time, represent a direct time line sequence of events, which can be analyzed during the execution. For any given process, this sequence can be large or relatively small depending on what system resources it is trying to access. The *GSR* is contained within the sequence produced by a malicious process and it could be dispersed throughout that sequence.

Since none of the system calls alone can be considered malicious, only the particular sub-sequences of calls can form the *GSR*. As per [3], the *GSR* is described using the concept of building blocks, where each block performs a part of the chosen self-replication procedure. This concept is illustrated in Fig. 1. Most of the building blocks involved in malicious self-replication activity can individually be performed by any piece software for a variety of legitimate reasons. Only when integrated into larger structures and based on their inter-functional relationships, these building blocks are indicative of attempts to self-replicate.

The *GSR* can be composed of such blocks in various ways. Therefore its structure can be viewed as a regular sentence being built up by concatenating phrases, where phrases are built up by concatenating words, and words are built up by concatenating characters.

One of the major reasons for applying such a syntactic approach to describing the *GSR* is to facilitate the recognition of sub-patterns. This implies the recognition of smaller building blocks first, establishing their relevance and contribution to the replication, and then considering the next sub-pattern. This process is consistent with text analysis, which includes recognizing characters first, then concatenating them into words, running a spell checker on an entire word to check for mistakes, then continue concatenating words into phrases and sentences checking for correct grammar and punctuation. The syntactic description of the *GSR* provides a capability for describing and detecting large sets of complex patterns by using small subsets of simple pattern primitives. It is also possible to apply such a description any number of times to express the basic structures of a number of *gene mutations* in a very compact way.

Following the concept of syntactic description the *GSR* structure could be represented using the grammar definition notations [4]:

$$G = \{V_N, V_T, P, S\} \tag{1}$$

where,

G	- gene of self-replication
V_N	- non-terminal variable
V_T	- terminal variable
P	- finite set of rules
S	- starting point of the *gene*

Assuming, that the *GSR* is represented by the pyramidal structure (Fig.1), the non-terminal variable V_N in the expression above can be expressed as:

$$V_N = \begin{cases} \langle \text{Gene\_of\_self\_replication} \rangle, \langle \text{File\_Search\_Block} \rangle, \langle \text{File\_Copy\_Block} \rangle, \\ \langle \text{Directory\_System\_Call} \rangle, \langle \text{Open\_File\_System\_Call} \rangle, \langle \text{Create\_File\_System\_Call} \rangle, \\ \langle \text{Write\_File\_System\_Call} \rangle \end{cases} \tag{2}$$

The terminal variable V_T represents the *GSR* sequence:

$$V_T = \{ZwQueryDirectoryFile(...), ZwOpenFile(...), ZwCreateFile(...), ZwWriteFile(...)\} \tag{3}$$

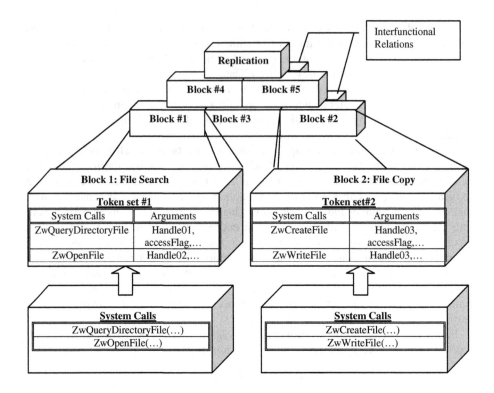

Fig. 1. *GSP* pyramidal structure

The sum of V_N and V_T forms the complete vocabulary $V(G) = V_N \cup V_T$, and the intersection of V_N and V_T is indeed an empty set, $V_N \cap V_T = O$.

The set of rules P is expressed as $\alpha \rightarrow \beta$, where α and β interconnections in V so that α involves at least one simplest block in V_N.

Finally, $S \in V_N$ represents the starting point in V_N, which corresponds to the $\langle Gene\_of\_self\_replication \rangle$ in the structure above.

3.2 Details

In spite of the apparent simplicity of the above structure, in order to accurately describe the *GSR* the relations between different blocks and system calls could be very complex. Our research shows that in some cases, the margin between malicious activity and normal behavior is quite narrow and the differentiation requires fine-tuning of inter-functional relations.

Normally, a single system call has a unique CID that identifies it to the kernel, a number of input arguments, a number of output arguments to be generated upon completion of the system call execution, and the indicator of the result of the execution. Also, every system call carries IDs of the process (PID) and the thread (TID) from where the call has been originated. The structure of the system call is depicted below:

PID	TID	CID	Input Arguments	Output Arguments	Result

Input arguments, as well as output arguments may include any data structures, allowed by the system, such as numerical values, flags, object handles, and data strings. Some of these arguments indicate direct relations among different system calls that could be utilized to bind system calls together to define the *GSR*. The following is an example of binding two system calls together by their arguments to form a single building block of the *GSR*:

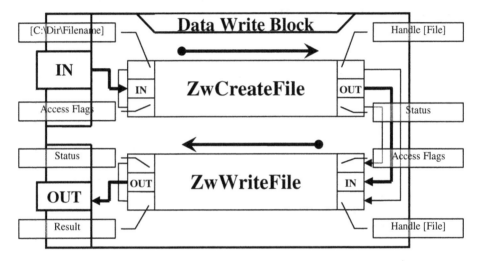

Fig. 2. *GSR* Building Block Internal Structure

In this case, "Data Write Block" is derived from two basic system calls ZwCreateFile and ZwWriteFile. The unit is responsible for writing specific data into a newly created file. System calls inside the block are linked together by several key parameters. For this particular block we consider the following three parameters to play the key role in identifying the correct pair of block's internals:

- Object Name / Path
- Object Access Flags
- Object Handle

The file system operates on files in a number of different ways, but with only a few system calls. Therefore, it needs to define strict regulations for every key system call, specifying what exactly that system call is expected to do with the file. A number of flags are supported by almost every system call; most of these flags are designed to specify Access Rights to be applied by the system call onto the target object, the file in this particular case. For example, in order to create a file for writing, the "Generic

Write" flag has to be set to "HIGH". There are also several other important flags to be set, such as File Attributes Flag "Normal" – specifies an attribute for a newly created file to Normal, Share Access "Write" – specifies the limitations on sharing the file, File Create Disposition flag defines what to do with the file in case it already exists, etc.

Another important link parameter is the Object Handle. Files, as well as many other resources, are considered to be an Object type by the operating system. Therefore, every time a process creates a new object, it receives a unique access handle, which facilitates fast access to this object within the process and by other processes as well. The usage of this handle is obvious, since it is created by a system call and it links to an object, any time another system call uses this handle, it is trying to gain access to the object, and therefore, the given system calls are related. In the case of Data Write Block, ZwCreateFile creates the handle upon completion of the call execution. Later, this handle (Handle [File]) is used by another call, ZwWriteFile, in order to write data into a file, represented by that handle.

Finally, when two system calls are properly linked together, the inputs of the first system call become the inputs of the entire block, and likewise the block inherits the outputs of the last system call. Then, the structure forms one solid block of the pyramid with its own inputs and outputs, and is ready to be included as a unit into a larger structure.

While defining connections between different blocks or system calls, it is important to realize, that some of the larger blocks, created as a result of this combination, are likely to serve legitimate purposes of any regular program. This is expected, since computer viruses tend to employ the same kind of techniques for accessing operating system infrastructure. However, regular computer programs would never call these blocks in a particular order with particular input parameters. At the same time, some blocks are very typical for computer viruses. These considerations provide the basis for the *GSR* definition.

3.3 Detection Mechanism

Since the *GSR* structure is defined in terms of sub-patterns similar to the structure of a sentence with its phrases, words and characters, the automata theory for text recognition is applicable for *GSR* detection.

A finite-state machine A represents a quintuple $A = \{\Sigma, Q, \delta, q_0, F\}$

where,

Σ - finite set of simple input blocks

Q - finite set of states

δ - mapping of $\Sigma \times Q$ into Q_{n+1}

q_0 - the initial state, such that $q_0 \in Q$

F - set of final states, such that $F \subseteq Q$

According to [4], it is possible to define a finite-state automata $A = \{V_T, V_N \cup \{T\}, \delta, S, F\}$ with $T(A) = L(G)$, if $G = \{V_N, V_T, P, S\}$, defined above, is a finite-state *GSR* expression. Since P always contains relation rule for S when detecting a *GSR*, the set of final states F contains S, such that $F = \{S, T\}$. Therefore, the finite-state machine can be constructed for *GSR* detection purposes, so that all replication combination that are accepted by the automata are, in fact, in the state space of a phrase-structure language defined as $L(G)$. This language is to be generated by the *GSR* grammar in the following way:

$$L(G) = \{x \mid x \in V_T\}, \text{ such that } S \xrightarrow[G]{} x, \tag{4}$$

Where, x is a replication building block, and $S \xrightarrow[G]{} x$ implies that x is directly derived by another building block S, such that both x and S follow the rule P by yielding $S = \omega_1 \alpha \omega_2$ and $x = \omega_1 \beta \omega_2$, where $\alpha \to \beta$ by the definition of P.

A complex computer operating system such as Microsoft Windows XP receives hundreds of calls every second from many different processes. Most of the function calls, produced by an application in *user mode* deal with secure objects and hardware resources such as File System, Processes and Threads, Graphical System Services, System Registry, etc., are transferred into the Kernel mode of the operating system for further execution in secure environment. During this process, function calls are processed into system calls for unification, compatibility, security and other reasons. At the Kernel level, system calls are processed by System Service Dispatcher (SSD) and routed to a designated service. The internal structure of system call dispatching is even more complex and is not a subject of this paper.

The Operating System in question provides us with almost no support for monitoring its Kernel level for security reasons; therefore such a software monitor has to be created. While it is not a trivial task, as it requires very low-level system design and implementation, the very basic idea for the monitor is shown in figure 3.

When Kernel receives a function call from user mode, it has to decide which Kernel interface to call to process this function. The API Processing Unit also known as System Service Dispatcher (KiSystemService) is responsible for making this decision by looking up an appropriate system call handler in its System Service Table (SST), which stores handlers to every system call supported by the Kernel, and invoking it. However, if the handler to a particular system call in SST is replaced with a fake one pointing to other memory location, System Service Dispatcher will simply execute a different function at that location. This extra function can be designed to gather information about the system call, its parameters and the origin. When all needed information is collected, the function calls the original system call and the entire system proceeds as usual.

All system calls, once invoked at the Kernel level, are expected to produce a result, whether it was successful or not. This result is represented by the output arguments of the system call, as well as the return value that confirms successful execution, or indicates errors. All system calls, intercepted by the monitor, appear in two parts: system call with input arguments and system call with output arguments.

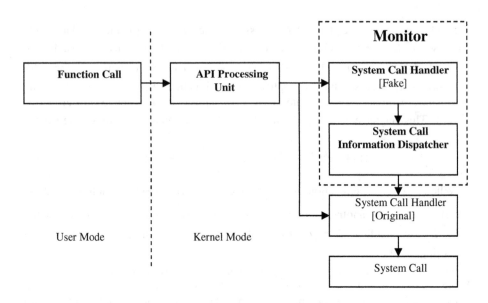

Fig. 3. Functionality of the System Calls Monitor

Table 1. Typical system call layout

Process ID			1023
Thread ID			1
System Call			NtCreateFile
Input Arguments	Access Mask		11000000000100000000000 010000000 (bin)
	Object attributes	Length	24
		Dir pointer	12
		Object Name	"virus.exe"
		Attributes	1000000 (bin) (Obj_Case_Insensitive)
		Security Descriptor	0
		SecurityQoS	0
	Allocation Size		0
	File Attributes		10000000 (bin) (NORMAL)
	Share Access		0
	Create Disposition		1 (FILE_OPEN)
	Create Options		1100000 (bin)
	Buffer		NULL
	Buffer Length		0
Output Arguments	File Handle		56
	Status Block	status	0
		info	1 (FILE_OPENED)
Result			0 (SUCCESS)

Our research shows, that sometimes the information a system call returns as a result of its execution is even more important than incoming arguments for the purpose of virus detection. Table 1 shows a typical system call layout as it goes through our monitor.

Having the information, observed by the monitor, it is possible to conclude, that Thread #1 that belongs to Process #1023 invoked a system call named NtCreateFile for the purpose of opening a file named "virus.exe". Upon completion of call execution, the file was successfully opened and a unique handle,56, was assigned for further access to that file.

In order to detect if such a call belongs to any parts of the virus' self replication, we have to consider most of its input and output arguments. While obviously, any system call by itself with all possible combinations of input/output arguments cannot be considered as a threat, we believe that certain APIs called with certain arguments when combined do present a clear pattern of self replication.

During the *GSR* detection process, every system call intercepted by our monitor comes right into the Replication Detector, where it goes thought a complete range of different detection and filtration mechanisms. Following the concept of decoupling of *Gene* definition, presented in the previous part of this paper, the detection process is also highly decoupled to ensure compatibility and to reduce false detections. Just like the *GSR* is formed from many different building blocks, the detection mechanism observes and makes decisions regarding every block separately, until it finally reaches the top of the *GPR* pyramid structure and declares the alarm state. Below is a brief diagram of detection algorithm for a single block:

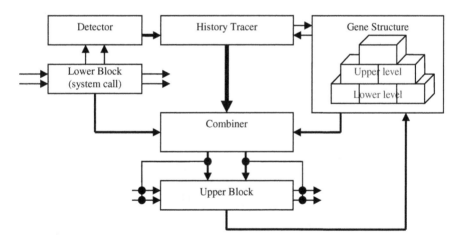

Fig. 4. Detection Algorithm for abnormal behavior

As soon as a system call is detected, the History Tracer communicates with the database, where the GSP Structure is defined, to determine whether or not this system call can be combined with any other lower level blocks to form a larger structure. When such combination is possible, the Combiner takes two chosen lower level blocks and forms a single upper level block so that its inputs are identical to the inputs of the Lower Block taken from the history, and the outputs are inherited from the newly detected Lower Block. When new Upper Block is finally formed, the history is updated and the algorithm repeats itself, but with regards to this newly created block. At every repetition, the detection is taking place at a higher level, as though climbing up the pyramidal structure.

4 Experiments

The concept of *GSR* definition explained earlier requires building a pyramidal structure with basic system calls at the bottom, combinations of calls represented by Blocks in the middle, and the *GSR* itself at the top. While usually replication is not a very complicated process, it may involve a number of steps, and among them the system calls dominate greatly. Therefore, the complexity of *GSR* definition depends on several facts:

– The number of unique system calls involved.
– The number of inter-functional relations among system calls.
– The complexity of inter-functional relations.

Table 2. Replication schemes for major types of computer viruses

Replication Type	Details	Replication Scheme
Overwriting	Virus overwrites an existing executable by replacing its content with the body of the virus	1. Read "Virus.exe" 2. Open "Host.exe" 3. Write "Virus.exe" into "Host.exe" 4. Close "Host.exe"
Companion	Virus renames an existing executable and replaces the original with itself	1. Read "Host.exe" name 2. Rename "Host.exe" into "Host.ex" 3. Rename "Virus.exe" into "Host.exe"
Parasitic	Virus attaches itself to an existing file by injecting its code into the body of the executable and replacing code entry points	1. Open "Virus.exe" 2. Read "Virus.exe" Code 3. Open "Host.exe" 4. Inject Code into "Host.exe" 5. Patch "Host.exe" Entry point

Since the margin between malicious and normal behavior can be small, it is important to keep the complexity of the *GSR* at the high level whenever possible in order to avoid misdetections. On the other hand, some flexibility when connecting blocks of the *GSR* is needed as well; otherwise the approach becomes less generic.

Computer viruses, implemented as executables have enough flexibility when interfacing with the operating system to replicate in several different ways. In our experiments we consider three basic types of virus replication:

- Overwriting existing files (Overwriting viruses).
- Creating new look-alike files (Companion viruses).
- Attaching to existing files (Parasitic viruses).

These three types of replication are sorted by simplicity of implementation, with Overwriting viruses being the simplest. Table 2 presents details for every type, as well as their simplified replication schemes.

All viruses, falling under these categories, require low-level access to system resources, and therefore are detectable. However, categories have to be identified first and described in terms of the *GSR*. A way to establish the *GSR* is to acquire samples of a real live virus, extract self-replication behavior and process the leads. Viral behavior acquisition was done in an isolated controlled environment running Windows XP operating system, under surveillance of our system calls monitoring system. Apart from maintaining a sufficient system security level, one of the acquisition problems we have encountered was the elimination of noise from other concurrently running processes. The most suitable solution found was to introduce a per-process monitoring and detection scheme, where every signal detected by the monitor gets traced back to its origin, the process ID. Therefore, every signal is associated with a unique process so that signals coming from different sources do not mix.

As an example virus with parasitic behavior, we consider a classic internet worm "I-Worm.Xanax". This is a small worm, capable of replicating onto Windows system executable files. When executed, the worm searches for .EXE files in the Windows directory and replicates onto them while changing the entry point of the file. The virus follows the replication algorithm accordingly, and makes a total of 639 calls to the operating system. As it passes through the monitor, we observe some replication related activity among many others, such as self-access by consequently opening the source directory "Virlab" on local disk "C":

```
NtOpenFile  100020h,    {24,    0,    42h,    0,    0,      1
"\??\c:\Virlab\"}, 3, 33 ... 12, 0h, 1) result = 0
```

The execution of this call completed successfully, introducing a new directory handle. Later, this handle is used when accessing the contents of this directory. Indeed, after throwing some garbage into the system, the virus invokes another suspicious command by trying to open itself for reading:

```
NtCreateFile 80100080h, {24, 12, 42h, 0, 1243404,       2
"xanax.exe"}, 0h, 128, 3, 1, 96, 0, 0 ... 68, 0h,
1) result = 0
```

Once again, upon successful execution, a new handle, #68, is created, which points itself. According to our definition of the structure for the *GSR*, we may bind these two calls and form a larger structure representing a *File Access Block*. These calls are then bound by several different important parameters such as the directory handle and input flags shown in grey above. When bound, the new structure inherits input parameters from its first component, as well as output parameters from its second component.

In the same manner, after locating a target host file, the virus is expected to open it and append the viral body to the host so that the control over code execution gets passed over to the viral code. In our experimental run of the virus, it was able to locate the "Windows" directory, a very common target for viruses due to a very high probability of infecting the most important and frequently run system files and utilities. While searching for a host to infect, the virus invokes another pair of system calls to locate an executable. This pair forms another replication block called *Host Search Block*:

Table 3. Virus searching for executable file in Windows folder

System Call	Input Arguments	Output Args	
NtOpenFil[File Extension]4, 0, 0x40, 0, 0, ??\C:\WINDOWS\""}, ⌐, 46417		12, {0x0,1}	3
NtQueryDirectoryFile 12	0, 0, 0, 1243364, 616, 3, 1, "<.exe", 0	{0x0,110 }	4

The next step in the replication is to read itself and append itself to the host file. Since the virus knows perfectly well its own location (output handle # 68 of File Access Block), it easily executes yet another pair of system calls to map itself into a memory location 980000h:

Table 4. Virus maps its body into memory

System Call¤	Input Arguments¤	Output Args¤	¤	¤
NtCreateSect⌐ 0xf001f¤ [Virus Handle¶]0h, 0h, 2, 7728, 68¤		72¤	5¤	¤
NtMapViewOfSection 72¤	-1, 0h, 0, 0, {0, 0}, 0, 1, 0, 2¤	0x980000, 0,0,36864¤	6¤	¤
	Section Handle¶			

The memory mapping routine pair allows for defining another replication building block named *Memory Mapping Block*. Since this block requires a file handle as an input parameter, which in turn is provided by the File Access Block constructed earlier, these two blocks are bound into a new higher-level structure named *File-in-Memory Block*. As usual, the block inherits inputs and outputs of the two parenting structures.

Finally, when the virus is in memory and the victim file is identified, another set of system calls is required for completing a successful replication, the set that is responsible for actually writing the viral code into the host body. However, since overwriting the host with the virus code would trigger an alarm for to the user, clearly implying that something is going wrong with the system, it is much more elegant to append viral body to the host and change code entry pointers in such a way that the viral code gets executed first, then passing control back to the original host, allowing for regular file execution. Therefore, the virus in question needs to open the host, locate the correct section for viral code injection and finally append its code by executing an NtWriteFile system call:

Table 5. Virus injects its code into the host

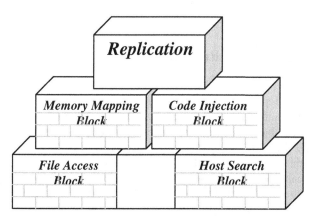

System Call	Input Argum Victim file	Output Args
NtCreateFile 0x40110080	{24, 0, 40h, 0, 124⟋ 58, "\??\C:\WINDOWS\calc.exe" }, 0h, 32, 0, 5, 100, 0, 0	52, {0h,3}
NtSetInformationFi le 52	1241948, 8, 20 End Of File	, 0}
NtWriteFile 52	0, 0, 0, "MZ\220\0\3\0\0\0\4\0\0\0 ⟋77\37..... \0\0\0". 33792, Viral Code 0h, 0 Code Size	{0h, 33792}

This set of calls, while being the last sequence in replication, also form the final block for GSR Pyramid, called the *Code Injection Block*. It inherits its input parameters from its first system call NtCreateFile, while the outputs of NtWriteFile become its output arguments. These four blocks form the final structure — *The Gene of Self Replication*:

Fig. 5. Final replication behavior structure of a virus

The graph below shows the replication timeline along with the system calls related to the replication for Xanax worm. There are two visible replication attempts, one of which has been successful, reaching the top of the pyramid – the replication point.

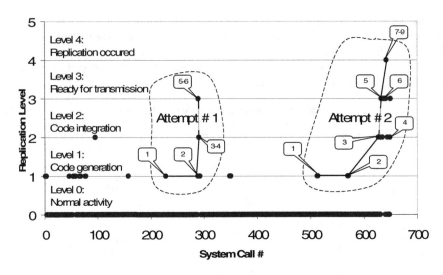

Fig. 6. Sample Virus Replication Data (648 points, 2 attempts)

There are certainly other ways to follow exactly the same algorithm and execute a successful replication, such as using virtual memory for data swapping instead of the direct memory access, etc. Also, there are still two more types of replication (see Table 2) to be covered. There could be many attempts to obfuscate virus code for the purpose of misleading the detector (i.e. changing object handles on-the-fly before), however these attempts are easily traceable by the detector since they are also implemented at a low level with the use of system calls. Finally, the block structure of the *GSR* allows for detection of many different replication sequences of the same Gene by simply rearranging building blocks in the *GSR* definition.

5 Parts of Gene of Self Replication in Legitimate Code

While most computer viruses and worms capable of self-replication are believed to be detectable by their replication activity, there is always a considerable number of non-viral, fully legitimate pieces of software that have to pass through the monitor undetected and be able to continue their legitimate actions. After all, the system calls used to identify the *GSR* are all created to serve these "good" programs. Our major assumption in this research is that this legitimate software never tries to replicate itself through any means of communication, either through local disk propagation or remote network communication. This means that the GSR has to be designed in such a way that it only incorporates replication blocks from the beginning to the end, as legitimate code is never supposed to follow replication completely. However, it is expected, that legitimate software may contain some parts of the *GSR*, and this can and should be detected in case that the software starts expressing suspicious behavior.

Testing the detector on legitimate processes was a part of the experiment. In this attempt we were trying to show how close to detection a regular non-infected process can get. Windows native service process svchost is a good common example of a regular system process running constantly in the background. This process is actually a generic host process name representing different services currently running, and therefore can do virtually any operation within the system including access to files, networks, internet, etc. Upon invocation, svchost interacts with the system in order to load a file into memory, the algorithm and implementation of such an action is very similar to the virus described above, however there are some differences:

```
NtCreateFile 80100080h, {24, 0, 40h, 0, 14678832,  | 2
"\??\C:\WINDOWS\Prefetch\CMD.EXE-087B4001.pf""}, 0h,
0, 0h, 1, 96, 0, 0, ... 2080, 0h, 1) result = 0
```

Here the file is opened with the same system call and even the same access mask (80100080h), however the file object does not propagate its handle to any children processes (flag 40h), nor is it opened with "Read" and "Write" share access flags (0h). But the main difference in these two system calls is that svchost, being a legitimate process, does not open itself, instead it is working with other files within the system.

There is a definite similarity between two processes when it comes to working with memory objects, which is a normal procedure, and most processes are expected to have it done in the same manner:

Table 6. Memory operation in a legitimate program

System Call	Input Arguments	Output Args	
NtCreateSection 0xf0005	0h, 0h, 2, 134217728, 2080	4080	5
NtMapViewOfSection 4080	-1, 0h, 0, 0, {0, 0}, 0, 1, 0, 2	0xf70000, 0,0,8192	6
	Section Handle		

Therefore, there is a probability for the Memory Mapping Block above to be detected even in non-malicious programs, but this one block, as well as many other blocks in *GSR* structure such as Code Injection Block, by itself in no way represents the entire *GSR* Pyramid.

Finally, the graph below represents the timeline for the legitimate process svchost as it goes through approximately 240 instructions, many of which in one way or another relate to some parts of the *GSR* structure. However, process actions never reach the replication level.

While comparing these two graphs representing two different processes, the difference in their behavior is obvious. It is expected from a legitimate process to generate a behavior similar to that of a virus when operating on files and directories, as they have to use the same API. However the malicious process clearly goes all the way to the end of the replication procedure on its second attempt, while the legitimate process, expressing normal behavior, never goes beyond Level 2 no matter how many "attempts" it makes.

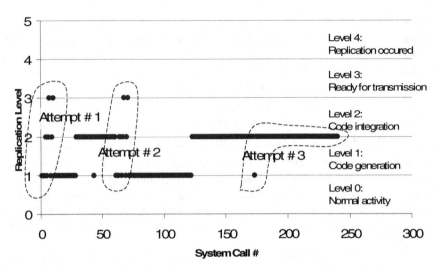

Fig. 7. Sample legitimate code activity graph 240 points, (3 attempts)

5.1 Replication over the Local Network and the Internet

Ever since computers started communicating with each other using local networks, virus writers have exploited this feature. Indeed, networking opens endless possibilities for a virus to replicate itself to as many computer systems as it possibly can within the network instead of just infecting a limited number of files on a host machine. Such a remote replication is possible with the use of specific network protocols administrated by the operating system.

Theoretically speaking, replication over the network is almost identical to local replication with the only difference being the necessity for a computer virus to enumerate available network resources before it can access target files on a remote computer. Therefore, a complete algorithm of virus replication for a parasitic virus, which attaches itself to an existing file by injecting its code into the body of the executable and replacing code entry points, would look as follows:

1. Open "Virus.exe"
2. Read "Virus.exe" Code
3. Enumerate network resources
4. Open remote "Host.exe"
5. Inject Code into "Host.exe"
6. Patch "Host.exe" Entry point

Hence, it is only required to add one block into the Gene's syntax describing Network resources enumeration in order for the detector to recognize the behavior. However, enumeration can be accomplished in several different ways such as:

- Sockets
- Remote Procedure Calls
- Named pipes
- NetBIOS
- Other networking APIs

A very good example of network communication via Named Pipes can be observed in the behavior of a family of parasitic viruses named EfishNC[1] [5], the "C" version of this virus uses named pipes when trying to communicate to other computers on the network. While the actual source code for resource enumeration via named pipes is only a couple of lines, the operating system has to take care of most of the communication. Thus, the algorithm for named pipes from the OS' point of view would be as follows:

1. Open a pipe as a file object
2. Set appropriate information affecting the pipe
3. Send a request for resource enumeration to the pipe
4. Receive enumerated shares of a remote computer
5. Proceed with regular replication

All the events listed above are accomplished by consequently invoking regular file management system calls with specific parameters as illustrated in table 7.

Communication through the means of Named Pipe "PIPE\srvsvc" presented above requires several valid handles to be produced during sequence execution. First, a file object has to be created with NtCreateFile pointing to a remote machine (BU-SY46Q9D3MCQ2), this file object is assigned with a handle (228). As soon as the handle is returned, the file object is set to represent a pipe that is later involved in communication with the remote machine to obtain its available resources. NtFsControlFile sends a packet containing the enumeration request to remote computer (BU-SY46Q9D3MCQ2) returning a list of all available resources including standard Windows administrative resources such as "IPC$" and "Admin$", as well as a single file share directory named "fake". For the purpose of the experiment, this directory contains a fake copy of the "Windows" system folder allowing viruses to safely replicate onto critical operating system components – the most hunted targets.

From the point of view of networking through named pipes, Internet communications work almost identically with a single difference in remote machine naming convention. Specifically, when opening a named pipe to access a remote machine over the Internet, its IP address is used as the UNC instead of the computer's actual name. For example, the following system call would try to open a named pipe connection on a PENTNET remote computer.

Replication over the Internet is usually more complicated than the local network attack, partially due to the fact that remote machines with direct Internet access are less vulnerable. Longer response times and a much broader range of computers to scan can make such virus activity obvious for a skilled user. Computer viruses have to conduct a variety of tests on every single computer they attack in order to detect, recognize and exploit vulnerability so that replication can be possible. However, such activities are hard to predict and they should not be accounted for when defining this

---

[1] W32.EfishNC is a memory-resident infector of all Windows Portable Executable applications. It infects files in all folders on all local and mapped network drives. It also infects files in folders on network shares and IP addresses that are shared with write access. It uses entry-point obscuring (EPO) and an encryption method that is both very simple to implement and very hard to decrypt without the key. [Symantec Security Response]

Table 7. Network resources enumeration via a Named Pipe

Pipe file object handle

System Call	Input Arguments	Output Args
NtCreateFile 0xc0100080	24, 0, 40h, 0, 4060988, "\??\UNC\BU-SY46Q9D3MCQ2\PIPE\srvsvc", 0h, 4194368, 0, 0	228,0h, 1
NtSetInformation File 228	4061044, 8, Pipe	0h, 0, 0
NtSetInformation File 228	4061036, 8, Completion	0h, 0, 0
NtFsControlFile 228 INPUTS	19... "\ \ 22\0\0 \0B\0U \0S\0Y\04\06\0Q\09\0D\03\0M\0 C\0Q\02\0\0\0\1\0\0\0\1\0 \0\0\0\0 0\0\0\0",	See Input Args below
NtFsControlFile 228 OUTPUTS	"...15\0\0\0R Qm\0o\0t\0e \0A\0d\0m\0i\0n\0 0P\0\5\0\ 0\0\0\0\0\0\5\0\0\0f\0a\0k\0e \0\0\0e\0\1\0\0\0\0\0\0\0\1..."	336, 259
NtOpenFile 100001h	24, 0, 40h, 0, 0, "\??\UNC\BU-SY46Q9D3MCQ2\fake\", 3, 16417	232,0h,1 ,0

(Callout annotations on the table read: "Remote Computer", "Pipe "srvsvc"", "Set "Pipe" object", "Request "BU-SY46Q9D3MCQ2" for available resources", "Request returned: open directory "fake"", "No more data is available")

part of the *GSR*. A virus, looking for an IP on the network is by itself is a suspicious activity that may or may not lead to a complete successful replication.

System Call	Input Arguments	Output Args
NtCreateFile 0xc0100080	24, 0, 40h, 0, 4060988, "\??\UNC\134.11.4.132\PIPE\srvsvc", 0h, 0, 3, 1, 4194368, 0, 0	228,0h, 1

The sequence of events described above represents a perfect example of a well bound structure where every system call produces a result that is vital for the subsequent execution and such dependencies are very traceable. Therefore, such a sequence can be syntactically described as part of replication and can form another component of the *GSR*. Such a component is called ***Pipe Enumeration Block*** and is connected to other blocks of the Gene right before the ***File Access Block.***

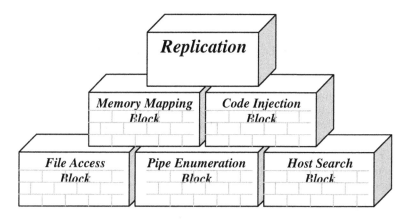

Fig. 8. Final replication behavior structure of a virus with networking capabilities

6   Results

The experiments have shown that most blocks of the *GSR*, being described in a generic form, do express the behavior of many well-known as well as yet undetermined viruses. The detection mechanism, implemented as a finite-state machine, allows for successful tracking and detection of such behavior. Table 8 below shows detection system response to several viruses as well as some legitimate processes expressing similar "viral" behavior from the replication point of view. Only the most vital blocks of self-replication are shown.

Table 8. Detection system response to various malicious and legitimate processes

	Host Search	File Access	Networking	Memory	Injection/ infection	Replication (total)
W32.Alicia	100 %	100 %	100 %	32.4 %	100 %	100 %
W32.Bogus	100 %	100 %	5.3 %	3.7 %	100 %	100 %
W32.Crash	100 %	100 %	0 %	100 %	100 %	100 %
W32.Neo	100 %	100 %	7.0 %	100 %	100 %	100 %
W32.Linda	100 %	100 %	4.3 %	100 %	100 %	100 %
W32.Stream	100 %	100 %	32.5 %	100 %	100 %	100 %
Svchost.exe	26.3 %	100 %	79.4 %	100 %	36.0 %	78.4 %
Explorer.exe	14.5 %	92.1 %	100 %	84.5 %	47.4 %	86.2 %
Acrobat.exe	75.0 %	89.0 %	53.5 %	100 %	87.1 %	89.8 %

Since the approach is generic in its nature, many legitimate applications may trigger some of the Gene's building blocks. It can be seen from the table that some of the blocks, being more generic, are detected at a rate very close or even equal to 100 % for non-malicious applications tested. A process "svchost", for example, indeed expressed behavior identical to a virus when working with system memory objects. However, the host search routine has only been presented by partial detection directory listing, therefore earning only 26 % of the entire host search behavior.

Similarly, not all computer viruses have to incorporate every possible mean of self-replication in a single body. Companion virus W32.Bogus, for example, did not show any signs of replication over the network or the Internet, neither it actually deals with system memory object. However, the replication for this particular virus is proven by other very strong arguments, such as host search and code injection.

The authors realize that no detection method is 100 % perfect and it is expected that some viruses may express different behavior that are not yet described in terms of the *GSR*. However, all viruses have to follow the most generic rules of replication. In the case of a false positive detection of a block in the replication pyramid, provided that other blocks are detected correctly, the protection system may conclude that the replication rate for the given process is achieved to a certain degree, while it is still lower than 100 %. In this case, the threshold can be set to suspend a suspicious process from any further action and alarm the user. However, such a threshold should not be set below 90 %, as it can be seen from the table, a high rate of false positives will be generated under such conditions.

7 Conclusion

In this paper we proposed an advanced approach to software behavior recognition with specific application to the detection of malicious behavior in computer viruses. The reason for choosing the mechanism of self-replication as the detection criteria is that non-malicious codes have no reason to disseminate themselves, while self-replication is crucial for deploying widespread information attacks. One of the primary strengths of the proposed approach is its ability to detect previously unknown viruses with a very low false-positive rate. In addition, it is independent of the style of the programmer, programming language, and compiler (assembler) used. Malicious behavior detection is done at a very low level, in the operating system, where the most important activities can be monitored. This prevents the detection system from getting overflowed with useless calls that can be accomplished at a higher, more vulnerable level, while still allowing for the monitoring all activities of processes accessing vital operating system facilities. The detection is implemented as a runtime monitor – a detector system allowing for immediate detection and termination of any number suspicious of processes currently running on the system.

Of course, no method of detection is perfect. Although this paper presents an attempt to detect and account for all existing methods of self-replication, there may be some new techniques in virus writing that will thwart this effort. The authors are aware of the feasibility of multi-processing self-replication that could be implemented by a very sophisticated attacker and intend to address this threat in future research. However, most information attacks require the use of less sophisticated programming techniques to ensure successful execution on a wide range of computer systems, assuring the success of the proposed technology.

Acknowledgement

The authors are grateful to the Air Force Office of Scientific Research for funding the project "Recognition of Computer Viruses by Detecting Their Gene of Self Replication" that has resulted in findings presented in this paper.

The authors are also grateful to Prof. Scott Craver of Binghamton University for his valuable suggestions and insights.

References

1. Skormin V. at al.: "BASIS: A Biological Approach to System Information Security", Proceedings of the International Workshop Mathematical Methods, Models and Architectures for Computer Network Security, Lecture Notes in Computer Science, Vol. 2052, Springer Verlag (2001) 127–142
2. Tarakanov, A., Skormin, V., Sokolova, S.: Immunocomputing. Theory and Applications. Springer-NY (2003) pp. 210
3. Skormin, V., Summerville, D., Moronski, J.: "Detecting Malicious Codes by the presence of their *Gene of Self-Replication*", "Computer Network Security", Lecture Notes in Computer Science, Vol. 2776, Springer (2003)
4. Fu, K.S.: Syntactic Methods in Pattern Recognition. Academic Press Inc., NY (1974)
5. Symantec Security Response
   http://securityresponse.symantec.com/avcenter/venc/data/w32.chiton.gen.html
6. Ludwig, M.A.: The Giant Black Book of Computer Viruses. 2nd Ed., American Eagle Publications (1998)
7. Russinovich M.E., Solomon, D.A.: "Microsoft Windows Internals, Fourth Edition: Microsoft Windows Server 2003, Windows XP, and Windows 2000", Microsoft Press (2005)
8. Nebbett, G.: "Windows NT/2000 Native API Reference", Macmillan Technical Publishing, IN (2000)
9. Poor, H.V.: An Introduction to Signal Detection and Estimation. 2nd Ed., Springer (1994)
10. Skormin, V., Summerville, D., Moronski, J., McGee D.: "Biological Approach to System Information Security (BASIS): A Multi-Agent Approach to Information Security", Lecture Notes in Computer Science, Vol. 2691, Springer-Verlag Heidelberg (2003)
11. Weaver, N., Paxson, V., Staniford, S., Cunningham, R.: "A Taxonomy of Computer Worms", Proc. ACM CCS Workshop on Rapid Malcode (October 2003)
12. Kienzle, D., Elder, M.: "Recent Worms: A Survey and Trends", Proc. ACM Workshop on Rapid Malcode (October 2003)
13. Aho, A.V., Sethi, R., Ullman, J.D.: Compilers: Principles, Techniques, and Tools. Addison-Wesley (1986)
14. Grune, D., Jacobs, J.H.: Parsing Techniques: A Practical Guide. Ellis Horwood (1990)
15. Whalley, I., Arnold, B., Chess, D., Morar, J., Segal, A., Swimmer, M.: An Environment for Controlled Worm Replication and Analysis. IBM TJ Watson Research Center (Sept 2000)
16. Weaver, N., Paxton, V.: A worst case worm. 3rd Annual Workshop on Economics and Information Security (WEIS04), May 13–14, 2004 University of Minnesota, Digital Technology Center
17. Schechter, S.E., Smith, M.D.: "Access for Sale: A New Class of Worm", The ACM CCS Workshop on Rapid Malcode (WORM 2003), Washington, DC (October 2003)
18. Ellis, D.: "Worm anatomy and model", Proc. ACM CCS Workshop on Rapid Malcode, (October 2003)
19. Arnold, W., Tesauro, G.: Automatically Generated Win32 Heuristic Virus Detection. Virus Bulletin Conference (2000)

Calibrating Entropy Functions Applied to Computer Networks

Duncan A. Buell

Department of Computer Science and Engineering,
University of South Carolina,
Columbia, South Carolina 20209
buell@cse.sc.edu
http://www.cse.sc.edu/ buell

Abstract. It has been suggested that the problem of determining the state of a network could be solved by computing entropy functions based on the dynamic connections that are made among the nodes of that network. In this paper we will attempt to calibrate, in a quantitative way, the computation of those entropy functions on simulated data that we believe should resemble real data. Our purpose is to understand how one might use the entropy functions to signal that the state of a network is undergoing a significant change, perhaps due to an attack on the network or an attack emanating from the network. Our results are, we believe, either inconclusive or negative. Specifically, we believe that our simulations suggest either that these entropy functions are not sufficiently indicative of anomalous behavior in a network as to be usable for this purpose or that conversely in order for them to be used to detect anomalous behavior, the underlying "normal" behavior of the network would have to be more stable than we might expect it to be.

1   Introduction

It has been suggested [1,3] that the problem of determining the state of a network could be solved by computing entropy functions based on the dynamic connections that are made among the nodes of that network. In this paper we will attempt to calibrate, in a quantitative way, the computation of those entropy functions on simulated data that we believe should resemble real data. Our purpose is to understand how one might use the entropy functions to signal that the state of a network is undergoing a significant change, perhaps due to an attack on the network or an attack emanating from the network.

We are attempting to model the behavior of a network, which we assume comprises at least hundreds if not thousands or tens of thousands of nodes. A large university campus, for example, has on the order of $10,000$ nodes connected to its network. From the traffic on the network, we can construct a *connectivity matrix C* that represents the dynamic connections of the network as defined by the traffic in the time interval during which data has been gathered.

We note that the *physical* network topology is not of interest here. Physical connections are not relevant to the state of the network unless they are actually

V. Gorodetsky, I. Kotenko, and V. Skormin (Eds.): MMM-ACNS 2005, LNCS 3685, pp. 76–87, 2005.

used. What is of interest is the logical set of network connections, that is the set of point-to-point connections of which use has been made. We thus let the connections of the network be defined by the data and not by a predetermined description of the underlying hardware.

We also note two characteristics of the matrix C that we will deal with later, but that we mention only in passing in this introductory discussion. The first is the fact that the dynamic connections of the network, as defined by its traffic, are time-varying, but we cannot hope (for reasons of computational efficiency, if for no other reason) to view them as connections that vary continuously. We will of necessity deal with the network data in discrete, perhaps overlapping, time intervals in order to obtain a sequence of snapshots of the network.

Second, the matrix C can be defined in many ways, depending on one's concept of "network traffic." Perhaps the simplest definition is that it is simply the adjacency matrix of nodes of the network, representing an undirected graph (and thus a symmetric matrix) in which nodes are connected if they have exchanged a message (in either direction) during the time interval during which data has been collected, and not connected otherwise. More complicated matrices can be constructed by weighting the adjacency matrix to reflect the number of messages sent, the number of bytes sent, and so forth. Later in this document, when we discuss the issues of entropy, we will normalize the entries so that the sum of all entries is 1.

Finally, we must deal with the diagonal entries of C. In keeping with the proposal made by Gudkov, Johnson, Madamanchi, and Sidoran [3], we place in the diagonal entries of the matrix the negative of the row (or column, since the matrix is assumed symmetric) density off the diagonal. This is done by Gudkov et al. so as to obtain a matrix that represents a Markov process and thus to be able to argue that a deeper analysis based on the theory of Markov processes is relevant. In what follows here we in fact never use the diagonal entries of the matrix, so the actual values assigned to them are not relevant.

The matrix C will change over time as the dynamic connections change. If we were to view the network as a graph, and we had a sequence of matrices, then we could (in theory) view the graphical images of the graphs over time and detect changes in the network that would represent anomalous behavior and/or intrusions. The proposal of Gudkov et al. is that one can apply entropy functions to these matrices, and that the changes in the entropy functions will reflect changes in the matrix (and by extension, the network) in a useful way.

Caveats About the Real World

There are a number of assumptions about the real world that may or may not be true and which would affect the ability of an entropy metric as mentioned here to detect anomalous situations in a network. On the one hand, verifying that these assumptions were true would be important if one were to determine that this version of an entropy approach were viable for detecting anomalies in a network. On the other hand, if our analysis suggests that the approach is not viable even if the assumptions were true, then the matter of verifying the assumptions becomes moot.

One assumption is that anomalous situations might result in clusters of connections among nodes. This was the initial assumption of Gudkov et al., but there is reason to believe that a cluster is not what one would expect from an anomaly. A worm, for instance, that was scanning IP addresses for vulnerable computers, would be indicated not by a cluster in the matrix but by a high density of nonzeros in the row and/or column for that node. A collection of nodes infected with a worm would be indicated by a set of denser "lines" in a set of rows and columns, but not a cluster. On the other hand, the entropy change from a cluster will be greater than that from a small list of lines, so if changes caused by clusters cannot be detected reliably, then changes caused by sets of lines will be even harder to detect.

The argument of the previous paragraph can also be made regarding the question of what kinds of attacks might be detectable by this approach. An attack includes some set of machines involved in higher-than-normal communication with other machines. The extreme end of higher-than-normal communication is not just a cluster but a solid block of nonzero entries for the nodes involved in the attack either as attacking or attacked machines.

Further concerns about the utility of this approach come from questions about whether it would be feasible to collect the everything-to-everything connectivity data in a real network. It would be difficult–indeed probably impossible–to gather data from every node in a network. Further, the return of that data to a central node for processing would in itself look very much like an anomalous event. Also, normal traffic is almost certainly not just the random sending of messages among nodes; there will be daily and weekly fluctuations, bursts of events, broadcasts to all users, and such. With a very short time window one would be hard pressed to distinguish an administrative communication to all machines on a net from an infected machine searching all machines to find those that might be vulnerable.

Again, we do not attempt to address these questions. If under ideal situations there is insufficient ability to distinguish anomalies from normal behavior with the proposed entropy metric, then there is little reason to worry about whether anomalies could be detected under less-than-ideal conditions.

Finally, this paper describes an experiment based on simulated data. We are in the process of gathering real data for processing. In the event that this approach shows promise, then it would be necessary to verify simulation results against real data. However, in an experimental mode it is necessary to begin with real data so that the input to the processing can be predictable and the presence and severity of an anomaly can be measured.

2   Entropy Functions

Following the method by which Gudkov et al.[3] address the question of entropy in the network, we first normalize the connectivity matrix C so that $\sum_{i,j} C_{ij} = 1$. For convenience, we will abuse notation and also refer to this as C in this section.

Although our matrix is symmetric, reflecting an undirected graph, we will intuitively view the values C_{ij} in what follows as representing connections from node (row) i to the node (column) j. The sum $P_i = \sum_{j=1}^{n} C_{ij}$ is thus the probability of a connection from node i to the other nodes in the network, and we can define a row-wise *Shannon entropy*

$$H(row) = -\sum_{j=1}^{n} P_i \log P_i. \tag{1}$$

We note that we could just as well consider a column-wise entropy $H(column)$ and that $H(row) = H(column)$ since the matrix is assumed to be symmetric.

The *Shannon mutual information*, or negative Shannon entropy, contained in the matrix C is

$$I(C) = H(row) + H(column) - H(column|row) = \sum_{j=1}^{n} C_{ij} \log \frac{C_{ij}}{P_i P_j}. \tag{2}$$

We note that $I(C)$ is independent of the labelling of the nodes of the network.

A more general *Rényi entropy of kind q* [6] can be defined as follows.

$$H_q(row) = \frac{1}{1-q} \log \sum_{j=1}^{n} P_j^q. \tag{3}$$

The Rényi information of the first kind ($q = 1$) is identical with Shannon information [2,7]. One can in fact view Rényi information as a generalization of Shannon information. The Rényi formulas above follow as the only formulation of entropy/information that is consistent with axioms set forth by Kolmogorov and Nagumo [4,5].

Since Rényi entropy is a generalization of Shannon entropy, we can consider the entropy of equation (3) and the associated

$$H_q(column|row) = \frac{1}{1-q} \log \left(\sum_{i,j} C_{ij}^q \right). \tag{4}$$

From these we can compute the Rényi mutual information $I_q(C)$ for a connectivity matrix in a manner analogous to that for Shannon information.

One suggestion made by Gudkov *et al.* is that instead of computing the entropy functions alone, we could compute the *difference* between the Rényi entropies of the second and first kinds as a way of measuring the state of a network.

3   Calibration

The proposal has been made to use entropy functions to measure the state of a network. The work of Gudkov *et al.* has shown that a qualitative change in the entropy function does arise from a change in the connectivity matrix derived from traffic data. To use the entropy functions in a viable system for detecting anomalous behavior, one must calibrate these functions to determine their predictive capability. In an operational setting, one could imagine a constant recomputation of entropies and a comparison of the values computed against a baseline of "normal" behavior. The goal would be to know that abnormal behavior would change the values computed in a definable, measurable, predictable, way so that such changes could be used to trigger the alarm bells and the necessary responses to what would be presumed to be an attack or other anomaly.

All software was developed and run on a Red Hat Linux system and the `gcc` compiler. This is relevant only in that the random numbers used were generated by the built-in `rand()` function. We acknowledge that this sequence of pseudo-random numbers may not satisfy high-grade tests for randomness. Some of our tests were done again with a better random number generator, and the change in the results was too small to be considered relevant to our basic conclusion at the end of this paper.

3.1   Assumptions

In order for the entropy functions of the previous section to be applicable, it is necessary that the underlying input data be compatible with the computation of these entropies. Specifically, we assume for the purposes of calibrating these functions that we have a matrix of n rows and columns, representing n nodes on the network, and with $n \approx 10000$ as a ballpark estimate. We would expect $n < 5000$ to be too small to be of interest and $n > 50000$ to be perhaps too large. The entropy measures are global measures of network behavior; absent an incremental approach or a method for rapidly determining a subset of the connectivity matrix on which to focus, we would expect an $O(n^2)$ or worse computation for $n > 50000$ to be prohibitive for real time. We assume also that there is a background density of connections between nodes, and we take that density to be in the range of 5% to perhaps 15%. Finally, the underlying assumption in the use of these entropies is that, when properly viewed, the matrix will have a nonrandom structure. In Gudkov *et al.* and in this work we look at clusters that could be seen (with an appropriate permutation of the node subscripts) as denser blocks along the diagonal. Anomalies that scanned, for example, all the nodes in a subnet local to the infected machine would result in rows and/or columns of the matrix that were much denser than the background.

We admit that the assumptions of the previous paragraph are in fact just assumptions. In another part of the larger project of which this work is a part we are studying real data from networks to determine whether the above assumptions are justified and how the simulated data would have to change in order to be more realistic. But these assumptions must be expressed in order to understand why the parameters of our experimental data have been chosen as they have been. We postulate, however, for the purpose of initial study, that we could calibrate these entropy functions by studying the following independent variables.

1. The overall size of the network. This is the number of rows (also of columns) in the matrix C. We will study sizes ranging from approximately 100 up through approximately 10000.
2. The background density. This is the probability that one node will be connected to another at random. We will assume until shown to be in error that these probabilities will fall in the range 0.05 to about 0.15.
3. The number of clusters in the network.
4. The sizes of the clusters.
5. The densities of the clusters.

It is the latter three variables that require justification. We assume that in a large network, such as a university, that departments, colleges, and other units will appear in the connectivity matrix as clusters, because the nodes in these units will have reasons to be communicating with each other more frequently than would be observed for the background random activity. If one were to have complete information about the network traffic (this would require an NP-complete computation to be done), then one could, for any chosen threshold that would define a cluster, rearrange the matrix C into a block-diagonal form. In the absence at present of any real data contradicting the assumption, we will assume that the number of clusters of a given size will have a Zipf-like distribution and will vary inversely with the size of the clusters, and we will generate simulated data accordingly. For our initial experiments we have chosen cluster densities in the range of 0.50 to 0.90. We have chosen initially to study two types of cluster structure. The first is a single cluster of varying size that could in fact be the entire network. This follows the mode of Gudkov *et al.* in looking at difference of entropies for a single cluster as it grows from a small size eventually to become the entire network. The second study is motivated by an assumption about how C might change for a network experiencing an anomaly. We begin with a series of clusters of decreasing size, computing the entropies as we go, to establish the parameters for a "normal" state. We then introduce a moderately large cluster (on the order of 10% of the entire network) that we might postulate to arise from a newly-infected computer that has begun an attack.

3.2 The Software Artifact

A brief description of the software is in order. Our program takes as input a set of parameters that includes the matrix size, the background density, and the number, size, and density of the clusters to be simulated. Calls to `rand()` are made to fill in the background of a symmetric matrix of the appropriate density, and the background entropy is computed. Following this, the simulated clusters are added one at a time and the entropy recomputed. An overall outer loop controls the number of such tests to be made. Any of the entropy calculations themselves are simply effected by a double loop through the rows and columns of the matrix (which is for programming convenience represented in dense matrix form). The code was written for simplicity and flexibility, not for performance, and since even for the larger matrices the running times were at worst in minutes, we made no attempt to improve the efficiency of the code if that would have added complexity and/or decreased the flexibility.

3.3   Variability Due to Sampling

One first question to be addressed is whether the entropy functions are stable from one randomly-generated matrix to another, a fundamental question of the signal-to-noise ratio of the functions being studied. To this end, we have run two experiments.

- In the first experiment, we assume a background density of 5% for random connections, we assume overall network sizes of 1000 to 10000 nodes in increments of 1000 nodes, and we assume a cluster size of 1000 nodes with a cluster density of 80%.
- In the second experiment, we assume a network size fixed at 10000 nodes, a single cluster of 1000 to 5000 nodes in increments of 1000 nodes, and the same background and cluster densities as in the first experiment.

In both cases we do ten iterations and compute the Shannon entropy (equation (1)), the Rényi entropy (equation (3)), the mutual Shannon entropy for $q = 2$ (equation (2)), the mutual Rényi entropy for $q = 2$ (equation (4)), and the difference between the latter two mutual entropies.

We did not conduct a thorough statistical analysis, because this did not seem necessary. If we naively compute the difference between the maximum and minimum values and divide by the average value with each parameter setting, we obtain a measure of the relative error from using different random samples but with all other variables held constant.

The result of both experiments seems to be that the differences arising from sampling are very small. There were a few instances in which this relative error was as large as 2.0×10^{-4}, but for the most part the relative errors were even smaller than this, often less than 10^{-6}. As long as the predictive use of entropy as an indicator of anomaly is based on observed changes significantly larger than 1 in 10000, say, we would not expect sampling variations to have a significant effect.

3.4   The Entropy Functions Themselves

We turn next to the entropy functions themselves.

Single-Cluster Matrices: In our first simulation we computed entropies for all matrices with

- network size 100 to 1000 in increments of 20, with constant background density 0.05
- a single cluster of size 20 to 1000 in increments of 5
- cluster densities from 0.50 to 0.80 in increments of 0.10

We present a plot that provides a heuristic view of the functions. Figure 1 is of the standard Shannon entropy for cluster densities 0.80. The plot is quite similar for different cluster densities and for the Rényi entropy for various densities. As one would expect, the entropy is high for networks in which either few or most

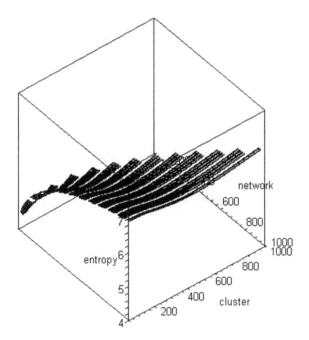

Fig. 1. Shannon entropy, cluster density 0.80

nodes are not in a cluster, and the entropy is smaller for networks in which roughly half the nodes are in a cluster. What is to be noted, however, and is also to be expected, is that the variation between high and low decreases, for a fixed pair of densities, as the network size increases. This bodes ill for the scalability of this approach to detecting network anomalies.

In Figure 2 we present the difference between Shannon and Rényi entropies of the second kind for cluster density 0.80. We present the view from a slightly different angle and with a slightly different view so as to expose the shape of the surface.

Multiple-Cluster Matrices the initial experiment: For our second experiment, we have constructed a single matrix of 10000 nodes with a background density of 0.05. To this we have then added five clusters of 500 nodes each (that is, 5% of the total matrix size for each cluster), four clusters of 300 nodes (3%), three clusters of 200 nodes (2%), and seven clusters of 100 nodes (1%), all with a density of 0.80. This represents a total of 50% of the matrix contained in clusters, and this we take to be the matrix in "normal" state. To this we then add one final cluster of 500 nodes to simulate a new hot spot in the network.

The plot of the entropy differences is shown in Figure 3. An initial tentative conclusion from this experiment is that these entropy measures may not be sufficiently sensitive to be used to predict behavior. Although we do observe a drop in the mutual entropy when the hot spot is introduced, the change is not obviously so great as to be convincing that such a change could be detected in an operational situation.

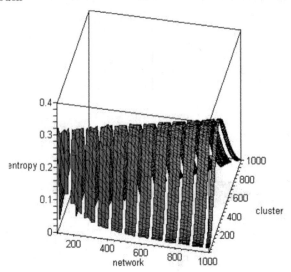

Fig. 2. Entropy difference, cluster density 0.80

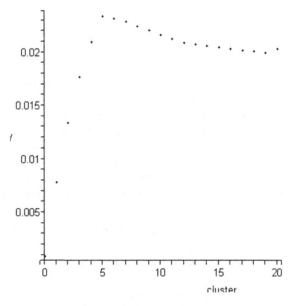

Fig. 3. Entropy difference

A more general test: For our final experiment, we used a network of $10,000$ nodes with a background density of 0.05. We then added clusters, with densities all at 0.80, whose node counts summed to $5,000$, or half the total network. To this mix we then add one cluster of 1000 nodes, or 10% of the entire network. The sequences of clusters added were of the percentages of the total network indicated in Table 1. For example, the first experiment used a single cluster that

Table 1. Clusters used in the large experiment

```
e 50 10
f 45  5 10
g 40  5  5 10
h 35  5  5  5 10
i 30  5  5  5  5 10
j 30 10  5  5 10
k 25  5  5  5  5  5 10
l 25 10  5  5  5 10
m 25 10 10  5 10
n 20  5  5  5  5  5  5 10
o 20 10  5  5  5  5 10
p 20 10 10  5  5 10
q 20 10 10 10 10
```

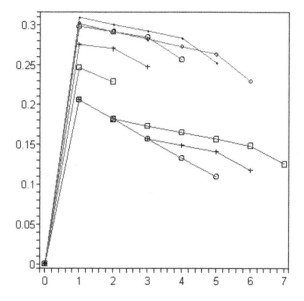

Fig. 4. Difference of entropies, experiments e through i, o through q

was 50% of the entire network, to which a subsequent cluster of size equal to 10% of the network was then added. In the last experiment, we began with a single cluster that was 20% of the network and then added three clusters each of size equal to 10% of the network before adding a final cluster of size 10%.

We apologize for less-than-optimal plotting capability in this version of the paper, but present the results below. Figures 4 and 5 contain the differences of mutual entropy of Shannon and Rényi, and is thus a generalization of Figure 3. Although the sequences are somewhat hard to distinguish, the lines representing entropy values are in essentially reverse order, top to bottom, as the cluster sequences are presented in Table 1. The upper grouping in Figure 4 is of experiments i through e, top to bottom, and the lower grouping is of experi-

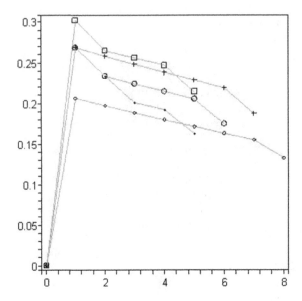

Fig. 5. Difference of entropies, experiments j through n

ments q through o, top to bottom. In Figure 5 the sequence top to bottom is of experiments n through j.

Our analysis of this very preliminary data suggest that it may well be difficult to distinguish the presence of a new cluster, even one so large at 10% of the entire network, on the basis of entropy values. This conclusion is based on the fact that, although there is a decided bend in the graphs when the last cluster is added, the ranges of values that we observe with the last cluster fall well within the ranges we would expect with a different sequence of normal clusters. In order to use the "kink" of the last cluster as a predictor of anomalous behavior, it would probably be necessary for the network in steady state to have an extremely fixed structure. We suspect that computer networks might well be more dynamic than would be necessary to use these small changes in entropy as predictors.

4   Conclusions and Future Work

We believe we can draw three conclusions from the experiments presented here.

- We believe that the entropy functions suggested in Gudkov *et al.* are robust under statistical variations in random number generation.
- We observe noticeable qualitative changes in the entropy functions due to the addition of clusters in the connectivity matrix on the order of 5% to 50% of the entire matrix.
- We are unsure as to the predictive capability of these entropy functions for detection of anomalies. Although a change in the entropy functions can be observed when a cluster of size 10% of the matrix is added, that change

is well within the range of what would be "normal" changes depending on the prior addition of clusters of similar sizes. We remark that to be effective in detecting anomalies, a system would have to respond to changes in time windows certainly not much larger than five minutes, if even that large. Normal changes might be observed from diurnal work habits, lunch breaks, morning broadcast of messages, and the like, and it is unclear whether or not such changes would mask, in something like a five-minute window, the effect of an anomaly.

To resolve the question left open in the third bullet above, we are refining our simulation software. We are generating background and anomaly data based on statistical characteristics actually observed in real traffic so that we might better understand the range of changes in the background that would mask the effects of an anomaly.

Acknowledgements

We are grateful to the Joe Johnson and Vladimir Gudkov for assistance in making sure that our computations were a correct implementation of the functions suggested.

References

1. Buell, D.A., Huang, C.-T., Janies, J., Gudkov, V., Johnson, J.E.: Introductory material. Prepared for a DARPA workshop 18-20 October 2004, Kiawah Island, South Carolina.
2. Brillouin, L.: Science and Information Theory. Academic Press. New York (1956)
3. Gudkov, V., Johnson, J., Madamanchi, R., Sidoran, J.L.: Monitoring of network topology dynamics. Proceedings, NATO Symposium on Adaptive Defence in Unclassified Networks. (2004) To appear
4. Kolmogorov, A.N.: Sur la notion de la moyenne. Atti della Reale Accademia Nazionale dei Lincei, Serie VI, Vol. 12. (1930) 388–391
5. Nagumo, M.: Über eine klasse der mittlewerte. Japanese Journal of Mathematics, Vol. 7 (1930) 71–79
6. Rényi, A.: Probability Theory. North-Holland. Amsterdam and London (1970)
7. Shannon, C.: A mathematical theory of communication. Bell System Technical Journal, Vol. 27 (1948) 379–423, 623–656

A Passive External Web Surveillance Technique for Private Networks

Constantine Daicos and Scott Knight

Royal Military College of Canada,
PO Box 17000, Station Forces Kingston, Ontario Canada K7K 7B4
cdaicos@gmail.com, knight-s@rmc.ca

Abstract. The variety and richness of what users browse on the Internet has made the communications of web-browsing hosts an attractive target for surveillance. We show that passive external surveillance of web-browsing hosts in private networks is possible despite the anonymizing effects of NATs and HTTP proxies at the gateway. These devices effectively anonymize the origin of communication streams, and remove many identifying features, making it difficult to group web traffic into mutually disjoint same-host single user sets called sessions. Sessions offer a complete picture of each user's web browsing experience. Without them, passive external surveillance is of little use. This paper offers a content analysis technique called Link Chaining that aids the sessionization process by recovering large pieces of sessions called session fragments. The technique is based on the knowledge that the majority of downloaded web resources are clicked-to from other web pages. By following hyperlinks in the bodies of HTTP messages in passively collected trace data, web traffic can be be coalesced into session fragments and used by human analysts to isolate individual users' sessions. The technique gives the human analyst a significant advantage over manual methods. The implementation presented here has been tested on accumulated local data and demonstrates the feasibility of the scheme.

1 Introduction

Given a raw trace of web traffic collected from the outside of a private network, an adversary performing surveillance can be expected to take three steps:

1. Reconstruct TCP/IP connections from raw packets
2. Organize the connections into user sessions
   (mutually disjoint same-host sets)
3. Browse the web content of each session to gather intelligence

Without the effects of gateway devices, the second step is trivial. The adversary logging packets from the outside can group them by the original host's IP address and produce user sessions. With (network address translation (NAT) and HTTP proxies however, the original IP address and other identifying information is absent, making it very difficult for to group traffic into user sessions.

V. Gorodetsky, I. Kotenko, and V. Skormin (Eds.): MMM-ACNS 2005, LNCS 3685, pp. 88–103, 2005.

Without any sophisticated techniques, an adversary performing surveillance on the outside of any of these devices would be able to reconstruct individual TCP/IP connections, but would be unable to group those connections into user sessions. The adversary would be forced to sessionize them manually. This would involve evaluating the web content of every single connection and making a best guess at which ones belong together. The problem is akin to accurately assembling the pieces of many jigsaw puzzles jumbled together in one box.

The Link Chaining Attack (LCA) of this research aids the adversary by automatically organizing TCP connections into groups we call session fragments. Fragments are formed by following HTML hyperlinks across multiple TCP connections. These fragments are much larger than individual connections, and allow the adversary to assemble sessions more quickly.

1.1   Related Work

The are three types of devices that pose increasing levels of difficulty to the problem of grouping traffic into user sessions (mutually disjoint same-host sets).

1. NAT
2. Plain HTTP Proxy
3. Anonymizing HTTP Proxy

Although none are designed specifically for surveillance, existing techniques [4] [5] can be used to sessionize traffic collected from the outside of NATs and plain HTTP proxies, but not anonymizing HTTP proxies. The LCA was designed to operate under the strict conditions of anonymizing HTTP proxy. There is no known existing technique for doing this. The following three sections will explain why.

1.2   NAT

With NAT in place, a large number of private addresses are mapped to a small number of public addresses (often just one), so all traffic looks like it is coming from a single host. When all communication is with the same IP, there is no obvious way to differentiate the streams of traffic generated by individual hosts.

Existing attacks like Bellovin's IPid technique [4] can be re-purposed to group NATed web traffic into user sessions. These attacks exploit the fact that most NAT devices are configured to re-write only the IP address of packets. Other fields are left untouched, passing through NAT unchanged from their originating host. Bellovin traces the unchanged IPid field to reveal which packets come from the same host.

1.3   Plain HTTP Proxy

Web proxies are middlemen that fulfill transactions on the client's behalf. Without a web proxy, HTTP clients talk directly to HTTP servers. With a web proxy, two separate TCP connections are established: one between the client and HTTP proxy, and one between the proxy and server. The use of this intermediary means that, unlike NAT, the TCP/IP packet headers contain no identifying features to differentiate streams emanating from different hosts. This renders attacks like Bellovin's IPid technique useless.

Original host information can still be found however, in the HTTP headers of outgoing requests. Plainly configured HTTP proxies pass these headers to the web server unchanged. If browsers in a network are not all configured identically, these headers can be used [5] to resolve at least some of the HTTP traffic to same-host sets. Of course, this assumes that the headers are present, and have not been scrubbed by an anonymizing proxy.

1.4   Anonymizing HTTP Proxy

The HTTP Anonymizing Proxy performs the same functions as a plain proxy, but scrubs all non-essential headers from outgoing requests. Without any headers to uniquely identify distinct hosts, keying on HTTP headers is not at all effective.

The Link Chaining Attack can be an effective technique under the conditions of an anonymizing web proxy because it operates on the HTTP message body. Although HTTP headers can be changed by intermediate devices, the web content itself cannot be changed in any meaningful way without affecting the browsing experience. The Link Chaining Attack takes advantage of this by reconstructing individual web pages from the traffic stream and following the links they contain forward in time to chain TCP connections into user session fragments.

1.5   Research Goals

The aim of this work is to develop a technique that aids the analyst's manual sessionization by grouping TCP connections into fragments that are as large and accurate as possible. The technique follows the hyperlinks in HTTP messages to identify the TCP connections that belong together. The theory is described in section 2 and the experiment is outlined in section 3. Before presenting the results in section 5 we propose some metrics to evaluate the quality of fragments isolated by our technique. In the analysis of section 6 we validate the work by establishing a lower bound on the effective analyst speedup.

2   Theory

The Link Chaining technique coalesces independent TCP connections into same-host groups by following hyperlinks in web pages. By matching the URLs contained in the body of an HTTP response of one connection to the URLs in the HTTP requests of all other connections, and judiciously removing impossible or improbable links, it is possible to assemble fragments of user sessions.

The TCP connection is the basic building block in this process. Figure 1 depicts the HTTP requests and responses of two independent TCP connections.

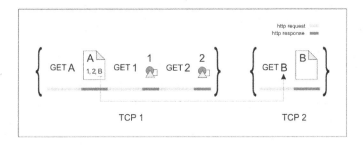

Fig. 1. Chaining Two Independent TCP Connections

The figure illustrates how the independent connections TCP 1 and TCP 2 can be chained by matching URLs. The hyperlink B in the first HTTP response of the first connection is matched with the URL B in the first HTTP request of the second connection.

The four phases of the Link Chaining technique are: Naive Chaining, Impossible Link Removal, Unlikely Link Removal, and Session Fragment Isolation. The first phase produces a tangled mass of edges and nodes representing all possible links between all connections. The two subsequent phases chip away at this mass, selectively removing impossible and unlikely links. By traversing the edges of the isolated graphs that remain, connection nodes are aggregated into groups. These groups of connections form session fragments. The process is summarized in Figure 2.

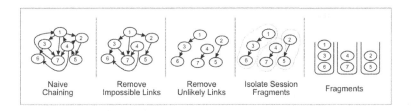

Fig. 2. Four Phases of the Link Chaining Attack

The raw inputs to the LCA are reconstructed TCP streams, HTTP messages, and the HTML hyperlinks they contain. Although these inputs are extracted from logged packets using known methods, the difficulty of this process should not be discounted. Before links can be extracted from web pages, the pages must be accurately reconstructed from individual packets. In many cases, the pages must also be decoded, uncompressed, parsed, and normalized. Relative links must then be resolved to their absolute form, stored with contextual meta data like timestamps and connection origin, and indexed appropriately for use in the LCA. For link extraction to be comprehensive and accurate, the software must also accomodate imperfect implementations of web protocols. These specifications essentially require the development of TCP/IP assembly and HTTP parsing facilities comparable to those of a full-fledged web browser.

2.1   Naive Chaining

The first step of the Link Chaining technique is to naively match all response URLs with all request URLs across all connections. A "URL match" is defined as a literal match between a URL in any response of one connection (e.g. in a web page) and a URL in the first line of any request in another connection (e.g. in a GET request). The complete set of URL matches can be represented as a list of adjacencies (ordered pairs) forming one or more directed graphs, where each node is a TCP connection.

Naive chaining identifies every single adjacency. This includes adjacencies representing link traversals that never actually occurred. By including all adjacencies, naive chaining produces a set of comprehensive starting graphs for the Link Chaining Attack. Many edges must be removed from these graphs before individual user session fragments can be isolated.

2.2   Removing Impossible Adjacencies

In the second phase of Link Chaining, the impossible edges in the graphs are removed. An edge is considered impossible if the link traversal it represents could never happen. The TCP and HTTP protocol mechanisms impose structural and temporal constraints on the traversal of links. Certain connections cannot be chained because it would imply an impossible link traversal. Two impossibilities are defined based on these constraints:

1. Connections Chained Backward in Time
2. URLs Chained Backward in Time

Each is discussed in turn.

Connections Chained Backward in Time. When a page containing URL pointers to other resources is downloaded, it is followed by a flurry of requests. Some of these are due to the browser automatically requesting resources associated with the page, others are due to a user's clicking of a hyperlink. These are implicit and explicit requests respectively. In terms of HTTP protocol specification, no distinction is made between implicit and explicit requests.

If the requested resources are on the same server, and the web server and browser are so configured, HTTP requests may be issued on the same, already open TCP connection used to download the initial page. Otherwise, a new connection is opened to issue the request. HTTP requests can also be sent on older connections to the same server that are still open. This flexible connection reuse policy is made possible by HTTP/1.1 [2], and it affords us only one temporal constraint on the chaining of connections:

Constraint 1: For any two TCP connections A and B, if B is closed before A is opened, A cannot be chained to B.

URLs Chained Backward in Time. The second important temporal constraint is due to the fact that a resource request cannot be made if the URL pointer to that resource has not yet appeared in a response. For implicit requests, this simply means the browser cannot request a URL that has not yet been downloaded. For explicit requests, it means that users cannot click on URL hyperlinks that have not yet appeared on screen. This constraint is summed up as follows:

> **Constraint 2**: A link traversal is impossible if the request URL appears before the response URL. A URL Match representing such a traversal is invalid. Two connections cannot be chained if every URL Match between them is invalid.

Since the packets of connections are interleaved on the wire, the content of connections is interleaved in time. To determine the validity of a URL Match, the timestamp of the request URL must be compared with the timestamp of the response URL. In a timing diagram, HTTP events in a connection might look like Figure 3.

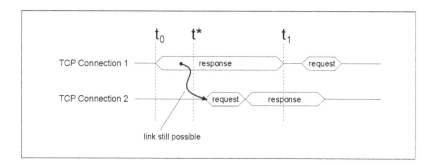

Fig. 3. Chaining Two Independent TCP Connections

Assuming a URL in the response of connection 1 matches the URL in the request of connection 2 in the figure, we must decide whether it is temporally possible that the request in connection 2 was initiated from 1. If not, the connections cannot be chained. To do this, URLs must be tagged with the time their containing packet appeared in the traffic stream.

2.3 Marking Likely Adjacencies

The preceding step identifies adjacencies that are definitively impossible, and can therefore be removed from the connection graphs. The remaining adjacencies cannot be removed this easily. Since they do not violate any of the constraints, every remaining adjacency is a potential candidate for inclusion.

To accurately isolate user session fragments, the most likely of the remaining adjacencies must be identified. A time oriented heuristic was developed to do this. The heuristic is based on the time between the appearance of a URL, and the request for the resource it points to. This time is called think time, and it is defined differently for browsers and users.

User Think Time (Δ_e): Length of time between a page download and a hyperlink click (explicit request). User think time includes the browser's parsing and rendering time.

Browser Think Time (Δ_i): Length of time between a page download and an ancillary, automatic request (implicit request). Browser think time includes browser parsing time.

Think time corresponds exactly to the length of time between matching URLs in distinct connections. It can be represented by a label on each edge in a TCP connection graph. An example of this is shown in Figure 4.

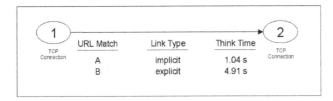

Fig. 4. Think Times for Two Links between Two Connections

The figure shows two potential URL matches linking connections 1 and 2. The first URL match implies an implicit request (an ancillary request made automatically by a browser fetching embedded content), while the second implies an explicit request (a request resulting from a human user click). Think times are calculated for every URL match, including matches implying link-traversals that never occurred. The marking of likely adjacencies is based on the length of these think times.

The time oriented heuristic is a simple set of think time limits outside which link traversals are deemed unlikely and removed. Link traversals (represented by URL matches) are removed according to the following rules:

Implicit URL Match (Browser Request): if think time $t_t > \Delta_i$, remove.
Explicit URL Match (User Request):   if think time $t_t > \Delta_e$, remove.

Borrowing from the traditional sessionization techniques of web analytics [5], the values of Δ_i and Δ_e are 20 seconds and four minutes respectively.

The heuristic is only applied to those connection nodes having an indegree greater than one. That is, nodes with multiple incoming edges that imply the node was linked-to from more than one other connection. An example is shown in Figure 5.

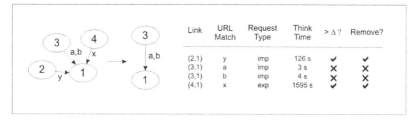

Fig. 5. Removing Unlikely Adjacencies from a Multi-Indegree Node using the Time Oriented Heuristic

Multi-indegree nodes (MINs) are an ideal target for edge removal because they are over-represented in the adjacency graphs. Although naive chaining produces lots of them, MINs only happen for real when requests initiated from multiple connections are being issued on a single, already open, connection. This is a connection reuse scenario that web browsers do not experience often. MONs (multi-outdegree nodes), on the other hand, happen all the time. They represent the situation where multiple connections are being initiated from the same connection, like when a flurry of implicit requests are made for objects embedded in a page.

Because it focuses only on MINs, the time oriented heuristic is consistently optimistic. It leaves most out-links intact. The only out-links it removes are those associated with MINs.

2.4 Fragment Isolation

The Link Chaining process begins as a tangled graph of naively chained connections. This graph is then processed to remove the impossible and unlikely adjacencies. The remaining graphs of connected nodes form the fragments that the analyst will use to assemble user sessions. The fragments are isolated by simply tracing the edges of each graph and aggregating the connection nodes.

3 Experimental Setup

Network traffic was collected passively from the inside of a live campus network with a high volume (2 GB/hour) of web traffic and later written to a database. The logging point was situated at the gateway before any NAT or proxy so that individual host IP addresses were visible. A real attack would tap external to this gateway, but IP address visibility was necessary here to validate the results. All traffic features that would not normally appear in the presence of NAT or proxy were selectively ignored for each experiment. The tap and network under test are illustrated in Figure 6.

Traffic collection was performed using Snort 2.0. Snort is an open source network intrusion detection system, capable of performing real-time packet sniffing,

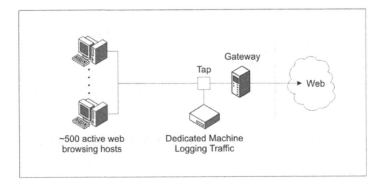

Fig. 6. Network Under Test

analysis, and logging on IP networks [6]. In this experiment, it was used exclusively for its packet sniffing and packet logging capabilities. The tool was configured to break out packets into their constituent fields and write them to a MySQL [8] database.

Figure 7 shows the three tools used to prepare the data. The first tool labels all packets by TCP connection and removes broken or empty connections. The second reconstructs the contents of every TCP connection while preserving the relationship of those contents with their underlying packet features. The final tool parses all relevant HTTP features and statistics from each TCP stream. The results from each of these steps are written back to the database.

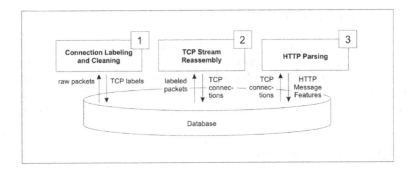

Fig. 7. Three Data Preparation Steps

These tools process the raw packets to produce multiple views of the data across all relevant protocols. They provide a convenient, granular, and relational breakdown of every traffic feature of interest. All tools were written in C++ and made extensive use of MySQL++ [8], an object oriented API used to access the database. The API allows queries and query results to be handled as STL Containers. Shell scripts were used to drive the compiled tools. Perl was employed for some ancillary tools.

The TCP reassembler reconstructs TCP streams accurately despite packet retransmissions or out-of-order delivery. The reassembler operates on a database of packets (as opposed to a raw log) and preserves the mapping between a stream's content and its constituent packets.

The HTTP Parser extracts information from the HTTP transactions in reassembled TCP stream files. It parses individual HTTP headers as well as the web resources contained in the bodies of HTTP responses. For example, the parser can rebuild sounds, images, and documents from the HTTP stream. It can also inflate or unzip HTML web pages that have been compressed by web servers. This is necessary for extracting the valuable hyperlinks that allow the Link Chaining Attack to chain TCP connections together into user sessions. The parser very much emulates the parsing functionality of a web browser.

Data preparation constituted a significant effort before the Link Chaining Attack could be applied.

3.1 Experimental Inputs and Procedure

The experiment was performed for five sets of Port 80 traffic data. Each set was collected in the same hour on different week days. In raw TCPdump [9] format, the data sets were roughly 550Mb each. They each contained about 30 minutes of traffic generated by approximately 500 active hosts. Each set contained about 750,000 packets, 25,000 TCP connections, and 100,000 HTTP messages.

3.2 Two Versions of Fragment Isolation

Fragment isolation was performed in two ways for each data set. In the first, fragments were isolated from all possible adjacencies. In the second, fragments were isolated only from those adjacencies marked as likely by the heuristic. The two tests were labelled A and B respectively.

Fragment Isolation Tests
A - All possible adjacencies
B - Adjacencies marked as likely by the heuristic

Both tests are versions of the Link Chaining Attack. Test A should be considered a naive implementation. It was conducted to establish a baseline for the performance of the heuristic in test B.

4   Link Chaining Evaluation Metrics

For session fragments to be useful to a human analyst, they must be as large and accurate as possible. The evaluation of the Link Chaining Attack is based on a series of metrics that measure how the test fragments compare to actual whole user sessions. Actual user sessions are complete sets of same-host connections, organized by IP address. The IP address of every TCP connection is recorded in the experiment so that actual user sessions can be isolated and easily compared with fragments.

The measures for fragment quality are based on the degree to which actual sessions are reconstructed by fragments. These measures consider the number of TCP connection elements in the intersection of a fragment and an actual session. They are described in the following sections.

4.1 Coverage

Coverage is the degree of overlap between the connection elements in fragments and actual sessions. Coverage measures the size of the fragment in relation to the size of the actual session. For a given fragment f and actual session s, coverage C is given by:

$$\text{Coverage} \quad C = \frac{|f \cap s|}{|s|} \tag{1}$$

4.2 Accuracy

The fraction of fragment elements that have been correctly assigned. It is calculated as follows:

$$\text{Accuracy} \quad A = \frac{|f \cap s|}{|f|} \tag{2}$$

Ideally, the Link Chaining attack would reproduce entire user sessions. That is, it would produce fragments of unit coverage and accuracy. This is highly unlikely. Instead, the goal is to consistently isolate non-trivial session fragments of high accuracy. Regardless of their size, non-trivial fragments decrease the session assembly time for an analyst as long as they are accurate.

4.3 Matching Fragments to Actual Sessions

There are always more session fragments than actual user sessions. Before applying any metrics, each fragment must be matched to the user session of which it is a part. The best matching user session is the one that shares the largest number of connection elements with the fragment. For a given fragment f, and the set of all user sessions S, the matching session m, is given by:

$$\text{Matching Session} \quad m = \left\{ m \epsilon S \middle| |f \cap m| = max\{|s \cap f| \big| s \epsilon S\} \right\} \tag{3}$$

4.4 Ambiguous Fragments

Some fragments will match multiple sessions. Such fragments are inaccurately chained and contain equal numbers of connections from two or more sessions. For example, the following fragment f matches sessions s_1 and s_2 equally:

$$f = \{1, 2, 3, 4\} \quad s_1 = \{1, 2, 5, 9, 13\} \quad s_2 = \{0, 3, 4, 12, 26, 52\}$$

To evaluate these fragments effectively, they must be assigned to, and compared with, a single whole session. There is no way to do this meaningfully. Such an assignment would be essentially arbitrary. Fragments that are too ambiguous to evaluate in the context of this experiment would be similarly confusing to the analyst in practice. Measuring the quality of such fragments is pointless; they are all bad. For this reason, the metrics are not applied to ambiguous fragments. Instead, the fragments are counted separately, and presented as an index of ambiguity, indicating one aspect of the performance of the LCA overall.

$$Ambiguity = \frac{AmbiguousFragments}{AllFragments} \tag{4}$$

4.5 Trivial Fragments

By definition, fragments made up of one connection element always match one session and have unit accuracy. Their effect is to increase the aggregate accuracy in a meaningless way. For example, if half of all fragments are trivial, the aggregate accuracy is guaranteed to be at least 0.5. This is an unnaturally inflated score that does not represent the accuracy of non-trivial fragments. To correct this, accuracy is not measured for trivial fragments, and aggregate results are presented with a triviality score.

$$Triviality = \frac{TrivialFragments}{AllFragments} \tag{5}$$

5 Results

5.1 Trivial and Ambiguous Fragments

Trivial fragments accounted for 5.25% to 9.33% of all fragments in Test A and 12.81% to 16.81% in Test B. The larger number of trivial fragments in Test B is to be expected, as the naive method of Test A chains connections into fragments much more readily than the discerning heuristic of Test B. It is important to mention that some fragments were small because the sessions themselves were small. Specifically, 3.48% to 7.21% of actual user sessions were trivial.

Ambiguous fragments accounted for 2.25% to 4.41% of all fragments in Test A and 1.14% to 4.02% in Test B. There was no statistically significant difference in ambiguity between the two methods.

5.2 Coverage

The distributions of coverage scores for Tests A and B are shown in Figure 8 and 9. The coverage of the fragments isolated by the heuristic appear to be exponentially distributed, with about 75% of them having session coverage less than 25%. The naively isolated fragments are distributed much differently, with generalized peaks at coverages less than and greater than 50%.

5.3 Accuracy

The distribution of fragment accuracy for Tests A and B is shown in Figures 10 and 11. The figures show clearly that the heuristic isolates fragments that are much more accurate than those of the naive method.

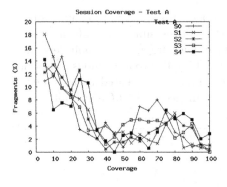

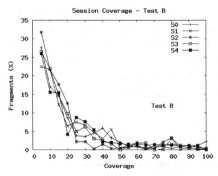

Fig. 8. Distribution of Session Coverage of Fragments (Test A)

Fig. 9. Distribution of Session Coverage of Fragments (Test B)

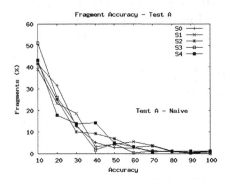

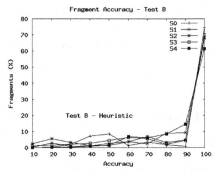

Fig. 10. Distribution of Accuracy Scores, Naive Chaining (Test A)

Fig. 11. Distribution of Accuracy Scores, Heuristic (Test B)

6 Analysis

The previous section showed that the Link Chaining Attack was able to group TCP connections into non-trivial fragments with moderate success. The inde-gree heuristic proved to be far more accurate than naive chaining, although the fragment sizes it produced were much smaller. The averages for each metric are summarized in Table 1 below.

Table 1. Summary of Link Chaining Performance Averages

Test	Fragment Size	Coverage	Accuracy	Triviality	Ambiguity
A. Naive	58.67	31.48	24.15	6.96	3.28
B. Heuristic	10.62	12.63	88.41	14.3	3.32

This research has been predicated on the notion that it is desirable for human analysts to group the contents of passively logged TCP connections into user sessions for the purpose of surveillance. The above results are now used to show how Link Chaining aids this process.

6.1   Modeling Sessionization Time

Without Link Chaining, or a similar technique, the largest unit of network traffic that can be rebuilt from the stream automatically and reliably is the TCP connection. After TCP connections are rebuilt, it is assumed the analyst would sessionize them by analysing hyperlinks, content, semantics etc. Since no real data on human sessionization time is available, the time t_s, to sessionize n connections is modeled as follows:

$$\text{Sessionization Time Model 1}\quad t_s = t_c\frac{n(n-1)}{2} \qquad (6)$$

Where the time to compare one connection or fragment to another, t_c, is constant, and is multiplied by the maximum number of comparisons required (i.e. the comparison of all possible connection pairs or $\binom{n}{2}$). This is a conservative model.

Modeling sessionization time without empirical data is admittedly clumsy. The following relationship is used to model the best case sessionization time achievable by an analyst, $t_s^\star$, which is linear with respect to the number of connections. It is impossible to argue that a human (or even a computer) can do better than compare all connections in one pass simultaneously, so the model is used as an ultra-optimistic benchmark.

$$\text{Sessionization Time Model 2}\quad t_s^\star = n \cdot t_c \qquad (7)$$

6.2   Time Savings

The average size of fragments isolated by the heuristic in the Link Chaining Attack was 10.62 connections. Based on this average, the number of pieces, n, that an analyst would have to sessionize is reduced to $\frac{n}{10.62}$. Figures 12 and 13 illustrate the effect of such a reduction on sessionization time using both models M1 and M2.

The first model shows that based on the average fragment size of the experiments, a human analyst working with fragments (as opposed to individual TCP connections) would experience a speedup of greater than 100 when based on a conservative model of analyst efficiency. When based on an optimistic model for analyst efficiency, the LCA represents a ten-fold speedup. Since the optimistic model represents the best possible case for a human analyst's unaided performance, it is expected that the actual speedup would be significantly better than the indicated ten-fold speedup.

The amount of content visible in each fragment has a definite impact on sessionization speed. Individual TCP connections offer only a small window onto

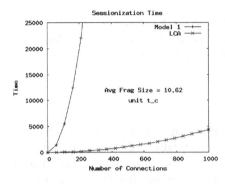

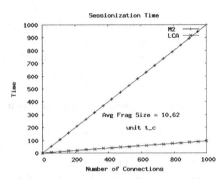

Fig. 12. Sessionization Time Functions, Original and With LCA, Model 1

Fig. 13. Sessionization Time Functions, Original and With LCA, Model 2

a user's browsing sessions, while fragments made up of multiple connections offer a much larger window. This larger window provides the analyst with much more semantic context, allowing him to infer user sessions more easily than he could with individual TCP connections.

For example, some of the fragments in this experiment were rendered in a web browser. These fragments revealed stock research pages, online education seminars, and shopping pages. In a few cases, whole webmail sessions were contained in one fragment and could be rendered in their entirety, including email attachments.

7   Conclusion

By reducing the high cost of sessionizing connections manually, the Link Chaining Attack makes passive external surveillance of private networks a real possibility. The results suggest a minimum ten-fold speed improvement for a human analyst with acceptable accuracy. This number may be closer to 100 when using a reasonable model of human sessionization speed.

The fact that the indegree heuristic performed more accurately than the naive method of fragment isolation demonstrates that web traffic contains an exploitable relationship that is more descriptive than that marked by hyperlinks alone. Web browsing is governed by a discernible pattern of user and browser think times that can be used — together with tracing hyperlinks — to group connections.

The Link Chaining Attack capitalizes on navigation and time oriented heuristics to sessionize fragments of user sessions. Proposed improvements include the tuning of user and browser think time thresholds, the identification of new impossibilities for link removal, and the discovery of impossible event sequences spanning multiple connections. A method for assessing the likelihood of a link based on a recursive calculation of the likelihood of its adjacent links is also being considered.

It is believed that evolved versions of the technique will take advantage of these small improvements to enable the uncomplicated passive external surveillance of private networks — despite the anonymizing effects of NATs and HTTP proxies.

References

1. Clarke, F., Ekeland, I.: Nonlinear oscillations and boundary-value proeblems for Hamiltonian systems. Arch. Rat. Mech. Anal. **78** (1982) 315–333
2. Clinton Wong: HTTP Pocket Reference. O'Reilly, July 30 (2000)
3. Gourley, David et al.: HTTP: The Definitive Guide. O'Reilly, Cambridge, September (2002)
4. Bellovin, S.M.: A Technique for Counting NATed Hosts. www.research.att.com/ smb/papers/fnat.pdf, AT&T Labs Reseach (2003)
5. Berendt, B., Mobasher, B., Spiliopoulou, M.: Web Usage Mining for E-Business Applications. ECML/PKDD-2002, 19 August (2002)
6. Snort IDS. http://www.snort.org/about.html
7. MySQL. http://www.mysql.com/
8. MySQL++. http://tangentsoft.net/mysql++/
9. TCPdump. http://tcpdump.org/

A Secure Way to Combine IPsec, NAT & DHCP

Jacques Demerjian[1], Ibrahim Hajjeh[2], Mohamad Badra[3], and Salim Ferraz[4]

[1] GET-Télécom Paris, 46 Rue Barrault 75013 Paris, France
demerjia@enst.fr
[2] ESRGroups, 17-19 Rue Barrault 75013 Paris, France
ibrahim.hajjeh@esrgroups.org
[3] UQAM, H3C 3P8 Montréal, Canada
mohamad.badra@uqam.ca
[4] LIP6, 8 Rue du Capitaine Scott 75015 Paris, France
salim.ferraz@etu.upmc.fr

Abstract. This paper examines the use of NAT with IPsec as a transparent security mechanism. It discusses the security needs and solutions that define how to combine IPsec and NAT. Because of the inherent limitations of current proposed solutions, this paper proposes an end-to-end security architecture using IPsec in the NAT/DHCP environment with a formal validation to the proposed architecture using an automatic protocol analyser called Hermes. This paper is builds upon works previously published.

1 Introduction

NAT (Network Address Translation) [30] is widely used in security architectures. It was originally developed as an interim solution to combat IPv4 [27] address depletion by allowing globally registered IP addresses to be re-used or shared by several hosts [24]. NAT provides transparent routing mechanism to end hosts trying to communicate from disparate address realms, by modifying IP and transport headers en-route. By providing this mechanism, NAT has become of vital importance in the implementation of network security.

The use of NAT has been the savior as well as the doom-maker for IP network deployment. At the same time that it solved address space issues and enabled the deployment of private IP networks, favoring address reuse, it has introduced major issues, breaking some of Internet's protocols and applications. IPsec (IP Security) [18] might be considered one of the main protocols that NAT has broken, even if there are currently solutions in order to "make" IPsec work when NAT devices are in place, the truth is, IPsec deployment is seriously hindered. However, IP security end-to-end from any host to any other host in the Internet is yet far from a reality.

In this paper, we propose a solution for assuring the end-to-end security using IPsec in the NAT/DHCP [8] environment. This solution is built upon [6, 7] and [32], works previously published.

The remainder of this paper is structured as follows: Section 2 describes known incompatibilities between NAT and IPsec, section 3 explores some existing solutions that define how to combine IPsec and NAT, and exposes their limits. Section 4 illus-

V. Gorodetsky, I. Kotenko, and V. Skormin (Eds.): MMM-ACNS 2005, LNCS 3685, pp. 104–118, 2005.
© Springer-Verlag Berlin Heidelberg 2005

trates our proposed solution for assuring the end-to-end security using IPsec in the NAT/DHCP environment and validates it using an automatic protocol analyser called Hermes. Section 5 presents some security consideration related to our solution. Section 6 concludes this paper and gives directions for future work.

2   IPSEC/NAT Incompatibilities

This section describes known incompatibilities between NAT and IPsec. The use of IPsec, or any other security protocol with "NAT" which uses IP addresses as part of a SA (Security Association), for communications that span multiple routing realms is problematic. NATs clearly limit the scope where IPsec could be applicable (or vice versa, IPsec could limit the scope where NATs could be applicable). IPsec techniques which are intended to preserve the endpoint addresses of an IP packet will not work with NAT enroute for most applications in practice [29]. Techniques such as AH (Authentication Header) [19] and ESP in tunnel mode (Encapsulation Security Payload) [20] protect the contents of the IP headers (including the source and destination addresses) from modification. Yet, NAT's fundamental role is to alter the addresses in the IP header of a packet. IPsec supports two "modes". Transport mode provides end-to-end security between hosts, while tunnel mode protects encapsulated IP packets between security gateways.

In IPsec transport mode, both AH and ESP have an integrity check covering the entire payload. When the payload is TCP [26] or UDP [25], the TCP/UDP checksum is covered by the integrity check. When a NAT device modifies an address the checksum is no longer valid with respect to the new address. Normally, NAT also updates the checksum, but this is ineffective when AH and ESP are used. Consequently, receivers will discard a packet either because it fails the IPsec integrity check (if the NAT device updates the checksum), or because the checksum is invalid (if the NAT device leaves the checksum unmodified).

Note that IPsec tunnel mode ESP is permissible so long as the embedded packet contents are unaffected by the outer IP header translation. If the transport endpoint is under our control, we might be able to turn off checksum verification. In other words, ESP can pass through NAT in tunnel mode, or in transport mode with TCP checksums disabled or ignored by the receiver. IPsec tunnel mode AH doesn't suite NAT because whole packet is authenticated (including header) hence leaving no space for NAT to modify the IP header. Thus, co-existence of NAT and IPsec (using AH) in either of the operational modes is not feasible due to functional architecture of AH. If we stick to ESP in tunnel mode or turn off checksums, there's still another obstacle: the IKE (Internet Key Exchange) [14].

IPsec-based VPNs (Virtual Private Networks) use IKE to automate security association setup and authenticate endpoints. The most basic and common method of authentication in use today is preshared key. Unfortunately, this method depends upon the source IP address of the packet. If NAT is inserted between endpoints, the outer source IP address will be translated into the address of the NAT router, and no longer identify the originating security gateway. To avoid this problem, it is possible to use another IKE "main mode" and "quick mode" identifier (for example, user ID or fully qualified domain name).

It may be of interest to note that IKE is a UDP based session layer protocol and is not protected by network based IPsec security. Only a portion of the individual payloads within IKE are protected. As a result, IKE sessions are permissible across NAT, so long as IKE payload does not contain addresses and/or transport IDs specific to one realm and not the other. Given that IKE is used to setup dynamic IPsec associations, the majority of current solutions propose a ways of making IPsec work through a NAT function.

In the next section we explore some of those solutions that define how to combine IPsec and NAT, and expose their limits.

3 Existing Solutions

End-to-end network layer security via IPsec cannot operate with an intervening NAT device. One simple solution is to have a single device for performing NAT and IPsec tunnelling. [28] is a useful resource that describes a security model with tunnel-mode IPsec for NAT domains.

There are a variety of solutions being proposed for the NAT-IPsec compatibility problem [1]. A number of them recommended as intermediate solutions pending the wide-spread adoption of IPv6. Those solutions [1] are:

3.1 IPsec Tunnel Mode

In a limited set of circumstances, it is possible for an IPsec tunnel mode implementation, such as that described in [8], to traverse NA(P)T successfully [28]. However, the requirements for successful traversal are sufficiently limited so that more general solution must meet the following requirements [1]:

1. *IPsec ESP.* IPsec ESP tunnels do not cover the outer IP header within the message integrity check, and so will not suffer Authentication Data invalidation due to address translation. IPsec tunnels also need not be concerned about checksum invalidation.
2. *No address validation.* Most current IPsec tunnel mode implementations do not perform source address validation so that incompatibilities between IKE identifiers and source addresses will not be detected.
3. *"Any to Any" SPD (Security Policy Database) entries.* IPsec tunnel mode clients can negotiate "any to any" SPDs, which are not invalidated by address translation. This effectively precludes use of SPDs for the filtering of allowed tunnel traffic.
4. *Single client operation.* With only a single client behind a NAT, there is no risk of overlapping SPDs. Since the NAT will not need to arbitrate between competing clients, there is also no risk of re-key mis-translation, or improper incoming SPI or cookie de-multiplexing.
5. *Active sessions.* Most VPN sessions typically maintain ongoing traffic flow during their lifetime so that UDP port mappings are less likely be removed due to inactivity.

3.2 RSIP

Described in [3] and [4], includes mechanisms for IPsec traversal, as described in [23]. By enabling host-NA(P)T communication, RSIP addresses issues of IPsec SPI de-multiplexing, as well as SPD overlap. By enabling hosts behind a NAT to share the external IP address of the NA(P)T (the RSIP gateway), this approach is compatible with protocols including embedded IP addresses. By tunnelling IKE and IPsec packets, RSIP avoids changes to the IKE and IPsec protocols, although major changes are required to host IKE and IPsec implementations to retrofit them for RSIP-compatibility. It is thus compatible with all existing protocols (AH/ESP) and modes (transport and tunnel). In order to handle de-multiplexing of IKE re-keys, RSIP requires floating of the IKE source port, as well as re-keying to the floated port. As a result, interoperability with existing IPsec implementations is not assured. RSIP does not satisfy the deployment requirements for an IPsec-NAT compatibility solution because an RSIP-enabled host requires a corresponding RSIP-enabled gateway in order to establish an IPsec SA with another host. Since RSIP requires changes only to clients and routers and not to servers, it is less difficult to deploy than IPv6 [1].

3.3 6to4

6to4, as described in [5] can form the basis for an IPsec-NAT traversal solution. In this approach, the NAT provides IPv6 hosts with an IPv6 prefix derived from the NAT external IPv4 address, and encapsulates IPv6 packets in IPv4 for transmission to other 6to4 hosts or 6to4 relays. This enables an IPv6 host using IPsec to communicate freely to other hosts within the IPv6 or 6to4 clouds. While 6to4 is an elegant and robust solution where a single NA(P)T separates a client and VPN gateway, it is not universally applicable. Since 6to4 requires the assignment of a routable IPv4 address to the NA(P)T in order to allow formation of an IPv6 prefix, it is not usable where multiple NA(P)Ts exist between the client and VPN gateway. For example, NA(P)T with a private address on its external interface cannot be used by clients behind it to obtain an IPv6 prefix via 6to4. While 6to4 requires little additional support from hosts that already support IPv6, it does require changes to NATs, which need to be upgraded to support 6to4. As a result, 6to4 may not be suitable for deployment in the short term [1].

3.4 NAT-Traversal in the IKE

[21] describes how to detect one or more Network Address Translation devices (NATs) between IPsec hosts, and how to negotiate the use of UDP encapsulation of IPsec packets [16] through NAT boxes in IKE.

For NAT Traversal to work properly, two things must occur. First, the communicating VPN devices must support the same method of UDP encapsulation. Second, all NAT devices along the communication path must be identified.

According to [21], IPsec devices will exchange a specific, known value to determine whether or not they both support NAT Traversal. If the two VPN devices agree on NAT Traversal, they next determine whether or not NAT or NAPT occurs anywhere on the communications path between them.

NAT devices are determined by sending NAT-D (NAT Discovery) packets. Both end points send hashes of the source and destination IP addresses and ports they are aware of. If these hashes do not match, indicating that the IP address and ports are not the same, then the VPN devices know a NAT device exists somewhere in between.

All NAT Traversal communications occur over UDP port 500. This works great because port 500 is already open for IKE communications in IPsec VPNs, so new holes do not need to be opened in the corporate firewall.

NAT Traversal is the long-awaited solution to one of the major issues with IPsec VPNs, but it does not solve everyone's problems.

NAT-T (NAT Traversal) has the following limitations:

1. NAT-T imposes approximately 200 bytes of overhead during IKE negotiation and about 20 bytes of additional overhead for each packet. Depending on the amount of available bandwidth and processing power, the difference in throughput may in some instances be measurable.

   Because AH transforms actually authenticate packet header as well as packet payloads, and because NAT Traversal provides a mechanism by which packet headers can be modified in transit, AH and NAT-T do not function together; NAT-T operates only on ESP-transformed packets.

   Because of this authentication deficiency, the trust level between hosts using NAT-T is greatly reduced; NAT-T should not be used when the greatest level of host-based authentication is required.

2. NAT-T works only when the IKE initiator is the system behind the NAT box. An IKE responder cannot be behind a NAT box unless the box has been programmed to forward IKE packets to the appropriate individual system behind the box [31].

3. The NAT box does not use special processing rules. A NAT box with special IPsec processing rules might interfere with the implementation of NAT-T [31].

Next, we shall present our solution for assuring the end-to-end security using IPsec in the NAT/DHCP environment.

4   Proposed Solution

Because of the inherent limitations of current solutions proposed for the NAT-IPsec compatibility problem, it proves to be necessary to find solution answering effectively this legitimate security preoccupation.

Given that IKE can be used to setup dynamic IPsec associations, we propose a new way of making IPsec work through a NAT function. This solution is built upon [6, 32] and [8], works previously published.

Before developing our proposition, the following section starts with an overview of E-DHCP (Extended-Dynamic Host Configuration Protocol) solution then the IKE protocol issue at NAT environment.

4.1   Overview of E-DHCP

The DHCP (Dynamic Host Configuration Protocol) [8] provides a framework for passing configuration information to hosts on a TCP/IP network.

DHCP itself does support neither an access control for a proper user nor the mechanism with which clients and servers authenticate each other.

In [6] we have proposed an extension to DHCP protocol called E-DHCP (Extended-Dynamic Host Configuration Protocol) in order to allow a strict control on the equipments and users through a strong authentication process. [6] defines a new DHCP option (fig.1) based on the use of certificates.

The definition of new DHCP options [11] is possible because the options field envisages the implementation of new options [10].

This option provides simultaneously the authentication of entities (DHCP client and server) and DHCP messages. The technique used by this option is based on the use of public key cryptography [17], X.509 identity certificates [15] and AC (Attribute Certificates) [12]. On the other hand, E-DHCP allows an improved access control to the DHCP system by using AC.

Fig. 1. Authentication option structure

In E-DHCP proposal (fig. 2), DHCP server is leaned on an AA (Attribute Authority) server [12] that creates a client Attribute Certificate (client AC), which ensures the link between the client identity certificate and the allocated IP address. Therefore, the use of AC confirms client's ownership of the allocated IP address.

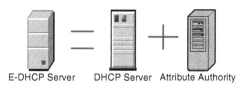

E-DHCP Server   DHCP Server   Attribute Authority

Fig. 2. E-DHCP Server

In a typical E-DHCP scenario (fig.3), the client broadcasts a DHCPDiscover message on its local physical subnet. This message includes the proposed authentication option.

The client specifies its identity certificate URI (Uniform Resource Identifiers) [2] in DHCPDiscover message, then in response, the server specifies its identity certificate URI in DHCPOffer message.

In all the transactions, on one side the sender (client/server) encapsulates the value of the encrypted signature of DHCP message, and on the other side, the corresponding receiver (server/client) checks signature's authenticity.

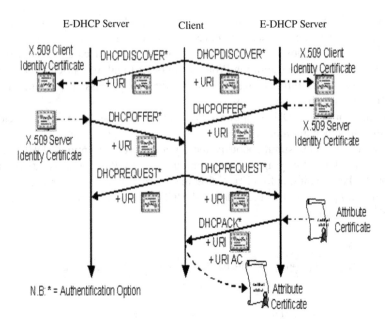

Fig. 3. E-DHCP Scenario

Information included in X.509 identity certificates will be used by the client and the server in signature validation for the rest of the transaction. When the server receives the DHCPRequest message, it will create the client's AC and save it in a database. The server specifies the AC URI in the DHCPACK message. This URI is used by the client to extract its AC from the database.

4.2 IKE Protocol issue at NAT Environment

4.2.1 IKE Protocol Overview
The Internet Key Exchange Protocol version 1 allows two entities (i.e. network hosts or gateways) to derive session keys for secure communication via a series of messages. These exchanges provide authentication and/or encryption for some messages, and various degrees of protection against flooding, replay, and spoofing attacks.

Currently, the IETF is developing a new version of the IKE protocol that is coming up in more simplified and efficient way than the existing IKE protocol.

The Internet Key Exchange Protocol version 2 presents a greatly simplified IKE protocol. IKE v2 is an attempt to simplify the standard, remove the un-needed requirements, and incorporate new standard IPsec functionalities currently contained within other documents. Unlike IKE v1, which is documented within three separate documents, IKE v2 is completely described within a single document.

The important difference between IKE v1 and IKE v2 is the reduced number of round trips required to implement identity protection, the number of possible Phase 1 exchanges is reduced from eight to one. IKE v1 aggressive mode is no longer supported. In addition, the establishment of SA (Security Association) for other security protocols (IPsec) can be piggybacked on the Phase 1 IKE exchange.

From authentication's schemes point of difference, digital signature is the only supported mechanism for certificate based authentication. Shared secret authentication is still supported.

Thus, IKE v1 and v2 relies on the same mechanisms that power most network security systems: public and private key cryptography, and keyed hash functions. They also allow the use of AC (Attribute Certificate) within a Public Key and a Privilege Management Infrastructures (PKI/PMI).

Even that version 2 of IKE does not interoperate with version 1, but it has enough of the header format in common that both versions can unambiguously run over the same UDP port.

4.2.2 IKE v1 Negotiation Issue at NAT and E-DHCP Environment

Generic IPsec process starts with the IKE negotiation which establishes SA and key agreement (fig.4). The main mode of IKE continues with the negotiation of NONCE values in the IKE nonce payloads and the DH (Diffie-Hellman) public parameters in the KE payloads. Now both initiator and responder create the master secret and its derived keys.

At this point, all payloads (without the HDR payload) will be encrypted with the derived key protecting ID authentication against ID spoofing attack. The two entities can exchange identity information using a digital signature algorithm to authenticate themselves.

The digital signature is not applied to the IKE message. Instead it is applied to a hash on all information available to both entities. All this information is carried in an identity payload, authentication payload and a certificate payload.

The second phase of IKE establishes the SA agreement for IPsec treatment for the IP payloads. Using the SA and key information agreed through the IKE negotiation, IPsec ESP or AH modes are applied to support confidentiality or integrity of the IP datagrams.

In the NAT environments, however, applying IPsec transport mode causes a problem due to the datagram conversion at the NAT server on route to the destination node. The problem happens at the first phase of the IKE negotiation and at the mode of IPsec AH operation. In fact, at the fifth and sixth steps of the main mode operations of IKE (fig.4), both nodes exchange the ID information and hash values (HASH_I and HASH_R) verifying some information including the ID values. The IP addresses are usually used as the ID values in this procedure.

The IP translation at the NAT server causes the ID authentication to fail, because the IP node at the destination is ignorant of the IP translation at the NAT server, and the verification of the hash value (HASH_I) based on the translated IP address fails. Thus, the whole IKE negotiation procedure fails.

To inform the responder of the IP address masked behind the IP translation, we propose to correlate the masked IP address and the IP translated address through an AC generated by the E-DHCP server. AC was integrated in the ISAKMP (Internet

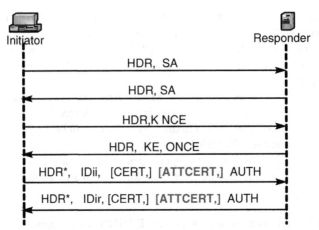

Fig. 4. IKE v1 main mode

Security Association and Key Management Protocol) [22] and the IKE v1 standards and now in the IKE v2 proposition allowing access control and service delegation. In addition, the flexibility of this type of certificate is what motivate us to use it with current IPsec implementation and in particular with NAT. We have developed X.509/XML AC with its PMI (Privilege Management Infrastructure) in E-DHCP proposition. In the last IKE v1 exchange, the node behind the NAT Server can send its AC in the authentication phases. The X.509/XML AC is signed through the E-DHCP server and contains both:

1. The Identity (IP address) of the "client or node" which was allocated by the E-DHCP Server.
2. The Identity (IP address) of the NAT Server. This will allow end entity to verify that the NAT Server which he negotiates is the pretending NAT that hides the original IP address of the client.

Upon receiving this certificate from the responder (an end entity node or even a NAT server), this entity verifies the authentication message and the AC by verifying the digital signature of the PKI/PMI certificate authority. Once verified, the responder can verify all IPsec Packets by replacing the NAT address by the masked IP address send in the AC. The following lines present an example of the XML AC.

```
<?xml version="1.0" encoding="UTF-8"?>
<!DOCTYPE AttributeCertificate SYSTEM "Applica-
tion1.dtd">
<AttributeCertificate Version="1">
  <Issuer>....</ Issuer >
  <ApplicationName>Application1
  </ApplicationName >
  <NetworkConnexion>
  <NetworkName>VPNdialer</NetworkName>
  <NetworkConnexionType>Unlimited
   </NetworkConnexionType >
  <NATaddress>137.194.192.2-137.194.192.50
```

```
    </NATaddress >
    <Bandwidth>2 Mbits/s</Bandwidth>
   </NetworkConnexion>
  <PersonnalInfo>
   <Holder>… DN + SN ….</ Holder >
   <PrivateIPaddress>137.194.192.2
    </PrivateIPaddress >
   <DNS>serveraix.ftcom.com</DNS> …
 </PersonnalInfo>
  <Validity>
   <From>2004.12.12.12.12</From>
   <To>2005.12.12.12.12</To>
  </Validity>
   <SerialNumber>1012313281</ SerialNumber >
 </ AttributeCertificate>
```

4.2.3 IKE v2 Negotiation Issue at NAT and E-DHCP Environment

The IKEv2 is very similar to IKEv1 in performing mutual authentication and establishing security associations. IKEv2 first replaces the eight possible phase 1 exchanges with a single exchange that provides identity protection and is based on either public signature or shared secret keys. In addition, IKEv2 is the only proposal that was conceived to be simply extensible. In a simple manner, IKEv2 proposes adapting a simple hash function over all payloads, no matter which authentication methods is used [13]. As shown in (fig.5), and Like IKEv1, IKEv2 allow authentication throw AC that can be used to negotiation all NAT parameters.

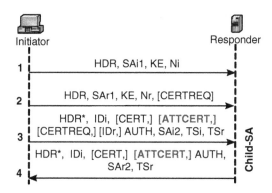

Fig. 5. IKE v2 negotiation

In the first exchange, the two entities negotiate a list of proposed cryptographic algorithm in the SA payload, their DH public values (KE) and random nonces (Ni, Nr). At this point, the two endpoints begin generating the master secret SKEYSEED and the derived keys SK_e, SK_a and SK_d. Now, all messages in the second round trip (except the HDR payload) will be encrypted using the encryption key. The initiator can now send his identity with the ID (Identity) payload, and a hash of the first round trip messages using the Authentication (AUTH) payload. The initiator can now send his X509 identity certificate containing his public key that proves his real identity and his X.509/XML AC that proves his real IP address masked with the NAT server. The initiator can also send a certificate request and the identity of the responder that can host multiple services. The second exchange contains also the SA2 that can serve for the child-SA negotiation and the TS (Traffic Selector) payloads. In the last message the responder will assert his identity in the IDr (IDentity Responder) payload, his CERT (Certificate) payload that contain his public key, hash the 3 messages in AUTH payload to assure an integrity protection and complete the negotiation of a child SA. TSi and TSr are used to assure the description of traffic to be sent.

4.3 IKE Validation with Hermes

In this section, we propose a formal validation of our proposed protocol using a model checking tool, called Hermes [33] [36]. Hermes computes an invariant of the intruder knowledge to check whether the defined secrets within a protocol may be revealed. The result is obtained without any restriction on the number of parallel sessions, the number of participants and the size of exchanged messages. The research around Hermes has also been supported by the EVA RNTL project [35] that aims at providing a toolbox for verifying cryptographic protocols using a protocol specification language called LEAVA [36].

Presenting EVA abstract model is out of the scope of this paper [33]; we only provide here a high level specification of our protocol in LEVA language. This specification is then automatically translated to an intermediate representation used as an entry point to Hermes which compiles and verifies our proposition.

We illustrate our scenarios as a negotiation between two principals A, B that represent respectively the IPSec initiator and responder. Our goal is to open an IKE v1 phase 1 negotiation with identity protection based on X.509 identity and attribute certificates.

```
IKEv1_Identity_Protection_Signature
alg : asym_algo
everybody knows alg
  A, B,CA,EDHCP: principal
  basetype key
  keypair^alg SK, PK (principal)
  SAi,SAr,Ca,Cb,Na,Nb,certreq: number
  //Ks(number, number, number) : number
  p, g, Xa, Xb: number  // valeur publique DH éphémère
  Ks: key  // clé dérivée des valeurs DH et des autres
paramètres.
  alias certB = { CA, B, PK(B) }_SK(CA)^alg
  alias certA = { CA, A, PK(A) }_SK(CA)^alg
  alias Attcert = { A, EDHCP }_SK(EDHCP)^alg
// Inital Knowledge
everybody knows alg
 A knows A, SK(A), PK(A), PK(CA), certA, Ks,
EDHCP,PK(EDHCP),Attcert
  B knows B, CA, SK(B), PK(B), PK(CA),certB,
Ks,EDHCP,PK(EDHCP)
//Message Knowledge
```

```
{
    1. A -> B : Ca,SAi
    2. B -> A : Cb,SAr
    3. A -> B : Ca, Cb, p,g,Xa, Na, certreq
    4. B -> A : Ca, Cb,p,g,Xb, Nb, certreq
    5. A -> B : Ca,Cb, {{A,certA,Attcert,
Na,Nb,p,g,Xa,Xb, certreq}_(SK(A))^alg}_Ks
    6. B -> A : Ca,Cb, {{B,certB,Nb,Na,p,g,Xa,Xb, cer-
treq}_(SK(B))^alg}_Ks
    }
//Sessions and properties
    s. session* {Ca,Cb,Na,Nb,p,g,Xa,Xb,Ks} A=A, B=B
    assume secret (SK(B)@s.B),
            secret (SK(A)@s.A),
            secret(Ks@s.A),
            secret(Ks@s.B)
```

We can divide the first phase of IKE v1 protocol into five parts. In the first part, Principals (A, B, EDHCP for Attribute Authority and CA for Certificate Authority) and variables (called numbers, algo and, key) are explicitly declared. It contains the definition of all necessary Diffie Hellman parameters like n, g and the public DH values Xa,Xb, are for the principals A, and B respectively. The two principals A and B will be authenticated using their two constructors PK and SK that represent respectively the public and private key of each principal.

The X.509 certificates of A and B concatenate the identity and the public key of each principal under a signature. The signature is done using the private key SK(CA) of a trusted certificate Authority (CA). The attribute certificate of the principal A is signed with the private key of the E-DHCP attribute certificate.

The second part (commented by initial knowledge) specifies the initial knowledge of each principal. It indicates also that some variables could be defined as public values under the 'everybody knows' syntax.

In the third part (describing the messages to be exchanged) comes a sequence of message that is exchanged between the two principals. A message in the sequence is expressed in the form A -> B: M, meaning that entity A sends the message M to entity B. Typically cryptographic algorithms with special representation are required to construct the messages that are exchanged. For example, {M}_SK(H) means that the message M is signed with the private Key of H but {M}_K means that the message M is encrypted with the secret key K.

The extended IKE protocol is represented with six steps providing a protection against replay attacks, message authentication, secure session negotiation and dual entity authentication. In the first four messages, the two entities A and B exchange cookies (Ca, Cb), nonces (Na and Nb), security associations (SAa and SAb) and their ephemeral public DH values n, g, Xa and Xb) that represents the group module of DH. The two entities send also the message *certreq* forcing the use of certificates in authentication. In the last exchange the two entities will authenticate each other with a signature on all exchanged data. A should also send his attribute certificate explained previously that contains all its attributes. All data except the cookie messages will be encrypted using an encryption Key (Ks) derived from the DH and Nonces.

The fourth part (assumptions and claims) considers an unbounded number of sessions in parallel, and the final part provides the secrecy hypothesis that is exploited in the Hermes's reasoning [33]. It defines keys unknown to the intruder which can be used to safely encrypt messages. secret (K@s.H) means that the key K in session s should be treated as a secret from H's point of view.

Table 1. Result of IKE phase 1 with digital signature

Secrets: SK(h);Ks; (h represent a Principal)	
GoodPatterns: {xs}_PK(h); {xs}_Ks	BadPatterns: Vide

Using the Online Hermes's tool [34], our specification was correctly compiled and verified regarding secrecy properties. As output, Hermes provides the sequence of rules leading to each new secret or bad pattern.

The previous table summarizes the result obtained on the first phase of IKE protocol with digital signature. In table 1, "GoodPatterns" means that, all message encrypted with one of the three secrets (Ka, shr and SK) can be securely exchanged [33]. No attack was identified with "BadPatterns". Moreover, Hermes provides online, a graphical tree proof that can be exploited for understanding attacks and protocol certification.

5 Security Consideration

This paper describes how to solve IPsec security issue at NAT/DHCP environment. Since this proposition does not change or discard any of the IPsec security itself, the security of this paper is exactly the same as that of the IPsec functionality.

However, the use of this proposition will be limited to the presence of a PKI infrastructure. This is due to the fact that this proposition is based on the use of attribute certificate in correlation with X.509 certificate in IKE authentication schemes.

6 Conclusion and Future Work

NAT removes the end-to-end significance of an IP address. Therefore, end-to-end network layer security via IPsec cannot operate with an intervening NAT device. This is significant problem with NAT, particularly considering the increase in demand for IPsec and VPN-based solutions.

This paper has presented the incompatibilities between NAT/IPsec, exposed some existing solutions that define how to combine NAT/IPsec and illustrated the limits of those solutions. We have proposed a safely new way of making IPsec work through a NAT function. Our proposed solution assures end-to-end security using IPsec in the NAT/DHCP environment. We point out that this solution is built upon [6] and [8], works previously published. This proposition has several advantages compared to alternative solutions:

1. The integration of AC (Attribute Certificate) in IKE protocols for access control will allow all IPsec entities to bypass NAT servers without any change in the current IPsec functionalities. These ACs are always protected against identity spoofing attacks under a secured tunnel.
2. Use the IKE standards UDP ports (500 or 4500 for IKE v2). Doing so, avoids poking new holes in firewall rules and packet filters.
3. Transparently to IPv4 or IPv6 networks.

A future direction of this research is to validate this proposition through the development and the establishment of real scale tests.

References

1. Aboda. B., Dixon, W.: IPsec-Network Address Translation (NAT) Compatibility Requirements, IETF, RFC 3715 (2004)
2. Berners-Lee, T., Fielding, R., Masinter, L.: Uniform Resource Identifiers (URI): Generic Syntax, IETF, RFC 3986 (2005)
3. Borella, M., Lo., J., Grabelsky, D., Montenegro, G.: Realm Specific IP: Framework, IETF, RFC 3102 (2001)
4. Borella, M., Lo., J., Grabelsky, D., Taniguchi, K.: Realm Specific IP: Protocol Specification, IETF, RFC 3103 (2001)
5. Carpenter, B., Moore, K.: Connection of IPv6 Domains via IPv4 Clouds, IETF, RFC 3056 (2001)
6. Demerjian, J., Serhrouchni, A., Achemlal, M.: E-DHCP: Extended Dynamic Host Configuration Protocol, IETF, Internet Draft (2004)
7. Demerjian, J., Serhrouchni, A., Achemlal, M.: Certificate-based Access Control and Authentication for DHCP. In ACM/IEEE ICETE'04. International Conference on E-Business and Telecommunication Networks. ICETE Conference, Setúbal, Portugal (2004)
8. Demerjian, J., Serhrouchni, A.: DHCP authentication using certificates. In SEC'04, 19th IFIP International Information Security Conference. SEC Conference, Toulouse, France (2004)
9. Droms, R.: Dynamic Host Configuration Protocol, IETF, RFC 2131 (1997)
10. Droms, R., Alexander, S.: DHCP Options and BOOTP Vendor Extensions, IETF, RFC 2132 (1997)
11. Droms, R.: Procedure for Defining New DHCP Options, IETF, RFC 2489 (1999)
12. Farrell, S., Housley, R.: An Internet Attribute Certificate Profile for Authorization, IETF, RFC 3281 (2002)
13. Hajjeh, I., Serhrouchni, A., Tastet, F.: New Key Management Protocol for SSL/TLS. In IEEE-IFIP NETCOM'03. Network Control and Engineering for QoS, Security and Mobility. NETCOM Conference, Muscat, Oman (2003)
14. Harkins, D., Carrel, D.: The Internet Key Exchange (IKE), IETF, RFC 2409 (1998)
15. Housley, R., Polk, W., Ford, W., Solo, D.: Internet X.509 Public Key Infrastructure Certificate and Certificate Revocation List (CRL) Profile, IETF, RFC 3280 (2002)
16. Huttunen & al.: UDP Encapsulation of IPsec ESP Packets, IETF, RFC 3948 (2005)
17. Jonsson, J., Kaliski, B.: Public-Key Cryptography Standards (PKCS) #1: RSA Cryptography Specifications Version 2.1, IETF, RFC 3447 (2003)

18. Kent, S., Atkinson, R.: Security Architecture for the Internet Protocol, IETF, RFC 2401 (1998a)
19. Kent, S., Atkinson. R.: IP Authentication Header (AH), IETF, RFC 2402 (1998)
20. Kent, S., Atkinson. R.: IP Encapsulating Security Payload (ESP), IETF, RFC 2406 (1998)
21. Kivinen, T., Swander, B. Huttunen, A., Volpe, V.: Negotiation of NAT-Traversal in the IKE, IETF, RFC 3947 (2005)
22. Maughan, D. Schertler, M., Schneider, M., Turner, J.: Internet Security Association and Key Management Protocol (ISAKMP), IETF, RFC 2408 (1998)
23. Montenegro, G., Borella, M.: RSIP Support for End-to-end IPsec, IETF, RFC 3104 (2001)
24. Phifer, L.: IP Security and NAT: Oil and Water?, ISP-Planet (2000)
25. Postel, J.: User Datagram Protocol, IETF, RFC 768 (1980)
26. Postel, J.: Transmission Control Protocol, IETF, RFC 793 (1981)
27. Postel, J.: INTERNET PROTOCOL, IETF, RFC 791 (1981)
28. Srisureh, P.: Security Model with Tunnel-mode IPsec for NAT Domains. IETF, RFC 2709 (1999)
29. Srisureh, P., Holdrege. M.: IP Network Address Translator (NAT) Terminology and Considerations, IETF, RFC 2663 (1999)
30. Srisureh, P., Egevang. K.: Traditional IP Network Address Translator (traditional NAT), IETF, RFC 3022 (2001)
31. Sun Microsystems: System Administration Guide: IP Services [Electronic version], Part No: 816-4554-10. Retrieved from docs.sun.com, Web site: http://docs.sun.com/app/docs/doc/816-4554/6maoq020v?a=view (2005)
32. Demerjian, J., Hajjeh, I., Serrhrouchni, A., Badra, M.: Network security using E-DHCP over NAT/IPsec, In WTAS'05. International Conference on Web Technologies, Applications and Services. IASTED Conference, Alberta, Canada (2005)
33. Bozga, L., Lakhnech, Y., Périn, M.. Hermes: A tool verifying secrecy properties of unbounded security protocols. In CAV'03. 15th International Conference on Computer-Aided Verification. Lecture Notes in Computer Science, Springer Verlag, July 2003 (2003)
34. Herme's tool, url: www-verimag.imag.fr/~Liana.Bozga/eva/hermes.php
35. French National Projet EVA (Explication et Vérification Automatique pour les Protocoles Cryptographiques). url : www-eva.imag.fr
36. Le Metayer, D., Jacquemard, F. : Langage de spécification de protocoles cryptographiques de EVA : syntaxe concrète. Technical Report EVA-1-v3.17, Trusted Logic, November 2001. Available from http://www-eva.imag.fr

A Generic Model
for Analyzing Security Protocols*

Yonggen Gu, Yuxi Fu, Farong Zhong, and Han Zhu

BASICS, Department of Computer Science and Engineering,
Shanghai Jiao Tong University, Shanghai 200030, China
{gyg68, fu-yx, zhong-fr, zhu-h}@sjtu.edu.cn

Abstract. Formal methods have proved useful in the analysis of security protocols. The paper proposes a generic model for the analysis of the security protocols (GSPM for short) that supports message passing semantics and constructs for modelling the behavior of agents. GSPM is simple, but it is expressive enough to express security protocols and properties in a precise and faithful manner. Using GSPM it is shown how security properties such as confidentiality, authentication, non-repudiation, fairness, and anonymity can be described. Finally an example of formal verification is illustrated.

1   Introduction

Security protocols are playing an increasingly important role and have become an essential ingredient of communication infrastructures. They are designed to provide properties such as confidentiality, authentication, non-repudiation, fairness, and anonymity for users who wish to exchange messages through a medium over which they have little control. However the design of a security protocol is a difficult and error-prone task. Many popular and widely used security protocols have been shown to have flaws. For this reason, the use of formal methods for the verification of security protocols has received increasing attention.

Since the security protocols themselves often contain a great deal of combinatorial complexity, it is extremely difficult to model them and verify their properties. Over the past few years various modelling languages, for instance logics and process algebras, have been proposed for the systematic and tool-supported analysis of the security protocols. Formal methods have proved useful in the analysis of the security protocols. A popular approach is to model a protocol as a system of concurrent processes, described using an appropriate language like CSP [9]. In [10] Lowe found a new attack to Needham-Schroeder public-key protocol [13] by encoding and analysing it in CSP. Following this initial work, numerous other calculi have been studied for the purpose of modelling and analyzing security protocols. For example, VSPA [8] is a value passing variant of CCS [11] extended to incorporate two security levels; The spi calculus [2]

---

* The work is supported by The Young Scientist Research Fund (60225012),The Natural Science Fund (60473006) and The National 973 Project (2003CB316905).

V. Gorodetsky, I. Kotenko, and V. Skormin (Eds.): MMM-ACNS 2005, LNCS 3685, pp. 119–128, 2005.

extends the pi calculus [12] with cryptographic primitives [3]; The applied pi calculus [1] extends the pi calculus with a general notion of terms; $L_Y S_A$ [4] is a variant of the spi calculus with pattern matching. An obvious strength of process calculus approach is their inherent mechanism for handling concurrency and communication.

Since there is no general formal framework for the analysis of security protocols, we intend to devise the GSPM to state various security properties, as expressed explicitly in a formal specification, and model the protocols in a precise and faithful manner. GSPM stems from concepts well established in the field of process calculi (such as CSP, pi calculus and ambient [5] etc.). We discard the notion of channel and don't explicitly model the intruder, yet our simple model is powerful.

The next section presents GSPM. Section 3 defines formally some security properties such as confidentiality, authentication, non-repudiation, fairness, and anonymity based on our model. Section 4 illustrates an example. Section 5 discusses our future work and concludes.

2   GSPM

In this section we present the main aspects of our model. The motivation for the model is to be more explicit about the activities of the participants in a protocol and those of possible attackers, and to express various security properties in a formal specification.

2.1   The Abstract System Model of Security Protocols

In this subsection we outline how the abstract system model of the security protocols are constructed in GSPM. Our approach provides a GSPM description of the Dolev-Yao assumption [7]: the communication medium is entirely under the control of the enemy, who can block, re-address, duplicate, and fake messages. In [16], the roles of the passive medium and of the active intruder are described using different processes. In our framework we see the combination of the intruder and the medium as a single entity (we call it active environment). Let Id_i stand for the ith participant of a security protocol. The resulting system model of the protocol is shown in the Figure 1.

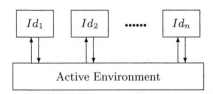

Fig. 1. The abstract system model of security protocols

The rest of this subsection will give a deeper insight into the abstract system model.

Message space. The message space we used for the analysis of security protocols is as follows:

$$
\begin{array}{llll}
k & ::= & Public\ key \mid Private\ key \mid Symmetric\ key & \text{Keys} \\
a & ::= & k \mid Nonces \mid Plaintext & \text{Atomic messages} \\
M & ::= & a \mid M.M \mid \{M\}_k \mid Hash(M) & \text{Messages}
\end{array}
$$

Plaintexts, nonces and keys are atomic messages. The other messages are composite. Like in [16] we have rules defining how messages may be generated from existing ones. We write $\mathcal{M} \vdash M$ to mean that the message M may be derived from the finite set of messages $\mathcal{M}$. The following rules define the generated relation $\vdash$:

$$M \in \mathcal{M} \implies \mathcal{M} \vdash M \tag{1}$$

$$\mathcal{M} \vdash M_1 \wedge \mathcal{M} \vdash M_2 \implies \mathcal{M} \vdash M_1.M_2 \tag{2}$$

$$\mathcal{M} \vdash M_1.M_2 \implies \mathcal{M} \vdash M_1 \wedge \mathcal{M} \vdash M_2 \tag{3}$$

$$\mathcal{M} \vdash M \wedge \mathcal{M} \vdash k \implies \mathcal{M} \vdash \{M\}_k \tag{4}$$

$$\mathcal{M} \vdash \{M\}_{Publickey} \wedge \mathcal{M} \vdash privatekey \implies \mathcal{M} \vdash M \tag{5}$$

$$\mathcal{M} \vdash \{M\}_{Symmetrickey} \wedge \mathcal{M} \vdash Symmetrickey \implies \mathcal{M} \vdash M \tag{6}$$

$$\mathcal{M} \vdash M \implies \mathcal{M} \vdash Hash(M) \tag{7}$$

Let $el(\mathcal{M})$ be the set of the elements of the message base $\mathcal{M}$. We can obtain the $el(\mathcal{M})$ by iteration as follows:

Do while $\mathcal{M}$ is not empty, we get a message M from $\mathcal{M}$

(1) When M is atomic message, we put M into $el(\mathcal{M})$;

(2) When $M = M_1.M_2$, we put M_1 and M_2 into $\mathcal{M}$;

(3) When $M = \{M_1\}_k$, if $k^{-1} \notin \mathcal{M}$ and $k^{-1} \notin el(\mathcal{M})$ (k^{-1} is the k's corresponding key) then we put M into $el(\mathcal{M})$ else we put M_1 into $\mathcal{M}$.

Enddo.

Theorem 1. *Let $\mathcal{M}$ is a message base, and M is a message, then $\mathcal{M} \vdash M$ is decidable.*

Proof. It can be proved by induction on the structure of message.

(1) If M is atomic message or hash message, then $\mathcal{M} \vdash M$ only when $M \in el(\mathcal{M})$;

(2) If $M = M_1.M_2$, then $\mathcal{M} \vdash M$ only when $el(\mathcal{M}) \vdash M_1$ and $el(\mathcal{M}) \vdash M_2$.

(3) If $M = \{M_1\}_k$, then $\mathcal{M} \vdash M$ only when $M \in el(\mathcal{M})$ or $\mathcal{M} \vdash k$ and $el(\mathcal{M}) \vdash M_1$.

Protocol participants. For each protocol participant there are a set of processes and a message base IM. Each process of a participant corresponds to an instance of the participant involved in a particular execution of the protocol. All the processes work asynchronously and concurrently. The concurrency is simulated by non-deterministic interleaving of process running.

Active environment . The active environment also is an intruder. It reads all message outputs of protocol participants, and can output any message which it generates to any protocol participant that allows for honest message passing, redirecting messages, replaying messages, and inventing new messages. The intruder can also be a legitimate protocol participant. In our model we are only interested in the active environment's message capability, and describe the messages the active environment posses as EM. We let EM_0 stand for the active environment's initial messages.

2.2   The Syntax of GSPM

In order define GSPM we need the syntactic sets defined below:

- N: an infinite set of names, ranged over by $n, m, k, Id, Id_1 \cdots, x, x_1, \cdots$. A name is plaintext, participant's name, nonce, key, or atomic name variable etc.; A key k is either public key (Pub_N), or a private key (Prv_N), or a shared/secret key $(SecKey)$.
- Variables over messages $\varphi, \psi, \psi', \psi_1, \cdots$.
- $\{.\}_k$ represents symmetric encryption, $\{.\}_{+k}$ represents asymmetric encryption, $\{.\}_{-k}$ represents asymmetric decryption.

$$M \quad ::= \quad N \mid \varphi \mid (M_1, M_2) \mid \{M\}_k \mid \{M\}_{+k} \mid H(M) \qquad \text{Message expr.}$$
$$Patt \quad ::= \quad M \mid ?x \mid ?\varphi \mid (Patt_1, Patt_2) \mid \{Patt\}_k \mid \{Patt\}_{-k} \quad \text{Pattern expr.}$$

The grammar for processes is similar to that of the pi calculus, except that here messages may contain terms (rather than only names) and that the notion of channel is absent:

$$
\begin{array}{lll}
P, Q, R ::= & & \text{process} \\
& \mathbf{0} & \text{null process} \\
& in(patt(\tilde{x}\tilde{\varphi})).P & \text{message input} \\
& out(new\tilde{x}M).P & \text{message output} \\
& P \mid Q & \text{parallel composition}
\end{array}
$$

In the above definition $\tilde{x}$ for example abbreviates some possibly empty list $x_1, \cdots, x_l$. An informal explanation of the GSPM is similar to the one in [6]. The null process $\mathbf{0}$ does nothing; $in(patt(\tilde{x}\tilde{\varphi})).P$ awaits an input that matches the pattern for some binding of the pattern variables $\tilde{x}\tilde{\varphi}$ and resumes as P under this binding. Here $patt(\tilde{x}\tilde{\varphi})$ represents that there may be some variables $\tilde{x}\tilde{\varphi}$ in the pattern. $out(new\tilde{x}M).P$ chooses fresh, distinct names $\tilde{n} = n_1, \cdots, n_l$ and binds them to the variables $\tilde{x} = x_1, \cdots, x_l$. Then the message $M[\tilde{n}/\tilde{x}]$ is output to the network and the process resumes as $P[\tilde{n}/\tilde{x}]$. The communication is asynchronous in the sense that the action of output does not await input. The *new* construct is like that of Pitts and Stark [15] and abstracts out an important property of a value chosen randomly from some large set.

Furthermore we extend processes with the location to agent:

$$
\begin{array}{lll}
A, B, C ::= & & \text{Agents} \\
& Id[P, IM] & \text{Agent } Id \text{ performs } P \text{ with } IM \\
& A\|B & \text{parallel composition}
\end{array}
$$

We take $fv(M)$, $fv(patt(\tilde{x}\tilde{\varphi}))$, $fv(IM)$ to be the set of variables appeared free in M, $patt(\tilde{x}\tilde{\varphi})$, IM. The free variables of process terms are defined as follows:

$$fv(out(new\tilde{x}M).P) = (fv(P) \cup fv(M))\backslash\{\tilde{x}\}$$
$$fv(in(patt(\tilde{x}\tilde{\varphi})).P) = (fv(P) \cup fv(patt(\tilde{x}\tilde{\varphi})))\backslash\{\tilde{x}, \tilde{\varphi}\}$$
$$fv(P|Q) = fv(P) \cup fv(Q)$$
$$fv(Id[P, IM]) = fv(P) \cup fv(IM)$$
$$fv(A|B) = fv(A) \cup fv(B)$$

2.3   A Transition Semantics

The semantics of the GSPM is given in terms of a transition relation $\longrightarrow$. Similar to the approach in [3], we model the state of the protocol system as a pair $\langle s, System \rangle$, where s records the current environment's message base EM (Because the environment has 'seen' the sequence of messages traveling on the network up to the moment), and $System$ is the protocol agent composed of some agents. An action is a term of the form $Id[in(M)]$(input action) or $Id[out(M)]$(output action), which means a participant Id inputs or outputs a message M. The set of actions $\mathcal{A}$ is ranged over by $\alpha, \beta, \cdots$, while the set $\mathcal{A}^*$ of strings of actions is ranged over by $s, s', \cdots$. String concatenation operator is written as '$\cdot$'. We denote by $act(s)$ and $msg(s)$ the set of actions and messages, respectively, appearing in s. A string s is closed if $fv(s)$ is nil. In what follows, we write $s \vdash M$ for $EM \vdash M$ ($EM = msg(s) \cup EM_0$).

We now define paths, sequences of actions that may result from the interaction between an agent and its environment. In paths, each message received by a agent can be synthesized from the knowledge the environment has previously acquired. A path is a closed string $s \in (\mathcal{A})^*$ such that for each s_1, s_2 and $Id[in(M)]$, if $s = s_1 \cdot Id[in(M)] \cdot s_2$, then $s_1 \vdash M$.

A configuration, written as $\langle s, system \rangle$, is a pair consisting of a path s and a *system*. Configurations are ranged over by $C, C', \cdots$, and C_0 stands for the initial configuration. The transition relation on configuration is defined by the following rules:

(input)
$$\frac{EM \vdash patt(\tilde{n}\tilde{M})}{\langle s, Id[in(patt(\tilde{x}\tilde{\varphi})).P, IM] \rangle \xrightarrow{in(patt(\tilde{n}\tilde{M}))} \langle s \cdot Id[in(patt(\tilde{n}\tilde{M}))], Id[P[\tilde{n}/\tilde{x}, \tilde{M}/\tilde{\varphi}], IM \cup patt(\tilde{n}\tilde{M})] \rangle}$$

(output)
$$\frac{IM \vdash M[\tilde{n}/\tilde{x}] \qquad (\ \tilde{n}\ are\ fresh\ in\ s\ )}{\langle s, Id[out(new\tilde{x}M).P, IM] \rangle \xrightarrow{out(M[\tilde{n}/\tilde{x}])} \langle s \cdot Id[out(M[\tilde{n}/\tilde{x}])], Id[P[\tilde{n}/\tilde{x}], IM \cup \tilde{n}] \rangle}$$

(internal par)
$$\frac{\langle s, Id[P, IM] \rangle \xrightarrow{\alpha} \langle s', Id[P', IM'] \rangle}{\langle s, Id[P|Q, IM] \rangle \xrightarrow{\alpha} \langle s', Id[P'|Q, IM'] \rangle}$$

$$\text{(external par)} \quad \frac{\langle s, A \rangle \xrightarrow{\alpha} \langle s', A' \rangle}{\langle s, A \| B \rangle \xrightarrow{\alpha} \langle s', A' \| B \rangle}$$

The symmetric rules have all been omitted.

3   Properties of Security Protocols

Properties of security protocols, such as confidentiality and authenticity, are the very objects which security protocols want to guarantee. GSPM provides a suitable language in which they can be formally addressed and it is easy to verify whether a security protocol has them as it is supposed to.

3.1   Confidentiality

Confidentiality means that a secret will not leak to those who are not designed to know it while the protocol is running. Since we use message base to describe a participant's knowledge, it is natural for us to use $\mathcal{M} \vdash m$ to express the meaning that a participant with message base $\mathcal{M}$ "knows" m. Usually the secret is shared between proper participants of the protocol, so a violation of confidentiality can be seen as the leakage of a secret to the active environment, which leads to the following definition:

Definition 1. *Let C_0 be the initial configuration, if for all paths s generated from C_0, $s \nvdash m$, then the system satisfies the confidentiality of m.*

3.2   Authenticity and Integrity

What authenticity guarantees is that a message supposed to be from a certain participant is indeed originated by that participant. According to correspondence assertion, participant A has sent a relevant message desired by participant B before B receives it, we say that B authenticates A. In order to define it more precisely, we need some auxiliary definitions:

Definition 2. *Let α and β be two actions and s a path. We say that α occurs prior to β in s if we have $\alpha \in act(s_1)$ whenever $s = s_1 \cdot \beta \cdot s_2$, and denote it by $s \models \alpha \hookleftarrow \beta$.*

Definition 3. *Let C_0 be the initial configuration, if all paths s generated from C_0, we have $\alpha \hookleftarrow \beta$, then we say that the configuration C_0 satisfies $s \models \alpha \hookleftarrow \beta$, and denote it by $C_0 \models \alpha \hookleftarrow \beta$.*

Now we can express authenticity as follows: (note that $out(B \ auth. \ A \ by \ m)$ is an auxiliary action for B to make authenticity more explicit)

Definition 4. *If $C_0 \models A[out(F(m))] \hookleftarrow B[out(B \ auth. \ A \ by \ m)]$ (here $F(m)$ is a composite message generated by A who is the only one to know m), then B authenticates A.*

Integrity also can be easily expressed by the notion of $\alpha \hookleftarrow \beta$. Since it usually requires that data cannot be corrupted or at least that any corruption will always be detected. In other words, the input message should match the output message.

Definition 5. *Integrity means that for all M, $C_0 \models [out(M)] \hookleftarrow [in(M)]$.*

There is no participant ID before the action for we don't care about who is the actor.

3.3   Non-repudiation and Fairness

Non-repudiation and fairness mainly concern electronic commerce protocol, which provides services among participants that don't trust each other [17]. In [16] Schneider discusses the non-repudiation in his CSP model.

Firstly, we give the definitions of two evidences used in analysis: NRO and NRR. Non-Repudiation of Origin (NRO) is an evidence intended to protect the receiver from the deliberate denial of the other participant of having sent a message; Non-Repudiation of Receipt (NRR) is another evidence intended to protect the sender from the deliberate denial of the other participant of having received a message.

Definition 6. *Let C_0 be the initial configuration, if for all paths s generated from C_0, $(msg(s) \cup EM_0 \cup IM_R) \vdash NRO$ (i.e. the receiver Id_R possesses NRO), then the protocol is said to have the sender non-repudiation property; $(msg(s) \cup EM_0 \cup IM_O) \vdash NRR$ (i.e. the sender Id_O possesses NRR), then the protocol is said to have the receiver non-repudiation property.*

Fairness can be seen as the combination of two non-repudiation properties, for at no point in a protocol's run one participant will have any advantage over another. In other words, none of the participants can get his or her evidence while the other cannot.

Definition 7. *Let C_0 be the initial configuration, if for all paths s generated from C_0, $(msg(s) \cup EM_0 \cup IM_R) \vdash NRO \wedge (msg(s) \cup EM_0 \cup IM_O) \vdash NRR$ or $((msg(s) \cup EM_0 \cup IM_R) \nvdash NRO) \wedge ((msg(s) \cup EM_0 \cup IM_O) \nvdash NRR)$ always holds, the protocol is fair.*

3.4   Anonymity

Anonymity is another property that mainly concerns electronic commerce protocol and it seems to have been hardly explored from a formal point of view. Intuitively a system is anonymous over some set of events E means that even though an observer can deduce that an event from E has occurred but he or she should not be able to identify which.

Definition 8. *Let C_0 be the initial configuration, if for all paths s generated from C_0, $(msg(s) \cup EM_0 \cup IM_A) \nvdash m$, we say that the protocol has anonymity over message m for participant A.*

4   An Example

We consider the Needham-Schroeder public-key protocol. This protocol aims to establish mutual authentication between an initiator A and a responder B, and share with the secret nonces. Every participant Id has a private key Prv_{Id} and a corresponding public key Pub_{Id}. We will write $\{m\}_k$ for the message m encrypted with the key k. Any participant can encrypt a message m using A's public key Pub_A to produce $\{m\}_{Pub_A}$; only A can decrypt this message. The protocol also uses nonces: random numbers generated with the purpose of being used in a single run of the protocol. We denote nonces by N_{AX} and N_{BY}: the subscripts are intended to denote that the nonces were generated by A and B are sent to X and Y, respectively. The complete protocol involves seven steps. Here we consider a simplified version with only three steps. This version is related to the assumption that each agent initially has the other's public key. The simplified protocol can be described as:

$$
\begin{array}{ll}
1. & A \longrightarrow B: \{N_{AB}, A\}_{Pub_B} \\
2. & B \longrightarrow A: \{N_{AB}, N_{BA}\}_{Pub_A} \\
3. & A \longrightarrow B: \{N_{BA}\}_{Pub_B}
\end{array}
$$

The three protocol participants are named A, B, I. Here I is a malicious insider: in other words, the hostile environment has registered itself as a legitimate participant having name I, private key Prv_I and public key Pub_I. We add an action '$out(\{X \ auth. \ Y \ by \ m\})$' that the participant X performs when he believes to have successfully authenticated the participant Y by message m. The formal description of the protocol is as follows:

$$
A \stackrel{\text{def}}{=} A[\Pi_{X \in \{I,B\}}(out(newN_{AX}\{N_{AX}, A\}_{Pub_X}).in(\{N_{AX}, ?N_x\}_{Pub_A})
$$
$$
.out(\{A \ auth. \ X \ by \ N_{AX}\}).out(\{N_x\}_{Pub_X}), \{Pub_A, Pub_B, Pub_I, Prv_A\}]
$$

$$
B \stackrel{\text{def}}{=} B[\Pi_{Y \in \{I,A\}}(in(\{?N_y, Y\}_{Pub_B}).out(newN_{BY}(\{N_y, N_{BY}\}_{Pub_Y}))
$$
$$
.in(\{N_{BY}\}_{Pub_B}).out(\{B \ auth. \ Y \ by \ N_{BY}\}), \{Pub_A, Pub_B, Pub_I, Prv_B\}]
$$
$$
System \stackrel{\text{def}}{=} A \| B
$$

In order to make the description more readable some obvious meta-notation is used. In particular we have abbreviated '$P_1 | \cdots | P_n$' to '$\Pi_{i \in 1, \cdots, n} P_i$'.

This version of the protocol is subject to a subtle form attack [10]. In this protocol, the initiator A and the responder B authenticates each other by exchanging nonce, and only A and B know the exchanging nonces. Formally the authentication goal is that

$$
C_0 \models B[out(\{N_{AB}, N_{BA}\}_{Pub_A})] \hookleftarrow A[out(\{A \ auth. \ B \ by \ N_{AB}\})]
$$

and

$$
C_0 \models A[out(\{N_{BY}\}_{Pub_B})] \hookleftarrow B[out(\{B \ auth. \ A \ by N_{BY}\})]
$$

hold. But this is not that case for the latter. The attack is that, A tries to establish a session with the intruder I, while I impersonates A to establish a false session with B. The attack involves two interleaved executions of the protocol, one in which the intruder I acts as the responder and one in which it acts as the initiator.

Theorem 2. *The NSPK protocol does not satisfy the authentication and Confidentiality properties. There exists a path s don't such that*

$$A[out(\{N_{BA}\}_{Pub_B})] \hookleftarrow B[out(\{B \ auth. \ A \ by \ N_{BA}\})]$$

thus

$$C_0 \models A[out(\{N_{BY}\}_{Pub_B})] \hookleftarrow B[out(\{B \ auth. \ A \ by N_{BY}\})]$$

don't hold. i.e. B can not authenticate A by the correspondence assertion; and $s \vdash N_{BA}$, i.e. the protocol does not satisfy the confidentiality property.

Proof. We know $EM_0 = \{Pub_A, Pub_B, Pub_I, Prv_I\}$. C_0 generates the path $s = \alpha_1 \cdots \alpha_8$, where :

$$\alpha_1 = A[out(\{N_{AI}, A\}_{Pub_I})]$$
$$\alpha_2 = B[in(\{N_{AI}, A\}_{Pub_B})]$$
$$\alpha_3 = B[out(\{N_{AI}, N_{BA}\}_{Pub_A})]$$
$$\alpha_4 = A[in(\{N_{AI}, N_{BA}\}_{Pub_A})]$$
$$\alpha_5 = A[out(\{A \ auth. \ I \ by \ N_{AI}\})]$$
$$\alpha_6 = A[out(\{N_{BA}\}_{Pub_I})]$$
$$\alpha_7 = B[in(\{N_{BA}\}_{Pub_B})]$$
$$\alpha_8 = B[out(\{B \ auth. \ A \ by \ N_{BA}\})]$$

It is clearly that the path s do not satisfy $A[out(\{N_{BA}\}_{Pub_B})] \hookleftarrow B[out(\{B \ auth. \ A \ by \ N_{BA}\})]$, and $(msg(s) \cup EM_0) \vdash N_{BA}$. Thus the protocol does not satisfy the authentication and Confidentiality properties.

5   Conclusion and Further Work

In this paper we present a generic model (GSPM) for security protocols that allows one to reason about formal definitions of a variety of security properties. In GSPM one does not explicitly model intruders. We have formulated security properties such as confidentiality, authentication, non-repudiation, fairness, and anonymity in GSPM. We have taken the Needham-Schroeder public-key protocol as a case study to demonstrate the expressive power of GSPM. We plan to construct an automatic tool to help analyzing the security protocol using GSPM. However we have to consider the following questions:

1. The active environment possesses infinite messages. Since the protocol participant must receive the matched messages, we are ready to take into account the symbolic method.

2. There are infinite sessions between the participants. Because the LTS semantics of our model is based on structural induction, we'll adopt the approach similar to Paulson's inductive method [14].

As for future work, we plan to define formally other security properties based on our model, and analyze the protocols such as Kerberos, SET etc.

References

1. Abadi, M., Fournet, C.: Mobile values, new names, and seucre communication. Proceedings of the 28th ACM Symposium on Principles of Programming Languages. ACM Press (2001) 104-115
2. Abadi, M., Gordon, A.D.: A calculus for cryptographic protocols: The spi calculus. Information and Computation. 148(1) (1999) 1-70
3. Boreale, M.: Symbolic trace analysis of cryptographic protocols. Proceedings of the 28th International Colloquium on Automata, Languages and Programming. LNCS 2076, Springer-Verlag (2001) 667-681
4. Bodei, C., Buchholtz, M., Degano, P., Nielson, F., Nielson, H.R: Automatic validation of protocol narration. Proceedings of the 16th Computer Security Foundations workshop. IEEE Computer Society Press, (2003) 126-140
5. Cardelli, L., Gordon, A.D: Mobile ambients. Foundations of Software Science and Computational Structures. LNCS 1378, Springer-Verlag, (1998) 140-155
6. Crazzolara, F., Winskel, G.: Events in security protocols. Proceedings of the 8th ACM conference on Computer and Communications Security. ACM Press (2001) 96-105
7. Dolev, D., Yao, A.C: On the security of the public key protocols. IEEE Transcations on Information Theroy. 29(2) (1983) 198-208
8. Focardi, R., Gorrieri, R.: The compositional security checker: A tool for the verification of information flow security properties. IEEE Transactions on Software Engineering. 23(9) (1997) 550-571
9. Hoare, C.A.R.: Communicating Sequential Processes. Prentice Hall (1985)
10. Lowe, G.: Breaking and fixing the Needham-Schroeder Public-key protocol using FDR. Proceedings of Tools and Algorithms for the Construction and Analysis of Systems. LNCS 1055, Springer-Verlag (1996) 147-166
11. Milner, R.: Communication and Concurrency. Prentice Hall (1989)
12. Milner, R., Parrow, J., Walker, D.: A calculus of moblie processes(I and II). Information and Computation. 100(1) (1992) 1-77
13. Needham, R., Schroeder, M.: Using encryption authentication in large networks of computers. Communications of the ACM. 21(12) (1978) 993-999
14. Paulson, L.C.: The inductive approach to verifying cryptographic protocols. Journal of Computer Security. 6, (1998) 85-128
15. Pitts, A.M., Stark,I.: Observable properties of higher order functions that dynamically create local names, or: What's new? Proceedings of the 18th International Symposium on Mathematical Foundations of Computer Science. LNCS 711, Springer-Verlag (1993) 122-141
16. Schneider, S.A.: Security properties and CSP. Proceedings of the IEEE Symposium on Security and Privacy. IEEE Computer Society (1996) 174-187
17. Zhou, J., Gollmann, D.: Towards verification of non-repudiation protocols. Proceedings of the International Refinerment Workshop and Formal Methods Pacific. Springer-Verlag (1998) 370-380

Networks, Markov Lie Monoids, and Generalized Entropy

Joseph E. Johnson

University of South Carolina,
Department of Physics,
Columbia, South Carolina 29208
jjohnson@sc.edu

Abstract. The continuous general linear group in n dimensions can be decomposed into two Lie groups: (1) an n(n-1) dimensional 'Markov type' Lie group that is defined by preserving the sum of the components of a vector, and (2) the n dimensional Abelian Lie group, A(n), of scaling transformations of the coordinates. With the restriction of the first Lie algebra parameters to non-negative values, one obtains exactly all Markov transformations in n dimensions that are continuously connected to the identity. In this work we show that every network, as defined by its C matrix, is in one to one correspondence to one element of the Markov monoid of the same dimensionality. It follows that any network matrix, C, is the generator of a continuous Markov transformation that can be interpreted as producing an irreversible flow among the nodes of the corresponding network.

1 Introduction

There is a broad spectrum of mathematical problems that involve the general theory of networks and the associated classification, optimization, and potentially even their dynamical evolution. By a network we mean a set of n nodes (points), some pairs of which are connected with a representative non-negative weight or strength of connection. Such a network can be represented by a connection (or connectivity, or adjancy) matrix C_{ij} whose off-diagonal elements give the non-negative 'strength' of the connection between nodes i and j in the network. Often that 'strength' or 'weight' is as simple as a '1' for a connection and a '0' otherwise. A network can be 'undirected' or 'directed' depending upon whether C_{ij} is symmetric or not thus indicating respectively a symmetric or asymmetrical connection between i and j. There may or may not exist a well defined 'metric distance' between the nodes or, equivalently, positions for the points in a metric space of some dimensionality, such as airports for airline networks, or substations for power or utility distribution networks. It is well known that the classification of different network topologies cannot be accomplished with just the eigenvalue spectra of the connectivity matrix as there are topologically different networks with as few as five nodes that have the same eigenvalue spectra. One root of the network problem is that although the network is exactly defined by the C matrix, there are n! different C matrices that correspond to the same topology because different C matrices result from different

V. Gorodetsky, I. Kotenko, and V. Skormin (Eds.): MMM-ACNS 2005, LNCS 3685, pp. 129–135, 2005.

nodal numbering orders. Most network problems become computationally intractable for more than a few hundred nodes.

We are interested in seeking useful metrics (functions of the C matrix) for the description of the topology of large networks such as sub-nets of the internet which might have from a hundred to a million nodes, and thus perhaps a trillion connection matrix values. To be useful, the metrics must be (a) rapidly computable, (b) intuitively meaningful, (c) should holistically summarize the underlying topology with a few variables, and (d) ideally would offer meaningful expansions that would provide increasing levels of topological detail. Mathematically, they should be (e) invariant under the permutation group on node numbering. We are specifically interested in the information flows of which originating node sends email or data to which destination node; and we are not initially interested in the underlying physical connectivity nor the path which the information traverses. Internet transmissions are extremely dynamic and thus to achieve some form of continuity, we envision constructing the C matrix with the summation of information transfers, over some time window δ, surrounding a time t for C(t, δ) thus representing the time evolution of the connection matrix. Given the number of connections, this problem resembles the representation of a physical gas in terms of thermo dynamical variables (such as temperature, volume, pressure, heat, and entropy). Generally, in such internet environments there is no meaningful location or position metric and distance is not usefully defined. As such pressure and volume, do not have a clear meaning without a distance function. Nor is it clear that what equilibrium is being approached, if any, and thus heat and temperature do not offer clear meanings. However, we suggest that the concept of both Shannon and generalized Renyi entropies [1, 2] can be well defined and summarize the order and disorder in the underlying topological structure.

Initially, how to define entropy on the connection matrix is not clear since both Shannon and Renyi entropies are defined as the log of the sum of the powers of the components of a vector, x_i, representing probabilities: $S = c \log_2 (b(\Sigma x_i^a))$ where $\Sigma x_i = 1$ and where a, b, and c are constants. As such these entropies represent the disorder in the underlying probability distribution. The disorder is a maximum with an even probability distribution and is a minimum when all the probability is in one cell with others having a value of zero. But the connection matrix columns or rows cannot be used as probability distributions since the diagonal of C is totally arbitrary. Even if we make some arbitrary choice of the diagonal values of C and normalize the columns, it is not clear what underlying topological 'disorder' we are measuring. In this work, we utilize our past work on the decomposition of the general linear group in order to answer both of these objections and to gain insight into how one might define these entropy metrics in useful ways that satisfy the requirements a-e above.

2 Background on Markov Lie Groups and Monoids

We had previously shown [3] that the transformations in the general linear group in n dimensions, that are continuously connected to the identity, can be decomposed into two Lie groups: (1) an n(n-1) dimensional 'Markov type' Lie group that is defined by preserving the sum of the components of a vector, and (2) the n dimensional Abelian Lie group, A(n), of scaling transformations of the coordinates. To construct the Markov type Lie group, consider the k,l matrix element of a matrix L^{ij} as a basis for n x n matrices, with off-diagonal elements, as $L^{ij}_{kl} = \delta^i_k \delta^j_l - \delta^j_k \delta^j_l$ with i =/= j. Thus the ij basis matrix has a '1' in position ij with a '-1' in position jj on the diagonal. These n(n-1) matrices form a basis for the Lie algebra of all transformations that preserve the sum of the components of vector. With this particular choice of basis, we then showed that by restricting the parameter space to non-negative values, λ^{ij} >=0, one obtains exactly all Markov transformations in n dimensions that were continuously connected to the identity as M = exp (s λ^{ij} L^{ij}) where we summarize over repeated indices and where s is a real parameter separated from λ^{ij} to parameterize the continuous evolution of the transformation. In other words λ^{ij} L^{ij} consists of non-negative coefficients in a linear combination of L^{ij} matrices. This non-negativity restriction on the parameter space removed the group inverses and resulted in a continuous Markov monoid, a group without an inverse, in n dimensions, MM(n). The basis elements for the MM algebra are a complete basis for n x n matrices that are defined by their off-diagonal terms. The n dimensional Abelian scaling Lie algebra can be defined by $L^{ii}_{kl} = \delta^i_k \delta^i_l$ thus consisting of a '1' on the i,i diagonal position. When exponentiated, A(s) = exp (s λ^{ii} L^{ii}), this simply multiplies that coordinate by e^s giving a scaling transformation. In what follows, we will show that all networks exactly correspond (one to one) to a combination of this Abelian transformation group and the Markov monoid transformations.

3 Connecting Markov Monoids to Network Metrics

The essence of this paper is the simple observation that (1) since the non-negative off diagonal elements of an n x n matrix exactly define a network (via C) and its topology with that node numbering, and (2) since a Markov monoid basis is complete in spanning all off-diagonal n ½ n matrices, then it follows that such networks are in one to one correspondence with the elements of the Markov monoids. Thus each connection matrix is the infinitesimal generator of a continuous Markov transformation and conversely. This observation connects networks and their topology with the Lie groups and algebras and Markov transformations in a well defined way. Since the Markov generators must have the diagonal elements set to the negative of the t sum of the other elements in that column, this requirement fixes the otherwise arbitrary diagonal of the connection matrix to that value also (sometimes referred to as the Lagrangian).

It now follows that this diagonal setting of C generates a Markov transformation by M= $e^{\lambda C}$. One recalls that the action of a Markov matrix on a vector of probabilities (an n-dimensional set of non-negative real values whose sum is unity), will map that vector again into such a vector (non-negative values with unit sum). The next observation is that by taking λ as infinitesimal, than one can write M = I + λC by ignoring order 12 and higher order infinitesimals. Here one sees that the bandwidth of the connection matrix between two nodes, now give that M matrix element as the relative transition rate between those two components of the vector. Thus it follows that given a probability distribution xi distributed over the n nodes of a network, then M gives the Markov transition (flow) rates of each probability from one node to another. Thus it follows that the connection matrix gives the infinitesimal transition rates between nodes with the bandwidth reflecting that exact topology.

Specifically, if the hypothetical probability vector is $x_i = (1,0,0,0\ldots0)$ then the first column of the M matrix will give the concentration of probability at the ith node after that infinitesimal time period. Thus the first column of M is the probability distribution after an infinitesimal time of that part of the probability that began on node 1 and likewise for all other nodes thus giving a probability interpretation to each of the columns of M. Thus each column of M can be treated as a probability distribution associated with the topology connected to that associated node and supporting an associated entropy function that reflects the inherent disorder (or order) after a flow λ. Thus the columns of M support a meaningful definition of Renyi entropies which in turn reflect the Markov transformation to disorder of the topology near the node for that column. Thus this Renyi entropy on this column can be said to summarize the disorder of the topology of the connections to that node. It follows that the spectra of all nodes reflects in some sense the disorder of the entire network. When sorted in descending order, it represents a spectral curve independent of nodal ordering and thus independent of the permutations on nodal numbering. That spectral curve can be summarized by the total value for the entropy of all columns (since entropy is additive and the column values are totally independent). The structure of the spectra can also be summarized by the entropy of the entropies in the spectra thus giving a second variable summarizing the entire topology.

If the connection matrix is symmetric then the graph (network) is said to be undirected, but if there is some asymmetry, then the graph is at least partially directed where the flow from i to j is less or greater than the converse flow. If the connection matrix is not symmetrized then one can capture this asymmetry by resetting the diagonal values of C to be equal to the negative of all other row values in that row. Then upon expansion of $M = I + \lambda C$, the rows are automatically normalized probabilities that in turn support entropy functions for each row. These row entropy values form a spectrum which could be sorted by the same nodal values (in order) that is used to order the column values. This will result in a different spectral curve that is not necessarily in non-decreasing order for the row entropies. One also can compute the total row entropy and the entropy if these row entropies as we have done from columns. If two columns have the same entropy then one can sometimes partially remove this degeneracy by the values of the associated row entropies.

Thus we suggest that the column and row spectral entropy curves, and the column and row total entropy and entropy of entropy values, distil essential disorder and order from the network topology – from n^2 values down to 2n (spectral) values, and finally to 4 values for the entire network – constitute a set of entropy metrics for the network, all of which are independent of the nodal ordering (numbering) in the network and thus indicative of the underlying topology. This analysis is expansive in two ways: (1) These two spectra and four values can be computed to higher order in λ thus including higher orders of the C matrix approximation for M and thereby incorporating connections of connections into the metric values. It is with higher powers of C via larger values of λ that we unfold more complex aspects of the network topology. (2) One can also compute these metric values for each of the Renyi entropy values. Work by V. Gudkov [4] has found that the order of the Renyi entropy is equivalent to the Hausdorf dimensionality equation. This opens the possibility that higher order entropy reveals connections of a 'higher dimensionality' in the network structure [4, 5].

4 Expansion of Second Order Renyi Entropy as a Taylor Series

Let us assume that C is symmetric (an undirected graph) thus $C = C^T$. If one considers the expansion of a vector of probabilities from state $\lambda=0$, $|x(0)>$, to another vector at a later state λ, $|x(\lambda)>$ by the continuous Markov transformation $M = e^{\lambda C}$ then $|x(\lambda)> = e^{\lambda C} |x(0)>$ and thus the entropy is given by:

$$S = \log_2(n\Sigma x_i^2) = \log_2(n<x(\lambda)|x(\lambda)>)= \log_2(n<x(0)|\ e^{\lambda C})^T (e^{\lambda C})|x(0)>)$$

or rearranging and defining R we get:

$$R(\lambda) = 2^S/n = <x(0)|\ e^{2\lambda C} |x(0)>)\ \text{ since } C = C^T$$

and then expanding the exponential we get:

$$R(\lambda) = <x(0)|\ (I + 2\lambda C + (2\lambda C)/2! + \dots\ )\ |x(0)>$$

Thus this power of the second order Renyi entropy consists of two times the diagonal values of the powers of the connection matrix, plus the unit matrix as shown. From this one can see that as λ becomes larger and larger, one must take more and more of the topology connections into consideration. This in fact gives a hierarchical expansion of this entropy that gradually 'explores and includes' higher and higher order connectivity. If the row and column entropies are computed to include these higher orders, then they will begin to take into account more complex aspects of the networks interconnectedness. When there is asymmetry a similar equation can be obtained.

5 General Diagonal Values and Eigenvalues

The previous results can be generalized to include totally general diagonal values for C, by utilizing the diagonal transformations available in the n-parameter Abelian scaling group. This group simply multiplies any node value by a scaling factor via $M= e^{\lambda C}$. There is a natural interpretation to the actions of this group in terms of network probability flows as introducing a source or sink of probability at the node which is acted upon. That action removes the conservation of probability that was maintained by the Markov monoid, but since such flow was simply used to encapsulate the topological structure of the network, we can accept this lack of conservation. Thus one can add to any diagonal of C, any positive or negative value representing the scaling value of that coordinate and one will still have a valid network as all off diagonal values of C are unchanged and the M matrix will still give the indicated flows. This allows one to see the previous arbitrary allocations of '1' or '0' of the C diagonals in a new light, especially for the eigenvalue computations.

When C is diagonalized, with the values leading to the Markov transformations, or to the more general values of the diagonals of the last paragraph, one automatically gets a diagonalization of the M matrix. The interpretation of the eigenvectors is now totally obvious as those linear combinations of nodal flows that give a single eigenvalue (decrease when the transformation is Markov) of the associated probability, for that eigenvector. This follows from the fact that all Markov eigenvalues are less than one except the one value for equilibrium which has eigenvalue unity for equilibrium. That means that each of these eigenvalues of C reflect the decreasing exponential rates of decrease of the associated eigenvector as the system approaches equilibrium as λ approaches infinity in $M = e^{\lambda C}$. This insight allows us to see that all of the Renyi entropy values are increasing as the system approaches equilibrium, which is normally the state of all nodes having the same value of this hypothetical probability. The use here of this 'artificial flow of probability under M' provides us with more than just a method of encapsulating the topology with generalized entropy values, it also gives an intuitive model for the eigenvectors and eigenvalues for C and sheds light on the graph isomerism problem (different topologies having the same eigenvalue spectra).

6   Conclusion. Potential Applications to Large Internet Networks

Based upon the arguments above, we suggest that for real networks such as the internet, that the appropriate connection matrix be formed, from source and destination information transfers, where both asymmetry and levels of connection are to be maintained in the C(t) matrix values during that window of time about that time instant. Specifically, this means that if a connection is made multiple times in that time interval, then that C element should reflect the appropriate weight of connectivity as this adds substantial value to the entropy functions. We then suggest that at each instant, the column and row entropy spectra be computed along with the total row and column entropy and entropy of entropies and that this be done for lower order Renyi entropies as well as lower order values in the expansion of the Markov parameter λ that includes higher order connectivity of the topology. We are currently performing tests to see how effective these entropy metrics are in detecting abnormal changes in topologies that could be associated with attacks, intrusions, malicious processes, and system failures. We are performing these experiments on both mathematical simulations of networks with changing topologies in know ways, and also on real network data both in raw forms and in forms simulated from raw data. The objective is to see if these metrics can be useful in the practical sense of monitoring sections of the internet and other computer networks. In addition to the two values of total entropy and entropy of entropy that summarize the column (or row) spectral distribution, we are looking at other natural expansions of this function in terms of functions or orthogonal polynomials that summarize the general behavior in useful ways thus providing other summary metric variables for the entropy spectra.

Acknowledgements

The author benefited from extensive collaborations and conversations with Dr. Vladimir Gudkov.

References

1. Renyi, A.: Probability Theory, North-Holland Series in Applied Mathematics and Mechanics, North-Holland Pub. Co (1970) 670 pages.
2. Renyi, A.: Selected Papers of Alfred Renyi, Akademia Kiado, Buadapest, Vol. 2 of 3 volumes (1976)

3. Johnson, J.E.: Markov-type Lie Groups in GL(n, R). Journal of Mathematical Physics 26 (1985) 252–257
4. Gudkov, V., Johnson, J.E.: Network as a complex system: information flow analysis, arXiv:lin.CD/0110008v1 (2001) 10 pages
5. Gudkov, V., Johnson, J.E.: Chapter 1: Multidimensional network monitoring for intrusion detection, arXiv: cs.CR/020620v1 (2002) 12 pages

Trust by Workflow in Autonomic Communication

Mikhail I. Smirnov

Fraunhofer FOKUS,
Kaiserin-Augusta-Allee 31, 10589 Berlin, Germany
Mikhail.Smirnov@fokus.fraunhofer.de

Abstract. Autonomic network elements cooperate for media and media signalling delivery; the paper demonstrates how these nodes can elaborate significant trust and achieve self-organisation by the exchange of blueprints of their internal packet processing workflows. We outline a model of an etiquette for the above exchange under the governance of a locally computed community fitness. We concentrate on the etiquette design using extended protocol expressions as the notation for behaviours, and ad hoc communication example for the demonstration of design steps. We show that properly defined fitness can be used as a meta-rule modifying the etiquette towards wider or deeper trust within the community.

1 Introduction

Current progress in the design of wired and wireless network elements demonstrates the clear trend towards more flexible, finer grained and self-managing packet processing. Self-management [1] is a top of a pyramid comprised of other self-properties: self-awareness, self-[re]configuration, self-optimization, self-healing, self-protection, self-adaptation, self-description, and finally self-implementation, or self-* for short. The autonomic communication research initiative [2] intends to apply self-* to all facets of communication.

Autonomic Communication studies the individual network element as it is affected by and affects other elements and the often numerous groups to which it belongs as well as network in general. The goals are to understand how desired elements behaviours are learned, influenced or changed, and how, in turn, these affect other elements, groups and network. Autonomic communication intends during the design phase to embed into a system such features that will facilitate right decision making at runtime, likely involving cross-layer interactions between protocol stack entities. Autonomic decision making will be assisted by locally perceived and processed community state under the governance of community fitness.

Trust is the primary issue in IP communication, it is often achieved off path. Fundamental lack of security in the Internet is the inherent consequence of its main architectural principle, known as End-To-End [3, 4] that forbids in-network functionality placement, thus keeping network open. As it is noted in [22], "closed networks are a waste of public money, but open networks are a huge risk." Facilitating end-user creativity and rapid deployment of new application level services the E2E has created

V. Gorodetsky, I. Kotenko, and V. Skormin (Eds.): MMM-ACNS 2005, LNCS 3685, pp. 136–150, 2005.

at the same time possibilities for multiple exploits of Internet technology that are visible at higher levels but rooted at the bottom of its protocol stack.

The self-* properties of autonomic communication promise to change existing balance between feature rich network edges and stupid core. The hope is to eliminate many if not all security threats found currently in IP-based networks by eliminating possible exploits. An autonomic network element empowered by self-* capabilities will not only able to detect an attack but also to act cooperatively with other elements of a trusted community against the reason. The power of autonomics is in community awareness; however community building and maintenance requires some sort of hose keeping — in-network information exchange between lower protocol layers.

Alike routing — the dominant Internet house-keeping information exchange for topology and connectivity awareness, we propose packet processing information exchange between network nodes for trust awareness. Similar approaches were proposed recently: forensic [5] and wafer-thin control plane [6] efforts aim at de-anonymisation of attackers by correlating seemingly disjoint events collected from network observations. Here we go one step further — enable network itself to support this.

Like telephone networks are designed with Trust By Wire principle in mind, the main principle we want to investigate is the Trust By Workflow, meaning that autonomic nodes that cooperate at media delivery level can eventually elaborate significant trust based on successful history of common work. Observing that network nodes are performing very repetitive work, and following the *routing with a clue* motivation [7] we generalise this principle for potentially any network function.

Workflow information is readily available in network nodes. Media processing in a node uses a lot of local state data for decision making: Where to forward this datagram? Is this micro flow admitted to EF service class? Is this port number allowed for the requesting host? Is this peer allowed to upload a file on another peer's computer? After a decision is made the result is usually dropped or at best logged.

Most challenging, yet possible is trust in ad hoc communication scenario, with no infrastructure to host trusted third party, etc. When a pair of nodes realises that they belong to the same path shared by significant traffic volume they start exchanging their workflows for served traffic with the aim to agree on an optimization of a common service. This pair-wise process leads to a bootstrapping of a community (e.g. per path) of nodes; it starts with *confirmation of the obvious*. Exchange of workflows pertaining to a common media flow — information with firmly verifiable evidence, can be advanced after trust is achieved. We propose to use content adaptation: the more advanced is the trust the finer grained details are exchanged. Thus the amount of data exchanged is very close to constant, subject to media traffic volumes served.

The paper is not about a trust establishment protocol, or fitness function calculation, though those are sketched as means to demonstrate our concepts; it's rather about a new paradigm of in-network community communication that enables trust and immunity. The rest of the paper is organized as follows. Section two builds a model of node's functionality and describes the vision of autonomic network, it introduces also the basic notation of protocol expressions that is used and extended throughout the paper to describe behaviours. Section three starts with a example, introduces some reasonable etiquette rules for cooperation, and picks some reasonable fitness function. It concludes with considerations of bootstrapping and finally demonstrates self-organisation of etiquette based on community context. Section four summarises our main claims.

2 Functional Models

2.1 Design Considerations

We treat the self-* requirement as a meta-level non-functional one that supersedes other, often overlooked non-functional requirements such as security, manageability, and testing. By this we avoid partitioning of a system under design into separately handled concerns that later might require integration. Also, possible replication of features might be avoided. Finally, we hopefully meet all other non-functional requirements within the same design paradigm.

The most benefits can be achieved at the finest possible granularity of node's function. Following the traditional telecommunication definition of a functionality found in [8] we model node's function F as a triple

$$F = <component, resources, controls>, \tag{1}$$

where *component* is to denote the identity of autonomic node, device or functionality that hosts internal *resources* with local *controls,* we assume that local controls are represented by fully specified policies (see section 3.2). Inputs for F are media and media signalling; usually signalling inputs are destined to local controls, while media inputs are resource requests. Both inputs might have certain safeguards, preventing known to be unwanted inputs. An example of media safeguard is filtering of so called Martian addresses on router interface; an example of media signalling safeguard is filtering of attempts to contact network side signalling agents by non-authenticated roaming signalling user agents [9]. SMTP filtering of spam messages differs from the above examples in one important respect — it learns, but the process of learning is typically under the governance of a human [10]. There are also two types of outputs of F — media and its signalling, with optional safeguards on outputs, e.g. to ensure in-profile transmission of outbound media.

Functional safeguards play paramount role in the proposed cooperative defence of the infrastructure: locally triggered safeguard is an important source of vulnerability information that cooperating entities learn from the workflow and use for pressing back at potential attacker.

2.2 Node Model

Without loss of generality we model any network node media or media signalling function as an input-output relay with possible transformation. We no longer distinguish between media and media signalling, the both types of payloads will be treated as media, contrary to a new type of communication we aim to design. Thus, we can conceptually represent all node's functionality as a matrix (2)

$$\Phi = \left[F_{i,j} \right]_{i = \overline{1, n}; j = \overline{1, m}}, \tag{2}$$

where media flows arriving at n inputs are transformed by Φ to m outputs. The interpretation of model (2) to represent, for instance forwarding is straightforward — Φ is then forwarding information base that defines in-node processing path from input i to output j. A number of different media datagrams processing types, that are termed — generic functions (g_l) found in most advanced Internet routers is around ten [11]; they are receiving and transmitting, forwarding, SSL processing, IPv4/IPv6 interoperability, header compression, classification, metering, scheduling, shaping, etc. — relatively small number of g_l makes workflow exchange feasible.

In-node processing of a particular datagram instantiates and chains as required these generic functions per micro flow. Note, the micro flow awareness is no longer a scalability concern, new router designs are emerging that take advantage of flow awareness, e.g. a truly autonomic cross-protect router by J. Roberts [12].

A workflow W_k is a chain of generic functionalities for a single micro flow; each workflow is a sequence of functions from (2) for the k-th micro flow as shown in (3), where a dot sign is sequential order within a k-th workflow, square brackets are for repetition. Workflow's sequence starts with the receiving of a datagram at the i-th physical interface, continues with processing by function $F_{i,j}$ that defines the next function $F_{j,p}$, and so on until the datagram leaves the node's protocol stack.

$$W_k = F^k_{i,j} \bullet [F^k_{j,p}] \tag{3}$$

In-node datagram processing as modelled by Φ is an in-node hammock — directed acyclic graph interconnecting physical interfaces; matrix Φ being asymmetric and triangular. Figure 1 shows an example (adopted from [13]) of a datagram processing hammock composed of five generic functions: g_1 — receiving of a datagram from a link; g_2 — optional datagram header decompression, g_3 — forwarding with optional interoperability processing between IPv4 and IPv6, g_4 — optional header compression, g_5 — queuing and transmission to a link.

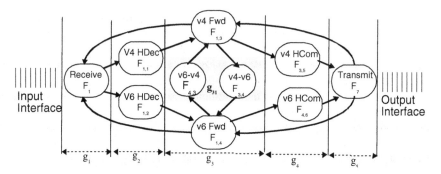

Fig. 1. In-node datagram processing hammock

A number of workflows can be instantiated from a hammock in Fig1. For example, expression (4) outlines a workflow of a router that receives IPv4 datagrams from a wireless link, decompresses their headers, converts to IPv6 and sends over to wireless link with new headers compressed.

$$W_1 = F^1_{1,1} \bullet F^1_{1,3} \bullet F^1_{3,4} \bullet F^1_{1,4} \bullet F^1_{4,6} \qquad (4)$$

Forwarding is the key to the trust by workflow — any meaningful workflow will have forwarding in it; this ubiquity makes forwarding a universal source of information on trustworthiness of network nodes. To speed up forwarding a routing cache stores recently used entries, and is consulted before the forwarding tables. If the kernel finds a matching entry during route cache look up, it will forward the packet immediately and stop traversing the forwarding tables [14]. Fig. 2 demonstrates a case of RC implemented as a compact binary trie data structure (only tails are shown) with leaves, being destination IP addresses labelled by a timestamp of last usage, outgoing port, error condition, if any was generated, and a source address of forwarded datagram, thus RC provides the evidence of performed forwarding. The rightmost icon shows how a compact tree is being expanded when a new entry is cached.

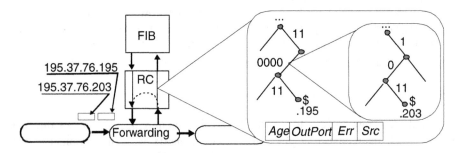

Fig. 2. Fast forwarding path (FIB — Forwarding Information Base; RC — Routing Cache; *Age* — time to expire for an RC entry; *Err*- error condition; $- leaf of a trie structure)

2.3 Network Model

The Internet of today handles media and media signalling flows, orthogonal to them management and control flows, when and if midcom infrastructure is available [15] as well as some in-network generated and consumed house-keeping flows, e.g. routing. We describe another house-keeping information exchange — autonomic communication.

An autonomic network is an in-lay of a media network; each node is a first-class citizen; no distinction is being done intentionally between user, access, edge, backbone, etc. node types. We assume that autonomic communication is done by exchange of messages with no visible relation between message sequences, i.e. there is no notion of autonomic communication flow. Message source and destination are not necessarily always applications, the model allows nodes to exchange messages on the discretion of protocol stack entities, like it is done in ICMP [16] and IGMP [17]. This might look similar to exchange of messages between roles as proposed in role-based architecture [18], however we do not want to hard-code in role-specific headers sources and destinations of our messages.

A message has a payload and a header: payload represents sender's media behaviour, expressed in workflows, header has message source and indirects the destination by what is called here a concern — a predicate on the behaviour — to a concerned community. Messages do not disclose to communicating peers sender's internal structure and algorithms, but only behaviour choices.

Community behaviours are observed locally through message boxes. Processing of messages in autonomic nodes is FCFS, it follows the arrivals of messages in node's message box. We assume that a node is able to create a message box per concern; this message box shall contain both sent and received messages pertaining to the concern. There are no assumptions on reliability of message delivery.

To represent contents of message boxes and consequently behaviours reflected in these messages we shall use and extend the notation of protocol expressions following the seminal work on protocol validation by G. Holzmann [19]. Small Latin characters represent received messages; characters, written as denominators of a fraction represent own sent messages; a dot represents FCFS ordering of messages; a plus sign between two messages represents alternatives; bracketed message sequence taken to the power of N represents N or more repetitions of the same message sequence; 1 stands for empty box, and ш — for a deadlock.

A cross operation ($[B_1] \otimes B_2[...]$) applied to one or more message boxes verifies the soundness of message exchange; the exchange is sound if it is deadlock free and there are no residuals in message box[es]. As axiomatically suggested in [19] the properties (re-write rules) of protocol expression as in (5) should hold.

$$a = \frac{a}{1}; \ a \bullet \frac{1}{b} = \frac{a}{b}; \ \frac{1}{a \bullet b} = \frac{1}{a} \bullet \frac{1}{b}; \ \frac{a+b}{c} = \frac{a}{c} + \frac{b}{c}; \ \frac{a}{b+c} = \frac{a}{b} + \frac{a}{c} \tag{5}$$

3 Autonomic Communication Models

3.1 An Example of Etiquette

Using the above models we show how autonomic node behaviours are induced by certain rules reflecting common community concern. To distinguish these rules from other rules (policies) we shall term them etiquette rules (e-rules), where etiquette is a complete ruleset reflecting the concern in question. As an example of a shared concern we consider trust establishment in ad hoc communication environment, where nodes use/ donate each other's resources to relay media datagrams with no infrastructure. Etiquette can be used in parallel with e.g. reputation schemes [20], or with inferring trust from control exchange, e.g. routing [21].

Consider the set of workflows (6) implemented by three nodes A, B, and C, and expressed in terms of functionalities (3) as introduced in Fig. 1.

$$a \to W_a = F_{1,3}; \quad b \to W_b = F_{1,4}; \quad c \to W_c = F_{1,3} \bullet F_{3,4} \bullet F_{1,4};$$
$$d \to W_d = F_{1,4} \bullet F_{4,3} \bullet F_{1,3} \tag{6}$$

Semantics of (6) and their distribution between nodes A, B, and C is represented in Fig. 3, where dotted line is a boundary between IPv4 and IPv6.

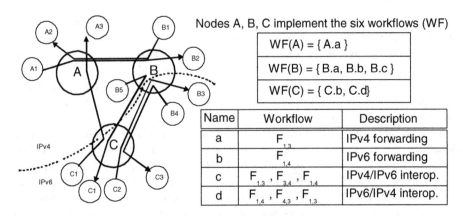

Nodes A, B, C implement the six workflows (WF)

WF(A) = { A.a }
WF(B) = { B.a, B.b, B.c }
WF(C) = { C.b, C.d}

Name	Workflow	Description
a	$F_{1,3}$	IPv4 forwarding
b	$F_{1,4}$	IPv6 forwarding
c	$F_{1,3}, F_{3,4}, F_{1,4}$	IPv4/IPv6 interop.
d	$F_{1,4}, F_{4,3}, F_{1,3}$	IPv6/IPv4 interop.

Fig. 3. Sample communication scenario

Let all the nodes having trust establishment as a common concern to have the following etiquette rules, refined from the purpose of community communication:

- E0: autonomic communication message heard by a node is consumed if message header represents actual node's concern;
- E1: each active workflow is advertised to the concerned community;
- E2: every heard advertisement of a remote workflow that is locally active is consumed and notified; every consumption notification is consumed (by remote peer);
- E3: the trust per workflow is considered to be established between peers after a certain number of notifications (N_n) is exchanged;
- E4: trust relationships are to be evaluated and progressed in the direction of increasing community fitness.

Consumption of messages is caching and processing of messages per concern. For the concern of trust the processing of messages is applying the cross operator to each node's message box; this hides sound behaviours. We extend the notation by overlying consumed message: $\bar{a}$ denotes consumption of a and $1/\bar{a}$ is the notification to the sender. We reserve to mean: z -no trust, t — established trust, x — trust in progress.

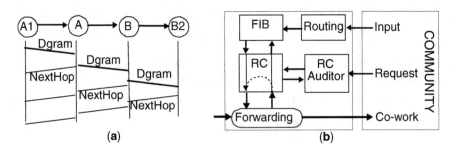

Fig. 4. Examples of auditing

Etiquette creates prerequisites for auditable trust. Relaying of a micro flow from Fig. 3 that is presented in Fig. 4 (a) is accompanied by sending back a NextHop notification, optionally forwarded to the source. Every receiver of a NextHop notification will be in the position to audit the delivery and eventually to discover any black or grey hole [21] along the path.Auditing is just inspecting contents of routing cache of other members, as in Fig. 4 (b) to see whether datagrams have been really relayed. This kind of auditing is a natural step in community collaboration: recall that FIB is being computed by a node based on routing information offered by community members. Of course access to private parts of RC can be protected by access control rules.

Following etiquette rules the nodes shall exhibit their active workflows; for simplicity we assume that all potential workflows from Fig. 3 are being simultaneously active. Expressions (7) through (9) present etiquette behaviours induced by E1 — E3 as observed in message boxes. Etiquette shall eventually establish trust between $A.a$ and $B.a$ within IPv4 connectivity, and between $C.b$ and $B.b$ within IPv6 connectivity, as reflected in Fig. 5. The behaviours are partial in a sense that message sequences outlined in (7)–(9) will appear in the same message box of each node due to the assumption of them having one message box per concern.

Assuming that trust was established, we apply a cross operator and re-write rules (5) to each node's message box that results in certain residuals as in (10). The (10) shows that certain workflows due to their incompatibility cannot be used to establish a trust based on the proposed etiquette; for example there is no trust between nodes A and C. However as it is obvious from Fig. 2 it might be possible for A and C to use node B as a trusted third party.

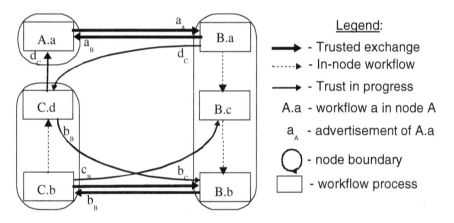

Fig. 5. Sample etiquette communication graph

This will require modification of etiquette rules, i.e. introducing a new e-rule allowing trust delegation or trust transfer, which might be regarded in general as a non-desired feature from security viewpoint. In case one of the nodes is a malicious one, e.g. acting as a black hole the cross operator applied to message boxes of the nodes whose media datagrams would have been dropped will result in more residuals and no trust.

$$A_{E1} \to 1/a_A \bullet (a_B + d_C) \; ;$$
$$B_{E1} \to 1/a_B \bullet 1/c_B \bullet 1/b_B \bullet (a_A + d_C + b_C) \; ;$$
$$C_{E1} \to 1/d_C \bullet 1/b_C \bullet (b_B + c_B + a_A) \; .$$

$$(7)$$

$$A_{E2} \to a_B \bullet 1/\overline{a_B} + \overline{a_A} \; ;$$
$$B_{E2} \to a_A \bullet 1/\overline{a_A} + b_C \bullet 1/\overline{b_C} + d_C + \overline{a_B} + \overline{b_B} \; ;$$
$$C_{E2} \to b_B \bullet 1/\overline{b_B} + c_B + \overline{b_C} \; .$$

$$(8)$$

$$A_{E3} \to (a_B \bullet 1/\overline{a_B} \bullet 1/x_B)^{N_n} \bullet 1/t_B + \overline{x_A} + \overline{t_A} \; ;$$

$$B_{E3} \to (a_A \bullet 1/\overline{a_A} \bullet 1/x_A)^{N_n} \bullet 1/t_A + \ldots$$
$$\ldots + (b_C \bullet 1/\overline{b_C} \bullet 1/x_C)^{N_n} \bullet 1/t_C + \overline{x_B} + \overline{t_B} \; ;$$

$$C_{E3} \to (b_B \bullet 1/\overline{b_B} \bullet 1/x_B)^{N_n} \bullet 1/t_B + \overline{x_C} + \overline{t_C} \; .$$

$$(9)$$

$$A_{E1} \otimes A_{E2} \otimes A_{E3} = d_C + \overline{t_B} \; ; \quad B_{E1} \otimes B_{E2} \otimes B_{E3} = 1/c_B + d_C + \overline{t_A} + \overline{t_C} \; ;$$
$$C_{E1} \otimes C_{E2} \otimes C_{E3} = 1/d_C + c_B + \overline{t_B}$$

$$(10)$$

3.2 Fitness Function

We consider e-rule E4 together with node's fitness as a meta-rule that can be used to modify etiquette rules to safely adapt to network situation or context, how the trust establishment etiquette itself can be modified to progress trust. The rationale behind is that of community leadership expressed in local preferences for decision making; if the community is active, stable (conflict-free), and mutually trusted then the behaviour choices of every node can be streamlined, and, on contrary, when community is inactive, unstable or disappears, the behaviour choices of every node should follow largely the principles of self-protection, survivability, etc. Natural metrics of community's activity are the number of served workflows and the number of trusted or trust-in-progress node pairs within the community. On the other hand, an autonomic node should preserve certain balance between the amount of served workflows and the relative amount of community members producing/consuming these workflows. The rationale for this is to avoid DoS and DDoS scenarios, where relatively small fraction of community is generating unrealitsically high volumes of workflows destined for a node.

We claim that an optimal fitness function can be found for a given communication scenario, and given community, sets of etiquette rules, and concerns. Our goal is not to find an optimal fitness function but to demonstrate how a fitness function can be used as a mean for self-adaptation, in particular in autonomic adaptation of etiquette rules to situation changes. For demonstration purposes only we shall use (11)

$$F_\varphi(i) = \frac{N_t(i) + \omega \cdot N_x(i)}{N} \cdot \frac{n_w(i)}{\overline{n_w}} \qquad (11)$$

where $F_\varphi(i)$ — fitness function value computed by the i-th autonomic node; $N_t(i)$ and $N_x(i)$ are respectively the number of nodes, with which node i has trust, including i itself, or trust in progress relation per advertised workflow, N — total amount of community nodes the i-th node is aware of, including i itself; ω, $\omega \in [0, 1]$ — relative importance of trust as compared to trust in progress; $n_w(i)$, $\overline{n_w}$ — the number of workflows advertised by the i-th node and the total number of community workflows the i-th node is aware of, including i-th own workflows. Note, that for the example in section 3.1 in the state reflected by (10) nodes would have computed their fitness as in the second column of Table 1.

This sample calculation demonstrates an interesting property, node fitness is a function of community awareness. Just two nodes having established trust for all advertised workflows will have maximum fitness 0,50. The (11) shows that the fittest node should have some community information beyond current communication scenario; this information can be treated as community context, as degrees of freedom that can be used for adaptation. For example, as shown in (10) and (11) nodes B and C are fit not only because they have more trust relationships with other nodes than node A but also because they have more residuals in (10).

Community fitness (12) is a generalisation of (11). Maximal community fitness is always higher than that of a single node. The function (12) for a community (C^o) is non-linear (see table below) with regard to contributions of community members. Thus we propose that nodes compute their weighted fitness as (13); this computation for the situation (10) is presented in Table 1, last column.

$$F_\varphi(C^o) = \frac{[N_t(i) + \omega \cdot N_x(i)] - N}{n_w(i)} \quad ; i = \overline{1, N} \; , \; F_\varphi \in [0, 1] \qquad (12)$$

$$F_{\varphi, w}(i) = 1 - F_\varphi \, \tilde{C}^o \cdot F_\varphi(i) \quad ; i \not\subset \tilde{C}^o \qquad (13)$$

Table 1. Weighted fitness for situation (10)

Node	Node Fitness	Community Fitness		Node Fitness Weight	Weighted Node Fitness
		All nodes	Without		
A	0,22	0,67	0,40	k_A=0,60	0,13
B	0,50		0,00	k_B=1,00	0,50
C	0,50		0,50	k_C=0,50	0,25

Fitness function must be evaluated continuously, starting from a boot process; at boot the only etiquette behaviour that a node can complete is the one defined by E1, it returns initially zero fitness. Evaluation of a local fitness function (that is easy to associate with the processing of local etiquette message box) might be programmed to generate fitness function events — either reaching threshold values, or every change. We shall now demonstrate, starting with node's bootsrapping how fitness function can help to modify e-rules towards increasing fitness of a node and a community.

3.3 Bootstrapping

On boot a node is assigned default role[s] and a purpose, this is done by enforcing locally the two rule sets — policy and etiquette. Policy set is node's role refined into a set of fully specified policies — rules defining node's functional behaviour choices. Etiquette is the refinement of node's purpose with regard to autonomic communication; the purpose is enforced by a set of etiquette rules defining choices in node's community behaviour. Role and purpose are local names persistently identifying boot configuration of a node; these names unambiguously point to node's storage areas where fully parametrised policy set and yet behaviour-independent etiquette rule sets are stored.

The boot manager keeps the values of role (*Role*) and purpose (*Purpose*), passes them for kernel initialisation and writes in a bootstrap log file the two values. After kernel initialisation is done, the log file is appended by the refinement of role — policy and by the refinement of purpose — etiquette. There is no assumption that boot configuration is conflict free, especially with regard to the agreement between *Purpose* and *Role*; it is assumed however that role-defined *Policy* rules have higher priority than purpose-defined *Etiquette*. The assumption is motivated by the fact that *Etiquette* might need to be further refined (constrained) by policies depending on a situation in concern; the result of this refinement process is a set of e-rules — fully specified etiquette rules. Thus, e-rules and policy rules form a consistent and locally conflict-free set of rules, however only until the need for further refinement is identified.

Consider node D with a bootsrap purpose defined by E0 – E3, it is refined to a bootsrap etiquette (14), with square brackets to denote optional extensions

$$D_{E1} \rightarrow 1/y_{D,1} \bullet [1/y_{D,2}] \; ;$$

$$D_{E2} \rightarrow y_{D,1} \bullet 1/\overline{y_{D,1}} + [y_{D,2} \bullet 1/\overline{y_{D,2}}] + [\ldots] + \overline{y_{Y,1}} + \overline{[y_{Y,2}]} \; ; \qquad (14)$$

$$D_{E3} \rightarrow (y_{D,1} \bullet 1/\overline{y_{D,1}} \bullet 1/x_Y)^{N_n} \bullet 1/t_Y + [\ldots] \; ,$$

where $y_{D,1}, y_{D,2} \cdots$ are variables to be instantiated with D's workflows as defined by policies, note that these variables are generic functionalities ($g_1, g_2,\ldots$ in Fig. 1); $y_{Y,1}, y_{Y,2} \cdots$ are variables to be instantiated by similar workflows of not yet known community member Y.

Each policy from a policy set is represented as <event: condition, action>, where action is one of the node's functions, as in (6). A mapping from the policy set to the set of workflows returns a list of workflow identifiers that are the values that instantiate all variables in (14), thus the etiquette is refined by the mapping into a fully specified set of e-rules. In other words, the mapping function identifies for e-rules all workflows that are managed by policies, i.e that are potentially changeable by context.

We consider the two types of boot behaviour: normal boot and soft boot. In normal boot a node completely suspends all its operations on media, media signalling and community communication; it drops all previously accommodated soft state and starts anew. On soft boot a node suspends only etiquette defined behaviour and drops only etiquette related state. Immediately after a normal boot a network element does not have any active workflow; it needs to receive either media or media signalling to launch one. However, etiquette behaviours are fully specified by the refinement process above and can be used right after any type of boot, for example to collect community context. On soft boot a network element has no memory on trust establishment, all even on-going workflows are considered as fresh, i.e. the e-rules within a policy set consider these workflows as just being started. In both boot cases we are interested in booting of the etiquette behaviour only, thus we no longer distinguish between the two types of bootstrapping. We introduced soft boot to reflect the process of a new node joining a community, thus soft boot can also be regarded as booting to a community.

Community communication that can be done for a number of concerns must be performant and scalable. Our approach is to use progressive communication patterns that will gradually evolve to serve more complex tasks by morphing under already achieved progress within the concerns of interest. Trust establishment is a primary concern on boot, should follow easy to discover, or standard patterns like those sketched in E0 – E3. However, after initial trust is established, community peers could launch etiquette communication for other concerns (QoS, interoperability, auto-configuration, etc.) using trusted peers — this substitution of etiquette messages (7) – (9) by messages of another concern we dub etiquette progression. Progression can be continued with deeper or wider trust establishment itself using fitness function events to modify etiquette messages as in the next section.

3.4 Evolving to Fit the Community

Situation outlined by (10) will be noted by each community member as stability of their message boxes and existing etiquette will be perceived as no longer productive. While trust is the permanent concern the peers will attempt to use progression as situative re-refinement of e-rules using basic etiquette and fitness function. Figure 6 summarises a possible internal organisation of an autonomic node.

After initial trust as in (10) is established between pairs of community peers the rule E4 — progression of the etiquette — will be triggered by the local fitness function event $F_\varphi(i) = const|_\tau$, meaning that node's fitness is unchanged during time interval τ. Natural etiquette progression suggested here is the exchange between trusted peers of summaries of established trust relations together with summaries per workflows. This way, trusted peers can compute [sub-]community fitness and distribute back to peers their trust connectivity. There is no need to make any additional computation for this, sufficient will be to distribute to peers residuals as in (10).

The re-refined etiquette is the exchange of residuals from cross operation on local message boxes between trusted nodes that results in a new state, e.g. (15)

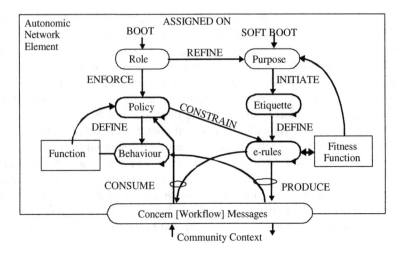

Fig. 6. Autonomic Node Architecture

$$A \to (d_C + \overline{t_B}) \bullet (1/c_B + d_C + \overline{t_A} + \overline{t_C})\big|_B \; ;$$

$$B \to (1/c_B + d_C + \overline{t_A} + \overline{t_C}) \bullet \left[(d_C + \overline{t_B})\big|_A + (1/d_C + c_B + \overline{t_B})\big|_C \right] \; ; \qquad (15)$$

$$C \to (1/d_C + c_B + \overline{t_B}) \bullet (1/c_B + d_C + \overline{t_A} + \overline{t_C})\big|_B \; ,$$

where $(\ldots)\big|_i$ denotes a residual received from the i-th trusted peer. After (15) all trusted nodes share trusted sub-community state information including weighted node fitness values (Table 1, last column), and in accordance with the purpose shall try to increase their fitness and, consequently the fitness of the community. Each node according to E4 shall attempt to achieve wider trusted connectivity based on the contents of its message box. In our example only A succeeds: A that previously was aware of node C (because of (d_C) advertisement) concludes from (15) that its trusted peer node B is in trust with node C, it's only possibility to enhance its fitness. Node A re-refines its E1 induced etiquette $A_{E1} \to 1/a_A \bullet (a_B + d_C)$ to advertise to the community the following intended behaviour

$$A_{E1'} \to (1/a_A \bullet d_C) \, \| \, (1/c_B \bullet 1/b_B)\big|_B \, \| \, (b_C \bullet d_C) \qquad (16)$$

where $\|$ is the intended concatenation of local behaviours of community members. Expression (16) is a payload of etiquette message, its concern is yet improved trust in the community, with message header signalling to community members that node A is proposing certain behaviour. Basically, (16) suggests trusted concatenation of local workflows: IPv4 forwarding from A to B, IPv4 to IPv6 interoperability at B and IPv6 forwarding from B to C; reverse IPv6 to IPv4 interoperability at C. Though this sample scenario might look artificial, it shows that community concerns taken locally and opportunistically may yield improvements to community fitness.

4 Conclusions

Design of autonomic communication systems and their elements is complicated by a large number of interdependencies between different concerns and requirements. The real challenge is not to attempt to solve associated problems at system design phase but to embed such features into a system that will facilitate solutions at run-time. We demonstrate this with soft-boot, run-time, local and context sensitive etiquette refinement approaches. Autonomic network elements will likely to be much more flexible than current hosts and routers in cross-layer interactions between entities of their protocol stack; we try to capture this feature by the notion of a workflow — chromosome characterisation of node's behaviour — the payload of proposed etiquette communication.

Etiquette is a mechanism for community building and community self-management that is achieved through locally perceived and processed community state under the governance of community fitness. We select trust establishment in ad hoc networking as an example of non-functional requirement to be able to demonstrate throughout the paper abstract concepts with examples; despite this demonstration purpose the future work will address more realistic scenarios for trust and intrusion detection based on the principles of autonomic communication.

References

1. Autonomic Computing Overview, IBM, on line at http://www.research.ibm.com/autonomic/overview/elements.html
2. Autonomic Communication: Research Agenda for a New Communication Paradigm, white paper, Fraunhofer FOKUS on-line at http://www.autonomiccommunication.org/publications/doc/WP_v02.pdf (2003)
3. Blumenthal, M.S., Clark, D. D.: Rethinking the design of the Internet: The end to end arguments vs.the brave new world, ACM Transactions on Internet Technology 1(1) (2001)
4. Kempf, J., Austein, R. (Eds.): The Rise of the Middle and the Future of End-to-End: Reflections on the Evolution of the Internet Architecture, IAB. http://www.ietf.org/rfc/rfc3724.txt (2004)
5. Sekar, V., Xie, Y. Maltz, D., Reiter, M., Zhang, H.: Toward a Framework for Internet Forensic Analysis, HotNets-III (2004)
6. Rexford, J., Greenberg,A., Hjalmtysson,G., Maltz,D., Myers,A., Xie,G., Zhan,J., Zhang, H.: Network-Wide Decision Making: Toward A Wafer-Thin Control Plane, HotNets-III (2004)
7. Afek, Y., Bremler-Barr, A., Har-Peled, S.: Routing with a Clue, Proceedings of ACM SIGCOMM'99 (1999)
8. ATIS Telecom Glossary 2000. T1.523-2001, ATIS Committee T1A1 Performance and Signal Processing, on-line at http://www.atis.org/tg2k/ (2000)
9. Kroeselberg, D.: SIP security requirements from 3G wireless networks, Internet Engineering Task Force, work in progress <draft-kroeselberg-sip-3g-security-req-00.txt> (2001)

10. Guardian Digital Secure Mail Suite, User Guide. Guardian Digital, Inc. http://infocenter.guardiandigital.com/manuals/SecureMail/EnGarde-MAIL-1.0.html (2004)

11. Hegde, H.: Building an IPv6 Router. Proceedings of 2002 Communications Design Conference, Network Processing Forum, on-line at http://www.npforum.org/pressroom/Building_an_IPv6_Router.ppt (2002))

12. Roberts, J.: Towards a Traffic Theory Friendly Internet: the Cross-Protect Router, invited talk at QofIS 2003, Stockholm, Sweden. http://www.imit.kth.se/info/LCN/qofis2003/slides/WelcomeANDkeynote/QofIS_Roberts. pdf (2003)

13. Kokku, R., Riche, T., Kunze, A., Mudigonda, J., Jason, J., Vin, H.: A Case for Run-time Adaptation in Packet Processing Systems, ACM SIGCOMM Computer Communication Review, Volume 34, Issue 1 (2004)

14. Brown, M.A.: Guide to IP Layer Network Administration with Linux, Version 0.4.4, on-line at http://linux-ip.net/html/routing-cache.html

15. Srisuresh, P., Kuthan, J., Rosenberg, J., Molitor, A., Rayhan, A.: Middlebox communication architecture and framework, IETF Request for Comments: 3303 (2002)

16. Postel, J.: Internet Control Message Protocol. IETF Request for Comments: 792 (1981)

17. Deering, S.: Host Extensions for IP Multicasting, IETF Request for Comments: 1112 (1989)

18. Braden, R., Faber, T., Handley, M.: From Protocol Stack to Protocol Heap -- Role-Based Architecture, HotNets-I, Princeton, NJ (2002)

19. Holzmann, G. J.: A Theory for Protocol Validation, IEEE Trans. on Computers. Vol C31, No 8 (1982) 730–738

20. Garg, A., Battiti, R., Costanzi, G.: Dynamic Self-management of Autonomic Systems: The Reputation, Quality and Credibility (RQC) Scheme, Proceedings of WAC 2004, LNCS 3457 (2004) 165–179

21. Pirzada, A. A., McDonald, C.: Establishing Trust In Pure Ad-hoc Networks, Proc. 27th Australian Computer Science Conference, New Zealand (2004)

22. Hutchison, D., Bhatti, S., Wakeman, I., Crowcroft, J., et al: Communications Research Challenges for the 21st Century, unpublished memo, on-line at http://www.cl.cam.ac.uk/~jac22/out/crc.txt

An Ontology-Based Approach to Information Systems Security Management

Bill Tsoumas, Stelios Dritsas, and Dimitris Gritzalis[*]

Dept. of Informatics, Athens University of Economics and Business,
76 Patission Ave., Athens GR-10434, Greece
{bts, sdritsas, dgrit}@aueb.gr

Abstract. Complexity of modern information systems (IS), impose novel security requirements. On the other hand, the ontology paradigm aims to support knowledge sharing and reuse in an explicit and mutually agreed manner. Therefore, in this paper we set the foundations for establishing a knowledge-based, ontology-centric framework with respect to the security management of an arbitrary IS. We demonstrate that the linking between high-level policy statements and deployable security controls is possible and the implementation is achievable. This framework may support critical security expert activities with respect to security requirements identification and selection of certain controls and countermeasures. In addition, we present a structured approach for establishing a security management framework and identify its critical parts. Our security ontology is being represented in a neutral manner, based on well-known security standards, extending widely used information systems modeling approaches.

Keywords: Security Management, Security Policy, IS Security, Security Ontology.

1 Introduction

Modern information systems offer organizations and individuals a lot of benefits. The advances in information and communication technologies (ICT) offer dramatic cost savings and can introduce new capabilities in order to support new and diverse services to organizations and/or end users. A combination of conventional networks and wireless- and sensor-aware devices with traditional installations such as mainframes, becomes more and more popular. The dynamic character of IS exacerbates the security risks innate in any IS; the lack of effective security requirements inclusion during the system development is the most important reason, which is further stressed by the rush of commercial competition. In addition, new technologies face several categories of risks; a number of these risks are similar to those of a conventional IS, while others are introduced by the new technologies' immaturity and the lack of efficient integration with conventional ones. As an example, we might consider the vulnerabilities introduced by wireless where the use of the airwave as the underlying communication medium it might be an easy target to malicious users.

---

[*] Corresponding author.

V. Gorodetsky, I. Kotenko, and V. Skormin (Eds.): MMM-ACNS 2005, LNCS 3685, pp. 151–164, 2005.

In this context, the organizations should be aware of the risks introduced by the dynamic nature of information systems which support the business functions; thus, the maintenance, management and administration of such network infrastructures should be a continuing process, which requires greater effort compared to conventional networks [1], [2]. IS security requirements might stem from the stakeholders and the environment of the organization (market trends, data protection acts). Therefore, there is a need for the identification and implementation of robust security controls to ensure that information resources are protected against potential threats. By the term *"Security Control"* we mean the applicable, low-level technical countermeasures, which can be applied directly to the IS devices. Traditionally, the requirements of such controls come up as a result of an Information System (IS) Risk Analysis (RA) study, given the thorough intervention of a (possibly group of) security expert(s). Furthermore, the formulation of a generic security policy, which is linked with and exploits the RA results, is a usual addition to the RA process. In all cases such a process, either assisted through computerized tools or not, renders the security expert(s) responsible for the following tasks: a) capturing the security control requirements of the IS, b) translating organizational input to a set of semiformal security rules, c) transforming the security rules into an effective set of security controls, d) deploying and managing the security controls over the IS and, e) establish a risk management process over the effectiveness and efficiency of the security controls in place (optional).

To accomplish the above tasks, security experts usually deal with high-level statements from various sources (e.g. output of RA tools, policy statements expressed in a managerial level, Service Level Agreements), combined with IS technical information. This is often an effort-consuming intervention – especially for large organizations – which has not yet been properly assisted by automated processes. We argue that we may employ a structured approach to support the process leading from informal, high-level statements found in policy and RA documents to deployable technical controls. The outcome of this process will be a knowledge-based, ontology-centric security management system, eventually bridging the IS risk assessment and organizational security policies with security management.

This paper aims to provide the foundations of a framework for supporting the above procedure. More specifically, the proposed framework will encapsulate IS security management through the linking between high-level policy statements and explicit, low-level security controls adaptable and applicable in the IS environment. Additionally, in the specific paper we propose an architecture that will facilitate the implementation of the above framework (scheme). Our overall approach is outlined as follows;

1. Identify and define the necessary components and mechanisms of the framework.
2. Gather the security requirements that stem from the policy statements and express them in an information-rich manner.
3. Associate security requirements with appropriate risk mitigation actions (i.e. specific countermeasures).
4. Provide deployment mechanisms to the IS infrastructure.
5. Define an architecture for security management of the IS.

It should be noted that the paper deals with the description of the total framework and respective architecture, and as such, does not research into implementation details of certain parts of the architecture; in addition, its' modular structure permits independence of implementation, provided that the interfaces between the architecture modules are well-defined.

The rest of this paper is organized as follows: the next section gives an overview of the prerequisite information about IS management standards and the ontological paradigm, which will be the enablers for our approach. In section 3 we define an architecture and its components, while in section 4 we present the IS security management framework. In section 5 we present related work to our research and, finally, our conclusions and further work in section 6.

2 Background

2.1 Common Information Model

The Common Information Model (CIM) [3] is a conceptual information model, which developed by Distributed Management Task Force (DMTF) for describing computing and business entities in Internet, enterprise and service provider environments. The CIM is a hierarchical, object-oriented architecture that makes it comparatively straightforward to track, and depict the complex interdependencies and associations among different managed objects. Such interdependencies may include those between logical network connections and underlying physical devices, or those of an e-commerce transaction and the web and database servers on which it depends. The CIM does not require any particular instrumentation or repository format, attempting to unify and extend the existing instrumentation and management standards (SNMP, DMI, CMIP, etc.) using object-oriented constructs and design. While CIM is an evolving standard, there are several commercial implementations from vendors like HP and Dell [3].

Management schemas are the building blocks for management platforms and management applications, such as device configuration, performance management, and change management. The CIM Schema supplies a set of classes with properties and associations that provide a well-understood conceptual framework, within which it is possible to organize the available information about the managed environment. The CIM Schema is the combination of the Core and Common Models.

Core Model: The core model captures notions that are applicable to all areas of management. The core model is a set of classes, associations, and properties that provide a basic vocabulary for describing managed systems, representing a starting point for determining how to extend the common schema.

Common Models: The Common Models are information models that capture notions that are common to particular management areas, but independent of any particular technology or implementation. Examples of common models include systems, applications, networks and devices. The classes, properties, associations and methods in the common models are intended to provide a view of the area that is detailed enough to use as a basis for program design and, in some cases, implementation.

Extension Schema: Extension schemas represent extensions of the common models. It is expected that the common models will evolve as a result of the promotion of objects and properties defined in the extension schemas [3].

CIM is advantageous for our approach in that the model can be mapped to structured specifications such as OWL [4].

2.2 Ontologies: Their Use in Knowledge Modeling

An ontology is "an explicit specification of a conceptualization" [5]. Ontologies are discussed in the literature as means to support knowledge sharing and reuse [6]. This reusability approach is based on the assumption that if a modeling scheme - i.e. ontology - is explicitly specified and mutually agreed by the parties involved, then it is possible to share, reuse and extend knowledge. It is obvious that there is no "silver-bullet" ontology - in other words, it is unlikely that there will be a single, common ontology for all domains of human activity. This led to the concept of newsgroup metaphor or domain specific ontology, in order to define the terminology for a group of people that share a common view on a specific domain [6]. Ontologies can be used to describe structurally heterogeneous information sources of different levels of abstraction, such as found on security policy documents and RA outputs, helping both people and machines to communicate in a concise manner, a manner which is based not only on the syntax of security requirements, but on their semantics as well.

An ontology is comprised by three major building blocks: *concepts, relationships* and *constraints*. Concepts are abstract terms, which are typically organized in *taxonomies*. Hierarchical concepts are linked with an *"is-a"* relationship. Furthermore, concepts can have *properties* (or *attributes*), which help establishing relationships between non-hierarchical concepts. Attributes may have a specific type like STRING, INTEGER, BOOLEAN, etc. *Axioms* are rules that are valid in the modeled domain, finally constraining the possible (i.e. meaningful) interpretations for the defined concepts. There are simple symmetric, inverse or transitive axioms and complex rules consisting of several relations. Ontologies provide for *inheritance* in an object-oriented manner, with *instances* being concrete occurrences of abstract concepts.

Ontologies are a vital part of our framework, which is described next.

3 Proposed Security Architecture

In the following paragraphs we present a generic architecture for IS security management based on an ontology-centric approach. The main idea is to associate the security requirements (*"what"*) stemming from the security knowledge sources with the appropriate actions (*"how"*) and eventually deploy them to the IS. To accomplish these tasks, four main phases exist: a) building the SO in order to simulate the underlying IS, b) capturing the IS security requirements (*"what"*) from high-level policy statements into appropriate instances of the SO concepts, c) matching every security requirement with the appropriate technical security control (*"how"*) that effectively produces a population of (*what, how*) pairs for every IS device instance, and d) the actual deployment of the identified actions to the IS, which can be accomplished by piping the necessary data to a policy-based management platform, such as Ponder [7]. Figure 1 depicts the architecture under consideration, whereas a detailed description of required steps is given in section 4.

Our approach is modular enough, in such a way that enhancements in any given component(s) can be applied with a minimal overhead to the architecture. The proposed security architecture is based on the combination of several methods, techniques and enablers such as knowledge representation, information extraction, IS management standards, and best practices from wide accepted security standards. The (vague) security knowledge that is present to high-level policy statements is transformed through successive steps into applicable security countermeasures. For simplicity, with the term *"policy statements"* hereafter we refer to RA outputs, lists of security controls requirements, organization policy statements and SLA requirements.

In the next sections we present the components of our architecture, as well as the necessary steps that demonstrate the framework establishment.

3.1 Sources of Security Knowledge

A number of security-related knowledge information sources exist that influence in a direct or indirect way the security expert so as to implement the security controls. Direct sources are bound to the specific IS and include organization policies and SLAs, RA outputs and IS infrastructure information. Indirect sources are implicitly associated with the given IS and include security and risk management standards [8] [9], technical best practices [10], security advisories from vendors [11] and security portals [12], security mailing lists [13] and vulnerability catalogues such as CVE [14].

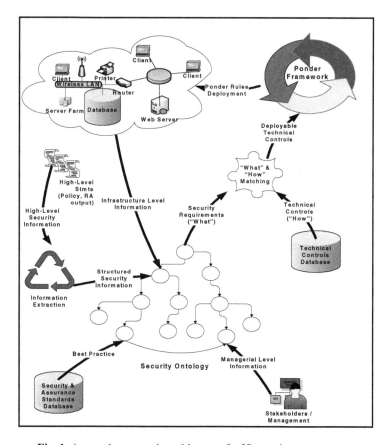

Fig. 1. An ontology-centric architecture for IS security management

An indirect source of security information, usually neglected by the experts is business decisions made by the organization stakeholders (e.g. *"Company's IT systems should support the Sales process"*). This may raise certain IS security considerations (e.g. *"the sales application must be accessible by the salesmen with wireless laptops during business hours"*).

Furthermore, these sources of security knowledge can be *classified* among a number of criteria: the *ambiguity of contained information*, the *relevance to the specific IS environment*, the *nature of the information* therein - e.g. *requirement* (*"what"*) or *implementation* (*"how"*) - the *target of appliance* (e.g. applies to all IS assets or to a subset of them), etc. Figure 2 depicts a classification of certain security knowledge sources against the first two points of view, namely: *ambiguity* of contained information, and *relevance* to the specific IS environment. The depicted sources of security knowledge that span from high to low relevance reflect the existence of specific, still irrelevant information to the IS under question, due to diversity of technologies present in some knowledge sources such as mailing lists.

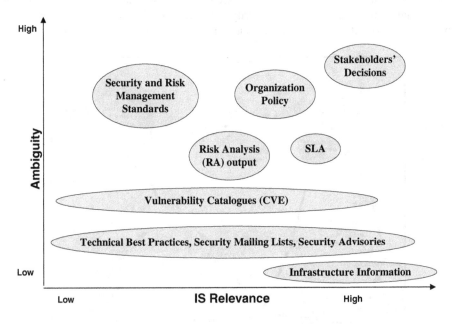

Fig. 2. A classification of IS security knowledge sources

In conclusion, it is evident that the complexity, the different way of representation and the diverse nature of abovementioned sources turns the work of security expert(s) into a challenging and time-consuming task. The modeling and extraction of security-related information from different information sources can be addressed with standardization initiatives such as OVAL [15] and CVE [14], with separate information extraction modules for each definition [16] [17], etc; our knowledge-based system which will exploit this vast, but still unstructured wealth of security information is a valuable tool in the arsenal of security experts.

3.2 Security Ontology

In this section, we define a generic Security Ontology (SO), as "*an ontology that elaborates on the security aspects of a system*". In the sequel, the terms "Security Ontology" and "Ontology" will be used interchangeably.

Ontology languages such as OWL [18] provide for formal logic support like Description Logics, a particular decidable fragment of first order logic (i.e. OWL DL version), which has desirable computational properties for reasoning systems. It is true that, OWL comparing to pure formal logic models expressing security issues may lack in expressiveness (issue which is expected to be supported with the evolution of tools compliant with OWL Full version), but ontologies have several advantages: a) ontologies are more close to human mentality expressing a world model, in contradiction with formal languages which are difficult to understand and use by humans, b) the formal models deal with access control issues mainly which can be expressed mathematically and they lack support for more soft actions such as countermeasure selection, c) comparing to formal languages, ontologies are more well-suited for expressing approximations and decision support systems via semantic support and inferencing mechanisms, d) the query mechanisms which can be applied to OWL ontologies.

Our SO extends CIM meta-model in order to capture the security requirements of an arbitrary IS. The SO is formulated as a CIM extension schema enriched with ontological semantics, modeling the security management information; in addition, it is linked with the legacy CIM concepts in order to access the already modeled information for the IS resources. The SO acts as a container for the IS security requirements ("*What*"), as they will be extracted from the available information sources. While there is no standard method for ontology development [19], we followed the collaborative approach for ontology design described in [20]. The idea is to build an ontology by a group of people in an iterative way, improving the ontology in every round. During design, well-known security standards and the design criteria in [5] were taken into account. SO development is achieved through the following steps:

Step 1 - *Consideration of ontology design criteria [1] as a framework for the development process*;

Step 2 – *Identification of core security concepts from security standards and best practice*; from a literature review of wide-accepted standards such as ISO/IEC 17799 [8], British Standard 7799 Part 2 [21], Australian Standard Handbook of Information Security Risk Management (AS/NZS 4360) [22], and Common Criteria framework [23], follows that there are recurrent and common used concepts including threats, vulnerabilities, risks, controls, assets, and impacts.

Step 3 – *Normalization of security vocabulary*; although recurrent and common used entities and concepts exist in all standards, the vocabulary of risk and security concepts in several cases is not identical (or even corresponding). Furthermore, different relationships between similar concepts exist, e.g. in AS/NZS 4360 vulnerabilities are linked directly to assets, whereas in CC vulnerabilities are linked to assets through risks. Thus, focusing to provide a common model for these informally recurrent concepts, a common vocabulary is established which will be used for the SO definition.

Step 4 – *Development of concept-centric partial ontologies*; in this step, in order to facilitate understanding, we developed partial ontologies which include a central security concept and relations with its direct neighbors so as to be able to approach the IS security concepts from different views and perspectives.

Step 5 – *Integration of the partial ontologies in a SO prototype*; in this step we integrate each partial ontology perspective into a wider ontology and extend the model with additional attributes and rules, if any.

Step 6 – *Refinement of vocabulary and normalization of the SO prototype*; we revise the vocabulary and adjust accordingly concept attributes and relationships in order to avoid redundancies.

Step 7 – *Evaluation and feedback*; the integrated model representing the SO is evaluated qualitatively through discussion and interaction among the participating individuals.

If the developed SO is not satisfactory, then the process is repeated from Step 2.

3.3 Knowledge Extraction Mechanisms

As analyzed in section 3.1, a variety of diverse sources concerning security knowledge is available to the security expert. The security knowledge can be acquired through several sources, namely:

- From *high-level policy statements*, which express the view of organization management on risk avoidance and mitigation issues, ideally aligned with business objectives and goals; for this task, information extraction tools with ontological support is used. Such information may be gathered through the use of tools and techniques such as [16] [17].
- From *widely accepted standards on security and assurance* that act as a reference model and provide a best practice perspective; a container database for security requirements according to these standards is used ("*Security and Assurance Standards Database*").
- From *system-specific information* from the organization domain, thereby facilitating the linkage of the model with the real world. Such information will be gathered twofold:
  - o From the *infrastructure level* through the use of system- and network-auditing tools and techniques such as Nmap [24] and NetStumbler [25]. These tools provide useful information for network mapping, identification of platforms and operating systems, available services and open ports;
  - o From the *managerial level* through dialog-based interfaces from the human owners of the system (e.g. justification of policy decisions in order to achieve the business objectives). In this case, the responsible individual enters the information through specific forms to provide the desired data. Typically, this kind of information refers to business applications' facts such as custom services / open ports etc.

The security knowledge extraction process is depicted in Figure.3. Although the detailed techniques of extracting the information from the aforesaid sources, as well as the process of the ontology concepts instantiation are beyond the scope of this paper, an overview is provided in section 4.

3.4 Database of Technical Controls

This component is the counterpart of the SO, and describes the technical actions ("How") in order to fulfill the security requirements identified in the SO ("What"), being actually a collection of security controls in a technical level; examples include executable programs and scripts, tools, secure configuration settings and security patches. These controls address, among others, the specific threats and vulnerabilities of IS and are *highly technology- and platform-dependent*. For instance, a script configuring a certain access device in order to enforce a given access control policy, may be inappropriate for different versions of the device software.

The idea is to provide customized, focused solutions in the technical level that address given security requirements of IS. These controls are organized in a relational database for easy retrieval and query support. Metadata of these security controls include, among others, the following attributes: target platform, operating system name and version, target domain, authorization level required, action performed, time constraints, prerequisite conditions for successful execution, clean-up actions, etc. The database of technical controls is by no means complete and/or static ; it should be updated in regular periods with the latest technical controls. The database schema definition, as well as the database management itself, is out of scope of this paper.

4 Security Management Framework

In this section we present a brief description of the necessary steps in order to establish the IS security management framework under examination. Four major phases can be identified throughout the process, namely: a) *Building of Security Ontology,* b) *Security Requirements Collection,* c) *Security Actions Definition, and* d) *Security Actions Deployment and Monitoring*. The steps in each phase are as follows:

1. Building of Security Ontology

I. *Get IS infrastructure data*; in this initial step, vital data concerning the network topology, technologies used, servers, wireless access points, services and active ports are located through the use of network scanning tools such as Nmap [24] and NetStumbler [25];

II. *Justify with organization managers and discuss business decisions*; management input entered into the knowledge system via dialog-based interfaces may influence dramatically the security of the IS, since it might affect network topologies, active services and open ports.

III. *Generate ontology concepts' instances from infrastructure data*; in this step there is enough information in order to generate instances from the correct concepts of the SO. Populate the instances with information from step I. The management of concepts' instances and population may be performed via ontology environments and tools, such as Protégé [26].

2. Security Requirements Collection

IV. *Extract security knowledge from the IS policy document*; perform information extraction work from the policy statements and populate the ontology concept instances with the extracted information, using tools such as GATE [16]. Eventually fill the gaps (if possible) in the instances from step II.

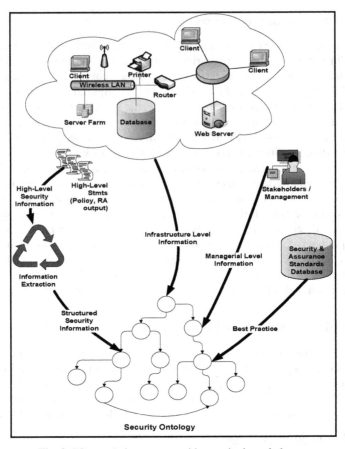

Fig. 3. SO population process with security knowledge

V. *Present the security requirements to management and security expert(s) for e-valuation*; if necessary, perform adjustments and/or corrections to security requirements. This step will help towards to the refinement and training of the information extraction process. The database of security and assurance standards may be used for enriching the security requirements, in case the information contained in the policy documents is deemed insufficient.

3. Security Actions Definition

VI. *Associate the security requirements with specific security controls;* this step performs the linking of requirements with deployable security controls (Database of Technical Controls), customized for the concept instance under question. In this task, valuable help will be utilized from the infrastructure data collected during step I.

VII. *Transform the controls identified into a Ponder-compatible input;* this step involves the transformation of the controls (actions) specified in step VI into a form that can be piped into Ponder rules. The Database of Technical Controls is not a part of Ponder or CIM framework, but rather an enabling repository of deployable security measures. The transformation to Ponder can be realized through an appropriate interface. The CIM-Ponder transformation/mapping is already discussed in [27] [28] [29].

4. Security Actions Deployment and Monitoring

VIII. *Deploy the Ponder rules over the IS infrastructure;* employ Ponder management framework in order to realize the security requirements (enforcing the policy statements that apply to technical controls) over the IS devices.

IX. *Iterate from step I in a timely basis;* in order to keep up with the changes in the IS environment and policy modifications, the whole process should be employed over certain periods of time.

Furthermore, reporting facilities should be in place so as to be able to monitor every step of the process. Additional capabilities, such as storage of the ontology in a suitable manner so as to be able to perform queries upon the ontology, are highly preferable. Moreover, the representation of the ontology should be available in a semantic web language, such as OWL [18], so as to promote reusability and exchange of security knowledge.

5   Related Work

Regarding previous work, two main directions exist: policy specification and (partial) security-related ontologies.

There is a research effort on different approaches to policy specification [7]; IETF/DMTF and the network component manufacturers are concentrating on information models [3] and condition-action rules focusing on the management of Quality of Service (QoS) in networks [30]. The security community has developed a number of models with respect to specification of mandatory and discretionary access control policies (e.g. such as Clark-Wilson), further evolving into work on role based access control (RBAC) and role based management where a role may be considered as a group of related policies pertaining to a position in an organization [31]. Finally, considerable work within the greater scope of management has already resulted in architectures and technologies that provide the basic infrastructure required to implement policy-based management solutions [32].

Although the need for a security ontology has been recognized by the research community [33] [34] [35], only partial attention has been drawn for a common solution. A loosely related to our work [34] [35] deal mainly with access control issues; Standards discussed include XML Signatures and integration with Security Assertions Markup Language (SAML), an XML-based security standard for exchanging authentication and authorization information [36]. Furthermore, work on KAON [37] focuses mostly on the managing infrastructure of generic ontologies and metadata, whereas in [38] authors present a policy ontology based on deontic logic, elaborating, among others, on delegation of actions.

Raskin et al. presented an ontology-driven approach to information security [39]. They argue that a security ontology could organize and systematize all the security phenomena such as computer attacks. Furthermore, the inherent ontology modularity could support the reaction in attacks by relating certain controls with specific attack characteristics, and finally, support attack prediction.

In general, we should mention that the policy languages which are represented using Semantic Web languages are, usually, defined in terms of ontologies. In this context the design of the KAoS [40, 41] policy ontology suggests the use of a description logic inference engine to analyze policy rules. The Rei [38] policy ontology requires the use of an F-Logic based interpreter to compute the defined policy restrictions and constraints. The policy analysis mechanism in the e-Wallet system [42] exploits the XSLT technology to translate policy rules from RDF to JESS rules and uses a JESS rule engine to compute policy restrictions. Furthermore, the SOUPA [43] policy language is similar to Rei in modeling a policy as a set of rules that defines restrictions on actions but the specific policy ontology has limited support for meta-policy reasoning and speech-acts (for a detailed description and comparison of policy representation and reasoning languages at the semantic level see [41]).

The legacy DMTF approach (i.e. the root of our SO), lacks a) the security management aspect (which we define as an Extension Schema), b) the centralized management of security management information, and c) the domain knowledge perspective, which we incorporate into our model enriching the Extension Schema with ontological support.

In addition, most of these approaches are related with specific aspects of security and particularly to specific application domains; our approach is generic enough to be applied in every information system, incorporating security knowledge from various sources. Furthermore, all aforementioned approaches lack the security standards support, which we use for modeling the security requirements.

6 Conclusions and Further Research

In this paper we set the foundations for establishing a knowledge-based, ontology-centric framework with respect to the security management of an arbitrary IS. We demonstrated that the linking between high-level policy statements and deployable security controls is possible and the implementation is achievable. This framework may support critical security expert activities with respect to security requirements identification and selection of certain controls that apply to a certain IS. In addition, we presented a structured approach for establishing a security management framework and identified its critical parts. Our security ontology is represented in a neutral manner, based on well-known security standards and can be used for security knowledge reusability and exchange.

Moreover, a reference representation for SO in OWL is underway, examining in parallel the possibility of integrations with other security standards, such as [44]. The combination of formal methods and an ontology-based semantic reference model is a very interesting direction and is under consideration. The standardization of security requirements in order to implement a standards-based, security requirements database (Security & Assurance Standards Database) is also investigated. Further steps of our work will include the practical implementation of the framework; a comprehensive set of attributes, relationships and constraints for the security ontology is under investigation. Additionally, we investigate ways of extracting security information from high-level documents (e.g. security policy and risk analysis documents) and from the infrastructure level of the organizational domain, as well.

Finally, open issues include conflict resolution on security requirements, compliance checking against desirable IS policy, automated development of IS audit programs; integration of the approach into a security/risk management framework; evaluation metrics of produced security controls; definition of a comprehensive matching algorithm between countermeasures in security ontology instances and technical security controls database. Other issues include storage and retrieval issues of security requirements, as well as development of a query-based system.

References

[1] Karygiannis T., Owens L., Wireless Network Security: 802.11, Bluetooth and Handheld Devices, NIST Special Publication no. 800-48, US Dept. of Commerce, USA 2002.

[2] PAMPAS ("Pioneering Advanced Mobile Privacy and Security") Project, EU-IST-2001-37763, Final Roadmap, Deliverable D4, www.pampas.eu.org/, May 2003.

[3] DMTF CIM Policy Model v. 2.81, available at http://www.dmtf.org/standards/published_documents.php (Feb. 2005).

[4] Clemente F., Perez G., Blaya J., Skarmeta A., Representing Security Policies in Web Information Systems, Policy Management for the Web - WWW2005 Workshop, 14th International World Wide Web Conference, May 2005, Chiba, Japan.

[5] Gruber T., "Toward principles for the design of ontologies used for knowledge sharing". In *Formal Ontology in Conceptual Analysis and Knowledge Representation*, Kluwer Academic Publishers, 1993.

[6] Decker S., et al., "Ontobroker: Ontology based access to distributed and semi-structured information". In R. Meersman et al. (Eds.), *DS-8: Semantic Issues in Multimedia Systems*. Kluwer Academic Publishers, 1999.

[7] Damianou N. et al., "The Ponder Policy Specification Language". In Workshop on Policies for Distributed Systems and Networks, Springer-Verlag LNCS 1995, 2001, pp. 18-39.

[8] ISO/IEC 17799 (2000-12-01), Information technology - Code of practice for information security management, ISO.

[9] COBIT 3rd Edition Control Objectives, IT Governance Institute, 2000.

[10] BSI, IT Baseline Protection Manual, Germany available at http://www.bsi.bund.de/english/index.htm (Mar. 2005).

[11] Cisco Security Advisories, http://www.cisco.com/go/psirt/ (Mar. 2005).

[12] SecurityFocus security portal, (http://www.securityfocus.com (Mar. 2005).

[13] Seclists. Org Security Mailing List Archive (http://seclists.org (Mar. 2005).

[14] Common Vulnerabilities and Exposures (http://www.cve.mitre.org/ (Mar. 2005).

[15] OVAL--Open Vulnerability Assessment Language (http://oval.mitre.org/) (Mar. 2005)

[16] Cunningham H., et al., "GATE: A Framework and Graphical Development Environment for Robust NLP Tools and Applications". Proc. of the 40th meeting of the Association for Computational Linguistics (ACL'02). USA, July 2002.

[17] Bontcheva K., et al., Evolving GATE to Meet New Challenges in Language Engineering. Natural Language Engineering (to appear).

[18] Dean M., et al., OWL Web Ontology Language Reference W3C Recommendation, http://www.w3.org/TR/owl-ref/ (Mar. 2005)

[19] Noy N., McGuiness D., "Ontology Development 101: A Guide to Creating Your First Ontology", Stanford Knowledge Systems Laboratory Technical Report KSL-01-05 and Stanford Medical Informatics Technical Report SMI-2001-0880, March 2001.

[20] Holsapple C., Joshi K., "A collaborative approach to ontology design", Com. of the ACM, 45(2):42-47, 2002.

[21] British Standard 7799, Part 2 (1999), Information Technology - Specification for Information Security Management System, BSI.

[22] Standards Australia and Standards New Zealand, Australian/New Zealand Standard for Risk Management 4360 (1999).

[23] ISO/IEC 15408-1, 2, 3:1999 Information technology - Security techniques - Evaluation criteria for IT security - Part 1: Introduction and general model, Part 2: Security functional requirements, Part 3: Security assurance requirements.

[24] Nmap scanner, available at http://www.insecure.org/nmap (Mar. 2005).

[25] Netstumbler 802.11 network scanner, available at http://www.stumbler.net (Mar. 2005).

[26] Protégé Ontology Development Environment, at http://protege.stanford.edu/ (Mar. 2005)

[27] Andrea Westerinen, Julie Schott "Implementation of the CIM Policy Model Using PONDER", 5th IEEE International Workshop on Policies for Distributed Systems and Networks (POLICY 2004), 7-9 June 2004, Yorktown Heights, NY, USA. IEEE Computer Society 2004, ISBN 0-7695-2141-X

[28] L. Lymberopoulos, E. C. Lupu, M. S. Sloman "Ponder Policy Implementation and Validation in a CIM and Differentiated Services Framework". Presented at NOMS 2004, Seoul, April 2004.

[29] Oscar Diaz Alcantara, Morris Sloman, "QoS policy specification - A mapping from Ponder to the IETF", Department of Computing, Imperial College, 180 Queen's Gate, London SW7 2BZ,

[30] Hewlett-Packard, A Primer on Policy-based Network Management, September 14, 1999.

[31] ANSI INCITS 359-2004, "Information Technology - Role Based Access Control", 2004.

[32] Hegering H.-G., Abeck S., Neumair B., Integrated Management of Network Systems: Concepts, Architectures and Their Operational Application, 1999: Kaufmann Publ.

[33] Donner M., "Toward a Security Ontology", In IEEE Security and Privacy, Vol. 1, No. 3, pp. 6-7, May 2003.

[34] Denker G., Access Control and Data Integrity for DAML+OIL and DAML-S, SRI International, USA, 2002.

[35] Denker G., Security Mark-up and Rules, SRI International, CAIn: Dagstuhl Seminar on Rule Markup Techniques, 2002.

[36] OASIS Security Service TC. Security Assertion Markup Language (SAML), http://www.oasis-open.org/committees/security/ (Mar. 2005)

[37] Bozsak E., Ehrig M., Handschub S., Hotho J., "KAON – Towards a Large Scale Semantic Web", in: Bauknecht, K., et al. (Eds.): Proc. of the 3rd International Conference on e-Commerce and Web Technologies, EC-WEB-2002, 2002, pp. 304-313.

[38] Kagal L., et al., "A policy language for a pervasive computing environment". In 4th IEEE International Workshop on Policies for Distributed Systems and Networks, 2003.

[39] Raskin V., et al., "Ontology in Information Security: A Useful Theoretical Foundation and Methodological Tool". In V. Raskin, et al. (Eds.), Proc. of the New Security Paradigms Workshop, ACM, USA, 2001.

[40] Uszok A., et al., "KAoS: A Policy and Domain Services Framework for Grid Computing and Semantic Web Services", Proc. of the Second International Conference on Trust Management, 2004.

[41] Tonti G., et al., "Semantic Web Languages for Policy Representation and Reasoning: A Comparison of KAoS, Rei and Ponder", Proc. of the 2nd International Semantic Web Conference, 2003.

[42] Gandon F. L., Sadeh M. N., "Semantic web technologies to reconcile privacy and context awareness". Web Semantics Journal, 1 (3), 2004.

[43] Chen H., et al., "SOUPA: Standard ontology for ubiquitous and pervasive applications", Proc. of the First International Conference on Mobile and Ubiquitous Systems: Networking and Services, 2004.

[44] XACML Specification (2003), eXtensible Access Control Markup Language, v. 1.1, available at http://www.oasis-open.org (Mar. 2005).

Safety Problems in Access Control with Temporal Constraints

Philippe Balbiani and Fahima Cheikh

Université Paul Sabatier,
Institut de recherche en informatique de Toulouse,
31062 Toulouse Cedex 09, France
Philippe.Balbiani@irit.fr

Abstract. Most of access control mechanisms use the matrix model to represent protection states of computer systems. We present a variant of the access control matrix model obtained by incorporating temporal constraints saying that "subject s has right r on object o since at least duration d". In connection with this enriched model, we also discuss the decidable and undecidable cases of one of the major themes of computer security, namely the classical safety problem for access control matrices.

1 Introduction

The need for protection arises in any computer system where several users share multifarious data and resources. The protection state of a computer system is the set of all values of memory locations of the computer system that deal with protection. Protection models provide a foundation for the representation of protection states of computer systems. They are usually defined in terms of subjects, objects, and rights between subjects and objects. In the matrix model introduced by Lampson [9], rows represent subjects and columns represent objects. Each element of the matrix is a set of rights. On most computer systems, "subject s has right r on object o" if and only if r belongs to the element (s, o) of the matrix. The access control model formalized by Harrison, Ruzzo, and Ullman [8] was the first model to propose a language for administrating protection in terms of propagation of rights. Within the HRU model, a protection system consists of a set of commands. As commands are executed, the protection state of the computer system, i.e. its access control matrix, changes. Protection models based on the HRU language must consider the well-known safety problem: given a right r, a protection system Π, and a protection state Δ, is there a protection state containing r and reachable from Δ in a finite number of Π-steps? The safety problem is undecidable for generic protection systems but it becomes decidable if protection systems are restricted in some way. Can the borderline between decidable and undecidable cases of the safety problem be drawn sharply and on the basis of which criteria? This matter is analysed in [7,8]. See also [2] in this connection.

Additional topics related to the HRU model include results concerning a number of interesting variants obtained by extending HRU in various ways. Re-

V. Gorodetsky, I. Kotenko, and V. Skormin (Eds.): MMM-ACNS 2005, LNCS 3685, pp. 165–178, 2005.

visiting the results obtained so far, Sandhu [11] and Soshi [14] expanded the HRU model by typing subjects and objects. The papers [3,5,12] formulated role-based access control, RBAC, a model within which the right for a subject to have access to an object depends both on the roles assigned to the subject and on the permissions allocated to the object. In this connection see also [4]. RBAC has recently attracted a great deal of attention. However, nothing is known about role-based protection systems for which the safety problem is decidable. An interesting extensions of HRU is HRU with explicit prohibitions saying that "subject s has not right r on object o". The essential ingredients of this variant of the HRU model have been introduced by Sandhu and Ganta [13]. Nevertheless, nothing is known about protection systems with explicit prohibitions for which the safety problem is decidable. In [10], an access control mechanism based on Boolean expression evaluation, BEE, is presented. This mechanism defines elements of the matrix to be sets of pairs of the form (r, B) where r is a right and B is a Boolean expression. Whenever subject s attempts to r-access object o, the Boolean expression associated with r in element (s, o) of the matrix is evaluated: if it is true, access is allowed. Yet, nothing is known about protection systems with Boolean expression evaluation for which the safety problem is decidable.

In practice, computer systems provide primitives such as "date" which corresponds to the current date and "time" which corresponds to the current time. Incorporating them into access decisions based on BEE would afford an excellent example of an access control matrix whose elements depend on temporal requirements. Since temporal requirements are involved in every aspect of human activity and computing, it becomes essential to develop protection systems which can take temporal constraints into account. The temporal role-based access control model proposed by Bertino, Bonatti, and Ferrari [1] provides support for periodic role enabling and disabling whereas the temporal data authorization model proposed by Gal and Atluri [6] is able to express access control policies based on the temporal characteristics of data. In this paper we investigate the description of a HRU model incorporating temporal constraints saying that "subject s has right r on object o since at least duration d". The bulk of this paper is devoted to the problem of trying to characterize the borderline between decidable and undecidable cases of the safety problem for HRU with temporal constraints. Before we proceed with the next sections, let us briefly describe their contents. Section 2 presents the concept of protection state in matrix form and defines a set of primitive operations that alter the access control matrix of computer systems. Section 3 deals with HRU protection systems and examines under what conditions the classical safety problem for access control matrices becomes decidable. Section 4 expands the HRU model by incorporating temporal constraints and extends the concept of safety defined within the context of HRU protection systems to the concept of timed safety. Section 5 considers under what conditions the timed safety problems defined within the context of timed protection systems become decidable.

Table 1. Protection state Δ

A	o_0	o_1
s_0	$\{r_1, r_2\}$	$\{r_0, r_1, r_2\}$
s_1	$\{r_0, r_1, r_2\}$	$\{r_1, r_2\}$
s_2	$\{r_1, r_2\}$	$\{r_1, r_2\}$

2   Protection States

Let R be a finite set with typical member denoted r, r' etc, possibly with subscripts. Its elements are called rights. The rights of our abstract model correspond, for instance, to those of the Unix system: *read*, *write*, etc. Let SC be a countable set of individuals of type subject with typical member denoted s, s' etc, possibly with subscripts, and OC be a countable set of individuals of type object with typical member denoted o, o' etc, possibly with subscripts. Individuals will also be denoted by the letters a, a', etc, possibly with subscripts. Elements of SC will also be called subjects and elements of OC will also be called objects. The set of subjects is the set of active entities, such as human beings. The set of objects is the set of passive entities, such as files. To characterize the connection between subjects and objects, we present the concept of protection state. A protection state (S, O, A) has three components: a finite subset S of SC, a finite subset O of OC, and a function A assigning to each subject s in S and each object o in O a subset $A(s, o)$ of R. With each finite subset S or O we associate its cardinality, denoted by $|S|$ or $|O|$. Let $|R|$ be the cardinality of the finite set R. For subject s in S and object o in O, the relationship "r is in $A(s, o)$" means that subject s has right r on object o. Protection states will be denoted by the letters Δ, Δ', etc, possibly with subscripts. Table 1 illustrates a simple protection state Δ presented in a matrix form. The entries in the matrix specify the rights that each subject has on each object. Seeing that entities such as processes can be treated as both subjects and objects, we will assume that for all protection states (S, O, A), S is included in O. Let SV be a countable set of variables of type subject with typical member denoted σ, σ' etc, possibly with subscripts, and OV be a countable set of variables of type object with typical member denoted ω, ω' etc, possibly with subscripts. Variables will also be denoted by the letters X, X', etc, possibly with subscripts. There are 6 primitive operations which are used to modify protection states:

- "create subject σ" and "destroy subject σ",
- "create object ω" and "destroy object ω",
- "enter r into $A(\sigma, \omega)$" and "delete r from $A(\sigma, \omega)$".

Primitive operations will be denoted by the letters π, π', etc, possibly with subscripts. Substitutions replace individuals for variables. Hence they are finite sets of the form $\{X_1/a_1, \ldots, X_n/a_n\}$ where each X_i is a variable, each a_i is an individual, and the variables X_1, ..., X_n are pairwise distinct. We will always consider that substitutions are balanced, i.e. for all i in $\{1, \ldots, n\}$, X_i and a_i are of the same type. Substitutions will be denoted by the letters θ, θ', etc, possibly with subscripts. Each primitive operation modifies the current protection state in a way which is peculiar to what its name implicitly means. To make things perfectly clear, it is convenient to consider the concept of state derivability. Let θ be a substitution and π be a primitive operation. Suppose there is no variable in $\theta(\pi)$, i.e. every variable in π is replaced by an individual through the use of θ. If $\Delta = (S, O, A)$ and $\Delta' = (S', O', A')$ are protection states then we shall say that Δ' is derivable from Δ in one step using θ and π, in symbols $\Delta \longrightarrow^{\theta}_{\pi} \Delta'$, iff one of the following conditions is satisfied:

- π is "create subject σ", $\theta(\sigma)$ is not in S, and the only difference between Δ and Δ' is that $S' = S \cup \{\theta(\sigma)\}$,
- π is "destroy subject σ", $\theta(\sigma)$ is in S, and the only difference between Δ and Δ' is that $S' = S \setminus \{\theta(\sigma)\}$,
- π is "create object ω", $\theta(\omega)$ is not in O, and the only difference between Δ and Δ' is that $O' = O \cup \{\theta(\omega)\}$,
- π is "destroy object ω", $\theta(\omega)$ is in O, and the only difference between Δ and Δ' is that $O' = O \setminus \{\theta(\omega)\}$,
- π is "enter r into $A(\sigma, \omega)$", $\theta(\sigma)$ is in S, $\theta(\omega)$ is in O, and the only difference between Δ and Δ' is that $A'(\theta(\sigma), \theta(\omega)) = A(\theta(\sigma), \theta(\omega)) \cup \{r\}$,
- π is "delete r from $A(\sigma, \omega)$", $\theta(\sigma)$ is in S, $\theta(\omega)$ is in O, and the only difference between Δ and Δ' is that $A'(\theta(\sigma), \theta(\omega)) = A(\theta(\sigma), \theta(\omega)) \setminus \{r\}$.

Consider again the protection state Δ shown in table 1. If primitive operations π_1, π_2, π_3, and π_4 are "create object ω", "enter r_0 into $A(\sigma, \omega)$", "enter r_1 into $A(\sigma, \omega)$", and "enter r_2 into $A(\sigma, \omega)$" and substitution θ is $\{\sigma/s_2, \omega/o_2\}$ then $\Delta \longrightarrow^{\theta}_{\pi_1} \circ \longrightarrow^{\theta}_{\pi_2} \circ \longrightarrow^{\theta}_{\pi_3} \circ \longrightarrow^{\theta}_{\pi_4} \Delta'$, where Δ' is the protection state defined by table 2. If primitive operation π_5 is "enter r_3 into $A(\sigma', \omega)$" and substitution θ is $\{\sigma'/s_0, \omega/o_2\}$ then $\Delta' \longrightarrow^{\theta}_{\pi_5} \Delta''$, where Δ'' is the protection state defined by table 3. If primitive operation π_6 is "enter r_4 into $A(\sigma', \omega)$" and substitution θ is $\{\sigma'/s_1, \omega/o_2\}$ then $\Delta'' \longrightarrow^{\theta}_{\pi_6} \Delta'''$, where Δ''' is the protection state defined by table 4. If primitive operation π_7 is "enter r_5 into $A(\sigma'', \omega)$" and substitution θ is $\{\sigma''/s_2, \omega/o_2\}$ then $\Delta''' \longrightarrow^{\theta}_{\pi_7} \Delta^{(4)}$, where $\Delta^{(4)}$ is the protection state defined by table 5.

3   HRU Protection Systems

Within the context of HRU protection systems, primitive operations can be invoked indirectly via HRU commands of the form:

Table 2. Protection state Δ'

A	o_0	o_1	o_2
s_0	$\{r_1, r_2\}$	$\{r_0, r_1, r_2\}$	$\emptyset$
s_1	$\{r_0, r_1, r_2\}$	$\{r_1, r_2\}$	$\emptyset$
s_2	$\{r_1, r_2\}$	$\{r_1, r_2\}$	$\{r_0, r_1, r_2\}$

Table 3. Protection state Δ''

A	o_0	o_1	o_2
s_0	$\{r_1, r_2\}$	$\{r_0, r_1, r_2\}$	$\{r_3\}$
s_1	$\{r_0, r_1, r_2\}$	$\{r_1, r_2\}$	$\emptyset$
s_2	$\{r_1, r_2\}$	$\{r_1, r_2\}$	$\{r_0, r_1, r_2\}$

- "if C_1 and ... and C_i then begin π_1; ...; π_j end",

where $C_1, \ldots, C_i$ are elementary conditions like:

- "r is in $A(\sigma, \omega)$",

and $\pi_1, \ldots, \pi_j$ are primitive operations. The number of elementary conditions is i, a non-negative integer, and the number of primitive operations is j, a positive integer. A HRU command is invoked by replacing all variables in it with individuals of the appropriate types. After that, if the elementary conditions C_1, ..., C_i are evaluated to true in terms of the current protection state then the primitive operations $\pi_1, \ldots, \pi_j$ are executed. HRU commands will be denoted by the letters α, α', etc, possibly with subscripts. By a HRU protection system, we simply mean a finite set $\{\alpha_1, \ldots, \alpha_k\}$ of HRU commands. We shall say that a command is conditional iff it contains at least 1 elementary condition. A HRU protection system is monotonic iff none of its HRU commands contain a primitive operation of the form "**destroy**" or "**delete**". It is monoconditional iff none of its HRU commands contain more that 1 elementary condition whereas it is mono-operational iff none of its HRU commands contain more that 1 primitive operation. HRU protection systems will be denoted by the letters Π, Π', etc, possibly with subscripts. For all $i \in \{0, 1, 2, \infty\}$ and for all $j \in \{1, 2, \infty\}$, let $\mathcal{C}_{HRU}(i, j)$ be the class of all HRU protection systems such that none of their HRU commands contain more than i elementary condition or more than j primitive operations and $\mathcal{C}^+_{HRU}(i, j)$ be the class of all monotonic HRU protection systems in $\mathcal{C}_{HRU}(i, j)$. For example, the HRU protection system Π shown in table 6 is in the class $\mathcal{C}^+_{HRU}(2, \infty)$. Let θ be a substitution and C be an elementary condition. Suppose there is no variable in $\theta(C)$, i.e. every variable in C is

Table 4. Protection state Δ'''

A	o_0	o_1	o_2
s_0	$\{r_1, r_2\}$	$\{r_0, r_1, r_2\}$	$\{r_3\}$
s_1	$\{r_0, r_1, r_2\}$	$\{r_1, r_2\}$	$\{r_4\}$
s_2	$\{r_1, r_2\}$	$\{r_1, r_2\}$	$\{r_0, r_1, r_2\}$

Table 5. Protection state $\Delta^{(4)}$

A	o_0	o_1	o_2
s_0	$\{r_1, r_2\}$	$\{r_0, r_1, r_2\}$	$\{r_3\}$
s_1	$\{r_0, r_1, r_2\}$	$\{r_1, r_2\}$	$\{r_4\}$
s_2	$\{r_1, r_2\}$	$\{r_1, r_2\}$	$\{r_0, r_1, r_2, r_5\}$

Table 6. HRU protection system Π

begin create object ω; enter r_0 into $A(\sigma,\omega)$; enter r_1 into $A(\sigma,\omega)$; enter r_2 into $A(\sigma,\omega)$ end
if r_0 is in $A(\sigma,\omega)$ then enter r_3 into $A(\sigma',\omega)$
if r_0 is in $A(\sigma,\omega)$ then enter r_4 into $A(\sigma',\omega)$
if r_3 is in $A(\sigma,\omega)$ and r_4 is in $A(\sigma',\omega)$ then enter r_5 into $A(\sigma'',\omega)$

replaced by an individual through the use of θ. If $\Delta = (S, O, A)$ is a protection state then we shall say that θ makes C true at Δ, in symbols $\Delta \models_\theta C$, iff the following condition is satisfied:

- C is "r is in $A(\sigma, \omega)$", $\theta(\sigma)$ is in S, $\theta(\omega)$ is in O, and r is in $A(\theta(\sigma), \theta(\omega))$.

It follows from the definition that if substitution θ is $\{\sigma/s_2, \omega/o_2\}$ and elementary condition C is "r_0 is in $A(\sigma, \omega)$" then $\Delta' \models_\theta C$, where Δ' is the protection state defined by table 2. As well, if substitution θ is $\{\sigma/s_0, \sigma'/s_1, \omega/o_2\}$ and elementary conditions C' and C'' are "r_3 is in $A(\sigma, \omega)$" and "r_4 is in $A(\sigma', \omega)$" then $\Delta''' \models_\theta C'$ and $\Delta''' \models_\theta C''$, where Δ''' is the protection state defined by table 4. Let Π be a HRU protection system. If $\Delta = (S, O, A)$ and $\Delta' = (S', O', A')$ are protection states then we shall say that Δ' is derivable from Δ in one step using Π, in symbols $\Delta \longrightarrow_\Pi \Delta'$, iff there exists a substitution θ and a HRU command $\alpha \in \Pi$ with elementary conditions $C_1, \ldots, C_i$ and primitive operations $\pi_1, \ldots, \pi_j$ such that:

- $\Delta \models_\theta C_1, \ldots, \Delta \models_\theta C_i$,
- $\Delta \longrightarrow^\theta_{\pi_1} \circ \ldots \circ \longrightarrow^\theta_{\pi_j} \Delta'$.

It is obvious from the definition that $\Delta \longrightarrow_\Pi \Delta' \longrightarrow_\Pi \Delta'' \longrightarrow_\Pi \Delta''' \longrightarrow_\Pi \Delta^{(4)}$ where Δ, Δ', Δ'', Δ''', and $\Delta^{(4)}$ are the protection states defined by tables 1, 2, 3, 4, and 5 and Π is the HRU protection system defined by table 6. Let Π be a HRU protection system and Δ be a protection state. Π is said to be unsafe for r with respect to Δ iff there exists a sequence $\Delta_0 = (S_0, O_0, A_0), \ldots, \Delta_n = (S_n, O_n, A_n)$, $\Delta_{n+1} = (S_{n+1}, O_{n+1}, A_{n+1})$ of protection states such that:

- $\Delta_0 \longrightarrow_\Pi \circ \ldots \circ \longrightarrow_\Pi \Delta_n \longrightarrow_\Pi \Delta_{n+1}$,
- the following conditions are satisfied for some individual s ot type subject and for some individual o of type object:
  - if s is in S_n and o is in O_n then r is not in $A_n(s, o)$,
  - s is in S_{n+1}, o is in O_{n+1}, and r is in $A_{n+1}(s, o)$,
- $\Delta_0 = \Delta$.

We also say that the sequence $\Delta_0 = (S_0, O_0, A_0), \ldots, \Delta_n = (S_n, O_n, A_n)$, $\Delta_{n+1} = (S_{n+1}, O_{n+1}, A_{n+1})$ leaks r with respect to Π and Δ. For example, with respect to Δ, the HRU protection system Π defined in table 6 is unsafe for r_0, r_1, r_2, r_3, r_4, and r_5, where Δ is the protection state defined by table 1. Let $\mathcal{C}_{HRU}$ be a class of HRU protection systems. The most basic problem on HRU protection systems in $\mathcal{C}_{HRU}$ is the following decision problem:

Problem: SAFETY($\mathcal{C}_{HRU}$),

Input: a right r, a HRU protection system $\Pi \in \mathcal{C}_{HRU}$, and a protection state $\Delta = (S, O, A)$,

Output: determine if Π is unsafe for r with respect to Δ.

The above is a planning problem. Abstractly, we have an initial protection state and certain HRU commands that can be performed in a given protection state if it satisfies certain conditions. Performing a HRU command with respect to a protection state brings about a new protection state. The goal is to bring about a protection state leaking the right r and the task is to find a sequence of HRU commands that achieves this end.

Theorem 1. 1. SAFETY($\mathcal{C}_{HRU}(\infty, 1)$) is decidable,
2. SAFETY($\mathcal{C}^+_{HRU}(1, \infty)$) is decidable,
3. SAFETY($\mathcal{C}^+_{HRU}(2, \infty)$) is undecidable.

Proof. See [7,8].

4 Timed Protection Systems

Within the context of HRU protection systems, the mechanism granting and revoking access of subjects to objects is based on the execution of commands. This mechanism tends to restrict our thinking about access control to just the ordering between protection states in a transition $\Delta \longrightarrow_\Pi \Delta'$ rather than to the duration that elapse between protection states in the transition $\Delta \longrightarrow_\Pi \Delta'$. At a more sophisticated level, it is not enough that the computer system is in such or such protection state. For some positive real number d, we must additionally ensure either that the computer system has remained in such or such protection state since at least duration d or that the computer system has remained in such or such protection state since at most duration d. For instance, we might wish to force the protection system either to wait at least d units of time before granting access or to wait at most d units of time before revoking access. We are primarily concerned with the temporal aspect of state derivability. The central point of this paper is to demonstrate that adding temporal requirements to protection systems can be achieved. For this purpose, we have developed a new HRU model incorporating temporal constraints saying that "subject s has right r on object o since at least duration d", leaving aside for another paper temporal constraints saying that "subject s has right r on object o since at most duration d". Hence, within the context of timed protection systems, primitive operations can be invoked indirectly via timed commands of the form:

- "if C_1 and ... and C_i then begin π_1; ...; π_j end",

where C_1, ..., C_i are now elementary conditions like:

- "r is in $A(\sigma, \omega)$ since at least duration d" where d is a positive real number.

Table 7. Timed protection system Π'

begin create object ω; enter r_0 into $A(\sigma, \omega)$; enter r_1 into $A(\sigma, \omega)$; enter r_2 into $A(\sigma, \omega)$ end
if r_0 is in $A(\sigma, \omega)$ since at least duration 2 then enter r_3 into $A(\sigma', \omega)$
if r_0 is in $A(\sigma, \omega)$ since at least duration 2 then enter r_4 into $A(\sigma', \omega)$
if r_3 is in $A(\sigma, \omega)$ since at least duration 3 and r_4 is in $A(\sigma', \omega)$ since at least duration 3 then enter r_5 into $A(\sigma'', \omega)$

The concept of timed protection system and the adjectives conditional, monotonic, monoconditional, and mono-operational are defined as in section 3. For all $i \in \{0, 1, 2, \infty\}$ and for all $j \in \{1, 2, \infty\}$, let $\mathcal{C}_{timed}(i, j)$ be the class of all timed protection systems such that none of their timed commands contain more than i elementary condition or more than j primitive operations and $\mathcal{C}^+_{timed}(i, j)$ be the class of all monotonic timed protection systems in $\mathcal{C}_{timed}(i, j)$. For example, the timed protection system Π' shown in table 7 is in the class $\mathcal{C}^+_{timed}(2, \infty)$. A timed history is a mapping that assigns to every non-negative real number a protection state. Timed histories will be denoted by the letters h, h', etc, possibly with subscripts. We are interested in non-Zeno timed histories, i.e. timed histories changing at most a finite number of times in any finite interval. Hence, we assume that for all timed histories h, there exists a strictly increasing sequence v_0, v_1, ... of real numbers such that:

- $v_0 = 0$,
- $\lim_{n \to \infty} v_n = \infty$,
- for all non-negative integers n, there exists a protection state Δ_n such that $h(v) = \Delta_n$ for all $v \in [v_n, v_{n+1}[$.

We shall say that the sequence (v_0, Δ_0), (v_1, Δ_1), ... is a timed sequence for h. In such sequences, the three components of protection state Δ_n will be denoted S_n, O_n, and A_n for each non-negative integer n. To gain some intuition, the reader may easily see that the sequence $(0, \Delta)$, $(1, \Delta')$, $(2, \Delta')$, $(3, \Delta'')$, $(4, \Delta''')$, $(5, \Delta''')$, $(6, \Delta''')$, $(7, \Delta^{(4)})$, $(8, \Delta^{(4)})$, ... is a timed sequence for the timed history h shown in table 8, where Δ, Δ', Δ'', Δ''', and $\Delta^{(4)}$ are the protection states defined by tables 1, 2, 3, 4, and 5. Let θ be a substitution and C be an elementary condition. Suppose there is no variable in $\theta(C)$, i.e. every variable in C is replaced by an individual through the use of θ. If h is a timed history with timed sequence (v_0, Δ_0), (v_1, Δ_1), ... and v is a non-negative real number then we shall say that θ makes C true in h at v, in symbols $h, v \models_\theta C$, iff the following condition is satisfied:

- C is "r is in $A(\sigma, \omega)$ since at least duration d", $d \leq v$, and for all non-negative integers n, if $v_n < v$ and $v - d < v_{n+1}$ then $\theta(\sigma)$ is in S_n, $\theta(\omega)$ is in O_n, and r is in $A_n(\theta(\sigma), \theta(\omega))$.

It follows from the definition that if substitution θ is $\{\sigma/s_2, \omega/o_2\}$ and elementary condition C is "r_0 is in $A(\sigma, \omega)$ since at least duration 2" then $h, 3 \models_\theta C$, where h is the timed history defined by table 8. As well, if substitution θ is $\{\sigma/s_0, \sigma'/s_1, \omega/o_2\}$ and elementary conditions C' and C'' are "r_3 is in $A(\sigma, \omega)$ since at least duration 3" and "r_4 is in $A(\sigma', \omega)$ since at least duration 3" then $h, 7 \models_\theta C'$ and $h, 7 \models_\theta C''$, where h is the timed history defined by table 8. The concept of timed history is used to model the behaviour of timed protection systems. We shall say that timed history h is a model for timed protection system Π, in symbols $h \models \Pi$, iff there exists a timed sequence (v_0, Δ_0), (v_1, Δ_1), ... for h such that for all non-negative integers n, there exists a substitution θ_n and a timed command $\alpha_n \in \Pi$ with elementary conditions $C_n^1, \ldots, C_n^{i_n}$ and primitive operations $\pi_n^1, \ldots, \pi_n^{j_n}$ such that:

- $h, v_{n+1} \models_{\theta_n} C_n^1, \ldots, h, v_{n+1} \models_{\theta_n} C_n^{i_n}$,
- $\Delta_n \xrightarrow[\pi_n^1]{\theta_n} \circ \ldots \circ \xrightarrow[\pi_n^{j_n}]{\theta_n} \Delta_{n+1}$.

We shall say that the sequence $(v_0, \Delta_0, \theta_0, \alpha_0)$, $(v_1, \Delta_1, \theta_1, \alpha_1)$, ... is a dynamic timed sequence for h. It is obvious from the definition that the timed history h shown in table 8 is a model for the timed protection system Π' of table 7. It is now time to get more precise concerning the question of safety in timed protection systems. Let Π be a timed protection system and Δ be a protection state. If d is a positive real number then Π is said to be d-unsafe for r with respect to Δ iff there exists a timed history h with dynamic timed sequence $(v_0, \Delta_0, \theta_0, \alpha_0)$, $(v_1, \Delta_1, \theta_1, \alpha_1)$, ... such that:

- $h \models \Pi$,
- the following conditions are satisfied for some individual s of type subject and some individual o of type object:
  - if s is in S_n and o is in O_n then r is not in $A_n(s, o)$,
  - s is in S_{n+1}, o is in O_{n+1}, and r is in $A_{n+1}(s, o)$,
- $\Delta_0 = \Delta$,

for some non-negative integer n such that $v_{n+1} \leq d$. We shall also say that d is a waiting period of Π for r with respect to Δ. For example, with respect to Δ, the timed protection system Π' defined in table 7 is 1-unsafe for r_0, 1-unsafe for r_1, 1-unsafe for r_2, 3-unsafe for r_3, 4-unsafe for r_4, and 7-unsafe for r_5, where Δ is the protection state defined by table 1.

Table 8. Timed history h

v	$h(v)$
$v \in [0, 1[$	Δ
$v \in [1, 3[$	Δ'
$v \in [3, 4[$	Δ''
$v \in [4, 7[$	Δ'''
$v \in [7, \infty[$	$\Delta^{(4)}$

5 Some Mathematical Results

Consider a timed protection system Π. If Π' is a timed protection system obtained from Π by modifying all or part of its timed constraints "since at least duration d" then, obviously, Π and Π' leak the same rights, possibly at different points in time. Hence, $HRU(\Pi)$ denoting the HRU protection system obtained from Π by removing all its timed constraints "since at least duration d", the following lemma should not come as a great surprise.

Lemma 1. *Let Δ be a protection state. The following conditions are equivalent:*

- *there exists a positive real number d such that Π is d-unsafe for r with respect to Δ,*
- *$HRU(\Pi)$ is unsafe for r with respect to Δ.*

Let $\mathcal{C}_{timed}$ be a class of timed protection systems. The most basic problem on timed protection systems in $\mathcal{C}_{timed}$ is the following decision problem:

Problem: UNIVERSAL TIMED SAFETY($\mathcal{C}_{timed}$),
Input: a right r, a timed protection system $\Pi \in \mathcal{C}_{timed}$, and a protection state $\Delta = (S, O, A)$,
Output: determine if there exists a positive real number d such that Π is d-unsafe for r with respect to Δ.

Like all decision problems, UNIVERSAL TIMED SAFETY($\mathcal{C}_{timed}$) must have a countable set of instances. As a result, hereafer, we will always assume that for all positive real numbers d, if a timed protection system $\Pi \in \mathcal{C}_{timed}$ contains the timed constraint "since at least duration d" then d is rational.

Theorem 2. *1. UNIVERSAL TIMED SAFETY($\mathcal{C}_{timed}(\infty, 1)$) is decidable,*
2. UNIVERSAL TIMED SAFETY($\mathcal{C}_{timed}^{+}(1, \infty)$) is decidable,
3. UNIVERSAL TIMED SAFETY($\mathcal{C}_{timed}^{+}(2, \infty)$) is undecidable.

Proof. The corresponding results for SAFETY with respect to HRU protection systems have been proved by [7,8]. Lemma 1 now finishes the proof.

Let r be a right, $\Pi \in \mathcal{C}_{timed}$ be a timed protection system, and Δ be a protection state. Suppose that the set of all waiting periods of Π for r with respect to Δ is nonempty. Hence, it has a greatest lower bound d_{glb}. What is the crucial observation we need to make about d_{glb}? Simply this: in view of the fact that the timed constraints in Π are rational, d_{glb} must be rational. This suggests the following optimization problem:

Problem: MIN TIMED SAFETY($\mathcal{C}_{timed}$),
Input: a right r, a timed protection system $\Pi \in \mathcal{C}_{timed}$, and a protection state $\Delta = (S, O, A)$,
Output: if the set of all waiting periods of Π for r with respect to Δ is nonempty then find its greatest lower bound.

Let us observe that it need not be the case that d_{glb} is a waiting period of Π for r with respect to Δ. To see this, let us consider the timed protection system Π' shown in table 7. It is easy to see that for all positive real numbers d, $5 < d$ iff d is a waiting period of Π' for r_5 with respect to the protection state Δ defined by table 1 whereas Π' is not 5-unsafe for r_5 with respect to Δ.

Theorem 3.   *1. MIN TIMED SAFETY$(\mathcal{C}_{timed}(\infty, 1))$ is solvable,*
  2. MIN TIMED SAFETY$(\mathcal{C}^+_{timed}(1, \infty))$ is solvable,
  3. MIN TIMED SAFETY$(\mathcal{C}^+_{timed}(2, \infty))$ is unsolvable.

Proof. (1) To prove that MIN TIMED SAFETY$(\mathcal{C}_{timed}(\infty, 1))$ is solvable, let $HRU(\Pi)$ be the HRU protection system obtained from Π by removing all its timed constraints "since at least duration d". If the sequence $\Delta_0 = (S_0, O_0, A_0)$, $\ldots$, $\Delta_n = (S_n, O_n, A_n)$, $\Delta_{n+1} = (S_{n+1}, O_{n+1}, A_{n+1})$ of protection states leaks r with respect to $HRU(\Pi)$ and Δ then following the line of reasoning suggested by Harrison, Ruzzo, and Ullman [8], we may assume that $n \leq (|S| + 1) \times (|O| + 1) \times |R| + 1$, where $\Delta = (S, O, A)$ is the given protection state. The corresponding waiting period necessary if one wants to reach Δ_n from Δ_0 by performing timed commands in Π is computable in linear time. To finish the proof we only need to note that the number of requisite waiting periods that we should compute and compare is finite.
(2) To prove that MIN TIMED SAFETY$(\mathcal{C}^+_{timed}(1, \infty))$ is solvable, let $HRU(\Pi)$ be the HRU protection system obtained from Π by removing all its timed constraints "since at least duration d". If the sequence $\Delta_0 = (S_0, O_0, A_0)$, $\ldots$, $\Delta_n = (S_n, O_n, A_n)$, $\Delta_{n+1} = (S_{n+1}, O_{n+1}, A_{n+1})$ of protection states leaks r with respect to $HRU(\Pi)$ and Δ then following the line of reasoning suggested by Harrison and Ruzzo [7], we may assume that $n \leq 3 \times |R|$, where $\Delta = (S, O, A)$ is the given protection state. The corresponding waiting period necessary if one wants to reach Δ_n from Δ_0 by performing timed commands in Π is computable in linear time. To finish the proof we only need to note that the number of requisite waiting periods that we should compute and compare is finite.
(3) If we had an algorithm A for solving MIN TIMED SAFETY$(\mathcal{C}^+_{timed}(2, \infty))$ then we would be able to derive an algorithm for deciding UNIVERSAL TIMED SAFETY$(\mathcal{C}^+_{timed}(2, \infty))$: given input (r, Π, Δ), we would be able to decide whether there exists a positive real number d such that Π is d-unsafe for r with respect to Δ by simply telling whether $A(r, \Pi, \Delta)$ is defined. Since UNIVERSAL TIMED SAFETY$(\mathcal{C}^+_{timed}(2, \infty))$ is undecidable, then MIN TIMED SAFETY$(\mathcal{C}^+_{timed}(2, \infty))$ is unsolvable.

Sometimes it is less important to know the greatest lower bound of the set of all waiting periods of timed protection system $\Pi \in \mathcal{C}_{timed}$ for right r than to know given a positive rational number d, that there is no history h modelling Π and leaking r between time points 0 and d. This observation leads us to the following decision problem:

Problem: BOUND TIMED SAFETY$(\mathcal{C}_{timed})$,
Input: a right r, a timed protection system $\Pi \in \mathcal{C}_{timed}$, a protection state $\Delta = (S, O, A)$, and a positive rational number d,
Output: determine if Π is d-unsafe for r with respect to Δ.

Theorem 4. *1. BOUND TIMED SAFETY($\mathcal{C}_{timed}(\infty, 1)$) is decidable,*
2. BOUND TIMED SAFETY($\mathcal{C}_{timed}^{+}(1, \infty)$) is decidable.

Proof. (1) The proof that BOUND TIMED SAFETY($\mathcal{C}_{timed}(\infty, 1)$) is decidable is an adaptation of the proof that MIN TIMED SAFETY($\mathcal{C}_{timed}(\infty, 1)$) is solvable.
(2) The proof that BOUND TIMED SAFETY($\mathcal{C}_{timed}^{+}(1, \infty)$) is decidable is an adaptation of the proof that MIN TIMED SAFETY($\mathcal{C}_{timed}^{+}(1, \infty)$) is solvable.

We do not know at present whether BOUND TIMED SAFETY($\mathcal{C}_{timed}^{+}(2, \infty)$) is undecidable. However, considering regular timed protection systems in $\mathcal{C}_{timed}^{+}(\infty, \infty)$ makes a limited variant of the BOUND TIMED SAFETY question decidable. A timed protection system Π is regular iff there exists a positive real number d_Π such that for all positive real numbers d, if Π contains the timed constraint "since at least duration d" then $d = d_\Pi$. Let $\mathcal{C}_{timed}^{\oplus}(\infty, \infty)$ be the class of all regular timed protection systems in $\mathcal{C}_{timed}^{+}(\infty, \infty)$.

Theorem 5. *The following decision problem is decidable:*

Input: *a right r, a timed protection system $\Pi \in \mathcal{C}_{timed}^{\oplus}(\infty, \infty)$, a protection state $\Delta = (S, O, A)$, and a positive rational number d such that $d < 2 \times d_\Pi$,*
Output: *determine if Π is d-unsafe for r with respect to Δ.*

Proof. Let r be a right, $\Pi \in \mathcal{C}_{timed}^{\oplus}(\infty, \infty)$ be a timed protection system, $\Delta = (S, O, A)$ be a protection state, and d be a positive rational number such that $d < 2 \times d_\Pi$. Without loss of generality, we may assume that $S \neq \emptyset$ and $O \neq \emptyset$. If Π is d-unsafe for r with respect to Δ then there exists a timed history h with dynamic timed sequence $(v_0, \Delta_0, \theta_0, \alpha_0), (v_1, \Delta_1, \theta_1, \alpha_1), \ldots$ such that:

- $h \models \Pi$,
- the following conditions are satisfied for some individual s of type subject and some individual o of type object:
  - if s is in S_n and o is in O_n then r is not in $A_n(s, o)$,
  - s is in S_{n+1}, o is in O_{n+1}, and r is in $A_{n+1}(s, o)$,
- $\Delta_0 = \Delta$,

for some minimal non-negative integer n such that $v_{n+1} \leq d$. The key arguments we need are embodied in the following lemmas.

Lemma 2. *If the sequence $\alpha_0, \ldots, \alpha_n$ contains at least 1 conditional command then the command α_n is conditional.*

Proof. Suppose that the sequence $\alpha_0, \ldots, \alpha_n$ contains at least 1 conditional command. If the command α_n is not conditional then $n \geq 1$. Moreover, there exists a timed history h' with dynamic timed sequence $(v_0', \Delta_0', \theta_0', \alpha_0'), (v_1', \Delta_1', \theta_1', \alpha_1'),$ $\ldots$ such that:

- $h' \models \Pi$,
- the following conditions are satisfied for some individual s' of type subject and some individual o' of type object:

- if s' is in S_0' and o' is in O_0' then r is not in $A_0'(s', o')$,
  - s' is in S_1', o' is in O_1', and r is in $A_1'(s', o')$,
- $\Delta_0' = \Delta$,

contradicting the minimality of n.

Lemma 3. *The sequence* α_0, ..., α_n *contains at most 1 conditional command.*

Proof. If the sequence α_0, ..., α_n contains at least 2 conditional commands then the command α_n is conditional and there exists a non-negative integer p in $\{0, \ldots, n-1\}$ such that the command α_p is conditional. Moreover, there exists a timed history h' with dynamic timed sequence $(v_0', \Delta_0', \theta_0', \alpha_0')$, $(v_1', \Delta_1', \theta_1', \alpha_1')$, ... such that:

- $h' \models \Pi$,
- the following conditions are satisfied for some individual s' of type subject and some individual o' of type object:
  - if s' is in S_{n-1}' and o' is in O_{n-1}' then r is not in $A_{n-1}'(s', o')$,
  - s' is in S_n', o' is in O_n', and r is in $A_n'(s', o')$,
- $\Delta_0' = \Delta$,

contradicting the minimality of n.

How do such ideas bear on theorem 5? By lemmas 2 and 3, there are two possibilities:

- the commands α_0, ..., α_n are not conditional,
- the commands α_0, ..., α_{n-1} are not conditional and the command α_n is conditional.

In the first case, n is equal to 0. In the second case, n is less than or equal to the number of elementary conditions in α_n. This completes the proof of theorem 5.

6   Conclusion

Temporal constraints allow the security administrator to clearly express the desired temporal requirements that must satisfy the successive alterations of the protection state of a computer system. The critical issue is the characterization of classes of timed protection systems for which the safety problems considered in section 5 are decidable. A key feature of access control with temporal constraints is its extensibility. The form of elementary conditions is not fixed. We could, for example, explore the effects of allowing testing in an access control matrix for the presence of rights since at most duration d as opposed to testing for the presence of rights since at least duration d which the model described in this paper does. The intensive study of the issues relating to the support of such conditions in our timed protection systems is still to be done.

Acknowledgments

Thanks to the project "Développement de systèmes informatiques par raffinement des contraintes sécuritaires" of the action "Sécurité informatique" for partly financing our research.

References

1. Bertino, E., Bonatti, P., Ferrari, E.: TRBAC: a temporal role-based access control model. ACM Transactions on Information and System Security **4** (2001) 65–104
2. Bishop, M.: Computer Security: Art and Science. Addison-Wesley (2003)
3. Ferraiolo, D., Barkley, J., Kuhn, D.: A role-based access control model and reference implementation within a corporate intranet. ACM Transactions on Information And System Security **2** (1999) 34–64
4. Ferraiolo, D., Kuhn, D., Chandramouli, R.: Role-Based Access Control. Artech House (2003)
5. Ferraiolo, D., Sandhu, R., Gavrila, S., Kuhn, D., Chandramouli, R.: Proposed NIST standard for role-based access control. ACM Transactions on Information And System Security **4** (2001) 224–274
6. Gal, A., Atluri, V.: An authorization model for temporal data. In: Proceedings of the 7th ACM conference on Computer and Communications Security. ACM Press (2000) 144–153
7. Harrison, M., Ruzzo, W.: Monotonic protection systems. In: Foundations of Secure Computation. Academic Press (1978) 337–363
8. Harrison, M., Ruzzo, W., Ullman, J.: Protection in operating systems. Communications of the ACM **19** (1976) 461–471
9. Lampson, B.: Protection. Operating Systems Review **8** (1974) 18–24
10. Miller, D., Baldwin, R.: Access control by Boolean expression evaluation. In: Fifth Annual Computer Security Conference. IEEE Computer Society Press (1990) 131–139
11. Sandhu, R.: The typed access matrix model. In: 1992 IEEE Computer Society Symposium on Research in Security and Privacy. IEEE Computer Society Press (1992) 122–136
12. Sandhu, R., Coyne, E., Feinstein, H., Youman, C.: Role-based access control models. Computer **29** (1996) 38–47
13. Sandhu, R., Ganta, S: On testing for absence of rights in access control models. In: The Computer Security Foundations Workshop VI. IEEE Computer Society Press (1993) 109–118
14. Soshi, M.: Safety analysis of the dynamic-typed access matrix model. In: Computer Security — ESORICS 2000. Springer-Verlag, Lecture Notes in Computer Science **1895** (2000) 106–121

A Modal Logic for Role-Based Access Control*

Thumrongsak Kosiyatrakul, Susan Older, and Shiu-Kai Chin

EECS Department, Syracuse University, Syracuse, New York 13244, USA
skchin@syr.edu

Abstract. Making correct access-control decisions is central to security, which in turn requires accounting correctly for the identity, credentials, roles, authority, and privileges of users and their agents. In networked systems, these decisions are made more complex because of delegation and differing access-control policies. Methods for reasoning rigorously about access control and computer-assisted reasoning tools for verification are effective for providing assurances of security. In this paper we extend the access-control logic of [11,1] to also support reasoning about role-based access control (RBAC), which is a popular technique for reducing the complexity of assigning privileges to users. The result is an access-control logic which is simple enough for design and verification engineers to use to assure the correctness of systems with access-control requirements but yet powerful enough to reason about delegations, credentials, and trusted authorities. We explain how to describe RBAC components such as user assignments, permission assignments, role inheritance, role activations, and users' requests. The logic and its extensions are proved to be sound and implemented in the HOL (Higher Order Logic version 4) theorem prover. We also provide formal support for RBAC's static separation of duty and dynamic separation of duty constraints in the HOL theorem prover. As a result, HOL can be used to verify properties of RBAC access-control policies, credentials, authority, and delegations.

1   Introduction

The ubiquitous use of inter-networked computers makes controlled access to information and services simultaneously essential and complex. Access is ultimately granted based on establishing a relationship between a principal and her privileges with respect to a particular object. In networked systems, requests and authority may be delegated. This complicates the task of establishing the identity and authority of principals behind access requests.

One interesting specialty logic for reasoning about access-control policies and decisions is the access-control logic of Abadi and colleagues [11,1]. This modal logic brings clarity and consistency to reasoning about access requests because it provides a formal model of principals, statements, credentials, authority, trust,

---

* Partially supported by the CASE Center at Syracuse University, a New York State Center for Advanced Technology supported by the New York State Office of Science Technology and Academic Research.

and delegations. However, this logic lacks the capability for specifying and reasoning about role-based access control (RBAC) [4,6]. RBAC policies are particularly well-suited for large-scale computing systems, because they reduce the administrative complexity of associating users with permissions by decoupling the two: users are authorized for *roles*, and permissions are assigned to roles. RBAC also supports a decentralized view of access control.

Our objective is to unify within a single logic the ability to describe and reason about access-control requests and decisions based on the relationships between principals, statements, and trusted authorities while accounting for credentials, delegation, and RBAC roles. We therefore extend the access-control logic of Abadi to encompass three major RBAC components: (1) user-role associations, (2) role-permission associations, and (3) role-inheritance relations. We express user-role associations as delegations (roles delegate their authority to users to act on their behalf); role-permission associations and role-inheritance relations are expressed as relations among principals and sets of statements by which certain statements of one principal may be attributed to another principal. With these extensions, we can (1) model RBAC policies within the access-control logic, and (2) reason about RBAC-based access-control decisions.

Other researchers have used modal logic for describing security policies and properties [8,2]. Those frameworks are more general than ours, but require a high level of sophistication on the part of users. Our objective was to identify a simple logic accessible to engineers that nonetheless could describe a wide variety of access-control concerns. Our experiences teaching the Abadi logic to computer science and engineering Master's students indicate that the logic meets those criteria [12,13].

To verify the soundness of the access-control logic and its extensions, we use the HOL (Higher Order Logic version 4) theorem prover [7,10]. Defining the access-control logic within HOL serves several purposes. First, HOL is used to verify the soundness of the access-control logic. Second, because HOL is an open system, all of our proofs can be easily checked by third parties. Finally, the existence of an executable and verifiable access-control logic implemented in HOL makes both the access-control logic and a means for formal verification available to design and verification engineers.

In addition to user-role associations, role-permission associations, and role hierarchies, RBAC allows the specification of constraints that prevent users from (1) being assigned to roles that are in conflict (static separation of duty), and (2) activating certain roles simultaneously (dynamic separation of duty). These constraints are outside the direct scope of the access-control logic, which focuses on access-control decisions for a specific policy. In contrast, the separation of duty constraints impose limits on what should be considered a well-defined or consistent policy in the first place. However, like the access-control logic, these constraints can be described and verified within the higher-order logic of HOL. Hence, we are able to use higher-order logic to verify the consistency of a specific RBAC policy prior to using the access-control logic to reason about access-control decisions based on that policy.

The rest of this paper is organized as follows. Section 2 provides a brief RBAC tutorial. Section 3 describes the syntax and and semantics of our logic, which builds on the work of Abadi and colleagues [11,1]. Section 4 explains how RBAC relations are described in our extended logic. Section 5 presents the HOL definitions of static and dynamic separation of duty constraints. Finally, our conclusions are in Section 6.

2 Role-Based Access Control (RBAC)

Role-Based Access Control (RBAC) [5,4,6] replaces direct user-permission associations in traditional access control through a combination of user-role and role-permission associations. Rather than assigning individuals specific permissions that may change as their duties and status change, an RBAC policy assigns users to roles and grants permissions to roles. In RBAC, an access request q made by a user U will be granted if and only if U is authorized to act in a role R that has been granted the permission q.

RBAC policies involve three essential entities: a set of users, a set of roles, and a set of permissions. RBAC also defines a set UA of user assignments and a set PA of permission assignments: $(U, R) \in UA$ means that user U has the right to act in role R, and $(p, R) \in PA$ means that permission p is assigned to role R.

2.1 Role Inheritance

RBAC also includes a partial order over roles called *role inheritance*. When role R_1 inherits role R_2, denoted $R_1 \succeq R_2$, every user U explicitly assigned to role R_1 is also implicitly assigned to role R_2; likewise, every permission p explicitly associated with role R_2 is implicitly associated with role R_1. The sets *authorized_users*(R) and *authorized_permissions*(R) define the authorized users and authorized permissions of a role R are given respectively:

$$authorized\_users(R) =$$
$$\{U \in USERS \mid \exists R' \in ROLES. \ (R' \succeq R) \wedge ((U, R') \in UA)\}$$
$$authorized\_permissions(R) =$$
$$\{p \in PRMS \mid \exists R' \in ROLES. \ (R \succeq R') \wedge ((p, R') \in PA)\}.$$

From these definitions, it is straightforward to verify the following two properties:

1. If $R_1 \succeq R_2$, then *authorized_users*(R_1) $\subseteq$ *authorized_users*(R_2).
2. If $R_1 \succeq R_2$, then *authorized_permissions*(R_2) $\subseteq$ *authorized_permissions*(R_1).

2.2 Separation of Duty

RBAC also supports constraints such as separation of duty. Static separation of duty provides a way to specify mutually exclusive roles (i.e., roles that should never have authorized users in common). In RBAC, static separation of duty is

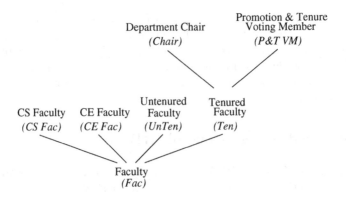

Fig. 1. Role Hierarchy Structure

represented by a set SSD of pairs (rs, n), where rs is a set of mutually exclusive roles and $n \geq 2$. When (rs, n) is in SSD, no users should be authorized to act in n or more of the roles in rs.

Note that static separation of duty constrains the role hierarchy as well as the user-role assignment UA. For example, if a user U is authorized to act in role R_1 and R_1 inherits R_2, U is also authorized to act in role R_2. Thus, both UA and $\succeq$ must be checked to ensure that they satisfy the SSD constraints.

Dynamic separation of duty constrains the combinations of roles that users may *activate* at any given instant, and is specified by a set DSD of pairs similar to SSD. When (rs, n) is in DSD, a user cannot have n or more roles in rs simultaneously activated. When a user activates a set of roles, the set of roles constitutes a *session*. The function *session_roles*(s) determines the set of activated roles associated with the session s. In an RBAC system, the role-activation monitor denies any role-activation requests that would violate the DSD constraints.

2.3   RBAC Example

As an example of an RBAC policy, consider a hypothetical academic department that houses both Computer Science (CS) and Computer Engineering (CE) programs. The department includes both tenured and untenured faculty, and every faculty member is associated with at least one of the two academic programs. In addition, the department has a chairperson and a Promotion & Tenure (P& T) committee. Thus, there are seven relevant roles for this example:

$ROLES = \{Fac, Ten, UnTen, CS\ Fac, CE\ Fac, Chair, P\&T\ VM\}.$

Figure 1 provides a Hasse diagram representing a plausible role-inheritance relation for this scenario (e.g., the roles *Chair* and *P&T VM* both inherit *Ten*).

The standard academic situation is that no one can be both tenured and untenured, and hence the roles *Ten* and *UnTen* should be mutually exclusive. Furthermore, the department's bylaws mandate that the chair cannot be a P&T

voting member. These constraints can be represented by the following static separation-of-duty relation:

$$SSD = \{(\{\mathit{Ten}, \mathit{UnTen}\}, 2), (\{\mathit{P\&T\ VM}, \mathit{Chair}\}, 2)\}.$$

Because the roles *Chair* and *P&T VM* both inherit the *Ten* role, these two constraints also prevent untenured faculty from being department chair and from being voting members of the P&T committee.

The department's bylaws also require the P&T Committee to contain a fixed number of representatives from each of the CS and CE programs. Thus, for the purposes of P&T deliberations, no faculty member can simultaneously represent both the CS and CE programs, although she may be associated with both programs. This constraint can be represented by the following dynamic separation-of-duty relation:

$$DSD = \{(\{\mathit{CS\ Fac}, \mathit{CE\ Fac}, \mathit{P\&T\ VM}\}, 3)\}.$$

Thus, no one may simultaneously act as CS faculty, CE faculty, and a P&T voting member, although they may authorized for all three roles and may act in any two of those roles simultaneously.

We have not explicitly given the user-role and permission-role assignments. However, suppose that the permission *read student grade reports* is associated with the faculty role *Fac* (i.e., (*read student grade reports, Fac*) ∈ *PA*), and that *Alice* is explicitly assigned to the role *Chair* (i.e., (*Alice, Chair*) ∈ *UA*). First of all, note that the *SSD* relation prohibits any user from being authorized for both the *Ten* and *UnTen* roles. Thus, the role hierarchy prevents *Alice* from being assigned to the *UnTen* role, as her assignment to *Chair* also implicitly authorizes her for the *Ten* role. Second, the role-inheritance relation also authorizes *Alice* to act in the role *Fac* (*Alice* ∈ *authorized_users(Fac)*), and hence she is entitled to adopt either the *Fac* or *Chair* roles to *read student grade reports*.

Having described the key concepts of RBAC, we now introduce a modal logic for access control in which RBAC relationships can be described.

3   A Logic for Reasoning About Access Control

The access-control logic of Abadi and colleagues [11,1] incorporates a calculus of principals into a standard multi-agent modal logic. The result is a set of logical rules for manipulating formulas that provides a tool for reasoning about access control, delegation, and trust.

Principals are entities (e.g., people, machines, encryption keys, and processes) that make statements. Principals can be either a simple name (e.g., "*Alice*") or compound principals (e.g., "*Alice and Carol*"). Statements are the things that principals say, such as "read file *foo*" or "*Alice* can read file *foo*."

In this section, we extend the Abadi logic with a few constructs that will allow us to reason about requests in the context of RBAC.

3.1 Syntax

We start out by introducing a collection of principal expressions, ranged over by P and Q. Letting A range over a countable set of simple principal names, the abstract syntax of principal expressions is given as follows:

$$P ::= A \mid P \& Q \mid P|Q \mid P \text{ for}_A Q$$

The principal $P \& Q$ represents a compound principal who makes exactly those statements made by both P and Q. $P|Q$ represents an abstract principal corresponding to principal P quoting principal Q. $P \text{ for}_A Q$ represents a principal P acting on behalf of principal Q: $P \text{ for}_A Q$ is syntactic sugar for $P|Q \& A|Q$, where A is a principal that vouches for P's authorization to make statements on Q's behalf [1].

For the logic itself, we let p range over a countable collection of primitive propositions and define the abstract syntax for the logic as follows:

$$\varphi ::= p \mid \neg\varphi \mid \varphi_1 \wedge \varphi_2 \mid \varphi_1 \vee \varphi_2 \mid \varphi_1 \supset \varphi_2 \mid \varphi_1 \equiv \varphi_2 \mid P \text{ says } \varphi \mid P \Rightarrow Q$$
$$\mid P \rightarrowtail_T Q \mid P \text{ serves}_T^A Q \mid P \succcurlyeq_T Q$$

Here, T ranges over sets of formulas that include only formulas of the forms included on the first line (e.g., not involving $\rightarrowtail_T$, serves_T^A, or $\succcurlyeq_T$); the forms involving T are our extensions.

Primitive propositions are used to represent requests and permissions, while the formula $P \text{ says } \varphi$ represents principal P making the statement φ. In turn, $P \Rightarrow Q$ represents a relationship between principals P and Q through which statements of P can also be attributed to Q. The formula $P \rightarrowtail_T Q$, pronounced as "P is mimicked by Q on T," is our extension to the logic, inspired by Howell and Kotz's *restricted speaks for* relation $\overset{T}{\Rightarrow}$ [9]. This *restricted mimics* formula represents a weaker relation than $P \Rightarrow Q$, in part because only P's statements from the set T can be attributed to Q. Finally, $P \text{ serves}_T^A Q$ (the *restricted serves* relation) and $P \succcurlyeq_T Q$ (the *restricted inherits* relation) are syntactic sugar for $P|Q \rightarrowtail_T A|Q$ and $(P \Rightarrow Q) \wedge (Q \rightarrowtail_T P)$, respectively.

3.2 Semantics

The semantics of the logic is based on Kripke structures. A Kripke structure is a triple $\mathcal{M} = \langle W, I, J \rangle$, where W is a set of possible worlds, I is an interpretation function that maps each primitive proposition to a set of worlds, and J is an interpretation function that maps each primitive principal to a binary relation over W. We extend J to a function $\tilde{J}$ over arbitrary principal expressions as follows:

$$\tilde{J}(A) = J(A)$$
$$\tilde{J}(P \& Q) = \tilde{J}(P) \cup \tilde{J}(Q)$$
$$\tilde{J}(P|Q) = \tilde{J}(P) \circ \tilde{J}(Q)$$
$$= \{(w_1, w_3) \mid \exists w_2.\ (w_1, w_2) \in \tilde{J}(P) \wedge (w_2, w_3) \in \tilde{J}(Q)\}.$$

$$\mathcal{E}_{\mathcal{M}}[\![p]\!] = I(p)$$
$$\mathcal{E}_{\mathcal{M}}[\![\neg\varphi]\!] = W - \mathcal{E}_{\mathcal{M}}[\![\varphi]\!]$$
$$\mathcal{E}_{\mathcal{M}}[\![\varphi_1 \wedge \varphi_2]\!] = \mathcal{E}_{\mathcal{M}}[\![\varphi_1]\!] \cap \mathcal{E}_{\mathcal{M}}[\![\varphi_2]\!]$$
$$\mathcal{E}_{\mathcal{M}}[\![\varphi_1 \vee \varphi_2]\!] = \mathcal{E}_{\mathcal{M}}[\![\varphi_1]\!] \cup \mathcal{E}_{\mathcal{M}}[\![\varphi_2]\!]$$
$$\mathcal{E}_{\mathcal{M}}[\![\varphi_1 \supset \varphi_2]\!] = \mathcal{E}_{\mathcal{M}}[\![\neg\varphi_1]\!] \cup \mathcal{E}_{\mathcal{M}}[\![\varphi_2]\!]$$
$$\mathcal{E}_{\mathcal{M}}[\![\varphi_1 \equiv \varphi_2]\!] = \mathcal{E}_{\mathcal{M}}[\![\varphi_1 \supset \varphi_2]\!] \cap \mathcal{E}_{\mathcal{M}}[\![\varphi_2 \supset \varphi_1]\!]$$
$$\mathcal{E}_{\mathcal{M}}[\![P \text{ says } \varphi]\!] = \{w \mid \tilde{J}(P)(w) \subseteq \mathcal{E}_{\mathcal{M}}[\![\varphi]\!]\}$$
$$= \{w \mid \{w' \mid (w,w') \in \tilde{J}(P)\} \subseteq \mathcal{E}_{\mathcal{M}}[\![\varphi]\!]\}$$
$$\mathcal{E}_{\mathcal{M}}[\![P \Rightarrow Q]\!] = \begin{cases} W & \text{if } \tilde{J}(Q) \subseteq \tilde{J}(P) \\ \emptyset & \text{otherwise} \end{cases}$$
$$\mathcal{E}_{\mathcal{M}}[\![P \rightarrowtail_T Q]\!] = \begin{cases} W & \text{if } \forall s \in T. \ P \text{ says } s \supset Q \text{ says } s, \\ \emptyset & \text{otherwise} \end{cases}$$
$$\mathcal{E}_{\mathcal{M}}[\![P \text{ serves}_T^A Q]\!] = \mathcal{E}_{\mathcal{M}}[\![P|Q \rightarrowtail_T A|Q]\!]$$
$$\mathcal{E}_{\mathcal{M}}[\![P \succcurlyeq_T Q]\!] = \mathcal{E}_{\mathcal{M}}[\![(P \Rightarrow Q) \wedge (Q \rightarrowtail_T P)]\!].$$

Fig. 2. The meaning functions $\mathcal{E}_{\mathcal{M}}[\![-]\!]$

We then define a family (indexed by Kripke structures $\mathcal{M}$) of extended meaning functions $\mathcal{E}_{\mathcal{M}}[\![-]\!]$, which map arbitrary formulas to the sets of worlds in which they are considered true. The definition of $\mathcal{E}_{\mathcal{M}}[\![-]\!]$ appears in Figure 2. We write $(\mathcal{M}, w) \models \varphi$ if and only if $w \in \mathcal{E}_{\mathcal{M}}[\![\varphi]\!]$, and we say that $\mathcal{M}$ satisfies φ provided that $(\mathcal{M}, w) \models \varphi$ for all $w \in W$. We say that φ is *valid* if every Kripke structure $\mathcal{M}$ satisfies φ.

3.3   Logical Rules

The Kripke structures provide a precise semantics for the logic, but it is not convenient to reason at that level. Thus, we introduce a collection of logical rules for manipulating logical expressions. These rules, given in Figure 3, are sound with respect to the Kripke semantics: for every formula φ, if φ is derivable (i.e., $\vdash \varphi$), then φ is valid (i.e., satisfied in all Kripke structures).

3.4   Our Extensions to the Access-Control Logic

The original Abadi logic is unable to adequately describe RBAC for two reasons: its notion of roles conflicts with the RBAC concept, and it provides no way to express the role-permission associations. Specifically, the Abadi logic includes a special class of principals called *roles*, and arbitrary principals can adopt roles to make requests (e.g., "(*Alice* as *Fac*) says φ"). However, adopting roles is at the principal's discretion, and the effect is a *reduction* of privileges (e.g., *Alice* as *Fac* has fewer privileges than *Alice* does). In contrast, an RBAC user is granted privileges purely through the adoption of roles, and only when the user has been authorized to adopt a given role. Thus, reasoning about RBAC requires us to

$$\frac{}{\vdash \varphi} \quad \text{if } \varphi \text{ is an instance of a propositional-logic tautology}$$

$$\frac{\vdash \varphi \quad \vdash \varphi \supset \varphi'}{\vdash \varphi'} \qquad \frac{\vdash \varphi}{\vdash P \text{ says } \varphi} \quad \text{(for all } P)$$

$$\frac{}{\vdash (P \text{ says } (\varphi \supset \varphi')) \supset (P \text{ says } \varphi \supset P \text{ says } \varphi')}$$

$$\frac{}{\vdash \varphi} \quad \text{if } \varphi \text{ a valid formula of the calculus of principals}$$

$$\frac{}{\vdash P \text{ says } (\varphi_1 \wedge \varphi_2) \equiv (P \text{ says } \varphi) \wedge (P \text{ says } \varphi)}$$

$$\frac{}{\vdash (P \mid Q) \text{ says } \varphi \equiv P \text{ says } Q \text{ says } \varphi}$$

$$\frac{}{\vdash (P \Rightarrow Q) \supset ((P \text{ says } \varphi) \supset (Q \text{ says } \varphi))} \quad \text{(for all } \varphi)$$

$$\frac{}{\vdash (P \rightarrowtail_T Q) \supset ((P \text{ says } \varphi) \supset (Q \text{ says } \varphi))} \quad \text{(for all } \varphi \in T)$$

Fig. 3. Logical rules for the derivability predicate $\vdash$

$$\frac{}{\vdash (P \rightarrowtail_T Q) \wedge (Q \rightarrowtail_T R) \supset (P \rightarrowtail_T R)} \qquad (\rightarrowtail \text{ Trans})$$

$$\frac{}{\vdash (P \rightarrowtail_{T_1} Q) \supset (P \rightarrowtail_{T_2} Q)} \quad \text{(for all } T_2 \subseteq T_1) \qquad (\rightarrowtail \text{ Sub})$$

$$\frac{}{\vdash (P \rightarrowtail_T Q) \supset (R|P \rightarrowtail_T R|Q)} \qquad (\rightarrowtail \text{ Mon})$$

$$\frac{}{\vdash (P \text{ serves}_T^A Q) \wedge (P|Q \text{ says } s) \supset (P \text{ for}_A Q \text{ says } s)} \quad \text{(for every } s \in T) \quad (\text{Role Del})$$

$$\frac{}{\vdash P \succcurlyeq_T P} \qquad (\succcurlyeq \text{ Ref})$$

$$\frac{}{\vdash (P \succcurlyeq_{T_1} Q) \wedge (Q \succcurlyeq_{T_2} R) \supset (P \succcurlyeq_{T_1 \cap T_2} R)} \qquad (\succcurlyeq \text{ Trans})$$

$$\frac{}{\vdash (Q_1 \succcurlyeq_{T_2} Q_2) \wedge (P \text{ serves}_{T_1}^A Q_1) \supset (P \text{ serves}_{T_2}^A Q_2)} \quad \text{(for all } T_2 \subseteq T_1) \quad (\text{Role Sub})$$

Fig. 4. Logical rules related to $\rightarrowtail_T$, serves_T^A, and $\succcurlyeq_T$

model role-permission associations, which relate roles (principals) with sets of permissions (sets of statements).

We can model these RBAC notions in our logic using our three extensions: the *restricted mimicked by* relation, the *restricted serves* relation, and the *restricted inherits* relation. We explain how to do so in the next section. For now, we introduce to our logical system some additional rules related to these relations. These rules (see Figure 4) are all sound with respect to the Kripke semantics.

4   Describing RBAC Policies in the Access-Control Logic

When a user U acts in a role R and makes a request q, a reference monitor makes an access-control decision based on UA and PA. The request will be granted if the user has the right to act in role R (i.e., $U \in authorized\_users(R)$) and q is a permission associated with role R (i.e., $q \in authorized\_permissions(R)$).

For the logic to support reasoning about a specific RBAC policy, it must provide ways to express the following components: (1) RBAC entities (e.g., users, roles, permissions), (2) role activation and user requests, and (3) the role-inheritance relationship. We consider these components in turn.

4.1   Describing RBAC Entities

We represent users and roles as principals in the logic, and we represent *permissions* as primitive propositions. *UA* and *PA* are jointly represented in the logic as statements of the form

$$U \text{ serves}_{ap(R)}^{RA} R,$$

where RA represents a role authority that certifies that the user U has the right to act in the role R, and $ap(R)$ is the set of propositions corresponding to the permissions in the set *authorized_permissions*(R).[1] Simply put, U serves$_{ap(R)}^{RA} R$ indicates that user U is an authorized user of role R and may make requests involving permissions associated with R.

The reference monitor's ultimate decision on whether to grant a request q is based on a series of access-control list (ACL) entries, each of which can be expressed as

$$((U \text{ for}_{RA} R) \text{ says } q) \supset q,$$

where $U \in$ *authorized_users*(R) and $q \in$ *authorized_permissions*(R). That is, if the reference monitor can verify that (1) a user U is making the request q while activated in the role R, and (2) q is a permission associated with role R, then the reference monitor will grant the request.

4.2   Describing User Requests

In RBAC, all requests by users are made within the context of a role. The result is that two principals—the user and the role—are involved in all requests.

We use quoting to describe role assertions (e.g., $U|R$) and the says operator to represent the actual requests. For example, a user U asserting role R and making a request q is represented as $U|R$ says q. Multiple requests can be expressed through conjunction, as in $U|R$ says $(q_1 \wedge q_2)$ or $(U|R_1$ says $q_1) \wedge (U|R_2$ says $q_2)$.

Note that the statement $U|R$ says q does not guarantee that U is *authorized* for role R: it merely states that U is *claiming* to be acting in role R. There is no danger, however that an inappropriate request will be granted: the ACL entry requires the reference monitor to deduce (via Role Del) that $(U \text{ for}_{RA} R)$ says q, which is possible only when U is authorized for role R.

4.3   Describing Role Inheritance

The relationship $R_1 \succeq R_2$ is expressed in the logic by the formula $R_1 \succcurlyeq_{ap(R_2)} R_2$, which is syntactic sugar for $(R_1 \Rightarrow R_2) \wedge (R_2 \rightarrowtail_{ap(R_2)} R_1)$.

---

[1] Henceforth, we shall blur the distinction between actual permissions and the primitive propositions that are associated with them.

It is important to confirm that this formulation accurately captures all of the important properties of inheritance: reflexivity, transitivity, and the subset relationships between related roles' authorized users and authorized permissions. That is, we must ensure that the logical rules (and thus the logic's semantics) validate the following properties:

- For all roles R, $\vdash R \succcurlyeq_{ap(R)} R$.
  This rule is an instance of the $\succcurlyeq$-reflexivity rule ($\succcurlyeq$ Ref) from Figure 4.
- For all roles R_1, R_2, R_3,

$$\vdash (R_1 \succcurlyeq_{ap(R_2)} R_2 \wedge R_2 \succcurlyeq_{ap(R_3)} R_3) \supset R_1 \succcurlyeq_{ap(R_3)} R_3.$$

Recall that, whenever $R_2 \succeq R_3$, $authorized\_permissions(R_3)$ is a subset of $authorized\_permissions(R_2)$, and thus $ap(R_3) \subseteq ap(R_2)$. Therefore, $ap(R_3) = ap(R_3) \cap ap(R_2)$, and the desired rule is simply an instance of the $\succcurlyeq$-transitivity rule ($\succcurlyeq$ Trans) from Figure 4.
- For all roles R_1 and R_2, users U, and role authorities RA,

$$\vdash (R_1 \succcurlyeq_{ap(R_2)} R_2 \wedge U \text{ serves}^{RA}_{ap(R_1)} R_1) \supset (U \text{ serves}^{RA}_{ap(R_2)} R_2).$$

That is, if U is an authorized user of R_1 and R_1 inherits R_2, then U is also an authorized user of R_2. Once again, we rely on the relationship $ap(R_2) \subseteq ap(R_1)$ to see that the desired rule is simply an instance of the role-subsumption (Role Sub) rule from Figure 4.

4.4   Reasoning About Access-Control Decisions

To demonstrate the use of the logic in reasoning about access-control decisions, we return to the example from Section 2. We temporarily ignore the separation-of-duty constraints, and focus on the access-control aspects of the example.

Recall that the permission *read student grade reports* is associated with the role *Fac*: we use *rsg* as the primitive proposition corresponding to this permission. For simplicity, we also assume the permission *rant* (proposition *rt*) is assigned to the *Ten* role; there are no other explicit permission assignments.

Thus, the role hierarchy shown in Figure 1 can be described as follows:

$$(CS\ Fac \succcurlyeq_{\{rsg\}} Fac) \wedge (CE\ Fac \succcurlyeq_{\{rsg\}} Fac) \wedge (UnTen \succcurlyeq_{\{rsg\}} Fac) \wedge$$
$$(Ten \succcurlyeq_{\{rsg\}} Fac) \wedge (Chair \succcurlyeq_{\{rsg,rt\}} Ten) \wedge (P\&T\ VM \succcurlyeq_{\{rsg,rt\}} Ten).$$

Recall that *Alice* is explicitly assigned to the role *Chair*. This fact can be represented in the logic by the statement $Alice\ \text{serves}^{RA}_{\{rsg,rt\}}\ Chair$. This statement, along with the description of the role hierarchy above, provide the basis for reasoning about whether *Alice* should be allowed to read student grade reports.

More specifically, we interpret *Alice*'s attempt to read student grade reports as a statement $Alice|Fac\ \text{says}\ rsg$. Ultimately, the reference monitor must be able to deduce that $(Alice\ \text{for}_{RA} Fac)\ \text{says}\ rsg$, in which case the request will be granted.

Table 1. Mapping from RBAC to Access-Control Logic

RBAC	Access-Control Logic
A permission q is associated with role R	$p \in ap(R)$
User U is authorized to act in role R.	U serves$_{ap(R)}^{RA}$ R
Role R_1 inherits role R_2 $(R_1 \succeq R_2)$	$R_1 \succcurlyeq_{ap(R_2)} R_2$
User U asserting role R makes a request q.	$U|R$ says q
User U, acting in authorized role R, makes a request q.	U for$_{RA}R$ says q

From above, we know that $(Chair \succcurlyeq_{\{rsg,rt\}} Ten) \wedge (Ten \succcurlyeq_{\{rsg\}} Fac)$. Role transitivity allows us to conclude $Chair \succcurlyeq_{\{rsg\}} Fac$. Taken together with

$$Alice \text{ serves}_{\{rsg,rt\}}^{RA} Chair,$$

Figure 4's role-subsumption rule (Role Sub) lets us deduce $Alice$ serves$_{\{rsg\}}^{RA}$ Fac.

From $Alice|Fac$ says rsg and $Alice$ serves$_{\{rsg\}}^{RA}$ Fac, we can use the Figure 4's role-delegation rule (Role Del) to deduce $(Alice$ for$_{RA}Fac)$ says rsg as needed. As a result, $Alice$'s request can be granted.

4.5 Summary

Table 1 summarizes how RBAC concepts are translated into formulas of the access-control logic, providing a guideline for describing RBAC policies in the logic. The logical rules in Figure 4 provide the basis for reasoning about access-control decisions. Specifically, to determine whether a request $U|R$ says q should be granted, it suffices to determine whether the statement $(U$ for$_{RA}R)$ says q can be deduced from the logical rules.

5 Formal Specifications of RBAC Constraints

RBAC's separation-of-duty constraints do not directly affect access-control decisions, in that they are not checked at the time a decision is made. Rather, they impose additional restrictions on the initial specification of an RBAC policy. Therefore, we have not incorporated them into our access-control logic. However, it is desirable to be able to verify that a given policy is consistent: its user-role assignment and role hierarchy should not conflict with the stated separation-of-duty constraints.

For this reason, we have formalized RBAC constraints in the Higher-Order Logic (HOL) theorem prover. The result is a tool which one can verify the consistency of RBAC policies. Because the access-control logic has also been implemented and proved sound in HOL, we can easily convert RBAC policies which has been proved consistent in HOL into the access-control logic for reasoning about access-control decisions.

5.1 Static Separation of Duty

The role-inheritance relationship between roles R_1 and R_2 $(R_1 \succeq R_2)$ is a partial order and thus reflexive, transitive, and antisymmetric. In RBAC, the role hierarchy is generally represented pictorially by a Hasse diagram. We implement Hasse diagrams in HOL as a set HSD of pairs, with $(R_1, R_2) \in HSD$ precisely when there's an explicit edge between R_1 and R_2 in the Hasse diagram. It is then straightforward to define $\succeq$ as the reflexive, transitive closure of HSD, relative to the set $ROLES$ of roles:

$$rhRel\ HSD\ ROLES = \{(R_1, R_2) \mid (R_1 \in ROLES) \wedge (R_2 \in ROLES) \wedge$$
$$(RTC\ (CURRY\ HSD)\ R_1\ R_2)\},$$

where $(CURRY\ HSD)\ R_1\ R_2$ is equivalent to $(R_1, R_2) \in HSD$ and the predicate RTC (defined in HOL's *Relation* theory) identifies the elements in the reflexive, transitive closure of a relation.

For example, the Hasse diagram from Figure 1 can be represented by a set HSD as follows:

$$HSD = \{(Chair, Ten), (P\&T\ VM, Ten), (Ten, Fac),$$
$$(CS\ Fac, Fac), (CE\ Fac, Fac), (UnTen, Fac)\}$$

Letting $ROLES$ be the set $\{Chair, P\&T\ VM, Ten, UnTen, CS\ Fac, CE\ Fac, Fac\}$, the inheritance relation $\succeq$ is given by:

$$rhRel\ HSD\ ROLES =$$
$$HSD \cup \{(R, R) \mid R \in ROLES\} \cup \{(Chair, Fac), (P\&T\ VM, Fac)\}.$$

The set of users authorized for a role R depends on both the user-role assignments (UA) and the inheritance relation $\succeq$; likewise, the set of permissions associated with a role depends on the permission assignments (PA) and $\succeq$. Thus, we define predicates *authorized_users* and *authorized_permissions* as follows:

authorized_users $R\ UA\ HSD\ ROLES =$
$\{U \mid \exists R'. (R \in ROLES) \wedge ((R', R) \in rhRel\ HSD\ ROLES) \wedge (U, R') \in UA\}$,
authorized_permissions $R\ PA\ HSD\ ROLES =$
$\{p \mid \exists R'. (R' \in ROLES) \wedge ((R, R') \in rhRel\ HSD\ ROLES) \wedge (p, R') \in PA\}$.

It is straightforward to prove that, whenever $R_1 \succeq R_2$—that is, when (R_1, R_2) is in $rhRel\ HSD\ ROLES$—the following two properties hold:

$$(authorized\_users\ R_1\ UA\ HSD\ ROLES) \subseteq$$
$$(authorized\_users\ R_2\ UA\ HSD\ ROLES)$$
$$(authorized\_permissions\ R_2\ PA\ HSD\ ROLES) \subseteq$$
$$(authorized\_permissions\ R_1\ PA\ HSD\ ROLES).$$

As described in Section 2, static separation-of-duty constraints are given by a set SSD: each pair $(rs, n) \in SSD$ represents a constraint to prevent users from being authorized for n or more roles in rs. Because the set of authorized users for a given role depends on both the user assignment *and* the role hierarchy, we must consider both when determining whether a particular RBAC policy is consistent with its separation-of-duty constraints. The predicate *isConsistent* verifies that a given user assignment *UA* and role hierarchy (given as a Hasse diagram *HSD* and a set of *ROLES*) do not violate the *SSD* constraints:

$$\forall \ UA \ SSD \ HSD \ ROLES. \ isConsistent \ UA \ SSD \ HSD \ ROLES =$$
$$\forall \ rs \ n. \ (rs \subseteq ROLES) \supset (FINITE \ rs) \supset (n \geq 2) \supset (rs, n) \in SSD \supset$$
$$(\forall \ t. \ (t \subseteq rs) \supset (CARD \ t \geq n) \supset$$
$$(\neg \exists \ U. \ \forall r. \ (r \in t) \supset (U \in authorized\_users \ r \ UA \ HSD \ ROLES))),$$

where *CARD t* returns the number of elements in the finite set *t* and *FINITE s* returns true if the set *s* is a finite set.

[4] identifies several properties that should hold of consistent RBAC policies, such as that if two roles are mutually exclusive, then no nonempty role can possibly inherit both of them. We have verified that these properties do hold in our HOL implementation, which provides additional assurance that we have accurately captured the definitions.

5.2   Dynamic Separation of Duty

Dynamic separation of duty imposes constraints on the roles that a user can have *activated* at any given instant. Like static separation of duty, these constraints are expressed as a set *DSD*: each pair $(rs, n) \in DSD$ represents a constraint that prevents a user from activating *n* or more roles in *rs* simultaneously.

In other words, if the set of roles associated with a user's session *s* is a subset of *rs*, the number of roles in *session_roles(s)* must be less than *n*. The predicate *SessionSatisfies* verifies that a session *s* satisfies the *DSD* constraints:

$$\forall \ s \ DSD \ ROLES. \ SessionSatisfies \ s \ DSD \ ROLES =$$
$$\forall \ rs \ n. \ (rs \subseteq ROLES) \wedge (FINITE \ rs) \wedge (n \geq 2) \wedge (CARD \ rs \geq n) \wedge$$
$$((rs, n) \in DSD) \supset$$
$$(\forall \ t. \ (t \subseteq rs) \wedge (t \subseteq session\_roles(s)) \supset (CARD \ t < n)).$$

As with static separation of duty, [4] also identified necessary consequences for dynamic separation of duty constraints, such as that, if two roles are mutually exclusive for activation, no session may involve both roles. We have verified that these properties hold of our HOL implementation.

6   Conclusions

Building information systems correctly is difficult—assuring information systems are secure is even more difficult. As the size, scope, and complexity of information systems is ever increasing, designers and verifiers of information systems face an ever more challenging task when assuring security. Many have observed that engineers must design security into systems from the start and that designs must be provably secure. An implication of this last point is the need for a simple, formal, and rigorous logic for reasoning about access control in a wide variety of forms and situations. Such a logic could be used by designers to reason about access-control decisions in ways that are analogous to how digital designers use propositional logic to reason about digital designs. Our conclusion is that such a logic is possible, based on our experience defining a modal logic capable of specifying and reasoning about access-control policies and decisions that utilize role-based access control (RBAC).

In our logic, user assignments, permission assignments, and role hierarchies are defined within the access-control logic. In so doing, we have soundly united in a single logic the ability to reason about privileges, authority, delegation, credentials, and RBAC. We are currently extending the logic to support the administration of RBAC roles with concepts such as administrative scope [14,3].

The requirement that engineers prove that their designs are correct and secure necessitates the development of automated tools and verification methods. To help meet this need, both the access-control logic and the consistency checks for static and dynamic separation-of-duty constraints are defined as conservative extensions to the logic of the Higher Order Logic (HOL) theorem prover [10]. The HOL extensions provide an executable implementation of the access-control logic, and the inference rules have been verified to be sound. Likewise, verification of static and dynamic separation-of-duty constraints of RBAC policies is also done in HOL. While we do not anticipate that theorem provers such as HOL will be routinely used by practicing engineers, the HOL definitions and theorems are a rigorous and provably correct basis for computer-assisted reasoning tools such as symbolic simulators, rewriting systems, and symbolic calculators. Such tools are accessible and familiar to engineers and do not carry the same burden of formal proof when compared to full-scale theorem proving systems such as HOL.

References

1. Abadi, M., Burrows, M., Lampson, B., Plotkin, G.: A Calculus for Access Control in Distributed Systems. ACM Transactions on Programming Languages and Systems, 15(4) (1993) 706-734
2. Cuppens, F., Demolombe, R.: A Modal Logical Framework for Security Policies. Proceedings of the 10th International Symposium on Foundations of Intelligent Systems, Lecture Notes in Computer Science, Vol.1325. Springer. (1997) 579-589
3. Cramton, J., Loizou, G.: Administrative Scope: A Foundation for Role-Based Administrative Models. ACM Transactions on Information and System Security, 6(2) (2003) 201-231
4. Ferraiolo, D.F., Barkley, J.F., Kuhn, D.R.: A Role-Based Access Control Model and Reference Implementation Within a Corporate Intranet. ACM Transactions on Information and System Security, 2(1) (1999) 34-64
5. Ferraiolo, D., Kuhn, R.: Role-Based Access Control. 15th NIST-NCSC National Computer Security Conference, Gaithersburg, MD (1992) 554-563

6. Ferraiolo, D.F., Sandhu, R.S., Gavrila, S.I., Kuhn, D.R., Chandramouli, R.: Proposed NIST Standard for Role-Based Access Control. ACM Transaction on Information and System Security, 4(3) (2001) 224-274
7. Gordon, M.J.C., Melham, T.F.: Introduction to HOL: A Theorem Proving Environment for Higher Order Logic. Cambridge University Press, New York (1993)
8. Glasgow, J., MacEwen, G., Panangaden P.: A Logic for Reasoning About Security. ACM Transactions on Computer Systems, 10(3) (1992) 226-264
9. Howell, J., Kotz, D.: A Formal Semantics for SPKI. Technical Report TR2000-363, Department of Computer Science, Dartmouth College, Hanover, NH 03755-3510 (2000)
10. International Computer Limited. Higher Order Logic (HOL) Theorem Prover Version 4 (Kananaskis-2) http://hol.sourceforge.net (2004)
11. Lampson, B., Abadi, M., Burrows, M., Wobber, E.: Authentication in Distributed Systems: Theory and Practice. ACM Transactions on Computer Systems, 10(4) (1992) 265-310
12. Older, S., Chin, S.-K.: Building a Rigorous Foundation for Assurance into Information Assurance Education. Proceedings of the 6th National Colloquium for Information Systems Security Education (2002)
13. Older, S., Chin, S.-K.: Using Outcomes-based Assessment as an Assurance Tool for Assurance Education. Journal of Information Warfare, 2(3) (2003) 86-100
14. Sandhu, R., Bhamidipati, V., Munawer, Q.: The ARBAC97 Model for Role-Based Administration of Roles. ACM Transactions on Information and System Security, 2(1) (1999) 105-135

Unique User-Generated Digital Pseudonyms

Peter Schartner and Martin Schaffer

University of Klagenfurt, Austria,
Computer Science · System Security Group
{p.schartner, m.schaffer}@syssec.at

Abstract. This paper presents a method to generate unique and never-theless highly random pseudonyms in a distributed environment. More precisely, each user can now generate his pseudonym locally in his personal security environment, e.g. in his smart card or his personal digital assistant. There is no need for any information interchange between issuing parties or global data (especially keys), except unique identifiers for each user and each device of the system. Additionally the holder can prove, that he generated a specific pseudonym without revealing his identity and he can reveal his identity by disclosing the pseudonym. Whereas the verifier of a disclosed pseudonym can be sure, that the presenter of the pseudonym is the holder of the pseudonym (i.e. the person which originally generated it). The identifier of the user and the identifier of the user's device will be used to generate unique pseudonyms, but to ensure pseudonymity, both components will be stored in the pseudonym in encrypted form.

1 Introduction

Pseudonyms (or nyms) are identifiers of subjects. The subject that may be identified by the pseudonym is the holder of the pseudonym (see [7,9]). From the technical point of view, a pseudonym is a bit string which is

- (locally or globally) unique as identifier and
- suitable to be used to authenticate the holder and his/her data (e.g. messages sent).

Most of the applications of pseudonyms have in common, that there should be no way to correlate data (of the pseudonym) stored in different applications or to link these data to the holder of the pseudonym and his identity. So another important aspect in the scope of pseudonyms is linkability, i.e. the knowledge of the relationship between the holder and his/her pseudonym. This linking may be known to third parties or only to the holder of the pseudonym.

Up to date, there are two ways to generate globally unique pseudonyms for a person (here called holder):

Centralized Generation: This approach employs a centralized third party, which generates the pseudonym on the user's behalf. This party can easily avoid duplicates and hence the generated pseudonyms are unique. On a larger scale, we

V. Gorodetsky, I. Kotenko, and V. Skormin (Eds.): MMM-ACNS 2005, LNCS 3685, pp. 194–205, 2005.

may employ several hierarchically organized issuing parties. In order to guarantee the uniqueness of the pseudonyms, these issuers either generate pseudonyms in a specific (previously specified) range, or they have to check the randomly generated pseudonym with all other issuers which causes immense communication efforts. Additionally, the holder of the certificate has to trust in the issuer, since the issuer knows the linking of the holders identity to his pseudonym.

Local (Holder-based) Generation: The other way is, that the user generates his pseudonym locally. Now, only the user knows the linking between his identity and his pseudonym. But again we need some sort of cross-checking to avoid duplicates.

In the approach presented in this paper, the holder locally generates globally unique pseudonyms, which are nevertheless highly random. There is no need for any information interchange between issuing parties or global data (especially keys), except unique identifiers for each user and each device of the system. Additionally the holder can prove, that he generated a specific pseudonym without revealing his identity and he can reveal his identity by disclosing the pseudonym. This disclosure is achieved by presenting some additional, previously unknown, information to the verifier. As a security feature, this information (the opening information) cannot be forged, so that the verifier retrieves an identity different from the identity used in the generating process of the pseudonym. Another feature of the proposed system is, that there is no way to disclose the pseudonym, if the holder does not cooperate. For several application scenarios this may seem to be a major drawback (e.g. the holder of a pseudonym has just won an auction, but does not want to pay). But there are others, where there is either no need for enforced disclosure, or where the holder of the pseudonym has a strong interest in disclosing his pseudonym at a certain point of time and hence will cooperate.

The application scenarios of pseudonyms (providing pseudonymity or anonymity), where the approach presented in this paper is suitable, include:

(Centralized) Register for Medical Records: Concerning medical records, there is a strong interest in privacy, i.e. to keep the connection between a person's name and his/her medical record(s) private. On the other hand many countries (like Austria and Germany) run centralized databases, in order to provide data for statistical studies. To achieve this, each medical record is sent to a Server, which keeps an anonymized medical history for each person. Hence the patients have to trust in this server, because it knows the relation between the patient's identifier and his/her (anonymous) record identifier. If the server has been compromised and the algorithm for mapping the patients name (or social insurance number) to his/her record identifer is publicly known, the privacy of all patients is at risk. In contrast to this, by applying our scheme for globally unique pseudonyms, the medical records are anonymized before sending them to the server. Hence, there is no way (except breaking the encryption algorithm) to re-map a pseudonym to a user of the system.

Online Gambling: Here, the player wants to stay anonymous during gambling. He participates in the game by using his pseudonym. In case of a win, he discloses his pseudonym. Since he wants to receive his prize, he will be cooperative and will not try to forge the disclosed identity.

Online Retrieval of Information: By correlating the different areas, where a certain person retrieves information (e.g. patents or conference papers), one may conclude the research topic (and the state of the research) of this person. Applying pseudonyms (actually anonyms) here, would solve the problem.

Electronic Voting: Here, the voter may use his unique identifier received during the setup phase of the voting scheme to choose his pseudonym locally. Unfortunately, by now there is no way to prove the binding between the identifier and the pseudonym without disclosing the pseudonym. Nevertheless, this approach may be useful within closed systems, where each participant in the system is a legitimate voter.

Other applications may be in the field of online-subscription of newspapers or temporary identifiers in the scope of mobile phones or RFID (radio frequency identification).

2   Generation of Pseudonyms

The method presented in this paper is based on the idea of generating unique keys (or key components like primes) within isolated instances [3] which has been refined in [4,5,6,14]. Figure 1 shows the operating principle of the original scheme. Here, we first generate unique identifiers $(EID_1||k_1$ respectively $EID_2||k_2)$ by means of symmetric encryption, where $EID = \mathrm{E}_k(UID||Data||PAD)$. The proof of uniqueness will be given later on in this paper. These identifiers are concatenated with some bits $(PP_1$ respectively $PP_2)$ in order to generate probabilistic primes. Finally, the primes are multiplied and the result gives the unique modulus of an RSA-Crypto-System consisting of two unique primes p_1 and p_2.

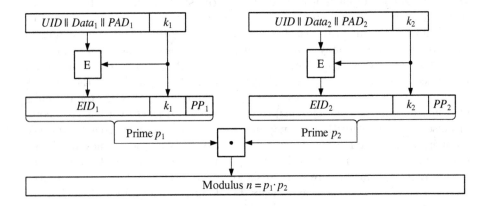

Fig. 1. Basic Idea – Generation of Unique Key Components

One may now directly use the unique Identifier $(EID_1||k_1)$ as a pseudonym. But it is obvious, that this pseudonym does not hide any information (especially the user identifier – UID) without additional measures. Given a pseudonym of this form, the ID of the user which has been used to generate the pseudonym can be easily retrieved by decrypting the block EID_1 with key k_1. Replacing the symmetric encryption by asymmetric encryption (in this paper RSA) solves that problem. For simplicity of our notation, we will only display the public and private exponents (e and d) of the public and private keys (e, n) and (d, n). So for example $E_e(m)$ represents the asymmetric encryption of message m with the public key (e, n).

More generally, a pseudonym P of an user identity (UID) is generated by use of a function f parameterized with at least two parameters: the user identity UID and a secret key k. In our approach, this function f has to be a bijective (one-to-one) one-way computation, more precisely an asymmetric encryption function, and the key k is the public key (e, n). Hence the pseudonym results in $P = f(UID, k) = E_e(UID)||k = E_e(UID)||e||n$.

Since the public key (and its components) are random, two different users may accidentally choose the same key. By concatenating $E_e(UID)$ and $e||n$ we ensure, that at least one of the components and hence the concatenation of the components is globally unique. For details see the proof of uniqueness given later on in this paper.

This scheme generates unique but nevertheless highly random pseudonyms in a distributed environment. More precisely, each user can now generate his pseudonym locally in his personal security environment (PSE), e.g. in his smart card or his PDA (personal digital assistant). There is no need for any global data (especially keys) or information interchange between issuing parties. The only requirement is a unique identifier (UID – user identifier) for each user of the system and a unique identifier for each PSE of the system, which may easily be managed by the use of a hierarchical issuing structure. If smart cards are used as a PSE, then the $ICCSN$ (integrated chip card serial number [10]) – a globally unique identifier which is stored in every smart card – can be used in the generating process. So we do not need to distribute or manage any IDs at all.

One problem with using the $ICCSN$ is, that this number may be used during the authentication of the smart card (e.g. to derive the individual authentication key of the card) or to manage black-lists of revoked or lost smart cards. In this case, the card has to hold a user identifier, which cannot be linked to the holder of the card. Nevertheless, by now only the need for a globally unique identifier shall be emphasized, one concrete mechanism for such an identifier will be presented in section 5.

The principle to generate unique and highly random pseudonyms is quite easy (see figure 2 and figure 3):

1. The user (respectively his PSE) generates a key-pair for an asymmetric encryption algorithm.

    For the ease of description, we will focus on the RSA-System [11] in the remainder of this paper. Other asymmetric encryption schemes will work as well. Hence the PSE generates the modulus n, the public exponent e, and the private exponent d. In the generation process, there is no need for the private exponent d. This parameter is only needed for later disclosure of the pseudonym.

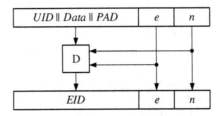

Fig. 2. Generation of a Unique Pseudonym

2. The unique identifier (UID) is concatenated with some additional data $(Data)$ and some padding (PAD) and is finally encrypted with the public-key (e, n). In the remainder of this paper we will call this block holding the user identifier the UID-Block.

   The data field has to contain a serial-number of the pseudonym, which has to be incremented automatically each time a pseudonym is generated by the PSE. If a user employs different PSEs, the data-field has to store a device identifier as well. By this, we can guarantee, that different devices generate different pseudonyms.

   Additionally, the data field may contain the (unique) identifier of the Application (AID) requesting the pseudonym. By this, the user holds different pseudonyms for different applications and there is no way for correlating data of different applications. If these application-specific pseudonyms are used, the PSE has to store the pseudonym along with the AID for later usage.

3. The result of this encryption process, the so called encrypted ID (EID), is concatenated with the public-key. In case of RSA this results in $EID||e||n$, which forms the unique and highly random pseudonym $P = EID||e||n$.

   The proof of uniqueness is given in the next section. Concerning the randomness of the pseudonym, it is obvious that the second half is completely random, because we chose e, p_1 and p_2 (and hence n) at random. The first half is an encrypted block. Since the key used for encryption was chosen at random, the encryption function works as a strong pseudo-random function.

2.1   Proof of Uniqueness

The proof of uniqueness of the generated pseudonyms is straight forward and is based on the following facts:

input : UID, Data
output: P
(1)   generate two random primes $p, q \in_R \mathbb{P}$
(2)   generate a random public key e with $((p-1)(q-1), e) = 1$
(3)   compute the private-key $d = e^{-1}$ MOD $(p-1)(q-1)$
(4)   generate the pseudonym $P = E_e(UID\|\|Data\|\|PAD)\|\|e\|\|n$
(5)   `return` P

Fig. 3. Generation of a Unique Pseudonym

Fact 1: Each issued user identifier (UID) is unique. A hierarchical structure of the identifiers may be used, in order to simplify the management of the identifiers.

Fact 2: $E_e(m_1) \neq E_e(m_2) \Leftrightarrow m_1 \neq m_2$, since $E_e(m)$ is a bijective (one-to-one) function for some constant public key (e, n).

To prove the uniqueness of the pseudonym generated by two different users, we have to distinguish two cases:

1. Both users (respectively their PSEs) accidentally generate (choose) the same public key (e, n). In this case, the second halves of the pseudonyms (namely $e\|\|n$) are equal for both users. But fact 1 and fact 2 guarantee, that the first halves, namely $E_e(UID_1\|\|Data_1\|\|PAD_1)$ and $E_e(UID_2\|\|Data_2\|\| PAD_2)$, differ in at least one bit, since UID_1 and UID_2 differ in at least one bit.
2. The second case is quite easy to prove: the users generate (choose) different keys, and hence, the second halves of the generated pseudonyms (namely $e_1\|\|n_1$ and $e_2\|\|n_2$) differ in at least one bit. So we do not need to care about the first halves, which may be accidentally equal (different plaintexts encrypted with different keys may result in the same ciphertext). *Note:* This proof obviously holds also for symmetric encryption (see [14]).

Pseudonyms generated by a specific user may either be generated by the use of the same PSE or by use of different PSEs:

1. Pseudonyms generated by the same PSE will differ in at least one bit, because the serial numbers of the pseudonyms will differ in at least one bit.
2. Pseudonyms generated by different PSEs will differ in at least one bit, because the device identifiers of the PSEs will differ in at least one bit.

3   Proof of Ownership

One central problem of pseudonyms is to prove, that a certain pseudonym has been generated by a certain person. In principle, this can be achieved straight forward by disclosing the pseudonym. In our case, we do not want to disclose our identity, we simply want to prove, that we have generated the pseudonym.

Since only the generator of the pseudonym knows the factorization of n, only he can calculate d. The verifier who holds a pseudonym $P = E_e(UID||Data||PAD)||e||n$ knows e and n and can simply run a challenge-response protocol, where the holder of the pseudonym has to prove the knowledge of d. To achieve this, the verifier encrypts some (random) challenge r with the public key (e, n) and sends $c = E_e(r)$ to the prover. The prover decrypts the encrypted challenge, retrieves $r' = D_d(c)$ and returns r' to the verifier. If r' matches r the verifier is convinced, that the prover has generated the pseudonym.

Since the verifier chooses the challenge, he might try to trick the prover by sending $c = E_e(UID||Data||PAD)$. In this case, the prover would return the value $r' = D_d(E_e(UID||Data||PAD)) = UID||Data||PAD$ which would reveal his identity UID. So the prover has to dismiss the encrypted challenge c if it matches $E_e(UID||Data||PAD)$.

Within our scheme of pseudonyms, two users may accidently choose the same public key (e, n) and hence the same value of d. In this case, they can obviously forge the proof of ownership of each other's pseudonym. Regarding key components of 1024 bits, this is a very rare scenario. To overcome this drawback, one may use the original scheme of generating unique key-components by use of trustworthy smartcards presented in [3] which has been refined in [4,5,6,14]. By applying this scheme, all primes and hence all public and private keys will be pairwise different (see also figure 1).

4   Disclosure of Pseudonym

In order to disclose his pseudonym (and to reveal his identity), the user simply presents his private exponent d. Now, the encrypted identifier EID may be decrypted and the resulting plaintext holds the user identifier UID (see figure 4 and figure 5).

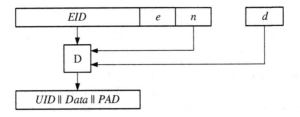

Fig. 4. Unique Pseudonyms – Disclosure

5   Forgery of Pseudonyms

Here we will investigate two attack scenarios and present solutions which prevent the following attacks:

input : pseudonym P, private exponent d	
output: $UID \parallel$ OK / NOK	
(1) retrieve EID and n form P	
(2) compute $UID = D_d(EID)$	// retrieve the UID
(3) **return** $UID \parallel$ OK	

Fig. 5. Disclosure of a Unique Pseudonym (1)

1. When disclosing his pseudonym, the user sends a modified value of his private exponent d' such that $UID' = D_{d'}(EID)$ and $UID' \neq UID$.
2. Another User (with identifier UID') who knows the identifier of a specific user (UID) generates a pseudonym $P = E_e(UID \| Data \| PAD) \| e \| n$ in order to impersonate the user with UID.

5.1   Disclosure of a False Identity

If somebody reveals a private key d (and the primes p and q building the modulus $n = p \cdot q$) to a verifier in order to disclose his pseudonym, this private key cannot be manipulated (forged) so that the verifier retrieves an identity different from the identity used to generate the pseudonym. This is simply given by the fact, that exactly one value of d fulfills the requirement $e \cdot d \equiv 1 \pmod{\varphi(n)}$, with $\varphi(n) = (p-1)(q-1)$.

Note: This is contrary to the variant that employs symmetric encryption, where the key may be changed (attack based on a plaintext-ciphertext-pair) in order to retrieve a different identity.

The complete procedure for disclosure of a pseudonym is given in the algorithm stated in figure 6. The algorithm runs on the inputs P, d, p and q and returns the user identifier UID if all checks concerning the correctness of d have been passed.

input : pseudonym P, private exponent d, primes p and q	
output: $UID \parallel$ OK / NOK	
(1) retrieve EID, e and n form P	
(2) **if** $(p \cdot q \neq n)$ **then**	// check the primes
(3) **return** $0 \parallel$ NOK	
(4) **if** $(e \cdot d \not\equiv 1 \pmod{\varphi(n)})$ **then**	// check the public exponent
(5) **return** $0 \parallel$ NOK	
(6) compute $UID = D_d(EID)$	// retrieve the UID
(7) **return** $UID \parallel$ OK	

Fig. 6. Disclosure of a Unique Pseudonym (2)

5.2 Forgery of a User's Pseudonym (Impersonation)

Another central problem of pseudonyms (presented in this paper) is, that a pseudonym which has been disclosed to a verifier may be used by the verifier to impersonate its original holder. This is possible, because after disclosure the verifier knows d, p, and q. Hence he can act like the original holder; he may use and disclose the 'stolen' pseudonym to proof the ownership, which enables him to impersonate the original holder.

A straight-forward solution for this problem is to sign the ID-Block ($UID\|$ $Data\|PAD$) and to replace the original ID-Block by the new ID-Block $UID\|$ $Validity\|Data\|\mathrm{SIGN}_{d_s}(UID\|Validity\|Data\|PAD)\|PAD$. Here $\mathrm{SIGN}_{d_s}(m)$ is the signature of the hash value of m using the private signing key (d_s, n_s) with the according public verification key (e_s, n_s). The value $Validity$ holds the time of generation (i.e. the time, the pseudonym was requested by some application) and the time-to-live of the pseudonym. These values may be used to check the freshness of a presented (and disclosed) pseudonym, after the signature has been verified by use of the public key which may be retrieved from a certificate issued by a trusted certification authority. A drawback of this approach is, that only the application that requested the pseudonym is able to verify the value of $Validity$. All other applications which also use the pseudonym do not know the point in time when the pseudonym has been requested (and generated). Hence, they cannot verify the freshness.

If the freshness of the pseudonym cannot be checked by the application using the pseudonym, we need some other mechanism to avoid the reuse of a previously disclosed pseudonym. Now, the verifier of the pseudonym simply checks if the presenter (i.e. the supposed holder) of the pseudonym has generated the signature within the pseudonym. This can again be checked by verifying, that the holder knows the according private key (d_s, n_s). As above, we will employ a challenge-response protocol to accomplish this proof.

The certificates used to sign the ID-Block, show a method to retrieve a unique user identifier. This identifier may be the distinguished name of the certificate issuer concatenated with the distinguished name of the owner of the certificate. It would be more practical to replace the distinguished name of the owner of the certificate by the serial number of the certificate. Since the verifier of a disclosed pseudonym knows the issuer and the serial number, he may retrieve the according certificate and use the public key to check (as described above), if the supposed holder of the pseudonym knows the private signing key. If we use this method, there is no need to include a signature in the pseudonym. In order to verify a presented pseudonym, it is sufficient to check that the presenter of the pseudonym knows the private key belonging to the certificate holding the identifier of the pseudonym's holder.

6 Analysis of the Proposed Scheme

For security reasons (i.e. to withstand factorization) the length of a modulus (which is the product of two primes) has to be significantly larger than 512 bit

(N.B. on December 3, 2003, the 174 digit (576 bit) RSA Challenge Number has been factored [12], whereas the next challenge, a 193 digit (640 bit) number has not been factored yet [13]).

Pseudonyms may be analyzed (and classified) according to the following criteria:

- Involved mechanisms (e.g. symmetric/asymmetric encryption, hash-function, MAC or digital signature)
- Pre-computation (Are pre-computations possible? Which values may be pre-computed?)
- Generation efforts (Which values have to be calculated at the time, the pseudonym is generated?)
- Length of pseudonym
- Proof of ownership (with or without disclosure)
- Disclosure (local/global, Key Escrow)
- Security (forging of pseudonyms, non-repudiation)

The last three points have been discussed in previous sections of this paper. Now we would like to analyze the length of the proposed pseudonyms and the (pre-)computation efforts.

Pseudonym: $P = \mathrm{E}_e(UID\|AID\|PAD)\|e\|n$
Involved Mechanisms: asymmetric encryption (here RSA)
Pre-computations: e, d, and n.
Generation Efforts: Needs one asymmetric encryption. This may be done in advance as well, if the pseudonym does not contain any data concerning the application which requests the pseudonyms (e.g. the application identifier AID).
Length: $|P| = |n| + |e| + |n| = 2|n| + |e|$, where $|n|$ is the block-length of the cipher (which is equal to the length of the modulus n) and $|e|$ is the length of the public exponent.

A variant of the proposed scheme uses a common public exponent e for all users of the system. Hence, there is no need to include e in the pseudonym, and the modified pseudonym results in $P = \mathrm{E}_e(UID)\|n$. The bit-length of this type of pseudonyms is only slightly smaller than the length above (N.B. e will be most commonly some small number, like 3, 17 or $2^{16} + 1$).

7   Resumee, Problems, Extensions and Future Research

In this paper we presented a scheme for generating digital pseudonyms, which does not apply any centralized issuers or any online-communications between issuers. The holder of the pseudonym can generate his pseudonym locally in his personal security environment (e.g. in his smart card or his personal digital assistant). The proposed method generates unique and nevertheless highly random pseudonyms in a distributed environment and with considerable computation efforts. On the one hand, the holder of a pseudonym can prove that he generated the pseudonym without disclosing it. On the other hand, the verifier of a disclosed pseudonym can be sure, that the presenter of the pseudonym is the original holder (i.e. the person who generated it).

However, there are still some open problems and possible extensions. These questions, which are scope of ongoing research include:

Enforcement of Disclosure: One of the major drawbacks of our approach is, that the disclosure of the pseudonym is completely under control of the holder. In specific application scenarios, this is an appreciated feature. In other scenarios we would like some mechanism which ensures, that a pseudonym can be disclosed under certain (previously specified) circumstances. Escrowing of the private key (d, n) is a straight-forward solution for this problem; but there may be better ones.

Certification of the Private Exponent d**:** A user may certify his private exponent d (note NOT his public key which would include n) at a certification authority. So he can later on prove that a specific pseudonym belongs to his identity.

Other Types of Pseudonyms: Different mechanisms and different types of common components influence the properties (pre-computations, generation efforts, length of pseudonym, proof of ownership, disclosure and security) of the generated pseudonym.

Pseudonyms by means of Unique Primes: Here, we will combine the original scheme of generating unique primes and the proposed scheme for unique pseudonyms in order to overcome the drawback discussed in section 3.

Proof of Binding between ID and Pseudonym: By now, the only way to prove the binding between the ID of a user presenting a certain pseudonym, is to disclose the pseudonym.

References

1. Chaum, D.: Untraceable electronic mail, return addresses, and digital pseudonyms. *Commun. ACM*, 24(2) (1981) 84–88
2. Heikkila, J., Holmstrm, U.: Secure digital pseudonyms for privacy and liability, Master Thesis, Pennsylvania State University, November 15 (2002)
3. Horster, P.: Dublettenfreie Schlüsselgenerierung durch isolierte Instanzen. *Chipkarten, DuD-Fachbeiträge, Vieweg Verlag* (1998)
4. Horster, P., Schartner, P.: Bemerkungen zur Erzeugung dublettenfreier Primzahlen. *Proceedings of Sicherheitsinfrastrukturen* (1998)
5. Horster, P., Schartner, P., Wohlmacher, P.: Key Management. *Proceedings of the IFIP TC11 14th international Information Security* (1998) 37–48
6. Horster, P., Schartner, P., Wohlmacher, P.: Special Aspects of Key Generation. *Information Technology: Science-Technique-Technology-Education-Health, Printed Scientific Works, Kharkov* (1998) 345–350

7. Lysyanskaya, A., Rivest, R.L., Sahai, A., Wolf, S.: Pseudonym systems. In *Selected Areas in Cryptography* (1999) 184–199
8. Mjolsnes, S.Fr.: Privacy, cryptographic pseudonyms, and the state of health. *Lecture Notes in Computer Science* 739 (1993)
9. Pfitzmann, A., Köhntopp, M.: Anonymity, unobservability, and pseudonymity — a proposal for terminology. In *Workshop on Design Issues in Anonymity and Unobservability* (2000) 1–9
10. Rankl, W., Effing, W.: *Smart Card Handbook, 3rd edition.* John Wiley & Sons (2003)
11. Rivest, R.L., Shamir, A., Adleman, L.: A Method for Obtaining Digital Signatures and Public-Key Cryptosystems. *Communications of the ACM*, 21 (1978) 120–126
12. RSA Laboratories. RSA-576 is factored!.
    http://www.rsasecurity.com/rsalabs/node.asp?id=2096
13. RSA Laboratories. The RSA Challenge Numbers.
    http://www.rsasecurity.com/rsalabs/node.asp?id=2093
14. Schartner, P.: *Security Tokens – Basics, Applications, Management, and Infrastructures.* IT-Verlag (2001)

A Probabilistic Property-Specific Approach to Information Flow

Danièle Beauquier[1,*], Marie Duflot[1,*], and Marius Minea[2,*]

[1] University Paris 12, France
{beauquier, duflot}@univ-paris12.fr
[2] Institute e-Austria Timişoara, Romania
marius@cs.utt.ro

Abstract. We study probabilistic information flow from a property-specific viewpoint. For a given property of interest, specified as set of traces, we examine whether different low-level observations imply different probabilities for the occurrence of the property. Quantifying over all properties in a given class (e.g., high-level traces, or high-level sequences separated by low-level events) we obtain different notions of information flow. We give characterizations of systems that are secure according to these definitions. We consider both properties that are expressed over whole traces and those that distinguish between past and future given a reference point. In this framework, we can express several classical definitions of possibilistic security, as well as giving a more detailed, quantitative measure of information flow.

1 Introduction

Several classical treatments of information flow exist in the literature. Trace-based approaches assume a set of observable low-level events L and a set of (not directly observable) high-level events H. The question is whether observing a certain low-level trace can give information about the occurrence of high-level events, either in a possibilistic sense (the possibility or impossibility of a certain high-level interleaving) or in a probabilistic sense, yielding quantitative information about high-level activity.

It is generally accepted that there is no single all-encompassing definition of information flow. Different notions are noninterference [5], generalized noninterference [11], noninference [14], generalized noninference and separability [13], depending on the kind of information about high-level behavior considered relevant. In these *possibilistic* approaches, information flow is prevented if the trace set corresponding to a low-level observation contains "enough" traces to make inferences about high-level behavior impossible. Indeed, there can be no information flow if all high-level behaviors of interest are possible, i.e., included in the set of traces corresponding to a low-level observation. Precisely which traces must be present depends on the individual notion of information flow.

---

* Partially supported by ECO-NET project No 08112WJ.

V. Gorodetsky, I. Kotenko, and V. Skormin (Eds.): MMM-ACNS 2005, LNCS 3685, pp. 206–220, 2005.

Subsequently, various frameworks for information flow [13,18,10], have been developed, attempting to unify the various existing definitions. McLean's introduction of selective interleaving functions [13] provides a way to reason about the relative strength of different security properties and their preservation under composition. Zakinthinos and Lee [18] propose "perfect security" as the weakest property on trace sets which guarantees absence of information flow (in a rather informally defined sense). In contrast, Mantel [10] argues the need for variety and modularity, and provides a library of basic security predicates from which common notions of security properties can be constructed.

In the same view, that an analysis of information flow must be flexible enough to be adapted to the specific features and needs of the considered application, we propose a *parameterized* view of information flow that develops a quantitative, probabilistic approach sketched in [17]. We define information flow with respect to a *property* (a set of system traces, possibly abstracted in its low-level part) which is deemed important for the system under scrutiny. The system has information flow with respect to the given property if there exist two low-level observations for which the chosen property has different probabilities of occurrence. In this case, the quantitative, probabilistic knowledge about the given property is sensitive to the observation which can be made, and so there is information flow in the system with respect to this property.

From this starting point, we define several generic notions of information flow, corresponding to different classes of properties of interest. These include *high-level* information flow, in which properties are sets of sequences of high-level events, and *sequential* information flow, in which properties can describe not only sequences of high-level events but also how these sequences are interrupted by the low-level, following the view of [12].

In examining information flow, we consider two views on the sequence of events in a trace. In the first, a *global* view, properties are simply sets of traces (infinite sequences of events). Alternatively, in a *relativized* view, the present timepoint splits a trace into a pair: a finite sequence of past events and an infinite sequence of future events. In this way, we can express properties that link the past behavior with the future behavior of the system; we have absence of information flow if such a behavior set is equiprobable regardless of the low-level observation up to the current timepoint. For instance, a property may state that if the last event before the time point is a then the next event is a' and if the last event before the time point is b then the next event cannot be a'.

We then give characterizations of systems that are secure according to these views of information flow, describing the structure of their trace sets in terms of high/low-level events and their probabilities.

Using this framework, and choosing appropriate sets of properties, we can express several classical definitions of possibilistic security: generalized noninterference [11], noninference [14], and separability [13]. At the same time, by supporting a user-defined choice of properties, we allow a finer granularity for the definition of information flow than previous approaches. In addition, for systems that are not secure according to one of these notions, the probabilistic approach allows us to give a quantitative measure of the appearing information flow.

An important issue when defining security properties is deciding what kinds of information flow are acceptable. In some existing definitions of information flow, such as noninference [14] or the perfect security property [18], covert channels already existent in the description of a system are allowed, such as auditing or copying low-level events on a high-level. Such definitions take a *causal* view, defining information flow as the fact that high-level behavior influences low-level behavior. Conversely, this means that viewing a string of low-level events may allow us to deduce something about the high-level events that have occurred in the past, prior to these observations.

In contrast, we take a purely *observational* view. Thus, if a low-level observation is compatible only with an interleaving of high-level events, but not with another, this constitutes information flow, regardless whether this knowledge is already present in the description (trace set) of the system. Indeed, the probability of a given interleaving of high-level events depends in this situation on the low-level observation, which corresponds to our definition of information flow.

Related Work

Work on tailoring security properties to the system under consideration originates with the string of different definitions for information flow [5,11,14,13]. Following the recognition that security is a property of trace sets rather than traces (e.g., [13]), in [18], security properties are defined uniformly by specifying a predicate that the low-level equivalent bunch of a trace has to satisfy. The approach is taken further in [10] by defining basic security predicates in terms of a restriction and a closure requirement on a trace set. The parameterization in the latter paper is given by the variants in which the basic operations of inserting and deleting high-level events in a trace (to keep their absence and presence, respectively, confidential) can be performed.

Probabilistic information flow has naturally been more difficult to treat than the possibilistic version. McLean [12] introduces the *flow model* which distinguishes mere correlation from actual causal influence. Gray [7] introduces probabilistic interference in a context of finite state machines and gives a more general information-theoretic framework, including probabilistic channel capacity [6]. Sabelfeld and Sands [16] define probabilistic noninterference in the context of schedulers for multithreaded programs, based on the concept of probabilistic bisimulation, and show compositionality properties. Lowe [9] treats quantitative information flow distinguishing probabilistic aspects from nondeterminism, which is handled from an adversarial worst-case perspective; the treatment is done in a discrete-time context, considering also the rate of information flow. A probabilistic process-algebraic approach is given in [1], focused on noninterference, generalizing the possibilistic variant and allowing formal reasoning about the amount of information flow.

All these approaches, whether possibilistic or probabilistic, treat general, system-independent notion of information flow. A framework which parameterizes information flow is defined in [8] by giving a definition of secrecy in multi-agent systems, using a modal logic of knowledge in a state-based model. This generalizes several existing approaches and can be extended to probabilistic security. Their parameterization stems from defining formulas (knowledge) of what must be kept secret, thus providing a fine-grained way of characterizing security requirements. Since the approach is state-based, our model appears complementary in that it can talk about both past and future evolution of the system.

Other perspectives on information flow include that of [2] which offers a variety of characterizations of non-interference, expressed in Hoare logics and CTL; however, the variety is not given by parameterization, but language aspects such as sequential vs. concurrent, or termination sensitivity. Closer to a parametric view is the approach of [4], where the parameter is an observable property (an abstraction) of the public observations of a program. Thus, the attacker is a data-flow analyzer, and can be specified in an abstract interpretation framework. Both approaches deal with much more specific systems, described in particular programming languages, and the class of expressed properties, though parameterized to some extent, is not as general.

Beyond the possibilistic approaches, [3] analyzes quantitative information flow for a simple imperative language from a semantic point of view, whereas [15] replace indistinguishability in the formalization of non-interference by similarity based on the notion of distance, in a process-algebraic setting. In comparison, we also define quantity of information flow based on the distance between the probability of a property given an observation.

Our approach to parameterization allows properties that range from the general to the entirely system-specific. Thus we can select the granularity (a particular trace set or even a single trace) with respect to which information flow is analyzed. Alternatively, quantifying over classes of such properties, we can still obtain and reason about several of the classic definitions of information flow.

Paper Outline. We first introduce the mathematical model of probabilistic event systems which we use throughout the paper. Section 3 gives property-based definitions for three classes of probabilistic information flow, and theorems characterizing systems that conform to these notions. These results are extended in Section 4 to properties which distinguish between past and future with respect to the reference point defined by the observation. Section 5 shows how some of the classic definitions of information flow can be expressed in this formalism.

2   Probabilistic Event Systems

Notations

Given a finite alphabet A, we let A^* (resp. A^ω) denote the set of finite (resp. infinite) sequences (or traces) over this alphabet. The set A^∞ is the union of A^* and A^ω. The empty sequence is denoted ϵ. Given a sub-alphabet $A' \subset A$ and a trace λ, $\lambda_{|A'}$ denotes the projection of λ onto this sub-alphabet. If λ is a finite non-empty trace, $last(\lambda)$ denotes the last letter of λ.

Let λ be a (finite or infinite) trace. We denote by $Pref(\lambda)$ the set of finite prefixes of λ. More generally, if Tr is a set of traces, $Pref(Tr) = \bigcup_{\lambda \in Tr} Pref(\lambda)$.

Let $u, v \in (A^*)^n$, $u = (x_1, x_2, \ldots, x_n)$, $v = (y_1, y_2, \ldots, y_n)$. We denote by $u \otimes v$ the *simple interleaving* of u and v defined as $u \otimes v = x_1 y_1 x_2 y_2 \ldots x_n y_n$.

If $U, V \subset (A^*)^n$, we denote by $U \otimes V$ the set: $U \otimes V = \{u \otimes v | u \in U, v \in V\}$.

If $U, V \subset (A^*)^\omega$, the definition of $U \otimes V$ is extended in a standard way.

The interleaving of two sequences x, y, denoted by $interl(x, y)$ is the set of sequences: $\{x_1 y_1 x_2 y_2 \ldots x_n y_n \mid x = x_1 x_2 \ldots x_n, n \in \mathbb{N}, y = y_1 y_2 \ldots y_n, x_i, y_i \in A^*\}$. This extends to sets of sequences: $interl(X, Y) = \{interl(x, y) | x \in X, y \in Y\}$.

Probabilistic Event System

The execution of a system is modeled by its set Tr of traces which are finite or infinite sequences of atomic events from a set E. A particular atomic event τ is distinguished which represents the halting of the system. For example, if λ is a sequence of atomic events, it is useful to distinguish between "λ has occurred but the system still executes", and "λ has occurred and the system has stopped". The latter case is modeled by the event $\lambda \tau$. To unify the presentation, it is convenient to use only infinite sequences, writing $\lambda \tau^\omega$ instead of $\lambda \tau$. Then, from now on, Tr is a set of infinite sequences which do not contain any occurrence of τ except when they are of the form $\lambda \tau^\omega$ where λ contains no occurrence of τ.

The set of atomic events E is divided into two disjoint sets, the set H of high-level atomic events and the set L of low-level ones. Depending on the situation, the stop event τ can be considered as a low-level or a high-level event. In this paper, we only consider the case when the low-level user can observe that the system has stopped, i.e., $\tau \in L$.

The set of traces Tr is equipped with a probability measure μ over the σ-algebra generated by the cylinders λE^ω, $\lambda \in E^*$, such that Tr is μ-measurable. The measure $\mu(X)$ of a measurable set X is denoted as $Pr_\mu(X)$, or shortly $Pr(X)$. Thus if we consider the infinite tree T built from Tr with edges labeled by atomic events, each edge of the tree is equipped with a non-zero probability. (We assume that every prefix of a trace in Tr has a non-zero probability).

Traditionally, an event is a measurable set in the theory of probabilities, so to avoid confusion, the atomic events of the system will be called actions.

We use the customary notation for conditional probabilities: if P and Q are two measurable events and $Pr(Q) \neq 0$, the conditional probability $Pr(P|Q)$ is $Pr(P \cap Q)/Pr(Q)$. Since we are interested only in traces of the system S we deal only with conditional probabilities relative to Tr. Thus, for each measurable event X we denote by $Pr_S(X)$ the probability $Pr(X|S)$ (assuming $Pr(S) > 0$).

Definition 1. *An event system S is a tuple (E, H, L, Tr, μ) where $E = H \cup L$, and H (resp. L) is the set of high-level (resp. low-level) actions, Tr is the set of traces of the system, and μ is a probabilistic measure on Tr.*

We assume that only low-level actions are observable on the low-level, i.e., for a trace λ the projection $\lambda_{|L}$ is observable by low-level users. More precisely, a finite prefix of $\lambda_{|L}$ is observable. Thus, from the observation of $u \in L^*$, the low-level user who is supposed to know the entire system can construct the *bunch* $B_S(u) = \{\lambda \in Tr \mid u$ is a prefix of $\lambda_{|L}\}$ and possibly deduce some information about what happened or what will happen at the high-level. When there is no ambiguity, we will write $B(u)$ instead of $B_S(u)$. For every u such that $B(u)$ is non empty, $B(u)$ is supposed to be measurable and without lost of generality the measure $Pr_S(B(u))$ is supposed to be positive. A projection $u \in L^*$ such that $B(u)$ is non empty is called *possible*.

3   Global Information Flow

Depending on the level of information we are interested in, we introduce an abstraction function $\phi : L \to L' \cup \{\epsilon\}$, where L' is some set with $|L'| \leq |L|$ and express properties as sets of infinite traces on $(H \cup L')^\omega$. We extend ϕ on H as the identity, and then on E^ω in a classical way. Notice that it is possible that an infinite trace of E^ω has an image which is finite.

A property of abstraction level ϕ is a subset of $(H \cup L')^\infty$. We consider only properties P such that $\phi^{-1}(P) \cap Tr$ is a measurable subset of Tr. By abuse of notation we write $Pr_S(P) =_{df} Pr_S(\phi^{-1}(P) \cap Tr)$, and write P instead of $\phi^{-1}(P) \cap Tr$ everytime we compute probabilities, e.g., in $Pr(P \cap A)$ or $Pr(P|A)$.

Definition 2. *Given a system S, the quantity of information flow for a property P of abstraction level ϕ is the value $IF(P,S) = max_{u,v}|Pr_S(P|B(u)) - Pr_S(P|B(v))|$ for all possible $u, v \in L^*$.*

A system S is without information flow for a property P of abstraction level ϕ if $IF(P,S) = 0$.

We can also consider a "qualitative" version of this definition:

Definition 3. *A system S is without qualitative information flow for a property P of abstraction level ϕ if for every $u \in L^*$ such that $B(u)$ is non-empty, $Pr_S(P) \neq 0 \to Pr_S(P|B(u)) \neq 0$.*

Definition 4. *A system is without information flow for a given abstraction level if it is without information flow for all properties of this level.*

We will consider three abstraction functions which are of interest in an obvious way. If $L = L'$ and ϕ is identity, i.e., there is no abstraction, we will speak of *general* information flow. If L' is a singleton $\{l\}$, and $\phi(l_i) = l$ for every $l_i \in L$, a trace on $(H \cup L')^\omega$ expresses what happens on the high-level, as well as whether two high-level events have been separated by a low-level event or not (the identity of this low-level event does not matter). In this second case we speak of *sequential* information flow. Finally, if $L' = \{\tau\}$ and $\phi(\tau) = \tau$, $\phi(l_i) = \epsilon$ for every $l_i \in L \setminus \{\tau\}$, that is we are interested only in the projection on the high-level of a trace, we will speak of *high-level* information flow.

The intuition behind this hierarchy of abstractions stems from the fact that we may be interested whether an event x is followed by an event y, in other words, in the presence of the pattern xy in a system trace.

If x and y are both high-level events, this property cannot be expressed using the definition of high-level information flow, since any intervening low-level events are projected out by the abstraction. However, it can be expressed as a sequential property: $(H \cup \{l\})^* xy (H \cup \{l\})^\omega$.

If one of the events (say x) is low-level and the other one high-level, the property can no longer be expressed by a sequential property, since the identity of y is lost by abstraction to l. However, the presence of the pattern xy can still be expressed as a general property: $(H \cup L)^* xy (H \cup L)^\omega$. This motivates considering properties which preserve full information for both high- and low-level events.

Another example to motivate our framework is the following. Consider a program where variables are classified as low (observable by low level users) or high. The system consists of the set of executions of the program. A regular property like "during every time duration t (the duration is measured by the number of events and t is a fixed integer), the high level variable x is updated at least once", in other words, it is impossible that there exists a time duration t without an update of variable x can be of interest, and one can require that the system does not suffer information flow for this property.

Let $L_0 = L \setminus \{\tau\}$.

We write $\mathcal{E} = (H \cup L_0)^\omega \cup (H \cup L_0)^* \tau^\omega$ for the set of all infinite words formed by actions from H and L. This is a superset of the set of system traces: $Tr \subseteq \mathcal{E}$.

In the following, low level actions are denoted $a, b, ...$, sequences of low-level actions $u, v, ...$, sequences of high-level actions $\alpha, \beta, ...$ and traces $\lambda, \lambda', ...$.

Let $S = (E, H, L, Tr, \mu)$ be a system and T be the associated probabilistic tree. We define:

$$H_n(Tr) = \{(\alpha_1, ..., \alpha_n) \in (H^*)^n | \exists a_1...a_n \in L \ \alpha_1 a_1 \alpha_2 a_2 ... \alpha_n a_n \in Pref(Tr)\}.$$
$$H_n^\omega(Tr) = \{(\alpha_1, ..., \alpha_n) \in (H^*)^{n-1} H^\omega | \exists a_1...a_{n-1} \in L \ \alpha_1 a_1 \alpha_2 a_2 ... \alpha_n \in Tr\}.$$
$$L_n(Tr) = \{(a_1, ..., a_n) \in L^n | \exists \ \alpha_1 ... \alpha_n \in H^* \ \alpha_1 a_1 \alpha_2 a_2 ... \alpha_n a_n \in Pref(Tr)\}.$$
$$Tr_n = \{\alpha_1 a_1 \alpha_2 a_2 ... \alpha_n a_n \in Pref(Tr) | \ \alpha_i \in H^*, \ a_i \in L\}.$$

We give below a characteristic property for a system S to be without sequential information flow. For this we need to introduce some technical terms related to the probabilistic tree T.

We color edges labeled by a high-level action black and edges labeled by a low-level action red. We are interested in the set of sequences of high-level actions (including the empty word) which can occur starting from a node x. To make this set of sequences more explicit we build for each such node x a "black" probabilistic tree T_x in the following way: we keep only the black edges reachable in T from x, and for each node y (including x) accessible from x by a black path, we add a node y' and an edge (y, y') labelled by ϵ and with a probability equal to the sum p of the probabilities of red edges starting from y in T. The tree T_x is a probabilistic tree which has the following meaning: the probability of a path in T_x starting from x labelled by α (without ϵ labels) is exactly the probability that the sequence of high-level actions α occurs from x; the probability of a path in T_x starting from x labelled by α and ending in a leaf is the probability that from x the sequence of actions α followed by a low-level action occurs.

A node has the color of the edge ending in this node. The root is red.

Two red nodes x and x' of T are H-*equivalent* if there exists an integer n such that the labels of the paths from the root to x and x' are respectively $\alpha_1 a_1 \alpha_2 a_2 ... \alpha_n a_n$ and $\alpha_1 b_1 \alpha_2 b_2 ... \alpha_n b_n$ where $\alpha_i \in H^*$ and $a_i, b_i \in L$.

We also need to state an equivalence property on L. Two nodes x and x' of T are L-*equivalent* if there exists an integer n such that the labels of the paths from the root to x and x' are respectively $\alpha_1 a_1 \alpha_2 a_2 ... \alpha_{n-1} a_{n-1} \alpha_n a_n$ and $\beta_1 a_1 \beta_2 a_2 ... \beta_{n-1} a_{n-1} \beta_n a_n$ where $\alpha_i, \beta_i \in H^*$ and $a_i \in L$.

A tuple (x, x', y, y') of red nodes of the tree T is H, L-*compatible* if x and x' are H-equivalent, y and y' are H-equivalent, x and y are L-equivalent and x' and y' are L-equivalent, i.e., there exist $(\alpha_1, ..., \alpha_n), (\beta_1, ..., \beta_n) \in H_n$, and $(a_1, ..., a_n), (b_1, ..., b_n) \in L_n$ such that the paths from the root to x, x', y, y' are labeled respectively by $\alpha_1 a_1 ... \alpha_n a_n$, $\alpha_1 b_1 ... \alpha_n b_n$, $\beta_1 a_1 ... \beta_n a_n$ and $\beta_1 b_1 ... \beta_n b_n$.

Let $p_1, ..., p_n, q_1, ..., q_n$ be the probabilities of edges labeled by $a_1, ..., a_n$ on the path from the root to x (resp. y). Let $p'_1, ..., p'_n, q'_1, ..., q'_n$ be the probabilities of edges labeled by $b_1, ..., b_n$ on the path from the root to x' (resp. y').

A H, L-compatible tuple (x, x', y, y') is *perfect* if for every $i = 1, ..., n$ we have $p_i / q_i = p'_i / q'_i$.

The systems we consider are supposed to satisfy:

(1) Tr is a closed subset of $\mathcal{E}$
(2) For each measurable subset X of Tr, the closure $\bar{X}$ is measurable and $Pr_S(X) = Pr_S(\bar{X})$.

We start by characterizing *sequential* information flow, where the identity of low-level events is abstracted out, and only their position in the sequence of events is preserved.

Theorem 1. *A probabilistic system S such that $Tr \not\subset H^\omega$ is without sequential information flow iff*

(1) $\forall n > 0 \ Tr_n = H_n(Tr) \otimes L_n(Tr)$.
(2) Every H, L-compatible tuple of the tree T is perfect.
(3) For every pair of H-equivalent nodes x, x' of T, the probabilistic trees T_x and $T_{x'}$ are isomorphic.
(4) For every $n > 0 \ (L_n(Tr) \neq \emptyset \rightarrow Pr_S(Tr \cap (H^*L)^{n-1} H^\omega) = 0)$.

The intuition behind this characterization is the following: we don't want the low-level traces to give any information on the interleavings with the high level. Then, if a sequential high-level trace is possible, this trace can occur whatever the trace on the low level is. Point (4) states that observing that k low-level actions have occurred doesn't give any additional information, since all traces of Tr have the same number of low-level events. Points (2) and (3) state that probabilities of certain subtrees have to be equal or in equal ratios.

We give here only a sketch of the proof.

If the system has no information flow, then we prove (1), (4) and, by contradiction, the existence of the same edges in T_x and $T_{x'}$ in (2). For the latter, we exhibit properties for which, if one edge is not in T then for some u, v,

$Pr(P|B(u)) > 0$ and $Pr(P|B(u)) = 0$. The probabilistic parts of (2) and (3) are proven by contradiction as well, assuming that there exist nodes with different ratios, considering the pair of nodes with the highest ratio and obtaining information flow for some property.

The converse is proven by considering basic cylinders for which it is possible to show that there is no information flow. Then we define measurable subsets P_n which are disjoint unions of cylinders and we prove that there is no information flow for these sets. Taking the limit of these sets we show that the absence of information flow follows for P.

Next, we characterize general information flow, which turns out to be a very strong property:

Theorem 2. *The only systems with $Tr \not\subset H^\omega$ which are without general information flow are those which have a projection on L reduced to a single trace.*

Proof. Suppose that the projection of Tr on L is a trace w. Since $Tr \not\subset H^\omega$ this trace w is different from ϵ and the finite non-empty low-level words u such that $B(u) \neq \emptyset$ are the finite prefixes of w. Moreover for such a trace u, we have $B(u) = Tr$ and in this case, the system is without general information flow.

Conversely, suppose that the projection on L of the trace set Tr contains two different traces w and w', and let u be their longest common prefix. Let $a \in L$ such that ua is a prefix of w'. Let P be the property which consists of the infinite sequences in Tr whose projection on L is equal to w. We have $Pr_S(P \mid B(u)) > 0$ and $Pr_S(P \mid B(ua)) = 0$. Therefore S has general information flow. ∎

To our knowledge, there is no simple characterization of systems which are without high-level information flow. It is immediate that any system without sequential information flow is without high-level information flow, since the definition of the latter has a coarser abstraction function. Also directly from the definition, it follows that the projection of any nonempty bunch $B(u)$ onto H must be the same, otherwise, for a high-level sequence $\alpha \in H^*$ distinguishing between $B(u)$ and $B(v)$ we can take $P = \alpha H^\omega$ and we have $Pr_S(P|B(u)) \neq Prb_s(P|B(v))$, since one is zero and the other one not.

4   Relativized Information Flow

The definitions of the previous section capture information flow, but provide no specific information about the time moment of the low-level observation and the events whose occurrence are linked to it. For a more refined and relativized view, one may wish to introduce the moment of observation in the property under consideration. For example a question of interest could be: observing some partial low-level trace at the current moment, what is the probability that the potential trace satisfies some past or future or more generally some relativized property? For example, what is the probability that starting from the current time, there is still one high-level action which will occur? Or, what is the probability that at current time, an event has occurred in the past, and will never occur in the future?

In this case, properties we are interested in are called relativized properties and are defined as subsets of $(\phi(H \cup L))^* \times (\phi(H \cup L))^\omega$, where ϕ is the abstraction function. The first component represents the past, and the second one the future.

A property P is a *past property* (resp. *future property*) if $P = R \times \phi((H \cup L)^\omega)$ (resp. $P = \phi((H \cup L)^*) \times R$) where $R \subset \phi((H \cup L)^*)$ (resp. $R \subset \phi((H \cup L)^\omega)$). We state the definition of information flow in this relativized situation.

Let $u \in L^+$ with $B(u) \neq \emptyset$. For a relativized property P we define $Pr_S(P, u) =$ $Pr_S(\{\gamma \in Tr | \ \gamma = \gamma_1 \gamma_2, \gamma_{1|_L} = u, last(\gamma_1) = last(u), (\gamma_1, \gamma_2) \in P\})/Pr_S(B(u))$.

The event $\{\gamma \in Tr | \ \gamma = \gamma_1 \gamma_2, \gamma_{1|_L} = u, last(\gamma_1) = last(u), (\gamma_1, \gamma_2) \in P\}$ corresponds to the situation when the low-level user observes u and the last action which occurred is a low-level action. We assume that P is well-behaved such that this event is a measurable set for every $u \in L^+$.

We can give now a definition of relativized information flow:

Definition 5. *A system S is without relativized information flow for a relativized property P of abstraction level ϕ if for every $u, v \in L^+$ such that $B_S(u)$ and $B_S(v)$ are nonempty, $Pr_S(P, u) = Pr_S(P, v)$.*

Definition 6. *A system is without relativized information flow for a given abstraction level if it is without relativized information flow for all relativized properties of this level.*

Again, one can use different levels of abstraction depending on the type of the events whose occurrence is of interest. For instance, consider the high-level event sequence xy, and assume one wishes to express that it occurs without any low-level event intervening after the last event of the low-level observation u. This can be expressed by the sequential relative property $(H \cup \{l\})^* \times H^* xy (H \cup \{l\})^\omega$. (A sequential property is needed to express the fact that x and y are not separated by low-level events). If now one of the interesting events (say y) is low-level, we need a general relative property so the identity of y is not abstracted away. For instance, $(H \cup L)^* \times (H \cup L)^2 xy (H \cup L)^\omega$ expresses that xy will occur with two intervening events after the last low-level event of the given observation.

Theorem 3. *The only systems such that $Tr \not\subset H^\omega$ which are without relativized general information flow are those which have a projection on L equal to τ^ω.*

Proof. Suppose that the projection of Tr on L is equal to τ^ω, then the only finite sequences $u \neq \epsilon$ such that $B(u)$ is non-empty are τ^n, $n > 0$, and in that case $Pr_S(P, \tau^n) = Pr_S(P, \tau^m)$ for all positive integers m, n for every relativized general property P. We conclude that the system S has no relativized general information flow.

Conversely, suppose that the projection of Tr on L contains a trace $w \neq \tau^\omega$. Then the first action a of w is different from τ, otherwise w would be equal to τ^ω. Consider the property $P = \{(\gamma_1 a, \gamma_2) \in E^* \times E^\omega \mid \gamma_{1|L} = \epsilon\}$. We have $Pr_S(P, a) > 0$ and $Pr_S(P, \tau) = 0$. Therefore S has a relativized general information flow. ∎

The next theorem characterizes the systems without relativized sequential information flow. Recall that in this case the abstraction function ϕ collapses all the low-level actions into a single one, the action l.

Theorem 4. *The only systems with $Tr \not\subseteq H^\omega$ which are without relativized sequential information flow are those which satisfy one of the following conditions:*

(1) the projection of Tr on L is reduced to τ^ω

(2) the projection of Tr on L is a subset M of L and $Tr = U \otimes (M \times \{\epsilon\})$ where $U = \{(\alpha_1, \alpha_2) \mid \alpha_1 l \alpha_2 \in \phi(Tr)\}$ and and for every pair of H-equivalent nodes x, x' of T, of depth one, the probabilistic trees $T(x)$ and $T(x')$ are isomorphic.

Proof. If the system S satisfies condition (1) it is easy to conclude like in Theorem 3 that S is without relativized sequential information flow.

If the system S satisfies condition (2), the only finite non-empty traces $u \in L^+$ such that the bunch $B(u)$ is non-empty are actions the $a \in M$. Clearly for every relativized sequential property P, $Pr_S(P, a) = Pr_S(P, b)$ for $a, b \in M$.

Conversely, let S be a system without relativized sequential information flow. Suppose that the projection of Tr on L is not reduced to τ^ω. We have to prove that S satisfies (2). The projection of Tr on L cannot contain a trace w with more than one action and different from τ^ω. Indeed suppose that $w = abw'$, $a, b \in L$. Then Tr contains a trace $\alpha a \beta b \lambda$, where $\alpha, \beta \in H^*$, and $\lambda \in (H \cup L)^\omega$. Consider now the relativized sequential property $P = \{al\} \times \{\beta l\}(H \cup \{l\})^\omega$. We have $Pr_S(P, a) \neq 0$ and $Pr_S(P, ab) = 0$. Contradiction. So the projection of Tr on L is a subset M of L. Let us prove that $Tr = U \otimes (M \times \{\epsilon\})$. Suppose that there exists $\alpha_1 l \alpha_2 \in \phi(Tr)$ and some $a \in M$ such that $\alpha_1 a \alpha_2 \notin Tr$. Then there is information flow for the property $P = \{al\} \times (H \cup \{l\})^\omega$: $Pr_S(P, a) = 0$ and there exists $b \in M$ such that $Pr_S(P, b) \neq 0$. Proving the other conditions of (2) is straightforward, following steps of the proof of Theorem 1.   ∎

The absence of relativized sequential information flow is a very strong property, and as seen from the conditions in Theorem 4, very few probabilistic event systems have this property. This stems from the fact that, in expressing the property P, a trace is split into two parts, just after the occurrence of a low-level event. If it is possible to observe more or fewer low-level actions in a trace than specified in the property, there is information flow.

But it is still interesting to consider low-level traces of the same length n, and examine if they give some additional high-level information (besides the fact that n low-level events have occurred). We are then interested in a weaker notion of "no information flow" for a relativized sequential property, namely:

Definition 7. *A system S is without information flow at each fixed step for a relativized property P if $Pr_S(P, u) = Pr_S(P, v)$ for every $u, v \in L^+$ such that $|u| = |v|$ and $B(u), B(v)$ are non-empty.*

In order to characterize the systems without sequential relativized information flow at each fixed step we need to introduce a new definition. In the probabilistic tree T of the system, the *red depth* of a node is the number of red edges on the path from the root to it.

Theorem 5. *A system S such that $Tr \not\subseteq H^\omega$ is without sequential relativized information flow at each fixed step iff*

(1) $\forall n > 0 \; Tr_n = H_n(Tr) \otimes L_n(Tr)$.
(2) $\forall n > 0$, all nodes of red depth n with outgoing red edges are equivalent
(3) For every H-equivalent nodes x, x' of $T(S)$, the probabilistic trees T_x and $T_{x'}$ are isomorphic.

The proof of this theorem is based on the lemma given below which links sequential relativized information flow at each fixed step with sequential relativized information flow. Then we can reuse the proof of Theorem 1.

Lemma 1. *Let $R\mathcal{E}'$ be a sequential property on traces where $R \subset (H \cup l)^*$ and $\mathcal{E}' = (H \cup l)^\omega \cup (H \cup l)^* \tau^\omega$. Then, for $P_R = \{(\gamma_1, \gamma_2) \mid |\gamma_{1|L}| = n, last(\gamma_1) = l, \gamma_1 \gamma_2 \in R\mathcal{E}'\}$, for every u of length n we have $Pr_S(P_R, u) = Pr_S(R\mathcal{E}'|B(u))$.*

5   Comparison with Some Classical Security Properties

In this section we restrict ourselves to finite systems, for which $Tr \subseteq (H \cup L)^* \tau^\omega$, and we suppose that $\tau \in L$. Denote by E_0 the set $H \cup L_0$, where $L_0 = L \setminus \{\tau\}$.

We identify an element of Tr with its shortest prefix ending with the action τ. Given a trace λ and a system S, the low-level user observing $\lambda_{|L_0}\tau$ can construct the set of system traces which correspond to the same observation, the *low-level equivalent set* [18] of λ:

For $\lambda \in E_0^* \{\tau\}$, $LLES(\lambda, S) = \{\beta \in Tr \mid \lambda_{|L_0} = \beta_{|L_0}\}$.

We will show that *separability*, *noninterference* and *noninference* can be expressed in our framework and correspond to the absence of information flow for some classes of properties.

1. Noninference

Noninference is a security property which was introduced by O'Halloran [14]. It requires that every trace λ of the system admits in its low-level equivalent set its projection $\lambda_{|L_0}$. As a consequence a low-level user cannot deduce from an observation the existence of any occurrence of a high-level action:

$Noninference(S) \equiv \forall \lambda \in Tr \; \exists u \in LLES(\lambda, S) \; u \in L_0^* \tau$.

Consider the property $NonInf = L_0^* \tau \subset (H \cup L_0)^* \tau$. A trace satisfies this property iff it does not contain high-level actions. Thus this property exactly focuses on the (non) existence of a high-level activity. It turns out that *noninference* can be expressed in terms of information flow for the property $NonInf$.

Theorem 6. *For a probabilistic system S, $Noninference(S)$ holds iff $Pr_S(NonInf) \neq 0$ and there is no qualitative general information flow for the property $NonInf$.*

Proof.   Suppose $Pr_S(NonInf) \neq 0$ and there is no qualitative general information flow for the property $NonInf$. Let λ be a trace $\in Tr$. Consider the projection $u = \lambda_{|L}$. Since $B(u)$ is non-empty, $Pr_S(NonInf) \neq 0$ and there is no qualitative general information flow for the property $NonInf$. So we have $Pr_S(NonInf, u) \neq 0$. It proves that $u \in Tr$ because $B(u) \cap NonInf = \{u\}$. Thus, $Noninference(S)$ is true.

Conversely, suppose that $Noninference(S)$ holds. Let $\lambda \in Tr$, and $u = \lambda_{|L}$. Then $Pr_S(NonInf) \neq 0$, since u is also in Tr. Suppose there exists some $v \in L^*$ such that $Pr_S(NonInf, v) = 0$ and $B(v)$ is non-empty. There exists some λ' in $B(v)$, and the projection w of λ' on L belongs to Tr and v is a prefix of w. So, $Pr_S(NonInf, w) > 0$, but $Pr_S(NonInf, v) > Pr_S(NonInf, w)$, a contradiction. No qualitative general information flow for the property $NonInf$ can occur. ∎

Moreover, we can quantify the degree of noninference by measuring the maximal value of $|Pr_S(NonInf) - Pr_S(NonInf|B(u))|$ for all non-empty $B(u)$, $u \in L^*$.

2. Separability

Separability is aimed to express a complete independence between the sequences of actions at high and low level:

$Separability(S) \equiv \forall \lambda \in Tr \; \forall \lambda' \in Tr \; interl(\lambda_{|L_0}, \lambda'_{|H})\tau \in Tr.$

Again this security property can be expressed in terms of qualitative sequential information flow for some set of properties. For each $\xi_1, ..., \xi_n \in H^*$, let $Sep_{\xi_1,...,\xi_n}$ be the following predicate defined on $(H \cup \{l\})^*$:

$Sep_{\xi_1,...,\xi_n}(\lambda)$ holds iff $\lambda = \xi_1 l \xi_2 l ... \xi_p l \xi_{p+1} \xi_{p+2}...\xi_n l$ for some $p \leq n$.

Theorem 7. *For a probabilistic system S, $Separability(S)$ holds iff for any property $Sep_{\xi_1,...,\xi_n}$, where $\xi_1...\xi_n \in Tr_{|H}$, $Pr_S(Sep_{\xi_1,...,\xi_n}) \neq 0$ and there is no qualitative sequential information flow for these properties.*

Proof.   Suppose $Separability(S)$ holds. Consider the property $Sep_{\xi_1,...,\xi_n}$ for some $\xi_1, ..., \xi_n \in Tr_{|H}$. Suppose $Pr_S(Sep_{\xi_1,...,\xi_n}) = 0$. Let $v = a_1 a_2...a_p$ be the projection on L of some trace in Tr. If $p \geq n$ then $\xi_1 a_1 \xi_2 a_2...\xi_n a_n a_{n+1}...a_p \in Tr$, and if $p < n$ then $\xi_1 a_1 \xi_2 a_2...\xi_p a_p \xi_{p+1}...\xi_n \in Tr$. The two cases contradict $Pr_S(Sep_{\xi_1,...,\xi_n}) = 0$. Suppose that for some $\xi_1...\xi_n \in Tr_{|H}$, there is qualitative sequential information flow for property $Sep_{\xi_1,...,\xi_n}$. This means that $Pr_S(Sep_{\xi_1,...,\xi_n}) \neq 0$ and there exists $u \in L^+$ with $Pr_S(Sep_{\xi_1,...,\xi_n} \mid B(u)) = 0$ and $B(u)$ is non-empty.

Let $v = a_1 a_2...a_p$ be the projection on L of some trace in $B(u)$. If $p \geq n$ then $\xi_1 a_1 \xi_2 a_2..., \xi_n a_n a_{n+1}...a_p \in Tr$ which contradicts $Pr_S(Sep_{\xi_1,...,\xi_n} \mid B(u)) = 0$. If $p < n$ then $\xi_1 a_1 \xi_2 a_2..., \xi_p a_p \xi_{p+1}...\xi_n \in Tr$ which contradicts again the fact that $Pr_S(Sep_{\xi_1,...,\xi_n} \mid B(u)) = 0$.

Conversely, suppose there is no qualitative sequential information flow for any property $Sep_{\xi_1,...,\xi_n}$, where $(\xi_1, ..., \xi_n) \in H_n(Tr)$ and there exists $\lambda, \lambda' \in Tr$ and $\nu \in interl(\lambda_{|L_0}, \lambda'_{|H})\tau$ such that $\nu \notin Tr$.

The trace ν can be written $\xi_1 a_1 \xi_2 a_2...\xi_{n-1} a_{n-1} \xi_n \tau$, where $\xi \in H^*$, and $a_i \in L_0$. Thus $Pr_S(Sep_{\xi_1,...,\xi_n} \mid B(a_1 a_2...a_{n-1}\tau)) = 0$ with $B(a_1 a_2...a_{n-1}\tau)$ non-empty since $a_1 a_2...a_{n-1}\tau = \lambda'_{|H}$. Therefore $Pr_S(Sep_{\xi_1,...,\xi_n})$ must be equal to zero since there is no information flow for this property. ∎

3. Noninterference

Noninterference is a security property introduced by Goguen and Meseguer [5] and generalized by McCullough [11]. It demands that a low-level user cannot infer that any sequence of high-level inputs has (not) occurred. Let $HI \subset H$ (resp. HO) is the set of high-level input (resp. output) actions. We have $HI \cap HO = \emptyset$.

$$\forall \lambda \in Tr \; \forall \gamma \in interl(HI^*, \lambda_{|L_0}) \exists \delta \in LLES(\lambda, S) \; \gamma = \delta_{|L_0 \cup HI}$$

For each $\mu_1, ..., \mu_n \in HI^*$ let $Noninter_{\mu_1, ..., \mu_n} = interl(HO^*, \mu_1 l \mu_2 l ... \mu_n l) \times (H \cup l)^\omega$. In a similar way to Theorem 7, one can prove

Theorem 8. *For a given probabilistic system S, $Noninterference(S)$ holds iff for each n, for each $\mu_1, ..., \mu_n \in HI^*$ $Pr_S(Noninter_{\mu_1, ..., \mu_n}, u) \neq 0$ for every $u \in L^n$ such that $B(u)$ is non-empty.*

6 Conclusion

We have studied probabilistic information flow from a point of view parameterized by user-specified properties of interest. A property is a set of system traces, possibly viewed through an abstraction function. Our definitions support a range of property classes, e.g., referring to high-level events only, or high-level sequences separated by low-level events. We also allow specifications where a distinction is made between the past and future fragments of a trace. In this way, we can define (absence of) information flow for a given property, or for an entire set of properties of a given class.

We have given theorems that characterize the structure of systems for which absence of information flow according to these notions is guaranteed: for instance, a certain isomorphism between probabilistic trees is needed for properties which can distinguish subsequences of high-level events separated by low-level ones. We have also shown how several classic notions of possibilistic information flow (noninference, noninterference and separability) can be expressed using qualitative versions of our definitions.

We believe that this property-specific fashion of characterizing information flow is useful because it can be adapted to the particularities of the system under analysis. In many cases, a mere division into high- and low-level events and a single definition of information flow policy may not be enough, whereas our approach allows for a finer granularity of reasoning depending on the property.

An issue for future research is to apply this framework in the case where systems and properties are explicitly given as Markov chains and regular languages, respectively, and to investigate the decidability of the above notions of information flow in this setting.

Acknowledgements. We are grateful to Anatol Slissenko for the numerous and fruitful discussions of the approach studied in this paper.

References

1. Aldini, A., Bravetti, M., Gorrieri, R.: A process-algebraic approach for the analysis of probabilistic noninterference. Journal of Computer Security, 12 (2004) 191–246
2. Barthe, G., D'Argenio, P.R., Rezk, T.: Secure information flow by self-composition. 17th IEEE Computer Security Foundations Workshop. IEEE Computer Society (2004) 100–114

3. Clark, D., Hunt, S., Malacaria P.: Quantified interference for a while language. Electronic Notes Theoretical Computer Science, 112 (2005) 149–166
4. Giacobazzi, R., Mastroeni, I.: Abstract non-interference: parameterizing non-interference by abstract interpretation. Proceedings of the 31st ACM SIGPLAN-SIGACT Symposium on Principles of Programming Languages. ACM (2004) 186–197
5. Goguen, J.A., Meseguer, J.: Security policies and security models. Proc. IEEE Symp. on Security and Privacy (April 1982) 11–20
6. James W. Gray III: Toward a mathematical foundation for information flow security. Proc. 1991 IEEE Symposium on Security and Privacy. IEEE Computer Society Press (1991) 21–35
7. J.W. Gray III: Probabilistic interference. Proc. IEEE Symp. on Security and Privacy (May 1990) 170–179
8. Halpern, J.Y., O'Neill, K.R.: Secrecy in multiagent systems. Proc. IEEE Computer Security Foundations Workshop (2002)
9. Lowe, G.: Quantifying information flow. Proc. IEEE Computer Security Foundations Workshop (June 2002) 18–31
10. Mantel, H.: Possibilistic definitions of security – An assembly kit. Proc. IEEE Computer Security Foundations Workshop (July 2000) 185–199
11. McCullough, D.: Specifications for multi-level security and hook-up property. Proc. IEEE Symp. on Security and Privacy (April 1987) 161–166
12. McLean, J.: Security models and information flow. Proc. IEEE Symp. on Security and Privacy (May 1990) 180–187
13. McLean, J.: A general theory of composition for trace sets closed under selective interleaving functions. Proc. IEEE Symp. on Security and Privacy (May 1994) 79–93
14. O'Halloran, C.: A calculus of information flow. Proc. of the European Symposium on Research in Security and Privacy (ESoRiCS'90) (1990) 180–187
15. Di Pierro, A., Hankin, C., Wiklicky, H.: Approximate non-interference. Journal of Computer Security, 12 (2004) 37–82
16. Sabelfeld, A., Sands, D.: Probabilistic noninterference for multi-threaded programs. Proc. IEEE Computer Security Foundations Workshop (July 2000) 200–214
17. Slissenko, A.: On probabilistic modeling of information flow. Talk at a working seminar of LACL (2004)
18. Zakinthinos, A., Lee, E.S.: A general theory of security properties. Proc. IEEE Symp. on Security and Privacy. IEEE Computer Society Press (1997) 74–102

Generalized Abstract Non-interference: Abstract Secure Information-Flow Analysis for Automata

Roberto Giacobazzi and Isabella Mastroeni

Dipartimento di Informatica - Università di Verona, Italy
roberto.giacobazzi@univr.it
mastroeni@sci.univr.it

Abstract. Abstract non-interference has been introduced as a weakening non-interference which models attackers as abstract interpretations (i.e., static analyzers) of programming language semantics. In this paper we generalize the notion of abstract non-interference to deal with tree-like models of computation. This allows us to widen the scope of abstract non-interference for modeling security properties in automata, timed automata as models of real-time systems, and concurrent systems. We show that well known definitions of non-interference in these models of computation can be viewed as instances of our generalization. This proves that abstract non-interference can reasonably be considered as a general framework for studying and comparing security properties at different levels of abstraction in both programming languages and systems. Moreover, the most precise harmless attacker of a system is systematically derived by transforming abstract domains, characterizing the security degree of automata and concurrent systems.

1 Introduction

Non-interference [15] is a key notion in language based security. The idea is that no information about confidential data can be obtained by observing public information. The standard methods used for preventing interference are based on access control, i.e. higher privileges are required in order to access files containing confidential data. The problem with these methods is that, after access, there is no further control on how confidential information flows during execution. Hence, many techniques for checking *secure information flows* in software and systems, ranging from standard data-flow/control-flow analysis techniques to type inference, are studied, based on non-interference (see [22] and [11] for excellent surveys). All these approaches are devoted to prove that a system as a whole, or parts of it, does not allow confidential data to flow towards public variables. Type-based approaches are designed in such a way that well-typed programs do not leak secrets. In a security-typed language, a type is inductively associated at compile-time with program statements in such a way that any statement showing a potential flow disclosing secrets is rejected [25,27,28].

V. Gorodetsky, I. Kotenko, and V. Skormin (Eds.): MMM-ACNS 2005, LNCS 3685, pp. 221–234, 2005.
© Springer-Verlag Berlin Heidelberg 2005

Similarly, data-flow/control-flow analysis techniques are devoted to statically discover flows of secret data into public variables [4,18,19,23]. In concurrency, bisimulation is used to prove equivalence between computations where private actions are hidden with respect to the same system's computations where these actions are avoided [10]. In real-time systems trace equivalence is used to prove that the computations where private actions are avoided are equivalent to the same system's computations where these actions are admitted with a minimum fixed delay, and then hidden to the attacker [2]. These notions are all based on the same principle, which is non-interference, but they can be hardly recognized as instances of a same construction. This is due to the fact that different aspects of the underlying computational models become crucial in order to provide expressive enough notions of secrecy in sequential, non-deterministic, concurrent and real-time systems. While in sequential programs we are mainly concerned with non-interference in input/output behavior, in concurrency and in real-time we are, respectively, mainly concerned with interleaving actions and time delays.

Standard non-interference is often too strict for any practical use in language-based security: most programs are rejected by static control/data flow analyzers or type checkers for non-interference. In order to adapt security policies to practical cases, it is essential to know how much an attacker may learn from a program by (statically) analyzing its input/output behavior. This idea led to the definition of the notion of *abstract non-interference* [14], which captures a weaker form of non-interference. Namely, non-interference is made parametric relatively to some abstract property, formalized as an abstract interpretation [7], of the input/output behavior. This notion however is not adequate to cope with more complex systems like concurrent and real-time systems. In particular, as stated in [14], abstract non-interference strongly relies upon a denotational model of computation, which is inadequate for modeling security protocols for instance.

Main Contribution and Related Works. In this paper, we prove that the notion of abstract non-interference introduced in [14] can be generalized in order to cope with many well-known models of secrecy in sequential, concurrent and real-time systems and languages. This is achieved by factoring abstractions in order to identify sub-abstractions modeling the different properties of the system on which the notions of non-interference are based. Abstract interpretation [7] and the theory of abstract domain transformers [8] plays a key role in this generalization: The abstraction represents here both what an attacker may observe about a computation (as in abstract non-interference [14]) and which aspects of the computation are relevant for checking non-interference. In this context, non-interference corresponds to asking that the behavior of the chosen relevant aspects of the computation is independent from what an attacker may observe. We prove that both narrow and abstract non-interference in [14] are instances of our generalized abstract non-interference (GANI). Then we prove that NNI (Non-deterministic Non-Interference), SNNI (Strong NNI), NDC (Non-Deducibility on Compositions), BNDC (Bisimulation NDC), BNNI (Bisimulation NNI), and BSNNI (Bisimulation SNNI) in [10] for Security Process Algebras (SPA), are all instances of GANI. Finally, we prove that decidable notions of non-interference introduced for timed automata in [2] are again instances of GANI. In all these constructions, the model of an attacker is specified as an abstract interpretation of the system semantics. This is a key point in order to introduce systematic methods for deriving attackers by transforming abstract domains. We generalize the method introduced in [14] to derive harmless attackers for GANI, i.e., abstractions of the semantics of systems which guarantee non-interference.

This is not the first attempt neither for deriving general schemes for security policies [12], nor for trying to bridge language-based and process-calculi security [13,16,20]. In particular, in [12] the authors provide a uniform method for defining computer security properties for process algebras, obtaining a quite flexible schema for reasoning about different properties. What we do in this paper is something similar since the aim is the same, but in a more general context which ranges from language based-security to process algebras, to timed automata. The problem of studying the link between language-based and process calculi security is well known in literature. In particular, recently [13] this problem has been approached by transforming imperative language in a CCS-like process calculus, and by defining a notion of BNDC which corresponds for imperative languages to the standard notion of non-interference. In our case, we don't have to transform programs, since we consider a general model that can cope with both imperative programming languages and process algebras.

2   Information Flows in Language-Based Security

Non-interference can be naturally expressed by using semantic models of program execution. This idea goes back to Cohen's work on *strong dependency* [5], which uses denotational semantics for modeling how information can be transmitted among variables during the execution of programs. Therefore non-interference for programs essentially means that *"a variation of confidential (high or private) input does not cause a variation of public (low) output"* [22]. When this happens, we say that the program has only *secure information flows* [3,5,9,18,26]. This situation has been modeled by considering the denotational (input/output) semantics $[\![P]\!]$ of the program P. In particular, we consider programs where data are typed as private (H) or public (L). Program states in Σ are functions (represented as tuples) mapping variables in the set of values $\mathbb{V}$. If $\mathtt{T} \in \{\mathtt{H}, \mathtt{L}\}$, $n = |\{x \in Var(P) | x : \mathtt{T}\}|$, and $v \in \mathbb{V}^n$, we abuse notation by writing $v \in \mathbb{V}^{\mathtt{T}}$ when v is a value for the variables with security type $\mathtt{T}$. Moreover, we assume that any input s, can be seen as a pair (h, l), where $s^{\mathtt{H}} = h$ is a value for private data and $s^{\mathtt{L}} = l$ is a value for public data. In this case, (standard) *non-interference* can be formulated as follows:

A program P is *secure* if $\forall$ input $s, t \,.\, s^{\mathtt{L}} = t^{\mathtt{L}} \;\Rightarrow\; ([\![P]\!](s))^{\mathtt{L}} = ([\![P]\!](t))^{\mathtt{L}}$.

This problem has been formulated also as a *Partial Equivalence Relation* (PER) [17,23]. In [14], the notion of abstract non-interference is introduced for modeling both weaker attack models, and declassification. The idea is that, instead of observing the concrete semantics of programs, namely the concrete values of

Table 1. Narrow and Abstract Non-Interference

$$[\eta]P(\rho) \text{ if } \forall h_1, h_2 \in \mathbb{V}^{\mathbb{H}}, \forall l_1, l_2 \in \mathbb{V}^{\mathbb{L}}. \ \eta(\{l_1\}) = \eta(\{l_2\}) \Rightarrow \rho(\{[\![P]\!](h_1, l_1)^{\mathbb{L}}\}) = \rho(\{[\![P]\!](h_2, l_2)^{\mathbb{L}}\})$$

$$(\eta)P(\phi \rightsquigarrow \rho) \text{ if } \forall h_1, h_2 \in \mathbb{V}^{\mathbb{H}}, \forall l \in \mathbb{V}^{\mathbb{L}}. \ \rho([\![P]\!](\phi(\{h_1\}), \eta(\{l\}))^{\mathbb{L}}) = \rho([\![P]\!](\phi(\{h_2\}), \eta(\{l\}))^{\mathbb{L}})$$

public data, the attackers can only observe *properties* of public data, namely *abstract semantics* of the program. For this reason we model attackers by means of abstract domains. Formally, the *lattice of abstract domains* of a concrete domain C is isomorphic to the lattice $uco(C)$ of all the upper closure operators on C [8]. An *upper closure operator* $\rho : C \rightarrow C$ on a poset C is monotone, idempotent, and extensive[1]. The *model of an attacker*, also called *attacker*, is therefore a pair of abstractions $\langle \eta, \rho \rangle$, with $\eta, \rho \in uco(\wp(\mathbb{V}^{\mathbb{L}}))$, representing what an observer can see about, respectively, the input and output of a program. The notion of *narrow (abstract) non-interference* (NANI), denoted $[\eta]P(\rho)$, is given in Table 1. It says that if the attacker is able to observe the property η of public input, and the property ρ of public output, then no information flow concerning the private input is observable from the public output. The problem with this notion is that it may introduce *deceptive flows* [14], generated by different public outputs due to different public inputs with the same η property. Consider, for instance, $[Par]l := l * h^2(Sign)^2$, then l can observe a variation of the output's sign due to the existence of both negative and positive even numbers, revealing flows not due to private data, since h cannot affect the sign of the result. Most known models for weakening non-interference (e.g., PER model [23]) and for declassifying information (e.g., robust declassification [29]) corresponds to instances of NANI [14,17]. In order to avoid deceptive interference we introduce a weaker notion of non-interference. In this case, the *set* of all the elements sharing property η is used as the public input. Moreover we consider also a property $\phi \in uco(\wp(\mathbb{V}^{\mathbb{H}}))$, modeling the private property that has not to be observed by the attacker $\langle \eta, \rho \rangle$. This notion, denoted $(\eta)P(\phi \rightsquigarrow \rho)$, is called *abstract non-interference* (ANI) and is defined in Table 1.

Note that $[\mathtt{id}]P(\mathtt{id})$ models exactly (standard) non-interference. Moreover, we have that abstract non-interference is a weakening of both, standard and narrow non-interference: $[\mathtt{id}]P(\mathtt{id}) \Rightarrow (\eta)P(\phi \rightsquigarrow \rho)$ and $[\eta]P(\rho) \Rightarrow (\eta)P(\phi \rightsquigarrow \rho)$, while standard non-interference is not stronger than the narrow version, due to deceptive interference. In [14], two methods for deriving the most concrete output observation for a program, given the input one, for both narrow and abstract non-interference are provided. In particular the idea is that of abstracting in the same object all the elements that, if distinguished, would generate a visible flow. These most concrete output observations, that are not able to get information from the program P observing η in input, are, respectively, denoted $[\eta][\![P]\!](\mathtt{id})$ and $(\eta)[\![P]\!](\phi \rightsquigarrow \mathtt{id})$, both in $uco(\wp(\mathbb{V}^{\mathbb{L}}))$.

---

[1] $\forall x \in C. \ x \leq_C \rho(x)$.
[2] Note that $Par \overset{\text{def}}{=} \{\top, ev, od, \bot\}$ and $Sign \overset{\text{def}}{=} \{\top, 0+, -, \bot\}$.

3   Generalized Abstract Non-interference

In this section, we introduce a generalization of abstract non-interference, called *generalized abstract non-interference* (shortly GANI), which subsumes many of the known notions of non-interference based on tree-like computations and automata. Abstract interpretation plays a key role in this generalization: The abstraction represents here both what an attacker may observe about a computation (as in abstract non-interference) and which aspects of the computation are relevant for checking non-interference, aspects determined by the specific notion of non-interference that we have to enforce on the system. Non-interference corresponds to asking that relevant (confidential) aspects of the computation have no effects on what an attacker observes of the computation. Moreover, what an attacker may observe is indeed composed by two aspects: what the particular notion of non-interference *allows* to observe, and what effectively the attacker *can* observe. In the following, we consider computational systems S modeled by their tree semantics $\{|S|\}$, i.e., the set of all the trees of computations of S. The corresponding trace and I/O denotational semantics are, respectively, denoted by $\langle|S|\rangle$ and $[\![S]\!]$.

We define generalized non-interference by means of three abstractions in the standard framework of abstract interpretation, i.e., additive functions, each one with a specific and precise meaning, depending on the given notion of non-interference, and depending on the attacker model. The chosen policy of non-interference decides two of these abstractions:

α_{OBS}: The first abstraction α_{OBS} abstracts the tree semantics in the model used in the notion of non-interference that has to be enforced. Note that, the abstraction level chosen for defining non-interference corresponds to *delegating particular parts* (i.e., aspects) *of the system to release information* [24]. For instance, if we want to check standard non-interference for imperative programming languages, then α_{OBS} corresponds to the denotational semantics abstraction of the computational tree. We call this abstraction the *observation abstraction*. Such an abstraction extracts always an observational property from semantic trees, e.g., all the computational traces, the I/O relations, etc.;

α_{INT}: The second abstraction α_{INT} characterizes the maximal amount of information that an attacker should observe, in the chosen policy. This abstraction *regulate what information may be released* [24]. For example, if we have to check non-interference in SPA [10], then we want the computations where private actions are hidden to be equivalent to the computations where private actions are avoided. Namely the set of all the computations where private actions are avoided is the maximal information that the attacker is allowed to observe. In this case α_{INT} selects only those computations where private actions are not executed. This abstraction, called *interference abstraction*, forgets about all information which should not be observed by an attacker. Such an abstraction always selects the subset of the possible computations that we allow the attacker to observe, namely it is such that for each X in its domain, $\alpha_{\text{INT}}(X) \subseteq X$.

These two abstractions tells us that, in general, non-interference holds whenever the amount of information that an attacker can grasp from a computation is precisely what, for the given notion of non-interference, that attacker *is allowed* to observe about it.

Finally, we have to model the observational capability of the *passive* attacker observing the system, and we consider a further abstraction α_{ATT}, called *attacker abstraction*, which characterizes the model of the attacker, namely what it can observe of the system behavior. In this case the attacker is passive since it cannot interfere with the execution of the program, and it cannot control the inputs of the system. By using these three abstractions we define generalized abstract non-interference for the system S as

$$\alpha_{\text{ATT}} \circ \alpha_{\text{OBS}}(\{|S|\}) = \alpha_{\text{ATT}} \circ \alpha_{\text{INT}} \circ \alpha_{\text{OBS}}(\{|S|\})$$

This equation says that, in the model chosen by α_{OBS}, the maximal amount of information that the attacker *is allowed to* observe, determined by $\alpha_{\text{ATT}} \circ \alpha_{\text{INT}}$, is exactly what the attacker *does* observe, determined by α_{ATT}. In other words, this definition of non-interference says that the attacker, modelled by the abstraction α_{ATT}, cannot distinguish between the observable computations (α_{OBS}) and the set of only those computations that the attacker should observe ($\alpha_{\text{INT}} \circ \alpha_{\text{OBS}}$).

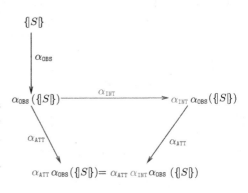

The Generalized Non-Interference Policy. It is worth noting that this definition of GANI in general is characterized by a *possibilistic* interpretation of equality and doesn't provide an explicit notion of non-interference. Indeed, in ANI [14], the non-interference policy states that all the computations with the same public input has to provide the same public outputs. We can think of generalizing the notion of non-interference by checking the equality of public observations of the outputs for all the computations sharing a common maximal partial execution, instead of sharing only the public input. Consider the tree semantics $\{|S|\}$ of the system S.

> A system S is *secure* if $\forall \sigma \in \alpha_{\text{INT}} \circ \alpha_{\text{OBS}}(\{|S|\}), \forall \delta \in \alpha_{\text{OBS}}(\{|S|\})$.
> $$\delta \preccurlyeq_{\max} \sigma \;\Rightarrow\; \alpha_{\text{ATT}}(\delta) = \alpha_{\text{ATT}}(\sigma)$$

where the relation $\preccurlyeq_{\max}$, specifies the maximal subtree which δ shares with an element in $\alpha_{\text{OBS}}(\{|S|\})$. The definition above clearly, depends on the subtree relation $\preccurlyeq$. Consider $\sigma \in \alpha_{\text{INT}} \circ \alpha_{\text{OBS}}(\{|S|\})$ and consider $\delta \in \alpha_{\text{OBS}}(\{|S|\})$: $\delta \preccurlyeq_{\max} \sigma$ if

$$\exists \pi \preccurlyeq \delta \,.\, \pi \preccurlyeq \sigma \,\wedge\, \forall \pi' \neq \pi \,.\, \pi \preccurlyeq \pi' \preccurlyeq \delta, \forall \sigma' \in \alpha_{\text{OBS}}(\{|S|\}) \text{ then } \pi' \not\preccurlyeq \sigma'$$

The definition above is based on the observation that if a *computation* has a maximal partial computation in common with what can be surely observed by the attacker, then it is in those points, where the common partial computations end, that some private action has interfered in the computation.

Example 1. Let A be a system, if $\alpha_{\text{OBS}}(\{\!|A|\!\}) = \{1 \to 2 \to 3, 1 \to 2 \to 4, 1 \to 3 \to 2\}$ and $\alpha_{\text{INT}} \circ \alpha_{\text{OBS}}(\{\!|A|\!\}) = \{1 \to 2 \to 3, 1 \to 3 \to 2\}$ then $1 \to 2 \to 3 \preccurlyeq_{\max} 1 \to 2 \to 3$, $1 \to 2 \to 4 \preccurlyeq_{\max} 1 \to 2 \to 3$ and $1 \to 3 \to 2 \preccurlyeq_{\max} 1 \to 3 \to 2$.

3.1   Abstract Non-interference as GANI

In this section, we show that abstract non-interference [14], which generalizes standard non-interference [5,15], is an instance of GANI. For deterministic programs the standard denotational semantics is given as the abstraction approximating traces with input/output relations (functions for deterministic programs) [6][3]. Let X be a set of traces, the denotational semantics is defined: $\alpha^{\mathcal{D}}(X) = \lambda \sigma_\vdash . \{ \sigma_\dashv \mid \sigma \in X, |\sigma| < \omega \} \cup \{ \bot \mid |\sigma| = \omega \}$, where $\sigma_\vdash$ and $\sigma_\dashv$ denote respectively the initial and the final states of the trace σ. Given two closures $\phi \in uco(\mathbb{V}^{\text{H}})$ and $\eta \in uco(\mathbb{V}^{\text{L}})$, we define the abstraction $\alpha^\eta_\phi : (\Sigma \to \Sigma) \longrightarrow \wp(\wp(\Sigma) \times \wp(\Sigma))$ such that for any $f : \Sigma \longrightarrow \Sigma$:

$$\alpha^\eta_\phi(f) = \{ \langle S_\vdash, S_\dashv \rangle \mid S_\vdash = \langle \phi(h), \eta(l) \rangle, h \in \mathbb{V}^{\text{H}}, l \in \mathbb{V}^{\text{L}} S_\dashv = f(\phi(h), \eta(l)) \}$$

The idea is to abstract denotational input/output semantics to the set of all the possible associations between the corresponding input/output abstract states. In this way, we model the observation made by the attacker, which consists precisely in the ability to observe input/output abstract values. Consider the function $\mathcal{C}_{\text{H}} : \wp(\mathbb{V}^{\text{H}}) \longrightarrow \mathbb{V}^{\text{H}}$ that uniquely chooses an element in the domain of values $\mathbb{V}^{\text{H}}$. Note that the equation $\forall h_1, h_2. \ \rho([\![P]\!](\langle \phi(h_1), \eta(l) \rangle)^{\text{L}}) = \rho([\![P]\!](\langle \phi(h_2), \eta(l) \rangle)^{\text{L}})$ is equivalent to the equation $\forall h. \ \rho([\![P]\!](\langle \phi(h), \eta(l) \rangle)^{\text{L}}) = \rho([\![P]\!](\langle \phi(\mathcal{C}_{\text{H}}(\mathbb{V}^{\text{H}})), \eta(l) \rangle)^{\text{L}})$. Therefore abstract non-interference can be formulated as follows:

$$\forall h \in \mathbb{V}^{\text{H}} . \ \rho([\![P]\!](\phi(h), \eta(l))^{\text{L}}) = \rho([\![P]\!](\phi(\mathcal{C}_{\text{H}}(\mathbb{V}^{\text{H}})), \eta(l))^{\text{L}})$$

At this point, we can define the *interference* abstraction $\alpha_{\text{ANI}} : \wp(\wp(\Sigma) \times \wp(\Sigma)) \longrightarrow \wp(\wp(\Sigma) \times \wp(\Sigma))$, which selects only the observation with the fixed private input, hence for any $\mathcal{F} \in \wp(\wp(\Sigma) \times \wp(\Sigma))$:

$$\alpha_{\text{ANI}}(\mathcal{F}) = \{ \langle S_\vdash, S_\dashv \rangle \in \mathcal{F} \mid \exists l \in \mathbb{V}^{\text{L}} . \ S_\vdash = \langle \phi(\mathcal{C}_{\text{H}}(\mathbb{V}^{\text{H}})), \eta(l) \rangle \}$$

In order to obtain abstract non-interference, we assume that the attacker may observe only the ρ abstraction of the low output. This process is encoded by the attacker abstraction, which depends upon the input/output abstractions $\eta, \rho \in uco(\wp(\mathbb{V}^{\text{L}}))$, i.e., $\alpha^{\rho\eta}_{\text{ATT}} : \wp(\wp(\Sigma) \times \wp(\Sigma)) \longrightarrow \wp(\wp(\mathbb{V}^{\text{L}}) \times \wp(\mathbb{V}^{\text{L}}))$ where

$$\alpha^{\rho\eta}_{\text{ATT}}(\mathcal{F}) = \{ \langle \eta(X_{\text{L}}), \rho(Y_{\text{L}}) \rangle \mid \langle \langle X_{\text{H}}, X_{\text{L}} \rangle, \langle Y_{\text{H}}, Y_{\text{L}} \rangle \rangle \in \mathcal{F} \}$$

Then, we can specify abstract non-interference in the following theorem.

---

[3] For deterministic systems the trace semantics coincides with the tree semantics.

Theorem 1. $\alpha_{\text{ATT}}^{\rho\eta} \circ \alpha_{\phi}^{\eta}(\llbracket P \rrbracket) = \alpha_{\text{ATT}}^{\rho\eta} \circ \alpha_{\text{ANI}} \circ \alpha_{\phi}^{\eta}(\llbracket P \rrbracket)$ *iff* $(\eta)P(\phi \rightsquigarrow_{\parallel} \rho)$.

Note here that the observation abstraction is the composition $\alpha_{\phi}^{\eta} \circ \alpha^{\mathcal{D}}$.

As far as the narrow case is concerned, we have to check if the possible executions with the high variable ranging on the whole concrete domain $\mathbb{V}^{\text{H}}$ and the low variables ranging on the set of values with the same property η are equal to the interference abstraction obtained by setting the high variable to $\mathcal{C}_{\text{H}}(\mathbb{V}^{\text{H}})$ and the low one to any fixed value in the given property of low variables. This means that we have to change the interference abstraction given above as follows, where $\mathcal{C}_{\text{L}} : \wp(\mathbb{V}^{\text{L}}) \longrightarrow \mathbb{V}^{\text{L}}$ is a function that uniquely selects an element from sets of values: $\alpha_{\text{NANI}} : \wp(\wp(\Sigma) \times \wp(\Sigma)) \longrightarrow \wp(\wp(\Sigma) \times \wp(\Sigma))$

$$\alpha_{\text{NANI}}(\mathcal{F}) = \left\{ \left. f \, \right| \begin{array}{l} \exists l \in \mathbb{V}^{\text{L}} . \, f = \langle\langle \mathcal{C}_{\text{H}}(\mathbb{V}^{\text{H}}), \eta(l) \rangle, S_{\dashv}\rangle \langle\langle \mathcal{C}_{\text{H}}(\mathbb{V}^{\text{H}}), l' \rangle, S_{\dashv}\rangle \in \mathcal{F} \\ l' = \mathcal{C}_{\text{L}}(\{\, y \in \mathbb{V}^{\text{L}} \, \big| \, \eta(y) = \eta(l) \,\}) \end{array} \right\}$$

Therefore, we can rewrite also narrow abstract non-interference (NANI).

Theorem 2. $\alpha_{\text{ATT}}^{\rho\eta} \circ \alpha_{\text{id}}^{\text{id}}(\llbracket P \rrbracket) = \alpha_{\text{ATT}}^{\rho\eta} \circ \alpha_{\text{NANI}} \circ \alpha_{\text{id}}^{\text{id}}(\llbracket P \rrbracket)$ *iff* $[\eta]P(\rho)$.

3.2   GANI in Concurrency

In [10], the authors introduced a classification of security properties for *security process algebras*. Since process algebras can be modeled by computational trees, we show how different security properties defined in [10] can be re-interpreted as instances of the generalized abstract non-interference. In the following we consider the process algebra SPA introduced in [10]. We only remind the reader that, if $L \subseteq Act$, then $P \backslash L$ can execute all the actions P is able to do, provided that they do not belong to L, $P \backslash_I L$ can execute all the actions P is able to do, provided that they do not belong to $L \cap I$, and P/L hides the actions in L.

Consider a process $P \in$ SPA, whose computational tree is $\{\!| P |\!\}$. We start by considering NNI (non-deterministic non-interference) which is defined by using the trace equivalence $\approx_{\text{T}}$ in the following way: $(P \backslash_I \text{H})/\text{H} \approx_{\text{T}} P/\text{H}$, where P/H means that all the action in H (high) are hidden, i.e., they are substituted by the internal action ε, while $P \backslash_I \text{H}$ means that all the actions in H which are input actions cannot be executed by P. Then, we can translate this definition as GANI. It is clear that the definition of NNI considers the concrete system P, this means that $\alpha_{\text{OBS}} \stackrel{\text{def}}{=} \text{id}$. On the other hand, we have that what an external user can observe is the system having the high actions hidden. Therefore, we have to define the attacker abstraction that hides high-level actions. In the following let $\mathbb{T}_{Act}$ be the set of all the semantic trees on the set of actions Act, while let $\mathbb{T}_{\text{L}}$ be the set of all the semantic trees where the private actions are hidden. Let $\tau \in \mathbb{T}_{Act}$ and consider the following function: $\text{low} : \mathbb{T}_{Act} \longrightarrow \mathbb{T}_{\text{L}}$ such that $\text{low}(\tau)$ is the tree where any label $\sigma \in$ H in τ is substituted by ε. Let $\{\!| P |\!\}$ the semantics of P specified as a computational tree. We define the function α_{low} as follows: $\alpha_{\text{low}}(\{\!| P |\!\}) = \{\, \text{low}(\tau) \, \big| \, \tau \in \{\!| P |\!\} \,\}$. This specifies the attacker abstraction in GANI and it is such that: $\{\!| P/\text{H} |\!\} = \alpha_{\text{low}}(\{\!| P |\!\})$. Moreover, we can note that NNI is defined by using trace equivalence, this means that the attacker can analyze traces of computations only. By definition two systems are trace equivalent if they accept the same language, therefore we have to make equal the α_T abstraction of the result, namely $\alpha_{\text{ATT}} \stackrel{\text{def}}{=} \alpha_T \circ \alpha_{\text{low}}$. Finally, consider the operation $P\backslash_I H$ which avoids high-level inputs. Let I be the set of input actions, then we can define the abstraction: $\alpha_L^I : \wp(\mathbb{T}_{Act}) \longrightarrow \wp(\mathbb{T}_{Act})$ such that for any $T \subseteq \mathbb{T}_{Act}$: $\alpha_L^I(T) = \{ \tau \in T \mid \forall \sigma \in \tau . \sigma \notin H \cap I \}$, where $\sigma \in \tau$ is a shorthand notation for σ being an action (node) in τ. Then we have that $\{P\backslash_I H\} = \alpha_L^I(\{P\})$. At this point, we can derive the NNI as:

$$\alpha_T \circ \alpha_{\text{low}}(\{P\}) = (\alpha_T \circ \alpha_{\text{low}}) \circ \alpha_L^I(\{P\})$$

Consider now the notion of *Strong Non-deterministic Non-Interference* (SNNI) defined in [10]: P satisfies SNNI iff $P/H \approx_T P\backslash H$. In order to define SNNI as an instance of the generalized abstract non-interference, we have to define the operator P/H, that hides all the high-level actions. Let $\alpha_L : \wp(\mathbb{T}_{Act}) \longrightarrow \wp(\mathbb{T}_{Act})$ be the map such that $\forall T \subseteq \mathbb{T}_{Act} : \alpha_L(T) = \{ \tau \in T \mid \forall \sigma \in \tau . \sigma \in L \}$. This defines the interference abstraction in GANI and it is such that $\{P\backslash H\} = \alpha_L(\{P\})$. The standard notion of SNNI introduced in [10] can be defined as

$$\alpha_T \circ \alpha_{\text{low}}(\{P\}) = \alpha_T \circ \alpha_{\text{low}} \circ \alpha_L(\{P\}).$$

At this point, since bisimulations are equivalence relations [21], they can be viewed as abstractions of computational trees, i.e., a tree is abstracted into the equivalence class of all the trees bisimilar to it, then we can model both BNNI and BSNNI. In this context, we obtain this by substituting to α_T, the abstraction α_B, corresponding to the given chosen bisimulation, which associates with a computation the set of all the computations bisimilar to the given one.

Consider now non-deducibility on compositions (NDC) and the bisimulation-based NDC (BNDC) notions of non-interference. NDC is: $\forall \Pi . P/H \approx_T (P||\Pi)\backslash H$, where Π is a process that can execute only high-level actions. In [10] it is proved that NDC=SNNI, therefore also NDC can be modeled as a generalized abstract non-interference. The situation is different when we consider BNDC, i.e., $\forall \Pi . P/H \approx_B (P||\Pi)\backslash H$, for the bisimulation relation B. In this case, we have that BNDC$\neq$BSNNI, and therefore we have to explicitly model it as generalized abstract non-interference. In [10] the authors also prove that BNDC can be equivalently formalized as: $\forall \Pi . P\backslash H \approx_B (P||\Pi)\backslash H$. At this point, we note that we have to consider $\alpha_B \circ \alpha_L$ as α_{ATT}, since in this definition it is only observable what a low-level user (i.e., a user that can execute only low level actions) can see, which is only the computation without high-level actions. Moreover, we have that α_{OBS} is the identity, since, in this case, non-interference is defined on computational trees. Finally, we define α_{INT} noting that the semantics (computational tree) of $P||\Pi$ contains the semantics of $P.\Pi$ (which doesn't execute synchronizations), therefore we can define $\alpha_{\text{INT}}(\{P||\Pi\}) = \{P.\Pi\}$, modeling BNDC as follows:

$$\forall \Pi . (\alpha_B \circ \alpha_L) \circ \alpha_{\text{INT}}(\{P||\Pi\}) = \alpha_B \circ \alpha_L(\{P||\Pi\}).$$

This is BNDC since in the right side of the equality α_L is applied to the semantics of $P.\Pi$, and therefore executes only the high-level actions of P.

Theorem 3. *Given a system P then:*
- *P satisfies SNNI iff $\alpha_T \circ \alpha_{1ov}(\{|P|\}) = \alpha_T \circ \alpha_{1ov} \circ \alpha_L(\{|P|\})$;*
- *P satisfies BNDC iff $\forall \Pi.(\alpha_B \circ \alpha_L) \circ \alpha_{INT}(\{|P||\Pi|\}) = \alpha_B \circ \alpha_L(\{|P||\Pi|\})$.*

3.3   GANI in Real-Time Systems

Let A be a timed automaton [1], $\{|A|\}$ the corresponding computational tree semantics, and $\mathcal{L} \overset{\text{def}}{=} \alpha_T(\{|A|\})$ the corresponding timed accepted language, i.e., the sequence of all the computational traces of states $\langle \sigma, t \rangle$, where σ is an action executed at the time t. In [2] a notion of non-interference for timed automata is introduced. Given a natural number n, the authors say that high-level actions do not interfere with the system, by considering minimum delay n, if the system behaviour in absence of high-level actions is equivalent to the system behaviour, observed on low-level actions only, when high-level actions can occur with a delay between them greater than n. Let Σ be the alphabet of actions of A. We suppose that Σ is partitioned into two disjoint sets of actions H and L: H is the set of the high-level actions, while L is the set of the low-level ones. Consider the following languages:

$$\mathcal{L}|_L \overset{\text{def}}{=} \left\{ \overline{\langle \sigma, t \rangle} \in \mathcal{L} \,\middle|\, \forall \langle \sigma_i, t_i \rangle \in \overline{\langle \sigma, t \rangle} \,.\, \sigma_i \in L \right\}$$

$$\mathcal{L}/H \overset{\text{def}}{=} \left\{ w \,\middle|\, \begin{array}{l} \exists \overline{\langle \sigma, t \rangle} \in \mathcal{L} \text{ such that } w \text{ is the projection of} \overline{\langle \sigma, t \rangle} \\ \text{on the pairs } \left\{ \langle \sigma, t \rangle \,\middle|\, \sigma \in L \right\} \end{array} \right\}$$

$$\mathcal{L}_H^n \overset{\text{def}}{=} \left\{ \overline{\langle \sigma, t \rangle} \in \mathcal{L} \,\middle|\, \begin{array}{l} \forall \langle \sigma_i, t_i \rangle, \langle \sigma_j, t_j \rangle \in \overline{\langle \sigma, t \rangle} \,.\, i \neq j, \\ \sigma_i, \sigma_j \in H \implies |t_i - t_j| \geq n \end{array} \right\}$$

So, $\mathcal{L}|_L$ avoids high-level actions, i.e., it takes only the traces of the system that make only low-level actions. On the other hand, $\mathcal{L}/H$ hides all the high-level actions, i.e., it executes them and then it hides them. Finally, $\mathcal{L}_H^n$ selects only those traces where the high-level actions are distant at least n. Then in [2] a system is said to be *n-non-interfering* iff $\mathcal{L}_H^n/H = \mathcal{L}|_L$.

Consider the example below [2]. This timed automaton have L = {begin-c,end-c} and H = {cloche,reset}. There is only one possible trace of only low-level actions:

$$\langle \text{begin-c}, 2 \rangle \langle \text{end-c}, 4 \rangle \ldots \langle \text{begin-c}, 2 + 4i \rangle \langle \text{end-c}, 4 + 4i \rangle \ldots$$

If more than one cloche action is executed and the time elapsed between them is less than 1, then it is possible to execute the action reset, which can change the moment of the execution of begin-c, and therefore in this case we have an interference.

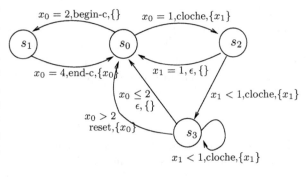

In particular, for example, we can have the trace

$$\langle\text{begin-c}, 2\rangle\langle\text{end-c}, 4\rangle\langle\text{cloche}, 5\rangle\langle\text{cloche}, 5.6\rangle\langle\text{cloche}, 6.3\rangle\langle\text{begin-c}, 8.3\rangle\ldots$$

whose projection $\langle\text{begin-c}, 2\rangle\langle\text{end-c}, 4\rangle\langle\text{begin-c}, 6.3\rangle\langle\text{end-c}, 8.3\rangle$, on the low-level actions, is not the one described above. This means that in this system there is interference.

Consider the attacker abstraction α_{low}, defined in Sec. 3.2, the interference abstraction α_{L} and the language $\mathcal{L}_{\text{H}}^n$. We define the family of abstractions α_n, with $n \in \mathbb{N}$, as follows:

$$\alpha_n(\mathcal{L}) = \left\{\, \tau \in \mathcal{L} \,\middle|\, \forall \langle\sigma_i, t_i\rangle, \langle\sigma_j, t_j\rangle \in \tau \,.\, i \neq j, \ \sigma_i, \sigma_j \in \text{H} \ \Rightarrow\ |t_i - t_j| \geq n \,\right\}$$

where each map α_n is additive and $\mathcal{L}_{\text{H}}^n = \alpha_n(\mathcal{L})$. Then the notion of non-interference introduced in [2] for timed automata can be specified as follows:

$$\alpha_{\text{low}} \circ \alpha_n(\mathcal{L}) = \alpha_{\text{low}} \circ \alpha_{\text{L}} \circ \alpha_n(\mathcal{L}),$$

where $\alpha_{\text{L}} \circ \alpha_n = \alpha_{\text{L}}$. Note that, in this case, $\alpha_{\text{OBS}} = \alpha_n \circ \alpha_{\text{T}}$.

Theorem 4. *A timed automaton, with timed language $\mathcal{L}$, satisfies n-non interference iff $\alpha_{\text{low}} \circ \alpha_n(\mathcal{L}) = \alpha_{\text{low}} \circ \alpha_{\text{L}} \circ \alpha_n(\mathcal{L})$.*

4 Deriving GANI Attackers

In this section, we generalize the construction to GANI of the most powerful attacker [14]. Let A be a system and let α_{OBS} and α_{INT} be abstractions defining the chosen notion of non-interference for which A results insecure whenever observed by the attacker modeled by α_{ATT}. As we said, α_{OBS} and α_{INT} depend on the definition of non-interference that we chose, while α_{ATT} depends on what we decide to observe about the computation. Therefore if non-interference is not satisfied, i.e., the system is not secure as regards the chosen notion of non-interference, we can think of further abstracting the attacker abstraction in order to achieve security. The resulting abstraction provides a certificate of the security level of the system A with respect to the fixed observation and private abstractions. In order to find an abstraction that makes equal the sets $\alpha_{\text{ATT}} \circ \alpha_{\text{OBS}}$ and $\alpha_{\text{ATT}} \circ \alpha_{\text{INT}} \circ \alpha_{\text{OBS}}$ we have to merge elements in both sets in order to make them contain the same new abstract objects. Hence, given a security policy determined by what is observable (α_{OBS}), and what at most the attacker should observe ($\alpha_{\text{INT}} \circ \alpha_{\text{OBS}}$), we derive *from the program* the most concrete harmless attacker α_{ATT} for the given policy. Namely, we derive the minimal abstraction necessary in order to make GANI hold. Note that, in abstract non-interference [14] there is a clear criterion for collecting elements in order to build the abstraction: abstracting to the same object all the elements resulting from computations that differ only for private inputs. The corresponding construction for GANI is provided by the relation $\preccurlyeq_{\text{max}}$ defined in the previous section. Hence, we use $\preccurlyeq_{\text{max}}$ for defining the sets of objects that need to have the same abstraction in order to achieve secrecy.

Hence, $\forall \sigma \in \alpha_{\text{INT}} \circ \alpha_{\text{OBS}}(\{|A|\})$ the following set collects all the trees that have to be indistinguishable from the tree σ:

$$\Upsilon(\sigma) = [\sigma] \stackrel{\text{def}}{=} \left\{ \delta \in \alpha_{\text{OBS}}(\{|A|\}) \,\middle|\, \delta \preceq_{\max} \sigma \right\}$$

Example 2. Consider a system A, if we have $\alpha_{\text{OBS}}(\{|A|\}) = \{1 \to 2 \to 3, 1 \to 2 \to 4, 1 \to 3 \to 2\}$ and $\alpha_{\text{INT}} \circ \alpha_{\text{OBS}}(\{|A|\}) = \{1 \to 2 \to 3, 1 \to 3 \to 2\}$ then $[1 \to 2 \to 3] = \{1 \to 2 \to 3, 1 \to 2 \to 4\}$, $[1 \to 3 \to 2] = \{1 \to 3 \to 2\}$. While, if we have $\alpha_{\text{OBS}}(\{|A|\}) = \{1 \to 2 \to 4, 1 \to 2 \to 3, 1 \to 5 \to 3, 3 \to 5 \to 4, 1 \to 2 \to 5, 1 \to 3 \to 2, 3 \to 2 \to 1\}$ and $\alpha_{\text{INT}} \circ \alpha_{\text{OBS}}(\{|A|\}) = \{1 \to 2 \to 3, 1 \to 3 \to 2, 3 \to 2 \to 1\}$ then $[1 \to 2 \to 3] = \{1 \to 5 \to 3, 1 \to 2 \to 3, 1 \to 2 \to 4\}$, $[1 \to 3 \to 2] = \{1 \to 5 \to 3, 1 \to 3 \to 2\}$ and, finally, $[3 \to 2 \to 1] = \{3 \to 2 \to 1, 3 \to 5 \to 4\}$.

Similarly to [14], we define the set $\mathbb{D}_{\{|A|\}}$ collecting all computations that may fail secrecy, and $\text{Irr}_{\{|A|\}}$ collecting all computations for which secrecy cannot fail.

$$\mathbb{D}_{\{|A|\}} = \left\{ [\sigma] \,\middle|\, \sigma \in \alpha_{\text{INT}} \circ \alpha_{\text{OBS}}(\{|A|\}) \right\}$$
$$\text{Irr}_{\{|A|\}} = \left\{ X \,\middle|\, \forall \sigma \in \alpha_{\text{INT}} \circ \alpha_{\text{OBS}}(\{|A|\}) . X \notin \Upsilon([\sigma]) \right\}$$

The predicate $Secr_{\{|A|\}}$, which characterizes all the elements that should be contained in the abstraction modeling the most concrete harmless attacker, is defined as

$$Secr_{\{|A|\}}(X) \text{ iff } \forall \sigma \in \alpha_{\text{INT}} \circ \alpha_{\text{OBS}}(\{|A|\}) . (\exists Z \in [\sigma] . Z \subseteq X \Rightarrow \forall W \in [\sigma] . W \subseteq X)$$

Following the construction in [14], we can prove that $\mathcal{S}\{|A|\} \stackrel{\text{def}}{=} \left\{ X \,\middle|\, Secr_{\{|A|\}}(X) \right\}$ is the most concrete abstraction that enforces the notion of GANI to hold, w.r.t. the relation $\preceq_{\max}$.

Theorem 5. *Let A be a system. $\mathcal{S}\{|A|\}$ is the most concrete abstraction such that $\forall \sigma \in \alpha_{\text{INT}} \circ \alpha_{\text{OBS}}(\{|A|\}), \forall \delta \in \alpha_{\text{OBS}}(\{|A|\}) . \delta \preceq_{\max} \sigma \Rightarrow \mathcal{S}\{|A|\}(\delta) = \mathcal{S}\{|A|\}(\sigma)$.*

Proposition 1. $\mathcal{S}(\{|A|\}) = \mathcal{S}(\Upsilon(\mathbb{D}_{\{|A|\}})) \cup \text{Irr}_{\{|A|\}}$.

5   Conclusion

We introduced GANI as a generalization of abstract non-interference for automata and concurrent systems. We believe that the combination of abstract interpretation and non-interference may provide advanced techniques for analyzing, in a *modular* way, how sub-components of complex systems interact during computation and how, analyses at different levels of abstraction can be combined in a useful way. On one side, abstract interpretation has been proved to be the most appropriate framework for reasoning about properties of computations at different levels of abstraction. On the other side, strong-dependency, and in particular non-interference, is the most appropriate notion to disclose information-flows among sub-components of a system, when a variation of some of them can be conveyed to the others. GANI is intended to bridge these two notions in order to provide adequate methods for studying properties of complex systems by analyzing the properties of computations that are conveyed among system sub-components. In this sense, GANI may provide a framework for studying the relation between different and interacting entities which may be reciprocally influenced by the action of computing, giving advanced techniques for systematically classifying the information leakage in the lattice of abstractions. Moreover, the advantage of specifying different notions of non-interference for sequential, concurrent and timed systems as GANI relies upon the possibility offered by abstract interpretation to systematically derive abstractions. This paper does not contain any tool support for the analysis, clearly such a tool would provide an evidence on how the framework can be used, and indeed this problem deserves further work. However, the definition of a general schema for defining security properties allows to study relationship among different properties. Moreover, by using a unique model and unique schema, parametric on the security policy and on the computational system, it is possible to develop more general theories which could then be applied to a number of definitions by simply instantiating them, in the same spirit as [12].

References

1. Alur, R., Dill, D.L.: A theory of timed automata. Theoretical Computer Science, 126(2) (1994) 183–235
2. Barbuti, R., De Francesco, N., Santone, A., Tesei, L.: A notion of non-interference for timed automata. Fundamenta Informaticae, 51 (2002) 1–11
3. Bell, D.E., LaPadula, L.J.: Secure computer systems: Mathematical foundations and model. Technical Report M74-244, MITRE Corp. Badford, MA (1973)
4. Clark, D., Hankin, C., Hunt, S.: Information flow for algol-like languages. Computer Languages, 28(1) (2002) 3–28
5. Cohen, E.S.: Information transmission in sequential programs. Foundations of Secure Computation (1978) 297–335
6. Cousot, P.: Constructive design of a hierarchy of semantics of a transition system by abstract interpretation. Theor. Comput. Sci., 277(1-2):47,103 (2002)
7. Cousot, P., Cousot, R.: Abstract interpretation: A unified lattice model for static analysis of programs by construction or approximation of fixpoints. Proc. of Conf. Record of the 4th ACM Symp. on Principles of Programming Languages (POPL '77). ACM Press, New York (1977) 238–252
8. Cousot, P., Cousot, R.: Systematic design of program analysis frameworks. Proc. of Conf. Record of the 6th ACM Symp. on Principles of Programming Languages (POPL '79). ACM Press, New York (1979) 269–282
9. Denning, D.E., Denning, P.: Certification of programs for secure information flow. Communications of the ACM, 20(7) (1977) 504–513
10. Focardi, R., Gorrieri, R.: A classification of security properties for process algebras. Journal of Computer security, 3(1) (1995) 5–33
11. Focardi, R., Gorrieri, R.: Classification of security properties (part i: Information flow). R. Focardi and R. Gorrieri, editors, Foundations of Security Analysis and Design, volume 2171 of Lecture Notes in Computer Science. Springer-Verlag (2001)
12. Riccardo Focardi and Fabio Martinelli: A uniform approach for the definition of security properties. World Congress on Formal Methods (1) (1999) 794–813

13. Riccardo Focardi, Sabina Rossi, and Andrei Sabelfeld: Bridging language-based and process calculi security. FoSSaCS (2005) 299–315
14. Giacobazzi, R., Mastroeni, I.: Abstract non-interference: Parameterizing non-interference by abstract interpretation. Proc. of the 31st Annual ACM SIGPLAN-SIGACT Symposium on Principles of Programming Languages (POPL '04). ACM-Press, NY (2004) 186–197
15. Goguen, J.A., Meseguer, J.: Security policies and security models. Proc. IEEE Symp. on Security and Privacy. IEEE Computer Society Press (1982) 11–20
16. Kohei Honda, Vasco Thudichum Vasconcelos, and Nobuko Yoshida: Secure information flow as typed process behaviour. ESOP (2000) 180–199
17. Hunt, S., Mastroeni., I.: The per model of abstract non-interference. Proc. of The 12th Internat. Static Analysis Symp. (SAS'05), Lecture Notes in Computer Science. Springer-Verlag (2005) To appear
18. Joshi, R., Leino, K.R.M.: A semantic approach to secure information flow. Science of Computer Programming, 37 (2000) 113–138
19. Laud, P.: Semantics and program analysis of computationally secure information flow. In Programming Languages and Systems, 10th European Symp. On Programming, ESOP, volume 2028 of *Lecture Notes in Computer Science*, Springer-Verlag (2001) 77–91
20. Mantel, H., Sabelfeld, A.: A unifying approach to the security of distributed and multi-threaded programs. Journal of Computer Security, 11(4) (2003) 615–676
21. Milner, R.: Communication and Concurrency. Prentice-Hall, Inc., Englewood Cliffs, New Jersey (1989)
22. Sabelfeld, A., Myers, A.C.: Language-based information-flow security. IEEE J. on selected ares in communications, 21(1) (2003) 5–19
23. Sabelfeld, A., Sands, D.: A PER model of secure information flow in sequential programs. Higher-Order and Symbolic Computation, 14(1) (2001) 59–91
24. Sabelfeld, A., Sands, D.: Dimensions and principles of declassification. Proc. of 18th IEEE Computer Security Foundations Workshop (CSFW-18). IEEE Comp. Soc. Press (2005)
25. Skalka, C., Smith, S.: Static enforcement of security with types. ICFP'00. ACM Press, New York (2000) 254–267
26. Volpano, D.: Safety versus secrecy. Proc. of the 6th Static Analysis Symp. (SAS'99), volume 1694 of Lecture Notes in Computer Science. Springer-Verlag (1999) 303–311
27. Volpano, D., Smith, G., Irvine, C.: A sound type system for secure flow analysis. Journal of Computer Security, 4(2,3) (1996) 167–187
28. Zanotti, M.: Security typings by abstract interpretation. Proc. of The 9th Internat. Static Analysis Symp. (SAS'02), volume 2477 of *Lecture Notes in Computer Science*. Springer-Verlag (2002) 360–375
29. Zdancewic, S., Myers, A.C.: Robust declassification. Proc. of the IEEE Computer Security Foundations Workshop. IEEE Computer Society Press (2001) 15–23

Detection of Illegal Information Flow

Alexander Grusho[1], Alexander Kniazev[2], and Elena Timonina[1]

[1] Russian State University for Humanity,
25 Kirovogradskaya, Moscow, Russian Federation
aaotee@mail.infotel.ru, eltimon@yandex.ru
[2] Russian Academy of Sciences Lebedev Institute of Precise Mechanics and
Computer Technology, 51 Leninsky Prospekt, Moscow, Russian Federation
avk@ipmce.ru

Abstract. Several types of statistical covert channels that break the informational system security policy ensuring a reliable information transfer between hostile agents can be detected by a competent warden. We introduce[1] the basic detection technique and analyze the conditions under which the warden with limited resources can perform his task successfully.

1 Introduction

Since [4] many papers dealing with statistical profiles of normal behavior in intrusion detection techniques have been published. Some methods proposed can be used as well for analysis of steganography methods or covert channels. We investigate the means to detect covert channels build up by hostile agents within an informational system. We assume that such covert channels will exploit for secure transmission a manipulation of the probability distribution parameters of the sent message sequence. We think that the most difficult problem here is to establish the proper correspondence between the reliability of analysis results and adequacy the chosen model of the message sequence probability distribution. In many cases a probabilistic description of informational system extremely simplifies the system behavior. Natural dependencies in message sequences are eliminated by the necessity to calculate probabilities.

The problem of mathematical exposure of data hiding was discussed in [1]. This work also pointed to existence of problem of adequate mathematical model choice. In [1] reasons were presented in the terms of Shannon entropies which suppose memoryless channels or channels with restricted memory. Usage of such models is a serious simplification of real command flow structure from one computer to another computer, for example from task manager of GRID to the computer where problems are solved. The main point of our paper is the research of data sequence from task control computer to the computer where tasks are solved. Adversary chances to manipulate this data sequence seem to be very limited. Adversary can use different dependencies. But he tries to use them without

---

[1] This work was supported by the Russian Foundation for Basic Research, grant 04-01-00089.

V. Gorodetsky, I. Kotenko, and V. Skormin (Eds.): MMM-ACNS 2005, LNCS 3685, pp. 235–244, 2005.

a define knowledge about the existence of such dependencies at the moment of transmission. It produces very complex probability models.

We use the term "system" in several senses. We think that the context determines the sense of the term "system" everywhere in the paper. The main sense of the term "system" means that there is a generator of data sequence from the task control computer to the computer where tasks are solved. This data sequence is unidirectional. Sometimes we say about computer systems to point that data generator in the task control computer is a complex system where independent hardware/software adversary agent can function besides task computation. The same can be said about the computer where tasks are solved.

We analyze the system with infinite sequences of messages and show that the final results of analysis are almost independent of the probability model. The word "almost" means that we need to have a probability measure of normal behavior being perpendicular to the probability measure of a covert channel. This assumption seems to be quite natural when we are dealing with the usage of statistical methods in signal detection. We prove also that under certain conditions the warden can construct consistent tests for covert channel detection. If the warden's capacities are limited we examine the possibilities for the warden to detect a covert transmission when a method of data hiding is known.

Likewise ideas were investigated in intrusion detection models, for example in [2,5]. But intrusion detection demands the quickest reaction to an attack. That means that the decision should be based on the shortest trace of entrance data. There are a lot of traces that should be considered as input of intrusion detection automaton. There is no decision rule that produces good detection of intrusion and a few false alarms. This fact is well known in mathematical statistics as the problem of large amount of short samples and also as detection of rare events in the sequence of homogeneous samples [3]. The best interpretation of this problem for intrusion detection systems is presented in [2]. We consider the problem which is likewise but different from intrusion detection. Warden can permit covert transmission to get enough information for proving covert channel existence (data hiding). Warden's problem consists of knowledge absence about a data hiding method. That means that he knows hypothesis H_0 but doesn't know alternatives. Our work solves theoretical problems and helps to understand weaknesses of statistical covert channels. It uses probability models and methods. That is why we cannot simultaneously consider construction of the practical tools for the warden. Nevertheless the proof of the existence of the consistent test is constructive. The hardness of the problem is to be researched.

The paper is structured as follows. In section 2 the proof of existence of a consistent test for hidden transfer detection is presented. Section 3 specifies conditions for the warden with the limited resources to detect a covert transmission. Section 4 presents the conclusions.

2   Existence of Consistent Tests

In the paper we analyze the simplest case of the system which consists of two computers connected by the only unidirectional link S.

Consider two computer systems KA and KB connected by link S. Let X, $X < \infty$, be a set of all possible messages, which can be sent from KA to KB through S. We describe the informational stream from KA to KB with a random infinite sequence of messages taken from X. Elements of any sequence are numbered with natural numbers N. Denote a sequence space: $\{\alpha = (x_{i_1}, x_{i_2}, ..., x_{i_n}, ...), \ x_{i_n} \in X\} = X^\infty$. Let $I_n(x_{i_1}, x_{i_2}, ..., x_{i_n}, ...)$ be an elementary cylindrical set in X^∞ and $\mathcal{A}$ be a minimal σ-algebra, which is generated by all cylindrical sets. Let

$$\{P_{0,t_1,...t_n}(x_{t_1}, x_{t_2}, ..., x_{t_n})\} - \tag{1}$$

be a consistent family of probability distributions on cylindrical sets. Then there is the only probability measure P_0 on measurable space $(X^\infty, \mathcal{A})$, generated by (1) which describes the normal behavior of the system. Imagine that adversary hardware/software agent KA' functions independently in computer system KA and tries to send illegally a message to his partner KB' in KB through the link S. It is not allowed and they need a covert channel [7] on the base of the legal transmission from KA to KB. We characterize the existence of transmission from KA' in legal traffic with a consistent family of probability distributions on cylindrical sets of X^∞

$$\{P_{1,t_1,...t_n}(x_{t_1}, x_{t_2}, ..., x_{t_n})\}, \tag{2}$$

which generates the only probability measure P_1 on measurable space $(X^\infty, \mathcal{A})$. When seeing the traffic from KA to KB to detect the signal from KA' agent KB' should test a hypothesis $H_0 : \{P_{0,t_1,...t_n}\}$ versus an alternative $H_1 : \{P_{1,t_1,...t_n}\}$.

Definition 1. There is a statistical covert channel from KA' to KB' in S if and only if measures P_0 and P_1 are mutually perpendicular [6]. That is $\exists A_0, \exists A_1, \ A_0, A_1 \in \mathcal{A}, \ A_0 \cap A_1 = \emptyset$,

$$P_0(X^\infty \setminus A_0) = 0, \ P_1(X^\infty \setminus A_1) = 0.$$

If P_0 and P_1 are mutually perpendicular then there exists a consistent testing of H_0 versus alternative H_1.

Considering Warden existence define a set of alternatives H_{11} instead of the single alternative H_1. It consists of all probability measures $\{P_{1\theta}, \theta \in \Theta\}$ where each $P_{1\theta}$ is perpendicular to P_0 (Θ is an arbitrary parameterization of alternatives in H_{11}). Let examine an existence of a consistent testing of H_0 versus alternatives H_{11}.

To prove an existence of the consistent tests we should consider more complicated model. It is convenient to see the finite set X as a topological space where every point is an open set and a closed set simultaneously. Then every subset of X is an open set and a closed set. Topological space X^∞ is a Tychonoff product [6], if its basis of open sets consists of cylindrical sets of X^∞. The topological space X is a separable space and compactum. Then the space X^∞ is compactum and Baire σ-algebra [6] on X^∞ equals to σ-algebra $\mathcal{A}$ [6]. Let us define a Borel

σ-algebra $\boldsymbol{A}$ on topological space X^∞. If P_0 and $\{P_{1\theta}, \theta \in \Theta\}$ are Baire measures [6] on compactum X^∞ then for each of them exists the only continuation [6] of the probability measure on $(X^\infty, \boldsymbol{A})$. As a result we can consider P_0 and $\{P_{1\theta}, \theta \in \Theta\}$ to be defined on $(X^\infty, \boldsymbol{A})$. From perpendicularity for every $\theta \in \Theta$
$$\exists A_0(\theta), \ \exists A_1(\theta), \ A_0(\theta), A_1(\theta) \in \mathcal{A}, \ A_0(\theta) \cap A_1(\theta) = \emptyset,$$

$$P_0(X^\infty \setminus A_0(\theta)) = 0, \ P_1(X^\infty \setminus A_1(\theta)) = 0.$$

It is easy to see that perpendicular measures on $(X^\infty, \mathcal{A})$ are perpendicular on $(X^\infty, \boldsymbol{A})$.

If we suppose that for every $\theta \in \Theta$ the set $A_0(\theta) \in \boldsymbol{A}$ and $A_0(\theta)$ is a closed set in Tychonoff product then the set

$$A_0 = \bigcap_{\theta \in \Theta} A_0(\theta)$$

is closed. Consequently, the set A_0 and $X^\infty \setminus A_0$ are measurable sets in $\boldsymbol{A}$.

Tychonoff product X^∞ is a topological space with countable basis. Then [8] a support S of the measure P_0 on $(X^\infty, \boldsymbol{A})$ exists, i.e. $S = \bigcap F$, where intersection of sets is such that every F is closed, $P_0(F) = 1$ and $P_0(S) = 1$. As for every $\theta \in \Theta$ we have $P_0(A_0(\theta)) = 1$ and $A_0(\theta)$ is closed, then

$$A_0 = \bigcap_{\theta \in \Theta} A_0(\theta) \supseteq \bigcap F = S.$$

As a result $P_0(A_0)) = 1$.

As every subset in X is closed then every cylindrical set is also closed.

We have already proved that if P_0 is perpendicular in $(X^\infty, \mathcal{A})$ to all $P_{1\theta}$, $A_0(\theta)$ is closed for $\theta \in \Theta$, then there is a measurable A_0 of $\boldsymbol{A}$ that for every $\theta \in \Theta$ $A_0 \cap A_1(\theta) = \emptyset$ and $P_0(X^\infty \setminus A_0) = 0$.

Let $B_1, B_2, \ldots$ be a decreasing sequence of cylindrical sets in which B_n is defined by all possible vectors from X^n, standing on as the first n elements of the sequences of A_0. Then

$$\lim_{n \to \infty} B_n = B.$$

It is clear that $A_0 \subseteq B$. We prove that $B \subseteq A_0$. Let $\omega \in B$. Then for every n the set $A(n)$, $A(n) \subseteq A_0$, is defined as a set of all sequences in A_0 for which their first n elements coincide with the first n elements of ω. One can see that $A(n) \neq \emptyset$ and $A(n)$, $n = 1, 2, \ldots$, is a decreasing sequence.

Projection π_n of the sequences of A_0 to the first n elements of the sequences is continuous as the inverse image of any open set D_n of X^n is the set $(D_n \times X^\infty) \cap A_0$. This set is open in topological space A_0 and closed in Tychonoff product X^∞. Then the inverse image of any closed set is closed in X^∞ and $\pi_n^{-1}(\omega_n) = A(n)$ - is a closed set in X^∞, where $\pi_n(\omega) = \omega_n$. Then

$$A = \bigcap_{n=1}^{\infty} A(n)$$

is closed set in X^∞ and ω is a limiting point of A in X^∞. It follows $\omega \in A$. We proved $B \subseteq A_0$. Then $B = A_0$. It follows that $X^\infty \setminus A_0$ and A_0 are elements of $\mathcal{A}$. We use that P_0 is continuous. Then

$$\lim_{n \to \infty} P_0(B_n) = 1.$$

We choose B_n and $P_0(X^\infty \setminus B_n) = 0$, so $X^\infty \setminus B_n$ can be taken as the set where we refuse to accept H_0. We have $A_0 \cap A_1(\theta) = \emptyset$ and

$$\lim_{n \to \infty} (X^\infty \setminus B_n) = X^\infty \setminus A_0.$$

Then for every $\theta \in \Theta$

$$\lim_{n \to \infty} P_{1\theta}(X^\infty \setminus B_n) = P_{1\theta}(X^\infty \setminus A_0) = 1.$$

We proved the following lemma.

Lemma 1. *If probability measures. P_0 and $P_{1\theta}$, $\theta \in \Theta$ are perpendicular on the measurable space $(X^\infty, \mathcal{A})$ and $A_0(\theta)$ are closed for all $\theta \in \Theta$ in Tychonoff product, then exist consistent tests of H_0 versus alternatives H_{11}.*

It can be proved that an arbitrary closed set can be represented as a limit of a decreasing sequence of cylindrical sets.

Lemma 1'. *If Probability Measures. P_0 and $P_{1\theta}$, $\theta \in \Theta$ are perpendicular on the measurable space $(X^\infty, \mathcal{A})$ and every $A_0(\theta)$ can be represented as a limit of a decreasing sequence of cylindrical sets, then exist consistent tests of H_0 versus alternatives H_{11}.*

3   Wardens with Limited Resources

Assume that the link S possesses an additional interface F for the warden U who can see either the whole sequence of messages in S or a part of it, depending on the properties of the new channel from KA to U which we denote $S(F)$. U has the task to find out whether a covert transmission from agent KA' to agent KB' takes place or not. Both U and KB' know P_0. KB' knows $P_{1\theta}$ as well, but U does not know $P_{1\theta}$. If U sees all messages in S, then lemma 1 shows when U can see the covert transmission from KA' to KB'.

Let us consider $S(F)$ that does not transmit to U the whole traffic of S, e.g. low level protocol messages are omitted in $S(F)$. Choose the set X_1, $X_1 \subseteq X$ and messages of X_1 are unseen to U. We have $X_0 \cup X_1 = X$, $X_0 \cap X_1 = \emptyset$. We have that messages of X_1 are taken away from the sequence of messages in S. As a result U sees the reduced sequence and draw his conclusions from it. Let $\mathcal{A}_1$ be σ-algebra which is generated by cylindrical sets of X_0^∞.

Let $\gamma \in X^\infty$. Denote by $\gamma \to \alpha, \beta$, $\gamma \in X^\infty$ the unique decomposition, where α is the subsequence of all elements of X_0 in γ, and β is the subsequence of all elements of X_1 in γ. One of the sequences α or β may be empty.

Denote $\widetilde{X} = \{\gamma : \gamma \rightarrow \alpha, \beta, \; \alpha \in X_0^\infty, \; \beta \in X_1^\infty\}$. Then $\Re = \{\widetilde{X} \cap A, A \in \mathcal{A}\}$ is σ-algebra on $\widetilde{X}$.

We can assume that only sequences from $\widetilde{X}$ are transmitted through S. Otherwise the warden sees too little or almost everything (this case has been discussed above in lemma 1). Then $S(F)$ defines a function $F : \; \widetilde{X} \rightarrow X_0^\infty$ the following way. If $\gamma \in \widetilde{X}$ and $\gamma \rightarrow \alpha, \beta$, then $F(\gamma) = \alpha$. Let KA' sends a covert message to KB' if it generates $\gamma \in \widetilde{X}$ using probability measure P_1 on $(\widetilde{X}, \Re)$ which is perpendicular to P_0. If F is $(\Re, \mathcal{A}_1)$ - measurable function then it defines two probability measures on $(X_0^\infty, \mathcal{A}_1)$:

$$\forall B \in \mathcal{A}_1, \; P_0'(B) = P_0(F^{-1}(B)), \; P_1'(B) = P_1(F^{-1}(B)).$$

Here P_0' is known to U and P_1' is unknown to U. But if P_0' and P_1' are perpendicular then since conditions of lemma 1 are satisfied, a consistent test to find the hidden message may exist. The fact is reflected in the next definition.

Definition 2. Statistical covert channel from KA' to KB' can be identified in $S(F)$ by U if and only if F is $(\Re, \mathcal{A}_1)$ - measurable and P_0' and P_1' are perpendicular.

To prove that F is $(\Re, \mathcal{A}_1)$ - measurable we investigate sets $F^{-1}(C)$, $C \in \mathcal{A}_1$.

Definition 3. For $\alpha \in X_0^\infty$, $\beta \in X_1^\infty$, we define an interleaved product of α and β as

$$\alpha \otimes \beta = \{\gamma : \gamma \rightarrow \alpha, \beta, \; \gamma \in X^\infty\}.$$

Definition 4. For $\alpha \in X_0^\infty$ an interleaved product of α and X_1^∞ is

$$\alpha \otimes X_1^\infty = \bigcup_{\beta \in X_1^\infty} \{\alpha \otimes \beta\}.$$

Definition 5. For $\in \mathcal{A}_1$ an interleaved product of and X_1^∞ is

$$C \otimes X_1^\infty = \bigcup_{\alpha \in C} \{\alpha \otimes X_1^\infty\}, \; C \neq \emptyset, \text{ or } C \otimes X_1^\infty = \emptyset, \text{ if } C = \emptyset.$$

The usefulness of the interleaved product is demonstrated by the following lemma.

Lemma 2. $\forall C \in \mathcal{A}_1, \; F^{-1}(C) = C \otimes X_1^\infty$.

Proof. If $C \neq \emptyset$ and $\gamma \in F^{-1}(C)$, then $\gamma \in \widetilde{X}$. Then there are the only $\alpha \in X_0^\infty$, $\beta \in X_1^\infty$ that $\gamma \rightarrow \alpha, \beta$, and $F(\gamma) = \alpha$. That means $\alpha \in C$. Then $\alpha \otimes \beta \subseteq C \otimes X_1^\infty$ and $F^{-1}(C) \subseteq C \otimes X_1^\infty$. If $C \neq \emptyset$ and $\gamma \in C \otimes X_1^\infty$, $C \in \mathcal{A}_1$, then by definitions 4 and 5 there are $\alpha \in C$ and $\beta \in X_1^\infty$, that $\gamma \in \alpha \otimes \beta$. Then $\gamma \rightarrow \alpha, \beta$, and $F(\gamma) = \alpha$. That means $F^{-1}(C) \supseteq C \otimes X_1^\infty$. That completes the proof.

Now we take an advantage from the fact that if the inverse image of any elementary cylindrical set of $\mathcal{A}_1$ belongs to $\Re$, then the inverse image of any set of $\mathcal{A}_\infty$ belongs to $\Re$. Let $C_n = (x_{i_1}, ... x_{i_n}) \times X_0^\infty$, $x_{i_j} \in X_0$, $j = 1, ..., n$, be an elementary cylindrical set of A_1. Denote $V_{k,n}$, $k \geq n$, a set of all vectors $(z_1, ..., z_k) \in X^k$, where $x_{i_1}, ...x_{i_n}$ is the sequence of all elements of X_0. It is clear that $V_{k,n} \times X^\infty$ is a cylindrical set of A.

Lemma 3. *If $C_n = (x_{i_1}, ...x_{i_n}) \times X_0^\infty$, $x_{i_j} \in X_0$, $j = 1, ..., n$, is an elementary cylindrical set of A_1, then*

$$C_n \otimes X_1^\infty = \bigcup_{k \geq n} \{V_{k,n} \otimes X^\infty\} \cap \tilde{X}.$$

Proof. By definition $C_n \otimes X_1^\infty \subseteq \tilde{X}$. Let $\gamma \in C_n \otimes X_1^\infty$, $\gamma \to \alpha, \beta$, $\alpha \in X_0^\infty$, $\beta \in X_1^\infty\}$, and α is represented as $\alpha = x_{i_1}, ...x_{i_n}, \alpha'$, where α' is a sequence of X_0^∞. Let $(z_1, ..., z_k)$, $k \geq n$, are the first k elements of γ, where $x_{i_1}, ...x_{i_n}$ is the sequence of all elements of X_0. Then $(z_1, ..., z_k) \in V_{k,n}$, and $\gamma \in V_{k,n} \times X^\infty$. That is why

$$\gamma \in \bigcup_{k \geq n} \{V_{k,n} \otimes X^\infty\} \cap \tilde{X}.$$

This is proof of

$$C_n \otimes X_1^\infty \subseteq \bigcup_{k \geq n} \{V_{k,n} \otimes X^\infty\} \cap \tilde{X}.$$

Prove the inverse implication of events. If $\gamma \in \tilde{X}$ and

$$\gamma \in \bigcup_{k \geq n} \{V_{k,n} \otimes X^\infty\} \cap \tilde{X},$$

then there is a set $V_{k,n}$, that the first k elements $(z_1, ..., z_k)$ of γ are in $V_{k,n}$ and all elements of X_0 in $(z_1, ..., z_k)$ are from the vector $x_{i_1}, ...x_{i_n}$. If $\gamma \in \tilde{X}$, then $\gamma \to \alpha, \beta$, $\alpha \in X_0^\infty$, $\beta \in X_1^\infty$ and the first n elements of α form the vector $x_{i_1}, ...x_{i_n}$. Then $\alpha \in C_n$, and $\gamma \in C_n \otimes X_1^\infty$. Here we proved

$$C_n \otimes X_1^\infty \supseteq \bigcup_{k \geq n} \{V_{k,n} \otimes X^\infty\} \cap \tilde{X},$$

and lemma is proved.

Corollary 1. $C_n \otimes X_1^\infty = A \cap \tilde{X}$, $A \in A$.

Proof. As $V_{k,n} \otimes X^\infty$ is a cylindrical set of A then

$$A = \bigcup_{k \geq n} \{V_{k,n} \otimes X^\infty\} \in A.$$

Corollary 2. $\forall C \in A_1$, $C \otimes X_1^\infty \in \Re$.

Theorem 1. *Function F is $(\Re, A_1)$ - measurable.*

Proof. The proof follows from lemmas 2 and 3 and corollary 2.

Let σ-algebra $\Im$ be generated by F. From lemma 2 we get that $\Im = \{C \otimes X_1^\infty, C \in \mathcal{A}_1\}$.

The next theorem shows how to use such a presentation of $\Im$. Let σ-algebra $\Im$ be generated by an arbitrary $(\Re, \mathcal{A}_1)$ - measurable function F, $\Im \subseteq \Re$.

Theorem 2. *Probability measures P_0' and P_1', which are generated by an arbitrary $(\Re, \mathcal{A}_1)$ - measurable function F, are perpendicular if and only if there are A_0 and A_1 of $\Im$, that $A_0 \cap A_1 = \emptyset$,*

$$P_0(\widetilde{X} \setminus A_0) = 0, \; P_1(\widetilde{X} \setminus A_1) = 0.$$

Proof. 1) *Sufficiency.* If A_0 and A_1 of $\Im$, then there are $B_0 \in \mathcal{A}_1$ and $B_1 \in \mathcal{A}_1$, that $A_0 = F^{-1}(B_0)$, $A_1 = F^{-1}(B_1)$. Then

$$P_0'(X_0^\infty \setminus B_0) = P_0(F^{-1}(X_0^\infty \setminus B_0)) = P_0(\widetilde{X} \setminus F^{-1}(B_0)) =$$

$$= P_0(\widetilde{X} \setminus A_0) = 0, P_1'(X_1^\infty \setminus B_1) = P_1(\widetilde{X} \setminus A_1) = 0.$$

It follows by definition $A_0 = F^{-1}(B_0)$, $A_1 = F^{-1}(B_1)$, $A_0 \cap A_1 = \emptyset$. Then $B_0 \cap B_1 = \emptyset$. The sufficiency is proved.

2) *Necessity.* If a statistical covert channel exists, then $B_0, B_1 \in \mathcal{A}_1, B_0 \cap B_1 = \emptyset$, $P_0'(X_0^\infty \setminus B_0) = 0$, $P_1'(X_0^\infty \setminus B_1) = 0$. Denote $F^{-1}(B_0) = A_0$, $F^{-1}(B_1) = A_1$. By definition

$$P_0(F^{-1}(X_0^\infty \setminus B_0)) = P_0(\widetilde{X} \setminus F^{-1}(B_0)) = 0,$$

$$P_1(F^{-1}(X_0^\infty \setminus B_1)) = P_1(\widetilde{X} \setminus F^{-1}(B_1)) = 0.$$

As far as $B_0 \cap B_1 = \emptyset$, then $F^{-1}(B_0) \cap F^{-1}(B_1) = \emptyset$. Consequently, there are A_0, A_1 of $\Im$, that $A_0 \cap A_1 = \emptyset$ and $P_0(X^\infty \setminus A_0) = 0$, $P_1(X^\infty \setminus A_1) = 0$. Theorem is proved.

According to definition 2 the theorem 2 states that U can detect the statistical covert channel from KA' to KB'.

Let us consider another case of $S(F)$, when the possibility of U to control the traffic in S is limited due to shortage of the computational resources or/and memory space available. As a result U has to draw his conclusions from some subsequences of messages.

Let μ be a binary sequence with an infinite number of 1 and an infinite number of 0, γ is the sequence of messages from KA to KB. U uses μ to make sampling in γ. Every element in γ is taken away if it is in the position, where 0 is in the sequence μ. Then U sees the sequence $\delta = F_\mu(\gamma)$, where $F_\mu : X^\infty \to X^\infty$.

Lemma 4. *For arbitrary sequence function F_μ is $(\mathcal{A}, \mathcal{A})$ - measurable.*

Proof. Let $B_n = (\delta_1, ..., \delta_n) \times X^\infty$ be an elementary cylindrical set of $\mathcal{A}$. Then $F_\mu^{-1}(B_n)$ is a cylindrical set of $\mathcal{A}$, where X^s there is between δ_i and δ_{i+1}. Here s denotes the number of binary zeros between i-th and $(i+1)$-th binary one position in μ. Lemma is proved.

Then for every μ the function F_μ generates probability measures P_0' and P_1' on $(X^\infty, \mathcal{A})$.

Theorem 3. *Measures P_0' and P_1' are perpendicular then $\exists A_0$, $\exists A_1$, A_0, $A_1 \in \mathcal{A}$, $A_0 \cap A_1 = \emptyset$,*

$$P_0(X^\infty \setminus A_0) = 0, \; P_1(X^\infty \setminus A_1) = 0,$$

and $F_\mu(A_0) \cap F_\mu(A_1) = \emptyset$.

Proof. The proof follows from the proof of the theorem 2.

Example. If P_0' and P_1' are not perpendicular then the warden U cannot detect a covert transmission reliably. Let μ be an arbitrary binary sequence and $P_0(\omega) = 1$, $P_1(\omega') = 1$, $\omega \neq \omega'$. Assume $F_\mu(\omega) = F_\mu(\omega')$. Despite P_0 and P_1 are perpendicular there is no consistent test for U to identify a hidden message from KA' to KB'. That means U can discover the hidden message if the agents do not use such P_1, that $\forall A_0$, $\forall A_1$, A_0, $A_1 \in \mathcal{A}$, $A_0 \cap A_1 = \emptyset$, if $P_0(X^\infty \setminus A_0) = 0$, $P_1(X^\infty \setminus A_1) = 0$, then $F_\mu(A_0) \cap F_\mu(A_1) \neq \emptyset$.

4   Conclusions

The obtained results show that the manipulation of the probability distribution of the messages in communicational link in order to send hidden messages can be revealed. The warden should know well enough the normal properties of the communication link and its probabilistic characteristics, e.g. in lemma 1'. Then it is possible to construct a consistent test for detection of hidden message. That is why it is a problem to make a statistical covert channel invisible for the warden. Even if the warden's resources are limited the detection of a hidden message most often can be done reliable enough.

We plan to research the necessary conditions to detect hidden transmission by the warden.

We didn't touch the problem whether the construction of a consistent test is a hard task. Most probably it is.

References

1. Anderson, R.J., Petitcolas, F.A.P.: On the Limits of Steganography. IEEE Journal of Selected Areas in Communications, 16(4) (May 1998) 474–481
2. Axelson S.: The Base-Rate Fallacy and its Implications for the Difficulty Of Intrusion Detection. Proc. of the 6th Conference on Computer and Communications Security (November 1999)
3. Grusho A.: Consistent revelation conditions for rare events search a sample from the uniform distribution. In: Probabilistic problems of discrete mathematic. Moscow Institute of Electronic mechanical engineering (1987) (in Russian)
4. Denning, D.: An Intrusion Detection Model. Proceedings of the IEEE Symposium on Security and Privacy (May 1986) 119–131
5. Lee W., Xiang D.: Information-Theoretic Meaasures for Anomaly Detection. IEEE Symposium on Security and Privacy (2001) 130–143

6. Prokhorov, U.V, Rozanov, U.A.: Theory of probabilities. Science, Moscow (1973) (in Russian)
7. Timonina, E.E.: The covert channels (review). Jet Info, Vol. 14(114) (2002) 3–11 (in Russian)
8. Vaxania, N.N., Tarielidze, V.I., Chobanian, S.A..: Probability distributions in Banach spaces. Moscow (1985) (in Russian)

Towards More Controllable and Practical Delegation

Gang Yin[1], Huaimin Wang[1], Dianxi Shi[1], and Haiya Gu[2]

[1] Department of Computer Science,
National University of Defense Technology, Changsha, China
[2] Agricultural Bank of China, Hunan Branch, China
jack_nudt@yahoo.com.cn, fayecoolbaby@163.com

Abstract. Delegation is essential to the flexibility and scalability of trust management systems. But unrestricted delegation may result in privilege proliferation and breach the privacy of information systems. The delegation models of existing trust management systems can not avoid privilege transition, and being lack of effective constraints on delegation propagation, which may easily lead to privilege proliferation. In this paper, we propose a generalized constrained delegation model (GCDM), which uses *typed privileges* to control potential privilege transition, and restricts the propagation scope of delegation trees by a novel delegation constraint mechanism named *spacial constraints*. This paper also designs a rule-based trust management language named REAL05 to express the policies and semantics for GCDM. REAL05 supports flexible delegation policies while can control the potential privilege proliferation in subsequent delegations. Comprehensive samples and simulation results show that our approach is more controllable and practical.

1 Introduction

Trust management (TM) is a promising approach to access control in environments where entities in different administrative domains want to share resources. Delegation is the core mechanism for transferring trust and authorization in TM systems, which greatly improves the flexibility and scalability of distributed access control. However, delegation may also easily lead to "privilege proliferation" and breach the privacy of information systems.

One important reason for privilege proliferation in TM systems is the transition between management-type permissions (MTP) and access-type permissions (ATP) during delegation process. B. S. Firozabadi etc have pointed out that privileges of these two types of privileges are essentially different [3], and use "authority" and "permission" to denote them respectively. In most TM systems however, delegation of MTP and ATP are expressed by the same sort of policy items, such as "condition" field in Keynote [8], "authorization tag" in SPKI [4], "base-atom" in DL [11], etc. For example, "read(file1)" and "isMember(?S, orgA)" are base-atoms in DL and used to express ATP and MTP respectively. Entities in these systems entitled with MTP may obtain the corresponding ATP simply by self-authorization; and the entities holding ATP are often allowed to re-delegate the ATP to others, which means they have been

V. Gorodetsky, I. Kotenko, and V. Skormin (Eds.): MMM-ACNS 2005, LNCS 3685, pp. 245–258, 2005.

inherently entitled with the corresponding MTP, and may lead to more speedy proliferation of privileges. This kind of privilege model also leads to inefficiency in specifying policies of more "pure" delegation of MTP or ATP, such as security administration policies in decentralized authorization and delegation of access capabilities in
proxy-based authentication systems [2, 6, 17].

The other reason for privilege proliferation in TM systems is inefficient control on
privilege propagation. Two typical constraints on delegation in existing TM systems
are boolean control and integer control. Boolean control includes two policies: no
further delegation or unrestricted delegation. SPKI [4] and RT [12] support this kind
of constraint. DL [11] supports integer control over delegation depth. Integer control
provides more flexibility than boolean control, but it supposes that the trust relationships are transitive within the upper-bound of delegation depth, which is too optimistic and may lead to undesired propagation of privileges. DL also supports constraints
on delegation width, but it has to use a temp key to sign the assistant policies to enforce such constraint.

In this paper, we propose a more controllable and practical delegation model
named GCDM (Generalized Constrained Delegation Model) to restrict the potential
proliferation of privileges during delegation while at the same time keep the inherent
strengths of delegation policies. GCDM uses typed privileges to control potential
privilege transition, and restricts the propagation scope of delegation trees by a novel
delegation constraint structure named spacial constraint. A rule-based policy language
is also introduced to specify the core policies and semantic rules for GCDM. The rest
of this paper is organized as follows. Section 2 defines the main components of
GCDM including a basic model, typed privileges and typed delegations, spacial constraint model and its control granularity. In section 3, we describe the syntax and
semantics of a rule-based specification language designed for GCDM. Implement
issues and simulation results are discussed in section 4. Section 5 give further discussion of related work and section 6 concludes this paper.

2   Generalized Constrained Delegation

In this section, we firstly define the basic and generalized part of our model. Then we
extend its privilege model and constraint model to support more controllable and
practical delegation and authorization policies.

2.1   Basic Model

The basic idea of delegation is that one entity delegates its privilege to another entity
to perform functions controlled by the privilege on behalf of the former. The core
components of GCDM are defined as follows.

Definition 1 (Authorization System). An authorization system (AS) is a 5-tuple (E,
P, F, $\ni$, $\propto$), where E, P and F are sets of all entities, privileges and functions in the
system respectively; $\ni$ and $\supset$ are relations where $\ni \subseteq E \times P$, $\propto \subseteq P \times F$. Given $e \in E$, $p \in P$
and $f \in F$, $e \ni p$ means e is entitled with p; $p \propto f$ means p controls f; e can perform the
function f iff $\exists p \in P$ ($e \ni p$ and $p \propto f$).

Definition 2 (Delegation Tree and Delegation Path). A delegation tree is a 5-tuple (p, dr, de, MD, DT), where $p \in P$, $dr \in E$, $de \in E$, $MD \subseteq E$, $DT \subseteq E$. p, dr, de, MD, DT are called delegated privilege, delegator, direct delegatee, set of mediate delegatees and set of delegation targets respectively. A delegation path in delegation tree (p, dr, de, MD, DT) is denoted as: $[dr \rightarrow de^{[0..n]} \rightarrow dt]_p$, where $n \geq 0$, $de_0 = de$, $de^{[0..n]} = de_0 \rightarrow de_1 \rightarrow \ldots \rightarrow de_n$, $de_i \in MD(i=1...n)$, $dt \in DT$. Here n is called *delegation depth* (n plus 1 is equal to the value of delegation depth defined in some TM systems such as DL [11]).

Fig.1 illustrates a sample delegation tree. When dr initiates a delegation by delegating p to de, de may re-delegate p to entities in MD, such as de_1, de_2, ..., de_5. de and the entities in MD may perform the functions controlled by p on the target entity in DT, such as dt_1 and dt_2. "$dr \rightarrow de \rightarrow de_1 \rightarrow de_3 \rightarrow dt$" is a delegation path whose delegation depth is 2.

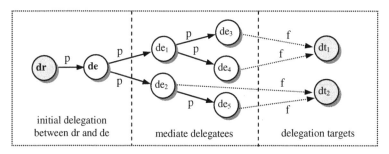

initial delegation between dr and de | mediate delegatees | delegation targets

Fig. 1. A Sample Delegation Tree

Definition 3 (Constraint Structure). A constraint structure is a 4-tuple $(DP, DC, \supset, \Rightarrow)$, where DP and DC are sets of delegation paths and delegation constraints respectively, $\supset$ and $\Rightarrow$ are relations where $\supset \subseteq DC \times DC$, $\Rightarrow \subseteq DP \times DC$. Given $c_1, c_2 \in DC$, $c_1 \supset c_2$ means c_1 *dominates* c_2. Given $dp \in DP$ and $c \in DC$, $dp \Rightarrow c$ means dp *satisfies* c. $\Rightarrow$ is monotonic: Given $c_1, c_2 \in DC$ and $c_1 \supset c_2$, if $dp \Rightarrow c_1$ then $dp \Rightarrow c_2$.

Given $dp = [dr \rightarrow de^{[0..n]} \rightarrow dt]_p \in DP$ and $c_i \in DC(i=0...n)$, we say dp is a *valid delegation path* iff $dp_i \Rightarrow c_i(i=0...n)$, where $dp_i = dr_i \rightarrow de^{[i..n]} \rightarrow dt$ $(i=0...n)$, $dr_0 = dr$, $dr_i = de_{i-1}(i=1...n)$, c_i is the delegation constraint specified by dr_i. If $dp = [dr \rightarrow de^{[0..n]} \rightarrow dt]_p$ is a valid delegation path and $dr \ni p$, then $de_n \ni p$ and de_n can perform function f, where $f \in F$ and $p \propto f$.

2.2 Typed Privileges

The privilege of the authorization system defined in section 2.1 is abstract and has no practical meaning. In this section, we reify it into two typical MTP and ATP, i.e., authority and capability, to express more specific authorization policies. The two types of privileges are strongly connected with one basic type of privilege named permission.

Definition 4 (Permission, Authority and Capability). PM is the set of all permissions, which are the privileges of accessing resources, such as read/write a file, invokes the functions of an object, etc. A is the set of all authorities, which are the privileges of managing the authorization of permissions in PM. C is the set if all capabilities, which are the privileges of exercising the activated permissions in PM. An entity must log on a server to activate some permission before it can obtain its capability.

Two more practical authorization systems (see def. 1) can be derived from above typed privilege model: (1) Management-level AS is a 5-tuple (E, A, E×PM, ∋, ∝), where A and E×PM are instances for P and F in AS. Given e∈E, a∈A, p∈PM, f=(e', pm)∈E×PM=F, if e∋a and a∝f=(e', pm), then e can perform f, i.e., e can perform the authorization of pm to entity e'; (2) Access-level AS is a 5-tuple (E, C, E×PM, ∋, ∝), where C and E×PM are instances for P and F in AS. Given e∈E, c∈C, p∈PM, f=(e', pm)∈E×PM=F, if e∋c and c∝f=(e', pm), then e can perform f, i.e., e can perform the access to resources identified by pm on entity e'.

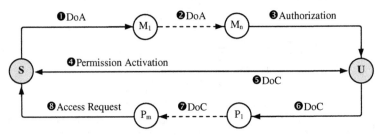

Fig. 2. Access Control Model based-on Typed Delegation

Delegation of authorities (DoA) and delegation of capabilities (DoC) can be used to construct access control models for widely distributed systems, as shown in fig. 2. S is a resource owner and wants to share resources with entity U across several administrative domains. In above access control model, S can make distributed authorization to U by DoA (❶❷) and direct authorization (❸). S can also enable proxy-based authentication for U by DoC (❺❻❼) and direct access request (❽). The path of DoA and the path of DoC are isolated by the process of permission activation (❹) on S requested by U. The policies for above scenarios will be further discussed and specified in section 3.3.

Permission activation is a basic mechanism for least privilege principles [9]. Here this mechanism is used to prevent the privilege transition: (1) before an entity can delegate its access permission (ATP) to another entity, it must activate the permission to obtain the capability from the server who is the source of the authority controlling the permission. Thus the privilege transition from ATP to MTP can be controlled by the server during activation. (2) on the other hand, if an entity entitled with some authority (MTP) authorizes a permission to an entity discretionally, then when the authorized entity activates the permission from the server, the server can check whether such activation should be allowed (so the transition from MTP to ATP can be controlled by the server).

In the paradigms of policy-based distributed systems management, privileges may be extended to responsibilities and obligations. Delegation of responsibilities and obligations are still hot problems in this area. One may reify GCDM to enforce the delegation policies for these paradigms. We will test these ideas in the future.

2.3 Spacial Constraint on Delegation

To restrict the privilege propagation in a delegation tree, the delegator can specify constraints from following aspects: (1) the scope of mediate delegatees in delegation tree; (2) the scope of delegation targets in delegation tree; (3) the valid time interval of all the delegation chains in the tree. The first two aspects care about the propagation scope of current delegation and called *spacial constraints*. The third aspect is called *temporal constraint*. This paper uses spacial constraints to enforce control on delegation.

Definition 5 (Spacial Constraint). The spacial constraint is a structure SC(*ds*, *dd*, *ts*), where SC is the type of the structure, and also denotes the set of all spacial constraints, $ds \subseteq E$, $dd \geq 0$ and $ts \subseteq E$ are attributes of the structure, and denotes the scope of mediate delegatees, upper-bound of delegation depth and the scope of delegation targets respectively. *ds* and *ts* are also called *trust scope* in our previous work [18]. Here the delegation depth is mainly used to avoid infinite delegation loops. The spacial constraint defines a kind of unitary control on delegation, as shown in fig.3-II.

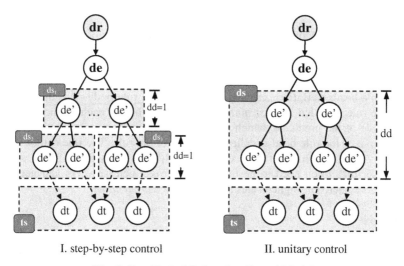

I. step-by-step control   II. unitary control

Fig. 3. Two Typical Delegation Control Model

The constraint structure defined in section 2.1 can be reified as (DP, SC, $\supset$, $\Rightarrow$). Here we can give more precise definition of the semantics for the relation $\supset$ and $\Rightarrow$:

$\supset$: Given sc_1, $sc_2 \in SC$, then $sc_1 \supset sc_2$ **iff** $(sc_1.ds \subseteq sc_2.ds) \land (sc_1.dd \leq sc_2.dd) \land (sc_1.ts \subseteq sc_2.ts)$.

$\Rightarrow$: Given $dp=[dr \rightarrow de^{[0..n]} \rightarrow dt]_p \in DP$, $sc \in SC$, then $dp \Rightarrow sc$ **iff** $(de_i \in sc.ds) \land (n \leq sc.dd) \land (dt \in sc.ts)$, where sc is specified by dr and i=1...n.

The delegator dr can specify spacial constraint when it begins a delegation to direct delegatee de, as shown in fig.3. In fact, dr can also specify constraints on each step of delegation, which is called step-by-step control, see fig.3-I. O. Bandmann etc adopted this kind of control in their delegation model [14]. The step-by-step control seems too detailed to be useful in practical systems and may raise much difficulty in constructing computation models [14].

According to the semantics of the relation ⇒ defined above, we can see that the spacial constraint adopts the unitary control model, as shown in fig.3-II. The unitary control model unifies the one-step constraint into more intuitionistic constraint and overcomes the deficiencies of step-by-step control, while still provides enough flexibility. Spacial constraint can be used both on DoA and DoC. Samples in section 4 will illustrate the advantages of such constraint model. The semantics of valid delegation path and relations of ⊃ and ⇒ will be defined by logic rules in section 3.

3   Rule-Based Policy Language

To validate the feasibility of our model, we design a policy specification language for GCDM named REAL05 (Role-based Extensible Authorization Language, 2005 Version). REAL05 is a declarative language based on Datalog^C [15], which can be used to specify policies as well as semantics.

Definition 6 (Rule). A rule in REAL05 takes the form of the following:

$$A.H \leftarrow A_1.B_1, A_2.B_2, \dots , A_n.B_n, \Psi,$$

where H, $B_1 \dots B_n$ are predicates with one or more parameters, A, $A_1, \dots A_n$ are entities. H is the rule head, $A_i.B_i$ (i=1…n) and Ψ constitute the rule body. Ψ is the constraint. If n=0, the rule is called a *constraint fact*. The entity before each predicate is called the *principle* of the predicate, which means the predicate is asserted by its principal. The principle of the rule head is called the *issuer* of the rule. The rule can be read as: to deduce A says H, we must deduce "A_1 says B_1", "A_2 says B_2", …, "A_n says B_n" and Ψ. The rules often need to be transferred across open networks and need to be signed by its issuer. The signed rules are often called *credentials*.

3.1   Syntax

REAL05 can specify authorization, delegation and constrained delegation policies. Table 1 shows the simplified syntax of REAL05. The undefined items such as ⟨user-defined-predicate⟩, ⟨entity⟩, ⟨name⟩, ⟨natural-number⟩ ⟨constant⟩ and ⟨var⟩ are user defined predicate name, entity, name of permission or role, natural number and variables respectively.

Privileges. The privileges in REAL05 include permission (5) and roles (6). Permissions have the same meaning as permissions defined in section 2.2. For example, **pm**(read, file-a) may represent the privilege to read the file named "file-a". The roles group related permissions together and can express more scalable policies. There are three types of roles in REAL05: dR, aR and sR.

Table 1. Core Syntax of REAL05

(1) Predicate Name ⟨pn⟩ ::= canRequest I canHold I canActivate I hasActivated IcanAdmin I canUse I ⟨user-defined-predicate⟩
(2) Predicate ⟨p⟩ ::= ⟨entity⟩.⟨pn⟩(⟨list of v⟩)
(3) Rule ⟨rule⟩ ::= ⟨p⟩. I ⟨p⟩ ← ⟨c⟩. I ⟨p⟩ ← ⟨list of p⟩. I ⟨p⟩ ← ⟨list of p⟩, ⟨c⟩.
(4) Query ⟨Query⟩ ::= ? ← ⟨p⟩.
(5) Permission ⟨pm⟩ ::= pm(⟨name⟩, ⟨list of var⟩)
(6) Role ⟨role⟩ ::= dR(⟨rv⟩) I aR(⟨rv⟩) I sR(⟨rv⟩)
(7) Role Variable ⟨rv⟩ ::= ⟨entity⟩, ⟨name⟩
(8) Parameter Vector ⟨v⟩ ::= ⟨constant⟩ I ⟨var⟩ I ⟨entity⟩ I ⟨permission⟩ I ⟨role⟩ I ⟨dc⟩
(9) List (macro) ⟨list of X⟩ ::= ⟨X⟩ I ⟨list of X⟩, ⟨list of X⟩
(10) Delegation Constraint ⟨dc⟩ ::= sc(⟨scope⟩, ⟨depth⟩, ⟨scope⟩) I ∅ I *
(11) Trust Scope ⟨scope⟩ ::= ⟨role⟩ I ⟨scope⟩ ∩ ⟨scope⟩ I {list of ⟨entity⟩} I { } I *
(12) Delegation Depth ⟨depth⟩ ::= ⟨natural-number⟩ I 0 I *
(14) Constraint ⟨c⟩ ::= ⟨e⟩ = ⟨e⟩ I ⟨e⟩ ≠ ⟨e⟩ I ⟨e⟩ ≤ ⟨e⟩ I ⟨e⟩ ≥ ⟨e⟩ I ⟨e⟩⊃⟨e⟩ I ⟨e⟩⊆⟨e⟩ I ⟨c⟩, ⟨c⟩
(15) Expression ⟨e⟩ ::= ⟨constant⟩ I ⟨var⟩ I ⟨dc⟩ I f(⟨list of var⟩) I ⟨e⟩ - ⟨e⟩ I ⟨e⟩ + ⟨e⟩ I ⟨e⟩ ∪ ⟨e⟩

- **dR** is a distributed role, e.g. **dR**(org, member) represents all the members in org. In the rest of this paper, roles denote distributed roles by default.
- **aR** is an administrative role, representing the authority defined in section 2.2, e.g. **aR**(org, member) is the administrative role for dR(org, member). Given a role dr, its administrative role is denoted as **aR**(dr).
- **sR** is a session role, representing the capability defined in section 2.2, e.g. sR(org, sid012) is the capability holding by the session identified by session ID "sid012". A user has to log on the server successfully before he can get a session role.

Delegation Constraint. The delegation constraint (10) is a logical term and defines the spacial constraint in section 2.3. Spacial constraint acts as parameters in predicates when specifying policies. ⟨scope⟩ and ⟨depth⟩ can be "*", which means no constraint. ⟨dc⟩ can be ∅, which is equivalent to the constant **sc**({ }, 0, *).

Constraint. The constraints (14) are composed of constraint expressions (15) and constraint predicates. The type of constants and variables in (15) can be integer, float, entity and set of entities. Constraint expression can also be delegation constraints and return values of functions. Constraint predicates include "=", "≠", "≤", "≥", "⊆" and "⊃", where "⊆" and "⊃" are binary predicates on entity sets and ⟨dc⟩ respectively.

Predicates. The predicates (2) are the policy items used to express authorization and delegation policies. REAL05 has six reserved predicates:

- x.canRequest(y, pm) means that x allows entity y to access the resources controlled by permission pm.
- x.canHold(dr, pm) means that x assigns role dr with permission pm.
- x.canActivate(y, dr) means that x allows entity y to activate the role dr, and y will be assigned with all the permissions hold by dr.
- x.hasActivated(y, dr) means that entity y has logged on x and activated the role dr successfully.

- x.canAdmin(y, ar, sc) means that x delegates the administrative role ar to entity y, where the delegation constraint sc is used to specify the special constraint on succeeding delegations initiated by y. The default value of sc is "∅". The predicate canAdmin is specifying DoA policies.
- x.canUse(y, sr, sc) means that x delegates the session role sr to entity y, where the delegation constraint sc is used to specify the special constraint on succeeding delegations initiated by y. The default value of sc is "∅". The predicate canUse is specifying DoC policies.

REAL05 also supports user defined predicates, which can be used to specify application dependent policies and constraints.

Rules. There are three kinds of rules in REAL05: policy rules, session rules and meta rules. (a) policy rules is the rules specified according to security requirements; (b) session rules are temporary rules within the context of a specific session. When the session is closed, its session rules are deleted; (c) meta rules are used to describe the general semantics that can not be expressed by policy rules and sessions rules.

3.2 Semantics

The semantics of REAL05 is defined by meta rules, as shown in Table 2. Meta-rules are used to describe rules with general purpose, such as the semantics of relations "⊃" and "⇒" defined in section 2.3.

Table 2. Meta Rules for REAL05 Semantics

[Meta Rules for Role-based Authorization]

① ?x.canRequest(?y, ?pm) ← ?x.canActivate(?y, dR(?x, ?n)), ?x.canHold(dR(?x, ?n), ?pm).

[Meta Rules for Delegation of Authority]

② ?x.doa(?y, ?ar, ?sc) ← ?x.canAdmin(?y, ?ar, ?sc'), ?sc ⊃ ?sc'.

③ ?x.doa(?z, aR(?x,?n), ?sc) ← ?y.canAdmin(?z, aR(?x, ?n), ?sc'), ?sc ⊃ ?sc', ?x.doa(?y, aR(?x,?n), sc({?z}∪?sc.ds, ?sc.dd+1, ?sc.ts)).

④ ?x.isMember(?z, dR(?x, ?n)) ← ?x.canActivate(?z, dR(?x, ?n)).

⑤ ?x.isMember(?z, dR(?x, ?n)) ← ?y.canActivate(?z,dR(?x, ?n)), ?x.doa(?y, aR(?x, ?n), sc({},0,{?z})).

[Meta Rules for Delegation of Capability]

⑥ ?x.doc(?y, ?sr, ?sc) ← ?x.canUse(?y, ?sr, ?sc'), ?sc ⊃ ?sc'.

⑦ ?x.doc(?z, sR(?x, ?s), ?sc) ← ?y.canUse(?z, sR(?x, ?s), ?sc'), ?sc ⊃ ?sc', ?x.doc(?y, sR(?x, ?s), sc({?z}∪?sc.ds, ?sc.dd+1, ?sc.ts)).

⑧ ?x.allowAccess(?y, ?pm) ← ?x.canRequest(?x, ?pm), doc(?x, ?y, sR(?x, ?s), sc({}, 0, {?x})).

[Meta Rules for Delegation Constraint Computation]

⑨ ?sc ⊃ ?sc' ← ?sc.ds ⊆ ?sc'.ds, ?sc.dd ≤ ?sc'.dd, ?sc.ts ⊆ ?sc'.ts.

REAL05 introduces four semantic predicates in meta rules: *isMember, doa, doc* and *allowAccess*, which are delegation-based extensions of predicates canActivate, canAdmin, canUse and canRequest respectively. The predicates *doa* and *doc* keep the status of delegation path within the delegation constraint structure of the last parameter, as shown by rules ③ and ⑦. The rule ⑨ expresses the semantics for constraint relation "⊃". The predicate "⊆" is used to check whether each entity in the left-side-parameter is belongs to the trust scope specified by right-side-parameter (also see its

Prolog implementation in section 4). During semantic inference, the left-side-parameter will be instantiated into a set of constant entities. The meaning of other meta rules in table 2 is easily read based on the introduction of predicates in section 3.1.

There are two kinds of queries need to be answered by the semantics of REAL05. The predicates in queries are *isMember* and *allowAccess* respectively. The query containing *isMember* will be raised when an entity tries to activate a role, and the query containing *allowAccess* will be raised when an entity tries to access resources.

Given a REAL05 rule set P, the computational complexity of P denotes the time needed to answer a given query Q based on P, i.e. $P \vdash Q$ or $P \not\vdash Q$. REAL05 is a subset of Datalog^C, its computational complexity lies on Datalog^C. The computational complexity of Datalog^C is closely connected with constraint domain it contains. The constraint domains that can be evaluated with safe Datalog in polynomial data complexity (PTIME) include: (1) equality constraints, order and inequality constraints over dense linear order domains [15], (2) linearly decomposable domain [13]. It's clear that REAL05 only contains these two constraint domains, and each rule in REAL05 has finite variables. Therefore we get the following result:

Proposition 1. Given a set of REAL05 rules P, its computational complexity is PTIME on size(P), where size(P) = $|P|*V$, $|P|$ is the number of the rules in P, V is the upper-bound of the sum of the variables in a rule.

3.3 Samples

A comprehensive example is introduced in this section to illustrate how REAL05 can be used to express more controllable delegation policies, both for DoA and DoC. The sample shares the same entity names and delegation paths in fig. 2.

Suppose S is an online digital library and wants to give 20% discount to the students of its cooperative universities. But these students must have papers indexed by S and can only download the discounted papers through the proxy servers of his/her certifying university. M_1 is a cooperative university of S. S only trusts M_1 and its branch campus to certify a student of M_1. M_n is one of the branch campuses of M_1. P_1 is a proxy server of M_1. U is a student of M_1 and studying at M_n. One of U's papers has been indexed by S. The above policies can be specified in REAL05 as follows.

    (1) **S.canHold(dR**(S, discount) , **pm**(download, 20%)).
    (2) **S.canActivate**(M_1, **dR**(S, co-university)).
    (3) **S.canActivate**(?x, **dR**(S, contributor)) ← **S**.author-of-indexed-papers(?x).

The rules (1, 2, 3) are basic authorization policies defined by S. The predicate "author-of-indexed-papers" is a user-defined-predicate, which will query database to answer whether S has indexed papers of an entity. The policies for ❶~❽ in fig. 2 are specified with following rules.

❶❷❸: The rules (4, 5) specify constrained DoA policies from S to M_1. The rules (6, 7) specify constrained DoA policies from M_1 to M_n. The rules (8, 9, 10, 11) define the authorization policies of M_1 and M_n. The rule (10) shows that M_n makes authorization based on the authority originated from S.

(4) **S.canAdmin**(?x, **aR**(S, trusted-proxy)) ← **S.canActivate**(?x, **dR**(S, co-university)).

(5) **S.canAdmin**(M_1, **aR**(S, discount), **sc**(**dR**(M_1, branch-campus), 1, **dR**(S,contributor)∩**dR**(M_1,student))).

(6) **M_1.canAdmin**(?x, **aR**(S, discount)) ← **M_1.canActivate**(?x, **dR**(M_1, branch-campus)).

(7) **M_1.canAdmin**(?x, **aR**(M_1, student)) ← **M_1.canActivate**(?x, **dR**(M_1, branch-campus)).

(8) **M_1.canActivate**(M_n, **dR**(M_1, branch-campus)).

(9) **M_1.canActivate**(P_1, **dR**(S, trusted-proxy)).

(10) **M_n.canActivate**(?x, **dR**(S, discount)) ← **M_n.canActivate**(?x, **dR**(M_1, student)).

(11) **M_n.canActivate**(U, **dR**(M_1, student)).

❹❺: When U wants to log on S with the role **dR**(S, discount), S transfers the login request to a query: "? ← S.isMember(U, dR(S, discount))". According to the semantics of REAL05, S will allow U to activate the role **dR**(S, discount) and create a session with an identity "sid001". The rule (12) defines the constrained DoC policy from S to the entity that has activated the discount role (here the entity is U). The function *curr-sid*() returns the current session id (now it is sid001). The rules (13, 14) are session rules. The rule (13) indicates that U has activated the discount role, and the rule (14) defines the permissions for the session "sid001".

(12) **s.canUse**(?x, **sR**(S, **curr-sid**()), **sc**(**dR**(S, trusted-proxy), 1, {S})) ← **S.hasActivated**(?x, dR(S,discount)).

(13) **S.hasActivated**(U, **dR**(S, discount)).

(14) **S.canRequest**(sid001, ?pm) ← **S.canHold**(**dR**(S, discount), ?pm).

❻❼❽: Now U logs on P_1 and begins to download papers from S. The rule (15) is session rule and defines the constrained DoC from U to P_1. Then P_1 makes a request to S to download the paper (here P_m is omitted in the sample).

(15) **U.canUse**(P_1, **sR**(S, sid001), **sc**({ }, 0, {S})).

S will transfer the request from P_1 to another query: "? ← S.allowAccess(P_1, pm(download, 20%))". According to the policies rules and semantics of REAL05, the query can be deduced and S will allow this request.

REAL05 can be used to express more sophisticated policies. But the discretional specification of policies may contain unrestricted delegations. For example, the rule "A.canActivate(?x, dR(A, r1)) ← B.canActivate(?x, dR(B, r2))" will implicitly defines the delegation of authority of dR(A, r1) to from A to B, and there is no control over this delegation. This kind of policy is also called distributed attributes inference [12], which may result in an unrestricted delegation chain. We can add some restrictions on the REAL05 rules (see def. 6) to avoid such delegation: $A=A_1=A_2=...=A_n$. We can omit the entities (i.e. A_1, A_2, ..., A_n) in the rule body because they are same to the issuer (i.e. A) of the rule, and denote a REAL05 rule with the form: A.H ← B_1, B_2, ..., B_n, Ψ. Note that the restriction will be enforced only when defining policy rules and session rules. The semantic rules (such as the meta rules in table 2) need not be controlled by this restriction.

4   Implementation

We use SICStus Prolog (SICSP) [5] as the inference engine of REAL05. The compound terms in SICSP are very suitable for expressing permissions, roles and spacial constraints in REAL05. List structures are suitable for expressing entity sets and trust scopes. The predicate symbols in REAL05 can be translated into SICSP predicates. For example, the predicate symbol "⊆" in rule ⑦ (see table 2) can be implemented as predicate "subspt", which is defined by following ❶~❻ SICSP predicates, where "isMember(E, X, dR(E, N))" is equivalent to "?y.canActivate(?x, dR(?e, ?n))" in REAL05.

❶ subspt(_, *). ❷ subspt(_, []).❸subspt([], []).❹ subspt([], _). ❺ subspt([X], [X]).
❻ subspt([X|ES], [dR(E, N)|TS]) :- isMember(E, X, dR(E, N)), subspt([X], TS), subspt(ES, [Y|TS]).

SICSP also provides a mapping mechanism between predicates and external functions. This mechanism allows the inference engine to make distributed query during local inference. When the predicate being evaluated is not asserted by local entity, the local inference engine will send a query containing this predicate to its principle. Each entity stores the delegation policies of the delegation trees that originated from it. The authorization policies are stored with subjects and will be submitted to server during login process. Note that the number of authorization policies is usually much more than that of delegation policies in the system. Therefore our policy distribution scheme is more attractive considering the efficiency of both policy retrieval and policy discovery. We have embedded such distributed inference mechanism into a middleware access control management (MACM) architecture, which is the central part of the security service in StarBus [16]. MACM covers multiple administrative domain, different domains exchange credentials and queries through a domain manger overlay network (DMON). DMON ensures the consistency and completeness of polices among all the domains participating in the overlay network. DMON also provides a new approach to realize negation policies within a specified domain, while enforcing negation policies in open decentralized systems is still very difficult and waits for more feasible solutions [11].

Our simulation system is the extension of the samples in section 3.3. There are 10 M_1 entities (treated as administrative domains), each M_1 has 10 P_1 and 10 M_n as its domain members, and each M_n has 100 U as domain members. The name of each entity is generated by a string randomizer. There are 1000 sessions on the server S. The system distributes over 10 PCs (CPU-2.0GHz, RAM-256M, LAN-100M) and the communication is protected by SSL. There are more than 10,000 rules (without signature yet) in the system. The average overhead of login is 0.26 seconds; the average overhead of each request is 0.12 seconds. This performance is acceptable for most large-scale distributed systems.

5   Related Work

The concept of trust management was firstly introduced by M. Blaze et al with PolicyMaker [7]. A large amount of work has been done on trust management, such as

Keynote [8], SPKI [4], DL [11], RT [12] and Cassandra [10]. In the introduction section, we have briefly reviewed some of the related work. Now we give further comparison of our work with some highly related work.

PolicyMaker allows arbitrary programs to be used in credentials and policies. Keynote uses a special assertion language to define delegation policies. However, both PolicyMaker and Keynote do not provide mechanisms to control the privilege proliferation during delegation. RT [12] is a family of role-based trust management languages whose semantics are built upon Datalog rules. RT supports boolean control over delegation of role authorities. The role intersections in RT can be viewed as a kind of constraint on the scope of delegation targets. However, RT can only enforce these delegation constraints for management-level AS. REAL05 supports the delegation constraints on the scope of mediate delegatees, upper-bound of delegation depth and the scope of delegation targets for both management-level AS and access-level AS.

RT^C [13] is a constrained version of RT for fine-grained control of structured resources, which adopts Datalog^C as the logical foundation. RT^C does not introduce new delegation constraints into existing RT framework. RT^C only supports equality and range constraints on role parameters. REAL05 supports inequality constraints as well as equality and range constraints on both role parameters and predicate parameters. The semantics of RT^C follows the approach in RT0, which translates each credential into a Datalog^C rule. REAL05 uses meta rules to capture the general semantics of policies, which can be extended to express more general constraints from the perspective of the whole system. Although the meta-rule approach will be a little more time-consuming than credential-rule-translating approach, our simulation results show that the performance is practically acceptable.

Cassandra [10] expresses policies in a language based on Datalog^C [15], which bears some similarities to our system. The expressiveness of Cassandra (and its computational complexity) can be tuned by choosing an appropriate constraint domain. The rules in Cassandra can refer to remote policies (for automatic credential retrieval and trust negotiation). However, Cassandra does not embed any delegation control mechanism in its reserved semantics. For example, the integer control on delegation is totally managed by security administrators in Cassandra, which will easily lead to mistakes in security management.

B. C. Neumann uses restricted proxy model [1] to support a variety of restrictions on authorization and delegation, including grantee, for-use-by-group, issued-for, quota, authorized, group-membership, accept-once. But the restricted proxy model does not provide restriction specification and semantics computation. Some of these restrictions can be expressed by REAL05. For example, the authorized restriction can be viewed as an access-level constraint on delegation targets. To support other restrictions such as accept-once, REAL05 need to be extended and collaborate with other security mechanisms such as session management facilities.

REAL05 can be viewed as a successor of REAL04 [18], a role-based extensible authorization framework proposed by the authors in 2004. REAL05 extends REAL04 to support many new features: (a) three types of roles to express the collections of permissions, authorities and session capabilities; (b) constraints on delegation targets and delegation depth; (c) using rules to define policies. The approaches to define the semantics of REAL04 and REAL05 are also different: REAL04 adopts the credential-rule-translating approach while REAL05 adopts the meta-rule approach. REAL05 is also powered by a clearly defined constrained delegation model named GCDM. Compared with REAL04, REAL05 are more flexible and extensible on both syntax and semantics.

6 Conclusion

"Trust can not be trusted." We aim to provide a more controllable and practical delegation model for TM systems, which could be used to specify delegation policies not only between entities that trust each other, but also between entities that (often have to) cooperate according to application requirements or security policies.

Contributions of this paper includes: (1) proposing a generalized constrained delegation model, giving clear definition of authorization system, delegation tree, delegation depth, delegation constraint, and the semantic model of constrained delegation. (2) proposing a typed privilege model based on permission activation mechanism, uncovering the essential difference between MTP and ATP, and provides means to avid undesired privilege transition. (3) using spacial constraint to restrict the shape of delegation trees, including mediate delegatees, delegation targets and upper-bound of delegation depth. (4) deigning a rule-based policy specification language, using meta rules to express general policy semantics, which provides a means to enforce more general policies (such as setting the upper-bound of the delegation depth for all the delegations in the whole system).

Future work includes: (i) extending GCDM with temporal constraints; (ii) integrating GCDM model with existing role-based TM systems such as RT [12] and Cassandra [10] to control the potential privilege proliferation in distributed attributes inference policies [12]; (iii) searching for more efficient credential distribution and distributed inference algorithms.

Acknowledgements

This research was sponsored by the National Natural Science Foundation under Grant No.90412011; the National High Technology Development 863 Program of China (No.2003AA115210; No.2004AA112020). The authors would also like to thank the anonymous reviewers for their valuable comments which greatly improve the quality of this paper.

References

1. Neumann, B.C.: Proxy-Based Authorization and Accounting for Distributed Systems. Proceedings of the 13th International Conference on Distributed Computing Systems, Pittsburgh, PA (May 1993)
2. Lampson, B., Abadi, M., Burrows, M., Wobber, E.: Authentication in distributed systems: Theory and practice. ACM Transactions on Computer Systems, 10(4) (November 1992) 265–310

3. Firozabadi, B.S., Sergot, M., Bandmann, O.: Using Authority Certificates to Create Management Structures. Proceeding of Security Protocols, 9th International Workshop, Cambridge, UK. Springer Verlag. In press (April 2001)
4. Ellison, C.M., Frantz, B., Lampson, B., Rivest, R., Thomas, B.M., Ylonen, T.: SPKI Certificate Theory. IETF RFC 2693 (1998)
5. Intelligent Systems Laboratory, Swedish Institute of Computer Science, SICStus Prolog User's Manual, Release 3.11.1 (February 2004)
6. Sollins, K.R.: Cascaded Authentication. Proceedings of the 1988 IEEE Symposium on Research in Security and Privacy (April 1988) 156–163
7. Blaze, M., Feigenbaum, J., Lacy, J.: Decentralized trust management. Proceedings of 17th Symposium on Security and Privacy, Oakland. IEEE (1996) 164–173
8. Blaze, M., Feigenbaum, J., John Ioannidis, and Angelos D. Keromytis: The KeyNote trust management system, version 2. IETF RFC 2704 (September 1999)
9. Schroeder, M.D., Saltzer, J.H.: The protection of information in computer systems. IEEE, 63(9) (September 1975) 1278–1308
10. Becker, M.Y., Sewell, P.: Cassandra: Flexible Trust Management, Applied to Electronic Health Records Proceedings of the 17th IEEE Computer Security Foundations Workshop (CSFW'04) (2004)
11. Li, N., Grosof, B.N., Feigenbaum, J.: Delegation logic: A logic-based approach to distributed authorization. ACM Transaction on Information and System Security (TISSEC) (2003)
12. Li, N., Mitchell, J.C., Winsborough, W.H.: Design of a role-based trust management framework. Proceedings of the 2002 IEEE Symposium on Security and Privacy. IEEE Computer Society Press (2002) 114–130
13. Li, N., Mitchell, J.C.: Datalog with constraints: A foundation for trust management languages. Proceedings of the 5th International Symposium on Practical Aspects of Declarative Languages (2003) 58–73
14. Bandmann, O., Damy, M., Firozabadi, B.S.: Constrained Delegation, Proceedings of the 2002 IEEE Symposium on Security and Privacy (S&P'02) (2002)
15. Kanellakis, P.C., Kuper, G.M., Revesz, P.Z.: Constraint query languages. Journal of Computer and System Sciences, 51(1) (1995) 26–52
16. Star middleware site, http://www.starmiddleware.net
17. Varadharajan, V., Allen, P., Black, S.: An Analysis of the Proxy Problem in Distributed systems. IEEE Symposium on Research in Security and Privacy. Oakland, CA (1991)
18. Gang, Y., Meng, T, Huai-min, W. etc: An Authorization Framework Based on Constrained Delegation, International Symposium on Parallel and Distributed Processing and Applications (ISPA'2004), Hong Kong, China, LNCS 3358, Springer Verlag (2004) 845–857

Policy-Driven Routing Management Using CIM

Félix J. García Clemente, Jesús D. Jiménez Re, Gregorio Martínez Pérez,
and Antonio F. Gómez Skarmeta

Departamento de Ingeniería de la Información y las Comunicaciones,
University of Murcia, Spain
{fgarcia, jdjimenez, gregorio, skarmeta}@dif.um.es

Abstract. Policy-based network management is intended to provide a system-wide and unified view of the network and its services and applications. This includes the combined management of network services as different as security, QoS or routing. However, while for IPsec and QoS there are clear models to define the semantics that a policy specification or language should implement, this is not equally true in the case of routing policies. This paper is intended to provide some results on the definition, modelling and deployment of routing policies using the Common Information Model (CIM). We also present the most relevant details of the implementation of our policy-driven routing management system, which has been successfully tested and used for the configuration of several relevant IPv6 IXes deployed as part of the three years Euro6IX (European IPv6 Internet Exchanges Backbone) EU IST research and deployment project.

1 Introduction and Motivation

One of the main goals of policy-based management is to enable network, service and application control and management at a high abstraction layer. Using a policy language, the administrator specifies rules that describe domain-wide policies which are independent of the implementation of the particular network node, service and/or application. It is, then, the policy management architecture that provides support to transform and distribute the policies to each node and thus enforce a consistent configuration in all the elements involved. This is a prerequisite for achieving a mean to dynamically constrain and regulate the behaviour of a system without the human cooperation.

Researchers have proposed multiple approaches for task-specific policy representation. They range from formal policy languages that a computer can easily and directly process and interpret, to rule-based policy notation using an if-then-else format.

The IETF provides information models for specifying policies that are independent of any implementation or encoding. In this sense, the IPsec Configuration Policy Information Model [1] presents an object-oriented information model for IP Security (IPsec) policies and the QoS Policy Information Model (QPIM) [2] presents a similar model for QoS policies. Both information models are based on the core policy classes defined in the Policy Core Information Model (PCIM) [3] and in the Policy Core

Information Model Extensions (PCIMe) [4]. Both, PCIM and PCIMe derive from and use classes defined in the DMTF Common Information Model (CIM) [5]. Moreover, the IPsec Model and QPIM define the semantics of IPsec policy and QoS policy, respectively. In fact, these models define the semantics that a policy specification or language should implement according to the IETF.

However, IETF lacks an information model for routing. Although it defines the Routing Policy Specification Language (RPSL) [6] which is a language to specify routing policies, is not based on any particular model and, moreover, there is no definition of a model to be used over it.

Thus, the definition, modeling and deployment of a model for routing policies based on a well-recognized standard, such as CIM, will enable the intra- and inter-domain management of different network services (such as, IPsec, QoS and routing) in a uniform manner.

This paper is intended to provide the results of modeling routing policies using CIM. It also describes how to take advantage of the Policy-based Network Management (PBNM) paradigm to develop such modeling. The last part of the paper is devoted to report on the development of the proposed modeling using for this some components deployed as part of the Euro6IX (European IPv6 Internet Exchanges Backbone) EU-funded IST project [8].

2 Representing Routing Policies in CIM

The Common Information Model (CIM) is an approach from the DMTF (Distributed Management Task Force) that applies the basic structuring and conceptualization techniques of the object-oriented paradigm to provide a common definition of management-related information for systems, networks, users, and services. The major benefit of specifying routing policy rules in this way is that an organization can utilize a common model that can be shared amongst all network nodes.

Policy model provides a framework for specifying configuration and operational information in a scalable way using rules composed of conditions and actions. It includes, among other elements, policy rules, policy groups, and policy conditions and actions, both in generic and vendor-specific form.

We propose a set of classes and associations to extend the CIM Policy Scheme to express routing policies (see Figure 1 for their representation in UML). Our proposal is based on the reposition of the class *RoutingPolicy* of CIM Network Scheme in CIM Policy Scheme.

RoutingRule is used to implement routing policies. It defines a common connection point for associating conditions such as *PacketFilterCondition* and *PolicyTimePeriodCondition*, and network actions (*RoutingAction*). One of the most important uses of this class is to change the routing policy by changing values of various attributes in a consistent manner.

RoutingAction is the base class for the various types of network actions. There are essentially three types of actions: forward the traffic unmodified, forward the traffic but modify either the attributes describing the route and/or other attributes that define how to adapt the traffic (e.g., its ToS –Type of Service– byte settings), or prevent the traffic from being forwarded. The class properties of *RoutingAction* correspond with the class properties of *RoutingPolicy*.

BGPRouteMapsInRoutingPolicy defines the *BGPRouteMaps* that are used by a particular *RoutingRule* object. *BGPRoutingPolicy* is a specialization of the *Dependency* association, and defines the relationship between a *BGPService* and the *RoutingRule* that control it. *FilteredBGPAttributes* is a specialization of the *Component* aggregation, which is used to define the set of BGP Attributes that are used by a particular *RoutingAction*.

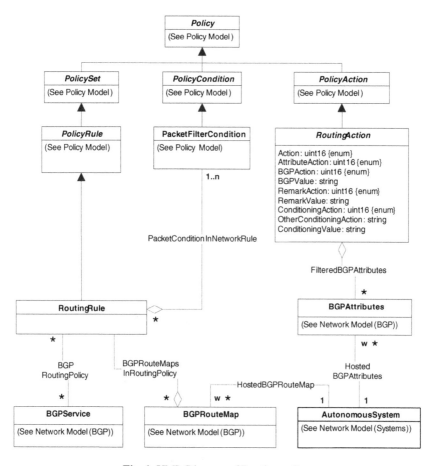

Fig. 1. UML Diagram of Routing policy

3 Mapping CIM to XML

The CIM schema is independent of any implementation. However, for an information model to be useful, it has to be mapped into some implementation. Thus, as Figure 2 shows, CIM can be mapped to (or represented as) several structured specifications. According to our approach, the CIM schema can be mapped to structured specifications such as XML, which can then be used to take advantage of XML technology and related tools. Other specifications such as MOF/CIM (Managed

Object Format/Common Information Model) for WBEM (Web-Based Enterprise Management), MIB (Management Information Block) for SNMP (Simple Network Management Protocol) and PIB (Policy Information Block) for COPS (Common Open Policy Service) are not considered because they do not use XML, which is a key requirement in the design of the overall routing policy management framework.

However, although policies are defined and managed initially in XML, they can be finally implemented and enforced in real devices using any of the other proposed formats, as the XML specification can be transformed to an equivalent MIB or PIB, for example, without loosing any semantics. This is because of the use of an information model that provides the semantics and basic conceptualization regardless the specific syntax in use.

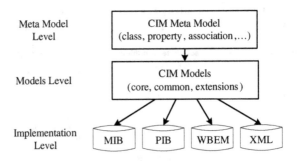

Fig. 2. CIM modeling levels

There are two main different models for mapping CIM into XML: schema mapping and metaschema mapping. DMTF defines a metaschema mapping for the representation of CIM elements and messages in XML [7]. This mapping defines a XML scheme that is used to describe the CIM metaschema, where both CIM classes and instances are valid XML documents for that schema. In other words the XML schema is used to describe in a generic fashion the notion of a CIM class or instance. In fact, in this approach CIM element names are mapped to XML attribute or element values, rather than XML element names.

The second approach, schema mapping, defines an XML Schema to describe the CIM classes; in this approach CIM Instances are mapped to valid XML documents for that schema. Essentially this means that each CIM class generates its own XSD fragment whose XML element names are the same that the corresponding CIM element names.

The metaschema mapping was mainly adopted by the DMTF, as it only requires one standardized DTD for the whole CIM regardless the version of this information model used in one particular implementation. However, our research identified several benefits related to the use of the schema mapping rather than the metaschema. The most important ones were more validation power and a more intuitive representation.

To build automatically such XML schema from any CIM version we designed an XML transformation using XSL Transformations (XSLT) [18]. XSLT is a language for transforming XML documents into other XML documents.

For our purpose, the main design principles identified as part of this mapping process were:

- Every CIM class generates a new XML element.
- Every CIM generalization (inheritance) generates the declaration of a new XML extension element.
- Every CIM key property generates a new XML <key> (or <unique>) element, which allows the unique identification of each XML element (i.e., CIM instance).
- Every CIM association is expressed in XML as entry references; this is the most suitable general-purpose mechanism currently available.
- A single XML database will host no more than one CIM implementation, and therefore the namespace is the same for all CIM instances stored in this database.

An example of the output of the mapping for a routing policy is presented in section 5.

4 Policy-Driven Routing Management System

We propose a policy-based routing management as depicted in Figure 3. This architecture was designed as an evolution of the IETF approach to policies, but providing some new features, as the complete use of XML-related technologies and tools in the policy life cycle.

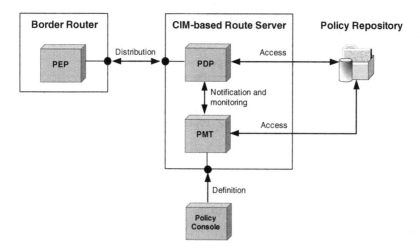

Fig. 3. CIM modeling levels

This architecture is composed by these four main functional elements:

- Policy Management Tool (PMT) that allows the administrator to develop routing policies making use of the Policy Console.
- Policy Repository that is used by the management tool (PMT) to store the policies and by the decision points (PDPs) to get them. The IETF suggests the use of a Lightweight Directory Access Protocol (LDAP). Due to our proposal

of use XML technologies, a more appropriate solution is to store routing policies in an XML native database, as such we will describe at section 6.

- Policy Decision Point (PDP) in charge of interpreting the policies stored in the policy repository, recuperating the set of rules for a particular PEP, transforming them into a format that can be understood by the PEP, and distributing them to the PEP.
- Policy Enforcement Point (PEP) is a component running on a border router that can apply and execute the different policies received from the PDP.

The proposed architecture is independent of any particular policy, so it could be used in the provision of security policies, QoS policies, or any other kind of policies.

5 Example of Routing Policy

The following example shows the mapping of the *RoutingAction* class of CIM Schema into XML Schema (which follows the general steps explained in section 3):

```
<xs:complexType name="CIM_RoutingAction" >
<xs:complexContent>
<xs:extension base="CIM_PolicyAction" >
<xs:sequence>
<xs:element name="Action" type="xs:string"/ >
<xs:element name="AttributeAction" type="xs:uint16" />
<xs:element name="BGPAction" type= xs:uint16" />
<xs:element name="BGPValue" type="xs:string" />
<xs:element name="RemarkAction" type="xs:uint16" />
<xs:element name="RemarkValue" type="xs:string" />
<xs:element name="ConditioningAction" type="xs:uint16" />
<xs:element name="OtherConditioningAction" type="xs:string" />
<xs:element name="ConditioningValue" type="xs:string" />
</xs:sequence>
</xs:extension>
</xs:complexContent>
</xs:complexType>
```

As it is shown, the CIM class is mapped in a XS type extending the type *CIM_PolicyAction*, and each class property is mapped into a different XS element. The *CIM_PolicyAction* and basic types (i.e., string and uint16) are defined in other XS documents.

A practical example of policy combining both routing concepts and QoS concepts is the following one:

If (IP source address = 155.0.0.0/8) and (IP source Port = 80)
then changing the DSCP value = 40

Differentiated Services Code Point (DSCP) value is related with differentiation of services in IPv4 and IPv6 network, as quality of services aspects. Therefore this rule implies that all web traffic (port 80) from the A class 155.0.0.0/8 network will be established to DSCP value equals to 40. Here the value 40 is just provided as a basic example, and there is no intention to mean any high-level business objective.

Since the routing policy is very verbose, we only present a fragment of the mapping.

```
<CIM_IPHeadersFilter>
<HdrIPVersion>4</HdrIPVersion>
<HdrSrcAddres>155.0.0.0</HdrSrcAddres>
<HdrSrcMask>255.0.0.0</HdrSrcMask>
<HdrSrcPortStart>80</HdrSrcPortStart>
<HdrSrcPortEnd>80</HdrSrcPortEnd>
</CIM_IPHeadersFilter>
<CIM_RoutingAction>
<RemarkAction>1</RemarkAction>
<RemarkValue>40</RemarkValue>
</CIM_RoutingAction>
```

The *RemarkAction* equals 1 identifies the value "Change DSCP" and the *RemarkValue* identifies the new value for the DSCP.

6   Deployment of a PBNM Framework for Routing Purpose

The design and implementation of the policy-based network management (PBNM) system now presented have been developed by the University of Murcia as part of the EU IST Euro6IX project [7]. The main objective of the project is to support the rapid introduction of IPv6 in Europe. In this sense, one of the UMU contributions to the project has been the development of a general PBNM functional architecture [8] (with IPv6 support) which allows the management of various kinds of network aspects, like VPN-IPsec, QoS and multihoming. The last contribution has been the integration of the routing model presented as part of this paper.

Figure 4 shows the general architecture and the elements which made up the implementation. The management architecture is composed of 5 main elements (Policy Console, PMT, Policy Repository, PDP and PEP) which are described as follows.

6.1   Policy Console

The policy console represents the entry point to the architecture. Our proposal is using a simple internet browser to access (i.e. Firefox, Netscape Navigator or Internet Explorer).

In order to protect the communication between the Policy Console and the Policy Management Tool, a secure connection is required, which provides confidentiality, data integrity, and a mutual authentication between the policy administrator using the Policy Console and the PMT server. HTTP protocol combined with SSL (i.e., HTTPS protocol) using X.509 certificates is a good approach to obtain these objectives and therefore PBNM system uses them for securing this communication.

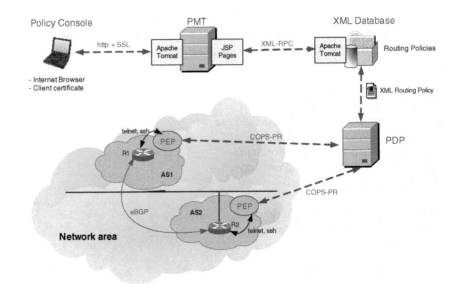

Fig. 4. PBNM deployment architecture

The policy administrator must present an X.509 certificate to gain access to the policy management tools. His private key and/or certificate could be stored in an encrypted file in his PC or in his smart card. This cryptographic information is issued previously by a valid Certificate Authority (CA). A Public Key Infrastructure (PKI) is necessary to provide support for it. The PBNM framework uses the UMU-PKI [10], although any other PKI software can be used.

6.2 Policy Repository

For storing XML policies, we have chosen to use a XML native database. The benefit of a native solution is that we do not need to worry about mapping XML policies to some other data structure (e.g., SQL). We also gain in flexibility through the semi-structured nature of XML and the schema independent model used by these databases. This is especially valuable when we have very complex XML structures (i.e., complex policies) that would be difficult to map to a more structured database.

Specifically, the UMU-PBNM uses Apache Xindice 1.1 database [11]. This version could be downloaded as a Tomcat Web Server Application (WAR) and therefore we have utilized the actual PMT infrastructure (Tomcat) for its installation.

One of the main advantages of Xindice according to our research is that it implements the concept of collections. Policies are stored in collections that can be queried as a whole, which increase the extensibility of the policy management as part of the DB.

Xindice uses XPath notation for its query language and XUpdate for its update language. Both PMT and PDP servers store/retrieve policies in/from the database using an interface based on XML-RPC and Java.

6.3 Policy Management Tool (PMT)

The PMT provides to the administrator the mechanisms for creating, modifying or deleting CIM policy documents. It is done by means of a high-level language or a graphical interface. In our case, we have developed a complete graphical web application that is accessible from the Policy Console Terminal. It has been implemented using JavaServer Pages (JSP), JavaBeans and Java Servlets technologies and it runs over Tomcat web server, which is IPv6-enabled and works well from its version 5 (previous versions have some problems when dealing with different IPv6 security realms).

Inside the PMT server, authorized network administrator can create, modify, and/or delete different types of CIM policies, and monitor how network end nodes are behaving.

Routing policies (in the same manner as IPsec, QoS and multihoming policies) could be created from the routing templates. The template concept represents a high-level representation and grouping of predefined policy values so the creation of new policies is easy.

Other interesting concept is the role. A role represents a logical group of network nodes that are managed in a similar way. PMT allows the network administrator to create, edit and/or delete network roles. Moreover allows the assignment of these roles to the current policies.

Clearly the main objective of PMT is the policies creation. With this objective in mind, PMT have been implemented by two main components as it is showed in Figure 5.

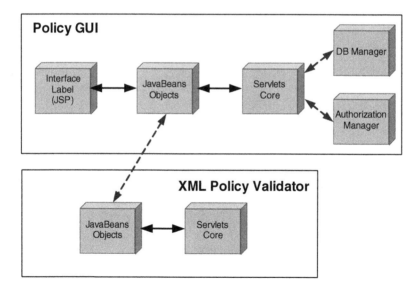

Fig. 5. PMT components

6.4   Communication Between PDP and PEP

Various alternatives have been analysed for the communication between the PDP and any PEP. A first approach is based on the use of Simple Network Management Protocol (SNMP). SNMP is an application layer protocol that facilitates the exchange of management information between network devices. In this case, our network components are the PDP and PEP elements. Although SNMP is a good protocol for implementing the outsourcing model and also for monitoring purposes, it lacks of appropriate mechanisms for implementing the provisioning model.

COPS-PR is the protocol recommended by the IETF to transport provisioning policy data between PDP servers and PEP clients. Therefore, as part of PBNM design and implementation, we have developed a complete COPS provisioning implementation, called UMU-jCOPS (University of Murcia Java COPS). It has been completely developed in Java, allowing the use of any operating system to run an implementation of PDP or PEP. Furthermore it is IPv6 enabled, so any operation can be performed using this new network protocol. Both the PDP and PEP contains UMU-jCOPS core libraries integrated inside.

6.5   Policy Decision Point (PDP)

The Policy Decision Point (PDP) is the PBNM component that applies the policy documents to the network nodes. It retrieves the CIM routing policies from the Policy Repository and uses them to generate the low-level policy decisions to be sent to PEPs.

PDP has been implemented using Java 1.4.x and XML technology. Figure 6 shows the internal PDP components.

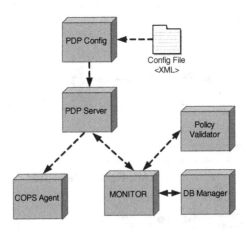

Fig. 6. Internal PDP components

The PDP obtains its configuration (i.e., type of policies, database path, digital certificate path, etc.) from an XML file. This file is store in memory by the PDP Config component. PDP Server launches the PDP Monitor and the COPS PDP Agent. The PDP Monitor component maintains a list of PEPs connected to a given PDP, whereas COPS PDP Agent, that is the integrated UMU-jCOPS implementation, performs communication with the set of PEP connected to it. The PDP monitor also takes decision about the specific policies to distribute to the PEP nodes. For that purpose, the PDP monitor component uses the DB Manager component allowing to access the Xindice policy database through XML-RPC requests. This components uses XML:DB API [12] for Java to access to Policy Repository.

The Policy validator module uses the XML schemas, which have been created previously, to validate a high-level policy after the PDP retrieves it from the XML policy database and starts generating policy decisions.

6.6 Policy Enforcement Point (PEP)

PEP clients enforce the policy decisions taken by the PDP to the policy-managed network nodes like PC Routers o CISCO Routers. The PEP Component could be integrated itself inside the Router or It could be placed outside of the router (playing the role of a PEP Proxy). In this case, a communication protocol between the PEP proxy and the router, such as SSH or Telnet is necessary to enforce the policy.

In the same way as the PDP server, PEPs controlling the Routing devices has been implemented using Java 1.4.x and XML technologies. Figure 7 shows the internal components of the PEP.

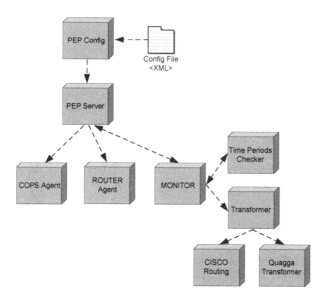

Fig. 7. Internal PEP components

The PEP (the IP Routing-based device) obtains its configuration (i.e., PEP role, PDP IP address, digital certificate path, etc.) from a XML file. This file is stored in memory by the PEP Config component. PEP Server, that is the core internal component, launches the PEP Monitor and the COPS PEP Agent. COPS PEP Agent, that is the integrated UMU-jCOPS implementation, performs communication with the PDP and obtains its Routing Policy.

PEP Monitor checks the current policy's validity. If policy is valid (TimePeriod Checker is the component to do it), then PEP Monitor launches the suitable PEP Transformer that it has to convert it to the specific configuration format used by the device that it is controlling. (CISCO Routing or Quagga Routing implementation [13]). PEP Transformer uses a set of XSL Transformation which has been developed to do the XML transformation to suitable configuration files. In this manner, every XSL (Extensible Stylesheet Language) contains a particular technology transformation for particular operating system architectures.

So far, we have created XSLT transformations for CISCO IOS Routers [14], Quagga BGP-4 protocol and Quagga Route Server model. Quagga implementation has been tested in PC Routers with Linux 2.6.x operating system and FreeBSD 5.x.

Quagga is a routing software suite, providing implementations of OSPFv2, OSPFv3, RIPv1, RIPv2, RIPv3 and BGPv4 [15][16] for Unix platforms, particularly FreeBSD, Linux, Solaris and NetBSD Routing Software Suite. The release tested is 0.98.0, although the latest releases can also be used.

If the PEP is not integrated inside the Router element (as it is the case of the CISCO Router) then Router Agent module takes care of communication with router using SSHv2 protocol (if router supports it) or through a telnet session.

7   Conclusions and Future Work

Policy-based network management (PBNM) is an emerging technology addressing open issues that are crucial for the deployment and evolution of network services and applications. For this the definition of common models indicating the semantics that a policy specification or language should implement regarding a network service is quite relevant. In the case of IPsec or QoS, for example, this issue has been mostly addressed during the last years, but in the case of routing policies just a few models have been defined. This paper provides a modelling for routing policies based on the CIM information model as well as the details of how it has been applied in a particular PBNM architecture.

Acknowledgements

This work has been partially funded by the EU Euro6IX (European IPv6 Internet Exchanges Backbone, IST-2001-32161) IST project and EU POSITIF (Policy-based Security Tools and Framework, IST-2002-002314) IST project.

References

1. Jason, J., Rafalow, L., Vyncke, E.: IPsec Configuration Policy Information Model, RFC 3585 (2003)
2. Snir, Y., Ramberg, Y., Strassner, J., Cohen, R., Moore, B.: Policy Quality of Service (QoS) Information Model, RFC 3644 (2003)

3. Moore, B., Ellesson, E., Strassner, J., Westerinen, A.: Policy Core Information Model - Version 1 Specification, RFC 3060 (2001)
4. Moore, B. (Ed.): Policy Core Information Model Extensions, RFC 3460 (2003)
5. Common Information Model (CIM) Standards, DMTF, http://www.dmtf.org/standards/cim
6. Alaettinoglu, C., Villamizar, C., Gerich, E., Kessens, D., Meyer, D., Bates, T., Karrenberg, D., Terpstra, M.: Routing Policy Specification Language (RPSL), RFC 2622 (1999)
7. Web-Based Enterprise Management (WBEM) Initiative Standards, DMTF, http://www.dmtf.org/standards/wbem
8. Euro6IX (European IPv6 Exchanges Backbone) IST Project, http://www.euro6ix.org
9. The University of Murcia Policy-Based Network Management System (UMUPBNM). http://pbnm.dif.um.es
10. The University of Murcia Public Key Infrastructure (UMU-PKI). http://pki.dif.um.es
11. The Apache Xindice XML database, http://xml.apache.org/xindice/
12. The XML :DB Initiative for XML Databases. http://xmldb-org.sourceforge.net/
13. Quagga Routing Suite. http://www.quagga.net
14. The CISCO Company. http://www.cisco.com/
15. Bates, T., et al.: Multiprotocol Extension for BGP-4, RFC 2858 (2000)
16. Rekhter, Y., Li, T.: A Border Gateway Protocol 4 (BGP-4), RFC 1771 (1995)
17. XML Schemas. http://www.w3.org/XML/Schema
18. XSL Transformations Version 1.0. http://www.w3.org/TR/xslt
19. Perez, G.M., Skarmeta, A.F.G.: Policy-Based Dynamic Provision of IP Services in a Secure VPN Coalition Scenario, IEEE Communications Magazine (2004)

Secure Hybrid Operating System
"Linux over Fenix"

Dmitry P. Zegzhda and Alex M. Vovk

Information Security Centre of Saint-Petersburg Polytechnical University,
P.O. Box 290, K-273, Saint-Petersburg, 195251
dmitry@ssl.stu.neva.ru

Abstract. The article discusses an approach to the construction of secure data processing systems based on the hybrid operating system technology, making it possible to use several different operating systems simultaneously on the same computer and arrange for an interaction between those. The Fenix secure operating system developed at the Software Security Laboratory(SSL) of the St. Petersburg State Polytechnical University (SPSPU) is proposed to be used as a host operating system, while the popular Linux OS — as a guest operating system, to ensure compatibility with commonly used applications.

1 The Problem of Integration Between the Facilities of Information Protection and Processing

In the course of their development information technologies infiltrate the areas where the most crucial demand to information processing is that of security. In order to entrust the information system with processing of confidential information whose protection is vital for the security of the country, a guarantee that the security features will function properly should be provided. And the only way of guaranteeing this is to make use of proprietary security features developed in-house, because it is only in this case that the full In this situation a problem emerges on the borderline between the information technologies and security features, both undergoing continuous development — *the problem of integration between the domestically produced facilities for information protection and the imported facilities for information processing.* This problem is of special importance for the software because the latter is developing at a very high rate — the operating systems serving as the environment for applications to function in, change every couple of years.

In this situation a problem emerges on the borderline between the information technologies and security features, both undergoing continuous development — *the problem of integration between the domestically produced facilities for information protection and the imported facilities for information processing.* This problem is of special importance for the software because the latter is developing at a very high rate — the operating systems serving as the environment for applications to function in, change every couple of years.

In order to deal with this problem the following contradictory requirements should be met:

V. Gorodetsky, I. Kotenko, and V. Skormin (Eds.): MMM-ACNS 2005, LNCS 3685,, pp. 272–285, 2005.
© Springer-Verlag Berlin Heidelberg 2005

1. in order that the security features could successfully function, performing the tasks assigned to them, it is imperative that they should have control over all information interactions in the system, with no exception;
2. in order that the information system could be successfully operated, it should both have the required functionality and meet the requirements to the modern IT products, i.e. it should be compatible with the solutions offered by other manufacturers, it should be user-friendly, it should be able to provide access to the resources of the World Wide Web etc.;
3. security features should not lag behind the data processing functions in the extent of their development, however, it is impractical to develop new protective measures for each novel information technology, since it will tie up enormous resources.

The solution for the outlined problem should be sought in the development of the system architecture which could combine various system and application components with security features in such a way that all the requirements formulated above would be met.

2 Security of Information Technologies Through Secure Operating Systems

For the modern computer systems the only way to ensure total control is to introduce security features at the operating system level. This method of solving the problem uses the systemic approach to the issue and guarantees results, though it involves certain expenses. However, in this case the funds will be spent directly on protective functions and not on the alterations made to the applications, which will inevitably reduce their functionalities, the applications themselves becoming obsolete in the process. On the contrary, the secure OS will be up-to-date as long as the problem of IT security persists, and the ready availability of the source codes and of the full set of design and operation documents will make it possible to monitor the security of software codes.

This approach has been implemented in the Fenix secure operating system[1] developed at the SSL of the SPSPU, making use of an original technology which allows both to eliminate the setbacks of existing systems and obtain a comprehensive mechanism of access control. The main objective of the project was to develop an original secure OS to meet the domestic requirements and information security standards, which could serve as the foundation for building a broad class of information systems for critical purposes.

The production of a secure OS is an indispensable precondition for the solution of the problem of IT security, however, it is not a final solution. The principal problem which all new OS face (and the secure ones in particular) when introduced, is the lack of a sufficient choice of user-defined application software which could be used in working with the protected resources. Writing new applications for such OS or importing the existing ones is a practically impossible task, in view of the time, funds, and intellectual resources needed.

This is why the only way out of this deadlock is the creation of a secure operating system to provide for the security of the processed information in conformity with the strictest requirements of domestic and international standards, at the same time designed for use together with the existing systems and applications in the way they are, without any changes or alterations. This approach alone will make it possible to deal with both special problems of protecting individual data processing complexes and to obtain a radical solution to the problem in the shape of a comprehensive secure OS serving as a basis for the construction of secure systems of various degrees of complexity.

3 Methods to Ensure Compatibility of the Secure OS with Popular Applications

There are several approaches to the problem of building a secure operating system capable of running applications of the commonly used OS, at the same time providing the required protection of the information resources used by these applications. Let us discuss these approaches, their advantages and disadvantages.

1. Attainment of a full binary compatibility of the secure OS and the popular OS at the level of the application code and the application programming interface (API). This is a task of ultimate complexity, because such compatibility cannot be found even among the products by well-known manufacturers, who have immense resources and capacities at their disposal. For example, no one has yet succeeded (despite numerous efforts) in achieving full compatibility of OS of UNIX and Windows families on the level of the binary code and the API. If such compatibility is ever attained, it will be only at the expense of reproducing the architecture of popular systems down to the minute details, inevitably receiving as the legacy all inherent problems and bottlenecks connected with the security issues, making it impossible to solve the problem in question — to create a secure system.
2. Emulation of the application programming interfaces of commonly used OS by the software of the secure OS. In this case re-compilation of applications for the new environment will be needed. If emulation is performed correctly, the application should not be able to notice that it is running in a foreign environment, since it will interact with the same API. Taking into account the sophisticated APIs of modern OS, this solution looks rather complicated and labor-intensive.
3. Embedding the security features in an open-source OS. This road looks very tempting because the results can be obtained quickly, but it will demand continuous reworking of the modified product, which will always stay behind the original version, losing in compatibility. In case the architecture of the original product is changed radically, there will be a stage when it will be impossible to introduce the required alterations. This is why this approach ultimately does not show much promise.
4. Hybrid OS. If the source codes of the OS are open, a much simpler and less labor-intensive solution, besides, allowing to achieve a better degree of compatibility, will be to modify the source code of the OS in such a way that it could be run as a common user process within the secure OS. This approach will provide for a full compatibility with the popular OS, because it will be used "as is", wholly with its architecture and APIs, and it will not involve extra expenses — what we need is to modify an open system in such a way that it could became operable in the process

environment of the secure OS. Since the popular OS now becomes an ordinary process within the framework of the secure OS, then from the standpoint of security this option looks like the preferred one.

Let us discuss what the hybrid OS technology consists in, and how it can be used for the construction of secure systems compatible with the applications of popular OS.

4   The Technology of Hybrid Operating Systems

The essence of the hybrid operating systems technology consists in the fact that within the framework of one operating system (called "host") an environment is created where another operating system (called "guest") can function, which makes it possible to start several different operating systems on the computer simultaneously and switch between them without rebooting the computer. The essence of the hybrid system technology is that there are one or several virtual machines set up on the computer running under the control of the basic ('host") operating system, and each of those makes it possible to run a ("guest") system of its own.

The virtual machine(VM) includes all the devices required for the operation of the guest OS: the processor, RAM, disc drives, network devices, I/O devices. These devices are emulated by the VM using the resources of the actual computer system through addressing the services offered by the host OS. The resources to be used by the VM are either delivered for the monopolist use by the VM and excluded from the main pool of resources (like RAM), or used by the host and the guest systems together — like it is with the processor, drives and the network. It is obvious that these opportunities can be offered at the expense of sharing the resources of the actual computer, so the requirements to the hardware will be higher.

In the hybrid system the host OS controls the hardware of the computer system, while the guest OS has no access to the hardware, interacting only with the VM. This way the host OS will be in full control of the operation of the guest OS, at the same time remaining fully transparent for the user of the guest OS.

The main purpose of the VM is to isolate the guest OS from the hardware and to create for it an appropriate computing environment on the basis of the application programming interface of the host OS. At that the VM will be able to set up various hardware configurations — for instance, it can be predetermined how much of RAM this or that VM will get and whether it will have access to the network.

5   Related Works

The central mechanism in our work is the VM, which allows secure OS to take control over the common OS and its applications. Extensive discussion of VMs and their properties is found in seminal work by Goldberg [2, 3] and more contemporary work on Disco [4] and VMware [5, 6]. More recently, Chen [7] argues for routine and extensive use of VMs for security purposes.

A more general argument about the inherently limiting nature of committing to a single OS abstraction has been made by the extensible OS community, perhaps most concisely in arguing for exokernels [8]. Exokernels and VMs are in many ways quite similar.

Grizzard in [9] proposes a Trusted Immutable Kernel Extension (TIKE) by way of a VM. Using a host operating system as a trusted platform, a self-healing system uses existing intrusion detection systems and corresponding self-healing mechanisms to automatically heal the guest operating system once a compromise has occurred.

Garfinkel presents a closed-box abstraction for trusted computing through the use of a VM monitor(*Terra*) for isolation and security [10].

Recently, the idea of isolated environments has become available in the form of commodity platforms implementing TCPA. [11], which related to our conception of combining trusted and untrusted components in one hybrid system. But TCPA is only a hardware mechanism for trusted computing, lacking a vision for support of trusted computing in operating systems.

In recognition of the need for OS support for trusted computing, Microsoft began development of its NGSCB (formerly Palladium) architecture [12, 13]. This work is the most similar to ours in that it provides a "whole system" solution to the problem of trusted computing. NGSCB works by partitioning the platform into two parts ("trusted" and "untrusted") each of which runs a different operating system. It achieves this through what can be seen as a very special purpose hybrid system that only supports two VMs. The untrusted(guest) is one of today's commodity operating systems (e.g. Windows) while the trusted(host) part is a dedicated trusted operating system (the "nexus" in NGSCB parlance).

NGSCB differs from Linux over Fenix most prominently in its security architecture. Linux over Fenix is a combination two full-power operating systems, in contrast, the trusted part of NGSCB is a dedicated operating system designed to run small, high-assurance programs called "agents." Agents work in conjunction with code on the untrusted side of the system, providing all of the security-critical functionality that programs on the untrusted side need (e.g. sensitive key storage).

6 "Linux over Fenix" Hybrid OS

The hybrid OS technology can be used for the construction of a secure operating system where the secure host OS would provide for the security, and the guest OS — for compatibility with applications and the user interface. What is required for this purpose is, first, the possibility of starting the guest OS as a common user process within the secure OS, and, second, the possibility of access by the applications of the guest OS to the resources of the secure OS under control of the embedded security features. Thus the multitude of applications of the secure OS is further expanded by both existing applications of the guest OS and those under development.

An example of a secure hybrid system is furnished by the solution developed by the Department of Information Security of the SPSPU School of Technical Cybernetics, which received the name "Linux over Fenix" secure hybrid system. The secure Fenix OS, having a special architecture and implementing a flexible model of access control to the information resources, plays the part of the secure OS. Within the environment provided by this OS, copies of the modified "Linux" kernel are run, adapted for operation in the user mode in the Fenix OS environment. Each user has at his disposal a personal copy of the Linux environment, fully isolated from the others. To access the information resources of the secure Fenix OS the driver of the file system of the modified Linux kernel is used, it redirects the calls for the resources of the Fenix secure OS, remaining under control of the Fenix security features.

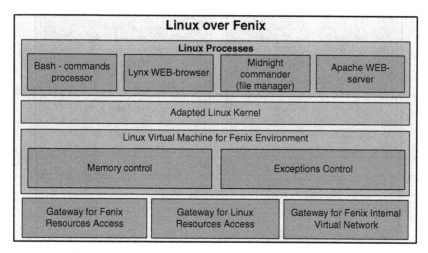

Fig. 1. The Structure of the "Linux over Fenix" Hybrid System

This solution makes it possible to expand the multitude of applications to be run under the Fenix with a vast multitude of applications for the popular Linux OS. This is how the problem of creating a secure system compatible with commonly used applications finds its solution, because all security functions are implemented with the Fenix, while all the Linux functionalities are open for application processes. The Linux OS functioning under continuous control of the Fenix security features, having no access to the hardware, and the security of the Fenix OS does not sustain any damage because the code of the Fenix security features was never changed.

6.1 "Fenix for Linux" Virtual Machine

Linux OS, functioning in the Fenix environment, is an ordinary Fenix OS process, which includes the "Fenix for Linux" VM, a modified Linux kernel and the Linux user processes (see Fig. 2). The Fenix VM for Linux includes:

1. A memory control module which makes it possible to map the required physical page to the required virtual address.
2. An exception and interrupt control module which can handle processor exceptions and interrupts in the user mode of the Linux VM.

At every particular moment of time in the virtual address space of the VM there are pages of the Linux OS kernel and the pages of the current Linux user process. For each Linux OS process a list of pages in use is kept, which is modified as the memory is allocated/freed. As soon as the time slice allocated for the current Linux process expires, the Linux kernel removes the pages belonging to the process being phased out from the virtual address space, and maps the pages which belong to the new process being switched over to, to the same addresses.

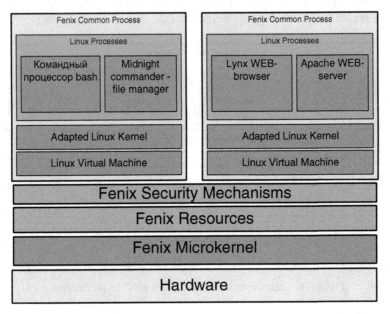

Fig. 2. The Architecture of the "Linux over Fenix" Secure Hybrid Operating System

The VM should handle certain processor exceptions and interrupts — for instance, timer interrupts or paging errors. When an exception or an interrupt related to the VM process occurs, the Fenix kernel transfers control to the VM, to handle the situation. In the case when the VM handles the interrupt or the exception incorrectly, the integrity and stability of the Fenix OS will not be damaged — the process of this VM will be terminated.

6.2 Security

Security features of the hybrid operating system should be dealing with the two main issues: they should protect the components of the operating systems (both kernels and processes) from interfering with each other, and control the access to the host system resources by the guest system applications.

In the Fenix environment Linux functions in the user mode as an ordinary user process. This means that Linux cannot disturb the operation of the Fenix OS kernel and of other applications run in the Fenix environment.

More than that, the Fenix VM for Linux using the mechanisms of segment boundaries, privileges and virtual memory can isolate the Linux kernel from the Linux user processes and the Linux user processes from one another. To deal with this problem the full scope of potentialities offered by the processors of IA-32 architecture is used for memory protection.

1. Protection of the Fenix kernel from the Linux kernel. The Fenix kernel is protected from the Linux kernel by the paged memory (the Fenix kernel is executed in

privileged pages, the Linux kernel — in user pages). The Linux VM is an ordinary process of the Fenix OS and does not have access to the internal structures of the Fenix OS kernel.

2. Protection of the Linux VM from the Linux processes. The Linux VM is protected from the Linux processes by memory segmentation and segments privileges.

3. Protection of the Linux processes from one another. The lower three gigabytes of the virtual address space of the VM are used to run Linux processes. Before switching from one process to another the memory used by the first process is removed from the virtual address space of the VM. The memory used by the new process is mapped to the same virtual address space, and only after that the control can go over to the new process. Thus, the Linux OS processes can have access only to their address space, without any access to the virtual address spaces of other Linux OS processes and, therefore, cannot interfere with their execution.

4. Protection of the Fenix kernel from Linux processes. The Linux OS processes are run at the third privilege level in the segment limited to three gigabytes, and have no access to the internal structures of the Fenix kernel; therefore, they cannot interfere with its operation or affect other Fenix processes.

5. Protection of applications of the secure Fenix OS from the Linux VM. Protection of the applications of the secure Fenix OS from both the Linux VM and Linux kernel is provided by the secure Fenix OS kernel, which isolates the address spaces of Fenix tasks and, respectively, the Linux VMs using segment and page protection of address spaces.

Thus, the components of the hybrid system form a hierarchy: "Fenix kernel" — "Linux VM" — "Linux process", where every component is in full control of the lower level components and protected from their interference.

The architecture of the secure Fenix OS, based on the concept of universal information resources and total control of interactions between all system components, makes it possible to deal with the problem of control over the access of Linux applications to all kinds of protected information resources under control of the secure Fenix OS using the built-in security features.

1. Control of the access to the terminals of the secure Fenix OS. The terminal which can display confidential information and accept commands from the user to process it, is one of the protected information resources controlled by the security features of the secure Fenix OS. The guest Linux OS does not have direct access to the secure Fenix OS terminal. The only way for Linux OS applications to display information or to receive a command from the user console is to access the programmable interface of the secure Fenix OS. Every such time the secure Fenix OS, after the appropriate authorization procedures, will make a decision on whether the access to the terminal for the Linux process will be granted or denied.

2. Control of the access to the information resources of the secure Fenix OS by the Linux OS and its applications. The file system driver of the modified Linux OS kernel is used as a gateway for the access to the information resources of the secure Fenix OS, it maps their file system in Linux and translates the events to the secure Fenix OS. Since from the standpoint of the secure Fenix OS architecture the Linux VM represents an ordinary user process, so, when these resources are accessed, a usual Fenix access control procedure takes place according to the security pattern

in operation within the system. Thus, this gateway allows the applications to run within the framework of the Linux VM, to access directories, files and other information resources located in the total namespace of the secure Fenix OS under the control of its security features.

3. Control of internetworking for the Linux OS and its applications. To ensure the computer system security it is essential to control not only the access to the local resources of the system, but also the internetworking. In Fig. 3 the architecture for a secure network of the hybrid "Linux over Fenix" OS is shown.

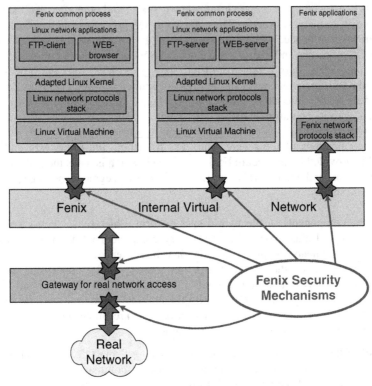

Fig. 3. The Architecture for a Secure Network of the Hybrid "Linux over Fenix" OS

The internal virtual network represents a hub combining network interfaces of Linux VMs and the network interface of the secure Fenix OS into a common virtual network which can be connected to the real external network via a special gateway performing all the functions of network security. Besides, network security features can be implemented on each virtual network interface connected to the internal network. Network security features include filtering the traffic at the level of TCP and IP; it is also possible to provide encryption and VPN facilities. Undesirable interactions both in the virtual network and with the external network can be prohibited. Thus, when Linux OS applications interact with a network, the security features of the secure Fenix OS will be in full control of all internetworking, both in the internal virtual network and in the external network.

Thus, the secure hybrid Linux over Fenix OS ensures both the security of all components of the host and the guest OS and the security of information resources under control of the secure host Fenix OS, as well as of internetworking of the guest Linux OS and its applications.

6.3 Compatibility

The Fenix for Linux VM has a high level of compatibility with the original Linux OS. This is achieved due to the fact that the Fenix for Linux VM does not attempt to emulate the Linux functionality, but represents a standard Linux 2.4 kernel, slightly modified to make it possible to run it as an ordinary secure Fenix OS process. These modifications involve a small number of modules and can be easily replicated in the later versions of the Linux kernel.

6.4 Power

Linux applications running in the Fenix for Linux VM demonstrate practically the same power level as they would if run in the original Linux OS. This is achieved because the responses to the system calls of the Linux kernel are not emulated, and they are executed in exactly the same way as when operating in the original Linux OS. The existing small overhead is associated only with the operation of the secure Fenix OS security mechanisms, but it becomes manifest only when an attempt to access protected resources is made, and not all the time while the Linux application is running. At that this overhead is not higher than in the case when this application is exported to the Fenix environment.

7   The Model of Access Control of the Secure Hybrid Linux over Fenix System

The access control mechanisms in the hybrid system are described by the following model:

The secure hybrid system G is the set tuple: $G = \{S, R, AC, CR, Op, P\}$, where:

S — the set of the subjects of the secure hybrid system. $S = S^F \cup S^L$, where S^F is the set of the subjects of the secure Fenix system, and S^L - the set of the subjects of the Linux operating system.

R is the set of the system resources. $R = \{R^F, R^L\}$, where R^F are multiple resources of the secure Fenix system, and R^L - the multiple resources of the Linux operating system. $R^L = \{Ri^L, Ro^L\}$, where Ri^L are the nonshared resources with the secure Fenix OS – multiple resources of the Linux operating system, inaccessible for the subjects S^F of the secure Fenix system, while Ro^L are the shared resources with the secure Fenix OS - multiple resources of the Linux operating system, accessible for the subjects S^F of the secure Fenix system. The secure hybrid Linux over Fenix OS incorporates a uniform system of access control of the subjects to the resources. And it does not matter what type the resource is — the access control system interacts with all types of resources in a uniform manner. Thus, the subjects are also resources $S^F \in R^F$ and $S^L \in R^L$.

AC is the set of algorithms of access control of subjects S to resources R. AC = {AC^F, AC^L}, where AC^F is the algorithm of access control to resources R^F of the secure Fenix OS, and AC^L — the algorithm of access control to resources R^L of the Linux OS.

The algorithms of access control in Linux over Fenix, in dependence of the types of objects and resources are shown in Fig 4.

	R^F	Ro^L	Ri^L
S^F	AC^F	$AC^F \wedge AC^L$	–
S^L	AC^F	AC^L	AC^L

Fig. 4. The Algorithms of Access Control in the Secure Hybrid Linux over Fenix OS in Dependence of the Types of Subjects and Resources

Op is the set of operations of the system. Op = {Op^F, Op^L}, where Op^F are multiple operations which can be performed by the subjects of the secure Fenix system S^F over the resources of the secure Fenix system R^F and the resources of the Linux operating system Ro^L, and Op^L — multiple operations which can be performed by the subjects of the Linux operating system S^L over the resources of the secure Fenix system R^F and the resources of the Linux operating system R^L. The set of operations Op^F = {deallocation, reading, writing, acquisition of security attributes, setup of security attributes, generation, deletion}. The set of operations Op^L = {deallocation, reading, writing, acquisition of security attributes, setup of security attributes, generation, deletion}.

P is the set of permissions. P = {P^F, P^L}, where P^F are multiple permissions which the subjects of the secure Fenix system S^F may have in regard to the resources of the secure Fenix system R^F and in regard to the resources of the Linux operating system Ro^L, while P^L are multiple permissions which the subjects of the Linux operating system S^L may have in regard to the resources of the secure Fenix system R^F and in regard to the resources of the Linux operating system R^L. $P^F = Pd^F \cap Pm^F$, where Pd^F are discretionary permissions, and Pm^F — mandatory permissions. Pd^F = {reading, writing, addition, execution}, Pm^F = {reading, writing}. P^L = {reading, writing, execution}.

CR is the resource container. All resources R^F and Ro^L are aggregated in resource containers. During authorization the access control algorithm interacts not with the resource directly, but with the container CR^R, where the resource R is aggregated. Access control algorithms are abstracted from both the types of resources aggregated in the containers and from the client requesting access to the resources. This makes it possible to ensure isomorphism of access control both from the client requesting access (secure Fenix OS application, or Linux OS application) and from the resources (resources of the secure Fenix OS or resources of the Linux OS).

This way the actions of the Linux VM are transformed into uniform requests to the resource containers controlled by the Fenix security features. All calls of the subjects S^L of the Linux VM for resources R^F of the secure Fenix OS, with no exception, are controlled by the access control algorithm AC^F of the secure Fenix OS. Linux OS operates under control of the secure Fenix OS security pattern and cannot bypass it.

In the secure hybrid Linux over Fenix OS multiple permissions which subject S has in regard to resource R can be written down as follows: P = AC(S, R, Op) = AC^F (S^F, R^F,Op^F) $\wedge$ AC^F (S^L, R^F,Op^L) $\wedge$ AC^L (S^L, R^L,Op^L) $\wedge$ AC^F (S^F, R^F,Op^F) $\wedge$ AC^L (S^F, R^F,Op^F). As the access to the resources can take place only through resource containers CR, a necessary condition for the access of subjects S to resources R is $\exists$ CR^R for the given type of resources R.

8   Using the Hybrid Secure Linux over Fenix OS

The hybrid secure Linux over Fenix OS can be employed as a platform for workstations and servers with several isolated environments for processing information of different confidentiality levels or gateways connecting information systems of different confidentiality levels.

As an example, let us discuss how the hybrid Linux over Fenix system can be used to solve the problem of setting up a workstation to process information of different confidentiality levels and arrange for its connection to Internet(Fig. 5). Several isolated from one another Linux VMs can be run on behalf of different users.

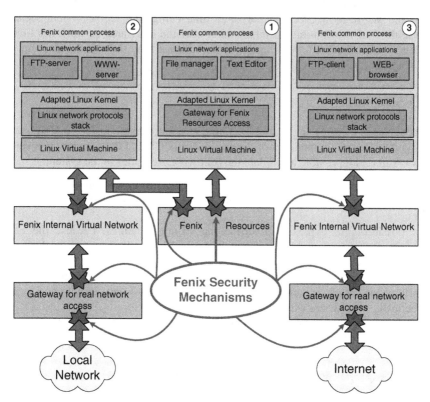

Fig. 5. A Workstation Based on the Hybrid Secure Linux over Fenix OS for Processing Confidential Information and Work with the Local Area Network and the Internet

For instance, one VM can be started with the permissions of a highly privileged user, enjoying full rights to process confidential information, and work in it, making use of the whole range of data processing facilities incorporated in the popular Linux OS. At that, to avoid leaks of confidential information, this VM should be fully banned from the network access (both to the intranet and the Internet).

Another VM could be run with the permissions of a not so highly privileged user, who will have limited access to the confidential information, and used for working with the resources of the local intranet — for example, for furnishing a restricted amount of information using Linux standard WWW- and FTP-services.

Finally, the third VM could be started with the permissions of an unprivileged user without any access to the confidential information, who can, therefore, freely work in the Internet using standard Linux features (like the Web-browser and ftp-client). This VM is used for the activities which can lead to the system being compromised and infiltrated by viruses and "Trojans". However, even in this situation only this VM will suffer damage, and the confidential information, inaccessible for this user, will remain intact.

This way we have succeeded in the construction of a system wherein the user can process confidential information, share it over the local area network at his discretion, access the World Wide Web, at the same time being sure of the system security, because the VM distributing the information over the local area network has limited privileges, and the VM working with the Internet is fully isolated from the confidential information.

9   Conclusion

The advantages of using the hybrid operating system technology for building secure information systems on the basis of the secure Fenix OS and the popular open-source Linux OS makes it possible to implant the following properties in the system:

1. Total control over all information interactions and information flows by the trusted security features from the secure Fenix OS range, thus providing a high level of security.
2. No possibility to bypass or override the security features, because the Fenix security facilities directly interact with the hardware platform, while the Linux facilities, on the contrary, do not have access to it.
3. The set of accessible applications can be expanded on the account of Linux applications, which makes it possible to use the Linux over Fenix hybrid system practically everywhere where Linux is used.
4. Minimum overhead for security — the only code run in addition to the commonly used Linux is the code of the secure Fenix OS security features.

References

1. Zegzhda, D.P., Stepanov, P.G., Otavin, A.D.: Fenix Secure Operating System: Principles, Models and Architecture // Proceeding of International Workshop on Mathematical Methods, Models and Architectures for Network Security Systems. Information Assurance in Computer Networks. Springer (2001) 207–218

2. Goldberg, R.: Architectural Principles for Virtual Computer Systems. PhD thesis, Harvard University (1972)

3. Goldberg, R.: Survey of virtual machine research. IEEE Computer Magazine, 7 (June 1974) 34–45

4. Bugnion, E., Devine, S., Rosenblum, M.: Disco: running commodity operating systems on scalable multiprocessors. In Proc. 16th ACM Symp. Operating Sys. Principles (Oct. 1997)

5. Sugerman, J., Venkitachalam, G., Lim, B.: Virtualizing I/O devices on VMware workstation's hosted virtual machine monitor. In Proc. 2001 Ann. USENIX Tech. Conf., Boston, MA, USA (June 2001)

6. Waldspurger, C.A.: Memory resource management in VMware ESX Server. In Proc. 2002 Symp. Operating Sys. Design and Implementation (December 2002)

7. Chen, P.M., Noble, B.D.: When virtual is better than real. In Proc. 2001 Workshop on Hot Topics in Operating Sys. (HotOS-VIII), Schloss Elmau, Germany (May 2001)

8. Engler, D., Kaashoek, M., O'Toole, J.: Exokernel: Anoperating system architecture for application-level resource managment. In Proc. 15th ACM Symp. on Operating Sys. Principles (Dec. 1995)

9. Grizzard, J., Dodson, E., Conti, G. Levine, J., Owen, H.: "Towards a trusted immutable kernel extension (TIKE) for selfhealing systems: a virtual machine approach," in Proc. 5th IEEE Information Assurance Workshop (June 2004) 444–446

10. Garfinkel, T., Pfaff, B., Chow, J., Rosenblum, M., Boneh, D.: "Terra: a Virtual Machine-Based Platform for Trusted Computing," in Proceedings of the nineteenth ACM Symposium on Operating Systems Principles, ACM Press (2003) 193–206

11. Trusted Computing Platform Alliance. TCPA main specification v. 1.1b. http://www.trustedcomputing.org/

12. Carroll, A., Juarez, M., Polk, J., Leininger, T.: Microsoft Palladium: A business overview. http://www.microsoft.com/PressPass/features/2002/jul02/0724palladiumwp.asp (August 2002)

13. Microsoft next-generation secure computing base—technical FAQ. http://www.microsoft.com/technet/treeview/default.asp?url=/technet/security/%news/NGSCB.asp (February 2003)

A Formal Description of SECIMOS Operating System*

Zhouyi Zhou[1,2,3], Bin Liang[4,5], Li Jiang[1], Wenchang Shi[1], and Yeping He[1]

[1] Institute of Software, Chinese Academy of Sciences, Beijing 100080, PRC
[2] Graduate School of the Chinese Academy of Sciences, Beijing 100049, PRC
[3] College of Computer and Communications, Hunan University,
Changsha HN 410082, PRC
[4] Department of Computer Science and Technology, Tsinghua University,
Beijing 100084, PRC
[5] Beijing Venus Info Tech Inc, Beijing 100081, PRC
{zhouyi04, jiangli02, wenchang}@ios.cn
liangbin@venustech.com.cn
yphe@ercist.iscas.ac.cn

Abstract. The application of formal methods in secure operating system experiences a procedure of development and maturity with the eminence and development of secure operating system itself. According to Common Criteria and United States Department of Defenses Trusted Computer System Evaluation Criteria (TCSEC), high security level secure operating system should introduce formal methods in the process development and evaluation. Security in Mind Operating System (SECIMOS) is a customizable secure operating system developed by Institute of Software, Chinese Academy of Science. In this work, we formally model the security policies using Z specification language and informally proved the correspondence between policies and top level functionalities. As a result, we summarize the gist to choose a formal description language for modeling a secure operating system and possibility of use Isabelle/HOL as a formal tool.

1 Introduction

Formal methods have played a more and more important role in the development of software and hardware systems. By describing some logic relations in a system using strict mathematical language, one can prove the system conforms to a given rule. Formal methods can also make reliability proofs on complex software and hardware system so as to discover design faults that can not be discovered by test and simulation previously. Formal methods can better control software and hardware products' development and provide a criterion for those products [1] [2].

* This work is jointly supported by National Basic Research Program of China (973) under Grant No. G1999035802, National Natural Science Foundation of China under Grant No. 60373054 and National High-Tech Research and Development Program of China (863) under Grant No. 2002AA141080.

V. Gorodetsky, I. Kotenko, and V. Skormin (Eds.): MMM-ACNS 2005, LNCS 3685, pp. 286–297, 2005.

The research of secure operating system begins in 1967's Adept-50 project. From that time on, the theories, technologies, and methods are established step by step. Adept-50 is also the first attempt to implement multi-level military secure mathematical model on running systems. A most influential result in the infancy stage of secure operating system research is Bell&LaPadula model (BLP) proposed by Bell and LaPadula in 1973. They give a formal description and an informal notation of BLP and the interpretation of its implementation in Multics system [3]. This is the beginning of application of formal methods in secure operating system. The UCLA Data Secure UNIX formally realizes BLP model later and uses XIVUS's theory prover to do formal proves. In the year 1985, United States' Department of Defense published the complete edition of Trusted Computer System Evaluation Criteria (TCSEC)[4]. TCSEC have 7 different security evaluation levels: D, C1, C2, B1, B2, B3 and A1. Each level corresponds to a set of particular security characters and insurances. United States Army Secure Operating System [5] is a family of operating system developed according to TCSEC. There are in fact two different systems: a TCSEC C2 level operating system and a TCSEC A1 level operating system. ASOS A1 operating system constructs formal specification and proofs in two levels: Abstract Security Model and Formal Top-Level Description. ASOS developed a flow analysis tool working in Gypsy Verification Environment to analysis convert channels in the system design. Another TCSEC A1 level secure operating system Logical Coprocessing Kernel (LOCK) [6] is developed by United States National Security Agency (NSA) also uses Gypsy specification language and GVE as its formal tool [7]. There is plenty of other secure operating systems use formal method to insure design consistence, but none of them has reached such a high security level as ASOS and LOCK do.

In the process of developing Security in Mind Operating System (SECIMOS), we use Z specification language to formalize the secure policy models and use ordinary English to describe top level security functionalities and informally prove the correspondence between the policy model and top level security functionalities. The rest of the paper is organized as follows, the basic architecture is discussed in section 2, the Z specification of the secure policy models is discussed in section 3, we compare several of formal tools and their potential for secure operating system use in section 4, and we conclude our paper in section 5.

2 Basic Architecture of SECIMOS

Security in Mind Operating System (SECIMOS)[8] is a customizable secure operating system developed by Institute of Software, Chinese Academy of Science based on Linux 2.6 kernel which has already absorbs LSM (Linux Security Module) framework as an indispensably part. This project makes uses of four security policies each of which is implemented as a separate module Fig. 1. These four modules are: module for Multilevel Security policy (MLS), module for Discretionary Access Control (DAC), module for Controlled Privilege Framework (CPF) (This is used to control the behaviors of Trusted Process), module for Privileged User (PUSER). To solve the policy conflicts, SECIMOS assign each module an unsigned 16 bit "order" and an unsigned 8 bit "type". The "order" field of each module indicates the module's invoking order of the policy module chain. The "type" field of each module has one of following value: null module which means the module does not make decision, grant module which means grant the access right even it is not allowed by the modules invoked later, constraint module which means the denial result be returned to the enforcement part immediately, grant-constraint module which means immediately return the decision to the enforcement part. SECIMOS enables runtime changing a module's type and order to resolve conflicts, and is an effective step towards the adaptive secure operating system. This paper doesn't discuss the principles of LSM and module coordinator further. We will introduce four policy models used SECIMOS rest of this section. In current implementation of SECIMOS all security policy modules are constraint modules. The system will deny an access request if any one of four modules denies the request. This greatly alleviate the job of formalization of SECIMOS as a whole because the security assurance is distributed in series.

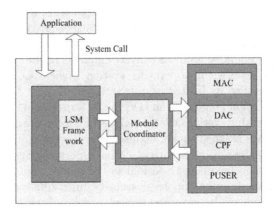

Fig. 1. Basic Architecture of SECIMOS

2.1   Mandatory Access Control (MAC) Policy Model

Our MAC policy model takes [9] approach which is a refinement of BLP model for networks [10]. Below, the set of security properties associated with our model are presented. Otherwise specially point out, the notions such as subjects set S, objects set O, set of access modes A , security level mapping function level are the same as in [10] or [3]. In our model, level function class f consists of four level functions: level(O), level(S), v-max(S) and a-min(S). Functions level(O) and level(S) are the same as before. However, the current-level(S) function is replaced by two new functions, v-max(S) and a-min(S). v-max(S) represents the maximum sensitivity at which a subject may view an object and a-min(S) represents the minimus sensitivity at which a subject may alter an object. It is required that for all subjects S: level(S) $\geq$ v-max(S) and v-max(S) $\geq$ a-min(S). The subset of security levels defined by inclusive range between v-max(S) and a-min(S) is denoted by the set ran(S). The set of trusted subjects are those subjects where v-max(S) $\neq$ a-min(S) and the set of untrusted subjects are those subjects where v-max(S) = a-min(S). The Tmach generalzation of the *-property is:

Definition 1. *A State* v = *(b, M, f) satisfies this generalization of the *-property iff, for each triple (S, O, $\underline{x}$)* $\in$ *b:*

1. $\underline{x}$ = $\underline{r}$ *or* $\underline{w}$ $\Rightarrow$ *v-max(S)* $\geq$ *level(O) and*
2. $\underline{x}$ = $\underline{a}$ *or* $\underline{w}$ $\Rightarrow$ *level(O)* $\geq$ *a-min(S).*

2.2 Discretionary Access Control (DAC)

Discretionary Access Control is based on identifier discrimination. The DAC decide whether or not to grant access right to certain object like file and directory etc to a subject according the object's owner and subject's identity. The DAC secure policy module (Fig. 2) of SECIMOS is constructed over the traditional DAC mechanism of Linux. It introduces Access Control List (ACL) to further strengthen the DAC mechanism.

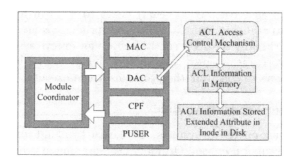

Fig. 2. Architecture of DAC Module

The ACL semantic rules are compatible with POSIX.1e+2c standard. Each ACL is composed of a group of rules to store the one subject or a group of subjects' access rights to a given object.

2.3 Controlled Privilege Framework (CPF)

To make a secure operating system usable, there must have some processes which is free of the control of Mandatory Access Control. These processes are named trusted processes. To regulate the behavior of trusted process, SECIMOS introduces a State-based trusted process restriction module: Controlled Privilege Framework [11]. By analysis the source code, CPF module divides the lifetime of the process into several so-called privilege states according to eight values: uid, euid, suid, suid, gid, egid, sgid and fsgid. CPF assign each privilege state of the process a set of capabilities and controlled system calls.

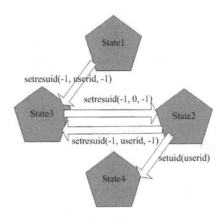

Fig. 3. Privilege States Transition of Wuftpd (CPF)

In the system test, we select Washington University's wuftpd as an example (Fig. 3). At the beginning, wu-ftpd's daemon process's user ids' are all 0 (root), this corresponds to State1 in figure 3. When there is a connect request, a new service process is established, after the user's identity has been authenticated, the new process's effective user id (euid) is set to login in user's id and the process transits to State3 in figure 3. When root privilege is needed, process will transit to State2. Finally State4 is sensitive state for execve system call. In this state, also the process is assigned the privilege to call execve, but there will be privilege parameters to constrain the programs it can execute.

2.4 Power User Security Module

In traditional Linux operating systems, there exist two kinds of users: the ordinary user and the super user root. Ordinary user has limited privilege, while root has sovereign power. Root can perform any operations on the objects in the system; use any resource in the system. This contradicts the basic security principle: the principle of minimal privilege. SECIMOS fine grain the root privilege into 10 privilege user roles. Each privilege role can only perform the allowed operation in predefined scope. We do not formalize the Power User Security Module.

3   Formal Description of Secure Policy Models

We choose Z specification language [12] to descript our secure policy models: MAC, DAC and CPF. Because the specification is very lengthy, we only describe the most instructive parts.

3.1   Formal Description of MAC Secure Policy Model

As mentioned in section 2, our MAC secure policy model uses the TMACH modification of original BLP model. According to TMACH, the set of subjects is made up of unshared sets of trusted subjects and untrusted subjects:

$$UnTSubject : \mathbb{P}\ Subject$$
$$TSubject : \mathbb{P}\ Subject$$

$$Subject = UnTSubject \cup TSubject$$
$$UnTSubject \cap TSubject = \emptyset$$

When a subject want to access a object, it must firstly get the access right from the decision subsystem of the policy. If granted, the subject, object and access type triple will add to current access set of system:

AddNewAccessTriple

$\Delta State$
$R? : Req1$

$b' = b \cup \{new : AccessTriple \mid$
$\qquad new.S = R?.S \wedge new.O = R?.O \wedge new.x = R?.x\}$
$f' = f$
$H' = H$

According to our policy, the subject can get the read access right to the object if and only if the subject's security level vmax dominates the object's security level.

ReadPass

$State$
$R? : Req1$

$R?.ra = get$
$R?.x = r$
$R?.S \in \operatorname{dom} f$
$R?.O \in \operatorname{dom} f$
$(f\ R?.S).vmax\ dominate\ (f\ R?.O).vmax$

As mentioned before, whenever a subject in system wants to access an object, it must first request the access right from decision subsystem. After validated the request, the decision subsystem will add the subject, object and access type access-triple into current access set, otherwise, the State keeps invariant.

$$Rule\_GetRead \mathrel{\widehat{=}} (ReadPass \wedge AddNewAccessTriple \wedge Pass)$$
$$\vee\ (ReadDeny \wedge Invariant \wedge Deny)$$
$$\vee\ (\neg\ (ReadPass \vee ReadDeny) \wedge Invariant \wedge Unknown)$$

In above definition, ReadDeny has the same structure as ReadPass while ReadDeny represents the condition that the get_read request should be rejected. Invariant is a schema which indicating that the system state is kept unchanged. Pass, Deny, Unknown are simply schemas represent answer to the get_read request.

There are many other rules in our formal specification. Because the limitation of space, we only list another rule ChangeObjectRange here. Under following condition, a subject's request of change a object's security level can be granted:

1. if the requesting subject is a trusted subject, or

2. the subject's security level dominate the object's security level and the goal security level's vmax equals amin (can not make the object a trusted subject) and the new security level should not violate the ∗-property of current access set and the new security level should keep the hierarchy rule that every object's security level should dominate its directory parent's security level.

__ *ChangePass* _____

State
$R? : Req3$

_____

$R?.ra = change$
$R?.S \in \text{dom} f$
$R?.O \in \text{dom} f$
$R?.O \notin Subject$
$(R?.range).vmax = (R?.range).amin$
$R?.S \in UnTSubject \Rightarrow (R?.range).vmax \ dominate \ (f \ R?.O).vmax$
$\forall \ Triple : AccessTriple \mid Triple \in b \wedge Triple.O = R?.O \ \bullet$
$\quad (Triple.x = r \Rightarrow (f \ Triple.S).vmax \ dominate \ (R?.range).vmax) \wedge$
$\quad (Triple.x = a \Rightarrow (R?.range).amin \ dominate \ (f \ Triple.S).amin) \wedge$
$\quad (Triple.x = w \Rightarrow$
$\quad\quad (\ (f \ Triple.S).vmax \ dominate \ (R?.range).vmax$
$\quad\quad \wedge (R?.range).amin \ dominate \ (f \ Triple.S).amin \ ))$
$\forall \ Opar : Object \setminus Subject \mid Opar \in \text{dom} f \ \bullet \ R?.O \in H(Opar) \Rightarrow$
$\quad (R?.range).vmax \ dominate \ (f \ Opar).vmax$
$\forall \ Ochd : Object \setminus Subject \mid Ochd \in \text{dom} f \ \bullet \ Ochd \in H(R?.O) \Rightarrow$
$\quad (f \ Ochd).vmax \ dominate \ (R?.range).vmax$

According to this rules, we can write security invariant and security theorems: A system's state is a secure state if and only if every access-triple in state's access set satisfy ∗-property:

__ *SecureState* _____

State

_____

$\forall \ p : AccessTriple \mid p \in b \wedge p.x = r \ \bullet$
$(f(p.S)).vmax \ dominate \ (f(p.O)).vmax$

$\forall \ p : AccessTriple \mid p \in b \wedge p.x = a \ \bullet$
$(f(p.O)).amin \ dominate \ (f(p.S)).amin$

$\forall \ p : AccessTriple \mid p \in b \wedge p.x = w \ \bullet$
$(f(p.S)).vmax \ dominate \ (f(p.O)).vmax$
$\wedge (f(p.O)).amin \ dominate \ (f(p.S)).amin$

Following theorem says that the rule ChangeObjectRangeSecure translate secure state to secure state:

theorem ChangeObjectRangeSecure

$Rule\_ChangeObjectRange \wedge SecureState \Rightarrow SecureState'$

The theorems like above in SECIMOS can all be proved using Z/EVES [13] tools. The proof scripts are lengthy and proof time is long (20 minutes to prove above theorem).

3.2 Formal Description of DAC Secure Policy Model

The state of DAC is made up of the current access set, a function ACL that represent the access control list in the system, a function Owner that maps an object to its owner.

State

$b : \mathbb{P}\, AccessTriple$

$ACL : OBJECT \rightarrow (USER \rightarrow \mathbb{P}\, PERM)$

$Owner : OBJECT \rightarrow USER$

The decision subsystem of ACL security model grant access permission, if and only if the request perm and the requestor: User is in the access control list of the object to be accessed.

PermApprove

State

$R? : Req1$

$R?.ReqPerm \in (ACL\ R?.O)(R?.User)$

GetAccess operation add to current access set new access-triple.

GetAccess

$\Delta State$

$R? : Req1$

$D! : Decision$

$ACL' = ACL$

$Owner' = Owner$

$b' = b \cup \{Triple : AccessTriple \mid Triple.User = R?.User \wedge$
$\qquad\qquad Triple.O = R?.O \wedge Triple.x = R?.ReqPerm\}$

$D! = Approve$

PermCheck is the state transition rule for DAC secure policy model.

$PermCheck \mathrel{\widehat{=}} (PermApprove \wedge GetAccess) \vee (\neg\, PermApprove \wedge AccessDeny)$

GivePerm and RescindPerm describe the rule for add a entry to object's access control list and remove a entry from object's access control list.

```
___ GivePerm _____
  ΔState
  R? : Req2
  _____
  R?.Caller ∈ PrivUser ∪ {Owner(R?.O)}
  R?.ra = give
  b' = b
  ACL' = ACL ⊕ {R?.O ↦ {R?.User ↦ (ACL R?.O)(R?.User) ∪ {R?.ReqPerm}}}
  Owner' = Owner
```

```
___ RescindPerm _____
  ΔState
  R? : Req2
  _____
  R?.Caller ∈ PrivUser ∪ {Owner(R?.O)}
  R?.ra = rescind
  b' = b
  ACL' = ACL ⊕ {R?.O ↦ {R?.User ↦ (ACL R?.O)(R?.User) \ {R?.ReqPerm}}}
  Owner' = Owner
```

3.3 Formal Description of CPF Secure Policy Model

As mentioned in section 2, CPF is a state based trusted process control framework. In the /etc/smos/cpf directory of SECIMOS operating system, there exists a configuration file prog.conf. In the file prog.conf, there will be a ProgPrivTableEntry for each privilege state of each trusted program. prog refers to the disk program like "wuftpd", pstate is the privilege state and priv_info is various of capabilities and operating parameters a process of program prog have in privilege state pstate.

```
___ ProgPrivTableEntry _____
  prog : Prog
  pstate : PState
  priv_info : ℙ(Priv × PParam)
```

On the other hand, the system state as a whole consists of the ProgPrivTable made up from ProgPrivTableEntries, b: the current access set and several of privilege mapping functions. For example, Proc_PState maps one of the process in system to the privilege state that process is current in.

```
___ State _____
  ProgPrivTable : ℙ ProgPrivTableEntry
  User_Priv : User → ℙ Priv
  Proc_PState : Proc → PState
  Proc_User : Proc → User
  Proc_Prog : Proc → Prog
  Proc_Creds : Proc → ℙ(Priv × ℙ PParam)
  b : ℙ AccessTuple
```

The description of secure state in CPF is lengthy, and we don't discuss it here. There are also many theorems about secure invariant of CPF secure policy model which can be proved by Z tools for example Z/EVES [13].

4   Comparison of Formal Methods for Secure Operating Systems

There are more than two hundred of formal tools existing today. According to the verification approach taken, they can be divided into two categories: Model Checking and Theory Proving. Model checking mainly depends on constructing the finite state model of system and verifying the desired property of the model. The verification of model checking is automatic and speedy. SPIN [14] and SMV [15] are the most famous tools of model checking. The above two model checking tools are used in NASA's space craft projects to check software fault. Model checking has the unconquerable shortcoming of combinatory exploding, and not suitable for complicated state transformation systems such as secure operating systems as a whole (model checking can apply the limited formalization on some parts of secure operating system). A theorem proving system includes a set of axioms and a set of induction rules, the verification produce is to prove given property of system start from system axioms using the induction rules. Theorem proving is usually human-machine interactive: people should give proof hints to machine during the proving steps. Theorem proving methods can describe and verify systems with infinite states. The most influential theorem proving tools is Gypsy specification language and GVE (Gypsy Verification Environment) [7]. The high security level operating systems ASOS and LOCK all use Gypsy and GVE as formal methods. The reason to choose Gypsy is that it clearly maps the specification to implementation. But GVE has shortcomings in secure theorem proving: GVE is not adaptable, after small change in specification, the proof procedure as whole needs to be rewrite from beginning, and Gypsy is not suitable for divide and conquer prove for large problem space. Z specification language gives a clean and punctual specification to state based systems, the Z/EVES has many nice features in proof management. On the other hand, Z/EVES's proof power is greatly impaired by its deficiency in handling of recursive date types and recursive function proving. Another formal tool, Isabelle/Isar [2] used mainly in protocol verification is a good candidate for formalizing secure operating systems. It is an open source project written by ML. It supports many computational logics such as HOL (High Order Logic) and FOL (classical and intuitionistic first order logic). Its good qualities on recursive definition and theorem proving reflect the characteristic of its underlining ML language. Following is a mutual recursive definition of Tmach [9] based secure lookup:

constdefs
```
ReadDirJudgement :: "States => Objects => ('a,'b,'c)env => uid ⇒  bool"
"ReadDirJudgement State1 AccessSubject file' Accessuid ≡
(snd (GetRead State1 ⦇SubjectinTriple = AccessSubject, ObjectinTriple =
 FileObject(attributes(file')), AccessMode = Readable ⦈ )) ∧
```

```
( Accessuid = 0 ∨
                    Accessuid = owner (attributes(file')) ∨
                    Readable ∈ others (attributes(file'))
)"
```

ReadDirJudgement is a isabelle description of function that judges if a subject is allowed to read a dir by MAC (Mandatory Access Control) and the usual Unix file permission constraint.

```
consts
  lookup_secure :: "States => Objects => uid ⇒ ('a,'b,'c)env  => 'c list =>
('a,'b,'c)env option × States"
  lookup_secure_option :: "States => Objects => uid ⇒ ('a,'b,'c)env option
=> 'c list => ('a,'b,'c)env option × States"

primrec (lookup_secure)
  "lookup_secure State1 AccessSubject AccessUid (Val a) xs = (if xs = [] then
(Some (Val a), State1) else (None, State1))"
  "lookup_secure State1 AccessSubject AccessUid (Env b es) xs = (let State3
= (GetReadTran State1
              AccessSubject  (Env b es) ); judgement = (ReadDirJudgement State1
AccessSubject  (Env b es) AccessUid)     in
    (case xs of
     [] => (Some (Env b es), State1)
     | y # ys =>
                 if (~judgement)
           then
                (None, State1)
           else
             lookup_secure_option  State3
                 AccessSubject AccessUid (es y) ys
))"
```

The function lookup_secure search recursively from the specified directory until the operation is not permitted or the string of path name is exhausted and the file is got. At the same time, the transition of system state is recorded.

Based on this definition, we can define many delicate theorems about recursive properties of system and prove them.

5   Conclusions

During the formalization of SECIMOS, we strengthen the idea that formal works is a indispensable part of developing secure operating systems. During the formalization procedure, we find some design faults in Linux Security Module and report the bugs to corresponding mailing-list. We write more than 30 security theorems and 40 auxiliary lemmas in order to prove them. The intermediate proof results are more than 150'000 lines long. We encountered many difficulties in theorem proofing; many of them are insurmountable using current Z tools. This is not expected in the pre-design stage of SECIMOS when we are investigating existing formal methods. From that experience and long-time re-investigation, we propose Isabelle/Isar as a good candidate in further developing of Chinese secure operating systems.

References

1. Leveson, N.G.: Geust Editor's Introduction: Formal Methods in Software Engineering. IEEE Transactions in Software Engineering. September (1990) 929–931
2. Wenzel, M.: Isabelle/Isar - A Versatile Environment for Human-Readable Formal Proof Documents. PhD thesis. Institute für Informatik, Technische Universität München. (2002)
3. Bell, D.E., La Padula, L.J.: Secure Computer System: Unified Exposition and Multics Interpretation. MITRE Report, MTR-2997 Rev.1. (1976)
4. CSC-STD-001-83, Department of Defense Standard. Department of Defense Trusted Computer System Evaluation Criteria. National Computer Security Center, Ft. Meade, MD. USA (1985)
5. Waldhart, N.A.: The Army Secure Operating System. 1990 IEEE Symposium on Security and Privacy (1990) 50–60
6. Saydjari, O.S.: LOCK: An Historical Perspective, 18th Annual Computer Security Applications Conference (2002) 96–108
7. Good, D., Akers, R., Smith, L.: Report on Gypsy 2.05. Tech. Rept. ICSCA-CMP-48. Institute for Computer Science and Computing Applications. The University of Texas at Austin (1986)
8. Wu, Y., Shi, W., Liang, H., Shang, Q., Yuan, C., Liang, B.: Security On-demand Architecture with Multiple Modules Support. Information Security Practice and Experience, First International Conference.Singapore (2005) 121–131
9. Mayer, F.L.: An Interpretation of a Refined Bell-La. Padula Model for the Tmach Kernel. Fourth Aerospace Computer Security Applications Conference (1988)
10. Bell, D.E.: Secure Computer Systems: A Network Interpretation. Second Aerospace Computer Security Conference (1986) 32–39
11. Liang, B., Liu, H., Shi, W., Wu, Y.: Enforcing the Principle of Least Privilege with a State-Based Privilege Control Model. Information Security Practice and Experience, First International Conference.Singapore (2005) 109–120
12. Spivey, J.M.: Understanding Z: A Spcification language and its formal semantics, volume 3 of Cambridge Tracts in Theoretical Computer Science. Cambridge University Press (1988)
13. Meisels, I., Saaltink, M.: The Z/EVES Reference Manual (for Version 1.5). Technical Report, TR-97-5492-03d. ORA Canada. (1997)
14. Havelund, K, Lowry, M., Penix, J.: Formal Analysis of A Space Craft Controller Using SPIN. IEEE Transactions on Software Engineering. Vol. 27, no. 8 (2001) 749–765
15. Pecheur, C., Simmons, R.: From Livingstone to SMV: Formal Verification for Autonomous Spacecrafts. In Proceedings of First Goddard Workshop on Formal Approaches to Agent-Based Systems. NASA Goddard (2000) 103-113

A Theoretical Model for the Average Impact of Attacks on Billing Infrastructures

Fabrizio Baiardi and Claudio Telmon

Dipartimento di Informatica, Università di Pisa,
L.go B.Pontecorvo 3, 56125 - PISA
{baiardi, claudio}@di.unipi.it

Abstract. The 0-delay is a mathematical model to evaluate the average impact of attacks on a billing infrastructure, that is an infrastructure that supports the billing of a set of users for some service. The model describes the search for vulnerabilities as a competition between a set of attackers and one of defenders, that are interested, respectively, in attacking and patching the infrastructure. As implied by its name, the model assumes that both the attack and the patching occur as soon as the vulnerability is discovered. The model assumes that the impact increases with the size of the vulnerability window, the time in between the discovery of the vulnerability by an attacker and by a defender and it relates this size to the numbers of attackers and of defenders. After describing the model, we describe some applications and generalizations.

1 Introduction

A billing infrastructure is any networked system deployed to bill a set of users for some service supplied either by the same system or by a distinct one. Well-known examples are public utility infrastructures such as those for the distribution of electric power or water, where a meter measures the amount of power or water distributed to the user. Through the infrastructure, the meter sends the running total to a database that is used to compute the user bill. The revenue of the infrastructure owner is the overall amount of the bills. The lifetime of a billing infrastructure is fairly long because most of its components are physically distributed on a wide area so that their update is expensive.

We assume a proactive attitude of the infrastructure owner that does not wait for someone else to find vulnerabilities and are interested in the definition of a mathematical model to drive the owner investment in the search and the elimination of vulnerabilities after the infrastructures has been deployed [1,2,3,5,7,12,13,14,15,17,19,25]. For these reasons, we are focused on vulnerabilities that enables attacks [3,5,7,19] resulting in losses in the revenue and neglect other impacts of attacks, such as denials of service. We assume that two sets of people compete in the search of vulnerabilities: attackers and defenders. The goal of a defender is to patch the infrastructure [10] to prevent an attack. Instead, attackers are interest in attacks to reduce the user bills. The number of

V. Gorodetsky, I. Kotenko, and V. Skormin (Eds.): MMM-ACNS 2005, LNCS 3685, pp. 298–310, 2005.

defenders depends upon the investment in security of the owner after the deployment. In a billing infrastructure, the loss of revenues due to a vulnerability V, i.e. the impacts of attacks exploiting V, depends upon the vulnerability window of V [8,26,27]. This window is the interval of time from when an attacker discovers V till when a defender finds V as well. The proposed model, 0-delay model, evaluates the loss in the revenue in terms of the window size and of the numbers of attackers and of defenders. As implied by its name, the model assumes that both the patching and the attacks are immediately executed as soon as either the defenders or the attackers find a vulnerability. The model may be integrated with game theory [21] to define an optimal allocation of attackers and defenders to the search of vulnerabilities. The model also enables the owner to determine whether to deploy the infrastructure even if some vulnerabilities have not been removed because he/she is willing to accept the average impact of the attacks enabled by the remaining vulnerabilities. Lastly, the model may be used to evaluate the advantages of open source components vs. proprietary ones with a "security through obscurity" approach [5,6].

The importance of a quantitative evaluation of attack impacts has often been stressed [5,17,18,23,25]. [25] presents a survey of current approaches and introduces the notion of market price of vulnerability. This notion cannot be immediately applied to a billing infrastructure where this price depends upon the service billed rather than the infrastructure components. [16] applies game theory to information warfare while [21] applies an insurance inspired methodology to optimally allocation a set of defenders to minimize the impact of a terrorist attack on a set of targets. The competition between defenders and attackers in the search for vulnerabilities has previously been considered in [9,23] but these works are focused on the disclosure policy rather than on attack impacts. Some of our assumptions are similar to those of [23] to compute the probability of finding a vulnerability. [9] considers the search for vulnerabilities and a social planner that decide when a vulnerability is disclosed. Coherently with the evaluation of disclosure policies, it assumes that a vulnerability is discovered by a benign user, i.e. a defender, rather by an attacker. Furthermore, most of the works on vulnerabilities and attacks considers general-purpose systems rather than billing infrastructure.

Sect. 2 introduces the 0-delay model and shows how it defines the average impact of an attack as a function of the numbers of attackers and defenders as well as of the vulnerability window. For the sake of simplicity, at first a simplified version of the model is introduced. Then, a more general version is defined by relaxing some of the constraints. Sect. 3 briefly outlines some alternative developments of our work. At first, we consider an infrastructure with several vulnerabilities and we show that, also in this case, the impact is always a function of the numbers of attackers and defenders searching for distinct vulnerabilities. Lastly, we show how our model may contribute to the debate on "security through obscurity" and on the adoption of open source components.

2   The 0-Delay Model

After discussing its main underlying assumptions and constraints, we present the 0-delay model in some details, Then, the model is generalized by removing some of the initial constraints.

2.1   Underlying Assumptions

Besides the one implied by its name, the most important assumptions underlying the 0-delay model concerns the existence of one vulnerability, denoted by V, and that the billing infrastructure is deployed even if V has not been removed. The former will be discussed in the next section. The latter, in general, it is satisfied because it may be not cost effective to deploy the infrastructure only after removing any vulnerability. Furthermore, the infrastructure owner has a proactive attitude towards the search for vulnerabilities. Given the existence of V and the proactive owner attitude, two sets of people are searching for V, the attackers and the defenders. The attackers search for V to define and implement an attack, the defenders, instead to patch the infrastructure.

In the 0-delay model, time is considered as a sequence of intervals with the same size δt, in the following *at time t* means *during the t-th interval*. If a defender finds V, in the same interval, the patch is defined and applied to the infrastructure. We assume that the time to develop a patch is independent of the number of defenders and that δt is larger than the time to start and complete the patching process. If a defender finds V at time t, any attack implemented after t fails. If, instead, an attacker finds V at time t before any defender, then at the same time the attack occurs and the loss begins. The loss ends only when, and if, the defender finds V and patches the infrastructure. Notice that δt depends upon the considered infrastructure and that it cannot be reduced at pleasure because it should suffice both to define and execute an attack and to define and apply the patch. The probability of discovering V is the same for any interval, although it may be different for an attacker and for a defender. This problem will be detailed in the following.

A further assumption concerns the absence of information exchange between the attackers and the defenders or within each set during the search. Hence, no information from other people is available to speed up the search. However, as soon as the attack has been discovered, it is immediately broadcast to anyone that can implement it and all the attacks are immediately executed. This is a worst-case for the defenders because any delay in the execution of attacks reduces the loss. Furthermore, if the attacks are not simultaneous, the detection of one attack may simplify the search of the defenders.

The model assumes that the impact of an attack is proportional to the size of the vulnerability window and that lifetime of the infrastructure is unbounded, i.e. the infrastructure is updated only to remove any vulnerability. The latter is realistic only for the long-term components of the infrastructure, such as the hardware of an ATM or a meter in the user house. Hence, the model should be applied to vulnerabilities of these components only. Notice that the two assumptions jointly imply that, in principle, there is no bound on the impact of a successful attack because this impact is proportional to the size of the vulnerability window but this size is unbounded if the defenders do not remove a vulnerability discovered by an attacker.

2.2   The 0-Delay Model

Here and in the following, the terms impact of attacks and loss in the infrastructure revenue are considered as synonymous and will be freely interchanged, The 0-delay model makes it possible to compute $I(na, nd)$, the impact of an attack as a function of na and nd, the numbers of attackers and of defenders. $I(na, nd)$ is positive if and only if the size of the vulnerability window is positive and it is proportional both to this size and to the number of successful attacks. This is summed up in the relation:

$$I(na, nd) = \begin{cases} nsa_A \cdot Uloss_A \cdot (td(nd) - ta(na)) \ if \ td(nd) - ta(na) \geq 0 \\ 0 \qquad\qquad\qquad\qquad\qquad\quad if \ 0 \geq td(nd) - ta(na) \end{cases}$$

where:

- $ta(na)$ is the time when one of the na attacker discovers both V and A, the attack enabled by V;
- $td(nd)$ is the time when one of the nd defenders finds V and patches the infrastructure,
- $td(nd)$ - $ta(na)$ is the size of the vulnerability window,
- ns_A is the number of instances of A that are successfully executed. ns_A is always larger than na, that is $ns_A = \psi \cdot na, \psi \geq 1$. In turn, ψ is a decreasing function of the resources and the skills to execute A and it reaches its maximum if A can be fully automated by proper programming tools [29]
- $Uloss_A$ is the loss in the infrastructure revenue for unit of time due to each attack that is an instance of A.

The 0-delay model assumes that $nsa \cdot Uloss_A$ is a constant.

If $Aver(R)$ denotes the average value of the random variable R, then

$$Aver(I(na, nd)) = ns_A \cdot Uloss_A \cdot Aver(td(nd) - ta(na))$$

In the following, we drop the dependency from the number of attackers or of defenders from both $ta(na)$ and $td(nd)$ and replace $td(nd)-ta(na)$ by either $td-ta$ or simply by vw. We are interested in the positive values of vw because these are the only cases where A is successfully executed. Instead, anytime $vw < 0$ there is no loss, because the loss is zero.

$Aver(vw)$, the average size of the vulnerability window depends upon $P(vw = i > 0|na, nd)$, the probability that $vw = i$ if there are na attackers and nd defenders. This probability is a function of both $Pd(nd,t)$ and $Pa(na, t)$ the probabilities that the attackers or the defenders find V exactly at time t i.e. that $td=t$ (or that $ta=t$). In turns, $Pd(nd,t)$ and $Pa(na, t)$ are a function of $Pd(nd)$ and $Pa(na)$, the probabilities that, respectively, at least one of the nd defenders, or one of the na attackers, finds V in a single time interval. Since both $Pd(nd)$ and $Pa(na)$ are time independent, we have that:

$$Pd(nd, t) = (1 - Pd(nd))^{t-1} \cdot Pd(nd)$$

$$Pa(na, t) = (1 - Pa(na))^{t-1} \cdot Pa(na)$$

Taking into account that each attacker and each defender works in isolation,

$$Pd(nd) = 1 - (1 - Pd(1))^{nd} \qquad Pa(na) = 1 - (1 - Pa(1))^{na} \qquad (1)$$

where $Pd(1)$ and $Pa(1)$ are, respectively, the probabilities that a defender and an attacker finds V in one interval of time. In the following, we assume that $Pd(1) = Pa(1)$ so that each attacker and each defender have the same probability of finding the vulnerability in one interval.

This assumption neglects that a defender can access an amount of the information on the infrastructure larger than the one of the attacker and that this asymmetry should, at least in principle, simplify the search of the defender. To model this asymmetry while preserving $Pd(1) = Pa(1)$, the number of defenders may be multiplied by a constant factor $\varphi, \varphi \geq 1$ before applying the 0-delay model. In the following, we assume that the number of defenders has already been multiplied by φ and drop the dependency of the probabilities from $Pd(1)$ and $Pa(1)$.

The previous consideration shows that the following relation holds:

$$P(vw = i | na, nd) = \lim_{N \to \infty} \sum_{ta=1}^{N-i} (1 - Pa(na))^{ta-1} \cdot Pa(na) \cdot (1 - Pd(nd))^{ta-1+i} \cdot Pd(nd)$$

This defines the probability that $vw = i$ as the limit of the sum of the probabilities of all the cases where:

1. an attacker finds V at ta,
2. the first defender find V at $td=ta+i$,
3. both ta and td belong to the range $1..N$.

Under these condition ta is, at most, equal to $N-i$ because td always belongs to $1..N$. Furthermore, we can consider the limit of the sum as N, the upper bound on td goes to infinity because we have assumed an unbounded life of the infrastructure. From a practical point of view, this introduce an error that is acceptable anytime the life of the infrastructure will be much larger than δt.

It can be proved that:

$$P(vw = i > 0 | na, nd) = Pa(na) \cdot Pd(nd) \cdot \frac{(1 - Pd(nd))^i}{1 - (1 - Pa(na))} \cdot (1 - Pd(nd))$$

Starting from this result, we can compute $P(vw = 0|na, nd)$, the probability that the size of the window is zero because the defenders discover the vulnerability before the attackers:

$$P(vw = 0|na, nd) = 1 - \sum_{i=1}^{\infty} P(vw = i|na, nd) = \frac{Pd(nd)}{(1 - (1 - Pa(na))) \cdot (1 - Pd(nd))}$$

Taking into account that a loss occurs if and only if $vw \geq 1$, we have that

$$Av(I(na, nd)) = Uloss_A \cdot ns_A \cdot \sum_{i=1}^{\infty} i \cdot P(vw = i|na, nd)$$

that can be further simplified to

$$Av(I(na, nd)) = Uloss_A \cdot ns_A \cdot Pa(na) \frac{1 - Pd(nd)}{Pd(nd) \cdot (1 - (1 - Pa(na)) \cdot (1 - Pd(nd)))}$$

By replacing $Pd(nd)$ and $Pa(na)$, according to (1), and then both $Pd(1)$ and $Pa(1)$ by p, we have that

$$Aver(I(na, nd)) = Uloss_A \cdot ns_A \cdot \frac{(1 - (1 - p)^{na}) \cdot (1 - p)^{nd}}{(1 - (1 - p)^{nd}) \cdot (1 - (1 - p)^{na+nd})}$$

Taking into account that p is fairly small because δt is small, we can exploit $(1 - q)^n \approx 1 - q \cdot n$ and rewrite the equation for the average impact as follows:

$$Aver(I(na, nd)) \approx Uloss_A \cdot \frac{1 - p \cdot nd}{p \cdot nd \cdot (1 + \frac{nd}{na})}$$

The approximation $(1 - q)^n \approx 1 - q \cdot n$ may be applied to the probability that no loss occurs as well. In this way, we can deduce that:

$$P(vw = 0|na, nd) \approx \frac{1}{1 + \frac{na}{nd}}$$

Hence, the probability that no loss occurs

- depends upon the ratio between the number of attackers and of defenders rather than upon both the number of attackers and the one of defenders
- is independent of the probability that an attacker or a defender finds V.

To increase the accuracy of the approximation, we can reduce δt so that p is reduced too. However, δt cannot be arbitrary small because it has to be larger than both the time to define and implement an attack and the one to patch the infrastructure.

By deriving $Aver(I(na, nd))$ with respect to nd and na, we can verify that lower number of defenders and/or larger number of attackers always result into larger impacts because of larger vulnerability windows.

2.3   Loss as a Function of the Time of the Discovery

The 0-delay model may be applied also to compute $Aver(I(na,\ nd,\ t))$the average loss as a function of the time t when a defender discovers V. This loss is interesting because it defines an upper bound on the owner investment in the checks to be executed to discover attacks that may have occurred before t, i.e. before patching the infrastructure [22]. These checks are the first step to recover the loss due to the attacks but, since they may be rather expensive, an estimate of the loss enable the owner to choose whether it is more convenient to simply accept any loss that may be occurred before t.

Because of the assumptions of the 0-delay model, we have that

$$Aver(I(na,nd,t)) = Uloss_A \cdot ns_A \cdot Aver(Svw(k|t,na,nd))$$

where $Uloss_A$ and ns_A have the usual meaning and $Svw(k|t,na,nd)$ is the probability that the size of the vulnerability window is k provided that the defenders have discovered V at time t.

$Aver(Svw(k\ |t,\ na,\ nd))$, the average size of the windows depends upon $P(vw = k > 0|td = t,na,nd)$, the probability that $vw = k$ provided that there are na attackers, nd defenders and $td{=}t$. Since $td{=}t$ and $vw{=}k$ jointly imply $ta{=}t{-}k$, because if the attackers discover V at t-k and the size of the vulnerability window is k, then the attackers have discovered V at time $t{-}k$, we have that

$$P(vw = k|td = t,na,nd) = P(ta = t - k|td = t,na,nd) \tag{2}$$

Since the probability that the attackers finds V is independent of the one that the defenders finds V, the following equality holds:

$$P(ta = t - k|td = t,na,nd) = P(ta = t - k|na,nd) \cdot P(td = t|na,nd)$$

By replacing the equality in the right hand size of (2), we have that

$$P(ta = t-k|td = t,na,nd) = (1-Pd(nd))^{t-1}\cdot Pd(nd)\cdot(1-Pa(na))^{t-k-1}Pa(na)$$

.

We apply now the 0-delay model to compute the average size of the vulnerability window. According to the model, $Aver(Svw(k|t,na,nd))$ is equal to

$$(1 - Pa(na)) \cdot (1 - Pd(nd))^{t-1} \cdot Pa(na) \cdot Pd(nd) \cdot \sum_{k=1}^{t-1} k \cdot \frac{1}{(1 - Pa(na))^k}$$

To simplify this expression, we exploit the fact that an estimate of the impact is important only when V has been discovered after a fairly long time from the infrastructure deployment. In fact, if the infrastructure is patched shortly after being deployed, the loss cannot be very large because the size of the window is bounded by the time from the deployment. Hence, we are interested in the loss if the value of ta is large and, in this case, the following approximation holds

$$\sum_{k=1}^{t-1} \frac{k}{(1 - Pa(na))^k} \approx \frac{1 - Pa(na)}{Pa(na)^2}$$

By applying this approximation, we have that

$$Aver(Svw(k|t, na, nd)) \approx ((1 - P(nd)) \cdot (1 - P(na)))^{t-1} \cdot Pa(na) \cdot Pd(nd) \cdot \frac{1 - Pa(na)}{Pa(na)^2}$$

Lastly, we exploit again (1) to replace the values of the probabilities that an attacker or a defender finds a vulnerability as well as the approximation $(1 - q)^n \approx (1 - nq)$. In this way, the formula for $Aver(Svw(k|t, na, nd))$ may be simplified as following

$$Aver(Svw(k|t, na, nd)) \approx (nd \cdot (t - 1) + na \cdot t) \cdot \frac{nd}{na} \approx (nd + na) \cdot \frac{nd}{na} \cdot t$$

Lastly, by exploiting the previous approximation, we have that

$$Aver(I(na, nd, t)) = Uloss_A \cdot (nd + na) \cdot nd \cdot t$$

2.4   Generalization of the Model

This section generalizes the 0-delay model by removing some of the constraints previously introduced.

At first, we consider the interval of time between discovering the vulnerability and patching of the infrastructure. In most cases, the time to produce and validate the patch or to update some components will be larger than zero. The associated delay increases with the number of the infrastructure components to be corrected. Consider, as an example, the vulnerabilities in the WEP authentication scheme. Hence, the delay DP between the discovery of the vulnerability and the complete patching of the infrastructure may be fairly larger than zero. We assume that DP is not fixed but that it does not depend upon other parameters of the model. Let M_{DP} be an upper bound on DP.

To take DP into account, we update the definition of the vulnerability window and properly increase its size. Hence, if the defenders discover the vulnerability at td and the infrastructure is patched at $td + M_{DP}$ then $vw = td - ta + M_{DP}$. Obviously, the average value of the new delay can be computed by adding M_{DP} to the previous one. Furthermore, any delay DA between the discovery of V and the execution of the attacks exploiting V can be handled in the same way. If M_{DA} is the upper bound on the time to discover an attack, in the most general case, we have that

$$vw = td - ta + M_{DP} - M_{DA} = td - ta - (M_{DA} - M_{DP})$$

To compute the corresponding average loss, we consider that now the probability of a window with a size equal to $td - ta - (M_{DA} - M_{DP})$ is the the same of a window with a size $(td - ta)$ in the 0-delay model.

The previous discussion shows that the framework of the 0-delay model can handle constant delays both in the patching and in the attack, provided that all the attacks are executed simultaneously. Hence, *constant delay* may be a more appropriate name for the model.

Let us consider now the constraint on the simultaneous execution of attacks. As already mentioned, this is a worst case for the defenders because any delay in the execution of attacks reduces the loss. By relieving this constraint, the overall number of attacks does not change but attacks may occur at distinct times. As an example, at each interval, someone could implement *Att* and then inform i other people so that the number of attacks at t is i times that at $t-1$. If V has been discovered at ta and $Natt(t)$ denotes the overall number of attacks executed at $t, t > ta$ we have that

$$NAtt(t) = \frac{i^{t-ta+1}}{i-1}$$

In the most general case, if $fa(t)$ is the number of attacks executed at $t, t > ta$

$$NAtt(t) = \sum_{tv=0}^{t-ta} fa \cdot (ta + tv)$$

δaa, the size of the interval to execute all the attacks, satisfies the following

$$NAtt(\delta aa + ta) = ns_A$$

To compute the loss, we notice that two cases have to be considered if $vw > 0$:

1. $td > ta + \delta aa$, if the defender discovers V after all the attacks have been executed,
2. $ta + \delta aa > td$, if the defender discovers V before all the attacks have been executed.

In case 1), the overall loss results from the sum of two components. The first one is the loss due to attacks in in the interval $(ta+\delta aa,\ td)$ that is equal to

$$Uloss_A \cdot ns_A \cdot (td - ta - \delta aa)$$

The other component is the loss in the interval $(ta,\ ta+stca)$ that is equal to

$$Uloss_A \cdot \sum_{t=0}^{\delta aa} fa(t) \cdot (\delta aa - t)$$

because it is proportional to $(\delta aa-t)$.

In case 2), the overall loss is

$$Uloss_A \cdot \sum_{t=0}^{td-ta} fa(t) \cdot (td - ta - t)$$

This shows that, as in the 0-delay model, we can pair each size of the vulnerability window with a loss. Then, the average impact can be computed if we take into account that the probability of a loss is the same of the size of the window.

In a further case, the overall number of attacks reaches ns_A asymptotically. As an example, the number of attacks in an interval of time sharply increases after discovering V and then approaches zero in a few intervals of time after this maximum. This behavior may be modeled by a Weibull distribution so that the number of attacks executed at $ta + \delta t, \delta t > 0$, is $ns_A * W(\delta t)$ where

$$W(\delta t) = 1 - e^{-(\frac{\delta t}{\alpha})^\gamma}$$

α and γ determine both the shape of W(t) and the standard deviation. The latter goes to zero as γ increases. In this case, the overall loss in the revenues may be approximated as

$$Uloss_A \cdot ns_A \cdot vw \cdot (1 - e^{-(\frac{vw}{\alpha})^\gamma})$$

Again, this value may be computed starting from the probability distribution of the window size.

3   Future Developments

This section briefly outlines some developments of our work by discussing the case of an infrastructure with several vulnerabilities. Then, we also how the 0-delay model can contribute to the debates on "security through obscurity" and on the security advantages of open source components. A further, fundamental, problem to be considered concerns the validation of the theoretical model results against those of some real billing infrastructure. Access to real data is fairly complex because it is well known that owners are not willing to reveal such data.

3.1   Infrastructure with Several Vulnerabilities

In an infrastructure with several vulnerabilities, the worst case for the defender is when the vulnerabilities are independent, because the discovery of one vulnerability does not improve that of discovering the other ones. In the case of such an infrastructure, we assume that attackers and defenders may be assigned to a vulnerability. This is not a contradiction even if no a priori information on the vulnerabilities is available, because we assume that each attacker and each defender consider just one component of the infrastructure. Hence, two defenders or two attackers are assigned to distinct vulnerabilities if they consider distinct components. This assumption implies that each vulnerability is always paired with exactly one component even if it arises because of the interactions among several components. The component a vulnerability V_i is paired with determines two important parameters namely the loss in the infrastructure revenue for unit of time due to attacks enabled by V_i and the probability p_i of finding V_i. If these parameters are known, the 0-delay model, or the constant-delay one, can be applied to compute the average loss due to V_i or the number of defenders to be assigned to V_i to reduce such a loss under some predefined threshold.

However, the most interesting problem to be solved is the relation among the loss due to each vulnerability and the overall allocation of attackers and defenders to the various vulnerabilities. Two cases have to be considered. In the first one the number of attackers allocated to a vulnerability is known when allocating the defenders to the same vulnerability, and the other way around. In the other, more interesting, case the allocations of attackers and of defenders are chosen simultaneously. In this case, the allocation of a resource, i.e. an attacker or a defender, to the search for vulnerabilities can be modeled as a strategy game with two players, the attacker and the defender. The attacker manages a pool with na resources, the attackers, while the defender, i.e the infrastructure owner, manages a pool with nd resources, the defenders. The move of each player defines a tuple with n integers, one for each vulnerability and the i-th integer of the tuple defines the resources allocated by the player to the corresponding vulnerability.

The complete definition of the game requires those of utility functions of both players. Both functions always depend upon the resources allocated to each vulnerability, but alternative definitions are possible. As an example, the utility of the attacker may be the average loss of the infrastructure, i.e. to the sum of the average impacts of attacks enabled by the vulnerabilities, while that of the defender may the inverse of this function. This defines is a zero sum game where the loss of a player is the utility of the other one. In other cases, the utility functions may be defined in terms of the probability that no loss occurs.

In all these cases, we can exploit the main results of game theory, starting from the Nash equilibrium, to define an optimal strategy for each player [22]. It is worth noticing that a worst case for the defender arises anytime the defender allocates a few resources to a vulnerability, say V_j and, simultaneously, the attacker allocates a large number of resources to the same vulnerability. The 0-delay model shows that these allocations result into a large impact due to V_j because of the large difference between the numbers of attackers and of defenders.

3.2 "Security Through Obscurity" and Open Source

The 0-delay model supports the introduction of some mathematical considerations into the discussion of "security through obscurity". This philosophy favors proprietary solutions with respect to open source ones, under the assumption that the lack of information on the infrastructure obstacles the search for vulnerabilities of the attacker. In this way, the attacker has to study a "live" system, which is much more dangerous. As discussed in the previous section. 0-delay models the asymmetry between the attackers and the defenders through the constant φ that multiplies the number of the resource of the defender so that we may assume that the probability of finding a vulnerability is the same for each resource. In a "closed" solution, and if the number of the resources of the attacker is constant, φ increases the number of the resources of the defender to take into account the larger amount of information these resources can access. As a consequence, in an infrastructure exploiting a proprietary solution, if the technical skills of the attackers and of the defenders are comparable, φ will be larger than one and inversely related to public information on the infrastructure or on the considered component.

Instead, the main advantage of the adoption of an open source, or at least an off-the-shelf, component, is that the number of resources searching for a vulnerability may become much larger than the pool managed by the defender. In fact. the search for the vulnerabilities may involve also other instances of the component in distinct infrastructures. As a counterpart, the number of attackers may increase as well, because other people may be interested in attacking distinct instances of the component. However, if the open source component is widely adopted, the defender is fairly sure that, independently of the strategy to allocate his/her resources, all the vulnerabilities in all the components will be covered because other people are searching for them. Hence, it is highly unlikely that very few defenders are searching for a vulnerability and that it will not arise the dangerous case considered at the end of Sect. 3.1 where a few defender resources are allocated to a vulnerability. We stress that an open source component cannot guarantee by itself the existence of a larger pool of resources for either the attacker or the defender because the sizes of these pools depend upon the adoption of the component in distinct systems, i.e. being open source is a necessary but not sufficient condition for larger pools of resources.

When adopting an off-the-shelf component, the number of resources searching for vulnerabilities may be actually so large that these numbers are almost independent of the pools managed by, respectively, the attacker and the defender. This may be a noticeable advantage with respect to a proprietary solution anytime the number of defenders cannot be very large. Consider, as an example, a small enterprise where the defenders may also have limited skills in this very specific field. Instead, if the expected number of attackers is low and they are low skilled, the adoption of an open source component may be a disadvantage.

Since it is defined in terms of φ, na and nd, i.e. the numbers of attackers and defenders, the 0-delay model makes it possible to compare in a quantitative way the advantages of a proprietary solution, i.e. a smaller number of attackers and defenders, against those of a widely adopted open source component, i.e. a larger numbers of both attackers and defenders. Even if the values of φ, na and nd that are used are just a rough approximation of the real ones, some general guidelines on the relative advantages of proprietary or open source components may be deduced from the mathematical framework underlying the 0-delay model.

References

1. Acquisti, A.: Privacy and security of personal information. Economic incentives and technological solutions, Workshop on Economics of Information Security, University of California, Berkley (2002)
2. Adkins, R.: An Insurance Style Model for Determining the Appropriate Investment Level against Maximum Loss arising from an Information Security Breach, Workshop on Economics of Information Security, University of Minnesota (2004)
3. Alberts, C.J., Dorofee, A.J.: An introduction to the OCTAVE method. http://www.cert.org/octave/methodintro.html
4. Anderson, R.J.: Why Information Security is Hard-An Economic Perspective, 17th Applied Computer Security Applications Conference (2001)

5. Anderson, R.J.: Security Engineering: A Guide to Building Dependable Distributed Systems. John Wiley & Sons, Inc., first edition (2001)
6. Anderson, R.: Security in Open versus Closed Systems - The Dance of Boltzmann, Coase and Moore, Conf. on Open Source Software Economics, Toulouse (France) (2002)
7. Anton, P.S., Anderson, R.H., Mesic, R., Scheiern, M.: Finding and fixing vulnerabilities in information systems: the vulnerability assessment and mitigation methodology, MR-1601, Rand Corporation (2003)
8. Arbaugh, W.A., Fithen, W.L., McHugh, J.: Windows of Vulnerability: A Case Study Analysis, IEEE Computer (2000) 52–59
9. Arora, A., Telang, R., Xu, H.: Optimal Policy for Software Vulnerability Disclosure. Workshop on Economics of Information Security, University of Minnesota (2004)
10. Beattie, S., Arnold, S., Cowan, C., et al.: Timing the Application of Security Patches for Optimal Uptime. 16th USENIX Sys. Administration Conf. (LISA 2002) (2002)
11. Burke, D.A.: Towards a game theory model of information warfare, Master Thesis, Air Force Institute of Technology (1999)
12. Carini, B.: Dynamics and Equilibria of Information Security Investments, Workshop on Economics of Information Security, University of California, Berkley (2002)
13. Deraison, R.: The Nessus Attack Scripting Language Reference Guide, www.nessus.org
14. Frey, B.S., Luechinger, S., Stulzer, A.: Calculating Tragedy: Assessing the Cost of Terrorism, Inst. for Empirical Research in Economics, University of Zurich (2004)
15. Gordon, L.A., Loeb, M.P.: The Economics of Information Security Investment, ACM Trans. on Information and System Security, Vol. 5. No. 4 (2002) 438–457
16. Hamilton, S.N., Miller, W.L., Ott, A., Saydjari, O.S.: The Role of Game Theory in Information Warfare. 4th Information Survivability Workshop, Vancouver, B.C., Canada (2002)
17. Hoo, K.S.: How Much Is Enough? A Risk Management Approach to Computer Security, Ph.D. Thesis, Standford University (2000)
18. Kannan, K., Telang, R.: An Economic Analysis of Market for Software Vulnerabilities. Workshop on Economics of Information Security, University of Minnesota (2004)
19. Krsul, I.V.: Software Vulnerability Analysis, Ph.D. Thesis, Purdue University (1998)
20. Major, J.A.: Advanced Techniques for Modelling Terrorism Risk. Journal of Risk Finance, Fall (2002)
21. Mercer, L.C.: Fraud detection via regression analysis. Computers & Security, Vol. 9, no. 4 (1990)
22. Owen, G.: Game Theory, Academic Press, 1995, Third Edition (1995)
23. Rescorla, E.: Is Finding Security Holes a Good Idea?, Workshop on Economics of Information Security, University of Minnesota (2004)
24. Schechter, S.E.: Quantitatively differentiating system security. Workshop on Economics of Information Security, University of California, Berkley (2002)
25. Schechter, S.E.: Computer Security Strength & Risk: A Quantitative Approach, Ph.D. thesis, Harvard University (2004)
26. Schneier, B.: Full disclosure and the window of vulnerability, Crypto-Gram http://www.counterpane.com/crypto-gram-0009.html (2000)
27. Schneier, B.: Closing the Window of Exposure: Reflections on the Future of Security, Securityfocus.com. http://www.securityfocus.com (2000)
28. Stoneburner, G., Goguen, A., Feringa, A.: Risk management guide for information technology systems, NIST, Special Publication 800–30 (2001)
29. Schudel, G., Wood, B.: Adversary work factor as a metric for information assurance, Workshop on New security paradigms, Ballycotton, County Cork, Ireland (2000) 23–30

Analyzing Vulnerabilities and Measuring
Security Level at Design and Exploitation Stages
of Computer Network Life Cycle

Igor Kotenko and Mihail Stepashkin

SPIIRAS, 39, 14 Liniya, St.-Petersburg, 199178, Russia
ivkote@iias.spb.su, stepashkin@computer.edu.ru

Abstract. Vulnerability detection and security level estimation are actual tasks of protecting computer networks. The paper considers the models and architectures of intelligent components intended for active analyzing computer network vulnerabilities and estimating its security level. The offered approach is based on simulation of computer attacks on different levels of detail and intended for implementation at various stages of computer network life cycle, including design and exploitation stages.

1 Introduction

According to CERT statistic [1] the quantity of attacks on computer networks, their complexity and extent of damage, caused by malefactor's attacks in the Internet, grows each year. The reason is a low security level of majority of systems connected to the Internet. The most common failures exist in operating system (OS) and applications software configuration, software maintenance, user management and administration, including improperly configured OS and applications, incorrect password policy and improper access control settings, existence of vulnerable or easily exploited services and malicious software (Trojans, worms, etc.). Therefore now vulnerability detection and estimation of security level of computer networks are actual tasks of information assurance.

A special class of systems exists for solution of these tasks —vulnerability assessment or security analysis systems (SAS) [18, 26]. The contemporary SAS destine to fulfill checking the system defended against the specified system configuration and security policy for non-compliance and identifying technical vulnerabilities in order to correct them and mitigate any risk posed by these vulnerabilities. The main objective of SAS components is to identify and correct the system management process and security policy failures that produced the vulnerabilities detected. The other important functions are security level estimation, supporting effective interface for control of scanning process, creating reports and automatic updating vulnerability signatures. The SAS components should scan system, update the system configuration according to the specified security policy and system configuration and also send inquiries to modify the security policy if it is necessary. It is a cycle that must be repeated

V. Gorodetsky, I. Kotenko, and V. Skormin (Eds.): MMM-ACNS 2005, LNCS 3685, pp. 311–324, 2005.
© Springer-Verlag Berlin Heidelberg 2005

continuously. Moreover, it is important to carry out vulnerability assessment and security analysis during the whole life cycle of computer networks, including initial stages of analysis and design.

The paper is *devoted to creating the models, architectures and prototypes of intelligent components of* vulnerability detection and security level estimation which allow expanding functional capabilities of existing SAS based on penetration testing and simulation. The main attention is devoted to design stage. We describe the architecture of security analysis system offered and models implemented in this system, including the models of attacks, analyzed computer network (estimating the attack results and the system's responses to attacks) and security level assessment. The rest of the paper is structured as follows. *Section 2* outlines the approach suggested and related work. *Section 3* describes the architecture of security analysis system developed and its implementation issues. *Section 4* gives an outline of generalized attack model used for vulnerability assessment and security level estimation. *Section 5* describes the model of analyzed computer network. *Section 6* presents the model of security level evaluation. *Section 7* gives an overview of case study used for checking the approach suggested. *Section 8* summarizes the main results and future research.

2   Related Work

In the paper we suggest the approach which is based on mechanism of automatic construction and replaying of distributed attacks scripts by combining known attacks fragments taking into account various intentions and experience level of malefactors. The results of attacks allow to calculate different security metrics which can be used for defining as the common security level of computer network (system) as well as security levels of its components. This approach can be used at different stages of computer network life cycle, including design and exploitation stages.

At the design stage, SAS should operate with the model of analyzed computer network generated from preliminary or detailed design specifications. The main approaches to vulnerability assessment and security analysis can be based on analytic calculation and imitation (simulation) experiments. Analytical approaches use as a rule different risk analysis methods [2, 11, 25, 28, 37, etc.]. Imitational approaches are based on modeling and simulation of network specifications, fault (attack) trees, graph models, etc. [9, 10, 11, 14, 17, 22, 32, 33, 34, 35, 38, etc.].

There are a lot of papers which consider different techniques of attack modeling and simulation: Colored Petri Nets [16], state transition analysis technique [12, 15], simulating intrusions in sequential and parallelized forms [5], cause-effect model [6], conceptual models of computer penetration [36], descriptive models of the network and the attackers [40], structured "tree"-based description [7, 20], modeling survivability of networked systems [19], object-oriented discrete event simulation [3], requires/provides model for computer attacks [39], situation calculus and goal-directed procedure invocation [8], using and building attack graphs for vulnerability analysis [13, 23, 29, 33, 38], etc.

As one can see from our review of relevant works, the field of imitational approaches for vulnerability assessment and security level evaluation has been delivering significant research results. [32] quantifies vulnerability by mapping known attack scenarios into trees. In [14] a system architecture injects intrusion events into a given network specification, and then visualizes the effects in scenario graphs. Using model checking, Bayesian analysis, and probabilistic analysis, a multifaceted network view of a desired service is provided. [17] suggests a game-theoretic method for analyzing the security of computer networks. The authors view the interactions between an attacker and the administrator as a two-player stochastic game and construct a model for the game. The approach offered in [34] is intended for performing penetration testing of formal models of networked systems for estimating security metrics. The approach consists of constructing formal state/transition models of the networked system. The authors build randomly constructed paths through the state-space of the model and estimate global security related metrics as a function of the observed paths. [38] analyzes risks to specific network assets and examines the possible consequences of a successful attack. As input, the analysis system requires a database of common attacks, specific network configuration and topology information, and an attacker profile. Using graph methods they identify the attack paths with the highest probability of success. [10] suggests global metrics which can be used to analyze and proactively manage the effects of complex network faults and attacks, and recover accordingly.

At the exploitation stage of computes systems two main groups of methods can be used: passive (by analyzing logs, configuration files, etc.) and active (based on penetration testing) [4, 21]. There are a lot of different SAS components which operate on the stage of exploitation. Examples are NetRecon, bv-Control for Internet Security (HackerShield), Retina, Internet Scanner, CyberCop Scanner, Nessus Security Scanner, etc. *The basic lacks of existing* SAS are as follows: (1) use of the scanner does not allow to answer to the main question concerning policy-based systems - "Whether what is revealed during scanning correspond to security policy?"; (2) the quality of obtained result essentially depends on the size and adequacy of vulnerability bases; (3) implementation of active vulnerability analysis on the computer system functioning in a regular mode can lead to failures in running applications. Therefore not all systems can be tested by active vulnerability analysis; (4) existing network security tools can essentially influence on the results generated by scanners. Quite often the protection level evaluated from the place where the scanner is located is wrongly considered as a protection level of the whole network from all types of threats.

3 The Architecture of Security Analysis System

The architecture of security analysis system offered contains the following components (fig.1): (1) user interface; (2) module of malefactor's model realization; (3) module of scriptset (attack scenarios) generation; (4) module of scenario execution; (5) data and knowledge repository; (6) module of data and knowledge repository updating; (7) module of security level assessment; (8) report generation module; (9) network interface.

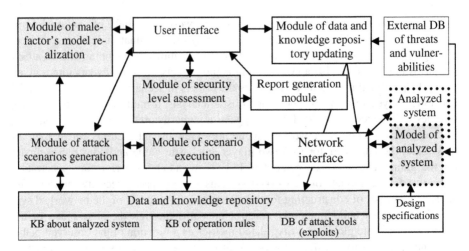

Fig. 1. Generalized architecture of security analysis system

At the design stage, the SAS operates with the *model of analyzed computer network (system)*. This model is based on design specifications. At the maintenance stage, the SAS interacts with a real *computer network (system)*.

Let us describe the functions of basic modules.

The module of malefactor's model realization determines a malefactor's skill level, a mode of actions and an attack goal.

The data and knowledge repository consists of a knowledge base (KB) about analyzed system, a KB of operation (functionality) rules, and a database (DB) of attack tools (exploits). This repository contains data and knowledge which are as a rule used by malefactor when he is planning and realizing attacks.

The knowledge base about analyzed system includes data about the architecture and particular parameters of computer network (for example, a type and a version of OS, a list of opened ports, etc) which are needed for scripts generation and attack execution. This data usually can be received by malefactor using reconnaissance actions and methods of social engineering.

The knowledge base of operation (functionality) rules contains meta- and low-level rules of "IF-THEN" type determining SAS operation on different levels of detail. Meta-level rules define attack scenarios on higher levels. Low level rules specify attack actions based on external vulnerability database. IF-part of each rule contains (meta-) action goal and (or) condition parts. The goal is chosen in accordance with a scenario type, an attack intention and a higher level goal (specified in a meta-rule of higher level). The condition is compared with the data from database about analyzed system. THEN-part contains the name of attack action which can be applied and (or) the link on exploit. An example of one of rules is *"IF GOAL = "Denial of service" AND OS_TYPE = "Windows_NT" AND OS_VERSION =4 THEN ping_of_death (PoD)"*. Each rule is marked with an identifier which allows us to determine the achieved malefactor's goal. For example, the rule mentioned above defines a denial of service (DoS) attack "ping_of_death".

The low-level rules of this database are generated on the basis of Open Source Vulnerability Database (OSVDB) [24]. For example, OSVDB vulnerability with id 6117 shown on fig.2 can be translated to the following rule: «*IF GOAL = "Buffer Overflow" AND PRODUCT_BASE_NAME = MDaemon AND PRODUCT_VERSION_NAME = "2.71 SP1" THEN HELLOEXPL.C*». This rule corresponds to the exploit *helloexpl.c* from the DB of attack tools (exploits).

```
<vuln    osvdb_id="6117"    osvdb_create_date="2004-04-08    22:45:51"
last_modified_date="2004-05-14 04:56:29">
    <osvdb_title>MDaemon Long HELO Overflow</osvdb_title>
    <disclosure_date>1998-03-11 00:44:45</disclosure_date>
    <discovery_date>0001-01-01 00:00:00</discovery_date>
    <exploit_publish_date>1998-03-11 00:44:45</exploit_publish_date>
    <location_remote>1</location_remote>
    <attack_type_dos>1</attack_type_dos>
    <impact_available>1</impact_available>
    <exploit_available>1</exploit_available>
    <vuln_verified>1</vuln_verified>
    <products>
        <product affected="Affected">
            <vendor_name>Alt-N Technologies</vendor_name>
            <base_name>MDaemon</base_name>
            <version_name>2.71 SP1</version_name>
        </product>
    </products>
    <ext_refs>
    ....
        <ext_ref type_name="Generic Exploit URL" indirect="0">
http://do wnloads.securityfo-
cus.com/vulnerabilities/exploits/heloexpl.c</ext_ref>
    </ext_refs>
    ...
    </vuln>
```

Fig. 2. OSVDB vulnerability of the MDaemon Long HELO overflow

The DB of attack tools (exploits) contains exploits and parameters of their execution. A choice of a parameter is determined by the data in KB about analyzed system. For example, the program of ftp brute force password cracking needs to know the ftp server port which can be determined by port scanning.

The module of scriptset (attack scenarios) generation selects the data about analyzed system from the data and knowledge repository, generates attack scriptset based on using operation (functionality) rules, monitors scriptset execution and scriptset updating at runtime, updates data about analyzed system.

The module of scenario execution selects an attack action and exploits, prognoses a possible feedback from analyzed computer network, launches the exploit and recognizes a response of analyzed computer network.

In case of interaction with a computer network a real network traffic is generated. In case of operation with the model of analyzed system two levels of attack simulation are provided: (1) at the first level each low-level action is represented by its label describing attack type and (or) used exploit, and also attack parameters; (2) at the second (lower) level each low-level action is specified by corresponding packets of the network, transport and applied level of the Internet protocols stack.

Network interface provides: (1) in case of operation with the model of analyzed system −transferring identifiers and parameters of attacks (or network packets under more detailed modeling and simulation), and also receiving attacks results and system reactions; (2) in case of interaction with a computer network −transferring, capturing and the preliminary analysis of network traffic. The preliminary analysis includes: (1) parsing of packets according to connections and delivery of information about packets (including data on exposed flags, payload, etc.) and connections; (2) acquisition of data about attack results and system reactions, and also values of some statistics reflecting actions of SAS at the level of network packets and connections.

The module of security level assessment is based on developed taxonomy of security metrics. It is a main module which calculates security metrics based on results of attack actions.

The module of database and knowledge repository update downloads the open vulnerability databases [30] (for example, OSVDB - open source vulnerability database [24]) and translates them into KB of operation (functionality) rules of low level.

4 Generalized Attack Model

Functioning of SAS is specified by the attack model implemented in the module of malefactor's model realization. The model is defined as hierarchical structure that consists of several levels (fig.3). Three higher levels of the attack model correspond to an attacks scriptset, a script and script stages. The *scriptset level* defines a set of general malefactor's intentions (high level goals). This level corresponds to realization of series of scenarios which can be implemented by a group of malefactors. The *script level* defines only one malefactor's intention. The set of *script stages* can contain the following elements: reconnaissance, implantation (initial access to a host), gaining privileges, threat realization, covering tracks and backdoors creation. Lower levels serve for malefactor subgoals refinement. The lowest level describes the malefactor's low level actions directly executing different exploits.

Two main methods of malefactor's goal achievement are used in the attack model: (1) forward and (2) backward inference. Both of these methods use database of functionality rules selecting an item in the hierarchy of a general attack model. *Forward inference* makes exhaustive or limited search of actions available on a current hierarchy level. Executing this inference method, SAS realizes all or limited number of available malefactor's low level actions for every script stage beginning from the first stage. *Backward inference* implies generation of optimized chain of actions based on definition of malefactor intention (goal) beginning from the last action in the line to the first action.

After definition of one or set of malefactor's intentions SAS goes to next level of generalized attack model and generates needed scenarios and attack actions.

The malefactor behavior strategy is defined by his model. In this model the malefactors are classified by knowledge and an experience level into three groups: (1) a low level ("novice"); (2) a middle level; (3) a high level ("professional"). "Novice" utilizes for goal achievement the exhaustive forward inference method, middle level malefactor −limited forward inference method and "professional" −the backward inference method.

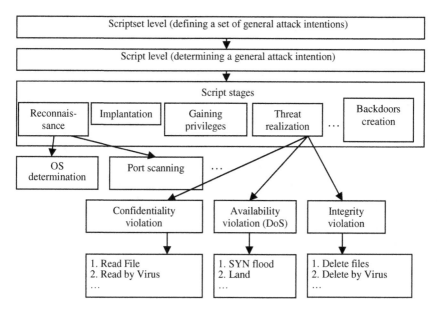

Fig. 3. Fragment of generalized attack model

5 Model of Analyzed Computer Network

The model of analyzed computer network (system) intends for evaluating attack results and defining system reaction. It contains the following basic components (fig.4):
network interface; module of malefactor actions recognition; module of attack result
evaluation; module of system response generation; database about analyzed system,
database of attack signatures.

Network interface provides: (1) receiving identifiers and parameters of attacks; (2)
transferring attack results and system reactions.

Module of malefactor actions recognition is necessary at realization of detailed attack modeling and simulation, i.e. when malefactor actions are represented as network
packets. Functioning of this module is based on a signature method – the data received from the network interface are compared to signatures of attacks from *database of attack signatures*. Outputs of the module are identifiers and parameters of
attacks.

The knowledge base about analyzed system is created from the specification of
analyzed system and structurally coincides with KB about analyzed system described
in section 3. The difference of these knowledge bases consist in the stored data: KB of
the model of analyzed system contains the results of translating the specifications of
analyzed system; KB related to the generalized architecture of SAS is initially empty
and is filled during the execution of attack scripts.

Formal representation of analyzed system includes the specification of computer
network structure, hosts resources and functions. The structure of a computer network
CN is determined as follows [9]: $M_{CN} = < A, P, N, C >$, where *A* is the network address; *P* is a family of protocols used (e.g., TCP/IP, FDDI, ATM, IPX, etc.); *N* is a set

$\{CN_i\}$ of sub-networks and/or a set $\{H_i\}$ of hosts of the network CN; C is a set of connections between the sub-networks (hosts) established as a mapping matrix. Each host H_i is determined as a pair $M_{Hi} = <A, T>$, where A is the host address, T is a host type (e.g., firewall, router, host, etc.). The network host resources and functionalities serve for representing the host characteristics that are important for attack simulation. These characteristics are represented as follows: $M_{Hi} = < A, M, T, N, D, P, S, DP, ASP, RA, SP, SR, TH$, etc.>, where A – IP-address, M – mask of the network address, T – type and version of OS, N – users' identifiers (IDs), D – domain names, P – host access passwords, S – users' security identifiers (SID), DP – domain parameters (domain, names of hosts in the domain, domain controller, related domains), ASP – active TCP and UDP ports and services of the hosts, RA – running applications, SP – security parameters, SR – shared resources, TH – trusted hosts.

The implemented algorithm for *module of attack result evaluation* is based on using a set of rules describing what kind of attacks, in what sort of conditions, and with what probability (possibility) do have success. The input for these rules is an attack identifier and a set of parameters defining current state of analyzed system. The output is a probability (possibility) of the attack successfulness.

If system description is sufficiently detailed, then the module of attack result evaluation can give as a rule univocal answer. But at the design stage the system description as a rule is incomplete. In this case we need to expand the model of attack result evaluation with meta-rules, or implement coefficients of probability (possibility) and evaluate the attack result utilizing these coefficients. For example, the rule which describes Ping of Death attack: "*IF ATTACK = PoD AND OS_TYPE = Windows_NT AND OS_VERSION = 4.0 AND ICMP_FILTERING = OFF THEN P= 0.8*", where PoD – an identifier of DoS-attack "Ping of Death", $P=0.8$ means that attack has success with probability (degree of possibility) 0.8. The OS type, OS version and the filtering condition are verified using the database about analyzed system.

Response of the information system model on malefactor attacks is a change of its state and (in some cases) a message directed to attacker (as a system reaction on attack). Each state can be characterized by the attributes describing accessibility of a system (as a whole one and its certain services), data integrity, data confidentiality, users and their privileges, etc. *The module of system response generation* fulfills a set of rules of the system reaction: $\{R^{SR}_j\}$, where R^{SR}_j: *Input -> Output & Post-Condition*,

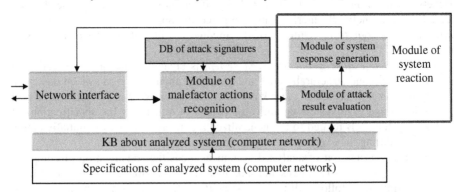

Fig. 4. Model of analyzed computer network

Input is the malefactor's activity, *Output* is the system reaction, *Post-Condition* is a change of the system state, & is logic connective "AND". Thus, the module produces the response of system to attack (for example, after successful attack on scanning ports the list of open ports is generated) and updates KB about analyzed system (for example, if a malefactor creates a new user in the group of administrators or starts a remote administration service, these changes are reflected in KB).

6 Model of Security Level Evaluation

The functionality of the module of security level evaluation is described by a corresponding model which uses a multi-level hierarchy of security metrics.

The taxonomy of security metrics is based on the attack model developed. The taxonomy contains as the notions of attack realization actions, as well as the notions of types and categories of assets (secured objects).

There are four levels of security metrics *sub-taxonomy based on attack realization actions* (fig.5): (1) an integrated level; (2) a script level; (3) a level of the script stages; (4) a level of the threat realization. Each higher level contains all metrics of lower levels (arrow in fig.5 shows the direction of metrics calculation). Examples of security metrics for this taxonomy are as follows: number of total and successful attack scenarios; number of total and successful stages of attack scenarios; number of total and successful malefactor attacks on the certain level of taxonomy hierarchy; number of attacks blocked by existing security facilities; number of discovered and used vulnerabilities; number of successful scenario implementation steps; number of different path of successful scenario implementation, etc.

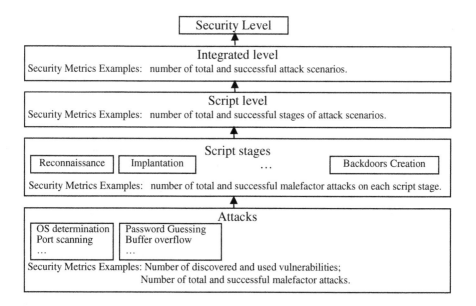

Fig. 5. Security metrics sub-taxonomy based on attack realization actions

Second sub-taxonomy is formed taking into *account types and categories of assets*. Assets are divided on the following types: (1) informational resources (confidential and critical information); (2) software resources (OS, DBMS, etc.); (3) physical resources (servers, workstations, etc.); (4) services (web, mail, ftp, etc). There are several approaches for assets categorizing. We use an approach which is based on dividing of assets into groups by confidentiality and criticality levels (fig.6). Examples of security metrics of this taxonomy are as follows: total score of confidentiality and criticality of assets that have been successfully attacked; number of confidential and critical assets that have been successfully attacked, etc.

Evaluation of these metrics is based on attacks results and reaction of the analyzed system.

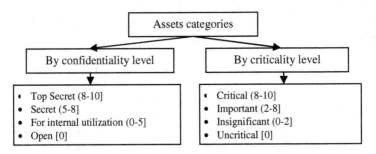

Fig. 6. Security metrics sub-taxonomy based on assets' categories

7 Case Study

For testing and evaluating our approach we specified, developed and deployed the computer network which configuration is shown in fig.7. The experiments were carried out using "VMWare Workstation 5.0", that allows to emulate the work of personal computers and to form a virtual computer networks.

The network consists of the following three subnets: (1) Internet area including hosts *Internet_host* and *ISP_DNS* with IP-addresses 195.19.200.*; (2) demilitarized zone including two servers with IP-addresses 192.168.0.*; (3) local area network with IP-addresses 10.0.0.*. The basic elements of the network are: (1) Internet host with SAS; (2) Firewall 1 – a firewall between Internet and demilitarized subnet; (3) File Server and (4) Mail Server – servers, located in the demilitarized subnet; (5) Firewall 2 – a firewall between local area network and demilitarized subnet; (6) DNS server – a local DNS server, which services the clients from LAN; (7) AAA Server – an authentication, authorization and accounting server; (8) Workstation 1..4 – workstations.

The generalized functional scheme of SAS prototype implemented is presented on fig.8.

The model of analyzed system uses specification of security policy and system architecture, defined on Security Policy Language (SPL) and System Description Language (SDL) [27]. SDL and SPL are represented in Common Information Model (CIM) format. The Common Information Model (CIM) is an approach from the DMTF to the management of systems, applications, networks and services that applies the basic structuring and conceptualization techniques of the object-oriented paradigm. SDL describes a computer network on the level of network topology and services. The network topology is described by the classes PhysicalElement, PhysicalLink, and the ElementsLinked association. The network services are described by classes ComputerSystem, Service, ProtocolEndpoint, ServiceAccessPoint, ServiceAvailableToElement, ProvidesEndpoint, HostedAccessPoint, BindsTo.

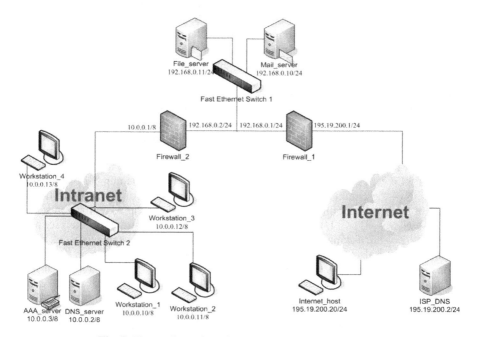

Fig. 7. The configuration of computer network for case study

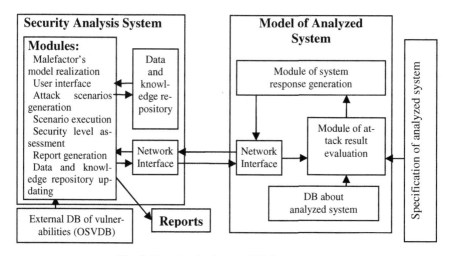

Fig. 8. Functional scheme of SAS prototype

Let us consider an example of using the SAS prototype for developed case study. Let we need to determine a security level of the file-server against attacks "denial of service" when the malefactor's experience level is a "novice". To do this we need to enumerate the necessary assets and its confidentiality and criticality levels (in brackets): (1) Information resources: the information about open ports on file-server (5,2); the information about used services on file-server (5,2); the information about operating system of file-server (5,8); the information about users on file-server – names and groups (5,8); the password of the user "admin" (10, 10); (2) Software resources: operating system (5,10); physical resources: server (0,10); (3) Services: file-server (0,10).

According to the malefactor's model realization SAS creates one script consisting of the following two stages: (1) reconnaissance and (2) threat realization (denial of service). At a first stage all accessible groups of actions are executed: port scanning, OS determination, services identification, etc. Actions of each group are executed until a positive result is reached, e.g. port scanning begins with "TCP SYN scan", in case of negative result the "TCP connect scan" is executed, and so on. If port scanning and identification of services are successfully completed by the first methods and three methods of OS determination and five methods of user logins enumeration are completed by failure, then the security metric of reconnaissance stage can be calculated as follows: $P_R=1 - N_{SA}/N_A=1 - 2/10=0.8$, where N_{SA} – the number of successful actions, N_A– the common number of actions. If at the stage of threat realization the usage of tenth vulnerability is successful, then the metric of thread realization stage is $P_{TR}=1- N_{SA}/N_A=1 - 1/10=0.9$. The security metric for the whole script is $(0.8+0.9)/2=0.85$. Taking into account that only one script has been generated, the integral metric is also equal 0.85. The value of security metric depends on the realization of malefactor's model. For example, in case of using backward inference method of malefactor goal achievement, the total number of actions is decreased; consequently the value of security metric is reduced.

Let us calculate a confidentiality and criticality levels of successfully attacked assets. At reconnaissance stage, the malefactor has received the information which total level of confidentiality is 10 and total level of criticality is 4. For the information which the malefactor tried to receive the appropriate levels are (20, 20). After normalization, the losses of confidentiality and criticality are (0.5, 0.2). At thread realization stage, the file-server has been successfully attacked (0 points of confidentiality and 10 points of criticality have been lost), therefore the appropriate losses are (0, 1). At script level the losses of confidentiality and criticality are as follows: ((0.5+0)/2, (0.2+1)/2) = (0.25, 0.6). The total security metric can be calculated as difference 1 and average value of the given coefficients: 1-0.43=0.57.

Let us select by expert evaluation the following security level scale: (1) "green" – if security level value in an interval [1, 0.8); (2) "yellow" – [0.8, 0.6); (3) "red" – [0.6, 0]. Then the value 0.57 acts as "red" level. As guideline on increase of security level, the report with instructions about vulnerability elimination is generated. Procedure of security level evaluation is repeated after eliminating detected vulnerabilities.

8 Conclusion

The paper offered the approach to vulnerability analysis and security level assessment of computer networks, intended for implementation at various stages of a life cycle of analyzed computer systems.

The basic components of suggested intelligent SAS are the knowledge base of functionality rules, the model of computer attacks and the model of security level assessment based on developed taxonomy of security metrics. The SAS prototype was implemented and the experiments were held based on the case-study developed.

The future research will be devoted to improving the models of computer attacks, the model of security level assessment, and comprehensive experimental assessment of offered approach.

Acknowledgement

This research is being supported by grant of Russian Foundation of Basic Research (№ 04-01-00167), grant of the Department for Informational Technologies and Computation Systems of the Russian Academy of Sciences (contract №3.2/03) and partly funded by the EC as part of the POSITIF project (contract IST-2002-002314).

References

1. CERT/CC Statistics 1988-2005. http://www.cert.org/stats/cert_stats.html
2. Chapman, C., Ward S.: Project Risk Management: processes, techniques and insights. Chichester, John Wiley (2003)
3. Chi, S.-D., Park, J.S., Jung K.-C., Lee J.-S.: Network Security Modeling and Cyber Attack Simulation Methodology. LNCS, Vol.2119 (2001)
4. Chirillo J.: Hack Attacks Testing – How to Conduct Your Own Security Audit. Wiley Publishing (2003)
5. Chung, M, Mukherjee, B., Olsson, R.A., Puketza, N.: Simulating Concurrent Intrusions for Testing Intrusion Detection Systems. Proc. of the 18th NISSC (1995)
6. Cohen, F.: Simulating Cyber Attacks, Defenses, and Consequences. IEEE Symposium on Security and Privacy, Berkeley, CA (1999)
7. Dawkins, J., Campbell, C., Hale, J.: Modeling network attacks: Extending the attack tree paradigm. Workshop on Statistical and Machine Learning Techniques in Computer Intrusion Detection, Johns Hopkins University (2002)
8. Goldman R.P.: A Stochastic Model for Intrusions. LNCS, V.2516 (2002)
9. Gorodetski, V., Kotenko, I.: Attacks against Computer Network: Formal Grammar-based Framework and Simulation Tool. RAID 2000. LNCS, V.2516 (2002)
10. Hariri, S., Qu, G., Dharmagadda, T., Ramkishore, M., Raghavendra C. S.: Impact Analysis of Faults and Attacks in Large-Scale Networks. IEEE Security & Privacy, September/October (2003)
11. Henning, R.: Workshop on Information Security System Scoring and Ranking. Williamsburg, VA: Applied Computer Security Associates and The MITRE Corporation (2001)
12. Iglun, K., Kemmerer, R.A., Porras, P.A.: State Transition Analysis: A Rule-Based Intrusion Detection System. IEEE Transactions on Software Engineering, 21(3) (1995).
13. Jha, S., Sheyner, O., Wing, J.: Minimization and reliability analysis of attack graphs. Technical Report CMU-CS-02-109, Carnegie Mellon University (2002)
14. Jha, S., Linger, R., Longstaff, T., Wing, J.: Survivability Analysis of Network Specifications. Intern. Conference on Dependable Systems and Networks, IEEE CS Press (2000)
15. Kemmerer, R.A., Vigna, G.: NetSTAT: A network-based intrusion detection approach. 14th Annual Computer Security Applications Conference, Scottsdale, Arizona (1998)

16. Kumar, S., Spafford, E.H.: An Application of Pattern Matching in Intrusion Detection. Technical Report CSDTR 94 013. Purdue University (1994)
17. Lye, K., Wing J.: Game Strategies in Network Security. International Journal of Information Security, February (2005)
18. McNab, C.: Network Security Assessment. O'Reilly Media, Inc. (2004)
19. Moitra, S.D., Konda, S.L.: A Simulation Model for Managing Survivability of Networked Information Systems, Technical Report CMU/SEI-2000-TR-020, December (2000)
20. Moore, A.P., Ellison, R.J., Linger, R.C.: Attack Modeling for Information Security and Survivability. Technical Note CMU/SEI-2001-TN-001. March (2001)
21. Nessus Network Auditing. Renaud Deraison. Syngress Publishing, Inc. (2004)
22. Nicol, D.M., Sanders, W.H., Trivedi, K.S.: Model-Based Evaluation: From Dependability to Security. IEEE Transactions on Dependable and Secure Computing. Vol.1, N.1 (2004)
23. Ortalo, R., Dewarte, Y., Kaaniche, M.: Experimenting with quantitative evaluation tools for monitoring operational security. IEEE Trans. on Software Engineering, 25(5) (1999)
24. OSVDB: The Open Source Vulnerability Database. http://www.osvdb.org/
25. Peltier, T.R.: Information security risk analysis. Auerbach 2001.
26. Peltier, T.R., Peltier, J., Blackley, J.A.: Managing a Network Vulnerability Assessment. Auerbach Publications (2003)
27. POSITIF Project leaflet. http://www.positif.org/idissemination.html (2004)
28. RiskWatch users manual. http://www.riskwatch.com
29. Ritchey, R. W., Ammann, P.: Using model checking to analyze network vulnerabilities. Proceedings of IEEE Computer Society Symposium on Security and Privacy (2000)
30. Rohse, M.: Vulnerability naming schemes and description languages: CVE, Bugtraq, AVDL and VulnXML. SANS GSEC PRACTICAL (2003)
31. Sademies, A.: Process Approach to Information Security Metrics in Finnish Industry and State Institutions. VTT Electronics, Espoo. VTT Publications (2004)
32. Schneier, B.: Attack Trees. Dr. Dobb's Journal, vol. 12 (1999)
33. Sheyner, O., Haines, J., Jha, S., Lippmann, R., Wing, J.M.: Automated generation and analysis of attack graphs. Proc. of the IEEE Symposium on Security and Privacy (2002)
34. Singh, S., Lyons, J., Nicol, D.M.: Fast Model-based Penetration Testing. Proceedings of the 2004 Winter Simulation Conference (2004)
35. Steffan, J., Schumacher, M.: Collaborative Attack Modeling. 17th ACM Symposium on Applied Computing (SAC 2002), Madrid, Spain (2002)
36. Stewart, A.J.: Distributed Metastasis: A Computer Network Penetration Methodology. Phrack Magazine, 9 (55) (1999)
37. Storms A.: Using vulnerability assessment tools to develop an OCTAVE Risk Profile. SANS Institute. http://www.sans.org
38. Swiler, L., Phillips, C., Ellis, D., Chakerian, S.: Computer-attack graph generation tool. DISCEX '01 (2001)
39. Templeton, S.J., Levitt, K.: A Requires/Provides Model for Computer Attacks. Proc. of the New Security Paradigms Workshop (2000)
40. Yuill, J., Wu, F., Settle, J., Gong, F.: Intrusion-detection for incident-response, using a military battlefield-intelligence process. Computer Networks, No.34 (2000)

A Temporal Logic-Based Model for Forensic Investigation in Networked System Security

Slim Rekhis and Noureddine Boudriga

CN&S Research Lab., University of the 7th Of November at Carthage, Tunisia
smr@certification.tn
nab@supcom.rnu.tn

Abstract. Research in computer and network forensic investigation has recently addressed the development of procedural guidelines, technical documents, and semi-automation tools. It has however omitted the need of formal proof. This work provides a novel approach that formalizes and automates the proof in digital forensic investigation. First, it brings out a formal logic-based language, called S-TLA$^+$, to enable reasoning on systems with uncertainty, by adding forward hypotheses to fulfill potential lack of details. S-TLA$^+$ is suitable for the description of evidences, as well as elementary scenarios fragments representing the investigators knowledge. Secondly, the proposal provides an automated verification tool, S-TLC, to prove the correctness of S-TLA$^+$ specifications. It checks whether there are possible hacking scenarios that meet the available digital evidences, and explores additional evidences. To demonstrate its effectiveness, the formalized analysis is applied on a compromised host.

1 Introduction

The growth of the number of digital security incidents and the sophistication of the intrusions techniques made it impossible to completely prevent attacks. Therefore, it becomes necessary to react efficiently to security incidents. Computer forensic investigation, defined as "preservation, identification, extraction, documentation and interpretation of computer data" [1], enables achieving these objectives while performing a post-incident examination: a) evidence collection; b) attack scenarios and relating security weakness determination; and c) result argumentation with methods and techniques that are well-tested and proved.

During the recent years, the literature has addressed two main themes: a) contribution to the development of technical documents specific to the investigation of various operating systems and b) writing of procedural guidelines for forensic investigation. It has omitted any need of formalization and proof automation in digital forensic investigation, reducing consequently the results accuracy, and analysis practicality. Formalization allows an explicit and unambiguous representation of forensic investigator's knowledge and observations. The proof automation makes the generated investigation deductions relevant even with a huge amount of data. It lets investigators argue about complex scenarios without a need for advanced skills, nor a priori knowledge about the incident causes.

V. Gorodetsky, I. Kotenko, and V. Skormin (Eds.): MMM-ACNS 2005, LNCS 3685, pp. 325–338, 2005.
© Springer-Verlag Berlin Heidelberg 2005

Formal digital forensic investigation has interested few works that differ according to the techniques and methodologies they used. [2] used Colored Petri Nets to model digital postmortems investigation as a time-line of events. It focused on determining the set of causes that enabled the security incident to success, so that the appropriate countermeasures can be foreseen. Nevertheless, the methodology does not model incident effects, and does not support hypotheses formulation when details are missing. [3] presented an automated diagnosis system that generates possible attacks sequences using a plan recognition technique, simulates them on the victim model, and performs pattern matching recognition between their side effects and log files entries. This technique assumes that attack activity is logged, which is in contradiction with the fact that complex attack scenarios may subvert logging daemon and alter logs before hackers leave the system. [4] used an expert system with a decision tree to search through evidences for potential violations of invariant relationship between digital objects. The methodology is useful in reducing the amount of data to be analyzed. Nevertheless, it roughly depends on the system time granularity and the degree of preciseness that the system uses to record time on objects.

This paper extends the work of [5]. First, it brings out a new logic-based language, entitled S-TLA$^+$. Using a temporal logic of security actions, it offers a important enhancement of the formal specification language TLA$^+$[6]. S-TLA$^+$ is founded on a logic formalism that let adding forward hypotheses whenever there is lack of details (information may be corrupted by hackers) to understand the system. Second, the proposal is completed with an automated verification tool, called S-TLC, to prove the correctness of S-TLA$^+$ specifications. The tool is based on the enhancement of the TLC model checker [6,7]. It is fitted to the automated diagnosis of digital security incidents.

Our contribution is straightforward. First, the proposed approach is completely independent from any computer security technology or incident. It allows arguing about sophisticated hacking scenarios as it tolerates potential lack of details. Second, S-TLA$^+$ takes advantage from the richness of the formal specification language TLA$^+$ to support advanced description of scenarios and evidences, namely using temporal modalities.

The remaining of this paper is organized as follows: First, the forensic investigation model is defined in Section 2. Next, Section 3 defines the novel S-TLA logic and emphasizes on the new concepts and modifications added to TLA. In Section 4, the formal specification language S-TLA$^+$ is defined and demonstrated how it can be used within forensic investigation. Section 5 presents S-TLC, explains how it represents states, and describes how hacking scenarios are inferred both using forward and backward chaining. In Section 6, the proposal is exemplified by a case study. Finally, the work is concluded in Section 7.

2   The Computer Forensic Investigation Model

Given a set of evidences collected further to the occurrence of a security incidents, the proposal aims to first reconstruct to potential hacking scenarios where hypotheses are advanced whenever needed, and secondly, provides any additional evidences. Alike [8], we consider a hacking scenario as a combination of more generic and reusable fragments, which are basically described in advance without an a priori knowledge about the whole hacking scenario that is looked for. Every scenario fragment is depicted by an optional set of hypotheses underlying the scenario-fragment occurrence, a set of pre-conditions that must be satisfied, and a set of actions to achieve a sub-goal of the whole scenario objective. The inclusion of hypotheses is due to the fact that investigation on sophisticated attack scenarios needs to be tolerant to potential lack of data. The latter is generated by intruders who want to alter any trace that could prove their identity or activity.

As the combination of scenario fragments leads to the accumulation of hypotheses, care need to be taken from inconsistency introduction. In fact, some hypotheses are contradictory with each other and could not arise in the same whole hacking scenario. Moreover as hypotheses are described by a set of relations between variables and values, two hypotheses using the same variable with different values might make no sense if grouped together in a scenario.

Figure 1 shows a set of attack scenarios relative to an unauthorized modification of access accounts on a remote server. The attack can be achieved after: 1) exploiting a remote vulnerability that grants privileged access; 2) escalating one's privilege via local vulnerability exploit, 3) Logging to the system from a trusted server. The node Log from a trusted server X is composed by a hypothesis stating that a trust relationship is established between servers S and X, a post-condition stating that the user Usr is being logged to the server X at that time and an action asserting a telnet connection by the user to the server S.

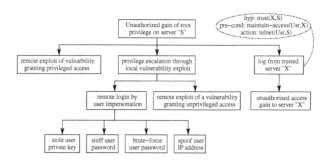

Fig. 1. Attack scenarios model

3   S-TLA: An Extension to the Temporal Logic of Actions

We provide in the following a Temporal Logic of Security Actions, S-TLA, as an extension to the Temporal Logic of Actions, TLA. We emphasize only on the new introduced concepts regarding TLA, as S-TLA embodies TLA and a TLA specification is indeed an S-TLA specification. TLA was introduced by Leslie Lamport for the specification of distributed and asynchronous systems [9].

Suppose, for instance, a formal system description that should involve a detail (value progress) of its n dependent variables, but some of them are unknown. To overcome such lack of details, it is conceivable to use a formalism that let enunciate hypotheses whenever needed. As denoted by Figure 2, we want to make TLA able to describe a system progress from a state s to a state t, further to the execution of an action $\mathcal{A}$ and under a hypothesis $H_{\mathcal{A}}$.

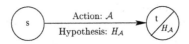

Fig. 2. State transitions under hypotheses

S-TLA Constrained Variables: We introduce a new set of variables, called constrained variables set V_C, to encompass the variables representing hypotheses. V_c is disjoint from sets V_F and V_R that represent flexible and rigid variables sets, respectively. Such separation is of great importance since we are looking during verification phase (c.f. section 5.1) to reach a given system state under a minimal set of hypotheses. Moreover as a hypothesis, once enunciated, might affect the system behavior, we assume that a constrained variable, whose value once set during a system state transition, could not be valued differently afterwards all through the system behavior.

S-TLA State: As in TLA, a state remains a valuation of all system variables. Precisely, it is an assignment from the collection *Val* of values to the set *Var* = $V_F \cup V_R \cup V_C$. A state can thus give information on the set of enunciated hypotheses that let it being reachable from the initial system state.

S-TLA Fictive Value ▽: As a state is a valuation of all variables, a constrained variable should have a value even if there is no enunciated hypothesis yet. To bridge this gap, a new fictive S-TLA value described by the symbol ▽ is introduced to represent the value of a constrained variable that up to the moment was not used to make a hypothesis. Broadly, a state with a constrained variable whose value is different from ▽ means that there is an enunciated hypothesis to reach the related state.

S-TLA Assumption Operator ″: We introduce a new S-TLA operator entitled assumption operator ″ to denote the value of a constrained variable in the new state. This operator is different from the TLA prime operator. It changes the value of a constrained variable only if its value is different from ▽. We define assumed and non-assumed variables to refer respectively to new and old state of constrained variables. In this way, we let $V_A \triangleq \{x" \mid x \in V_C\}$ be the set of assumed variables.

S-TLA Inconsistency: We define an S-TLA inconsistency as a predicate containing constrained variables, constants, and constants operators [9]. Informally, an inconsistency denotes a combination of hypotheses that must not be observed inside a system behavior. Semantically it is true or false for a state. If it is true for a state t , then the system transition on the way to that state should not be followed. Hereinafter, we denote an S-TLA inconsistency using the symbol $\bot$.

S-TLA Action and Hypothesis: An S-TLA action is a conjunct between two expressions. The former is optional, of type boolean, denotes some hypotheses, and contains assumed and non-assumed variables. The latter is the old TLA action containing primed and unprimed variables. Semantically, given an inconsistency $\bot$, an S-TLA action $\mathcal{A}$ is true for a pair of states $\langle s, t \rangle$ iff,

- $\mathcal{A}(\forall v \in V_F : s(v)/v, t(v)/v') = true$: By replacing each unprimed flexible variable in action $\mathcal{A}$ by $s(v)$; the value of v in state s, and each primed flexible one by $t(v)$, the boolean resultant expression equals true.
- $\mathcal{A}(\forall v \in V_C : s(v)/v, t(v)/v'') = true$: By replacing each non-assumed constrained variable v in the action $\mathcal{A}$ by $s(v)$ and each assumed constrained one v'' by $t(v)$, the boolean resultant expression equals true.
- $\forall v \in V_c / s(v) \neq \nabla : s(v)/v = t(v)/v$: The set of constrained variables whose values have been stated by a hypothesis (e.g. different from ∇) somewhere before, retain the same value in state s and t.
- $\bot (t) = false$: The predicate $\bot$ must not hold in the state t, that is $(t \nvDash \bot)$.

S-TLA Specification Formula: We introduce the predicate $IsTrue_{\mathcal{A}}(\bot)$ to be equal true if and only if $\bot$ is true further to the execution of action $\mathcal{A}$. We define $\mathrm{NI}_v(\mathcal{N}, \bot)$, *No Inconsistency* on action $\mathcal{N}$ as: $\mathrm{NI}_v(\mathcal{N}, \bot) \equiv$ ENABLED $\mathcal{N} \wedge \neg IsTrue_{\mathcal{N}}(\bot) \Rightarrow \langle \mathcal{N} \rangle_v$ to states: if action $\mathcal{N}$ is enabled and if its execution does not let inconsistency $\bot$ equal true, then action $\mathcal{N}$ occurs. We define ϕ as the system specification formula that generates an infinite behavior $\natural = \langle s_0, s_1, s_2, ... \rangle$ (denoting the system progression) where no inconsistency $\bot$ is holding in any state $s_i \in \natural$. The resultant form is as follows: $\phi \triangleq \exists x : Init \wedge \Box[\mathcal{N}]_v \wedge L \wedge \mathrm{NI}_v (\mathcal{N}, \bot)$. Except the quoted syntactically and semantically modifications, the remaining TLA notions including Fairness, stuttering, and temporal modalities are preserved.

4   S-TLA⁺: A Formal Language for Writing Specifications

We define S-TLA⁺ as a language for writing specifications in S-TLA, it embodies TLA⁺ [6] with some add-ons in the module structure (the lowest granular part of a TLA⁺ specification,) and in the constant and non constant operators. TLA⁺ is the high-level specification language that is based on TLA, and extended by notations of set theory (Zermelo Fraenkel set theory) and syntactic structuring mechanisms. To describe S-TLA⁺, we concentrate only on the introduced modifications as outlined hereinafter:

a) Module-Level constructs: The expression CVARIABLES $v_1, \ldots, v_n$ adds the declaration of constrained variables, distinguishing them from non-constrained ones, which remain declarable using VARIABLES statement.

b) Non constant S-TLA$^+$ operators: Given a constrained variable h, we denote by h'' the value of h in the next state. Moreover, UNTOUCHED h replaces the expression $h'' = h$

c) Constant S-TLA$^+$ operators: we denote by $\triangledown$ a fictive value to represent the constrained variable value, before a hypothesis is enunciated.

4.1   Standard Form of a S-TLA$^+$ Specification

The first part of Figure 3, [5], illustrates a typical S-TLA$^+$ specification, described by module *SpecExpl*. The specified system is described by formula *spec*, while the initial system state is described by predicate *Init* (no hypotheses are enunciated as constrained variables g and h are both equal to $\triangledown$). Action A, for instance, is true for a pair of states $\langle s, t \rangle$ if (1) the value that t assigns to x is 1 higher than the value that s affects to x, (2) under the hypothesis $g'' = 1$, and (3) without t being reached under the hypothesis $h'' = 2$ (by the definition of inconsistency predicate *Inc*). Finally, the predicate *Evd* describes a relevant S-TLA$^+$ system state (a valuation of some system variables) which is of capital importance especially in fulfilling forensic investigation objectives. Its use will be demonstrated afterwards in section 4.2.

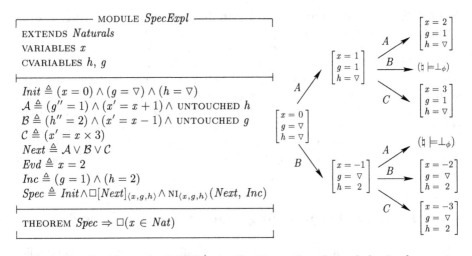

Fig. 3. Standard form of a S-TLA$^+$ specification and a relative behavior fragment

The second part of Figure 3 describes a fragment from the set of possible system behaviors relative to formula *Spec*. For a successive execution of A followed by B, two successive hypotheses are generated: $g'' = 1$ followed by $h'' = 2$.

This is an unacceptable execution as it drives to a state where the S-TLA inconsistency predicate *Inc* will be true. Besides, a successive execution of action *A* followed by *C* is legitimate.

4.2   Computer Forensic Investigation Using S-TLA$^+$

A scenario fragment component as modeled in Section 2 matches well the form of a S-TLA$^+$ action. In fact, pre-conditions, generated hypotheses, and actions which represent the context of a scenario fragment can be described respectively by state-predicates, relations between assumed and non-assumed variables, and relations between primed and unprimed variables.

A digital forensic evidence can take the form of a temporal property (e.g., a hacked system is issuing every so often an outbound connection to send sniffed passwords), or an undesirable state of a system component (e.g., an altered file is a violation of the integrity property). These two forms can be specified in S-TLA$^+$ using temporal formulas, and state predicates, respectively.

An expected hacking scenario is a disjunction of scenarios fragments (i.e., S-TLA$^+$ actions) denoting possible hacking events starting from a state representing a safe system and ending in a state satisfying the digital evidence(s). The core S-TLA logic works by infinitely selecting the suitable scenario fragment that copes with the attained system behavior, such that no inconsistency is holding and composing it with the previous ones into potential hacking scenarios.

5   S-TLC: A Model Checker for S-TLA$^+$ Specifications

To automate the proof in the context of forensic investigation, we propose S-TLC as an automated verification tool for S-TLA$^+$ specifications with a stress on the handling of hypotheses and an improvement in the states space representation. S-TLC is somehow an extension to the Model Checker TLC[6], which checks S-TLA$^+$ specifications for errors such as silliness, invariance properties violation, and deadlock [6, chapter 14]. In the following, we emphasize on the contributions and changes in S-TLC, namely state computation and scenario inference.

5.1   S-TLC's States Space Representation

Given two different states that represent respectively a valuation ($x = 1$) of the variable x under two possible sets of hypotheses ($h = 1 \land g = 2$) and ($h = 3 \land g = 3$). Representing a state as a valuation of all its variables (as in Figure 3) will involve a representation of two different states (($1,1,2$) and ($1,3,3$)) in the generated scenarios. We propose a more developed and optimal representation involving two notions: *node core* and *node label*. The core of a node represents a valuation of the entire non-constrained variables, and the node label represents the potential sets of hypotheses (a set of hypotheses is a valuation of the entire constrained variables) under which the node core is reached. The node label is represented and maintained in a way akin to the one used in the

Assumption Truth Maintenance System (ATMS [10]). Precisely, a node label is a set of environments and an environment is a set of hypotheses. The previous example will thus involve only one node represented by $1\{(1,2), (3,3)\}$ where 1 is the node core, $(1,2)$ and $(3,3)$ are both environments, and $\{(1,2), (3,3)\}$ is the node label. In the following, given a state t, we use t_n to denote its corresponding node core, t_c to describe its resulting environment, and $Label(G, t)$ to refer to its label in graph G.

5.2   Inferring Scenarios with S-TLC

The S-TLC Model Checker is described by Algorithm 1. It employs three data structures G, U_F and U_B. The first refers to the reachability directed graph under construction generated during forward chaining and backward chaining phase. The last two are FIFO queues, containing states whose successors have not being yet computed respectively during forward and backward chaining phases. The algorithm assumes that a configuration file is done as input, it includes statements denoting that $Init$ is the initial state predicate, $Next$ is the next state relation, $Invariant$ is a state-predicate to be satisfied by each reachable state, and Inc is the predicate to be equal false for all states of the system behavior, it represents the the set of S-TLA inconsistencies. Moreover, the specification is supposed to be made finite-state. To that effect the configuration file is presumed to include statements stating that $Constraint$ is a predicate that asserts bounds on the set of reachable states, and $EvidenceState$ is a predicate characteristic of a terminal state representing forensic evidences.

To append a node to the graph under construction, the algorithm uses function $Append(G, t, t \rightarrowtail s)$ to add a node t to graph G with a pointer to its predecessor state s. Besides, a state s is attached to a FIFO queue U using the function $Append(U, s)$ and detached using the function $Tail(U)$. Moreover, a node t is joined to an existing node s inside the graph G using the function $Join(G, t \rightarrowtail s)$. S-TLC works in three phases:

Initialization Phase: G, as well as U_F and U_B are created and initialized respectively to empty set $\varnothing$ and empty sequence $\langle \rangle$. During this step, each state satisfying the initial system predicate is computed and then checked whether it satisfies predicate $Invariant$. In that case, it will be appended to G after computing its label, and pointing it to the $null$ state. If the state does not satisfy $EvidenceState$, it will be attached to the unseen queue U_F, otherwise, it will be considered as a terminal state and appended to U_B in order to be retrieved in backward chaining phase.

Forward Chaining Phase: During this phase, the algorithm starts with U_F equal to the set of initial system states. Afterwards and until the queue becomes empty, state s (representing the tail of U_F) is retrieved and its successor states are computed. From the latter, for every state (denoted by t) satisfying $Constraint$, if $Invariant$ is not satisfied, an error is generated and the algorithm terminates, otherwise t is appended to G as follows:

- If t_n does not exist in $\mathcal{G}$, it is appended as a new node with a label equal to t_c and a predecessor equal to s_n. Then, t is appended to $\mathcal{U}_B$ if it satisfies *EvidenceState*, otherwise it is attached to $\mathcal{U}_F$.
- If there exists a node x in $\mathcal{G}$ which is the same as t_n and whose label includes t_c, then a conclusion could be made stating that t has been added previously to $\mathcal{G}$. In that case, a pointer is simply added from x to s_n.
- If there exists a node x in $\mathcal{G}$ that is the same as t_n, but whose label does not include t_c, then the node label is updated in the following manner:
  1. t_c is added to $Label(\mathcal{G}, x)$.
  2. Any environment from $Label(\mathcal{G}, x)$, which is a superset of some other environment in this label, is deleted to ensure hypotheses minimality. Formally, an environment E_1 is a superset of E_2 in the same environment iff: $E_1(x) = E_2(x) \vee E_2(x) = \nabla$, where $E(x)$ represents the xth value in E. An environment $(8, 1, 3)$ is for instance a superset of $(\nabla, 1, 3)$.
  3. If t_c is still contained in the label of state x (meaning that it was not deleted in step (2)) then node x is pointed to s_n and node t is appended to $\mathcal{U}_B$ if it satisfies *EvidenceState*. Otherwise, it is attached to $\mathcal{U}_F$.

Every node label is provided with the following four properties: 1) Soundness: a node x holds each environment E_i; 2) Consistency: None environment E_i in $Label(\mathcal{G}, x)$ is inconsistent, preventing *Inc* from holding; 3) Completeness: every environment E is a superset of some E_i; and 4) Minimality: no environment E_i is a proper subset of any other.

Forward chaining may generate many slices of global attacks scenarios, a great majority of them are useless due to further occurrence of inconsistencies or because they do not lead to evidence generation. Nevertheless, this may generate additional source of evidences and show the propagation steps of the attack.

Backward Chaining Phase: This phase helps obtaining potential and additional scenarios that could be the root causes for the set of available evidences. This phase starts with $\mathcal{U}_B$ holding the set of terminal states; the ones that satisfied *EvidenceState* in forward chaining phase. Afterwards, and until the queue becomes empty, the tail of $\mathcal{U}_B$, described by t, is retrieved and its predecessor states (the set of states s_i such that (s_i, t) satisfies action *Next*) which are not terminal states and satisfy *Invariant* (States that do not satisfy *Invariant* are discarded because this phase does not aim to check whether a specification is correct or not but simply to generate additional explanations) and *Constraint* are computed. Each computed s is appended to $\mathcal{G}$ as follows:

- If s_n does not exist in $\mathcal{G}$, a new node (set to s_n) is appended to the graph with a label equal to s_c. Afterwards, a pointer is added from t_n to s_n and s is appended to $\mathcal{U}_B$.
- If there exists a node x in $\mathcal{G}$ which is the same as s_n, and whose label includes s_c, then s was added previously to $\mathcal{G}$. In that case a pointer is simply added from t_n to s_n and s is appended to $\mathcal{U}_B$.
- If there exists a node x in $\mathcal{G}$ which is the same as s_n, but whose label does not include s_c, then the node label of x is updated in the following manner:

1. The environment s_c is added to $Label(\mathcal{G}, x)$, the label of state x.
2. Any environment from $Label(\mathcal{G}, x)$ which is a superset of some other environments in this label is deleted to ensure hypotheses minimality.
3. If s_c is still contained in the label of x then t is pointed to the predecessor state x and s is appended to $\mathcal{U}_B$.

The outcome of the three phases is a graph $\mathcal{G}$ of the potential scenarios that lead to the collected evidences. It embodies different initial system states apart from the ones described by the specification. In fact, in the context of forensic investigation, an attack scenario could start from a legitimate system state, as well as from a previous system incident or instability.

6   Case Study

To make concrete the use of S-TLA$^+$ and S-TLC in digital forensic investigation, we propose this case study which is an investigation of a standalone (disconnected from network) system that is compromised, where an illegal privileged access is detected. The system ran initially with two users accounts: a root and an unprivileged user. A straightforward examination by experts shows that the system security log is altered. The latter no longer contains more than a single unexpected record showing that the system root has closed its session.

6.1   S-TLA$^+$ Specification Description

The following set of S-TLA$^+$ actions is specified to represent hacking scenarios fragments. For the sake of readability, we ignore the fragments that will not be part of the whole expected scenarios.

– *LogAsUsr*: Using the hypothesis stating that the user password is a well-known word, an intruder guesses the password and gains access to the system, raising its privilege *localpr* from 0 to 1. Moreover, the pair $\langle$"*usr*", "*logon*"$\rangle$ is appended to the sequence *log* to log such event. Note that 0 means there is no granted access, while 1 lets a user execute any non administrative command. Finally, 2 refers to the root privilege.

$LogAsUsr \triangleq \wedge userhas'' = $ "weakpwd" $\wedge localpr = 0 \wedge localpr' = 1$
$\qquad\qquad\quad \wedge log' = Append(log, \langle$"usr", "logon"$\rangle)$

– *InstSoft*: A user who gained an unprivileged access can install its own software, particularly, a vulnerability exploit tool.

$InstSoft \triangleq localpr = 1 \wedge addsft = $ "" $\wedge addsft' = $ "exploit"

– *ExpLclVuln*: Hypothesizing that there is a vulnerability in one of the installed super-user commands that could grant a privileged access, if exploited, the current user exploits such vulnerability and rises its privilege from 1 to 2. The system kernel updates sequence *log* in order to log the event.

$ExpLclVuln \triangleq \wedge roothas'' = $ "vulnbin" $\wedge localpr = 1 \wedge addsft = $ "exploit"
$\qquad\qquad\qquad \wedge localpr' = 2 \wedge log' = Append(log, \langle$"root", "logon"$\rangle)$

Algorithm 1. S-TLC algorithm

Comment: *Initialization phase*
$\mathcal{G} \leftarrow \emptyset, \mathcal{U}_F \leftarrow \langle\rangle, \mathcal{U}_B \leftarrow \langle\rangle$
$S \leftarrow \{s_i \mid s_i \vDash Init\}$
For each $s \in S$

do $\begin{cases} \text{if } s \nvDash Invariant \textbf{ then } error, break \\ \text{if } s \vDash Constraint \textbf{ then } \begin{cases} Append(\mathcal{G}, s_n, s \rightarrowtail null), Label(\mathcal{G}, s_n) \leftarrow s_c \\ \text{if } s \vDash EvidenceState \textbf{ then } Append(\mathcal{U}_B, s) \textbf{ else } Append(\mathcal{U}_F, s) \end{cases} \end{cases}$

Comment: *Forward chaining phase*
While $\mathcal{U}_F \neq \langle\rangle$

do $\begin{cases} s \leftarrow tail(\mathcal{U}_F) \\ T \leftarrow \{t_i \mid ((s, t_i) \text{ satisfies the S-TLA}^+ \text{ action } Next) \wedge t \vDash Constraint\} \\ \textbf{For each } t \in T \\ \text{do} \begin{cases} \text{if } t \nvDash Invariant \textbf{ then } error, break \\ \text{if} \nexists x \in \mathcal{G} / t_n = x \\ \quad \textbf{then} \begin{cases} Append(\mathcal{G}, t_n, t_n \rightarrowtail s_n), Label(\mathcal{G}, t_n) \leftarrow t_c \\ \text{if } t \vDash EvidenceState \textbf{ then } Append(\mathcal{U}_B, t) \textbf{ else } Append(\mathcal{U}_F, t) \end{cases} \\ \text{if } (\exists x \in \mathcal{G} / t_n = x) \textbf{ and } t_c \subseteq Label(\mathcal{G}, x) \textbf{ then } Join(\mathcal{G}, x \rightarrowtail s_n) \\ \text{if } (\exists x \in \mathcal{G} / t_n = x) \textbf{ and } t_c \nsubseteq Label(\mathcal{G}, x) \\ \quad \textbf{then} \begin{cases} Label(\mathcal{G}, x) \leftarrow Label(\mathcal{G}, x) \cup t_c \\ \text{Delete any superset of hypotheses from } Label(\mathcal{G}, x) \\ \text{if } t_c \in Label(\mathcal{G}, x) \\ \quad \textbf{then} \begin{cases} Join(\mathcal{G}, t_n \rightarrowtail s_n) \\ \text{if } t \vDash EvidenceState \textbf{ then } Append(\mathcal{U}_B, t) \textbf{ else } Append(\mathcal{U}_F, t) \end{cases} \end{cases} \end{cases} \end{cases}$

Comment: *Backward chaining phase*
While $\mathcal{U}_B \neq \langle\rangle$

do $\begin{cases} t \leftarrow tail(\mathcal{U}_B) \\ S \leftarrow \{s_i \mid ((s_i, t) \text{ satisfies the S-TLA}^+ \text{ action } Next) \wedge (s_i \vDash Invariant, Constraint) \\ \qquad \wedge(s \nvDash EvidenceState)\} \\ \textbf{For each } s \in S \\ \text{do} \begin{cases} \text{if} \nexists x \in \mathcal{G} / s_n = x \\ \quad \textbf{then} \begin{cases} Append(\mathcal{G}, s_n, t_n \rightarrowtail s_n) \\ Label(\mathcal{G}, s_n) \leftarrow s_c \\ Append(\mathcal{U}_B, s) \end{cases} \\ \text{if } (\exists x \in \mathcal{G} / s_n = x) \textbf{ and } s_c \subseteq Label(\mathcal{G}, x) \textbf{ then } \begin{cases} Join(\mathcal{G}, x \rightarrowtail s_n) \\ Append(\mathcal{U}_B, s) \end{cases} \\ \text{if } (\exists x \in \mathcal{G} / s_n = x) \textbf{ and } s_c \nsubseteq Label(\mathcal{G}, x) \\ \quad \textbf{then} \begin{cases} Label(\mathcal{G}, x) \leftarrow Label(\mathcal{G}, x) \cup s_c \\ \text{Delete any superset of hypotheses from } Label(\mathcal{G}, x) \\ \text{if } s_c \in Label(\mathcal{G}, x) \textbf{ then } Join(\mathcal{G}, t_n \rightarrowtail s_n), Append(\mathcal{U}_B, s) \end{cases} \end{cases} \end{cases}$

- *OffBrForce*: Hypothesizing that the algorithm used to hash the account's passwords is weak, a user reads the file containing the password hashes and brute-forces the root password off-line (outside the current system). It succeeds thus in escalating its privilege.

$$OffBrforce \triangleq \wedge roothas'' = \text{``pwdhashcomp''} \wedge localpr = 1 \wedge localpr' = 2$$
$$\wedge log' = Append(log, \langle\text{``root''}, \text{``logon''}\rangle)$$

- *ChangeID*: Hypothesizing that the root password is equal to the user's, the user changes its identity to the root by providing the correct password. Consequently, its privilege rises from 1 to 2, and the event is logged.

$$ChangeID \; \stackrel{\Delta}{=} \; \wedge \; roothas'' = \text{``pwdequser''} \wedge localpr = 1 \wedge localpr' = 2$$
$$\wedge \; log' = Append(log, \langle \text{``root''}, \text{``logon''} \rangle)$$

- *ExtSoft*: Given a software installed on the system for security auditing purpose, the user copies one binary command from those that come with it to be used maliciously as an exploit tool.

$$ExtSoft \; \stackrel{\Delta}{=} \; localpr = 1 \wedge addsft = \text{``audittool''} \wedge addsft' = \text{``exploit''}$$

- *CleanLog*: A privileged user can clean the log file content.

$$ClaenLog \; \stackrel{\Delta}{=} \; localpr = 2 \wedge log \neq \langle \rangle \wedge log' = \langle \rangle$$

- *DelSoft*: A privileged user can delete the whole tools unexpectedly installed.

$$delSoft \; \stackrel{\Delta}{=} \; localpr = 2 \wedge addsft \neq \text{``''} \wedge addsft' = \text{``''}$$

- *Exit*: The user logs off, its privilege goes down to 0 and the event is logged.

$$Exit \; \stackrel{\Delta}{=} \; localpr = \wedge localpr' = 0 \wedge log' = Append(log, \langle \text{``root''}, \text{``logoff''} \rangle)$$

Inconsistency defined as: $userhas = \text{''weakpwd''} \wedge roothas = \text{''pwdequser''}$, states that a system state should not be reached under a conjunct of the following two hypotheses: a) the user password is a well-known word and b) the root password is equal to the user one. In fact, the forensic investigator is sure that the root password fulfills a strong password policy. The available evidence is described by predicate $EvidenceState \; \stackrel{\Delta}{=} \; Head(log) = \langle \text{''root''}, \text{''logoff''} \rangle$, which states that the finite sequence *log* encloses only one record equal to $\langle \text{``root''}, \text{``logoff''} \rangle$.

The system under investigation is specified by a S-TLA$^+$ formula *Spec* similarly to the form described in section 4.1, where *Init* describes the initial system state (empty log file, no unexpected tool installed, no granted access).

$$Init \; \stackrel{\Delta}{=} \; localpr = 0 \wedge log = \langle \rangle \wedge addsft = \text{``''} \wedge userhas = \nabla \wedge roothas = \nabla$$

6.2   Investigation Using S-TLC

Figure 4 describes the results generated by S-TLC until the forward chaining phase. It outlines two different system states (the ones which are encircled) satisfying predicate *EvidenceState*, where one of them shows a new generated evidence as an exploit tool installed by the malicious user to exploit a local vulnerability. These two evidences can be generated under two possible set of hypotheses: 1) the user password is weak and one of the installed system commands contains a vulnerability that grants a privileged access; and 2) the user password and the password hashing algorithm are both weak. Two main possible scenarios may be distinguished in this phase:

1. An intruder guesses the weak user password and gains an unprivileged access. Afterwards, it exploits a weakness in the password hashing algorithm and

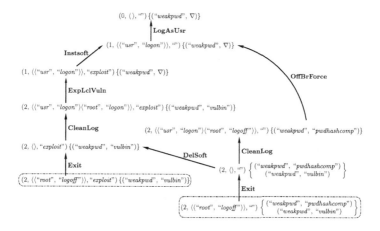

Fig. 4. Scenarios generated in forward chaining phase

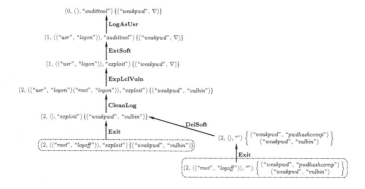

Fig. 5. Scenarios generated in backward chaining phase

succeeds in escalating its privilege by performing an offline brute-force of the root password. It cleans its logged activity and logs off from the system. Fortunately, the latter activity is logged.

2. An intruder guesses a weak user password and logs in to the system, gaining an unprivileged access. After that, it installs a malicious tool and exploits a vulnerability in one of the installed super-user commands, obtaining thus a privileged access. Before cleaning the log file and leaving the system, the intruder either deletes its installed tool or leaves such kind of evidence.

The generated scenario prevents inconsistency from occurring. In fact, action *ChangeID* does not belong to the scenario since it contains a hypothesis that is inconsistent with the one occurring in *LogAsUsr* according to the definition of predicate *Inconsistency*. The graph of Figure 5 is the graph generated after the execution of forward and backward chaining phases. For readability reasons, it shows only the new generated scenarios compared to the ones of Figure 4. Mainly, a new scenario is added. It strongly resembles to the second one generated in forward chaining phase, except that the system is initially housing a security auditing software and the hacker is using one of the commands that come with such software as an exploit tool, instead of installing its own one.

7   Conclusion

We proposed in this paper a novel formal logic-based language entitled S-TLA$^+$ to achieve a tremendous aspect in digital forensic investigation: the reconstruction of potential hacking scenarios and the providing of new evidences that could complement the available ones. S-TLA$^+$ uses a formalism that allows handling hypotheses whenever there is a lack of details to demonstrate some part of an attack scenario. We have also described S-TLC as a new automated formal verification tool that is able to handle S-TLA$^+$ specifications. Its main advantage lies in its robustness in managing hypotheses and representing states. Considering implementing and testing this tool represents a continuation of this work.

References

1. Kruse, W.G., Heiser, J.G.: Computer Forensics: Incident Response Essentials. Pearson Education (2001)
2. Stephenson, P.: Modeling of post-incident root cause analysis. International Journal of Digital Evidence, Vol. 2, No. 2 (2003)
3. Elsaesser, C., Tanner, M.C.: Automated diagnosis for computer forensics. tech. rep., The MITRE Corporation (2001)
4. Stallard, T., Levitt, K.: Automated analysis for digital forensic science: Semantic integrity checking. Proceedings of the 19th Annual Computer Security Applications Conference (2003)
5. Rekhis, S., Boudriga, N.: A Formal Logic-based Language and an Automated Verification Tool For Computer Forensic Investigation. Proceedings of the 20th ACM Symposium on Applied Computing (SAC 2005) (2005)
6. Lamport, L.: Specifying Systems: The TLA$^+$ Language and Tools for Hardware and Software Engineers. Addison-Wesley (2002)
7. Yu, Y., Manolios, P., Lamport, L.: Model checking TLA$^+$ specifications. Conference on Correct Hardware Design and Verification Methods (1999) 54–66
8. Keppens, J., Zeleznikow, J.: A model based reasoning approach for generating plausible crime scenarios from evidence. Proceedings of the 9th International Conference on Artificial Intelligence and Law (2003)
9. Lamport, L.: The temporal logic of actions. ACM Transactions on Programming Languages and Systems, Vol. 16 (1994) 872–923
10. de Kleer, J.: An assumption-based TMS. Artificial Intelligence, Vol. 28, No. 2 (1986) 127–162

Vulnerabilities Detection in the Configurations of MS Windows Operating System

Peter D. Zegzhda, Dmitry P. Zegzhda, and Maxim O. Kalinin

Information Security Centre of Saint-Petersburg Polytechnical University,
P.O. Box 290, K-273, Saint-Petersburg, 195251, Russia
{zeg, dmitry, max}@ssl.stu.neva.ru

Abstract. This paper addresses to the technique of the vulnerabilities detection. The proposed methodology is applicable to verify property of the operating system configurations safety. Using our technique it becomes possible to discover security drawbacks in any secure system based on access control model of 'state machine' style. We discuss the Vulnerability Criteria Processing Unit, the automated detection tool, working in MS Windows and calculating the set of vulnerable settings. Through our case study of model checking in Sample Vulnerability Checking (SVC), we show how the proposed technique is applied to verify system security.

1 Introduction

The most important aspect of the computer system is *secrecy* of information stored in a system. A secrecy violation was defined in [1] as "an unauthorized person is able to read or take advantage of information stored in the computer". Reasons of poor data protection are concealed at abundant errors that expose during system designing, coding, and administrating. The well-known lacks of security are those of programming origin, but they are successfully resolved with regular patches and service packs. At the same time, sophisticated analyses of the operating systems made by the world-renowned organizations, e.g. *CERT* or *Secunia*, testify to the 20 percents of vulnerabilities caused by incorrect security configuring and adjustment arranged by users or administrators. We consider errors made at the time of security administrating as reasons of *operating system configuration vulnerabilities (OSCV)*.

The OSCVs take place after:

- ignoring the security requirements, published by vendors or security experts;
- setting the different security adjustments that implicitly may conflict with each other or alternate other settings;
- keeping the security settings that may contradict to the company security policy.

The most typical examples of the OSCVs are using of default system security configuration, accidental folder permissions for the system files, and software installation to the default paths. For instance, in MS Windows 2000, if there is a shared folder created by administrator, the system grants '*Full Access*' to new object for '*Everyone*'. If administrator is a novice in security, she or he could miss such fault

V. Gorodetsky, I. Kotenko, and V. Skormin (Eds.): MMM-ACNS 2005, LNCS 3685, pp. 339–351, 2005.

and others could access to somebody's private files. Another example is that *Dr.Watson*, the built-in debugger in MS Windows, starts every time after system fault and creates the dump file *C:\Winnt\user.dmp*. Now imagine that *OE* falls down and *Dr.Watson* makes the dump. The dump corresponding to *OE* includes all mail accounts and passwords as plain text. Besides this, the NT file system (NTFS) creates a new file with default properties (with default access permissions among them) taken from the parent folder, e.g. *C:\Winnt*, and *'Everyone'* thus has *'Full Control'* over the dump file and consequently all private email passwords saved in the file. The Linux-style operating systems obtain the OSCVs of the same sort, e.g. they have a *SUID*-programs problem. Such mistakes in configuration of protection environment reduce every solid and well-engineered security to 'zero'.

To eliminate the OSCVs, administrator has to know and observe all of the system details on-the-fly, analyze the security bulletins and vulnerability reports, and apply the security reconfiguring operatively. Therefore, administrator needs to be in good knowledge of the system inside and control a countless number of the system securable objects. For instance, we can estimate a great many of the objects of security interest in the wide-spread MS Windows operating system. There are 36 types of the MS Windows entities that are used with access differentiation. Among them there are 9 entities of user level (e.g. group accounts, NTFS objects, system registry), and 27 kernel-level objects (e.g. jobs, processes, threads, objects of synchronization). Each object in MS Windows refers to the discretionary access control mechanism — the access control list (ACL). Every entry of ACL is a 32-bit access mask that provides the access rights. Users and groups obtain up to 37 privileges that allow control of their behavior in the system. What is more, 38 local security settings specify the computer-native security policy. Thus, even in the isolated station, a number of security setting combinations exceeds *tens of millions*. For administrator, it is an impracticable task to detect OSCVs in such a complex system as MS Windows. She or he could make a very hard work of analyzing and monitoring the security settings in 'step-by-step' mode for 'one-by-one' security setting, but it will take enormously long period. Consequently, to solve a task of security faultlessness in the operating system, we need a special facility for the system's vulnerability detection.

This paper discusses the theory and technique of the OSCVs detection in the secure operating systems. This paper is structured as follows. *Section 2* reviews the related works in security flaws detection conformably to the MS Windows safety. *Section 3* introduces our approach applied to the vulnerabilities searching. *Section 4* gives a brief review of our solution to search the OSCVs. Here we also explain an example of logical specification and OSCVs detection for Sample Vulnerability Checking (SVC) in MS Windows. Finally, *section 5* discusses conclusion of our work.

2   The Related Works

Most of the other works on security assurance in the computer systems relates to the evaluation of the system safety. CSP [2] is an example which allows a security of the fixed number of the system processes to be specified and evaluated. Each process is identified with a security label, and the system security is evaluated in a field of these labels. The security calculus is provided with a technique of a parallel programming language. This approach is useful for the vulnerabilities searching in the flow-related computer systems: network transactions [3], client-server communications.

In [3], there is presented the UML-based approach for the automated verification of the security requirements. They have demonstrated a conception of the verification routines for security constraints associated with the stereotypes of the UML security extension UMLsec [4]. To do so, the analysis routine extracts information from different diagram types (class, deployment, and statechart diagrams) that may contain specific security-related information. The system requirements can be formulated at the level of the system's security model. But for this work we need to obtain the UMLsec diagram. Unfortunately, it cannot be obviously built for MS Windows. To do this, we would have a need for special tool, which will automatically compose the UML-diagram for a huge number of MS Windows objects. Other ways, the UML-based approach could not be a reliable and efficient way to check the security vulnerabilities.

A group at Carnegie Mellon developed a security specification and checking system called Miro [6]. The Miro system consists of two languages and a collection of software tools. One specification language is for protection configurations and the other is for security policies. It is a general system, but the Miro system was accomplished for the UNIX operating system [7]. The UNIX-style systems are mostly the open source ones, they operate with a limit number of the objects to be protected. To investigate the UNIX security thus needs little mind and time expenses.

We have also observed characteristics of the MS Windows-oriented vulnerabilities detectors (Enterprise Security Manager, Symantec Corp.; Intrusion SecurityAnalyst, Intrusion Inc.; NetIQ Security Analyzer, NetIQ Inc.; XSpider, Positive Technologies; Microsoft Baseline Security Analyzer, Microsoft Corp., etc). After analyzes, we have made some conclusions (it is notable, that the following remarks are independent of developer's name and product version):

- no solution investigates the system inside. For example, the known products have an eye on the well-known file paths or the security-critical folders. No one looks at security of the kernel mode objects;
- no product allows composing the detection criteria. For example, the analyzed solutions use either the predefined checks or the scripts of the check sequence;
- no detector predicts an effect of the security settings upon the reachable states of the system.

Therefore, to our knowledge, the general problem of evaluation of security enforcement including weakness detection in such a complex operating systems as MS Windows has never been addressed by any author.

3 Vulnerabilities Detection

According to the fundamentals of computer system modeling, we look at the safety of the system through the safety of the system states. The *state* is characterized with the security configuration, which could (or not) contain the OSCV. To detect the OSCV in the state we need to analyze the security configuration corresponding to the given state. We consider the *security configuration* of the given state as a complex of subjects (the active system entities, e.g. users), objects (passive containers of information, that need a protection, e.g. files), and their security attributes (e.g. access rights). We add to this schema the term of *constraints* like a set of access restrictions given for the 'subject-object-attributes' triple. We call the system to be safe in the given state, i.e. "*something bad never happens in the given state*". In other words, there is no critical OSCV in the given state. In real-life systems, the constraints are imposed upon the system state through the scope of the system-related security configuration. Breaking the security configuration produces the OSCV. Criteria, that help us to delimit the secure and insecure states for the OSCVs checking, we will call as *OSCV-criteria*.

If security system has a problem in its security configuration, it means that the OSCV exists and secret information is leaked by unauthorized access. Assurance that system exploitation or the administrator's behavior does not result in the unauthorized access is fundamental for ensuring the system security. An important feature of an access control in the operating system is an ability to verify the correctness of security configuration. If the security configuration is set properly, then there is no OSCV in the system, and the system is thus secure in terms of the given vulnerabilities.

As we see, the OSCVs detection may be accomplished as checking of the security requirements fulfillment or, in opposite side, as checking of the definite insecure settings. Consequently, the criteria could be formulated either in terms of positive (required or "desirable") situation, or in form of negative (denied or "undesirable") situation. Verbally, in case of positive statement, the criterion specification starts with the words: "*System is secure, if ... [**security requirements that need to be in the system**] ...* ". In case of negative criteria, the specification of criterion starts with "*System is vulnerable, if ... [**vulnerability conditions that need not to be in the system**] ...* ".

To make the OSCVs detection a comfortable routine we need both specifications, because transformation from one mode to another is obvious mathematically but not trivial for complex computer systems. Let us demonstrate the example of 'negative-to-positive' transformation hardness. We have the following OSCV-criterion: "System is vulnerable, if *user U obtains right "w" for file F*" (fig. 1). We mathematically could use just a positive specification instead of both modes. To do this, we ought to transform negative description of OSCV to positive one. Thus, we need to specify four different positive situations.

The theory of security supplies us with the following basics of OSCVs detection.

R_{all} defines a set of all possible access rights that the user can obtain for the given type of securable object. R_{PA} denotes the "required" access rights, that user should have. If she or he has the "required" rights, the system will be thus secure. R_{PD} is a set of the "denied" rights, i.e. the access rights that should be forbidden to user. If those rights are banned to user, the system is considered to be secure. To take into account the system security settings, we need to introduce the set R_S, the number of access rights, range of which is allowed by the system security settings, $R_S \subseteq R_{all}$.

R_{excess} denotes the "excess" rights, i.e. a subset of rights which are not "necessary" but allowed by the security settings; and R_{miss} marks the "missed" rights, i.e. a subset of rights which are not enough for user to obtain all of the system-defined rights.

Rights mask R

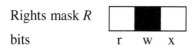

bits   r   w   x

<u>Negative specification (spec. of OSCV):</u>
- bit "w" is set

<u>Positive specification (spec. of security requirement):</u>
- bit "r" is set;
- bit "x" is set;
- bits "rx" are set;
- $\varnothing$ — no bits are set

Fig. 1. Criteria Enhancement in Specification Transformation

For positive specification of OSCV-criteria, we have declared three conditions of the system security.

Condition P1. Positive Equity. System is secure (according to the given criterion), if the set R_S of the system-provided rights coincides with the set R_{PA} of the "required" rights, $R_S=R_{PA}$ (fig. 2).

Condition P2. Positive Secrecy. System is secure (according to the given criterion), if the set R_S of the system-provided rights not exceeds the set R_{PA} of the "required" rights, $R_S \subseteq R_{PA}$ (fig. 3).

Condition P3. Positive Availability. System is secure (according to the given criterion), if the system allows the user to obtain all of the "required" access rights, $R_{PA} \subseteq R_S$ (fig. 4).

To detect the OSCV in positive case, we need to make the following calculus.

Test P1. $R_{excess} = R_S - R_{PA}$. If $R_{excess} \neq \varnothing$, the system is vulnerable, because the current security configuration allows the user to hold the unauthorized access rights (fig. 5).

Test P2. $R_{miss} = R_{PA} - R_S$. If $R_{miss} \neq \varnothing$, the system is vulnerable, because the current security configuration denies the user to possess the required access rights (fig. 5).

To explain the reasons of OSCV given in the form of 'Positive Equity', we need to make both tests. Thus, we will define inconsistency between the access rights completely. To check the 'Positive Secrecy', we need to make the Test P1. And to make 'Positive Availability', we need to accomplish the Test P2.

If R_{excess} is not empty, we can conclude that the system is vulnerable, because the system presents the user rights from R_{excess}. If R_{miss} is not empty, we can also show the vulnerable rights, because the user has no the required rights from R_{miss}.

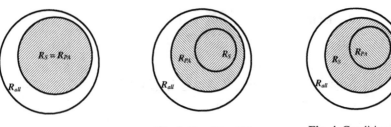

Fig. 2. Condition P1   **Fig. 3.** Condition P2   **Fig. 4.** Condition P3

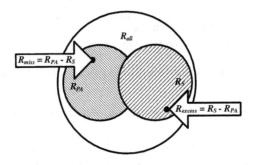

Fig. 5. Vulnerability Tests in Positive Mode

For negative specification of OSCV-criteria, we have declared another three conditions of the system security.

Condition N1. Negative Equity. System is vulnerable (according to the given criterion), if the set R_S of the system-provided rights coincides with the set R_{PD} of the "denied" rights, $R_S = R_{PD}$ (fig. 6).

Condition N2. Negative Secrecy. System is vulnerable (according to the given criterion), if the set R_S of the system-provided rights is not less than the set R_{PD} of the "denied" rights, $R_{PD} \subseteq R_S$ (fig. 7).

Condition N3. Negative Availability. System is vulnerable (according to the given criterion), if the system allows the user to obtain no more than the "denied" access rights, $R_S \subseteq R_{PD}$ (fig. 8).

To detect the OSCV in negative case, we need to make the following calculus.

Test N1. $R_{PD} \subseteq R_S$. In this case $R_{excess} = R_{PD}$. The system is vulnerable, for the current configuration does not denies the "denied" access rights (fig. 9).

Test N2. $R_S \subseteq R_{PD}$. We have $R_{miss} = R_{all} - R_{PD}$. If $R_{miss} \neq \emptyset$, the system is vulnerable, because the current security configuration does not allow to the user no one right from the set of the "required" access rights (fig. 9).

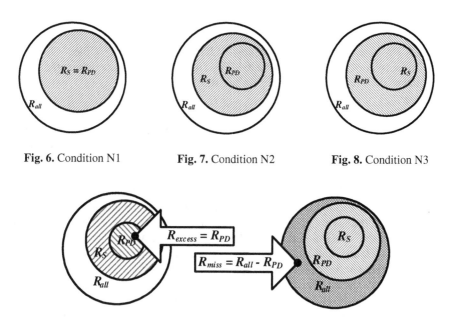

Fig. 6. Condition N1   **Fig. 7.** Condition N2   **Fig. 8.** Condition N3

Fig. 9. Vulnerability Tests in Negative Specification

As in positive case, here we need both tests when we check the 'Equity' condition. To check the 'Negative Secrecy' we need only Test N1. And we need to provide the Test N2 to check the 'Negative Availability'.

The above mentioned conditions and tests can be successfully extended to support users operations, because of granular nature of the sets to be compared.

Therefore, in positive case of OSCV detection, as well as in negative mode, we need to fulfill the following flowchart:

- parsing the criteria format specifications,
- comparing the sets of the security configurations (according to Conditions above),
- analyzing the results of the sets comparison (according to Tests above).

To make this algorithm a mechanical procedure, we have designed and built a vulnerability detection tool — the Vulnerability Criteria Processing Unit (VCPU).

4   The Criteria Calculus Procedure

Formal approaches are not intuitive. We do map our technique onto executive implementation. To automate the OSCVs detection according to the technique mentioned above, we have developed the *Vulnerability Criteria Processing Unit (VCPU)*. This utility is a *calculus facility* for the *Safety Problem Resolver*, the part of the *Safety Evaluation Workshop (SEW)*. Original conception of the SEW was presented in [8], and the current paper discloses the theoretical basis of the SEW's core component.

For its work VCPU uses:

- *Safety Problem Specification Language* (*SPSL*): allows to specify the system state, the access control rules, and the OSCV-criteria, and thus to obtain the formal model of the evaluated system for further resolving;
- *Scopes*:
  - *Model-related System Security State Scope* (*M3S-scope*): specifies the system security state in SPSL. For example, the scope for MS Windows 2000 contains the predicates describing all of the securable objects and their attributes, e.g. users, files, processes, ACLs, owners, hierarchy, memberships, etc. This scope is generated automatically with the Security Analyzer, the part of the SEW;
  - *Access Control Rules Scope* (*ACR-scope*): specifies the access control rules in SPSL. For example, in MS Windows 2000, this scope contains the rules that regulate the access control to the securable objects and that are realized in the *system reference monitor* (e.g. MS Windows SRM). Rules have a form of Prolog clauses and allow the state transactions resolving and computing of the authorized accesses for any user;
  - *State Security Criteria Scope* (*SSC-scope*): expresses the OSCV-criteria in SPSL. For example, in MS Windows 2000, this scope allows users to set checking of the Microsoft security requirements or the firm security policy. To construct this scope we use the Criteria Manager, the part of the SEW facility.

For easy understanding of security specification for the VCPU and OSCVs detection technique, we show a *Sample Vulnerability Checking* (*SVC*) applied in MS Windows 2000 Professional.

Like on office workstation, our sample computer has the MS Office installed. All of the MS Word templates of the user documents are located in the given folder, e.g. *C:\Documents and Settings\Administrator\Application Data\Microsoft\Templates*. Now let's imagine the situation when user named *'Administrator'* shares her template with other users. To do it, she grants the access to read and write the template for the MS Windows built-in group named *'Users'*. If the violator, the member of the *'Users'* group changes the *Normal.dot* template file in the given folder so it contains the malicious code (e.g. macro-virus). Thus, all new documents of *Administrator* will be infected. This is a sample of the OSCV: user has ignored or forgotten the recommendations to protect the MS Word templates.

Like in any theoretical security model, our security states are the collections of all entities of the system (subjects, objects) and their security attributes (e.g. ACLs). In our example, we assume that a target of OSCV-criteria is a *C:\Documents and Settings\Administrator\Application Data\Microsoft\Templates* folder. The system security states may be presented as the M3S-scope.

We have used the State Analyzer component of the SEW [8] to specify the SVC's security state. The following code example shows the M3S-scope for SVC.

```
..........[abbreviation].......
subj('s-1-5-21-73586283-484763869-854245398-500',
[type(user),name('administrator'),
```

```
privileges([security,...,remoteinteractivelogon]),
groups(['s-1-5-32-544'])]).
..........[abbreviation]........
subj('s-1-5-32-545',
[type(group),name(['users']),
privileges([shutdown,...,networklogon])]]).


..........[abbreviation]........
obj('c:\\documents and settings\\user\\application
data\\microsoft\\templates\\normal.dot',
[type(file),
owner(['s-1-5-21-73586283-484763869-854245398-
500']),inheritance(yes)],
[['s-1-5-21-73586283-484763869-854245398-
500',tnn,[0,1,2,3,4,5,6,7,8,16,17,18,19,20]],
['s-1-5-18',tnn,[0,1,2,3,4,5,6,7,8,16,17,18,19,20]],
['s-1-5-32-544',
tnn,[0,1,2,3,4,5,6,7,8,16,17,18,19,20]],
['s-1-5-32-545',tnn,[0,1]]]).
..........[abbreviation]........
```

We use the logic Prolog-style predicates to specify the state. This sample state specifies three entities: two subjects (one user with one group) and one object (the template file). Every entity is specified in the SPSL format. Each predicate declares the security attributes of the corresponding unit. For example, user '*Administrator*' owns SID equal to S-1-5-21-73586283-484763869-854245398-500, some system privileges, and membership in the '*Administrators*' group. The second predicate specifies the group named '*Users*', which is characterized with some system privileges only. The third expression declares the object, the template file *C:\Documents and Settings\Administrator\Application Data\Microsoft\Templates*, which is a goal of vulnerability evaluation. The attributes of this file are: the owner SID, inheritance flag, and the object's ACL. Each ACL is a set of access control entities, presented in the form of "*SID – 'rights delegation' – 'access bits'* ".

In the same manner, using the State Analyzer, we can gather all of the system objects of the user mode as well as of the kernel mode. For example, the following predicate specifies the COM-object and its security configuration:

```
obj('tlntsvr.exe',
[type(com), owner(['s-1-5-32-544']),
```

```
appID([' {b8c54a54-355e-11d3-83eb-00a0c92a2f2d}'])],
[['s-1-5-32-544',tnn,[0]],['s-1-5-4',tnn,[0]],
['s-1-5-18',tnn,[0]],
['s-1-5-18',tnn,[1]]]).
```

Access control rules express the restrictions on a system behavior. The system states transformation is able after the access authorized in kernel mode within the security subsystem of MS Windows by the system's reference monitor (access control mechanism). Using an object's ACL, it compares information about the client and the information about the object to determine whether the user has the desired access rights (for example, read/write permission) to that object (for example, a file). Depending on the outcome of this comparison, the security service will respond to the client, either serving the object or returning an access-denied failure.

To embody this mechanism, we have investigated the MS Windows inside (e.g. using the gray-box testing strategy) and looked through innumerous Microsoft Press. It made us able to re-compose the MS Windows protection subsystem in the form of logical clauses.

Such specification can be called as the ACR-scope. The following code example shows the ACR-scope of SVC. For want of paper space, we do not describe all of the MS Windows ACR-scope in SPSL. We have just prepared a sample of the read access checking with some comments describing the system reference monitor working:

```
..........[abbreviation].........
allow_file_read(U, F):-
% System security settings allow user U to traverse
% through containers of file F
    allow_traverse(U, F),
% EPL is effective permissions list
% for user U and file F
    effective_permissions(U, F, EPL),
% Get PL, the list of privileges granted to user U
    privileges_list(U, PL),
% Privilege "Backup files and directories"
% is granted to user U
    ( member(backup, PL), !;
% Permission "Read data" is granted to user U
    member(0, EPL),
% Permission "Read attributes" is granted to user U
    ( member(7, EPL),!;
```

```
% P is direct container of file F
   container_of_file(P, F),
% Permission "List folder" is granted to
% user U for direct container of file F
   group_permissions(U, P, 0) ),
% Privilege "Backup files" is granted to user U
   ( member(restore, PL), !;
% Permission "Synchronize" is granted to user U
   member(20, EPL) ) ).
.........[abbreviation].......
```

The 'read' access to the file is granted, if user has a 'traverse' permission for the file, or she has a 'Read Data' bit in her ACE referred to the file, or the user's group membership gives her some abilities to access the file.

The security criteria allow the customer or evaluator to delimit the secure and insecure states in security model. Criterion may have a form of constraint which states the necessary condition of the secure state (positive specification). The system is safe by the OSCV-criteria if all logical goals corresponding to the criteria are true. If some criterion goal is false, then system breaks the safety conditions specified in the criterion. In VCPU facility, security criteria can be noted as the SSC-scope. The special component of the SEW, the Criteria Manager, allows to compose and edit the vulnerability criteria [8]. The following code example shows the SSC-scope.

```
.........[abbreviation].......
criterion('Criterion #1: Users are not allowed to edit
the file Normal.dot',
mask,
[obj('c:\\documents and settings\\administrator\\
application data\\microsoft\\templates\\normal.dot'),
inheritance('tnn'),
's-1-5-32-544'(0,1,2,3,4,5,7,8,6,16,17,18,19,20),
's-1-5-18'(0,1,2,3,4,5,7,8,6,16,17,18,19,20)]).
.........[abbreviation].......
```

The logical predicate denotes one of the OSCV-criteria to be checked in MS Windows system. It refers to the *Normal.dot* file. It has the form of "required" access rights (positive mode of criteria specification). Type 'equity' pays our attention at an equity condition (**Condition P1**), i.e. there is the checking of the concrete access rights to the given *Normal.dot* object. There is also a condition of safe system: only

SYSTEM (its SID equals to S-1-5-18) and '*Administrators*' group (S-1-5-32-544) are allowed to do '*Full Access*' to *Normal.dot*. All other cases are considered to be vulnerable.

In the mentioned style, we can compose a full range of OSCV-criteria. It becomes able to handle even context-related conditions, such as "The system is vulnerable, if *Administrator* can modify object *X*, provided she is connected to the local console". Such conditions are indeed part of Microsoft Windows security model. From the point of security, all kinds of user's activity in the system (such as connection to the local console, applications running, etc) are mapped to Win32API functions calls operated with the Windows recourses. List of functions calls and set of resources maintained by the Windows security (so named as *securable objects*) are defined in MSDN. Because of monitoring a variety of operations over the securable objects, we can analyze the user's activity in the system.

We have the VCPU's input with a triple (M3S-scopc, ACR-scope, and SSC-scope) written in SPSL. Then we have run the resolving program for SVC. The VCPU makes calculus using our vulnerabilities detection technique. It takes the M3S-scope and finds the target object mentioned in the SSC-scope. Then it calculates the sets of the "pure" access rights taking into account all other security settings, e.g. privileges, ownerships, and etc. To do this VCPU uses the ACR-scope. Then it compares the rights sets, and makes the result tests for vulnerabilities using the SSC-scope and ACR-scope (**Test P1** and **Test P2**). After the running procedure, we have got a result file — the security evaluation *Report*. The following text example shows the report file for our SVC.

```
*** SYSTEM SAFETY RESOLUTION ***

CRITERION #1:

Users are not allowed to edit the file Normal.dot

>> VIOLATION DETECTED:

subject              group      <Users>

has unauthorized permissions

                     bits       [0,  1]

                                [Read Data,    Write Data]

for object(s)        file       c:\documents and settings\

                                administrator\

                                application data\

                                microsoft\templates\

                                normal.dot

.........[abbreviation]........
```

The result for checking *criterion 1* is the OSCV found. It means that there is some incorrectness in the security setup followed with security violation. After analyzing the unsafe state, VCPU discloses nature of security flaw, detecting subjects, objects, and their attributes that lead to protection weakness. The evaluation verdict is "*system is unsafe by the given criterion*", because members of '*Users*' have the '*Read Data*' and '*Write Data*' access in the ACL, corresponding to *Normal.dot*.

5   Conclusion

In this paper, we addressed to formal basics of OSCVs verification approach for secure operating systems. We discussed a technique of the vulnerabilities analysis and a formal processing tool, the VCPU. All these allow to specify the system security-related elements and proof the system safety.

The VCPU facility brings our vulnerability checking method to practice. The targets of its applications (being integrated into SEW toolkit) are the computer systems based on the granular security: the operating systems, DBMSs, and firewalls. Our approach is very useful for administrators and security officers to monitor the system securable resources (files, shared folders, printers, accounts, etc). It allows any user to discover security of her or his system in the depth, and thus open the 'holes' in the protection. The OSCVs, as mentioned, represent a very serious problem in the modern operating systems. Contemporary systems operate with a huge number of security settings, and the user needs some tools that could explain the whys and wherefores of security weaknesses. The VCPU utility makes this process closer to person than ever, because while logical resolving it marks the clause that caused fault of OSCV-criterion, and supplies user with a true reason of the security flaw.

References

1. Saltzer, J., Schroeder, M.: The Protection of Information in Computer Systems. Proceedings of the IEEE, Vol. 63(9) (1975) 1278–1308
2. Hoare C.A.R.: Communicating Sequential Processes. Communications of the ACM, vol. 21(8) (1978) 666–674
3. Banatre, J.-P., Bryce, C.: A Security Proof System for Networks of Communicating Processes, Irisa Research Report, #2042, 60 pp. (1993)
4. Jaurjens, J., Shabalin, P.: Automated Verification of UMLsec Models for Security Requirements. 7th International Conf. on the UML (2004) 365–379
5. Jaurjens, J.: UMLsec: Extending UML for secure systems development. UML 2002, Vol. 2460 (2002) 412–425
6. Heydon, A., Maimone, M.W., Tygar, J.D., Wing, J.M., Zaremski, A.M.: Miro: Visual Specification of Security. IEEE Transactions on Software Engineering, 16(10) (1990) 1185–1197
7. Heydon, A., Tygar, J.D.: Specifying and Checking Unix Security Constraints, In UNIX Security Symposium III Proc. (1992) 211–226
8. Zegzhda, P.D., Zegzhda, D.P., Kalinin, M.O.: Logical Resolving for Security Evaluation, MMM-ACNS (2003) 147–156

Hybrid Intrusion Detection Model Based on Ordered Sequences

Abdulrahman Alharby and Hideki Imai

Institute of industrial Science, The university of Tokyo,
4-6-1, Komaba, Meguro-ku, Tokyo, 153-8505 Japan
alharby@imailab.iis.u-tokyo.ac.jp
imai@iis.u-tokyo.ac.jp

Abstract. An algorithm for designing hybrid intrusion detection system based on behavior analysis technique is proposed. This system can be used to generate attack signatures and to detect anomalous behavior. The approach can distinguish the order of attack behavior, and overcome the limitation of the methods based on mismatch or frequencies, which performs statistical analysis against attack behavior with association rules or frequent episode algorithms. The preprocessed data of the algorithm are the connection records extracted from DARPA's tcp-dump data. The algorithm complexity is analyzed against a very known algorithm, and its complexity is decreased greatly. Using the proposed algorithm with transactions of known attacks, we found out that our algorithm describes attacks more accurately, and it can detect those attacks of limited number of transactions. Thus, any important sequence is considered and discovered, even if it's a single sequence because the extraction will cover all possible sequences combinations within the attack transactions. Four types of attacks are examined to cover all DARPA attack categories.

Keywords: intrusion detection, continuous pattern, discontinuous pattern, data mining.

1 Introduction

Over the past decade, the number as well as the severity of computer attacks has significantly increased. CSO magazine conducted a survey on the 2004 cyber crimes, the survey shows a significant increase in reported electronic crimes. Compared to the previous year, more than 40% of intrusions and electronic crimes are reported. Also, 70% of the respondents reported at least one electronic crime or intrusion was committed against their organization [1]. According to collected statistics, electronic crimes have an incredible impact on economy. Reports say that electronic crimes have cost more that $600 million in 2003.

IDSs are considered as powerful security tools in computer systems environments. These systems collect activities within the protected network and analyze them in order to detect intrusions. System activities are usually collected from

V. Gorodetsky, I. Kotenko, and V. Skormin (Eds.): MMM-ACNS 2005, LNCS 3685, pp. 352–365, 2005.

two main sources, network packet streams and host log files. Once the information is collected, the detection algorithm starts looking for any evidence for intrusions existence.

There are two general methodologies of detection used by IDSs: *misuse* and *anomaly* detection [2,3]. *Misuse* detection systems such as STAT [4] look for a known malicious behavior or signature, once it is detected an alarm is raised for further actions. While this type is useful for detecting known attacks, it can't detect novel attacks, and its signatures database needs to be upgraded frequently. The main feature of this model is its low false alarm rate. *Anomaly* detection models (e.g. IDES [5]) compare reference model of normal behavior with the suspicious activities and flag deviations as anomalous and potentially intrusive. Unlike *misuse* detection, *anomaly* detection systems identify unknown intrusions. The most apparent drawback of these systems is the high rate of false alarms. The two detection approaches can be combined to detect attacks more efficiently. There are various types of detection models (e.g. [6], [7], and [8]). Among these techniques, ADAM: Audit data analysis and mining, association rules data mining [9,10], and classification data mining [11,12,13] are the main used algorithms.

Following this introduction, we provide a background on the related work, and a briefing of our contribution. Section 2 then presents the proposed algorithm. In Section 3, the experiments are explained, including: data set model, details of learning and detection phases. Finally, Section 4 summarizes this paper's main conclusions.

1.1   Related Work

There has been extensive considerable work in representing and recognizing normal or malicious activities. Henry et al. in [14] proposed an approach that uses a time-based inductive machine (TIM) to generate rule-based sequential patterns that characterize the behavior of a user. This approach, to some extent, is similar to our approach in that both can be used to offer a simplified view of a set of complex data. There are, however, some fundamental differences between the two approaches: first, Henry's approach conducts a heuristic search to find the rules that satisfy certain given criteria, while our approach is mainly used for the evaluation of generated patterns. Second, Henry's model uses only continuous patterns, while our model combines both continuous and discontinuous patterns. Third, in the case of using our model as *Anomaly* detection, deviation from the norm in TIM is detected by matching the two sides of the rule, while in our model deviation is conducted by the summation weights of the matched patterns.

The most efforts that contribute to the current proposal are proposed by Kim and Wenke lee in [15] and in [16] respectively. While Kim proposed a new intrusion detection classification using data mining based on CTAR which considers temporal attribute of audit data. Wenke applied data mining with frequent episode algorithm, and structure statistic features. Wenke built his detection model based on RIPPER classifier. In the following, we summarize some drawbacks that have been noticed in these two approaches: First, although some intrusion behaviors depend on frequent episode or temporal attribute, analysis based on statistical features may not reflect the different features relationship in the context of time order. e.g., attacks with features appearing only once in the records, and attacks based on features that don't have frequent connection records or features that occur only once in an attack. Second, both detection methods of Wenke and Kim were designed to detect mainly Probe and DoS attacks. Current efforts of intrusion detection focus on detecting attacks with no clear evident features, such as application layer attacks or what are called in DARPA dataset remote to local and user to root attacks. Third. the most important, using statistical analysis would lead to lose order actions. Because attack evident features spread over many records, we need a technique to search the records vertically, and dig out the records for each single itemset sequences that may reflect attack features, that is continuous and discontinuous based data mining.

1.2 Our Contribution

The objective of this paper is to treat the systems ordered actions differently. Our approach uses the continuous and discontinues patterns to characterize the system behaviour. We used the proposed technique to extract some attacks signatures, and also to build an anomaly detection classifier. To classify a new sequence into either normal or intrusive, our proposed classifier converts the new sequence into a number of patterns and then calculates the similarity between these patterns and those of the training sequences. There are some advantages to applying this method to intrusion detection: First, without affecting the detection rate, limited and reasonable deviations from the norm are allowed, thus, false positive rate is significantly reduced. Second, foremost advantage is that this technique aims to discover all important possible patterns within the sequence. Third, in case of using this technique for building attack signature, it can deal with any kind of attack attributes such as time, numerical, categorical, and free-text.

2 Proposed Algorithm

2.1 Notations and Definitions

This section defines concepts that are central to this article, including the fundamental notions and definitions.

Definition 1 (Notions).

- $C(k,l)$: used to represent the set of candidate sequences of k elements and l stars.
- $L(k,l)$: The sequences set that have a support value bigger than the given minimal support where the sequence length is k and it has l stars.

- *SupL(k,l)*: The super large set, *SupL(k,l)*, used to store the list of all supported sequences of both types continuous and discontinuous.
- Pattern: also called sequence, it is a number of ordered actions. the pattern X can be shown as $(x_1, x_2, .., x_n)$, each x_j means an item or element.
- record: single instance of an attack. If an attack is involved in multi-instances, then we say attack records for all involved instances.

Definition 2 (continuous patterns). Suppose a pattern S_i extracted from the sequence $X_i = \{x_1, x_2, ..., x_m\}$ and contains some actions, that is, $S_i = \{s_1, s_2, ..., s_l\}$ which may reflect ordered commands executed by a program run on a computer machine. The pattern S_i can be classified as continuous pattern if all contained elements appear in consecutive positions of the sequence X_i, such that, there is an integer r such that; $s_1 = x_r$, $s_2 = x_{r+1}, ..., s_d = x_{r+l-1}$. For example, the continuous pattern (s_3, s_4) occurs in sequence: $X_1 = (s_1, s_2, s_3, s_4, s_5, s_6)$.

Definition 3 (discontinuous patterns). We say that S_i is a discontinuous pattern if the elements of that pattern don't appear in consecutive positions of the sequence X_i, that is, if there are existing integers $r_1 < r_2 < ... < r_l$ such that $s_1 = x_{r_1}$, $s_2 = x_{r_2}, ..., s_l = x_{r_l}$. For example, the pattern $(s_1, *, s_4)$ in sequence: $X_1 = (s_1, s_2, s_3, s_4, s_5, s_6)$ is a discontinuous pattern.

Definition 4 (star patterns). Star pattern is a pattern that contains one star or more as part of its elements. In a discontinuous pattern, hidden elements represented by star " $*$ " which is defined as a variable number of intermediate elements. The star pattern never starts or ends by " $*$ ". For example, if we have a sequence $X_i = \{x_1, x_2, x_3, x_4\}$, we may have these continuous patterns $(x_1, x_2), (x_2, x_3, x_4)$, and (x_1, x_2, x_3), or this discontinuous pattern $(x_1 * x_3, x_4)$. Because of the definition of the " $*$ ", the pattern $(x_1 * x_3, x_4)$ implicitly has two other patterns: (x_1, x_3, x_4), and (x_1, x_2, x_3, x_4).

2.2 Data Analysis and Patterns Generation

DARPA 1998 off-line data sets [17] developed to evaluate any proposed techniques for intrusion detection. These data prepared and managed by MIT Lincoln labs, sponsored by DARPA, and contain contents of every packet transmitted between hosts inside and outside a simulated military base. There were a collection of data including TCPDUMP and Basic security module (BSM) audit data of a victim Solaris machine. Both types are used in this work. While we used BSM data to model users normal behavior, we preprocessed and used tcpdump data set to model attack behavior. tcpdump records consist of a number of attributes as items of sequences, and these items include class attribute and other attributes, which are shown in Figure 1.

The aim of the proposed algorithm is to find out all frequent patterns from an attack records. Compared with CTAR or even with traditional Apriori algorithm, the proposed algorithm mines two types of sequences, one is continuous, and the

Service	Src Port	Dest Port	Src IP address	Dest IP address	Class Attack/Normal
http	1106	80	192.168.001.005	192.168.001.001	Normal
telnet	20504	23	172.218.117.069	172.016.113.050	loadmodule
...	...	...	...	...	...

Fig. 1. Dataset records, each one has a number of attributes. Class attribute has two categories, normal or attack. The rest of the attributes have many values.

other is discontinuous. The algorithm includes two steps, the first step is to search large-sequences of the first type of patterns, and the second step is to search the second type of patterns. In the following, the steps are summarized as follows:

- All attribute values in records database are considered as candidates to 1-element-zero-star-sequence-itemset, $C(1,0)$. After generating $C(1,0)$, the records database is scanned vertically. If the elements of $C(1,0)$ are contained in any instance, then the support of that element adds 1. Insert any element with support value greater than the given minimal support in 1-element-zero-star-sequence-large-itemset, $L(1,0)$, and store the results in a temporary database.
- Each two elements from two different attributes in $L(1,0)$ are combined to form 2-element-sequence-itemset-zero-star, $C(2,0)$. The records database is scanned for all patterns existing in $C(2,0)$. When the support value of a pattern exceeds the given minimal support it inserts in 2-element-sequence-large-itemset-zero-star, $L(2,0)$. We find out all k-element-large-zero-star $L(k,0)$ and store in a temporary database in turn. And then, we list all large-zero-star-sequence, $L(1,0)$, $L(2,0)$,..., $L(m,0)$, and store them in a common database called super large sequences set, $SupL$.
- After generating all possible $L(k,0)$, we extract all discontinuous patterns. First, from the temporary database of $L(3,0)$ we found out 2-element-1-star-sequence $C(2,1)$ by replacing the second item of the pattern by star. And then the records are scanned vertically for each pattern existing in $C(2,1)$, the patterns that have a support value exceeding the given minimal support are inserted in 2-element-zero-star-sequence-large-itemset, $L(2,1)$. We then found out all 2-element-l-star-large-itemset $L(2,l)$, and list all large-l-star-sequence, $L(2,1)$, $L(2,2)$, ..., $L(2,l)$. We do the same thing for all k-element-large-zero-star $L(k,0)$ in turn. The resulting sets add to $SupL$ database. These steps are shown in Figure 2.

In order to describe the algorithm clearly, we will take the example of an attack that includes 5 items and generate all possible sequences, which are shown in figure 3.

2.3   Complexity Analysis

The proposed algorithm is very different from Apriori algorithm [18]. First, discontinuous sequences are not considered in Apriori algorithm. Second, item-

Input: Extracted transactions from Original records.
Output: *SupL*; *L(k,l)* for all *k*s and *l*s

//Generate all possible candidate patterns of 1-element-sequence
C(1,0) = gen (Original records)
//Extract 1-element-sequences that have support value bigger than the min_support
L(1,0) = subset (C(1,0))
　　For (2 ≤ k ≤ m)
　　　　C(k,0) = gen (L(k-1,0))   //Generate all combinations of L(k-1,0)
　　　　L(k,0) = subset (C(k,0))   //Extract all supported continuous patterns
　　　　　　For (1 ≤ l ≤ m-2)
　　　　　　　　C(k,l) = gen (L(k,0))   //Generate all combinations L(k,0) with star
　　　　　　　　L(k,l) = subset (C(k,l))   //Extract all supported discontinuous patterns

Fig. 2. Proposed algorithm

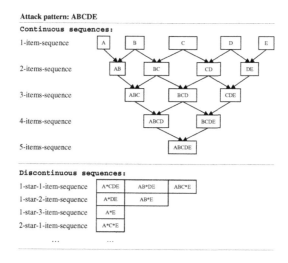

Fig. 3. Pattern extraction trees

record data is scanned vertically instead of horizontally. Among other steps, we found calculating the support value is the most time-consuming step, algorithm of support calculating is shown in Figure 4. Thus, the proposed algorithm reduces the complexity of continuous and discontinuous patterns mining greatly.

The Apriori algorithm built based on an iterative technique, where k-itemsets are used to generate $(k+1)$-itemsets. First, supported 1-itemset is generated, i.e. $L(1,0)$. Then, $L(1,0)$ is employed to generate the set of frequent 2-itemsets, i.e. $L(2,0)$, which is used to find $L(3,0)$, and so on until all supported k-itemsets are extracted. The next process consists of two actions; joining and pruning. First, the join step: To generate $L(k,0)$, a candidate set k-itemsets is extracted by joining $L(k-1,0)$ with itself, where items of $L(k-1,0)$ can be joined if their

```
Input: i=1, j=1, sequence x, pattern t
Output: sum, number of t included in x
  number(String[] x, int i, String[] t, int j){
    if (x[i]=("*")) i++; // If we have a star, skip it, it was already used
    // If the star was the last character, found another match.
    if (i = m AND x[i] = ("*")) return ++sum;
    if (j = n) {return sum;}
    if (i = 0 AND j = 0) sum = 0;

    // The " i > 0 " test simulates a starting star.
    if (i > 0 AND x[i - 1] ≠ ("*")) {
      if (x[i] = (t[j]) AND i = (m - 1)) { sum++;}
      else if (x[i] = (t[j])) { number(x, i + 1, t, j + 1); } }
    else {
      for (int p = j; p < n; p++) {
      if (x[i] = (t[p]) AND i = (m - 1)) {sum++;}
      else if (x[i] = (t[p])) { number(x, i + 1, t, p + 1); }
      }
  } return sum; }
```

Fig. 4. An algorithm to find out how frequent is each pattern within a certain number of records

first $(k\text{-}2)$ items are similar. This set of candidate is denoted $C(k,0)$. Second, the prune step: $C(k,0)$ is a superset of $L(k,0)$, that is, its elements may or may not be frequent, but all of the frequent k-itemsets are included in $C(k,0)$, even if $C(k,0)$ is very large. In fact any $(k\text{-}1)$-itemset that is not frequent cannot be a subset of a frequent k-itemset. Hence, if any $(k\text{-}1)$-subset of a candidate k-itemset is not in $L(k\text{-}1,0)$, then the candidate cannot be frequent either, and so, can be removed from $C(k,0)$. Suppose there are n records in the original data set, to find all n large sequences, the number of connection will be 2^n. To build the signature of an attack with around 100 records, this structure is not suitable.

In contrast, when we search for 1-itemsets candidate, $C(1,0)$, with our proposed algorithm, we need to scan the original records once and count all items, the same as the Apriori algorithm. When searching for frequent 1-itemsets, $L(1,0)$, instead of scanning original records, we only need to scan $C(1,0)$ which is composed of original records and much less than the original data. After generating all $L(k,0)$, we scan the original records once, and every $C(k,0)$ is also scanned once. In total, k times of scanning are performed. Since any $L(k,l)$ is extracted from the corresponding $L(k,0)$, we only need to scan the data stored in the temporary database instead of the corresponding $C(k,0)$ or original records. The data quantity is reduced evidently. And the most important, by taking out $C(2,0)$, and only scan the corresponding $L(1,0)$ which may compose the $C(2,0)$ in the temporary database. Then, the other $C(2,0)$ is taken out in turn.

Thus, for a limited number of attributes and more records, the proposed algorithm has proved more efficient compared to Apriori.

3 Experiments

3.1 Misuse Detection

For the sake of clarity, the algorithm is described through the example of number of attacks. Each attack includes a number of records, in some attacks tens of instances are collected, each record includes five attributes shown in table 1. We dig out continuous and discontinuous patterns of these attacks with the misuse intrusion detection algorithms. Results are shown in Figure 5.

The first examined attack is *Back* attack, which belongs to denial of service attack against the Apache web server. *Back* attack is fabricated by submitting frontslashes contained in URL's requests. The *Back* attack causes instances of the http process on the victim machine. As the server tries to process these requests it becomes unable to process other requests, consequently, the attack slows down the server. Attack signatures in Figure 5 show that the attacker https to the victim machine "172.016.114.050" from a certain machine. This flow of request consumes excessive processor time, when the original data was checked back, we found the attribute *Src port* has many values, none of them support the minimal given support value. Consequently, it is replaced by star in the patterns, and didn't appear in large-sequences $L(1,0)$ or in super-large-sequences, $SupL$.

The second simulated attack is the *ftp-write* attack, which belongs to R2U attack. It takes advantage of misconfiguration of an anonymous ftp, which allows the intruder to add files such as an rhosts file, and gain local access to the system. This is exactly what the patterns show in Figure 5. Regardless of the values of attributes: *Src port* and *dest port*, which are represented by star, the attacker anonymously ftps the victim machine, performs some tasks such as creating ".rhosts" file, and disconnects from the server. Then, as the second pattern shows, login to the victim machine by using rlogin to connect back to the server as ftp user, and finally performs some illegal actions on the victim machine.

An *eject* attack, the third simulated attack, belongs to U2R category. It exploits buffer overflow vulnerability of the distributed "eject" binary with Solaris 2.5. This vulnerability, if exploited, is used to gain root access on the attacked machine. As shown from the attack signature in figure 5, the attacker telnets the workstation "172.016.112.050", regardless of what source port is used, or from where the attack is launched, which explains the stars in the last three patterns. Then, telnet victim machine is exploited to distribute the malicious code. The implanted code, if compiled, can be run on the victim machine, as a command line session where the attacker can gain root access.

The last simulated attack is *ipsweep* which belongs to the probing attacks family. Attackers use this attack to search for vulnerable machines to determine which hosts are listening on a network. It can be performed by sending an ICMP Ping packets to every possible address within a subnet, listening machines will respond to the sender. The generated attack pattern shows that a Ping packet

Attack type	Generated patterns for chosen attacks
back (DoS) Week-2 Friday	Pattern 1: http (*service*) Pattern 2: 80 (*Des. port*) Pattern 3: 135.008.060.182 (*Src. IP*) Pattern 4: 172.016.114.050 (*Des. IP*) Pattern 5: http,*,80 Pattern 6: 135.008.060.182,172.016.114.050 Pattern 7: http,*,80,135.008.060.182 Pattern 8: http,*,80,135.008.060.182,172.016.114.050
ftp-write (R2U) Week-2,Friday	Pattern 1: ftp,*,195.073.151.050,172.016.112.050 Pattern 2: Login,*,195.073.151.050,172.016.112.050
eject (U2R) Week-6 Thursday	Pattern 1: telnet (*service*) Pattern 2: 23 (*Des. port*) Pattern 3: 172.016.112.050 (*Des. IP*) Pattern 4: telnet,*,23 Pattern 5: 23,*,172.016.112.050 Pattern 6: telnet,*,23,*,172.016.112.050
ipsweep (Probing) Week-3,Wednesday	Pattern 1: eco/i,7,7,202.077.162.213,*

Fig. 5. Number of chosen attacks, and their behavior as continuous and discontinuous sequences

"eco/i" is always sent from the same source "202.077.162.213", and the attribute *Dest IP address* is replaced by star " * " which explains that the Ping message is sent to a variety of destinations. That is exactly how the attack is performed.

The experiment indicates that the pattern we obtained is different from the command pattern, it is a new pattern. It can describe attacks more accurately, detect the attacks whose features appear only once, improve detection rate, and offer a new idea for the research of intrusion detection.

3.2 Anomaly Detection

Data Model and Preprocessing. In our experiments, and to evaluate the algorithm as an anomaly detector, we used the Basic Security Module (BSM) audit data collected by DARPA. Besides many attributes of BSM events, each session contains one or more system calls information that are generated by the programs running on the Solaris system. Also, each session is labelled with a related unique process number.

Programmatically, for each single process all related individual sessions are extracted, and then the complete set of ordered system calls spreading over the sessions are recorded. For our data model, we only recorded the names of the executed system calls ignoring other session attributes. And then, the algorithm is used to transform each process into its related continuous and discontinuous patterns. A sample of System calls generated by one user during two processes; 118 and 102 is shown in table 1.

Anomaly Model. Our implementation is based on normal programs behavior. Two stages have to be defined, the learning and detection stages. In the following, the two stages are presented in more details.

Table 1. Sample of ordered normal system calls included in two processes 118, and 102, Executed by the user named by: *franko* within the first day of the first week of the training 1998 DARPA data set

Process	System calls
118	stat stat stat stat chdir chdir lstat stat stat open chdir chdir lstat stat stat open pathdonf stat stat open chdir pathdonf stat open chdir pathdonf stat stat open chdir
102	stat stat stat stat access stat open open access stat open open

Learning Process. DARPA simulated BSM audit data set featured 6 users whose activity can be used to test anomaly detection systems. The users are named as: *franko, georgeb, janes, fredd, williamf,* and *donaldh*. The activity of those users remains consistent from day to day, but on some days, those users exhibit anomalous behavior in ways that should be detectable to an anomaly detection system. The anomalies that are introduced into the users' sessions include logging in from a different source, logging in at an unusual time, executing new commands, and changing identity. In the training data, all anomalies were introduced during the 6th week.

Among the seven weeks training period of DARPA data set, there are 6 weeks free of anomalous behaviour. Arbitrarily, 2 weeks (the first and the second) picked as a training data set, and left the sixth week for testing. We recorded only the names of the ordered system calls executed by those 6 users. Users names are usually found in two attributes: *path* or *mail*. Any process not related to any one of those users are ignored in either data sets, training or testing. The 2 weeks training data set consists of 17 intrusive instances and 17 clear or stealthy attacks. There are 7798 sessions within these 2 weeks. These normal training processes run only on Solaris machine. Once we have the training data set for the normal behavior, each single process is transformed to its related continuous and discontinuous patterns.

The proposed algorithm is used to generate all large-sequences $L(k,l)$ patterns that could be contained within one normal process. All system calls within one process are considered as a candidate to 1-element-sequence-itemset and stored in $C(1,0)$. This collection of patterns are used as a normal profile.

At a certain detector window size k, Large-sequences $L(1,0)$ patterns of only one process were generated in each run. A single process may contain a number of elements more than the detector window size, in this case, we applied the algorithm for the first k elements, and then moved to the next k elements until we covered all the elements included in the process.

We look for all normal processes separately and generate super-large- sequences, *SupL*. The resulting normal patterns are stored in a temporary data-

```
//build training normal patterns data set
Extract large-sequence L(k,l) of training dataset, and store in SupL_N;
for each process X in the testing data set Do
    extract all large-sequence L(k,l) patterns, and store in SupL_S;
    get value of n; // extracted programmatically
    compare SupL_N and SupL_S and get k_n;
    calculate k_n/n;
        if k_n/n ≥ threshold then
            The process X is normal;
        else then
            The process X is abnormal;
```

Fig. 6. An algorithm code for anomaly classifier

base called "normal pattern database" and denoted by $SupL_N$, and used later as a normal profile during monitoring and classifying testing processes.

Detection Process. This phase is intended to classify the testing processes to intrusive or normal. Once we have the training patterns data set for normal behavior, testing audit data is scanned for each new process associated with the same chosen 6 users. The new processes are also transformed to their related large-sequences patterns, $L(k,l)$. All possible patterns were generated for each testing process, and stored in a temporary database called "suspicious patterns database" and denoted by $SupL_S$. Then the similarity between patterns of the new process and the patterns of normal processes is calculated using similarity algorithm.

The similarity algorithm is described as follows: for any testing process that is needed to be classified, first, all corresponding large-sequence patterns $L(k,l)$ are extracted, and then each single generated pattern that is represented in $SupL_N$ database is given a weight $w = 1/n$, where n is the total number of all extracted patterns of that specific testing process. The value of n can be extracted programmatically. The value of w falls in the range $(0 \le w \le 1)$. By calculating the total summation weights (k_n) of all matches, strength of the normality signal can be determined. If the total weights summation exceeds a certain threshold, the testing process is classified as normal. Otherwise, it is an anomalous process. In Figure 6 an abstract of the pseudo code of the similarity algorithm is given.

Performance Measurements. Based on similarity function return value, the classifier makes the decision whether the process under investigation is intrusive or not. The first error that may occur is the false positive error which occurs when normal processes are classified as intrusions. The second error type is the false negative error which occurs when the real intrusive process is classified as normal, which is more serious.

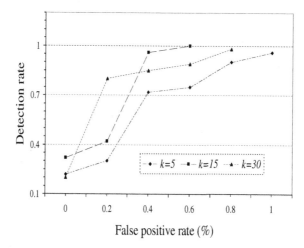

Fig. 7. Performance of the algorithm expressed in ROC curves. False positive rate vs attack detection rate for $k =$ 5, 15, and 30

Receiver Operating Characteristic (ROC) is a performance evaluation technique used to evaluate the intrusion detection algorithm [19]. It is related to the false error, and it is a trade off between detection rate and false alarms generated by the intrusion detection system. It can be obtained by varying the detection threshold and measuring the corresponding number of false alarms. This technique indicates how detection rate changes affect the raised false alarms. In our work, we used ROC metric to measure the performance of the proposed algorithm.

To evaluate the proposed algorithm as an anomaly detector, we formed a test data set from the DARPA BSM data of the 5 days of the sixth training week (none of the training data was chosen from this week). There are 53 intrusive sessions included in this testing data, and 14 distinct attacks included in these intrusive sessions. Also, 10 anomalous behaviors are included, such as unusual time logging in or from different source logging in, and new commands execution. Many of the attacks sessions were duplicated and appeared many times, like: *eject, neptune,* and *pod.* Duplicated sessions were not considered. Each process was classified to normal or intrusive, sessions associated with a single intrusive process was considered as an attack or anomalous sessions. The performance of the algorithm is evaluated as the detection rate versus false positive alarms. Detection rate and false positive alarm were built based on intrusive sessions detection and normal sessions misclassification. If one session is included in at least one intrusive process, it is counted as one attack. In our experiments, the presence of more than one intrusive process in one session does not affect the number of detection.

The proposed classifier can generate the related large-sequence patterns $L(k,l)$ of any length of sequences, this length may cover all the elements of the process, or just part of the process, and it is called the detector window size and denoted as k. A detector window size that is smaller than the length of the process would cause the detector to parse one process into many sequences resulting in a low anomaly signal. At the same time, a detector window size that is larger than the process would cause the detector to see only the one process sequences in the given instance resulting in a fair anomaly detection.

In the experiments, we varied $k's$ value from 5 to 30, most of the processes contained a number of system calls less than 30. Compared to the processes sequences, these values cover the possibilities of being equal, less, or greater than processes length. Precisely, this choice describes how does the value of k affect the performance of the classifier. Figure 7 shows the ROC curves for three different k values. For this particular training and testing data set, $k = 15$ is the best choice, with this value, the detection rate reaches 100% faster and at low false positive rate compared with the other two $k's$ values. For $k = 15$, the classifier algorithm can detect out of 10 anomalous sessions only 3 sessions with zero false positive rate. Reducing the similarity threshold leads to higher detection rate, but, this reduction has some cost in that the false positive rate becomes higher. For $k = 15$, and at threshold 0.81, the detection rate reaches 100% with false positive rate 0.6% (only 48 false positive detection out of 7798 normal sessions included in the training data set).

4   Conclusion

A new classifier has been proposed, it's built based on different treatments of patterns extraction. This type of classification is used for forming attacks signatures and to detect anomalous behavior. The experiments with DARPA data set have shown that the proposed algorithm can detect the intrusive behaviour effectively. The experiments indicate that the patterns that we obtained are different from the command patterns. They are new patterns, can describe attacks more accurately, detect the attacks whose features appear only once, and offer a new idea for the research of intrusion detection. Also, we found that continuous sequences reflect a clean occurred sequences, while discontinuous patterns represent the sequences mixed with undesirable noisy data.

References

1. The survey is available at: www.csoonline.com/releases/ecrimewatch04.pdf
2. Kumar, S., Spafford, E.H.: A Software Architecture to Support Misuse Intrusion Detection. Proceedings of the 18th National Information Security Conference (1995) 194–204
3. Forrest, S., Hofmeyr, S.A., Somayaji, A., Logstaff, T.A.: A Sense of Self for Unix process, Proceedings of 1996 IEEE Symposium on Computer Security and Privacy (1996) 120–128
4. Ilgun, K., Kemmerer, R.A., Porras, P.A.: State Transition Analysis: A Rule-Based Intrusion Detection System. IEEE Transactions on Software Engineering, 21(3) (1995) 181–199

5. Javitz, H.S., Valdes, A.: The SRI IDES Statistical Anomaly Detector. In IEEE Symposium on Security and Privacy, Oakland, CA. SRI International (1991)
6. Axelsson, S.: Research in intrusion-detection systems: A survey. Technical report TR 98-17, Gteborg, Sweden: Department of Computer Engineering, Chalmers University of Technology (1999)
7. Hofmeyr, S.A., Somayaji, A., Forrest, S.: Intrusion Detection using Sequences of System Calls. Journal of Computer Security Vol. 6 (1998)
8. Fox, K.L., Henning, R.R., Reed, J.H., Simonian, R.P.: A neural network approach towards intrusion detection. Proceedings of 13th National Computer Security Conference, NIST, Baltimore, MD (1999) 125–134
9. Barbara, D., Couto, J., Jajodia, S., Wu, N.: ADAM: A testbed for exploring the use of data mining in intrusion detection, ACM SIGMOD Record, 30 (4) (2001)
10. Barbara, D., Couto, J., Jajodia, S., Wu, N.: An architecture for anomaly detection. D. Barbara and S. Jajodia (Eds.), Applications of Data Mining in Computer Security, Boston: Kluwer Academic (2002) 63–76
11. Lee, W., Stolfo, S.: Data Mining Approaches for Intrusion Detection. Proc. of the 7th USENIX Security Symposium (1998)
12. Lee, W., Stolfo, S.: A Data Mining Framework for Building Intrusion Detection Models, IEEE Symposium on Security and Privacy (1999)
13. Barbara, D., Couto, J., Wu, N.: ADAM: Detecting Intrusion by Data Mining. Proc. of the 2th IEEE Information Assurance Workshop (2001)
14. Teng, H., Chen, K., Lu, S.: Adaptive Real-Time Anomaly Detection Using Inductively Generated Sequential Patterns, Proceedings, IEEE Symposium on Research in Computer Security and Privacy (1990)
15. Kim, J.S., Lee, H.G., Seo, S., Ryu, K.H.: CTAR: Classification Based on Temporal Class-Association Rules for Intrusion Detection, WISA 2003, Lecture Notes in Computer Science Publisher: Springer-Verlag, Vol 2908/2003 (2003) 84–96
16. Lee, W.: A Data Mining Framework for Constructing Features and Models for Intrusion Detection Systems, Ph.D. Thesis, Computer Science Department, Columbia University, New York, NY. June (1999)
17. DARPA data set:
    www.ll.mit.edu/IST/ideval/data/1998/1998_data_index.html
18. Agrawal, R., Imielinski, T., Swami, V.: Mining association rules between sets of items in large databases. P. Buneman and S. Jajodia, editors, Proceedings of the ACM SIGMOD Int. Conf. on Management of Data, Washington, D.C. (1993) 207–216
19. Lippmann, R.P.: Evaluating Intrusion Detection Systems: the 1998 DARPA Off-Line Intrusion Detection Evaluation. Proceedings of the 2000 DARPA Information Survivability Conference and Exposition, Vol. 2

Asynchronous Alert Correlation in Multi-agent Intrusion Detection Systems

Vladimir Gorodetsky, Oleg Karsaev, Vladimir Samoilov, and Alexander Ulanov

SPIIRAS, 39, 14-th Liniya, St.Petersburg, 199178, Russia
{gor, ok, samovl, ulanov}@mail.iias.spb.su

Abstract. This paper presents conceptual model, architecture and software prototype of a multi-agent intrusion detection system (IDS) operating on the basis of heterogeneous alert correlation. The latter term denotes IDS provided with a structure of anomaly detection–like classifiers designed for detection of intrusions in cooperative mode. An idea is to use a structure of classifiers operating on the basis of various data sources and trained for detection of attacks of particular classes. Alerts in regard to particular attack classes produced by multiple classifiers are correlated at the upper layer. The top-layer classifier solves intrusion detection task: it combines decisions of specialized alert correlation classifiers of the lower layer and produces combined decision in order to more reliably detect an attack class. IDS software prototype operating on the basis of input traffic is implemented as multi-agent system trained to detect attacks of classes *DoS*, *Probe* and *U2R*. The paper describes structure of such multi-layered intrusion detection, outlines preprocessing procedures and `data sources, specifies the IDS multi-agent architecture and presents briefly the experimental results received on the basis of DARPA-98 data, which generally confirm the feasibility of the approach and it's certain advantages.

1 Introduction

Currently, intrusion detection task is of great concerns and the subject of intensive research ([2], [4], [10], [11], [12], [13], [14], etc.). The contemporary studies show that advanced approaches to Intrusion Detection Systems (IDS) design are focused on data fusion ideas assuming use of multiple data sources and multiple classifiers operating in various feature representation spaces with the subsequent combining of their decisions [1]. Unfortunately, several specific properties of the intrusion detection system input make the above mentioned decision combining task very difficult. Among these properties, temporal nature, high-frequency dynamics and asynchronous character of input are of the primary importance. Other important issue of IDS input that is ignored in the most of research is information ageing resulting from the temporal nature and variety of frequencies of input data streams arriving from various sources.

The paper is devoted to the *heterogeneous alert correlation* approach to intrusion detection. The introduced term denotes an approach assuming that IDS is composed of a structure of classifiers and each classifier of this structure is trained for detection of attacks of a particular class, e.g. an attack of the class either *DoS*, or *Probe*, or

V. Gorodetsky, I. Kotenko, and V. Skormin (Eds.): MMM-ACNS 2005, LNCS 3685, pp. 366–379, 2005.

U2R. The second assumption of the approach is that several classifiers are trained for detection of the same attack class while operating with data of various sources and/or various feature representation spaces. Each of such specialized classifiers may produce decisions of two classes: "*Alert*" regarding to "its own" attack class (e.g. "*DoS alert*", "*U2R alert*", etc.) or "*Normal*" (without producing an alert). In the second layer, alerts of the same type (if any) produced by source-based classifiers are correlated and the results are sent to the top layer. The top-layer classifier solves intrusion detection task: it combines decisions of specialized alert correlation classifiers and produces combined decision in terms of particular attack class if any.

In the rest of the paper, section 2 outlines the IDS input data model and preprocessing procedures forming various data sources (representation spaces). It describes the structure of the interacting classifiers designed for heterogeneous alert correlation and event dynamics of the IDS operation. Section 3 describes a model of data ageing used in the developed IDS software prototype while Section 4 gives detailed specification of its architecture based on multi-agent framework. This architecture is specified in the style assumed by Gaia methodology [15] that is used in development of the IDS software prototype. Section 5 outlines experimental results received through testing of the developed prototype using DARPA data [3]. Conclusion summarizes the paper contributions and intentions for future research.

2 Conceptual Model of Multi-alert Correlation for Intrusion Detection

2.1 Input Data

The major peculiarity of IDS input data is their *temporal* nature. Indeed, input data perceived by sensors of IDS or produced by preprocessing procedures are mapped *time stamp,* which is considered as an important data attribute. Events of various data streams arrive into IDS classifiers *asynchronously.* Since averaged frequencies of various data streams are different, the data incoming to meta-level responsible for alert correlation possess finite life time, i.e. after elapsing certain time from the moment they are produced the data become of less relevance with regard to the current status of user activity and therefore less useful or useless for its assessment.

It is assumed that the input data model accounts the data streams resulting from the preprocessing of the network traffic represented in *TCP* dump. This traffic perceived by "*Data Sensor*" is further preprocessed according to the scheme presented in Fig.1. Traffic preprocessing procedures are aimed at extraction of various features resulting in creation of "secondary" data sources (feature representation spaces forming input for several source-based classifiers).

The developed traffic preprocessing procedures operate in the following order. First, events corresponding to new packets and new connections are identified. The information contained in the identified packets and connections is further processed in order to extract features and form secondary data sources. Network feature extraction procedure identifies events that indicate availability of newly arrived following data:

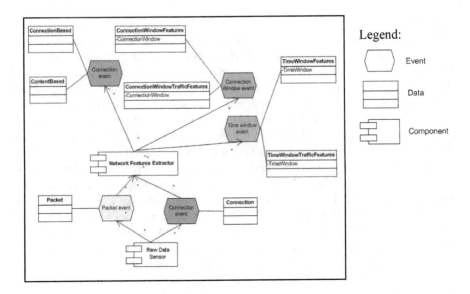

Fig. 1. Raw data streams and preprocessing procedures forming secondary data sources constituting input data streams of IDS

(1) *Connection–related* data that are used for extraction of connection-related features forming two data sources, i.e. *ConnectionBased* and *ContentBased* data sources.

(2) *Time window-related* data representing certain statistics averaged within sliding time window of the predetermined length and shift (in our case, *length= 5 sec.* and *shift=2 sec.*). These data are used for extraction of the features forming two secondary data sources, *TimeWindowFeatures*, and *TimeWindowTrafficFeatures*.

(3) *Connection window-related* data representing certain statistics averaged within sliding time window containing a user-assigned number of connections (in our case, this number is equal to 20 connections and shift is equal to 1 connection). These data are used for extraction of the features forming two more secondary data sources, *ConnectionWindowFeatures*, and *ConnectionWindowTrafficFeatures*.

Traffic preprocessing procedures were developed by authors. As the input of these procedures, the DARPA data [3] are used.

2.2 Heterogeneous Alert Correlation Structure

The primary factor influencing on the IDS architecture is the structure of interaction of the source-based classifiers and meta–classifiers. Let us comment it by example of the structure used in the developed case study illustrated in Fig. 2.

Each data source is attached several source-based classifiers. A peculiarity of these classifiers is that each of them is trained for detection of a fixed class of attacks and produces alerts regarding corresponding attack class. That is why the alerts produced are heterogeneous, i.e. correspond to different classes of attacks. Actually, each source-based classifier solves an anomaly detection task, but each "anomaly" alert corresponds to particular class of attacks. Thus, the IDS system in question solves intrusion detection task.

Connection–based data source is attached three specialized classifiers intended for detection *DNS CB*, *R2U CB* and *Probe CB* classes of attacks, i.e. these classifiers are trained to detect attacks of the classes "*Denial of Service*", *R2U* and *Probe* respectively. Each of the above connection-based data source classifiers transmit the produced decision to particular meta–classifier (see Fig.2).

ConnectionWindowFeatures data source forms input of two specialized classifiers, *R2U CW* and *Probe CW*, trained for detection of attacks of the classes *R2U* and *Probe* respectively. They also send their decisions to particular classifiers of the meta–level.

ConnectionWindowTrafficFeatures data source is attached three specialized classifiers, *R2U CWT*, *Probe CWT* and *NormalCWT* trained for detection of attacks of the classes of *R2U*, *Probe* and *Normal* activity (no attacks) respectively. They send their decisions to various classifiers of meta–level.

Time WindowFeatures data source forms input of three specialized classifiers, *DNS TW*, *R2U TW*, and *NormalTW* trained for detection of attacks of the classes *Denial of Service*, *R2U* and *Normal* activity (no attacks) respectively.

Time WindowTrafficFeatures data source is attached three classifiers, *DNS TWT*, *R2U TWT*, and *ProbeTWT* trained for detection of attack classes *Denial of Service*, *R2U* and *Probe* respectively.

At the meta–level, three specialized meta-classifiers are introduced. Each of them is responsible for combining decisions from source-based classifiers trained for detection of particular type of attack or *Normal* situation. They operate in asynchronous mode while making decision every time when an event and data from at least one source–based classifier arrives. A peculiarity of the decision making structure in question (Fig.2) is that, in it, one more decision combining layer, top layer, is used. It combines the inputs arriving from the specialized meta–classifiers thus solving the intrusion detection task.

2.3 Dynamics of IDS Operation

The data and event streams in the implemented IDS prototype are presented in Fig.1. Let us describe the dynamics of these streams in the process of IDS operation.

Dump of the network traffic is captured by sensor, *Raw Data Sensor*. It produces primary events of two types: (1) *PacketEvent* – receiving of an IP packet and *Packet* data, and (2) *ConnectionEvent* – completion of the connection and *Connection* data. Events and data input to the component *NetworkFeatureExtractor* intended for extraction of the features from raw data and generation of the secondary events, that are (1) *ConnectionEvent* and associated arrays of the features, *ConnectionBased* and *ContentBased*; (2) *ConnectionWindowEvent* indicating completion of a time window containing given number of connections and associated arrays of the features, *ConnectionWindowFeatures* and *ConnectonWindowTrafficFeatures*; (3) *TimeWindowEvent* indicating completion of the time window of a predefined duration and associated arrays of the features, *TimeWindowFeatures* and *TimeWindowTraficFeatures*.

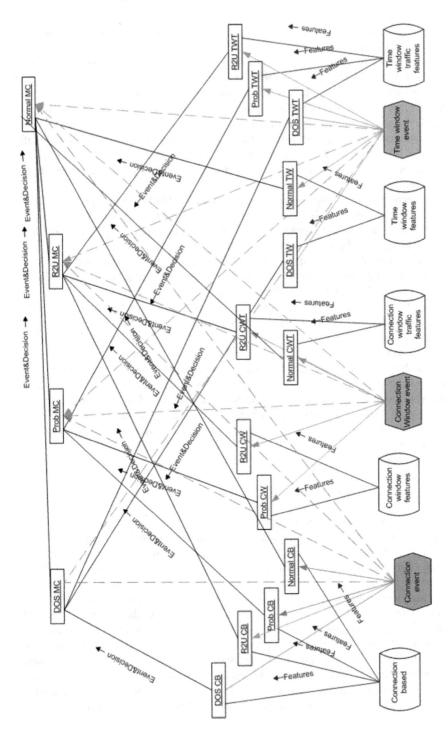

Fig. 2. The structure of decision making and decision combining implemented in the software prototype of multi-agent IDS

Table 1. Distribution of attack classes against types of operating systems

	Type of OS: *Redhat*	
Attack Class	Attack name	Number of cases
Denial of Service (DoS) Attacks	*back*	4
	land	22
	pod	35
	smurf	11
	teardrop	7
(*DoS*) attacks in total		79
Probes attacks	*ipsweep*	7
	portsweep	5
	satan	5
Probes attacks in total		17
Remote to User (R2U) attacks	*dict*	1
	guest	1
	imap	3
	phf	5
R2U attacks in total		10
User to Root attacks (U2R	*perl*	5

All classifiers of the source–based layer as well as meta–classifiers of the first and top layers were trained and tested based on DARPA data [3][1]. Generalized information about these data that are used for training and testing of the classifiers composing the decision structure depicted in Fig.2 is presented in Table 1.

3   Models of Data Ageing

According to the used alert correlation strategy, decisions of meta–classifiers are updated at any time when new input ("event") produced by some source–based classifier incomes. Let us recall that while receiving an updated decision from a source-based classifier, the meta-classifier updates its decision using the newly received decision and also on the decisions produced previously by other source-based classifiers at various time instants. The latter decisions have different "ages" and therefore different relevancies to the current computer security status. Thus, potential *data ageing* is one of the important peculiarities of the alert correlation system in question. Let us consider the models of data ageing.

Two data ageing models were explored. The *first* of them assumes that each data incoming to the alert correlation layer is assigned certain "age" at the moment of the computer security status update and if this "age" is less than a fixed threshold (it is individual for each data source) then the corresponding data are used in the alert correlation "as is". Otherwise, these data are assumed *missing*:

$$D_i(t_{k+1})) = \begin{cases} D(t_k), & \text{if } t_k \leq t_{k+1} \leq t_k + T_i^{Ag} \\ \varnothing, & \text{otherwise} \end{cases}.$$

where $D_i(t)$ –stands for the decision of a base classifier associated with the *i-th* data source produced at time instant t; t_k stands for the time instant at which the decision income into meta–classifier; T_i^{Ag} stands for the threshold value of life time of the decision D_i produced by the source # i; and $\varnothing$ stands for the missing value.

This model was experimentally investigated and the results were in full described in [5, 8]. The advantages of this model are twofold. On the other hand, this model is simple enough. On the other hand, if some sensors or data sources fail, i.e. do not

---

[1]   Training and testing procedures used in design of classifiers are not considered in the paper.

produce decision in required time instant then, nevertheless, the combined decision is produced because meta-layer classifier is capable to process data with missing values. The sound algorithm solving such task is described in [6]. A drawback of this model is that it is approximate and in some cases may be too rough.

The second model of data ageing assumes that the learning mechanism has to automatically determine dependence of informative power of the decision produced by a source classifier depending on "age". More strictly, this model assumes that each input of the alert correlation classifier is assigned an additional numerical attribute $\Delta_i(t_1,t_2)$, where $\Delta_i(t_1,t_2)$ is the "age" of input of i-th source-based classifier produced at the time instant t_1 if it is used in alert correlation procedure of meta-layer at the time instant t_2. Thus, when i-th source-based classifier produces and sends its decision to meta–level at a time instant t_β^i the age of this decision is equal to zero, $\Delta_i(t_\beta^i) = 0$. If decision of the alert correlation classifier is produced later, at the time instant t_α then the attribute $\Delta_i(t_\alpha^i)$ takes value $\Lambda_i(t_\alpha) = (t_\alpha - t_\beta^i)$.

The last model of data ageing is used in the intrusion detection system considered in this paper. It is important to note that for the model in question, no specific technique for learning of decision combining algorithm is necessary. Indeed, for this model, training and testing is a routine (but not trivial) procedure of learning based on dataset containing both binary and numerical attributes.

4   Architecture of Multi-agent IDS Software Prototype: An Outline

The architecture mentioned in the section title is described below in the style assumed by Gaia methodology implemented and extended within MASDK 3.0 software tool.

4.1   Basic Components of the Architecture

1. Roles
- *DataSensor*–source of the raw data; performs raw data preprocessing, computation of the features, translation of the primary events and generation of the secondary events associated with the data source.
- *ObjectDataReceiver*–acceptor of the network level features;
- *DecisionProvider*–source of decisions regarding the computer security status;
- *DecisionReceiver*–acceptor of the decisions produced by *DecisionProviders*;
- *ObjectMonitor*–acceptor of information presenting the host security status.

2. Protocols
- *DataTransmission*–the protocol transmitting features–related information;
- *DecisionTransmission*–the protocol transmitting decisions produced;
- *UpdateObjectInformation*–the protocol responsible for updating of the computer security status related information;

The aforementioned protocols are basic ones. The auxiliary ones are as follows:

- *AttackLogTransmission*–the protocol performing transmission of the attack log (the true labels of the attacks needed for the designed system testing);
- *OptionsProtocol*–the protocol performing adjusting of initial options determining the regime of the system operation.

3. Agent classes and roles to perform

The agent classes introduced in the IDS architecture and allocated the roles they have to perform are as follows:

NetLevelAgent–an agent class performing the *DataSensor* role intended for raw data preprocessing and extraction of the events and secondary features;

BaseClassifiers–an agent class assigned the *DecisionProvider* role performing source-based classification; it produces decisions when it receives an event from "its" source. This class is inherited by several subclasse that are as follows:

- *DOS_CB*: produces decisions when it receives the event *ConnectionEvent* using *ConnectionBased* features; it is trained to detect the *DoS* attack class;
- *DOS_TW*: produces decisions when it receives the event *TimeWindowEvent* and *TimeWindowFeatures* features; it is trained to detect *DoS* attack class;
- *DOS_TWT*: produces decisions after receiving *TimeWindowEvent* event and *TimeWindowTraficFeatures* features; it is trained to detect *DoS* attack class;
- *Prob_CB*: produces decisions after receiving *ConnectionEvent* event and *ConnectionBased* features; it is trained to detect attacks of the class *Probes*;
- *Prob_CW*: produces decisions after receiving the *ConnectionWindowEvent* event and *ConnectionWindowFeatures* features; it is trained to detect attacks of the class *Probes*;
- *Prob_TWTr*: produces decisions after receiving *TimeWindowEvent* event and *TimeWindowTraficFeatures* features; it is trained to detect attacks of the class *Probes*;
- *R2U_CB*: produces decisions after receiving t*ConnectionEvent* event and *ConnectionBased* features; it is trained to detect the attacks of the class *R2U*;
- *R2U_CW*: produces decisions after receiving the *ConnectionWindowEvent* event and *ConnectionWindowFeatures* features; it is trained to detect attacks of the class *R2U*;
- *R2U_CWT*: produces decisions after receiving the *ConnectionWindowEvent* event and *ConnectionWindowTraficFeatures* features; it is trained to detect the attacks of the class *R2U*;
- *R2U_TWT*: produces decisions after receiving the *TimeWindowEvent* event and *TimeWindowTraficFeatures* features; it is trained to detect attacks of the class *R2U*.

Metaclassifiers:–an agent class performing the roles *DecisionReceiver* and *DecisionProvider*; it is responsible for combining decisions produced by its child classifiers (Fig.2). It is replicated into the following instances:

- *DOS_MC*: an agent instance of the *Metaclassifier* class correlating alerts of the source-based classifiers trained for detection of *DoS* attack class;
- *Prob_MC*: an agent instance of the class *Metaclassifier* correlating alerts of the source-based classifiers trained for detection of *Probes* attack class;

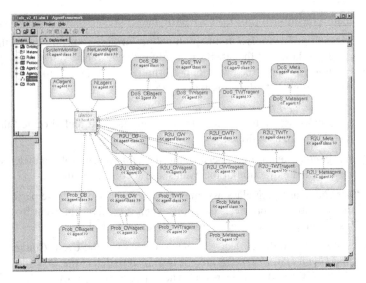

Fig. 3. IDS MAS agency configuration

- *R2U_MC*: an agent instance of the class *Metaclassifier* correlating alerts of the source-based classifiers trained for detection of *R2U* attack class;
- *Normal MC*: an agent instance of the *Metaclassifier* class combining alerts arriving from the meta–classifiers correlating alerts of particular attack classes;

SystemMontor–an agent class assigned the role *ObjectMonitor*; it provides visualization of the information about security status of the host depending on time.

The instances of the above agents are structured according to the conceptual heterogeneous alert correlation structure depicted in Fig.2. The above mentioned components represented graphically in Fig.3 determine configuration of the agents of the implemented multi-agent IDS.

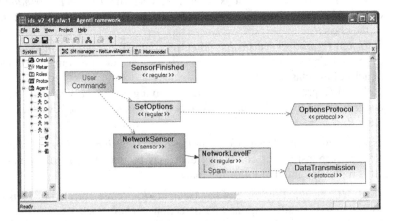

Fig. 4. Model of behavior of the agent class *NetLevelAgent*

4.2 Agent Classes Behavior Specification

Behavior of each agent class is specified in two layers. At the upper layer, the structure of the interaction of the state machines representing particular variants of the agent class behavior, which correspond to different agent services[2], is specified. At the lower layer, each such state machine is specified in details. Correspondingly, let us describe some of the agent class services distinguishing upper and lower layers.

4.2.1 *NetLevelAgent* Agent Class
The basic services of this agent class are the followings (Fig.4):

- *NetworkSensor*–provides monitoring of the network traffic and generation of the primary events associated with this data source. In other words, it is responsible for dispatching of input events and sequencing of its preprocessing;
- *NetworkLevelF*–provides computation of the connection-based features and generation of the secondary events;
- *Spam* – provides forwarding of the events and feature values to the source-based classifiers.

Interface of the options of the adjustment of the *NetworkSensor* service is shown in Fig.5.

Let us describe state machines implementing the services of the *NetLevelAgent* agent class. An example of the state machine corresponding to the *NetworkLevelF* service is presented in Fig.6. In the state *Get_Input_Data* the newly arrived data are analyzed. After detection of the type of the data arrived, the latter are processed according to their type: the packet data are processed in *Process_Packet* state, while connection–associated data are processed in the *Process_Connection* state. After this,

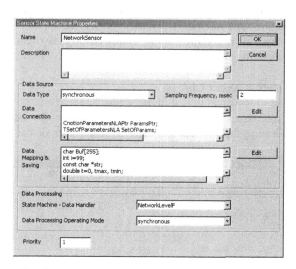

Fig. 5. Options of the service *NetworkSensor* adjusting

---

[2] Term "*agent service*" is used in multi-agent technology to denote an agent's functionality.

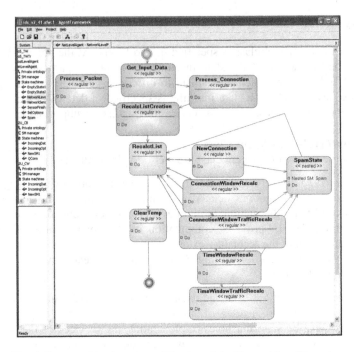

Fig. 6. State machine-based specification of the *NetworkLevelF* service

the list of all events, both primary and secondary, is formed (in the state *RecalcList-Creation*). Then, for each event stored in the aforementioned list, computation and updating of the features with the subsequent call of the service *SpamState* is carried out. This is done in the state *RecalcList*. In turn, the service *SpamState* performs forwarding the computed feature values to the source-based classifiers associated with the respective events in the above mentioned list.

4.2.2   Alert Correlation Agent Classes

In general, the agent classes mentioned in the subsection title are the same; they only differ (1) in their rule bases used for alert correlation, (2) in the lists of the source-based classifiers forming their inputs and also (3) in the lists of the receivers of the

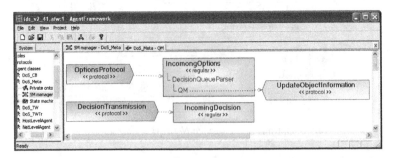

Fig. 7. Services of the agent classes responsible for meta–classification

decisions produced by alert correlation agents. The basic services of these agent classes structured as it is depicted in Fig.7 are the followings:

- *IncomingDecision*–service responsible for processing of the incoming decisions of the child classifiers of the lower layer;
- *IncomingOption* – service responsible for adjusting of the agent class options;
- *DecisionQueueParser* – service responsible for processing of the incoming decisions stored in the queue;
- *QM*–service implementing alert correlation (meta-classification functionality).

Detailed specification of the state machines implementing the aforementioned services is omitted due to the lack of the paper space.

4.2.3 Source-Based Classifier Agent Class
The basic services of *the Source–based classifier* agent class are as follows:

- *IncomingData*–service implementing the incoming events and data processing;
- *IncomingOption*–service responsible for adjusting of the agent class options;
- *ConnQueueParser*–service responsible for processing of the incoming decisions stored in queue (*Connection*-based, *Windows*-based);
- *QConn* – service responsible for producing decisions (*Alert* or *Normal*).

Like all the services, the aforementioned ones are specifies and implemented in terms of state machines, whose description is omitted. due to lack of the paper space.

5 Experimental Results

The multi-alert correlation IDS MAS designed according to the above described principles and architecture was implemented using MASDK 3.0 platform providing support of the MAS technology [7]. All the classifiers composing the proposed homogeneous alert correlation structure were trained using VAM [9] and GK2 [6] algorithms. The resulting system as a whole was tested using DARPA data [3].

Some testing results are illustrated in Fig.8. These figures present information about performance quality (probabilities of correct classifications and probabilities of false alarms and signal missing) of the alert correlation classifiers dealing with inputs produced by the source-based classifiers trained for detection of attacks of particular classes. At that, data used in training procedures as "counter class" include basically normal traffic. But, if, for a source-based classifier, the difference between the sums of the weights of rules voting in favor of *Alert* and *Normal* decision is less than a selected threshold (it is computed for each particular classifier experimentally in testing procedure) then the classifier refuses to classify input data. Analysis proved that as a rule, such kind of situation actually corresponds to some other class of attacks. Fig.8 illustrates the performance quality of the alert correlation meta-classifier destined for detection of the *DoS* class of attacks. It illustrates graphically the probability distributions of correct alert detection and various types of errors. An important observation is that even if the source-based classifiers operate not very precise, at the meta–layer, where the decisions of the particular source-based classifiers are combined, the

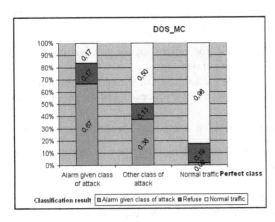

Fig. 8. Evaluation of the performance quality of the *DOS_MC* meta– classifier

quality of the *DoS* attack detection is increased. The same is valid for other alert correlation classifiers.

6   Conclusion

Though intrusion detection task is being a subject of intensive research during at least the last decade, it remains to be a problem; many important issues and peculiarities of this task have not been investigated in depth. One of the remarkable drawbacks of the existing approaches is simplified modeling of input data used in development of IDS. Indeed, along with multiplicity and heterogeneity of data sources to be taken into account, several other specific features of the intrusion detection system input are critical to fill in the gap between existing models used in IDS and reality. Among these features, temporal nature, high-frequency dynamics and asynchronous nature of input are of the primary importance. These factors result in the necessity to account such an important issue as information ageing caused by the fact that input data streams arrive in IDS with various averaged frequencies and asynchronously.

The input data model considered in this paper takes into account the aforementioned factors. For such model of IDS input, the paper proposes an approach called heterogeneous alert correlation. The major idea of the approach is to organize IDS system as a structured set of interacting classifiers dealing with data received from various data sources. The first layer of this structure is composed of classifiers operating with inputs of particular data sources. Each of them is trained for detection of attacks of a fixed class (in the developed IDS software prototype, the attack classes *DoS*, *Probe*, and *U2R* are considered). Each of such specialized classifiers produces decisions of two types: "*Alert*" in regard to the particular class of attacks (e.g. "*DoS alert*", "*U2R alert*", etc.) or "*Normal*". A peculiarity of such classifiers operation is that they produce decisions in different time instants. These decisions asynchronously arrive at the second layer responsible for correlation of the alerts produced by the first layer classifiers trained for detection of the attacks of the same class. In turn, the results of the alert correlations produced by the specialized classifiers of the second layer are asynchronously forwarded to the top layer. The top-layer classifier solves intrusion detection task: it combines heterogeneous alerts of specialized alert correlation classifiers and combines them producing decision it terms of particular attack class.

Two theoretical problems should be solved to implement the described approach: (1) development of data ageing model; and (2) development of specific techniques to train alert correlation classifiers to make decisions based on asynchronous input. In the developed IDS prototype the solutions proposed by the authors in previous research are used [5, 8]. This approach was implemented within multi-agent IDS dealing with three classes of attacks, *DoS*, *Probe* and *U2R*, and operating with input traffic. Architecture of the prototype and some experimental results are outlined.

The intended directions for future research will concern enrichment of the developed structure of interacting classifiers by the learning capabilities.

Acknowledgement

This research is supported by grant #1993P of European Office of Aerospace R&D and Russian Foundation for Basic Research (grant 04-01-00494a).

References

1. Bass, T.: Intrusion Detection and Multisensor Information Fusion: Creating Cyberspace Situational Awareness. Communication of the ACM, Vol. 43(4) (2000) 99–105
2. http://www.ll.mit.edu/IST/ideval/data/1998/1998_data_index.html
3. Cuppens, F., Miege, A.: Alert correlation in a cooperative intrusion detection framework. IEEE Symposium on Research in Security and Privacy (2002)
4. Debar, H., Wespi, A.: Aggregation and Correlation of Intrusion-Detection Alerts. RAID 2001, LNCS 2212 (2001) 85–103
5. Gorodetsky, V., Karsaev, O., Samoilov, V.: On-Line Update of Situation Assessment: Generic Approach. International Journal of Knowledge-Based & Intelligent Engineering Systems. IOS Press, Netherlands, 2005 (Accepted for publication)
6. Gorodetsky, V., Karsaev, O. Samoilov, V.: Direct Mining of Rules from Data with Missing Values. Studies in Computational Intelligence, T.Y.Lin, S.Ohsuga, C.J. Liau, X.T.Hu, S.Tsumoto (Eds.). Foundation of Data Mining and Knowledge Discovery, Springer (2005) 233–264
7. Gorodetsky, V., Karsaev, O., Samoilov, V., Konushy, V., Mankov, E., Malyshev, A.: Multi-Agent System Development Kit. R.Unland, M.Klusch, M.Calisti (Editors). "Multi-Agent Technology and Software Tools", Whitestein Publishers. Accepted for publication (2005)
8. Gorodetsky, V., Karsaev, O. Samoilov, V.: On-Line Update of Situation Assessment Based on Asynchronous Data Streams. 8th International Conference on Knowledge-Based Intelligent Information & Engineering Systems, LNAI, Vol. 3213, Springer (2004) 1136–1142
9. Gorodetski, V., Skormin, V., Popyack, L.: Data Mining Technology for Failure Prognostics of Avionics, IEEE Transactions on Aerospace and Electronic Systems. Volume 38, # 2 (2002) 388–403
10. Lazarevic, A., Ertoz, L., Kumar, V., Ozgur, A., Srivastava, J.: A Comparative Study of Anomaly Detection Schemes in Network Intrusion Detection. 3rd SIA Conference on Data Mining, San Francisco, CA (2003)
11. Morin, B., Debar, H.: Correlation of Intrusion Symptoms: An Application of Chronicles. RAID 2003, LNCS 2820, Springer-Verlag (2003) 94–112
12. Pietraszek, T.: Using Adaptive Alert Classification to Reduce False Positives in Intrusion Detection, RAID 04, LNCS volume 3224 (2004) 102–124
13. Song, T., Ko, K., Alves-Foss, J., Zhang, C., and Levitt, K.: Formal Reasoning About Intrusion Detection Systems, RAID 04, LNCS volume 3224 (2004) 278–295
14. 14 Valdes, A., Skinner, S.: Probabilistic Alert Correlation. W. Lee, L. Me, and A. Wespi (Eds.): RAID 2001, LNCS 2212, Springer-Verlag (2001) 54–68
15. Wooldridge, M., Jennings, N.R., Kinny, D.: The Gaia Methodology for Agent-Oriented Analysis and Design. Journal of Autonomous Agents and Multi-Agent Systems, Vol. 3. No. 3 (2000) 285–312

Behavior-Based Model of Detection and Prevention of Intrusions in Computer Networks

Victor Serdiouk

Department of Information Technologies,
"MATI" – Russian State Technological University, 121552, Orshanskaya 3, Moscow, Russia
vicsmati@online.ru

Abstract. The paper describes a new intrusion detection and prevention model, which is based on state machine-based formal grammar. This behavior-based model allows to detect computer attacks by means of normal network traffic modeling. The parameters of such normal network traffic are presented in a formal grammar. Each data packet that violates these parameters is considered as a part of intrusion and blocked by network filters. The described model was implemented in Intrusion Detection and Prevention System "Forpost" and successfully tested in a complex network environment.

1 Introduction

During last decade the number of successful network attacks has increased in many times [9]. The damage caused by these attacks is estimated in hundreds millions of dollars. At the same time current intrusion detection models seem incapable of dealing with many types of modern attacks. These factors lead to the necessity of development of new methods for the intrusion detection and prevention.

This paper describes a new approach for intrusion detection and prevention modeling, which uses state machine-based formal grammars. The rest of the paper is structured as follows. Section 2 describes the advantages and disadvantages of existing intrusion detection models. Section 3 presents new behavior-based intrusion detection model developed by the author. Section 4 describes practical implementation of developed model, which was integrated in Intrusion Detection and Prevention System "Forpost". Section 5 summarizes the main results of the paper.

2 Overview of Existing Intrusion Detection Models

Intrusion detection models formally describe the process of computer attacks detection. At present there are two complementary types of intrusion detection models — signature-based models and behavior-based models. The first type of models provides the search for evidence of intrusions based on knowledge accumulated from known attacks [2, 4]. Signature-based models present an attack in a form of so-called signature, which can be presented as a regular expression, semantic expression of specialized language, formal mathematical structure, etc. Behavior-

V. Gorodetsky, I. Kotenko, and V. Skormin (Eds.): MMM-ACNS 2005, LNCS 3685, pp. 380–393, 2005.

based models search for deviations from usual computer system behavior based on the observations of the system during a known normal state. Such deviations are considered as computer attacks.

2.1 Signature-Based Intrusion Detection Models

One of the most popular signature-based intrusion detection models is an expression matching model [7]. This model provides searching the source data (e.g. log entries, network traffic, etc.) for occurrence of specific patterns. These patterns are usually specified by means of regular expression syntax. For example, the pattern like ".*[Cc][Mm][Dd]\.[Ee][Xx][Ee].*" specifies the signature of an attack, aimed at the unauthorized execution of file "cmd.exe". Sometimes signatures are built on the basis of expression matching models, complemented by specialized programming languages like C/C++, Java, Perl, etc. In this case signatures are presented as a set of language operators. The example of attack "Land" signature, which is written in a specialized scripting language is cited below [3].

The example of attack "Land" signature, written in N-code programming language

```
filter pptp ip ()
{
  # If sender address is equal to receiver address then
  # the information about attack is written to log
  if (ip.src == ip.dest)
  {
     system.time,eth.src,ip.src,sth.dst to land_recrdr;
  }
}
```

Specialized languages like N-code allow to define more complex signatures, which can't be created by means of simple expression matching models. At present specialized languages is the most popular method for attack signature development.

Another type of signature-based intrusion detection model is a state-transition analysis model. This type of model presents attack as a finite state machine, which describes the transition of computer system from one state to another. The initial state of computer system in such machine corresponds to pre-attack state, the final state is associated with the last stage of the attack, which leads to the violation of confidentiality, integrity or availability of the system. The transition of computer system from one state to another is related to certain events like application execution, TCP connection establishment, shell-code transmission, etc. State-transition analysis model can be visualized by means of graphs or more complex mathematical structures like Petri-nets. The main disadvantage of described model is that it can represent only those attacks that are related to some visible changes in computer system.

Intrusion detection models, based on expert systems, allow to describe attack signatures on natural language with high level of abstraction. The expert system, which underlies this type of model, consists of a set of rules that describe attacks.

Usually all rules of such expert system are written in the following format: "if <certain conditions> then <certain actions>". The model also allows to create interdependent rules, in which the execution of one rule is possible only in the case of second rule execution. This model can be implemented on the basis of specialized program languages, such as Prolog. The disadvantage of intrusion detection models, based on expert systems, is in high complexity of initial rule set development.

The current state of signature-based intrusion detection models allows to make up a conclusion that existing models can rather effectively provide the detection of existing type of attacks. The detection of new types of attacks is achieved by means of behavior-based models, that are described below.

2.2 Behavior-Based Intrusion Detection Models

As was already mentioned above behavior-based models are used for the detection of deviations from normal computer system state. One of the most widely used models of this type are statistical models [3, 6]. According to the statistical models the computer system behavior is measured by a number of variables sampled over time. Examples of these variables include the user login and logout time, the amount of processor-memory-disk resources consumed during the session, etc. If current characteristics of the computer system deviate from the given statistical measures, then the attack is registered. Intrusion detection models, based on statistical models, can detect several types of attacks, that use extremely unusual commands. But in most cases statistical models can detect only the consequences of computer attacks, which lead to changes in statistical measures. Moreover the practical usage of these models is characterized by large number of false positives, because in many cases the deviations of statistical measures are caused by normal system work.

Another type of behavior-based intrusion detection models uses neural networks for detection of attacks. A neural network is a network of computational units that jointly implement complex mapping functions. Initially the neural network is trained with normal computer system behavior traces. After such training the network becomes capable of determining normal and anomalous system behavior on the basis of observed events analysis. Each detected anomaly in system behavior is considered as attack. At present the models, based on neural network, have a low level of efficiency because of long duration of network training, large number of false positives and high computational complexity.

Intrusion detection models, based on expert systems, are usually used for detection of anomalies in network packets during protocol verification. Such verification implies the check of data packet fields against established standards. All packets that violate the requirements of corresponding standards are considered as potentially dangerous. This type of models is implemented in number of commercial Intrusion Detection Systems. One of the main disadvantages of this model is the inability of protection against attacks, that use data packets which don't violate any standards.

Taking into consideration the disadvantages of existing behavior-based intrusion detection models a new model was developed. The description of this model is cited in Section 3.

3   Behavioral Intrusion Detection Model, Which Uses State Machine-Based Formal Grammars

As a result of conducted researches in the field of protection against network attacks a new behavioral intrusion detection model was developed. This model combines the functional capabilities of other models, based on expert systems and state transition analysis. The model is designed for the detection of anomalous network traffic that is used for informational attack realization. The developed model allows to detect the following types of potentially dangerous network packets:

– packets with syntax and semantics, that doesn't correspond to RFC-standards,
– packets, that addressed to non-existent informational resources,
– packets, which length exceeds the specified restrictions,
– packets with commands, which are not supported by computer system applications,
– other types of packets that violate the template of normal computer system traffic.

The developed model is based on finite state language L which describes the template of normal network traffic that is transmitted in computer system. Language L consists of strings, each string corresponds to normal network packet that can be correctly processed by computer system applications. Language L is specified by means of state machine-based grammar of the following type: $A = < S, X, Y, s_0, f_t, f_s, F, s_a>$, where S – the set of states, X – the set of input symbols, Y – the set of semantic operators that analyze the semantics of input data, $s_0 \in S$ – the initial state, $f_t: S \times X \to S$ – the state transition function, $f_s: S \times X \to Y$ – the semantic operator choice function, $F \subseteq S$ – the set of terminal states which indicate the correct recognition of input string as a element of language L, $s_a \in S$ – the terminal state which indicate that the input string is not the element of language L.

The algorithm of work of state machine A, that specifies language L, can be presented as follows. The state machine A processes the input string, which corresponds to an incoming data packet that must be processed by the protected computer system. If the state machine will reach one of the terminal states of set F it will mean that analyzed data packet doesn't pose any danger to the computer system and can be passed through. Otherwise, reaching the state s_a corresponds to the detection of network attack. In this case the data packet, which corresponds to the analyzed input string, should be blocked.

The practical usage of behavioral model can be illustrated with the example of state machine-based grammar A_{HTTP}, which was developed according to the described approach. This state machine is designed for the detection of network attacks on Web-servers, that interact with users by means of Hypertext Transfer Protocol (HTTP). The state-machine A_{HTTP} specifies the language L_{HTTP} which consists of strings, where each string corresponds to a normal HTTP-request, that can be correctly processed by the application software of Web-server. The state machine A_{HTTP} consists of the following modules (Fig. 1): the module of HTTP-method analysis, the module of Uniform Resource Locator (URL) analysis, the module of HTTP query analysis, the module of HTTP version analysis and the module of HTTP-headers analysis. Each of these modules provides the processing of a particular part of the HTTP-request.

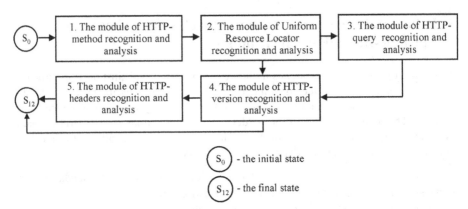

Fig. 1. The structure of finite state machine A_{HTTP}, designed for the detection of network attacks on Web-servers

During the analysis of HTTP-requests state machine A_{HTTP} uses the following auxiliary variables:

- $S_{methods}$ – one-dimensional string array with the list of allowed HTTP-methods,
- L_{URL} – numeric variable, that specifies the maximum allowed length of the URL (for example "www.mati.ru/scripts/example.exe" is an URL in the following HTTP-request "http://www.mati.ru/scripts/example.exe"),
- S_{URL} – one-dimensional string array with list of resources, stored on Web-server (this array can represent both static and dynamic Web-environment because of the ability to use regular expressions),
- L_{NQuery} – numeric variable, that specifies the maximum allowed number of parameters in a HTTP-query (for example "?var1=test1&var2=test2" is query in the following request "http://www.mati.ru/scripts/example.exe?var1=test1& var2=test2"),
- $L_{VarLength}$ – numeric variable, that specifies the maximum length of a variable name being passed via a HTTP-query (for example "var1" and "var2" are variable names in the following request "http://www.mati.ru/scripts/example.exe?var1=test1& var2=test2"),
- $L_{ValLength}$ – numeric variable, that specifies the maximum length of the data being supplied for a specific variable (for example "test1" and "test2" are variable data entries in the following request "http://www.mati.ru/scripts/example.exe? var1=test1&var2=test2"),
- $L_{NHeaders}$ – numeric variable, that specifies the maximum allowed number of headers in HTTP-request,
- $S_{Versions}$ – one-dimensional string array, that contains the list of HTTP protocol versions, supported by the protected Web-server,
- $S_{Headers}$ – one-dimensional string array with the list of allowed HTTP-headers,
- Z – temporary string variable, which is used for the storage of HTTP-request fragments,
- i, j, k – temporary numeric variables, that are used as counters.

The variables Z, i, j and k are initialized automatically during the work of state machine A_{HTTP}, whereas all other variables should be initialized by the operator before the start of state machine A_{HTTP} according to the RFC requirements and specific characteristics of the protected Web-server.

For the sake of simple graphical representations of state-machine modules we will use the following symbolic notations:

- A – set of English alphabet letters,
- N – set of numbers (0 - 9), symbols «.», «#», «?», «/», «%» and underline symbol,
- NOP – semantic operator, which doesn't perform any actions,
- "_" – space symbol,
- "CRLF" – symbol, which denotes carriage return and line feed.

The description of modules of state machine A_{HTTP} is cited below.

3.1 Module of HTTP-Method Analysis

The module of HTTP-method analysis starts the processing of input symbols of state machine A_{HTTP}. The module checks that the analyzed HTTP-request is based on one of the allowed HTTP-methods, which are defined in variable S_{method}. The graph model of this module is depicted in Fig. 2.

The first module consists of three states s_0, s_1, $s_2 \in S$ and three semantic operators y_0, y_1, $y_2 \in Y$, that are executed during the transition of the machine from one state to another. The description of these states and semantic operators of the module is cited in Table 1.

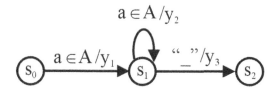

Fig. 2. The graph model of HTTP-method analysis module of finite state machine A_{HTTP}

Table 1. The description of states and semantic operators of HTTP-method analysis module

State transition	Transition condition	Semantic operator, which is executed during the transition
Transition from s_0 to s_1	The first input symbol is a letter of English alphabet $a \in A$	The semantic operator y_1 is executed. Operator y_1 clears the value of Z ($Z=$"") and initializes it with the first input symbol $a \in A$ ($Z=a$)
Transition from s_1 to s_1	The input symbol is a letter of English alphabet $a \in A$	The semantic operator y_2 is executed. This operator concatenates the value of Z with the input symbol a ($Z = Z + a$)
Transition from s_1 to s_2	The input symbol is a space symbol "_"	The semantic operator y_2 is executed. Operator performs the following check. If the value of Z corresponds to one of elements of $S_{methods}$ then the subsequent processing of input string is implemented by the module of URL analysis. Otherwise the processing of input strings is stopped because the analyzed HTTP-request contains the unsupported HTTP-method

3.2 Module of Uniform Resource Locator analysis

The module of URL analysis checks the length of the URL and verifies that the HTTP-request is addressed to one of the existing resources of the Web-server. The module uses two variables during the URL analysis – L_{URL} and S_{URL}. The graph model of the URL analysis module is presented in Fig. 3.

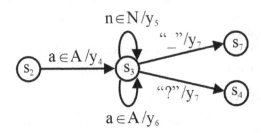

Fig. 3. The graph model of Uniform Resource Locator analysis module of state machine A_{HTTP}

Table 2. The description of states, transitions and semantic operators of URL analysis module

State transition	Transition condition	Semantic operator, which is executed during the transition
Transition from s_2 to s_3	The first input symbol is a letter of English alphabet $a \in A$	The semantic operator y_4 is executed. Operator y_4 performs the following actions: – clears the value of variable Z (Z="") and initializes it with the input symbol a ($Z = a$), – initializes variable i with "1" ($i = 1$)
Transition from s_3 to s_3	The input symbol is a letter of English alphabet $a \in A$	The semantic operator y_6 is executed. Operator y_6 performs the following actions: – concatenates Z with input symbol a ($Z=Z+a$), – increments the value of variable i ($i = i+1$), – performs the following check – if $i > L_{URL}$, then subsequent processing of input strings is stopped because the length of analyzed URL violates the specified restrictions
	The input symbol is a symbol $n \in N$	The semantic operator y_5 is executed. Operator y_5 performs the following actions: – concatenates Z with input symbol n ($Z = Z + n$) and increments the value of i ($i = i+1$), – performs the following check – if $i > L_{URL}$, then subsequent processing of input strings is stopped because the length of analyzed URL violates the specified restrictions
Transition from s_3 to s_7	The input symbol is a space symbol "_"	The state machine executes semantic operator y_7, which performs the following check. If Z is not equal to one of the elements of array S_{URL} then subsequent processing of input strings is stopped because the analyzed URL is addressed to non-existent resource of Web-server
Transition from s_3 to s_4	The input symbol is a symbol "?"	

The description of state transitions, transition conditions and semantic operators of the module is cited in Table 2.

If the URL analysis module reaches state s_4 it means that HTTP-request contains query parameters that must be processed by the module of HTTP query analysis. The transition to state s_7 means that URL is followed by the HTTP version field, which must be processed by the module of HTTP version analysis. In any other case the state machine A_{HTTP} is transferred to final state s_a.

3.3 Module of HTTP Query Analysis

The module of HTTP query analysis performs the following functions:

- checks the string length of the variable name being passed via a HTTP-query. The maximum length shouldn't exceed the value, specified in variable $L_{VarLength}$,
- checks the data value of a specific variable. The maximum length shouldn't exceed the value, specified in variable $L_{ValLength}$,
- checks the number of parameters in HTTP-query. The maximum number of parameters shouldn't exceed the value, specified in variable L_{NQuery}.

The graph model of HTTP query analysis module is shown in Fig. 4.

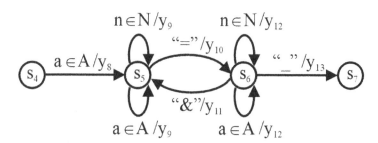

Fig. 4. The graph model of HTTP query analysis module of finite state machine A_{HTTP}

The description of state transitions, transition conditions and semantic operators of the HTTP query analysis module is cited in Table 3.

In the case of transition to state s_7 the state machine starts the processing of HTTP version number. In any other case the state machine A_{HTTP} is transferred final state s_a.

3.4 Module of HTTP Version Analysis

The module of HTTP version analysis checks that the version number equals to one of the elements of string array $S_{Versions}$. The graph model of this module is depicted in Fig. 5.

The first module consists of three states s_7, s_8, $s_9 \in S$ and three semantic operators y_{14}, y_{15}, $y_{16} \in Y$, that are executed during the transition of the machine from one state to another. The description of state transitions, transition conditions and semantic operators of the HTTP version analysis module is cited in Table 4.

Table 3. The description of state transitions, transition conditions and semantic operators of the HTTP query analysis module

State transition	Transition condition	Semantic operator, which is executed during the transition
Transition from s_4 to s_5	The first input symbol is a letter of English alphabet $a \in A$	The semantic operator y_4 is executed. Operator y_4 initializes the variables i, j, and k with zero values ($i = 0$, $j = 0$, $k = 0$). Variable i is used for query variable length calculation, j is used for the calculation of length of query variable data, k is used for the calculation of number of query variables.
Transition from s_5 to s_5	The input symbol is a letter of English alphabet $a \in A$	The semantic operator y_9 is executed. Operator y_9 performs the following actions: − increments the value of variable i ($i = i+1$), − performs the following check – if $i > L_{\text{VarLength}}$, then subsequent processing of input strings is stopped because the length of analyzed query variable violates the specified restrictions
	The input symbol is a symbol $n \in N$	
Transition from s_5 to s_6	The input symbol is a symbol "="	The semantic operator y_{10} is executed. Operator y_{10} reinitialize the variable i with zero value ($i=0$)
Transition from s_6 to s_6	The input symbol is a letter of English alphabet $a \in A$	The semantic operator y_{12} is executed. Operator y_{12} performs the following actions: − increments the value of variable j ($j = j+1$), − performs the following check – if $j > L_{\text{ValLength}}$, then subsequent processing of input strings is stopped because the length of analyzed data violates the specified restrictions
	The input symbol is a symbol $n \in N$	
Transition from s_6 to s_5	The input symbol is a symbol "&"	The semantic operator y_{11} is executed. Operator y_{11} performs the following actions: − initializes the variable j with zero value ($j=0$), − increments the value of variable k ($k=k+1$), − performs the following check – if $k > L_{\text{NQuery}}$, then subsequent processing of input strings is stopped because the number of query parameters violates the specified restrictions
Transition from s_6 to s_7	The input symbol is a space symbol " "	The semantic operator y_{13} is executed. Operator y_{13} performs the following actions: − increments the value of variable k ($k=k+1$), − performs the following check – if $k > L_{\text{NQuery}}$, then subsequent processing of input strings is stopped because the number of query parameters violates the specified restrictions

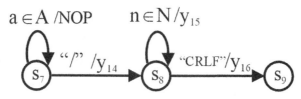

Fig. 5. The graph model of HTTP version analysis module of finite state machine A_{HTTP}

Table 4. The description of state transitions, transition conditions and semantic operators of the HTTP version analysis module

State transition	Transition condition	Semantic operator, which is executed during the transition
Transition from s_7 to s_7	The first input symbol is a letter of English alphabet $a \in A$	No semantic operators are executed
Transition from s_7 to s_8	The input symbol is a symbol "/"	The semantic operator y_{14} is executed. Operator y_{14} clears the value of variable Z ($Z=$"")
Transition from s_8 to s_8	The input symbol is a symbol $n \in N$	The semantic operator y_{15} is executed. Operator y_{15} concatenates the value of variable Z with input symbol n ($Z = Z + n$)
Transition from s_8 to s_9	The input symbol is a symbol "CRLF"	The semantic operator y_{16} is executed. Operator y_{16} performs the following check – if the value of Z is not equal to any of the elements of array $S_{Versions}$, then subsequent processing of input strings is stopped because the version of analyzed HTTP-request can't be correctly processed by the Web-server. In this case state machine A_{HTTP} is transferred final state s_a

3.5 Module of HTTP-Headers Analysis

The module of HTTP-headers analysis checks the length of query variables and values according to the restrictions, specified in variables $L_{VarLength}$ and $L_{ValLength}$. This module also checks that HTTP-request contains only allowed headers, that are specified in array $S_{Headers}$. The graph model of the module is depicted in Fig. 6.

The description of these states and semantic operators of the HTTP-headers analysis module is cited in Table 5.

The transition to state s_{12} means that the analyzed HTTP-request doesn't pose any danger to the computer system and can be passed through. In any other case the state machine A_{HTTP} is transferred to final state s_a and the packet must be blocked.

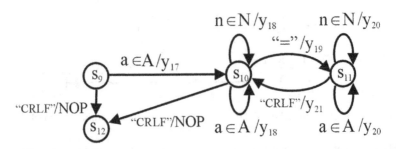

Fig. 6. The graph model of HTTP-headers analysis module of finite state machine A_{HTTP}

The described intrusion detection model can be used for the protection other network protocols such as SMTP, FTP, SNMP, SOAP, etc. This model can detect both known and new types of network attacks on computer systems. The model can also be easily extended by means addition of new parameters.

The developed model belongs to the class of specification or policy based intrusion detection techniques. In contrast to the existing models of this class, the behavioral intrusion detection model uses state machine-based formal grammars as a basic mathematical tool for attack detection. Such formal grammars allow more precise definition of parameters, that can be used for intrusion detection.

4   Practical Implementation of Developed Behavior-Based Intrusion Detection Model

The developed behavior-based intrusion detection model was implemented in Intrusion Detection and Prevention System (IPS) named "Forpost". IPS "Forpost" consists of the following components:

- network and server sensors, designed for the collection and analysis of information about network packets, transmitted in computer system,
- response module, that perform different types of responses depending on the types of detected attacks and administrator settings,
- informational database, designed for centralized storage of configurational data and results of IPS work,
- management module, which provides centralized remote management of IPS components over the network,
- coordination center, which provides the interaction between all other components of the IPS,
- software agents, that provide the transmission of data between sensors and coordination center.

Network sensors of IPS "Forpost" are implemented as appliances that can detect informational attacks in particular network segments. Network sensors can be installed in computer system by means of connecting sensors to hubs or SPAN-ports of switches. For security purposes network sensors are equipped with two network adapters, one of which is used as a management interface, and the other provides the collection of information about data packets [8, 1].

Table 5. The description of states and semantic operators of HTTP-headers analysis module

State transition	Transition condition	Semantic operator, which is executed during the transition
Transition from s_9 to s_{10}	The first input symbol is a letter of English alphabet $a \in A$	The semantic operator y_{17} is executed. Operator y_{17} performs the following actions: − initializes variables i, j, and k with zero values ($i = 0$, $j = 0$, $k = 0$). Variable i is used for header length calculation, j is used for the calculation of length of header variable data, k is used for the calculation of number of headers in HTTP-request, − clears the value of variable Z (Z = "") and initializes it with input symbol a.
Transition from s_{10} to s_{10}	The input symbol is a letter of English alphabet $a \in A$	The semantic operator y_{18} is executed. Operator y_{18} performs the following actions: − increments the value of variable i ($i = i+1$), − concatenates the value of Z with input symbol a or n ($Z = Z + a$ or $Z = Z + n$), − performs the following check − if $i>L_{\text{VarLength}}$, then subsequent processing of input strings is stopped because the length of analyzed header violates the specified restrictions
	The input symbol is a symbol $n \in N$	
Transition from s_{10} to s_{11}	The input symbol is a symbol "="	The semantic operator y_{19} is executed. Operator y_{19} performs the following actions: − reinitializes the variable i with zero value ($i=0$), − performs the following check − if the value of Z doesn't correspond to any of the elements of array S_{Headers} then subsequent processing of input strings is stopped because the analyzed HTTP-request contains forbidden header, − reinitializes Z with zero value ($Z=0$)
Transition from s_{11} to s_{11}	The input symbol is a letter of English alphabet $a \in A$	The semantic operator y_{20} is executed. Operator y_{20} performs the following actions: − increments the value of variable j ($j = j+1$), − performs the following check − if $j>L_{\text{ValLength}}$, then subsequent processing of input strings is stopped because the length of analyzed data violates the specified restrictions
	The input symbol is a symbol $n \in N$	
Transition from s_{11} to s_{10}	The input symbol is a symbol "CRLF"	The semantic operator y_{21} is executed. Operator y_{21} performs the following actions: − initializes the value of j with zero value ($j = 0$), − increments the value of variable k ($k = k+1$), − performs the following check − if $k>L_{\text{NHeaders}}$, then subsequent processing of input strings is stopped because the number of headers in HTTP-requests violates the specified restrictions
Transition from s_{10} to s_{12}	The input symbol is a symbol "CRLF"	No semantic operators are executed
Transition from s_9 to s_{12}		

Server sensors are installed on protected servers and provide protection of certain network services like HTTP, SMTP, POP3, etc. Several server sensors can be installed on one host. In contrast to network sensors, server sensors can prevent network attacks by means of filtering potentially dangerous data packets. Server sensors implement of intrusion detection model, which was described in Section 3 of the paper. The common structure of IPS "Forpost" is depicted in Fig. 7.

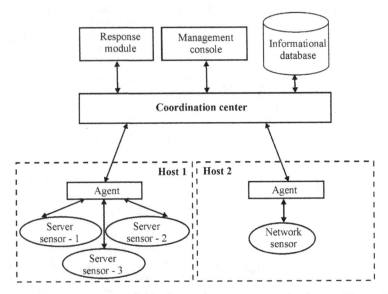

Fig. 7. Common structure of Intrusion Detection and Prevention System "Forpost"

The testing of IPS "Forpost" demonstrated that the developed intrusion detection model can effectively detect network attacks with low number of false negatives and false positives. The IPS was tested be means of specialized attack simulation tools [5] in heterogeneous network environment. At present IPS "Forpost" is successfully introduced in a number of computer systems of commercial and state enterprises such as Central Election Committee of Russia, Ministry of Justice, Committee of Financial Monitoring of Russian Federation, etc.

5 Conclusion

The development of intrusion detection models is currently one of the most rapidly evolving fields of information security. The main types of signature- and behavior-based models were considered in this paper. On the basis of existing models disadvantages a new intrusion detection model was developed. This model uses state machine-based formal grammars and allows to detect and prevent anomalous network traffic, related to informational attacks. Developed model can detect both known and new types of network attacks. The described approach was illustrated by an example of model, designed for the detection of attacks on Web-servers. The developed model was implemented in an Intrusion Detection and Prevention system "Forpost", which was successfully introduced in a number of computer systems.

References

1. Avdoshin, S., Serdiouk, V.: Some approaches to information security of communication networks. Vol. 26. Slovenia, Informatica. (2002) 1–10.
2. Cohen, F.B.: Information System Attacks: A Preliminary Classification Scheme. Computers and Security, Vol.16, No.1 (1997)
3. Debar, H., Dacier, M., Wespi, A.: Towards a taxonomy of intrusion-detection systems. Computer Networks. Vol. 31 (1999) 805–822.
4. Denning, D.: An intrusion-detection model. IEEE Transactions on Software Engineering. Vol. 13 (1987) 222–232.
5. Gorodetski, V., Kotenko I., Attacks against Computer Network: Formal Grammar-Based Framework and Simulation Tool: RAID 2002 (2002) 219–238.
6. Krsul, I.V.: Software Vulnerability Analysis, Ph.D. Dissertation, Computer Sciences Department, Purdue University, Lafayette, IN (1998)
7. Kumar, S., Spafford, E.:A pattern matching model for misuse intrusion detection, Proc. 17th National Computer Security Conf. October (1994) 11–21.
8. Serdiouk, V.: Methods of data collection by intrusion detection systems. BYTE/Russia, 54 (2003) 74–78
9. Serdiouk, V.: Prevention of computer attacks. Network Magazine. Russia. 2 (2003) 62-67.
10. Verwoerd, T., Hunt, R.: Intrusion detection techniques and approaches. Computer communications. Vol. 25 (2002) 1356–1365.

A Formal Immune Network and Its Implementation for On-line Intrusion Detection

Alexander O. Tarakanov, Sergei V. Kvachev, and Alexander V. Sukhorukov

St. Petersburg Institute for Informatics, Russian Academy of Sciences,
14th line 39, St. Petersburg, 199178, Russia
tar@iias.spb.su

Abstract. This paper presents a mathematical model of immune network specified for real-time intrusion detection. A software implementation of the model has been tested on data simulating a typical US Air Force local area network (LAN). The obtained results suggest that the performance of the model is unachievable for other approaches of computational intelligence. A hardware implementation of the model is proposed based on digital signal processor (DSP) of super Harvard architecture (SHARC).

1 Introduction

Immunological approach [2], [12], [13] looks rather constructive for information security assurance (ISA). For example, it is worth mentioning a mathematical notion of correlation immunity in cryptography [15], self-nonself discrimination in computer security [8], artificial immune systems as a new computational intelligence approach [4], [6], and immunocomputing (IC), which is based on mathematical models of information processing by proteins and immune networks [19].

An IC approach to ISA has been proposed in our previous papers [14], [16]. The present paper reports a mathematical model of spatial formal immune network (SFIN) specified for intrusion detection in LAN. The model has been implemented as a software emulator of the immunochip [17] and tested on data of the UCI KDD archive [1], which includes a wide variety of intrusions simulated in a military network environment.

2 Mathematical Model

2.1 Formal Immune Network

Definition 1. Cell is a pair $V = (c, P)$, where class c is natural number $c \in N$, whereas $P = (p_1,..., p_q)$ is a point of the q-dimensional Euclidian space: $P \in R^q$.

Fix some finite set of cells ("innate immunity"): $W_0 = (V_1,...,V_m)$.

Definition 2. Spatial formal immune network (SFIN) is a set of cells: $W \subseteq W_0$.

V. Gorodetsky, I. Kotenko, and V. Skormin (Eds.): MMM-ACNS 2005, LNCS 3685, pp. 394–405, 2005.

Let $d_{ij} = \|P_i - P_j\|_E$ be Euclidean distance between cells V_i and V_j. Let h be given threshold.

Definition 3. Cell V_i recognizes cell V_k if the following conditions are satisfied: $c_i = c_k$, $d_{ik} < h$, $d_{ik} < d_{ij}$, $\forall V_j \in W$, $j \neq i$, $k \neq j$.

Let us define the behavior of SFIN by the following two rules.

Rule 1 (Apoptosis). If cell $V_i \in W$ recognizes cell $V_k \in W$ then remove V_i from SFIN.

Rule 2 (Immunization). If cell $V_k \in W$ is nearest to cell $V_i \in W_0 \setminus W$ among all cells of SFIN: $d_{ik} < d_{ij}$, $\forall V_j \in W$, whereas $c_i \neq c_k$, then add V_i to SFIN.

2.2 Pattern Recognition

Definition 4. Pattern is any n-dimensional column-vector $Z = [z_1, ..., z_n]'$, where $z_1, ..., z_n$ are real values and (') is symbol of matrix transposing.

Definition 5. Pattern recognition is mapping $Z \to R^q$ and assigning to Z a class c of nearest cell of SFIN.

2.3 Training

Let $A_1, ..., A_m$ be n-dimensional training patterns with known classes $c_1, ..., c_m$.

Definition 6. Training is mapping of training patterns to cells of SFIN W_0: $A_1 \to V_1, ..., A_m \to V_m$, and application of the rules of Apoptosis and Immunization to all cells of W_0.

Let $A = [A_1, ..., A_m]'$ be training matrix of dimension $m \times n$. Consider singular value decomposition (SVD: see, e.g., [11]) of this matrix:

$$A = s_1 Y_1 X_1' + s_2 Y_2 X_2' + s_3 Y_3 X_3' + ... + s_r Y_r X_r', \tag{1}$$

where r is the rank of matrix A, s_k are singular values and Y_k, X_k are left and right singular vectors with the following properties: $Y_k' Y_k = 1$, $X_k' X_k = 1$, $Y_k' Y_i = 0$, $X_k' X_i = 0$, $i \neq k$, $k = 1, ..., r$.

Consider the following mapping $Z \to P \in R^q$ of any n-dimensional pattern Z:

$$p_k = \frac{1}{s_k} Z' X_k, \quad k = 1, ..., q. \tag{2}$$

According to [19], formulas (2) can be treated as "binding energies" between "formal proteins" Z ("antigen") and X_k ("antibodies").

2.4 Mathematical Properties of SFIN

Proposition 1. SFIN's projection $P = (p_1,..., p_q)$ of any training pattern $Z = A_i$, $i = 1,..., m$, lies within unit cube: $\max\{| p_1 |,...,| p_q |\} \leq 1$.

Let $Z' = A_i'$, $i = \{1,...,m\}$. Then, according to SVD (1):

$$Z' = s_1[Y_1]_i X_1' + s_2[Y_2]_i X_2' + s_3[Y_3]_i X_3' + ... + s_r[Y_r]_i X_r',$$

where $[Y_k]_i$ is i-th coordinate of left singular vector Y_k. Multiply both parts of this equation by X_k: $Z' X_k = s_k[Y_k]_i$, because $X_k' X_i = 0$, $i \neq k$. Substitution of this result to (2) leads to $p_k = [Y_k]_i$. Thus, $Y_k' Y_k = 1$ proves the proposition.

Proposition 2. SFIN W_0 without Apoptosis and Immunization recognizes any training pattern by zero Euclidian distance.

Let $W_0 = (V_1,...,V_m)$ be SFIN corresponded to training patterns $A_1,..., A_m$. Let $P_i = (p_{1i},..., p_{qi})$. Let $Z' = A_i'$, $i = \{1,...,m\}$. Then, according to the proof of Proposition 1, $p_k = [Y_k]_i = p_{ki}$, $k = 1,...,q$. Thus, $d_{ii} = 0$, which proves given Proposition 2.

3 Software Implementation

Based on the above mathematical model of SFIN, consider a description (in a pseudocode) of the IC algorithm of pattern recognition:

```
Training
{
    1st stage training // map data to SFIN
    {
        Get training patterns;
        Form training matrix;
        Compute SVD of the training matrix;
        Store q singular values // "binding energies"
        Store q right singular vectors; // "antibody-probes"
        Store left singular vectors; // cells of SFIN
    }
    2nd stage training // compress data by SFIN
    { // compute for all cells of SFIN:
        Apoptosis;
        Immunization;
    }
}
```

```
Recognition
{
    Get pattern; // "antigen"
    Map the pattern to SFIN;
    Find nearest cell of SFIN;
    Assign class of the nearest cell to the pattern;
}
```

This IC algorithm has been implemented in a version of the immunochip emulator using the following standard tools:

- MS Windows XP Operating System;
- MS Visual C++ 6.0 Developer Studio;
- OpenGL for three-dimensional (3D) visualization.

Screenshot of the emulator is shown in Fig. 1.

4 Test Data

The known UCI KDD archive has been used for testing the emulator. This is the data set used for The Third International Knowledge Discovery and Data Mining Tools Competition, which was held in conjunction with KDD-99 The Fifth International Conference on Knowledge Discovery and Data Mining. The competition task was to build a network intrusion detector, a predictive model capable of distinguishing between "bad" connections, called intrusions or attacks, and "good" normal connections.

The 1998 DARPA Intrusion Detection Evaluation Program was prepared and managed by MIT Lincoln Labs. The objective was to survey and evaluate research in intrusion detection. A standard set of data to be audited, which includes a wide variety of intrusions simulated in a military network environment, was provided. The 1999 KDD intrusion detection contest uses a version of this dataset.

Lincoln Labs set up an environment to acquire nine weeks of raw transmission control protocol (TCP) dump data for a LAN simulating a typical US Air Force LAN. They operated the LAN as if it were a true Air Force environment, but peppered it with multiple attacks.

The raw training data was about four gigabytes of compressed binary TCP dump data from seven weeks of network traffic. This was processed into about five million connection records. Similarly, the two weeks of test data yielded around two million connection records.

A connection is a sequence of TCP packets starting and ending at some well defined times, between which data flows to and from a source IP address to a target IP address under some well defined protocol. Each connection is labeled as either normal, or as an attack, with exactly one specific attack type. Each connection record consists of about 100 bytes.

Attacks fall into 4 main categories:

- DOS: denial-of-service (e.g. "syn flood");
- R2L: unauthorized access from a remote machine (e.g. "guessing password");

- U2R: unauthorized access to local superuser (root) privileges (e.g., various "buffer overflow"' attacks);
- probing: surveillance and other probing (e.g., "port scanning").

It is important to note that the test data is not from the same probability distribution as the training data, and it includes specific attack types not in the training data. This makes the task more realistic. Some intrusion experts believe that most novel attacks are variants of known attacks and the "signature" of known attacks can be sufficient to catch novel variants. The datasets contain a total of 24 training attack types, with an additional 14 types in the test data only.

Two data files from UCI KDD archive has been used for testing the emulator:

- File 1: kddcup_data_10_percent_gz.htm (7.7 MB);
- File 2: kddcup_newtestdata_10_percent_unlabeled_gz.htm (44 MB).

File 1 is the training data file. It contains 51608 network connection records. Any record (file string) has the following format, where parameters 2, 3, 4, 42 are symbolic, while other 38 parameters are numerical (real values):

```
1) duration, 2) protocol_type, 3) service, 4) flag, 5) src_bytes,
6) dst_bytes, 7) land, 8) wrong_fragment, 9) urgent, 10) hot,
11) num_failed_logins, 12) logged_in, 13) num_compromised,
14) root_shell, 15) su_attempted, 16) num_root, 17) num_file_creations,
18) num_shells, 19) num_access_files, 20) num_outbound_cmds,
21) is_host_login, 22) is_guest_login, 23) count, 24) srv_count,
25) serror_rate, 26) srv_serror_rate, 27) rerror_rate,
28) srv_rerror_rate, 29) same_srv_rate, 30) diff_srv_rate,
31) srv_diff_host_rate, 32) dst_host_count, 33) dst_host_srv_count,
34) dst_host_same_srv_rate, 35) dst_host_diff_srv_rate,
36) dst_host_same_src_port_rate, 37) dst_host_srv_diff_host_rate,
38) dst_host_serror_rate, 39) dst_host_srv_serror_rate,
40) dst_host_rerror_rate, 41) dst_host_srv_rerror_rate, 42) attack_type.
```

For example, two records (# 1 and # 745) of File 1 are as follows:

```
0,tcp,http,SF,181,5450,0,0,0,0,0,1,0,0,0,0,0,0,0,0,0,0,8,8,0.00,0.00,
0.00,0.00,1.00,0.00,0.00,9,9,1.00,0.00,0.11,0.00,0.00,0.00,0.00,0.00,
normal.
184,tcp,telnet,SF,1511,2957,0,0,0,3,0,1,2,1,0,0,1,0,0,0,0,0,1,1,0.00,
0.00,0.00,0.00,1.00,0.00,0.00,1,3,1.00,0.00,1.00,0.67,0.00,0.00,0.00,
0.00, buffer_overflow.
```

File 1.1 has also been prepared with the same 51608 records of the same format just without the last parameter 42) attack_type.

File 2 contains 311079 records of the same format as in File 1.1.

File 1.1 and File 2 are the test data files.

Note that KDD archive does not indicate the correct types of attack for none of the records of File 2. The only available information on possible attacks is gathered in Tab. 1 (column 'Code' is the emulator's code of attack). Nevertheless, we have used File 2 to test whether the emulator is able to detect unknown intrusions, which had not been presented in the training data of File 1.

Table 1. Attack types

Code	Attack type	File 1	File 2	Code	Attack type	File 1	File 2
0	normal	+	+				
1	apache2		+	16	pod	+	+
2	back	+		17	portsweep	+	+
3	buffer_overflow	+	+	18	rootkit	+	
4	ftp_write			19	saint		+
5	guess_passwd		+	20	satan	+	
6	imap			21	sendmail		+
7	ipsweep	+	+	22	smurf	+	
8	land	+		23	snmpgetattack		+
9	loadmodule			24	spy		
10	multihop		+	25	teardrop	+	
11	named		+	26	udpstorm		+
12	neptune	+		27	warezclient		
13	nmap			28	warezmaster		
14	perl			29	xlock		+
15	phf	+	+	30	xsnoop		+

5 Test Results

The results of training the emulator by File 1 are shown in Fig.1, where right-hand screen represents the initial population of SFIN in 3D space ($Z \to R^3$) after SVD (start cells = 51608), while left-hand screen shows the population of SFIN after

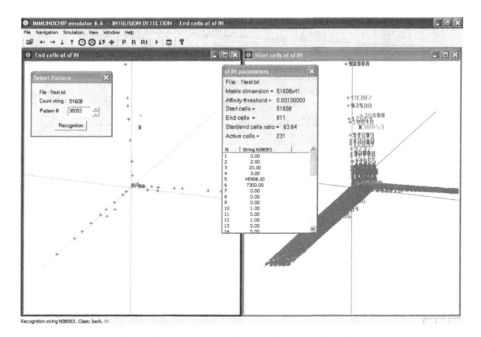

Fig. 1. Immunochip emulator for intrusion detection

Apoptosis and Immunization (h=0.001, end cells = 811). Total training time (for AMD Athlon 1.53 GHz) is 98.7 seconds including 8.03 s for the 1st stage (SVD) and 90.64 s for the 2nd stage (Apoptosis and Immunization).

During the recognition of the records of File 1.1 and File 2, the emulator writes test results into the output file in the format: Record # - attack_type. For example, four records (## 744-747) with test results for File 1.1 are as follows (see also Tab. 2):

```
744 - normal.
745 - buffer_overflow. !!!
746 - buffer_overflow. !!!
747 - normal.
```

The emulator also shows the on-line projection of any pattern to 3D SFIN (see bold skew cross in both screens) and write the recognition result on the bottom panel (see "Class: back !!!").

Test results in Tab. 2 correspond completely to the correct attack types (parameter 42) of File 1.

Table 2. Test results for File 1.1

Records ##	attack_type	Records ##	attack_type
745-746	buffer_overflow	38036-38051	ipsweep
3095-7373	smurf	38052-38151	back
9520-9523	buffer_overflow	38302-38311	ipsweep
9590-9591	rootkit	42498-42519	ipsweep
9928-10007	neptune	42548-42567	ipsweep
10072	satan	42593-42594	ipsweep
10320	phf	42706-42708	ipsweep
13340-13519	portsweep	42730-42761	ipsweep
13569	land	42762-42770	buffer_overflow
13845-13864	pod	42771-42772	land
16326-16327	pod	42773-43385	neptune
17446-37902	neptune	44451-44470	neptune
37929-37939	ipsweep	44800-48452	smurf
37959-37963	ipsweep	48453-48552	teadrop
38005-38012	ipsweep	All other	normal

Another test has been performed over File 2 to check whether the emulator is able to detect unknown intrusions, which had not been presented in the training data of File 1. The intrusion is treated as unknown if the projection of corresponding pattern to SFIN lies outside of the unit cube, according to Proposition 1. The emulator has recognized 13 unknown intrusions as the following records ## of File 2:

```
417, 12674, 97891, 139795, 170498, 176201, 177958, 232570, 236975,
296561, 296657, 96796, 297658.
```

According to Tab. 1, any unknown intrusion can correspond to one of the following types of attack that had not been presented in the training data:

```
apache2, guess_passwd, multihop, named, saint, sendmail, snmpgetattack,
udpstorm, xlock, xsnoop.
```

The recognition time per record is 15.7 ms for both tests of File 1.1 and File 2. This time includes not only computations but mainly reading the record from test file, visualization of the recognition result (projection of the pattern to 3D SFIN) in both screens of the emulator, and writing the result into output file.

6 Comparison with Neural Network

There is no possibility of direct comparison between immune and neural networks on the same data of File 1 and File 2, since none publication has been found on the training and testing any neural network on these data. Nevertheless, a comparison between SFIN and neural network has been performed using the sonar benchmark data available in the same KDD archive [1]. This is the data set used by [9] in their study of the classification of sonar signals using a neural network. The task is to train a network to discriminate between sonar signals bounced off a metal cylinder (i.e. submarine) and those bounced off a roughly cylindrical rock.

The KDD file "sonar.mines" contains 111 patterns obtained by bouncing sonar signals off a metal cylinder at various angles and under various conditions. The file "sonar.rocks" contains 97 patterns obtained from rocks under similar conditions. The transmitted sonar signal is a frequency-modulated chirp, rising in frequency. The data set contains signals obtained from a variety of different aspect angles, spanning 90 degrees for the cylinder and 180 degrees for the rock.

Each pattern is a set of 60 numbers in the range 0.0 to 1.0. Each number represents the energy within a particular frequency band, integrated over a certain period of time. The integration aperture for higher frequencies occurs later in time, since these frequencies are transmitted later during the chirp.

The label associated with each record contains the letter "R" if the object is a rock and "M" if it is a mine (metal cylinder). The numbers in the labels are in increasing order of aspect angle, but they do not encode the angle directly.

Two series of experiments have been reported in [9]: 1) an "aspect-angle independent" series, in which the whole data set is used without controlling for aspect angle, and 2) an "aspect-angle dependent" series in which the training and testing sets were carefully controlled to ensure that each set contained cases from each aspect angle in appropriate proportions.

A standard back-propagation network was used for all experiments in [9]. The network had 60 inputs and 2 output units, one indicating a cylinder and the other a rock. Experiments were run with no hidden units (direct connections from each input to each output) and with a single hidden layer with 2, 3, 6, 12, or 24 units. Each network was trained by 300 epochs over the entire training set.

Not surprisingly, the neural network's performance on the test set is somewhat better when the aspect angles in the training and test sets are balanced. These classification results of the neural network for "aspect-angle dependent" series are shown in Tab. 3.

It has been also reported that three trained human subjects were each tested on 100 signals, chosen at random from the set of 208 returns used to create this data set. Their responses ranged between 88% and 97% correct. However, they may have been using information from the raw sonar signal that is not preserved in the processed data sets presented here (according to [9]).

Table 3. Classification of sonar targets by neural network

Hidden units	% Right on Training Set	% Right on Test Set
0	79.3	73.1
2	96.2	85.7
3	98.1	87.6
6	99.4	89.3
12	99.8	90.4
24	100.0	89.2

According to [1], the authors of this work [9] further report that a nearest neighbor classifier on the same data gave an 82.7% probability of correct classification.

The immunochip emulator for intrusion detection has also been trained and tested by the "aspect-angle dependent" sets. Classification results of the immunochip emulator using only the 1st stage training (see Section 3) are shown in Tab. 4.

Table 4. Classification of sonar targets by immunochip emulator

Dimension of SFIN (q)	Training time (s)	% Right on Training Set	% Right on Test Set	Total Errors
3	0.02	100.0	76.9	24
5	0.03	100.0	84.6	16
7	0.03	100.0	89.4	11
8	0.06	100.0	90.3	10
9	0.08	100.0	93.2	7
10	0.08	100.0	92.3	8

Brief comparison between Tab. 3 and Tab. 4 shows that the best classification of the immunochip emulator (93.2%) is better than that of the neural network (90.4%). Besides, the emulator does not make mistakes on the training set (this is guaranteed by Proposition 2).

Note very low training time of the emulator in Tab. 4 (for AMD Athlon 1.53 GHz). Unfortunately, the training time of neural network in Tab.3 is unavailable from [1] or [9]. However, it can be estimated indirectly by the work [22], which uses the same sonar benchmark.

The authors of this work [22] report 58 s or 72 s (for Pentium 350 MHz) for their genetic algorithm applied to the neural networks with 3 or 4 hidden units respective and note that "This method is efficient because the time cost for evolution is about 2 or 3 orders less than that spent in training the networks." Such estimation confirms that the training time of the immunochip emulator is far lower than that of neural networks.

7   Hardware Implementation

A perspective way of hardware implementation of the immunochip can be provided by DSP of new TigerSHARC family. Such DSP is compatible with the standard PC, where it can be connected via PCI bus. Therefore, a hardware emulator of the immunochip can be implemented as a small standalone electronic board. A PC or PC compatible mobile computer (Notebook) can be used as a host workstation for user-friendly visualization of the results of processing, for debugging of algorithms, etc.

DSP provides, essentially, the application of mathematical operations to a series of digital samples representing physical world signals such as audio waves, or complex radar or sensor samples. DSP technology is nowadays common place in devices such as mobile phones, multimedia computers, video recorders, CD players, hard disc drive controllers and modems, and will soon replace analog circuitry in commercial TV sets and telephones. An important application of DSP is also in signal compression and decompression as well as encryption in the field of ISA [10].

The architecture of DSP allows overcome main drawbacks of general-purpose microprocessors. The program bus and the data bus are separate from each other, as are the program and data memories. These parallel buses allow instruction and data to be fetched at the same time. This separation of data and program busses characterizes the so-called Harvard architecture.

Analog Devices has introduced so-called super Harvard architecture (SHARC). The TigerSHARC 128-bit DSP is a high performance next generation version of SHARC. The TigerSHARC combines multiple computation units for floating-point and fixed-point processing.

Typically, real-time DSP systems require fast, deterministic input/output (I/O) and number crunching capability. Applications may range from basic processing of a small image with a single channel of incoming data (e.g. filtering or averaging) to a sonar system with hundreds of incoming data channels and a massive parallel processing requirement. The TigerSHARC has been designed to operate in the demanding world of telecommunications, but facilities that make it equally suitable for a wide range of applications, including aerial and maritime equipment (radar, avionics, sonar, etc.) and professional audio (mixers, digital effects, etc.).

Apparently, the TigerSHARC is the most effective fixed/floating-point device to date. The TigerSHARC is well suited to high-speed, low-power applications, involving large numbers of calculation and data I/O. The built-in link ports can transfer data between processors and provide fast interfaces to external hardware, yielding true system flexibility. Similarly, the dual compute blocks can handle mixed floating-point and fixed-point algorithms simultaneously, leading to very efficient and simplified software implementation. Overall, high-performance processing coupled with low power consumption (<1.5W) make the TigerSHARC DSP unbeatable for many applications. Since DSP algorithms permit a very high degree of parallelism, DSP chips can be used for super-computing with strong requirements like high performance and flexibility at very low power dissipation.

On the other hand, one of the main concerns when moving to a new chip is the effort involved in porting existing code to the new device. This can have a larger effect on the timescale of a project than the new hardware design, especially when software engineers have to learn a new development environment and a new assembly language. The TigerSHARC addresses both of these issues by keeping the same Visual DSP++ environment for all its processor families and maintaining a similar style of algebraic assembly programming.

Therefore, the choice of TigerSHARC architecture as a basis for the hardware implementation of the immunochip is caused by the following main reasons: 1) the

404 A.O. Tarakanov, S.V. Kvachev, and A.V. Sukhorukov

highest achievable performance for a large class of real-time floating-point applications and 2) the availability of rather advanced software tools for implementation of the developed algorithms.

According to our preliminary experiments, the TigerSHARC evaluation board EZ-KIT (ADSP-TS101S 250 MHz) works by 35 times faster than PC (Intel Celeron 400 MHz) while implementing an IC algorithm of recognition of results in immunoassay-based diagnostic arrays [18]. However, main advantage of the TigerSHARC implementation of the immunochip for on-line intrusion detection can be previewed in extracting of the recognizing pattern (network connection record) from the input flow (network traffic).

8 Conclusion

According to test results, SFIN reduces the storing patterns by 63.6 times using Apoptosis and Immunization without any loss of accuracy of recognition. Although this increases the training time (from 8 seconds to 1.5 minutes for AMD Athlon 1.53 GHz), nevertheless, more important is the decrease of the recognition time at least by 60 times per pattern (by decreasing number of the stored cells of SFIN to be compared with recognizing pattern).

It is also worth noting that so good performance of SFIN (error-free recognition with rather low training time) on the data of real-life dimension looks unobtainable for main competitors in the field of computational intelligence [7] like artificial neural networks (ANN) [5] and genetic algorithms (GA) [3]. According to our comparison in [20] and [21], SFIN trains by at least 40 times faster and recognizes by at least 2 times correctly than ANN and GA on the tasks of environmental monitoring and laser physics. These tasks have rather low dimension: 17×23×6 for ecological atlas and 19×5 for laser diode. However, the drawbacks of ANN and GA seem especially inadmissible for the task of intrusion detection with rather high dimension: 51608×41 and more.

The obtained results also show that the developing approach can successfully be applied to on-line intrusion detection in a typical US Air Force LAN (as simulated by the data of UCI KDD archive).

Acknowledgement

This work is supported by EOARD under project # 017007 "Development of mathematical models of immune networks intended for information security assurance".

References

1. Bay, S.D.: The UCI KDD Archive [http://kdd.ics.uci.edu]. Irvine, CA: University of California, Dept. of Information and Computer Science (1999)
2. de Boer, R.J., Segel, L.A., Perelson, A.S.: Pattern formation in one and two-dimensional shape space models of the immune system. J. Theoret. Biol. 155 (1992) 295–333

3. Buckles, B., Petry, F. (eds.): Genetic Algorithms. IEEE Computer Society Press, Los Alamitos CA (1992)

4. de Castro, L.N., Timmis, J. Artificial Immune Systems: A New Computational Intelligence Approach. Springer-Verlag, London (2002)

5. Cloete, I., Zurada, J.M. (eds.): Knowledge-Based Neurocomputing. MIT Press, Cambridge MA (2000)

6. Dasgupta, D. (ed.): Artificial Immune Systems and Their Applications. Springer-Verlag, Berlin (1999)

7. Fogel, D.B., Robinson, C.J. (eds.): Computational Intelligence: The Experts Speak. IEEE Press, Piscataway NJ (2004)

8. Forrest, S., Perelson, A., Aleen, L., Cherukuri, R.: Self-nonself discrimination in a computer. IEEE Symposium on Research in Security and Privacy. Oakland, USA (1994) 202–212

9. Gorman, R.P., Sejnowski, T.J.: Analysis of hidden units in a layered network trained to classify sonar targets. Neural Networks 1 (1988) 75–89

10. Hoang, X.D., Hu, J.: New encryption model for secure e-commerce transactions using DSP-host, board and server communication. IEEE Int. Conf. on Telecommunications 1 (2002) 166–170

11. Horn, R., Johnson, Ch.: Matrix Analysis. Cambridge University Press (1986)

12. Jerne, N.K.: The immune system. Scientific American 229/1 (1973) 52–60

13. Jerne, N.K.: Toward a network theory of the immune system. Annals of Immunology 125C (1974) 373–389

14. Melnikov, Y., Tarakanov, A.: Immunocomputing model of intrusion detection. Lecture Notes in Computer Science, Vol. 2776. Springer-Verlag, Berlin (2003) 453–456

15. Siegenthaler, T. : Correlation immunity of nonlinear combining functions for cryptographic applications. IEEE Trans. Inform. Theory 30 (1984) 776–780

16. Tarakanov, A.O.: Information security with formal immune networks. Lecture Notes in Computer Science, Vol. 2052. Springer-Verlag, Berlin (2001) 115–126

17. Tarakanov, A., Dasgupta, D.: An immunochip architecture and its emulation. NASA/DoD Conf. on Evolvable Hardware (EH'02). Alexandria, USA (2002) 261–265

18. Tarakanov, A., Goncharova, L., Gupalova, T., Kvachev, S., Sukhorukov, A.: Immunocomputing for bioarrays. 1st Int. Conf. on Artificial Immune Systems (ICARIS'02). Univ. of Kent at Canterbury, UK (2002) 32–40

19. Tarakanov, A.O., Skormin, V.A., Sokolova, S.P. Immunocomputing: Principles and Applications. Springer-Verlag, New York (2003)

20. Tarakanov A.O., Tarakanov Y.A.: A comparison of immune and neural computing for two real-life tasks of pattern recognition. Lecture Notes in Computer Science, Vol. 3239. Springer-Verlag, Berlin (2004) 236–249

21. Tarakanov A.O., Tarakanov Y.A.: A comparison of immune and genetic algorithms for two real-life tasks of pattern recognition. Int. J. Unconventional Computing 1/3 (2005) (in press)

22. Zhou Z.H., Chen S.: Evolving fault-tolerant neural networks. Neural Computing and Applications 11/3-4 (2003) 156–160

Foundation for a Time Interval Access Control Model

Francis B. Afinidad, Timothy E. Levin, Cynthia E. Irvine, and Thuy D. Nguyen

Computer Science Department, Naval Postgraduate School
Monterey, CA 93943, USA
{fbafinid, levin, irvine, tdnguyen}@nps.edu

Abstract. A new model for representing temporal access control policies is introduced. In this model, temporal authorizations are represented by time attributes associated with both subjects and objects, and a "time interval access graph." The time interval access graph is used to define constraints on the temporal relations between subjects and objects. Interval algebra is used to define and analyze the time interval access graph.

1   Introduction

In many commercial and military environments, time is often a critical factor for making decisions regarding authorization or access to information. The value or sensitivity of data and processes has become more dependent upon time attributes. Thus, future information systems will need to support system-wide security policies that incorporate time as a decision factor. To this end, a *Time Interval Access Control* (TIAC) model has been developed.

A significant contribution of the TIAC model is that it provides formal semantics to express temporal authorization policies, in which temporal attributes of subjects and objects are used to determine authorized accesses. The TIAC model differs from previously proposed models such as the *Temporal Authorization Model* by Bertino et al. [5, 6] and the *Temporal Data Authorization Model* by Gal and Atluri [4, 7], primarily in its ability to specify temporal relations between subjects and objects.

Another contribution of the TIAC model is that it is the first use of interval algebra [3] to express a temporal access control policy. This algebra provides the necessary expressive power to logically describe a temporal access control policy, and a precise and efficient way to computationally reason about the temporal relation between subjects and objects and associated access constraints. Policy enforcement mechanisms and the modeling of the effectiveness of those mechanisms with respect to the type of temporal authorizations describable in TIAC are outside of the scope of this paper (see [1]).

A brief discussion of interval algebra is presented in Section 2. Section 3 provides a description of the TIAC model, where we establish the definition of time intervals and discuss the formal semantics used for representing temporal authorizations and access requests. Finally, future work and conclusions are presented in Section 4.

V. Gorodetsky, I. Kotenko, and V. Skormin (Eds.): MMM-ACNS 2005, LNCS 3685, pp. 406–411, 2005.
© Springer-Verlag Berlin Heidelberg 2005

2   Background

Interval algebra [3] provides a means to represent time intervals associated with actions and entities and to computationally reason about their relationships. It defines the possible relations that can hold between two time intervals (see Table 1). These relations are mutually exclusive, in that only one is needed to describe the relative temporal placement of any two time intervals. Interval algebra assumes that the beginning and ending points (signified with "−" and "+" respectively) of an interval do not coincide. For each entry in Table 1, the first line shows the basic relation and the second line shows its inverse relation.

Table 1. Basic temporal relationships

RELATION	PREDICATE FORM	SYMBOL	RELATION ON ENDPOINTS	PICTORIAL MEANING
x before y y after x	BEFORE(x,y) AFTER(y,x)	$<$ $>$	$(x+ < y-)$	
x equals y y equals x	EQUALS(x,y) EQUALS(y,x)	$=$ $=$	$(x- = y-) \wedge$ $(x+ = y+)$	
x meets y y met by x	MEETS(x,y) MET_BY(y,x)	m mi	$x+ = y-$	
x overlaps y y overlapped by x	OVERLAPS(x,y) OVERLAPPED_BY(y,x)	o oi	$(x- < y-) \wedge$ $(x+ > y-) \wedge$ $(x+ < y+)$	
x during y y includes x	DURING(x,y) INCLUDES(y,x)	d di	$(x- > y-) \wedge$ $(x+ < y+)$	
x starts y y started by x	STARTS(x,y) STARTED_BY(y,x)	s si	$(x- = y-) \wedge$ $(x+ < y+)$	
x finishes y y finished by x	FINISHES(x,y) FINISHED_BY(y,x)	f fi	$(x- > y-) \wedge$ $(x+ = y+)$	

A set of time intervals and their required or allowed interrelationships can be represented using a directed graph (also known as an *interval algebra network*, or *IA network*), in which each vertex represents an individual time interval and each directed edge represents the relationship(s) between a pair of vertices.

3   TIAC Model

The TIAC model provides a formal semantic framework to extend existing authorization models with policies (e.g., restrictions) regarding the temporal relationships between subjects (e.g., user), objects (e.g., data) and the *time of access*.

In this section, a discussion of time and intervals provides a foundation for the TIAC model. Then the elements that make up the TIAC model are described. These elements are: 1) temporal entities, 2) the time interval access graph, 3) temporal authorizations, 4) access requests, and 5) the evaluation of access requests.

3.1   Time and Intervals

Time is assumed to be a set of discrete points, T, which is isomorphic to the natural numbers and is linearly ordered with respect to the $<$ relation. Points in T are used in representing time intervals.

Time intervals are represented using half-open intervals denoted as $\tau = [t\text{-}, t\text{+})$ where $t\text{-} < t\text{+}$. Half-open intervals are used so that there are no semantic ambiguities about the point where two time intervals meet. A *unit time interval* is the smallest expressible interval. It has a duration of one where $t\text{+} = t\text{-} + 1$. When referring to the *current* time a unit time interval is used. For discussion purposes, the current time will be referred to as *now. τ* where *now. $\tau = [now\text{-}, now\text{+})$*.

Time intervals are associated with subjects and objects, and temporal access control policies (restrictions regarding the relationships between intervals) are reasoned about using interval algebra.

3.2   Temporal Entities

Temporal entities are represented using the concept of subjects and objects similar to those discussed by Graham et al., Lampson, and Weissman [8, 9, 10]. Subjects and objects each have an associated time interval (attribute), which is used for making access control decisions.

In the following definitions, $S_\tau = \{s_1, s_2, ...s_n\}$ is the set of temporal subjects, and $O_\tau = \{o_1, o_2, ...o_n\}$ is the set of temporal objects (i.e., the passive entities that hold data or information and are accessed by temporal subjects).

Definition 1 (Temporal Object, Temporal Subject). *A temporal entity α is an object $o \in O_\tau$, or a subject $s \in S_\tau$, with which is associated a time interval $\tau = [t\text{-}, t\text{+})$ where:*

$\alpha.\tau$	*designates the time interval associated with α*
$\alpha.t\text{-}$	*designates the time point at the beginning of interval $\alpha.\tau$*
$\alpha.t\text{+}$	*designates the time point at the end of interval $\alpha.\tau$*

The time interval associated with a subject or object may be used to describe access constraints based on a temporal policy. For example, a time interval could be used to represent when a subject is valid or when an object may be accessed. Using interval algebra, it is possible to express policies regarding the temporal relations between a subject, an object, and a reference time interval such as *now. τ*.

3.3   Time Interval Access Graph φ

The TIAC model introduces the time interval *access graph, φ*. φ is a consistent instantiation of a three-vertex IA network that defines access constraints on the temporal relations between subjects and objects, and a reference time interval (τ_{ref}). A consistent version of any three-node access graph can be efficiently determined [1, 2, 3].

Definition 2 (Time Interval Access Graph φ). *The time interval access graph φ is a consistent instantiation of a three-vertex IA network* $G = (V, E)$ *where*:

V	$\{s.\tau, o.\tau, \tau_{ref}\}$
E	$\{(s.\tau, o.\tau), (\tau_{ref}, s.\tau), (\tau_{ref}, o.\tau)\}$
R	$\{<, >, d, di, o, oi, m, mi, s, si, f, fi, =\} \cup \varnothing$
$\gamma: E \rightarrow \wp(R)$	*a disjunctive set function that specifies the temporal relations allowed between a pair of vertices*

For example, φ could be instantiated with the following:

$s.\tau = [5, 20), o.\tau = [10, 15)$, and $\tau_{ref} = [11, 12)$
$\gamma(s.\tau, o.\tau) = \{includes\}, \gamma(\tau_{ref}, s.\tau) = \{starts \vee during\}$, and $\gamma(\tau_{ref}, o.\tau) = \{during\}$

3.4   Temporal Authorizations

Policies often distinguish between different "modes" in which a subject may access an object (e.g., observe, modify, execute, append). A *temporal authorization* A_{τ} is a mapping of a subject-object pair to a set of mode-φ pairs, which completely defines the temporal authorization policy for the subject with respect to that object. For simplicity of presentation, it is assumed herein that there is only one mode-φ pair per subject-object pair.

Definition 3 (Temporal Authorization). *A temporal authorization* A_{τ} *is defined as a 4-tuple (s, o, m, φ) where*:

$s \in S_{\tau}$	*temporal subject*
$o \in O_{\tau}$	*temporal object*
$m \subset M$	*allowed mode(s) of access*
φ	*time interval access graph that describes the temporal restrictions on the use of o*

A temporal authorization $\mathbf{A}_{\tau} = (s, o, m, φ)$ states that a subject *s* is allowed *m* access to object *o* as restricted by the time interval access graph φ. For a given policy instantiation, Ω_{τ} is the set of temporal authorizations.

3.5   Access Requests

A temporal subject, to gain access to a temporal object, initiates an *access request* for a given *mode* of access to occur at a particular time. In the most general form, temporal requests would specify an arbitrary time in the past, present and future. For simplicity in this discussion, requests will be characterized relative to *now.* τ . There are two types of access requests: *general access requests* and *duration access requests*.

Definition 4 (General Access Request). *A general access request $R_{g\tau}$ is a 4-tuple (s, o, m, now. τ) where:*

$s \in S_\tau$ *is a temporal subject*
$o \in O_\tau$ *is a temporal object*
$m \subset M$ *is a mode(s) of access*
now. τ is the time of access request

A general access request $R_{g\tau}(s, o, m, now. \tau)$ states that a subject s requests m access to object o at time *now. τ*. Implicit in this form of request is that the subject would be granted access for the maximum duration allowed by the access graph φ associated with s and o (if any exists).

Definition 5 (Duration Access Request). *A duration access request $R_{d\tau}$ is a 5-tuple (s, o, m, now. τ, δ) where:*

$s \in S_\tau$ *is a temporal subject*
$o \in O_\tau$ *is a temporal object*
$m \subset M$ is the mode(s) of access
now. τ is the time of the access request
δ *is the requested duration of access*

A duration access request $R_{d\tau}(s, o, m, now. \tau, \delta)$ states that a subject s requests m access to object o for a duration δ.

3.6   Evaluation of Access Requests

An access request is evaluated as follows: the set of temporal authorizations Ω_τ is searched for a matching subject-object pair. If no match is found, access is denied. If a match is found, the requested mode is compared to the allowed mode, and then the time interval access graph φ is interpreted relative to the requested interval, to grant or deny access. This process is specified in the boolean functions **Eval_g** and **Eval_d**.

Eval_g$(R_{g\tau}(s, o, m, now. \tau)) \Rightarrow \exists (s', o', m', \varphi) \in \Omega_\tau(s = s' \wedge o = o' \wedge m \subset m' \wedge \varphi =$ true when evaluated using $s.\tau, o.\tau,$ and *now. τ*)

Eval_d$(R_{d\tau}(s, o, m, now. \tau, \delta)) \Rightarrow \exists (s', o', m', \varphi) \in \Omega_\tau(s = s' \wedge o = o' \wedge m \subset m' \wedge \varphi =$ true when evaluated using $s.\tau, o.\tau,$ and *now. $\tau + \delta$*)

Note: *now. $\tau + \delta = [now\text{-}, now\text{-} + \varphi)$*

4   Conclusion and Future Research

In this short paper, we have presented the TIAC model as a novel way to specify temporal access control policies. This model is able to formally specify temporal constraints on time attributes associated with subjects and objects, and a reference time interval such as time of access.

Several areas related to TIAC are still being investigated. We are considering the formal semantics for creating and deleting temporal authorizations as well as the policy implications of the tranquility of temporal attributes associated with subjects and objects. In general, a *set* of mode-φ pairs can be associated with each subject-object pair in order to be able to express a different policy for each mode of access, but that extension to the TIAC model is left for future work.

We also plan to generalize this model so that it could specify an access request that uses a different reference time interval other than current time, which would allow the model to check for previous, current, and future authorizations. This research is also being extended to determine a set of useful temporal access control policies that can be expressed using the TIAC model. Finally, we are considering other enhancements to the TIAC model that involve extending the TIAC model concept to support the specification of event-based security policies.

References

1. Afinidad, F.B.: An Interval Algebra-Based Temporal Access Control Protection Architecture. Dissertation, Naval Postgraduate School, Monterey, CA (2005)
2. Afinidad, F.B., Levin, T.E., Irvine, C.E., and Nguyen, T.D.: Toward Building A Time Interval Access Control (TIAC) Model. Naval Postgraduate School, NPS Technical Report NPS-CS-05-006 (June 2005)
3. Allen, J.F.: Maintaining Knowledge About Temporal Intervals. Communications of the ACM, Vol. 26, no. 11 (November 1983) 832–843
4. Atluri, V. and Gal, A.: An Authorization Model for Temporal and Derived Data: Securing Information Portals. ACM Transactions on Information and System Security, Vol. 5, no. 1 (February 2002) 62–94
5. Bertino, E., Bettini, C. and Samarati, P.: A Discretionary Access Control Model with Temporal Authorizations. Proceedings of the 1994 Workshop on New Security Paradigms (1994) 102–107
6. Bertino, E., Bettini, C. and Samarati, P.: A Temporal Authorization Model. Proceedings of the 2nd ACM Conference on Computer and Communications Security (1994) 126–135
7. Gal, A. and Atluri, V.: An Authorization Model for Temporal Data. Proceedings of the 7th ACM Conference on Computer and Communications Security, November 1-4 (2000) 144–153
8. Graham, G.S. and Denning, P.J.: Protection – Principles and Practice. Proceedings of the Spring Joint Computer Conference, May 16–18 (1972) 417–429
9. Lampson, B.W.: Protection. Proceedings of the 5th Princeton Symposium on Information Sciences and Systems (March, 1971) pp. 437–443, reprinted in Operating Systems Review, Vol. 8, no. 1 (January 1974) 18–24
10. Weissman, C.: Security Controls in the ADEPT-50 Time-Sharing System. Proceedings of the Fall Joint Computer Conference, November 18–20 (1969) 119–133

Developing an Insider Threat Model Using Functional Decomposition

Jonathan W. Butts, Robert F. Mills, and Rusty O. Baldwin

Air Force Institute of Technology*, Dayton OH 45433, USA
`jonathan.butts@afit.edu`

Abstract. Addressing the insider threat using a systematic and formulated methodology is an inherently difficult process. This is because the problem is typically viewed in an abstract manner and a sufficient method for defining a way to categorically represent the threat has not been developed. The solution requires a security model that clearly identifies a process for classifying malicious insider activities. To be effective the model must compartmentalize the threat and attack it consistently. The purpose of this paper is to present a methodology for accurately defining the malicious insider and describe a process for addressing the threat in a systematic manner. Our model presents a definable taxonomy of the malicious insider and demonstrates a method for decomposing the abstract threat into a solvable and analyzable process.

1 Overview

The development of an insider threat model continues to be an elusive task. In August, 2000 an insider threat workshop of leading security professionals met to discuss the malicious insider and determined there is a specific need for a well-defined taxonomy and a comprehensive insider threat model [1]. To date, there has been little advancement by the security community in achieving these requirements. It is the goal of our research to address these issues by effectively defining the malicious insider and providing a model for determining the security of a system against this threat.

There has been relatively little work done in developing a model that encompasses the full spectrum of malicious insider activities. Previous work has focused on certain aspects of the problem but has not lead to a systematic method for defining the characteristics of an attack. To mitigate the malicious insider, it is necessary to have a comprehensive model that can be used to define the threat in a consistent and collaborated manner.

---

* The views expressed in this article are those of the authors and do not reflect the official policy or position of the United States Air Force, Department of Defense, or the U.S. Government.

V. Gorodetsky, I. Kotenko, and V. Skormin (Eds.): MMM-ACNS 2005, LNCS 3685, pp. 412–417, 2005.
© Springer-Verlag Berlin Heidelberg 2005

2   Related Work

When examining how to develop a model that can encompass the insider threat, one research area analyzed was attack tree methodologies [7]. Researchers have proposed that the attack tree is a sufficient tool for addressing the outside threat and assessing the security of a system against a compromise [4,5,8]. In the attack tree structure the goal of the attacker is the root node with the different ways to obtain the goals depicted as the leaf nodes.

Traditional attack trees are not capable of capturing the insider threat in an effective manner [2]. As shown by [3] they do not provide a comprehensive model for analysis of vulnerabilities. One of the more significant problems is that the insider may already have the required rights to perform their malicious actions. Additionally, the focus of the attack tree is on obtaining the goal represented by the root node. It is inherently difficult to quantify the motives or goals of the malicious insider in a truly analyzable manner because individual attributes are not measurable and may vary drastically from person to person.

In this paper, we propose a hierarchical tree approach capable of providing a complete malicious insider taxonomy by using a systems engineering approach rather than the goal oriented objectives associated with attack trees. The premise of our model is that it focuses on activities of the malicious insider and not their traits or attributes. Randazzo *et al.* demonstrates that malicious insiders do not share a common profile, so there must be a different tangible way to produce a taxonomy if measurable results are to be obtained [6]. The solution that we have chosen to implement is to methodically investigate possible actions through functional decomposition, which addresses the problems associated with modeling the insider threat using traditional attack trees. By exploring actions and not the individual or motives, no user is excluded from our model. Additionally, an action either occurs or it doesn't so the methodology is measurable and analyzable. This systematic approach produces a viable solution to the differences inherent with individuals and can effectively model their malicious behavior.

3   Methodology

To ensure the model adequately addresses the insider threat, it is necessary to clearly define the aspects that are being captured. In this context, an insider is any individual who has been granted any level of trust in an information system. This description does not limit the insider to specific borders such as Firewalls, Routers, or a Local Area Network. The system itself could be a conglomeration of networks. What is important is that once users have been granted any authorized explicit right to the information system, they are now considered an insider and are part of the system Protection State.

The Protection State is the manifestation of all trust rights for all users and objects in the information system. The Protection State encompasses all activities that are allowed according to organization policy or system access controls. Any change in privileges will transition it to a new state. The core basis of our model is capturing any unauthorized change in the Protection State. The malicious insider is any authorized user that utilizes inherent insider trusts to intentionally harm or alter the Protection State of the information system. Because the action must be intentional, this model does not view a user that accidently opens an attachment and launches a virus to be a malicious insider. Conversely, an individual who gains administrative rights and purposely deletes files is a malicious insider.

3.1 Model Implementation

The malicious insider is therefore someone who violates the Protection State of the system and is depicted as the root node of the tree representation, as shown in Fig.1. The four subordinate nodes are the specific types of *actions* a malicious insider may perform. It is possible to categorize any event into one of the four distinct *actions* through analysis of the Protection State. Because the Protection State is composed of system rights and we are focusing on the insider, we are interested in how a user can cause a change in the state. By definition of the Protection State, the possible ways this can occur can be defined as:

1. Change another user or object's rights (Alteration)
2. Leak user or object information to an unauthorized entity (Distribution)
3. Obtain protected information about another user or object (Snooping)
4. Change the rights on themselves (Elevation)

Each activity is considered unauthorized if it violates organization policy or system access controls. These *actions* capture the possible malicious events that can produce a transition in the Protection State.

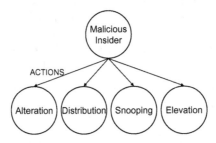

Fig. 1. The four *actions* represented in the first hierarchy of the tree

Alteration. Alteration encompasses modifying the information system structure in any unauthorized manner. The system structure is the collection of resources that comprise an information system, which includes computers, files, a user's rights or any other asset on the system that supports system functionality. The *action* of Alteration occurs when a malicious insider changes a user or object from one state to another in an unauthorized way. A case to represent this could be a user deleting a file from the system to purposely deny access or intentionally launching a virus that corrupts entities on the system.

Distribution. Distribution captures the transfer of protected information to an unauthorized entity. This occurs when a user has appropriate system rights and a need to know, such as access a file. The violation of the Protection State in Distribution occurs when a right or entity is transferred to someone or something that is not supposed to have them. The case of a user emailing a file to an unauthorized individual is an example of Distribution. This *action* can be the most difficult to detect because it typically mirrors normal activities. The malicious insider can be very evasive using this *action* because they may or may not be bound to a specific time constraint.

Snooping. Snooping addresses obtaining unauthorized information on a user or object. This *action* is similar to Distribution except the user has appropriate system rights without a need to know. This takes place when a user has permissions by the system access controls but the event should not take place because it violates organization policy. An example of this is an individual with administrative privileges who opens and reads another user's email in an attempt to gain information. Because they have accessed something their rights permit but organization policy states should be disallowed, they have violated the Protection State through Snooping.

Elevation. Elevation takes place when a user obtains unauthorized rights in the system. A classic example of this is someone trying to acquire administrative privileges. There are many different ways a malicious insider may try to accomplish this, from automated attacks to social engineering. Elevation addresses the notion of the malicious insider changing their permissions and encompasses the attempt to garner any rights that are not already allowed as defined by the Protection State.

3.2   Example

This model ensures every activity of the malicious insider can be specifically categorized in the context of the Protection State. This principle establishes the underlying framework that is necessary for identifying the malicious insider in a deterministic fashion. The distinction that each activity can be captured by one specific *action* is an important and definitive concept.

It is perhaps best to explore this notion through a practical example. If Mallory compromises an administrative password and then deletes Alice's email account, transitions to the Protection State take place. Mallory is a malicious insider because her activities were intentional and deliberate. In this scenario there are two distinct *actions* that occur to violate the Protection State and subsequently there are two transitions of the Protection State. The initial violation is through Elevation by gaining access to the administrator account. The second violation is by Alteration in destroying an email account and changing the system structure. Additionally, if Mallory then accesses a secure document another violation has occurred. Initially, when she captures the password through Elevation the Protection State has changed to allow her permission to the file. Although she now has these permissions in the context of the Protection State, Snooping has occurred because she still does not have an authorized reason (need to know) to view the file. Finally, if Mallory shares the document with Bob, Distribution has occurred because Bob has obtained rights to an object he shouldn't have. This example demonstrates the ability to compartmentalize the problem into distinct events. This concept will be built on in the next section.

3.3   Model Decomposition

Beginning with each *action*, the threats can be decomposed step by step down to the leaf nodes. This process is accomplished using a "how it can be performed" relationship between a parent and child node. The leaf node is the lowest level of abstraction and depicts the tool the malicious insider has used to accomplish the activity. A path from the malicious insider (root node) to a tool (leaf node) forms a completely decomposed activity. The model is developed in an hierarchical acyclic fashion, meaning a malicious activity can only follow one specific path from the root node to a leaf node. This indicates that each possible activity is capable of being explicitly defined.

The following is a simple example using this methodology for one Distribution *action* and is depicted in Fig.2. The Distribution *action* can be performed through file sharing, which can be accomplished through email, copying the file to storage media, online chat, or an electronic drop box. The email can be executed through a local account or web based account. In addition, copying the file to storage can be performed by floppy disk, CD-ROM or USB drive. An important concept in the configuration is the *actions* are limited to four distinct possibilities (Distribution, Snooping, Elevation, Alteration). The interim nodes, however, can use any number of children to expressively describe its parent. This notion allows for flexibility in the model to tailor it to the policies and specifics of the individual organization, while still providing an analyzable and decidable model.

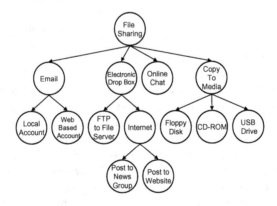

Fig. 2. An example decomposing the Distribution: file sharing

4   Summary of Model Attributes and Future Work

The fundamental concept underlying this model is expressing the malicious insider through distinct actions that are capable of being decomposed and analyzed. It presents a complete and well-defined taxonomy of the insider because the interest is in definable actions and not attempted categorization of individual attributes. Organizations can use this methodology to perform a cost/threat analysis to determine what acceptable risks exist and implement or develop countermeasures as appropriate. The model is scalable and has built-in flexibility for adapting to different organizations and information systems. These concepts present a process for effectively defining the malicious insider and providing the security community an effective tool for addressing the insider threat in a coordinated effort.

Further research for this methodology involves developing a fully decomposed baseline tree that addresses the majority of possible insider actions. This process should then lead to the automation of model development for the security professional and allow organizations to tailor the baseline tree for their specific system structure and policies.

References

1. Anderson, R., Bozek, T., Longstaff, T., Meitzler, W., Skroch, M., Van Wyk, K.: Research on Mitigating the Insider Threat to Information Systems. Proceedings of the Insider Workshop. CF-163-DARPA. Arlington, VA (2000)
2. Chinchani, R., Iyer, A., Ngo, H., Upadhyaya, S.: Towards a Theory of Insider Threat Assessment. Proceedings of the 2005 International Conference on Dependable Systems and Networks (DSN 2005), June 28–July 01, Yokohama, Japan (2005)
3. Daley, K., Larson, R., Dawkins, J.: A Structural Framework for Modeling Multi-Stage Network Attacks. Proceedings of the IEEE International Conference on Parallel Processing Workshops (2002) 5–10
4. Jha, S., Sheyner, O., Wing, J.: Two Formal Analyses of Attack Graphs. Proceedings of the 15th IEEE Computer Security Foundations Workshop (2002) 49
5. Phillips, C., Swiler, L.: A Graph-Based system for network vulnerability analysis.: ACM New Security Paradigms Workshop (1998) 71–79
6. Randazzo, M., Keeney, M., Kowalski, E., Cappelli, D., Moore, A.: Insider Threat Study: Illicit Cyber Activity in the Banking and Finance Sector. U.S. Secret Service and CERT Coordination Center/SEI (2004)
7. Schneier, B.: Secrets and Lies. Wiley Publishing (2000) 318–333
8. Sheyner, O., Haines, J., Jha, S., Lippman, R., Wing, J.: Automated Generation and Analysis of Attack Graphs. Proceedings of the IEEE Symposium on Security and Privacy (2002) 254–265

An XML-Seamless Policy Based Management Framework

Félix J. García Clemente, Gregorio Martínez Pérez,
and Antonio F. Gómez Skarmeta

Departamento de Ingeniería de la Información y las Comunicaciones
University of Murcia, Spain
{fgarcia, gregorio, skarmeta}@dif.um.es

Abstract. The great variety of policy representation forms currently existing (e.g., LDAP schemas, PIBs, MIBs, plain text, etc.) is leading to interoperability and manageability problems, mainly in inter-domain management environments, but also between the elements (i.e., PMTs, PDPs, and PEPs) dealing with and exchanging policies inside one particular management domain. The use of XML technologies provides a solution to this important limitation. This paper describes the seamless integration of XML technologies in a policy-based management framework. It includes a proposal for an XML-based management architecture, the definition of an XML PIB (Policy Information Base) and a new Java COPS (Common Open Policy Service) implementation supporting both XML-encoding and BER-encoding of the policy data exchanged between PDP servers and PEP clients. It also analyses the main techniques used to ensure the provision of security services to the management of policies.

1 Introduction and Motivation

Policies that are exchanged between the components of a PBNM (Policy-Based Network Management) system may assume different forms as they travel from a definition server to a repository or from a decision point to an enforcement point. At each step, policies are usually represented in a way that is convenient for the current task. It could be the case of policies defined as a text file by the administrator, stored in a directory according to a LDAP schema, distributed from a Policy Decision Point (PDP) to a Policy Enforcement Point (PEP) using a PIB (Policy Information Base) [1].

As this variety of forms could lead to important problems when trying to define interoperable and extensible multi-domain PBNM architectures, there is a clear need to consolidate a common technology to define policy languages and establish a common method for encoding policy data. XML technologies are a solution to this problem.

XML has also the advantage that it is widely accepted, which means that there are many tools available supporting the implementation of some of the management functionalities. In addition, XML facilitates the easy integration of different applications, something that is particularly important for the cooperation of different policy-based network and service management architectures in a multi-domain environment.

This paper describes in section 2 the design of an XML-seamless PBNM framework using XML technologies along the whole policy life cycle. XML technologies are used by all the components of the architecture to manage and monitor policies.

V. Gorodetsky, I. Kotenko, and V. Skormin (Eds.): MMM-ACNS 2005, LNCS 3685, pp. 418–423, 2005.

Moreover, the XML-seamless PBNM framework facilitates the integration of existing network nodes supporting the IETF protocols COPS (Common Open Policy Service) [2] and COPS-PR (COPS Usage for Policy Provisioning) [3]. We also present in section 3 one implementation of COPS and COPS-PR protocols in Java (named UMU-jCOPS) allowing the exchange of policy data using either XML- or BER-encoding (i.e., binary codification of the information). A preliminary implementation of this framework using UMU-jCOPS has been used in [4] and [5] to allow the dynamic provision of virtual private networks (VPNs) in different scenarios.

2 XML-Seamless Policy Based Management Framework

The PBNM framework presented here is based on the definition work undertaken by the IETF/DMTF, although in our case both the elements of the architecture and the policies themselves are based on the use of XML and its related technologies.

2.1 XML-Seamless Architecture

A general overview of the proposed elements of the architecture is provided in next sections. In them we will state the modules that need to be added for integrating XML technologies in a policy-based management architecture, paying special attention to the security measures applied in the design and implementation phases.

Policy Management Tool (PMT)
The PMT provides the administrator the mechanisms to create, modify or delete securely policy documents. It is done by means of a high-level language and a graphical interface. It is composed of two main XML-related components: a policy GUI, which is an editor that can generate or edit XML-based policy documents and an XML policy validator that validates every policy specification before it is stored in the XML policy database. This validation process is done using an XML Schema (XSD), which defines the high-level syntax of every network service or application being managed. This validation process also includes the verification of the digital signature of the administrator defining or modifying every policy.

XML Policy Database
The XML policy database is used as policy repository for storing high-level policies that are digitally signed. For it we propose the use of an XML native database. The benefit of a native solution is that we do not have to worry about mapping XML policies to some other data structures (as SQL for example). XML native database uses XPath notation for its query language and XUpdate for its update language.

Policy Decision Point (PDP)
The PDP is the PBNM component that applies the policy documents to the network nodes. It retrieves securely the high-level policies from the XML policy database and uses them to generate the low-level policy decisions to be sent to network nodes. The policy decisions are the response to the policy request sent by PEP clients or are a result of a PDP event (e.g., a change in a policy done by the administrator, a time condition verified, etc).

The PDP evaluates the policy request or the event and determines the policy decisions to be sent to the PEP clients. This is done securely using a TLS-based transport.

The PDP integrates different XML-based client-type specific modules according to the different kind of policies supported (e.g., IPsec, QoS, routing, etc). Each of these PDP modules has an XML schema defining its high-level policy representation.

Policy Enforcement Point (PEP)
PEP clients enforce the policy decisions taken by the PDP to the policy-managed network nodes. When a new PEP is active in the network or some events at the PEP occur, the PEP needs to get or update its internal configuration. In this moment the PEP will send a policy request to the default PDP server that it has configured.

PEP clients also integrate different XML-based client-type specific modules according to the type of policies supported. Additionally, PEPs can need to transform low-level representation to internal configuration that is specific to the vendor, operating system, and software release, and vice versa. PEP uses a Policy Configuration Transformer module to make it; it is based on XSLT (XSL Transformations).

2.2 XML-Seamless Policy Representation

The policy representation is defined at two levels. The first one represents high-level policies generated by the administrator in a Policy Management Tool (PMT) and stored in the XML Policy Database. The second level of representation defines low-level policies to be exchanged between the Policy Decision Points (PDPs) and the Policy Enforcement Points (PEPs) existing in the management architecture. Both policy representations have the following features in common:

- Based on the IETF Policy Core Information Model (PCIM) [6]
- Defined from an XML Schema
- Encoded in XML

For the low-level policy, we have defined an XML scheme from the PIB (Policy Information Base) definition that permits the XML-encoding of such structure (XML PIB). IETF uses ASN.1 format for the definition of PIB modules. Therefore, we use XER [7] to derive an XML scheme from the PIB definition in ASN.1, which is a mechanism for converting between ASN.1 encoded data structures and XML encoded data structures. When XER is applied to the ASN.1 expressions, data structures are encoded as character strings in the form of tag, value, and end-tag, whereas BER encodes data structures as octets in the form of tag, length, and value. Figure 1 shows how XER-encoded PIBs fit in the proposed management architecture.

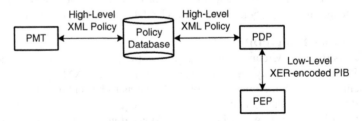

Fig. 1. XML-seamless policy representation

3 COPS and COPS-PR Protocols Supporting XML-Encoded Data

The proposed representation of low-level policy needs that the COPS and COPS-PR protocols support XML-encoded data. These protocols are independent of the type of policy carried, but they assume a data model based on the concept of PIB.

3.1 XML Encoded Data in the COPS and COPS-PR Messages

The COPS object descriptions use BER as the encoding type. But this encoding type is not unique, as additional encodings can be used. This is the case of XML.

COPS encapsulates data in request messages, decision messages and report messages. Request messages include the Named ClientSI (Named Client Specific Information) object for relaying specific information about the PEP. Decision messages made by the PDP send the Named Decision Data object in response to configuration requests. And report messages encapsulate Named ClientSI for reporting information from the PEP to PDP. The Named ClientSI and Named Decision Data objects are composed of one or more bindings. Each binding associates a PRID (Provisioning Instance Identifier) object and an EPD (Encoded Provisioning Instance Data) object. The PPRID (Prefix PRID) is used in the Remove Decisions and can also compose a Named Decision Data.

Furthermore, the PRID, PPRID and EPD objects encapsulate S-Num and S-Type identifier. The S-Num identifies the general purpose of the object, and the S-Type describes the specific encoding used for the object. The IETF documents usually use the BER as the encoding type (S-Type = 1).

In this context, we have defined an additional encoding to carry XML string-based XPath and XER as encoding type; the new value that we have assigned is S-Type = 2. We have also take the convention that the PRID and PPRID objects make use of XPath, and the EPD objects make use of XER encoding.

Provisioning Instance Identifier (PRID)
This object carries the identifier of a Provisioning Class (PRC) Instance. This identifier is encoded following the BER rules as a SNMP Object Identifier (OID). PRID is the OID of the Provisioning Class plus the Instance Identifier (InstanceId).

We propose to use XPath for XML encoding. This path has two parts: the first one identifies the PRC and the second one identifies the particular instance of this PRC.

Prefix PRID (PPRID)
PPRIDs are only used in the Remove Decisions command to identify a group of instances with the same PRID prefix and to avoid a sequence of individual Remove Decisions. PPRID is encoded following the BER rules as a SNMP Object Identifier (OID) like the PRID object commented before.

We also propose to use XPath for encoding PPRID in XML. For example, a PRID equal to the following path: *//iso/org/dod/internet/pib/frameworkPib/frwkBasePibClasses/frwkPibIncarnationTable/FrwkPibIncarnationEntry/** identifies all instances of the PRC called PIB Incarnation Table of the PIB Framework.

Encoded Provisioning Data (EPD)

This object carries the encoded value of a Provisioning Instance. This identifier is encoded following the BER rules as a set of TLVs (Tag-Length-Value) with the individual values of the attributes that comprise the Provisioning Class. We also propose to use XER for encoding in XML this kind of elements of the PIB.

3.2 Java Implementation: UMU-jCOPS

The University of Murcia Java COPS (UMU-jCOPS) protocol stack is a COPS-PR implementation that is one of the main components of the University of Murcia Policy-Based Network Management (UMU-PBNM) framework [5] used to perform dynamic provision and monitoring of configurations. The XML policy data model that we are presenting in this paper is supported by this COPS implementation. Its main features are:

- It is completely developed in Java, allowing the use of any operating system to run an implementation of PDP or PEP.
- It is IPv6 enabled, so any operation can be performed using this network protocol.
- It allows both BER and XML data encoding.
- It verifies PIB conformance with XML technologies.

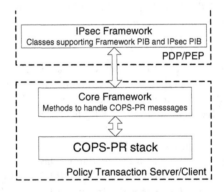

Fig. 2. Architecture of UMU-jCOPS

The basic architecture and set of layers of UMU-jCOPS are depicted in Figure 2. The UMU-jCOPS design presents two different layers: COPS-PR stack and core framework. On the one hand, the COPS-PR stack is the base COPS layer; it defines all COPS messages and provides the mechanism to exchange COPS messages between a PEP and PDP. This exchange can be done securely over a TLS channel. On the other hand, core framework was designed to be independent of the COPS client type and provides the COPS operations that need a PEP or PDP to be implemented.

4 Conclusions

There is a need to consolidate a common technology to define policies and establish a common encoding for policy data. In this paper we have presented an XML-seamless policy based management framework that uses XML technologies to define and encode policies during their whole life cycle (from the definition to the enforcement). The resulting XML-seamless policy based management framework shows an improvement in manageability, interoperability and extensibility over the PBNM architecture proposed by the IETF. Also security has been a priority during its design and later implementation.

Acknowledgments

This work has been partially funded by the EU POSITIF (Policy-based Security Tools and Framework) IST project (IST-2002-002314).

References

1. Sahita, R., et al.: Framework Policy Information Base. IETF, Request For Comments (RFC) 3318 (March 2003)
2. Durham, D., et al.: The COPS (Common Open Policy Service) Protocol. IETF, Request For Comments (RFC) 2748 (January 2000)
3. Chan, K., et al.: COPS Usage for Policy Provisioning (COPS-PR). IETF, Request For Comments (RFC) 3084 (March 2001)
4. Pérez, G. M., Skarmeta, A.F. G.: Policy-Based Dynamic Provision of IP Services in a Secure VPN Coalition Scenario, IEEE Communications Magazine, Vol. 47, No. 11 (2004) 118–124
5. UMU-PBNM (University of Murcia Policy-Based Network Management), University of Murcia, http://pbnm.dif.um.es/
6. Moore, B., et al.: Policy Core Information Model – Version 1 Specification. IETF, Request For Comments (RFC) 3060 (February 2001)
7. Information processing systems – Open Systems Interconnection, "XML Encoding Rules for Abstract Syntax Notation One (ASN.1)", International Organization for Standardization, International Standard 8825-4 (1988)

Statistical Covert Channels Through PROXY Server

Alexei Galatenko[1], Alexander Grusho[2], Alexander Kniazev[3],
and Elena Timonina[2]

[1] Moscow State University, GSP-2, Leninskie Gory,
Moscow, 119992, Russian Federation
agalat@msu.ru
[2] Russian State University for Humanity, 25 Kirovogradskaya,
Moscow, Russian Federation
aaotee@mail.infotel.ru
eltimon@yandex.ru
[3] Russian Academy of Sciences Lebedev Institute of Precise Mechanics and
Computer Technology, 51 Leninsky Prospekt, Moscow, Russian Federation
avk@ipmce.ru

Abstract. The paper[1] is devoted to creating a covert channel through
a PROXY server. The channel is based upon data permutation in server
buffer using the sequence of packets coming from the router connected to
the PROXY server. The resulting data flow allows to create a statistical
covert channel that transfers information by manipulating expectation
and dispersion of the number of increasing pairs in the sequence of network addresses.

1 Introduction

In [1,2] the problem of building an attack targeted at a secure global network
segment via a covert channel was investigated. The main tool for providing
security was IPSec protocol.

In this paper we consider security provided by a PROXY-server, which is
invulnerable to attacks and provides reliable data encryption. Like in [1,2], we
create a covert channel via modulating the address sequence in packets transmitted by the PROXY-server.

The rest of the paper is organized as follows. Section 2 describes the main
idea of covert channel creation. Section 3 shows how symbols 1, 0 and x can be
extracted from transmitted data with the help of statistical methods. Conclusions are provided in section 4.

2 Covert Channel Trough PROXY Server

Let us consider $m + 1$ local networks segments $S_0, S_1, ..., S_m$ containing workstations with local addresses and gateways connecting local networks with a

---

[1] This work was supported by the Russian Foundation for Basic Research, grant 04-
01-00089.

V. Gorodetsky, I. Kotenko, and V. Skormin (Eds.): MMM-ACNS 2005, LNCS 3685, pp. 424–429, 2005.

global network (e.g. Internet). Let $s_0, s_1, ..., s_m$ be gateway addresses for segments $S_0, S_1, ..., S_m$. Let workstations interconnect via a virtual private network (VPN). If some data from a workstation with address a in segment S_i needs to be transferred to a workstation with address b in segment S_j, the transmission is performed in the following way (fig. 1):

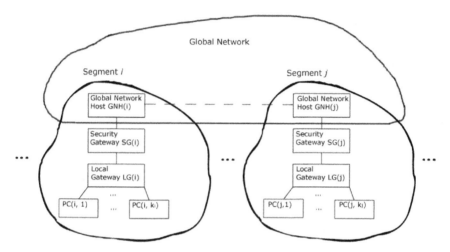

Fig. 1. System model

- the data from workstation a is first transferred to a Local Gateway LG(i) in S_i;
- then data is passed to a Security Gateway SG(i). Security Gateway operates as a PROXY server – it connects to workstation a, gathers data for workstation b, and collects data packets from S_i segment in a queue according to their arrival time. Then data is encrypted with a key of SG(j) – the Security Gateway of data recipient segment. Then SG(i) connects to SG(j) and transfers encrypted data:
  - SG(i) passes data to a Global Network Host GNH (i), which in turn passes data to a corresponding host GNH(j) via a global network;
  - data is then passed to SG(j). SG(j) collects packets for S_j segment and stores them in a queue.
- Packets in a queue are decrypted, SG(j) connects to a workstation b and transmits data via the internal gateway LG(j);
- LG(j) sends data to workstation b in S_j segment.

Every segment $S_0, S_1, ..., S_m$ contains software and/or hardware adversary agents. To work properly these agents need to receive some instructions from an adversary agent in a global network (AGN). Let us consider that AGN is in total control of GNH(j), $j = 0, 1, ..., m$, and adversary agents in $S_0, S_1, ..., S_m$

are in control of the corresponding internal gateways GNH(j), $j = 0, 1, ..., m$. Security Gateways SG(i) are considered to be totally secure, so they are out of adversary agent control. Sending instruction from AGN to local agents can be based on a channel from GNH(j) to LG(j), and information leak can be based on a channel from LG(j) to GNH(j).

We suppose that the only dependent packet parameters known both to GNH(j) and LG(j) are source addresses in case of incoming packets and destination addresses in case of outgoing packets. These dependencies can be expressed by a function $s = f(a)$ that maps internal addresses within a network segment to a global network address of the corresponding gateway.

LG(i) can affect the order in which the packets are transmitted in the following way. TCP protocol guarantees data recovery. If a packet is lost, TCP sends a request to retransmit lost data. Let PROXY server have two open connections with workstations a_1 and a_2 passing data A_1 and A_2 correspondingly. It is obvious that packets that were recovered earlier are put in SG(i) queue prior to packets that were recovered later. Let an adversary agent in LG(i) want to make SG(i) queue equal to A_1A_2. This goal can be achieved by the following procedure. If packets containing A_1 end earlier than packets containing A_2 (an adversary agent can delay packet transmissions to be sure that data transmission is over), the agent does not do anything. Otherwise the agent in LG(i) delays or drops one of the packets transmitted by a_2 (e.g. the final one). Then the agent waits till A_1 transmission is over and resends the delayed or dropped packet. So if the assumption that the packet sequence from a_1 to a single workstation in some other segment contained data of a single connection A_1, and the packet sequence from a_2 to a single workstation in some other segment contained data of a single connection A_2 is true, the above algorithm will change data ordering in SG(i) queue from the natural to the given order. A similar procedure is applicable to the incoming data flow and GNH(j) agents. Let us note that this procedure is stochastic because of randomness in packet arrival time — if SG(i) sent A_1 before A_2, A_2 can still arive earlier, especially if A_1 and A_2 are small.

It is obvious that the probability of a correct permutation is greater for long packet sequences transmitting large data segments.

Despite of possible errors we can construct a hidden language based on data permutation in queue. Let an agent in LG(0) pass data to an agent GNH(0) in a global network. The agent in LG(0) knows what data is being passed to the addresses s_j, $j = 0, 1, ..., m$ of SG(j). Let s_j be linearly ordered. Let $A_1A_2...A_k$ be the data queue of length k at LG(0), $s_{i_1}, s_{i_2}, ..., s_{i_k}$ be destination addresses. The output queue $B_1B_2...B_{2r}$ at SG(1) is produced in the following way:

- B_1B_2 is equal to A_1A_2, if $s_{i_1} < s_{i_2}$;
- B_1B_2 is equal to A_2A_1, if $s_{i_1} > s_{i_2}$;
- B_1 is equal to (or begins with) A_1A_2, if $s_{i_1} = s_{i_2}$ (A_1A_2 will be probably transmitted in a single connection). In this case if $s_{i_3} > s_{i_1}$, then $B_2 = A_3$. If $s_{i_3} = s_{i_1}$, then B_1 is equal to (or begins with) $A_1A_2A_3$ and $A_1A_2A_3$ will be probably transmitted in a single connection, etc.

The resulting sequence $B_1 B_2 ... B_{2r}$ consists of data such that every pair $B_{2i-1} B_{2i}, i = 1, ..., r$, contains increasing addresses. Let us consider $B_1 B_2 ... B_{2r}$ to encode 1 in the covert channel. The data in this sequence is split into packets. Packet sequences are transmitted to the corresponding addresses. These sequences can contain additional packets, e.g. for establishing other connections, so GNH(0) agent should not consider the additional packets, though some errors are possible. The received sequence is 1 of the covert channel. 0 is encoded by a sequence of decreasing address pairs of data. A sequence of unordered address pairs encodes a delimiter x. We use an assumption that the PROXY server establishes connections with other PROXY servers according to the addresses in data queue buffer, and packet block with the same destination address is transmitted in a single connection.

There emerge the problems of estimation of the value of r for reliable extraction of 1, 0 and x, and of investigation of transmitter fault tolerance. Due to the fact that data permutations in a queue are stochastic, and there exists a possibility of errors in address sequence in GNH(0), there exist the following errors in covert channels:

- data loss (loosing an address s in address sequence restored in GNH(0));
- data insertion.

3   Mathematical Model

Let $\bar{s} = (s(1), s(2), ..., s(2r))$ be the data address sequence determining one bit. To restore this bit taking into consideration possible errors we count all increasing and decreasing address pairs. The decision about the value of the bit is made by the means of mathematical statistics. In this paper we consider the problem of correct bit recognition by the sequence of data addresses. Bit recognition based upon packet sequence is not considered.

Let input data addresses be random values $\xi_1, ..., \xi_k$ that are produced independently with equal probabilities $P(\xi_j = s_i) = \frac{1}{m}$. Due to the fact that packets with the same source address are transmitted in a single connection, we delete all sequences with the same source address and replace them by a single representative. After this transformation we get a sequence $\eta_1, ..., \eta_{2r}$. This sequence is a simple Markov chain with the transition matrix

$$\| P(\eta_{i+1} = s / \eta_i = s') \|,$$

where

$$P(\eta_{i+1} = s / \eta_i = s') \text{ is equal to } \frac{1}{m - 1}, \text{ if } s \neq s', \text{ and } 0, \text{ if } s = s'.$$

The initial distribution is uniform, and transition matrix is twice stochastic, hence the Markov chain is stationary, with one acyclic ergodic class without insignificant states.

To transmit 1 the sequence $\eta_1, ..., \eta_{2r}$ is split into a sequence of pairs $(\eta_1, \eta_2), ..., (\eta_{2r-1}, \eta_{2r})$ and every pair is rearranged in ascending order. The number ν_r of increasing pairs for sequential count with possible overlaps in the output sequence $\varsigma_1, ..., \varsigma_{2r}$ is equal to

$$\nu_r = r + \sum_{i=1}^{r-1} I(\varsigma_{2i} \leq \varsigma_{2i+1}).$$

Let us consider stochastic values

$\mu(t)$ is equal to $I(\varsigma_{2i} \leq \varsigma_{2i+1})$, if $t = 2i + 1$, and 0, if $t \neq 2i + 1$.

It is obvious that for any t $E\mu^2(t) < \infty$ and $D\sum_{t=1}^{T} \mu(t) \longrightarrow \infty$ if $T \longrightarrow \infty$. So [3] the distribution of

$$\frac{\sum_{t=1}^{T} \mu(t) - \sum_{t=1}^{T} E\mu(t)}{\sqrt{D\sum_{t=1}^{T} \mu(t)}}$$

converges to Gaussian distribution with parameters 0 and 1 when $T \longrightarrow \infty$.

The situation with transmitting 0 is similar. A sequence $\eta_1, ..., \eta_{2r}$ is split into a sequence of pairs $(\eta_1, \eta_2), ..., (\eta_{2r-1}, \eta_{2r})$, and every pair is rearranged in descending order. The number ω_r of decreasing pairs for sequential count with possible overlaps in the output sequence $\varsigma'_1, ..., \varsigma'_{2r}$ is equal to

$$\omega_r = r + \sum_{i=1}^{r-1} I(\varsigma'_{2i} \geq \varsigma'_{2i+1}).$$

Like in the previous case, the random number $\omega_r - r$ after being centered and normed converges to Gaussian distribution with parameters 0 and 1.

If we consider ν_r calculated on the base of the original sequence $\eta_1, ..., \eta_{2r}$, after being centered and normed it will also converge to Gaussian distribution with parameters 0 and 1.

Let us find expectations of ν_r and ω_r when we transmit 1, 0 and x.

Let the transmitted value be 1. To evaluate the estimation ν_r let us consider stochastic values $\eta_{2i-1}, \eta_{2i}, \eta_{2i+1}, \eta_{2i+2}$. In our Markov chain

$$P(\eta_{2i-1} = s, \eta_{2i} = k, \eta_{2i+1} = l, \eta_{2i+2} = n) = \frac{1}{m(m-1)^3}.$$

So

$$E\mu(2i+1) = P(\max(\eta_{2i-1}, \eta_{2i}) \leq \min(\eta_{2i+1}, \eta_{2i+2})) =$$

$$= \frac{m^4 - m^3 - 9m^2 - 18m - 6}{6m(m-1)^3} = \frac{1}{6}(1 + O(\frac{1}{m})),$$

when the value of m is large. Then $E\nu_r = \frac{7}{6}r + O(\frac{r}{m})$.

Similarly for 0 we have $E\omega_r = \frac{7}{6}r + O(\frac{r}{m})$, and for x $E\nu_r = r + O(\frac{r}{m})$.

Due to the fact that ν_r and ω_r are asymptotically Gaussian, deviations of the above expectations are not greater than $\sqrt{r} \ln r$ with probability converging to 1. Hence we can recognize 1, 0 and x when r and m are large.

4   Conclusions

The paper considers the problem of building a covert channel through a PROXY server. The channel is based upon the permutation of data in PROXY server buffer using packet sequences coming through a router connected to the PROXY server. Such a permutation allows to create a statistical covert channel the data in which is being transmitted by manipulating expectation and dispersion of the number of increasing pairs in the sequence of data addresses. The paper does not consider the problem of data encoding by the sequence of packets (this problem will be addressed in one of the following papers).

References

1. Grusho, A., Timonina, E.: Construction of the Covert Channels. International Work-shop "Information Assurance in Computer Networks. Methods, Models, and Archi-tectures for Network Security". Springer, LNCS 2776 (2003) 428–431
2. Grusho, A.A., Timonina, E.E.: Estimation of the time needed to set up a covert channel. Discrete Mathematics and applications, **13**, 3 (2003) 257–263
3. Prokhorov, U.V., Rozanov, U.A.: Theory of probabilities. Moscow (1973)

Encoding Private Key in Fingerprint

Ernő Jeges[1], Zoltán Hornák[1], and Csaba Körmöczi[2]

[1] BME Department of Measurement and Information Systems, SEARCH Lab
[2] Guardware Systems Ltd
{jeges, hornak}@mit.bme.hu, kormoczi@guardware.com

Abstract. Electronic transactions require secure electronic signature techniques, which can provide the authentication of the signing individual, non-repudiation of the signature and protection of the integrity of the document using strong cryptographic methods. The weakest link in the chain in current electronic signature systems is the correspondence between the person and the secret key. The basic idea of our proposed method is to store the secret key encoded in a fingerprint in a way that it can only be retrieved using the fingerprint of its owner. This way it is much harder to steal the private key, since the creation of the signature requires the presence of the owner's fingerprint instead of the use of a PIN code in today's practice. Our scheme remains fully compatible with the existing Public Key Infrastructures (PKI), so it can be easily used in current applications that use asymmetric cryptography to verify digital signatures.

1 Introduction

The traditional hand-written signature is a simple but adequately effective method of proving the authenticity of a document in situations open to dispute, as it is reasonably hard to perfectly copy someone's handwriting.

Analogous to traditional signatures, digital signatures were introduced to ensure the authenticity of electronic documents. The digital signatures used today are based on a key pair, on a public and a private (secret) key. It is assumed that the secret key remains hidden from others, so that only the authenticated person can *possess* it. This assumption and the potential expropriation of the private key is the weakest link in such systems, so realizing this, several works have been published recently that suggest schemes to solve the convergence of the biometrics and cryptography [1][2].

In this paper we introduce a biometric method which fully relies on the public key infrastructure, but the biometric identification is embedded so deeply in the process of digital signing that the private key cannot be appropriated by stealing and cracking the chip-card, which is used to store the secret key in current practice.

2 Applying Biometrics in the Process of Digital Signing

The most frequently used identification method in automated identification systems is the *minutia-based method*. Minutia points are the endings, splits and various bifurcations of the ridges on fingerprints. As their positions, types, angles and curvatures are

V. Gorodetsky, I. Kotenko, and V. Skormin (Eds.): MMM-ACNS 2005, LNCS 3685, pp. 430–435, 2005.
© Springer-Verlag Berlin Heidelberg 2005

characteristic and unique to a particular finger, minutia-based identification systems decide the correspondence of two fingerprint samples by simply matching the positions of the minutia points.

There are several ways to involve biometric (e.g. fingerprint data) in document security. One can place biometric data in the document, and then digitally sign it to ensure its integrity [3]. It is also possible to incorporate biometric data in a PKI certificate [4], but the majority of systems involve biometrics only for controlling access to the private keys stored in the chip-card [5].

In our solution we also use an RSA private key to digitally sign documents, but in the proposed method biometrics is not only involved in controlling access to the stored private key, but the private key is *encoded in the biometric features* of the user's fingerprint. As an addition we can still store a part of the encoded information on a permanent storage medium (e.g. a chip-card), but – what is important – the secret key cannot be reconstructed in lack of any of these parts. Later on, if the private key is needed to sign a document, we can retrieve it by decoding the stored information, which is only possible via the fingerprint of the holder of the key.

In the next section we introduce the method we used to encode binary data using the minutia-point features of the user's fingerprint.

3 Storing Private Keys in Fingerprints

To digitally sign a document we need a key pair, the generation of which is based on cryptographically strong *random binary data*. Usually randomness is taken from random events like keystrokes and mouse movements, but if we are able to store this random data, we can regenerate the same key pair later. Theoretically, we can derive this sequence of bits from the fingerprint image itself, but as we need precisely the same sequence to be restored bit-by-bit every time, this method appears to be barely feasible. Also, we need the key pair to be revocable.

In light of this, the basic idea of our method is to generate a *binary codeword* by adding error correction parity bits to the random binary data, and to store it in the *challenge minutia vector* by means of data hiding. As for the data hiding scheme: on the one hand we construct the challenge minutia vector both from real minutia points from the registration sample and from generated fake minutia points, and on the other hand we change the minutia angles, depending on the codeword bits' values. Finally, the key pair is generated by feeding the binary codeword into the random pool used for key generation. Instead of biometric features or the private key itself, we only store the challenge minutia vector on a persistent store, for example a chip-card.

On the need for a private key, we can restore the binary codeword by matching the challenge minutia vector with the minutia points extracted from a sample fingerprint: we can determine whether a point is real or fake, and we can calculate the distortion of the original angle, thus recalculating the bits of the codeword. After error correction, we regenerate the key pair by again feeding the key generation random pool with the same random data, the binary codeword.

The method involves two main processes: registration and signing. During registration starting from a real random seed we generate a public/private RSA key pair, and create a certificate using the public key and the personal data of the user. We destroy the private key, but encode the random seed in the given fingerprint by generating a so called challenge minutia vector. In the process of document signing, we reconstruct the random seed using the challenge minutia vector and the actual fingerprint image, and re-executing the RSA key generation algorithm with the same random input we retrieve the private (and also the public) key.

The process of registration involves these steps: (1) Generating the *random binary data*; (2) Calculating a *binary codeword* by adding parity bits to random binary data4 (3) *Encoding*: generating the *challenge minutia vector* based on the binary codeword and the minutia points in the registered fingerprint sample; (4) Generating the *RSA key pair* and deleting the private key, the binary codeword and the random binary data afterwards; (5) Requesting a *certificate* that holds the registered person's personal data and the public key using a public key infrastructure.

To digitally sign a document, we have to accomplish these steps: (1) *Decoding:* matching of the fingerprint sample with the challenge minutia vector to reconstruct the original binary codeword; (2) *Error correction* of the binary codeword; (3) Retrieval of the original *RSA key pair* using the corrected codeword; (4) *Verification* of the regenerated public key, checking whether it is the same as the public key encapsulated in the certificate. Reporting an error if the public keys do not match, since it indicates incorrect decoding; (5) *Signature* of the document using the retrieved private key.

In the followings we introduce main problems and the given solutions during our research and the development of the frame system for the described method.

4   Encoding, Decoding and Error Correction

The process of encoding is basically the generation of the challenge minutia vector. In this process we generate the successive points of the challenge vector by processing the bits of the binary codeword five at a time.

Table 1. The five-bit runs in the encoding of a minutia point. We add a real or a fake minutia point to challenge vector depending on the 0th bit of a five-bit run, and the angle of a thus added minutia point is modified depending on the value of the next four bits (1...4) in the codeword.

0	1	2	3	4
Real / fake	Modification of the angle			

We assume the fake minutia angle to follow the curvature of the underlying ridges. This encoding method and the value with which the angle is modified (the added angle *dFi* modulo 180) is shown in figure 1.

For error correction, we decided to use the Turbo codes [6] , which are widely used in deep-space communication, where there are low signal-to-noise ratios, similar to those we met using the fingerprint as communication channel. The basic idea of Turbo coding is to use two (or even more) convolutional encoders, where each except the first one receives the permutated systematic bits. Turbo coding is easily scalable, as we don't have to transmit all of the bits; we can delete some of them following a deletion pattern, and the receiver can denote erasure errors following the same pattern before the encoding occurs. This way we can gain an arbitrary code rate.

Real ... Fake (figure)	Bits 1-4	dFi	Bits 1-4	dFi
	0000	0,00	1100	90,00
	0001	11,25	1101	101,25
	0011	22,50	1111	112,50
	0010	33,75	1110	123,75
	0110	45,00	1010	135,00
	0111	56,25	1011	146,25
	0101	67,50	1001	157,50
	0100	78,75	1000	168,75

Fig. 1. The encoding method and the encoding of the values added to angles. This is a Gray-coding of the angle modification values from 0° to 180° in steps of 11.25°, a feature of this coding being that the Hamming distance of the codes for two neighboring values is 1.

Decoding is done similarly to decoding of the convolutional codes [7]. We estimate the value of the sent bits depending on the received channel codes.

To make the previously introduced minutia point coding and decoding error-tolerant, we introduced the *Non-symmetric Binary Erasure Channel* (NBEC). This channel handles both simple and erasure errors, and is not symmetric, which means that it has different probabilities for different error types and bit values. Thus, the NBEC channel can be described by four parameters: p_{01} and p_{10} denote the probability that a simple error occurs, while p_{0x} and p_{1x} denote the probability that erasure occurs (e.g. the angle value is ambiguous) if the original bit is 0 or 1 respectively.

As we encode minutia points to five bits, and these bits are derived in different ways, we can define different error parameters for each bit position (0-4). Thus we modeled the fingerprint as an $NBEC_5$ communication channel, which is actually a set of five independent NBEC channels.

Applying an arbitrary channel model to Turbo coding can be done by isolating and modifying the function that returns the transfer probabilities of the channel, as described in [8]. The NBEC channel model and the measured transfer probabilities for different bits of the $NBEC_5$ channel using the above described minutia point coding are shown in figure 2.

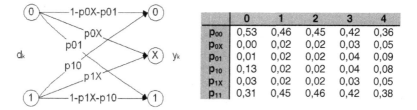

	0	1	2	3	4
p_{00}	0,53	0,46	0,45	0,42	0,36
p_{0x}	0,00	0,02	0,02	0,03	0,05
p_{01}	0,01	0,02	0,02	0,04	0,09
p_{10}	0,13	0,02	0,02	0,04	0,08
p_{1x}	0,03	0,02	0,02	0,03	0,05
p_{11}	0,31	0,45	0,46	0,42	0,38

Fig. 2. The Non-symmetric Binary Erasure Channel (NBEC) and the statistically determined transfer probabilities of $NBEC_5$

After several trials we selected to add 240 parity bits to 120 systematic bits, which meet the requirement for cryptographical strength, of having at least 100 random bits. As the distribution of minutiae in our database showed the average minutia point number to be 40, this choice satisfied the need for real minutia points from the registered samples for the coding of the 0th bit, as 120+240 bits encoded 360/5=72 minutia points, statistically having half of them, on average 36 chosen from real minutiae.

5 Finding the Best Fitting Transformation

When matching two fingerprints, the minutia vectors of one must be overlaid on the other to be able to check whether they fit. To find the best transformation, we introduced a goal function that would measure the quality of the fitting of points in the two minutia point sets. The domain of this function was the 3-dimensional space defined by the translation on the X and the Y axis, and the rotation angle α.

This goal function $f(\Delta x, \Delta y, \Delta \varphi)$ could be defined as following:

$$f(\Delta x, \Delta y, \Delta \varphi) = \sum_{i=0}^{M} \sum_{j=0}^{N} f_{ij}(d([x_i', y_i', \alpha_i'] [x_j, y_j, \alpha_j])) \tag{1}$$

where M is the number of challenge minutia points, N is the number of minutia points in the fingerprint sample and f_{ij} is the function that transforms the distance (d) of two minutia points (denoted by x, y and α). After testing several f_{ij} functions, we chose one that statistically showed the highest correlation between the maximum value of f and the restoration of the binary codeword:

$$f_{ij}(d) = \frac{100 - d^2}{100}, \text{ if } 0 < d < 10, \quad \text{otherwise } f_{ij}(d) = 0 \tag{2}$$

6 Conclusion

As in the case of other biometric systems, in a biometric digital signature system the most important quality parameters are the false rejection rate (FRR) and the false acceptance rate (FAR). Several tests were done on our sample database, having nearly 6000 fingerprint samples of around 600 fingers to measure the FAR and the FRR. The false acceptance rate was within the acceptable limit of 10^{-6}, but the best theoretically attainable false rejection rate appeared to be around 15%. The latter figure shows us that further improvements should be made in the scheme to lower the FRR.

From a cryptographical point of view, the information quantity that can be stored in a fingerprint using our method appeared to be enough to meet the requirement of having a cryptographically strong RSA key pair, as we use 120 randomly chosen bits to generate the private key.

In conclusion, we can state that our scheme to construct biometric digital signatures is feasible, but several further enhancements should be made. We plan to improve the image processing undertaken before minutia extraction to make it more accurate. In a remarkable number of cases false rejection was due to non-linear distortions, so we plan to introduce a new non-linear transformation of the challenge minutia set that fits the usual distortions of the sample fingerprints. Finding the parameters of this non-linear transformation will be an inspiring challenge for our further research.

References

[1] Bodo, A.: Method of producing a digital signature with aid of biometric feature, German Pat.

[2] Soutar, C., Roberge, D., Stoianov, A., Gilroy, R., Kumar, B.V.K.V.: Biometric Encryption. http://www.bioscrypt.com/assets/Biometric_Encryption.pdf

[3] Hefferman, S.: The Role of Biometrics within Document Security, TSSI Swindon, United Kingdom. http://www.afb.org.uk/downloads/pisec.pdf (1999)

[4] Lewis, J.W.: Biometrics for Secure Identity Verification: Trends and Developments. University of Maryland. http://faculty.ed.umuc.edu/~meinkej/inss690/lewis.pdf (2001-2002)

[5] Secure Personal Identification Systems: Policy, Process and Technology Choices for a Privacy-Sensitive Solution, A Smart Card Alliance White Paper. http://www.ibia.org/ membersadmin/whitepapers/pdf/11/secure_id_white_paper.pdf (2002)

[6] Berrou, C., Glavieux, A., Thitimajshima, P.: Near Shannon limit error-correcting coding and decoding: turbo codes. ICC Proceedings (1993)

[7] Ottoson, T., Agrell, E.: Decoding Convolutional Codes http://www.s2.chalmers.se/ graduate/courses/errctrlcoding/convcode_decoding.pdf (2003)

[8] Zhu, G.: Performance Evaluation of Turbo Codes. Queen's University, Kingston, Ontario, Canada. http://markov.mast.queensu.ca/Papers/zhu_proj98.ps (1998)

A New Scheme for the Location Information Protection in Mobile Communication Environments

Soon Seok Kim[1], Sang Soo Yeo[2], Hong Jin Park[3], and Sung Kwon Kim[2]

[1] School of Information and Communication Engineering,
Halla University, San 66, Heungup-Li, Heungup-myon, Wonjusi, Kangwondo, Korea
sskim@hit.halla.ac.kr
[2] School of Computer Science and Engineering,
Chungang University, 221 Huksukdong, Dongjakku, Seoul, Korea
ssyeo@alg.cse.cau.ac.kr, skkim@cau.ac.kr
[3] School of Computer Information and Communication Engineering,
Sangji University, Woosandong, Wonjusi, Kangwondo, Korea
hjpark1@sangji.ac.kr

Abstract. We propose a new scheme, protecting information about the location of a user against attacks from inside the mobile communication, especially the network providers. There have already been some proposals about how to protect location information in mobile communication environments. Among them, Kesdogan et al.[2,3] proposed a new method, using so-called temporary pseudonyms and also described protection method against passive and an active attacks. However, the protection method against an active attack is not clear. Moreover, there is an additional load in that it should append a reachability manager[1,6] to the proposed system. In this paper, we introduce a new scheme improving the method of Kesdogan et al. and analyze its security and effectiveness.

1 Introduction

There have already been some proposals[1,2,3,4] about how to protect location information in mobile communication environments. Federrath et al.[1] suggested firstly the concept of MIXes as introduced by Chaum[5]. However, Kesdogan et al.[2] pointed out some serious drawbacks: the encryption for the MIX has to exceed 512 bits which adds further load on the air interface. They also proposed a new method, using so-called temporary pseudonyms (TP). The basic idea of the TP method is originally based on the concept of trusted parties where, e.g., a home personal computer confidentially stores sensitive data (authentication keys, location information etc.) or even handles the complete location management, replacing the visited location register (VLR) in GSM network[5]. But, in [2], Kesdogan et al. protected location information of a user by saving her identity, instead of actual location information, within a home trusted device. To this end, the user is assigned a pseudonym, pseudo mobile subscriber identity (PMSI). As long as the user is registered under a pseudonym, the network provider may know that a user under a certain pseudonym currently is at a certain place, but he is not able to link the users

V. Gorodetsky, I. Kotenko, and V. Skormin (Eds.): MMM-ACNS 2005, LNCS 3685, pp. 436–441, 2005.

real identity with her present location[2]. In [3], Kesdogan et al. also identified some security flaws (including *passive attacks* and *active attacks*) of TP method and proposed a new method, using the distributed TP (DTP). This method can protect against passive attacks. However, the protection method against active attacks is not clear. A detailed explanation will be given in Section 2. In this paper we consider mainly some problems on an active attack in the TP method of Kesdogan et al.[3]. We also propose and analyze a new scheme solving them. Our scheme is more effective and secure than the previous ones.

We discuss about TP method in Section 2 and propose a new location management scheme in Section 3 and analyze it in Section 4. Finally, in Section 5 we describe concluding remarks.

2   Discussion of TP Method

Kesdogan et al. introduced attacks for the TP method in [3] as follows:

• **Active Attacks**: Active attacks of the network provider, i.e. attempts to find out the user location by periodically asking her home trust device, may be recognized because all requests are logged at the device. Hence, if there are many more requests at the device than actual calls, this points towards an active attack.

As a matter of course, this is able to detect the attempt of an attack by maintaining a log-file requested from the network provider in the trust device. However, it is not a reasonable proof of an the attack because the network provider may consider the log-file forged. They introduced only one solution, adding the functionality of a reachability manager[7] to the device, i.e. it could decide for each request whether the importance of the request justifies revealing the pseudonym. But this method would be rather an alternative than a solution. It is not clear about how to decide whether the request justifies a response. The problem lies upon the periodic request of network provider for the PMSI to the device without a reasonable reason, even though the external user did not call a request. In order to prepare for the attack of network provider, it is necessary to check the request of real calls from the external user and the real connection of the call setup that is received by the network provider to the user. In addition, it is surely needed for the function of surveillance for the real connection of calls by using the user and trust device. In addition, the existing reachability manager is not included in this function so far. Moreover, the attaching of the reachability manager system also adds further load. In the next section, we propose a new scheme improving on these problems and analyzing its security and effectiveness.

3   New Scheme for the Location Management

The basic idea of our scheme, protecting an illegal request from a malicious network provider, is to verify whether an external user actually has requested by giving an acknowledgement message ACK, as a proof that the user received a call request from the network provider. A scenario of the scheme is as follows: (1) If an external user requests a call using the initial addressing Message (IAM) and the MSISDN, (2) the network provider (especially, the GMSC) requests a current PMSI of user to the trust device using the ISDN number of user, MSISDN and (3) the trust device gives it. Then, (4) the GMSC stores the current PMSI in its table and sends a call setup message to the user. Next, (5) the user verifies the setup message and sends an acknowledgment message ACK as a proof to the trust device. (6) The trust device checks the ACK. If the trust device does not receive the ACK, then the trust device will decide that the network provider has attempted an illegal request to find out the user location. The notations to describe the proposed methods are as follows.

[Notations]
· PMSI_cur : the current value of PMSI periodically produced by the trust device according to the synchronization time with the MS
· ACK: an acknowledgment message transmitted to the trustdevice as a response that the user has asked to receive a call from the external user through the network provider. This value is a kind of combination message for the encrypted value of r, PMSI_cur, and t with the secret key K^1 and PMSI_cur. Here r is an arbitrary integer t is the time when the user is to send a message (This may become a time stamp signed by the user, if the architecture is based on the environments of public key.).
· PMSI_acked : the value of PMSI_cur is produced at the time when the user sends the ACK message, and the trust device stores it in its own table some time later where the initial value is null.
· PMSI_provided: the most recently provided value of PMSI, and it will be stored in the GMSC table in the network provider where the initial value is null.
· VAL: this is a bit of vector. If the trust device receives an ACK message from the MS, it will be the value of 1, otherwise it will be 0. At this moment, the value is stored in the trust device table where the initial value is null.
In case of the proposed method, a place, which is differed from the previous TP method, is needed for storing the mentioned values, such as PMSI_provided, PMSI_acked, and so on. Our proposed scheme assumed that the network provider (especially, the GMSC in the network provider) and trust device is maintained as a kind of table in its own server (See [Fig. 1]).
· MS: the mobile user, TD: the trust device, NP: the network provider.

[Step 1] the step for the call request from the external user (caller):
The external user sends the IAM and MSISDN message to the GMSC of NP in order to call with the MS.
[Step 2] the step for the current PMSI request from the GMSC:
The GMSC sends the MSISDN in the case that the value of PMSI_provided is null after the check-up on the value of PMSI_provided that is stored in it own table.

---

[1] It is a short term secret key between the MS and the TD and is independently calculated for each item. In addition, it is updated by the given period (In case of the real system application, it will be adjusted by one week in the short term or one month in the long term according to the required security level.) The secret key is defined as $K=F(K_{MT},T)$, where K_{MT} is a long term secret key between the MS and the TD, F is a single directional function of encryption, and T is a predefined synchronization time (periodically updated) between the MS and the TD.

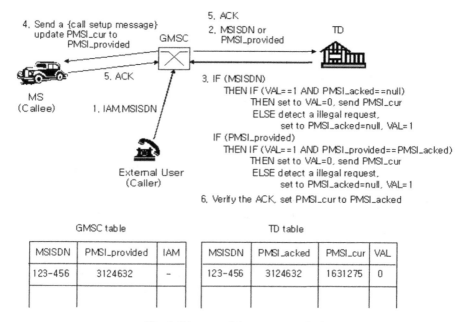

4. Send a {call setup message}
   update PMSI_cur to
   PMSI_provided

5. ACK

2. MSISDN or
   PMSI_provided

GMSC

TD

5. ACK

MS
(Callee)

1. IAM.MSISDN

3. IF (MSISDN)
    THEN IF (VAL==1 AND PMSI_acked==null)
        THEN set to VAL=0, send PMSI_cur
        ELSE detect a illegal request,
                set to PMSI_acked=null, VAL=1
  IF (PMSI_provided)
    THEN IF (VAL==1 AND PMSI_provided==PMSI_acked)
        THEN set to VAL=0, send PMSI_cur
        ELSE detect a illegal request,
                set to PMSI_acked=null, VAL=1

6. Verify the ACK, set PMSI_cur to PMSI_acked

External User
(Caller)

GMSC table

MSISDN	PMSI_provided	IAM
123-456	3124632	--

TD table

MSISDN	PMSI_acked	PMSI_cur	VAL
123-456	3124632	1631275	0

Fig. 1. Diagram of the request method

Otherwise it sends the value stored in the table to the TD in order to request the current PMSI.

[**Step 3**] the step for notifying the current PMSI after detecting the illegal attempt of the NP:

(1) In case of receiving the MSISDN, the TD checks the value of VAL in its own table is 1 at the same time as the fact that the PMSI-acked is null. If the values are 1 and null, the PMSI_cur will be sent to the GMSC after updating the value of VAL to 0. Otherwise, the stored value of the current PMSI_acked and VAL is to be reinitialized by null and 1 respectively after detecting the illegal attempt, and then raises an objection through off-line channels.

(2) In case of receiving the PMSI_provided from the GMSC, the TD checks the value of VAL in its own table is 1 at the same time as the fact that the PMSI_provided is the same as the PMSI_acked. If the values are 1 and null, the PMSI_cur will be sent to the GMSC after updating the value of VAL to 0. Otherwise the stored value of the current PMSI_acked and VAL is to be reinitialized by null and 1 respectively after detecting the illegal attempt, and then raises an objection through off-line channels.

[**Step 4**] the step for the connection setting to the MS:

The GMSC updates the value of PMSI_cur, which is received from the TD, to the value of PMSI_provided in its own table through the transmission of {call setup message} to the MS after setting the connection with the external user. There is a possibility that the PMSI, which is notified by the TD as the connection to the MS from the side of GMSC, does not exist in its own internal database of HLR and VLR. Because the MS has already updated in the process as the new value of PMSI or has not updated as the connection from the GMSC to the MS. Therefore, the GMSC is able to attempt to connect to the MS by using the updated PMSI with the request of the current PMSI once again to the TD. At this time, the TD notifies the other messages produced before or after by checking the synchronized time based on the PMSI, which has already been notified by the TD itself.

[Step 5] the step for the creation and updating for the ACK message of the MS:

The MS creates the acknowledgement message ACK after checking the {call setup message} and sends it to the TD through the GMSC. The value of PMSI_cur is the current value of PMSI, but it is a exact calculated value according to the synchronized time at the moment when the TD notifies it to the GMSC. In case the MS will renew the updating of PMSI just after receiving a call request from the GMSC, the value of PMSI_cur included in the ACK is to be used by the previous value of PMSI, that is, the value introduced by the synchronize time at the moment when the TD notifies it to the GMSC.

[Step 6] the step for the verification of ACK by the TD:

The TD updates the value of PMSI_cur after the encryption using the short term secret key K from the ACK message, which is encrypted by the MS, in its own table as the value of PMSI_acked.

If there is a normal call receiving request to the same MS from the external user after detecting the illegal attempt from the GMSC in [Step 3], the GMSC will also start from [Step 1] by reinitializing the value of PMSI_provided by null.

4 Analysis of the Proposed Scheme

The results for the comparison between the present method and the proposed method are shown in talbe 1 whether the location privacy of the MS is protected. As shown in table 1, the symbol Δ means that the passive attack is to be protected as the collusion between the disinterested party and the NP in the method of TP, but the active attack is not to be protected. Also, it is not perfect to protect for the attack by

Table 1. Comparison between the present method and the proposed method whether the position and location privacy of the MS is provided

		GSM[7]	TP Method[3]	TP Method+ Reachability Manager[6]	Proposed Method
Position Privacy Protection Method		Using TMSI	Using PMSI and TD	Using PMSI and TD	Using PMSI And TD
Location Privacy Protection	The 3rd Party	o	o	o	o
	Passive attack of the NP	×	o	o	o
	Active attack of the NP	×	×	Δ	o
	Collusion with the NP and 3rd Party	×	Δ	Δ	o

the reachability manager, where the NP will forge the personal information and call subject at the intermediate position from the external user. It disguises for a call request from the external user and is to send the personal information of the caller to the MS through the reachability manager.

5 Conclusions

In this paper we considered improvements of the TP method and proposed a new scheme, protecting an illegal attempt from the malicious network provider to find out location information. We also showed that the proposed scheme is secure against the active attacks through seven cases. Moreover, our scheme is more efficient than the previous schemes and is easily applicable in a current mobile network.

Acknowledgement. This work was supported by grant No. R01-2005-000-10568-0 from the Basic Research Program of the Korea Science & Engineering Foundation.

References

1. Federrath, H., Jerichow, A., Kesdogan, D., Pfitzmann, A.: Security in Public Mobile Communication Networks. Proc. IFIP/TC6 Personal Wireless Communications, Prague (1995) 105–116
2. Kesdogan, D., Federrath, H., Jerocow, A., Pfitzmann, A.: Location Management Strategies increasing Privacy in Mobile Communication Systems. Proc. of the 12th IFIP International Information Security Conference SEC96, Chapman & Hall (1996)
3. Kesdogan, D., Reichl, P., Junghartchen, K.: Distributed Temporary Pseudonyms: A New Approach for Protecting Location Information in Mobile Communication Networks. ESOROCS '98, LNCS, Vol. 1485 (1998) 295–312
4. Farber, D., Larson, K.C.: Network Security via Dynamic Process Renaming. Proc. of the 4th Data Communications Symposion, Quebec Canada (1975)
5. Chaum, D.: Untraceable Electronic Mail, Return Address and Digital Pseudonyms. Communications of the ACM, Vol.24, No.2 (1981) 65–75
6. ETSI, GSM Recommendations: GSM 01.02-12.21 (1993)
7. Reichenbach, M., Damker, H., Federrath, H., Rannenberg, K.: Individual Management of Personal Reachability in Mobile Communication. Proc. of the IFIP TC11 SEC 97. 13th International Information Security Conference (1997) 14–16
8. Beresford, R., Stajano, F.: Location Privacy in Pervasive Computing. IEEE Pervasive Computing, Vol.2, No.1 (2003) 46–55
9. Barkhuus, L., Dey, A. K.: Location-based services for mobile telephony: a study of users' privacy concerns. Proc. of the IFIP TC13 INTERACT 2003, 9th International Conference on Human-Computer Interaction (2003) 709–712
10. Gruteser, M., Grunwald, D.: Enhancing location privacy in wireless LAN through disposable interface identifiers: a quantitative analysis. Proc. of the 1st ACM international workshop on Wireless mobile applications and services on WLAN hotspots (2003) 46–55
11. Benjumea, V., Lopez, J., Montenegro, J. A., Troya, J. M.: A First Approach to Provide Anonymity in Attribute Certificates. Proc. of the PKC2004: 7th International Workshop on Theory and Practice in Public Key Cryptography, LNCS, Vol.2047 (2004) 12–28

Region Protection/Restoration Scheme
in Survivable Networks

Wojciech Molisz and Jacek Rak

Gdansk University of Technology, ul. Narutowicza 11/12,
80-952 Gdansk, Poland
womol@eti.pg.gda.pl, jrak@pg.gda.pl

Abstract. In this paper we propose the novel concept of a region protec-
tion/restoration, where one backup path protects a certain region of an active
path. We show that using the region protection/restoration we can keep both
restoration times and network resource utilization ratio at the reasonable level.

Since the optimization problem of finding working and backup paths is
NP-complete, we developed the heuristic algorithm. We show that in the worst
case our algorithm gave network resource utilization ratio only about 3.9 per-
cent higher compared to the optimal one returned by the CPLEX program. Results of the U.S. Long-Distance Network modeling show that region protection
gives a good compromise between path and link protection.

1 Introduction

We define survivability as the capability of a networked information system to fulfill
its mission, in the presence of attacks, failures, or intrusions. Protection and restoration [4], [5] have emerged as the two main techniques for fault management in survivable networks. We distinguish two basic approaches: path protection/restoration or
link protection/restoration against a single link or a single node failure (damage). Any
path/link protection can be dedicated or shared assuming that backup paths are link-
or node-disjoint with respective active paths [3], [4], [5].

In this paper we study various protection techniques and show that shorter restoration times imply greater network resource utilization ratio and vice versa. To find
a compromise, we propose a novel approach, which we call *region protec-
tion/restoration*. The key idea of our region protection is to protect a certain region of
an active path with help of one backup path. This concept offers a good trade-off
between restoration time and resource utilization ratio.

We call an individually protected area, the area of an active path that is protected
by a single backup path. In the path protection model (with backup paths being
link-disjoint[1] or node-disjoint[2] with active paths), the whole active path determines
the individually protected area. On the contrary, a single link of an active path is an

---

[1] By link-disjoint we mean that the backup path for a connection has no links in common with
the primary path for that connection.

[2] By node-disjoint we mean that the backup path for a connection has no nodes in common
with the primary path for that connection, except the source and destination nodes.

V. Gorodetsky, I. Kotenko, and V. Skormin (Eds.): MMM-ACNS 2005, LNCS 3685, pp. 442–447, 2005.
© Springer-Verlag Berlin Heidelberg 2005

individually protected area in a link protection technique. In this scheme a given backup path protects a single link of an active path (against the failure of a link) or two adjacent links of an active path (against the failure of a node).

In the region protection scheme each backup path protects a certain region of an active path. Size of this region is a compromise between appropriate lengths of individually protected areas in link and path protection schemes, respectively. Compared to the path protection, backup paths are expected to be shorter, which causes the faster restoration process. The level of resource utilization remains smaller than for the link restoration scheme, since for each connection less backup paths are needed.

The rest of the paper is organized as follows. Section 2 is devoted to ILP problem formulation, while Section 3 to the description of our heuristic algorithm. In Section 4 we compare our heuristic results of the US National Science Foundation (NSF) network modeling to the exact results of the CPLEX program. The convergence is almost ideal. Results of U.S. Long-Distance Network modeling for all three protection/restoration schemes are discussed in the concluding part of the paper.

2   ILP Model to Find Node-Disjoint Path Pairs (Dedicated Backup)

We consider a directed network $\Gamma(N,A)$, where: N – set of nodes; $|N| = N$; A - set of directed arcs; $|A| = M$. Each arc $e_m \in A$ is characterized by length, cost and offers L channels, each of a standard capacity. Source-destination pairs of nodes (sk, tk) (demands) are given, where: $k = 1, 2,\dots, K$; $1 < K \leq N \times (N-1)$.

It is to find paths transporting required flows from sources to destinations, protecting them against a single node failure and minimizing the linear cost:

$$\varphi(x) = \sum_{k=1}^{K} \sum_{l=1}^{L} \sum_{m=1}^{M} \kappa_{k,m} (x_{k,m}^{l} + y_{k,m}^{l}) \tag{1}$$

where: $\kappa_{k,m}$ = cost per unit flow of the k-th commodity on the arc $e_m \in A$;

$x_{k,m}^{l}$ ($y_{k,m}^{l}$) = k-th demand flow on the l-th channel on the arc $e_m \in A$ of a working (backup) path, respectively;

subject to:

−*flow conservation constraints for the l-th channel on working (backup)[3] paths:*

$$\sum_{\substack{m \in \{m:e_m \equiv (n,j) \in A; \\ j=1,2,\dots,N; j \neq n\}}} x_{k,m}^{l} - \sum_{\substack{m \in \{m:e_m \equiv (i,n) \in A; \\ i=1,2,\dots,N; i \neq n\}}} x_{k,m}^{l} = \begin{cases} 1 & if \quad n = s_k \\ -1 & if \quad n = t_k \\ 0 & otherwise \end{cases} \tag{2}$$

where: $e_m = (i, n)$ = arc incident into node n; $e_m = (n, j)$ = arc incident out of node n;
    $k=1, 2,\dots, K$; $l=1, 2,\dots, L$; $n=1, 2,\dots, N$;

−*finite arc capacity constraints:*

$$\sum_{l=1}^{L} \sum_{k=1}^{K} (x_{k,m}^{l} + y_{k,m}^{l}) \leq c_m = L \tag{3}$$

where: $m=1, 2, \dots, M$;

---

[3] Equations for backup paths are similar to (2) with $x_{k.m}^{l}$ replaced with $y_{k.m}^{l}$

– *constraints to ensure that every backup path is node-disjoint with its working path:*

$$\sum_{l=1}^{L} \sum_{\substack{m\in\{m:e_m\equiv(n,j)\in A; \\ j=1,2,...,N; j\neq n\}}} (x_{k,m}^l + y_{k,m}^l) \leq 1 \tag{4}$$

$$\sum_{l=1}^{L} \sum_{\substack{m\in\{m:e_m\equiv(i,n)\in A; \\ i=1,2,...,N; i\neq n\}}} (x_{k,m}^l + y_{k,m}^l) \leq 1 \tag{5}$$

where: $n\neq s_k$; $n\neq t_k$; for transit nodes (when both paths consist of at least two arcs);

$n\neq t_k$; for (4), when the working path consists of one direct arc;

$n\neq s_k$; for (5), when the working path consists of one direct arc;

– *nonnegativity constraints*
   all the variables should obtain nonnegative values

Unfortunately, the optimization problem (1) – (5) is NP complete [1]. For that reason we developed an efficient heuristic algorithm.

3   Heuristic SCRP Algorithm

In Fig. 1 we describe the SCRP algorithm finding survivable connections in the context of region protection. Each backup path is node-disjoint with a certain region of the active path. It's main advantage is the polynomial complexity.

SCRP ALGORITHM

Step 1. Find the active path Π_k between nodes (s_k, t_k), using Dijkstra's [2] algorithm.

Step 2. Set the source node s_k as the starting node b.

Step 3a. Find the shortest path tree T_k from t_k to b.

Step 3b. Start computing the backup path from b, using Dijkstra's algorithm, until the current node (say node x) reaches the tree T_k .

Step 3c. Determine the next part of the backup path as the fragment of the shortest path tree T_k from node x to the first node (say node y) that belongs both to the tree T_k and to the active path Π_k .

Step 3d. Accept the path between nodes b and y (calculated in steps *3b* and *3c*) as the backup path.

Step 3e. Set $b = z$ where z is a node of an active path, preceding the node y (i.e. placed upstream towards the source node).

Step 4. If $b <> t_k$ then go to step *3a* else return the paths for the connection.

Fig. 1. SCRP algorithm

4 Modeling Results

In this section we evaluate and compare restoration times and network resource utilization ratio obtained by both ILP and heuristic algorithm for the NSF network, shown in Fig. 2 We also modeled the U.S. Long-Distance Network [7], shown in Fig. 3, but, due to the size of the network, we applied only the heuristic algorithm.

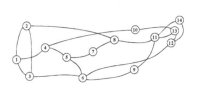
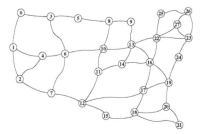

Fig. 2. NSF network   **Fig. 3.** U.S. Long-Distance Network

For each of the examined network, in each experiment, 30 logical topologies were generated. Each topology was determined by a graph having a fixed number of randomly chosen source-destination pairs of nodes. After establishing connections in each logical topology, single node failures were randomly generated. We assumed equal channel capacity and the same number of channels available in each link. For each connection we assumed protection against a single node failure, the distance metrics and no resource optimization in channel capacity allocation. Each demand of resource allocation was equal to the one channel capacity.

4.1 Accuracy of Heuristic Algorithm

We modeled the path protection in the NSF network to check the accuracy of our heuristic algorithm. Network resource utilization ratio per connection obtained with help of CPLEX program and our algorithm for 4-8 channels per link and 8 and 12 demands is shown in Table 1. Fig. 4 illustrates the rate of additional resource utilization ratio, obtained with help of heuristic algorithm, compared to the optimal results of CPLEX. Results prove that the heuristic algorithm is nearly as efficient as the optimal ILP approach. In particular, when increasing the number of available channels per link, the results for the heuristic approach tend to differ very little from the analogical ones for the ILP formulations.

Table 1. Network resource utilization ratio per one connection

number of demands per logical topology		8					12				
number of channels per link		4	5	6	7	8	4	5	6	7	8
resource utilization per connection [%]	(CPLEX)	3,62	2,90	2,42	2,07	1,81	3,58	2,88	2,42	2,07	1,82
	(heuristics)	3,70	2,93	2,44	2,09	1,83	3,72	2,97	2,45	2,09	1,83
95% confidence interval [%]	(CPLEX)	0,13	0,10	0,08	0,07	0,01	0,11	0,07	0,05	0,04	0,04
	(heuristics)	0,15	0,12	0,09	0,07	0,01	0,14	0,09	0,06	0,05	0,04

4.2   Comparison of the Three Protection Schemes

In this section we evaluate and compare results of our heuristic algorithm for path, link and region protection schemes for the U.S. Long-Distance Network. Here each link was assumed to have 32 channels; 30 demand pairs formed each scenario.

4.2.1   Network Resource Utilization Ratio

Fig. 5 shows the number of links as a function of percentage of link utilization ratio for all three protection schemes. Results from Fig. 5 prove that the smaller the individually protected area is, more network resources are necessary to protect a connection. Fig. 6 illustrates the relative network resource utilization ratio per connection. It shows that the region protection is almost as good as the path protection, giving about 60 % of the respective value for link protection. It is because the total number of links used by backup paths gets bigger when the size of individually protected area decreases. The region protection model leads to only insignificantly worse results regarding relative network resource utilization ratio per connection than those obtained by using the best model (i.e. path restoration), as shown in Table 2.

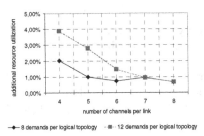

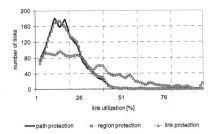

Fig. 4. Rate of additional resource utilization obtained by heuristic algorithm, compared to the optimal results of CPLEX

Fig. 5. Number of links as a function of percentage of link utilization ratio for all three protection schemes

Table 2. Link capacity utilization for three protection schemes

	path protection	region protection	link protection
network resource utilization [%]	18,30	20,01	30,56
95% confidence interval [%]	1,05	1,54	2,38

4.2.2   Restoration Times

Fig. 7 shows the cumulative distribution function of restoration times for all three protection schemes while Table 3 the respective average values.

Results show that the values of restoration times get smaller while decreasing the size of individually protected area. They represent values of time needed to restore a connection after a failure of a network component, according to the protocol taken from [5]. The lower the values of restoration time are, the smaller amount of data is lost within the period of restoration.

Table 3. Average restoration times for three protection schemes

	path protection	region protection	link protection
average restoration times [ms]	47,92	43,79	23,98
95% confidence interval [ms]	1,54	1,71	1,07

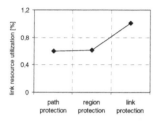

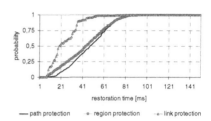

Fig. 6. Relative network resource utilization ratio per connection for all three protection schemes

Fig. 7. Cumulative distribution function of restoration time depending on protection model

5 Conclusions

Our results prove that region protection approach is the best way of keeping both restoration times and network resource utilization at the acceptable level.

Concluding the paper, we point out that one cannot simultaneously have the shortest restoration times and the smallest ratio of network resource utilization. One of these two factors plays against the second one and vice-versa. If they are of the same importance, the best solution is to use a region protection model, which provides the medium values of both restoration time values and network resource utilization.

References

1. Andersen, R., Chung, F., Sen, A., Xue, G.: On disjoint path pairs with wavelength continuity constraint in WDM networks. Proc. INFOCOM (2004) 524–535
2. Dijkstra, E.: A note on two problems in connection with graphs. Numerische Mathematik, 1, (1959) 269–271
3. Kodialam, M., Lakshman, T.V.: Dynamic routing of bandwidth guaranteed tunnels with restoration. Proc. INFOCOM (2000) 902–911
4. Ramamurthy, S., Mukherjee, B.: Survivable WDM mesh networks, Part I – protection. Proc. IEEE INFOCOM (1999) 744–751
5. Ramamurthy, S., Mukherjee, B.: Survivable WDM mesh networks, Part II – restoration. Proc. IEEE-ICC, Vol.3 (1999) 2023–2030
6. Suurballe, J.W.: Disjoint paths in a network. Networks, John Willey & Sons (1974) 125-145
7. Xiong, Y, Mason, L.G.: Comparison of two path restoration schemes in self-healing networks. Computer Networks 38 (2002) 663–674

Massive Data Mining for Polymorphic Code Detection

Udo Payer, Peter Teufl, Stefan Kraxberger, and Mario Lamberger

Institute of Applied Information Processing and Communications,
Inffeldgasse 16a, 8010 Graz, Austria
{Udo.Payer, Peter.Teufl, Stefan.Kraxberger,
Mario.Lamberger}@iaik.tugraz.at

Abstract. Driven by the permanent search for reliable anomaly-based intrusion detection mechanisms, we investigated different statistical methodologies to deal with the detection of polymorphic shellcode. The paper intends to give an overview on existing approaches in the literature as well as a synopsis of our efforts to evaluate the applicability of data mining techniques such as Neural Networks, Self Organizing Maps, Markov Models or Genetic Algorithms in the area of polymorphic code detection. We will then present our achieved results and conclusions.

1 Introduction

This paper is based on a set of known polymorphic shellcode generators (AD-MMutate [7], CLET [4], JempiScodes [17]) and will discuss the effectiveness of statistical methods like neural networks (NN) [5], Self Organizing Maps (SOM) [8] or finite Markov chains (MC) [20] for detecting malicious code. After analyzing existing polymorphic shellcode detection techniques (such as FNORD [16], APE [19] or Buttercup [12]), we have developed several possible approaches which have all in common, that they only make use of payload information without any use of additional information (e. g. header information).

For a good introduction on the concept behind shellcodes and polymorphic shellcodes we refer to [1] and [4].

2 Data Mining Approaches

2.1 Hybrid Detection Engine Using Neural Networks-HDE

In [13], we proposed a HDE which uses three phases to detect polymorphic shellcodes:

1. **NOP zone detection:** This phase searches the network traffic for consecutive chains of predefined NOP instructions (taken from ADMMutate and CLET). Whenever a chain exceeding a threshold length is found, the next phase is triggered. To overcome the problem with short or no NOP zones, this phase is scalable and can be turned off completely.

V. Gorodetsky, I. Kotenko, and V. Skormin (Eds.): MMM-ACNS 2005, LNCS 3685, pp. 448–453, 2005.
© Springer-Verlag Berlin Heidelberg 2005

2. **Search for execution chains**: This phase analyzes the data after the NOP zone by using a recursive function capable of following different execution chains in disassembled code. Whenever a controlflow instruction is detected, the function extracts the destination address and continues disassembling at this address. Depending on the instruction the function also follows the code directly after the instruction. For a similar approach we refer to [19].

3. **Neural network classification:** Whenever a termination criterion is met (see [13] for details), the recursive function stops to follow the code and starts neural network classification.

   The input for the neural network is the spectrum of encountered instructions along an execution path. (Here and in the course of this paper, by spectrum we mean a representation of the relative frequencies.) If the output of the neural network is larger than zero, a possible shellcode is reported.

   The features of the neural network were chosen by investigating the instructions used by the available polymorphic shellcode engines. These instructions were then used to create groups of similar instructions. Further instructions from the X86 set were then added to the groups. The groups are numbered and represent the features/inputs for the neural network. A complete list can be found in [13].

Results:

HDE was evaluated with six shellcode engines. There are three public available engines, that can be used to generate polymorphic shellcodes. These are ADM-Mutate [7], CLET [4] and JempiScodes [17]. With the knowledge we got from investigating these engines, we also made up our minds on alternative methods to generate polymorphism. As a result, we developed three independent shellcode engines which are based on different concepts.

In what follows, we will call these engines EE1, EE2 and EE3 (Experimental Engine). The purpose of these engines was to improve our detection mechanism by experimenting with concepts that could possibly evade HDE. EE1 was based on inserting junk instructions and XOR encryption. Such a mechanism was also proposed by the authors of [4]. EE2 uses the *Tiny Encryption Algorithm* (TEA) to encrypt the payload. EE3 uses random chains of simple instructions which are applied to the payload to transform the payload. The inverted instruction chain serves simultaneously as decryption engine and key.

Evaluation of HDE was made by training six neural networks (one for each polymorphic shellcode engine) and applying them to test data provided by the six engines and to real data known to be free of shellcodes. The results can be seen in table 1. To increase the detection accuracy for unknown engines, a new network was trained with positive training data used for the two best neural networks (ADMMutate and EE3) 2. In general, evaluation shows that HDE is able to detect engines not available during the training process.

2.2 Self-organizing Maps

Since we already applied the theory of Self-Organizing Maps in the context of traffic classification (cf. [14]), we also wanted to see them perform in anomaly detection. For the theory of SOMs, we refer to [8].

Table 1. Neural network performance

	ADMMutate	CLET	JempiScodes	EE1	EE2	EE3
ADMMutate	100%	38.8%	100%	79.2%	93%	75.9%
CLET	3.2%	100%	0%	1.7%	0%	3.5%
JempiScodes	26.6%	0%	100%	13%	0.1%	17.7%
EE1	17.4%	91.2%	0.8%	100%	100%	100%
EE2	2.3%	33%	0%	4.7%	100%	1.5%
EE3	20%	98.9%	0.8%	100%	97%	100%

Table 2. ADMMutate-EE3 network performance (30 NOPS)

ADMMutate	CLET	JempiScodes	EE1	EE2	EE3
100%	100%	71.4%	100%	98.3%	100%

Our SOM-based detection engine is virtually identical with the one described in Section 2.1, except that SOMs are used instead of a neural network. There are several reasons why choosing a SOM instead of a neural network could make sense:

- SOMs are based on unsupervised learning, neural networks use supervised learning
- SOMs can be trained with only positive examples
- SOMs can be used to visualize high dimensional data

This detection engine was not implemented for Snort^{TM}, because we only wanted to gather experience with SOMs. We made use of the SOMToolbox [6] for Matlab^{TM}, which we used for training and testing purposes.

Unfortunately, our achieved results lead to the conclusion that SOMs are incapable of replacing NNs for anomalous code detection, the detection rates were very poor even in simple test cases.

2.3   Finite Markov Chains

Another very promising approach in the field of abnormal code detection was the use of Finite Markov Chains (FMC). First, we trained the FMC-transition matrix by using "normal" network traffic. Thereafter, this transition matrix was used to calculate the probability of a dedicated Markov sequence, to find differences between the trained normal traffic and characteristic parts of a polymorphic shellcode.

By the knowledge of the intrinsic structure of the investigated engines, we were able to adjust the transition matrix manually. This lead to much better detection results. In addition, we applied some preprocessing functions due to efficiency and performance reasons (e.g. sequence preprocessing and NOP-filtering).

A substantial improvement of performance could be achieved be introducing the concept of **Genetic Algorithms** for the automatic training sequence of the FMC approach. Genetic algorithms are adequate tools if just little knowledge about the search space is available and the complexity of the problem is very hard (NP-complete).

The performance of a GA-improved transition matrix is shown in Figure 1.

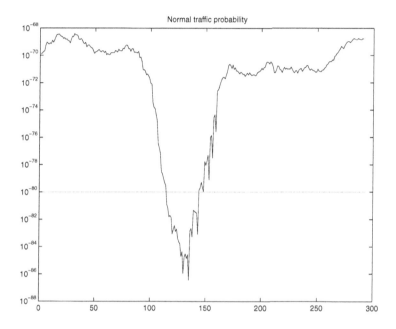

Fig. 1. Conditional probability of a 30-byte sequences with a GA-trained transition matrix

In Figure 1 we can see that the optimized transition matrix is highly qualified to detect deciphering engines. This is, since just deciphering-engines are used for the GA-algorithm.

Table 3 was generated by calculating the conditional probability of 37.785.600 30-byte sequences. After setting an empirically determined threshold we tested real network injected with shellcode examples. What we can see in Table 3 is that FMC produces no false-negatives. This is due to the fact that the GA-optimized transition matrix was tested by using the same category of shellcode as we used for the training process. We know that due to the relatively small number of test-sequences and the use of a single shellcode generator the presented results are not very significant. On the other hand, we just want to show that the number of false-positives can be reduced dramatically by the use of optimized transition matrices. Table 3 we can also reflects the fact that the GA modification process is much better than the manual process. (In Table 3, P1 denotes the case of a

Table 3. Markov model detection performance with different transition matrices

	P1	P2	P3
False negatives	0	0	0
False positives	33540	2540	13

learned transition matrix from normal traffic, P2 denotes the case of a manually manipulated transition matrix and P3 is the GA optimized transition matrix.)

3   Conclusions and Outlook

In this paper we give a short overview about three approaches to apply data mining techniques in the field of polymorphic code detection. The main idea was to find the most promising candidates which can be trained automatically. We think that commercial detection mechanisms can only be successful if they are based on automatic training mechanisms and do not require human interactions. We analyzed the concepts of NNs, SOMs, and FMCs by implementing SNORT^{TM}-plugins or simple Matlab^{TM} simulations - but always in combination with real network traffic.

The main difference between our approach and other solutions (found in the literature) is the exclusive use of payload information without any use of additional information (header information for instance).

In comparison, the NN-based approach showed very good results together with the most flexibility in detecting unknown shellcode. On the other hand, the Markov chain approach has the advantage of keeping the sequence information of the data. Our result can only be seen as a first glimpse on data mining techniques in malicious code detection. Clearly, the list of remaining tasks seems to be endless. Complexity-based comparison of proposed mechanisms and the search for possible new candidates are heading the list.

References

1. AlephOne: Smashing the stack for fun and profit. Phrack Magazine 49(14) (1996)
2. Biles, S.: Detecting the Unknown with Snort and the Statistical Packet Anomaly Detection Engine (SPADE).
   http://www.computersecurityonline.com/spade/SPADE.pdf retrieved on (2005)
3. Bishop, C.M.: Neural networks for pattern recognition. The Clarendon Press Oxford University Press, New York. With a foreword by Geoffrey Hinton (1995)
4. CLET team: Polymorphic shellcode engine. Phrack Magazine 61(9) (2003)
5. Duda, R., Hart, P., Stork, D.: Pattern classification. Wiley-Interscience, New York, second edition (2001)
6. Helsinki University of Technology. Som toolbox for matlab. http://www.cis.hut.fi/projects/somtoolbox/ (2005)
7. K2. Admutate 0.8.4. http://www.ktwo.ca. Retrieved (2004)
8. Kohonen, T.: Self-Organizing Maps. Springer (2001)

 9. Kraxberger, S., Payer, U.: Markov Model for Polymorphic Shellcode Detection. accepted at INC 2005. (2005)
10. Mathworks. Neural network toolbox. http://www.mathworks.com/products/neuralnet/ (2004)
11. NASM SourceForge Project. http://nasm.sourceforge.net (2005)
12. Pasupulati, A. Coit, Levitt, J., Wu, K., Li, S.F., Kuo, S.H., Fan, J.C.: Buttercup: on network-based detection of polymorphic buffer overflow vulnerabilities. Network Operations and Management Symposium, 2004. NOMS 2004. IEEE/IFIP, Vol. 1 (2004) 235–248
13. Payer, U., Teufl, P., Lamberger, M.: Hybrid Engine for Polymorphic Shellcode Detection. accepted at DIMVA (2005)
14. Payer, U., Teufl, P., Lamberger, M.: *Traffic classification using Self-Organizing Maps*. accepted at INC 2005 (2005)
15. Roweis, S.: *Levenberg-marquardt optimization*. http://www.cs.toronto.edu/~roweis/notes/lm.pdf (2005)
16. Ruiu, D.: Snort preprocessor - Multi-architecture mutated NOP sled detector. http://cansecwest.com/spp_fnord.c (2005)
17. Sedalo, M.: Polymorphic Shellcode Engine. http://www.shellcode.com.ar (2004)
18. Snort. Open Source Network Intrusion Detection System. http://www.snort.org (2005)
19. Toth, T., Kruegel, Ch.: Accurate buffer overflow detection via abstract payload execution. RAID 2002, Lecture Notes in Computer Science, Vol. 2516 (2002) 274–291
20. Weisstein, E.W.: Markov Chain. From MathWorld–A Wolfram Web Resource. http://mathworld.wolfram.com/MarkovChain.html

Key Escrow with Tree-Based Access Structure

Martin Schaffer and Peter Schartner

University of Klagenfurt, Austria, Computer Science · System Security
{m.schaffer, p.schartner}@syssec.at

Abstract. In this paper we propose a system in which a set of people is able to confidentially communicate using a common session key. Due to required governmental surveillance properties, this key will be escrowed using a multi-party version of the ElGamal cryptosystem. The resulting shares of the ciphertext are stored over a set of trusted servers to provide availability and to hamper ciphertext-based attacks. Using a particular tree-based multi-party decryption, the session key can be reconstructed by a tree-structured set of escrow agencies without reconstructing the private ElGamal key and the ciphertext.

1   Introduction

While monitoring people human rights are often neither protected by the government nor by other (private) organisations. Focused on this fact, it is very useful to store the monitored information confidentially. With the help of key escrow we are able to archive the corresponding key at a trusted third party. In this simple consideration we quickly find several problems. Firstly, we do not want to trust one single party that is able to recover the key. As a matter of fact, many solutions provide well defined access structures to the escrowed key (e.g. secret splitting/sharing or software solutions). Secondly, the escrow agencies require the availability of the database in which the key is stored. If we simply build redundant memories, this problem can be solved, but what happens if the access structure has been compromised? Another problem arises, if a communication process, such as a conferencing phone call between several instances, has to be monitored. For efficiency reasons only one key might have been generated in a fair way among users, but who is responsible for escrowing it?

The proposed key escrow system fulfils the following requirements:

- Fair distributed (tree-structured) generation of a private key d.
- Fair distributed generation of a session key k.
- Multi-party ElGamal encryption of k to provide its confidentiality.
- Distributed storage of the ciphertext (c_1 and shares of c_2) to provide availability, to avoid unauthorized encryption if d has been compromised and to hamper several ciphertext-based attacks.
- Tree-structured multi-party ElGamal decryption over c_1 and shares of c_2.

The proposed system consists of a set $\mathcal{P}$ of l monitored instances who generate and encrypt a common session key k for a confidential teleconference using multi-party ElGamal encryption. Furthermore, a set $\mathcal{S}$ of m ciphertext-servers exists

V. Gorodetsky, I. Kotenko, and V. Skormin (Eds.): MMM-ACNS 2005, LNCS 3685, pp. 454–459, 2005.

where c_1 and shares of c_2 are archived. Finally, a possibly tree-structured set $\mathcal{E}$ of escrow agencies exists, where each instance owns a (recursively generated) share of the private key d.

The tree-based access structure can be achieved by recursively using threshold cryptography. In order to be able to perform encryptions and decryptions in a distributed way, we need the concepts of secure multi-party computation (MPC) based on threshold security firstly introduced in [3]. There, any publicly known mathematical formula with secret inputs can be computed by a qualified set of instances (so called players) without revealing any information about the secrets but giving them enough power to compute and reconstruct the output. Basic solutions in this research field provide addition and multiplication of shared secrets as well as public constants (scalars). Due to the fact, that multiplication of two shared secrets is not very practical, we reduce our requirements to the exclusive usage of addition and multiplication with scalars. To provide a better understanding of our approach, the given protocols are only resistant against passive adversaries who always stand to the rules (for considerations with active adversaries we refer to our technical report [6]). Multi-party computation based on threshold security requires secret sharing in several stages, which is also required for availability reasons of the ciphertext. This heads to the output of the distributed encryption process which remains shared over $\mathcal{S}$. While performing a distributed decryption, the private key also always remains recursively shared by using ElGamal threshold decryption (likely proposed in [1]). Different from [1] we propose d to be tree-shared on the one hand and a very strong requirement on the other hand: decryptions are only allowed to be performed over shares of the ciphertext. As far as monitored instances are honest we can hamper several ciphertext-based attacks up to a particular grade.

2 Fundamentals

Due to the usage of the ElGamal cryptosystem and its system parameters p and q, every computational step in this paper is either reduced modulo q (within exponents) or modulo p (within bases). For sake of simplicity we use a multi-pseudo code that we developed especially for representing multi-party protocols. In order to run such a protocol in pseudo-code representation the participating input and output-players with the corresponding input and output-values (within brackets) have to be specified. Every direct successor of the root of the tree is called first-level-player (FLP). Although we shortly describe the used fundamentals, we assume the reader to be familiar with the basic ElGamal cryptosystem [2] as well as the paradigm of secure multi-party computation [4] and secret sharing [9] respectively.

2.1 Shamir's Secret Sharing and Reconstruction

A secret value s of group $\mathbb{Z}_q$ is shared among a set of n players by using Shamir's secret sharing [9] with threshold t (short: $s \mapsto (s_1, \ldots, s_n)$). For unique reconstruction of s we have to interpolate at least $t+1$ shares using the formula of Lagrange: $s = \sum_{i=1}^{n} s_i \cdot \lambda_{0,i}^s$, where $\lambda_{0,i}^s = \prod_{j=1}^{n} j \cdot (j-i)^{-1}$ is the weight of s_i corresponding to s. One big disadvantage of Shamir's secret sharing is the fact that incorrect shares head to the reconstruction of a wrong secret. Although we can never prevent from active misbehaviour of participating instances, it is possible to detect them up to a particular grade (for more information see [4]).

2.2   ElGamal Cryptosystem

Assuming the discrete-logarithm-based key generation has already taken place resulting in the public key e and the private key d the encryption of a session key k can be done by computing $c_1 = g^\alpha$ and $c_2 = k \cdot e^\alpha$, where $\alpha \in_R \mathbb{Z}_q$. The decryption can be done by computing $k = c_2 \cdot c_1^{-d}$.

2.3   Fair Tree-Shared Generation of a Private Key

In this paper we need a fair distributed generation of a (secret) value. We use a simplified version of the key generation protocol based on discrete logarithms proposed in [5]. The protocol in [5] is useful to generate a private key without reconstructing it. However, we need a fair tree-structured generation of the private key. Moreover, we need substitutability for every FLP within $\mathcal{E}$ in case of absence which can be realized by recursively sharing computations over the corresponding sub-trees. For lack of space we are forced to refer to our technical report [7].

3   Distributed Computation of the ElGamal Cryptosystem

Based on our strict requirement not using multiplication of two shared secrets we now try to split the ElGamal encryption and decryption function into several parts respectively so that it can be performed by different sets of players without revealing information about the session key k, the private key d, the ciphertext-part c_2 and randomness α up to a particular grade. We consider the ElGamal cryptosystem as one common multi-party computation where the computation-stage consists of three sub-stages: session key generation, encryption- and decryption. We assume, that d is already shared over $\mathcal{E}$ and players in $\mathcal{P}$ already know e.

Input. Each player P_i in $\mathcal{P}$ generates and shares two secret random values $k_i' \mapsto (k_{i1}', \ldots, k_{il}')$ and $\alpha_i' \mapsto (\alpha_{i1}', \ldots, \alpha_{il}')$ over $\mathcal{P}$.

Computation (Session Key Generation). Each player in P_i combines the received share-shares to a share of k [5]: $k_i = \sum_{j=1}^{l} k_{ji}' \cdot \lambda_{0,j}^{k_i}$.

Computation (Encryption). All players in $\mathcal{P}$ and $\mathcal{S}$ compute the encryption over the shares of k, α and the constant e^α resulting in c_2 that remains shared over $\mathcal{S}$. Protocol 1 (see fig. 1) starts with the combination of the received share-shares of α to a share of it. Then every player computes and broadcasts a share of e^α over $\mathcal{P}$. Now each player P_i is able to compute a share of c_2 by multiplying his share of k by e^α. Furthermore, he sends c_1 to $\mathcal{S}$. A resharing of c_2 results in c_2 shared over $\mathcal{S}$. First we have to proof, that any value z that is shared over x players can be reshared over a set of y players without reconstructing z:

Proof (of Correctness (xy-Resharing)).

$$\sum_{i=1}^{x} z_i \cdot \lambda_{0,i}^z = \sum_{i=1}^{x} \sum_{j=1}^{y} z_{ij} \cdot \lambda_{0,j}^{z_i} \cdot \lambda_{0,i}^z = \sum_{j=1}^{y} \sum_{i=1}^{x} z_{ji} \cdot \lambda_{0,i}^z \cdot \lambda_{0,j}^{z_i} = \sum_{j=1}^{y} z_j \cdot \lambda_{0,j}^{z_i} \quad (1)$$

$\square$

input: $(S_1[c_1, c_{21}], \ldots, S_m[c_1, c_{2m}], E_1[d_1], \ldots, E_n[d_n])$	**MPC:** $c_2 \cdot c_1^{-d}$
output: $(E_1[k_1], \ldots, E_n[k_n])$	

1.1	**for all** $i \in \{1, \ldots, m\}$ **do** // decryption stage 1 $(\mathcal{S}\ \&\ \mathcal{E})+$
1.2	$S_i: c_{2i} \mapsto (c_{2i_1}, \ldots, c_{2i_n})$
1.3	$\mathbf{send}(S_i[c_1, c_{2i_1}, \ldots, c_{2i_n}]) \rightarrow (E_1[c_1, c_{2i_1}], \ldots, E_n[c_1, c_{2i_n}])$
1.4	**for all** $i \in \{1, \ldots, n\}$ **do** // decryption stage 2 $(\mathcal{E})+$
1.5	$E_i: c_{1i}^* = c_1^{d_i}, \quad c_{2i}^* = \sum_{j=1}^m c_{2j_i} \cdot \lambda_{0,j}^{c_{2i}^*}$
1.6	$\mathbf{send}(E_i[c_{1i}^*]) \rightarrow (E_1[c_{1i}^*], \ldots, E_n[c_{1i}^*])$
1.7	**for all** $i \in \{1, \ldots, n\}$ **do** // decryption stage 3 $(\mathcal{E})+$
1.8	$E_i: k_i^* = c_{2i}^* \cdot (\prod_{j=1}^n c_{1j}^{*\lambda_{0,j}^d})^{-1}, \quad k_i^* \mapsto (k_{i1}^*, \ldots, k_{in}^*)$
1.9	$\mathbf{send}(E_i[k_{i1}^*, \ldots, k_{in}^*]) \rightarrow (E_1[k_{i1}^*], \ldots, E_n[k_{in}^*])$
1.10	**for all** $i \in \{1, \ldots, n\}$ **do** // decryption stage 4 $(\mathcal{E})+$
1.11	$E_i: k_i = \sum_{j=1}^n k_{ji}^* \cdot \lambda_{0,j}^{k_i}$

Fig. 1. Multi-Party Protocol 1: Distributed ElGamal Encryption

A proof of correctness of protocol 1 can be given referring to the proof of xy-Resharing and the lines of the encryption protocol:

Proof (of Correctness (Multi-Party Protocol 1)).

$$c_1 \stackrel{l.8}{=} \prod_{i=1}^{l} c_{1i}^{\lambda_{0,i}^\alpha} \stackrel{l.2}{=} g^\alpha, \quad c_2 = \sum_{i=1}^{m} c_{2i} \cdot \lambda_{0,i}^{c_2} \stackrel{(1)}{=} \sum_{i=1}^{l} c_{2i}' \cdot \lambda_{0,i}^k$$

$$\stackrel{l.5}{=} \sum_{i=1}^{l} k_i \cdot \left(\prod_{j=1}^{l} e_j^{\lambda_{0,j}^\alpha} \right) \cdot \lambda_{0,i}^k \stackrel{l.2}{=} \sum_{i=1}^{l} k_i \cdot \lambda_{0,i}^k \cdot e^\alpha = k \cdot e^\alpha$$

$\square$

Computation (Decryption). All players in $\mathcal{S}$ and $\mathcal{E}$ compute the decryption over c_1, the shares of c_2 and the shares of d resulting in k that remains shared among the players of $\mathcal{E}$ until reaching the output-stage (see fig. 2). $\mathcal{S}$ starts protocol 2 by resharing c_2 over $\mathcal{E}$ and sending c_1 to $\mathcal{E}$. Then each player E_i computes and broadcasts a share of c_1^d. Furthermore, he combines a share of c_2 and computes his part $c_{2i} \cdot c_1^{-d}$ of the main decryption (multiplication of a share with a scalar) resulting in a share of k. However, broadcasting this share enables every E_i to reconstruct c_2. Due to this fact, we blind c_2 by resharing k over $\mathcal{E}$.

input:	$(S_1[c_1, c_{21}], \ldots, S_m[c_1, c_{2m}], E_1[d_1], \ldots, E_n[d_n])$	**MPC:** $c_2 \cdot c_1^{-d}$
output:	$(E_1[k_1], \ldots, E_n[k_n])$	

1.1 **for all** $i \in \{1, \ldots, m\}$ **do**   // decryption stage 1 $(\mathcal{S}$ & $\mathcal{E})+$
1.2 S_i: $c_{2i} \mapsto (c_{2i_1}, \ldots, c_{2i_n})$
1.3   **send**$(S_i[c_1, c_{2i_1}, \ldots, c_{2i_n}]) \to (E_1[c_1, c_{2i_1}], \ldots, E_n[c_1, c_{2i_n}])$
1.4 **for all** $i \in \{1, \ldots, n\}$ **do**   // decryption stage 2 $(\mathcal{E})+$
1.5 E_i: $c_{1i}^* = c_1^{d_i}$, $c_{2i}^* = \sum_{j=1}^{m} c_{2j_i} \cdot \lambda_{0,j}^{c_{2i}^*}$
1.6   **send**$(E_i[c_{1i}^*]) \to (E_1[c_{1i}^*], \ldots, E_n[c_{1i}^*])$
1.7 **for all** $i \in \{1, \ldots, n\}$ **do**   // decryption stage 3 $(\mathcal{E})+$
1.8 E_i: $k_i^* = c_{2i}^* \cdot (\prod_{j=1}^{n} c_{1j}^{*\,\lambda_{0,j}^d})^{-1}$, $k_i^* \mapsto (k_{i1}^*, \ldots, k_{in}^*)$
1.9   **send**$(E_i[k_{i1}^*, \ldots, k_{in}^*]) \to (E_1[k_{i1}^*], \ldots, E_n[k_{in}^*])$
1.10 **for all** $i \in \{1, \ldots, n\}$ **do**   // decryption stage 4 $(\mathcal{E})+$
1.11 E_i: $k_i = \sum_{j=1}^{n} k_{ji}^* \cdot \lambda_{0,j}^{k_i}$

Fig. 2. Multi-Party Protocol 2: Distributed ElGamal Decryption

Analogous to protocol 1 a proof of correctness can be given as follows:

Proof (of Correctness (Multi-Party Protocol 2)).

$$k = \sum_{i=1}^{n} k_i \cdot \lambda_{0,i}^k \overset{(1)}{=} \sum_{i=1}^{n} k_i^* \cdot \lambda_{0,i}^{c_2^*} \overset{l.8}{=} \sum_{i=1}^{n} c_{2i}^* \cdot \left(\prod_{j=1}^{n} c_{1j}^{*\,\lambda_{0,j}^d} \right)^{-1} \cdot \lambda_{0,i}^{c_2^*}$$

$$\overset{l.5}{=} \sum_{i=1}^{n} c_{2i}^* \cdot \lambda_{0,i}^{c_2^*} \cdot c_1^{-d} \overset{(1)}{=} \sum_{i=1}^{m} c_{2i} \cdot \lambda_{0,i}^{c_2} \cdot c_1^{-d} = c_2 \cdot c_1^{-d}$$

$\square$

Output. Every player $E_i \in \mathcal{E}$ sends k_i to every player $E_j \in \mathcal{E}$. Then each E_j can reconstruct the session key by computing $k = \sum_{i=1}^{n} k_i \cdot \lambda_{0,i}^k$.

3.1 Performance and Security Analysis

The performance of the proposed protocols depends on the number of players in $\mathcal{P}$, $\mathcal{S}$ and $\mathcal{E}$. The following table shows the number of sent messages, performed multiplications and exponentiations of big integer values during the encryption and decryption-stages for one player (additions are not considered):

Player	Sent Messages	Multiplications	Exponentiations
P_i(encryption)	$O(l + m)$	$O(l + m)$	$O(1)$
S_i(encryption)	$-$	$O(l)$	$O(1)$
S_i(decryption)	$O(n)$	$O(n)$	$O(1)$
E_i(decryption)	$O(n)$	$O(n + m)$	$O(1)$

The security of the protocols lies in the difficulty of breaking the discrete logarithm problem and threshold multi-party computation with computational security (see [4]). An external adversary has to compromise at least $t + 1$ players in $\mathcal{S}$ to reconstruct c_2 and at least $t + 1$ FLP in $\mathcal{E}$ to reconstruct d in order to be able to decrypt k. The distributed storage of c_2 has two effects: firstly, the availability of ciphertext and secondly, the restriction of several ciphertext-based attacks. However, if an adversary is able to force any player in $\mathcal{P}$ to compute and publish c_2 the second advantage disappears. Considering the decryption of k, it is obvious that internal adversaries ($\mathcal{S}$ or $\mathcal{E}$) do not really have more power than external ones. Performing ciphertext-based attacks is not possible for up to t players in $\mathcal{S}$ and $\mathcal{E}$ (if $\mathcal{P}$ remains honest).

4   Conclusion

We proposed a key escrow system that fulfils the requirements stated in section 1 by using a particular version of distributed ElGamal to achieve several security-properties (discussed in section 3.1). For a detailed description of our proposal including more applications we refer to our technical report [8]. An extended version considering active adversaries can be found in our technical report [6].

References

1. Desmedt, Y., Frankel, Y.: Threshold Cryptosystems. Adv. in Crypt.: CRYPTO'89, Springer-Verlag (1990) 307–315
2. ElGamal, T.: A Public-Key Cryptosystem and a Signature Scheme Based on Discrete Logarithms. Adv. in Crypt.: CRYPTO'84, Springer-Verlag (1985) 10–18
3. Goldreich, O. et al: How to play any mental game – a completeness theorem for protocols with honest majority. Proc. 19th ACM STOC (1987) 218–229
4. Hirt, M.: Multi-Party Computation: Efficient Protocols, General Adversaries, and Voting. Ph.D. thesis. ETH Series in Information Security and Cryptography, Hartung-Gorre Verlag, Konstanz (2001)
5. Pedersen, T.: A threshold cryptosystem without a trusted party. Adv. in Crypt.: EUROCRYPT'91, LNCS, Vol.547 (1991) 522–526
6. Schaffer, M.: Hierarchical Key Escrow with Active Adversaries. Technical Report TR-syssec-05-03, University of Klagenfurt, Austria (2005)
7. Schaffer, M.: Tree-shared Generation of a Secret Value. Technical Report TR-syssec-05-01, University of Klagenfurt, Austria (2005)
8. Schaffer, M., Schartner, P.: Hierarchical Key Escrow with Passive Adversaries. Technical Report TR-syssec-05-02, University of Klagenfurt, Austria (2005)
9. Shamir, A.: How to share a secret. Comm. of the ACM, Vol.11 (1979) 612–613

Security Checker Architecture
for Policy-Based Security Management

Artem Tishkov, Igor Kotenko, and Ekaterina Sidelnikova

SPIIRAS, 39, 14 Liniya, St.-Petersburg, 199178, Russia
{avt, ivkote}@iias.spb.su, kittykate137@yandex.ru

Abstract. Policy-based management systems are now the object of steadfast attention in network security theory and applications. Due to a complex structure of subject role hierarchies, target grouping, and action mutual dependence the security policy conflicts are complicated to detect and resolve. Moreover, an initially consistent policy ruleset may lead to inconsistent or unenforceable rules during the system lifecycle. The paper presents the architecture of Security Checker module (intended for disclosure and resolution of policy conflicts) and illustrates conflict detection based on event calculus.

1 Introduction and Motivation

Recently, common standard for policy-based security architecture is the one provided by the IETF through several of its working groups, mainly policy framework (policy) WG [2]. Policy rules are stored in a repository and policy decision point (PDP) is separated from the policy enforcement point (PEP). Centralization of policy rules store allows to build separated (passive) software tool for verification of security policy as a whole. However, since verification process includes decision making in a conflict situations, the verification tool should provide a conflict resolution strategy used by PDP. PDP in turn sends decision to PEP which has to be appropriate to PEP capabilities. Therefore, the verification tool needs three kind of information: policy rules from repository, resolution strategy, and security capabilities of PEP.

Proposed policy-based framework which is under development in the Positif Project [10] contains two input languages: System Description Language (SDL) and Security Policy Language (SPL). SDL formally describes the information system. The language supports the description of (1) system topology as network elements and physical connections, (2) the network services offered and the applications supported for each network element, (3) the security functionality of element such as network filters, OS intrinsic controls, application-level ACL, etc. SPL specifies a security policy. The language is able to describe high-level and low-level security policy rules. High-level rules express a composite task that implies a number of actions to implement. For example, to enforce the rule "Split the network into two independent subnetworks", the system should perform gateway reconfiguration, change of IP addresses and subnet mask, and, possibly, addition of new filtering policies. Low-level rules are more specific and in most cases could be considered as atomic action. For example the rule "block any packet from network 195.19.200" would be

V. Gorodetsky, I. Kotenko, and V. Skormin (Eds.): MMM-ACNS 2005, LNCS 3685, pp. 460–465, 2005.

translated to one ACL item. One more kind of SPL rules defines decision algorithms. There might be Deny Take Precedence, Permit Take Precedence, More (Less) Specific Take Precedence, or another user-defined algorithm. Thus, policy rules and conflict resolution strategies are described in SPL, security capabilities of a network node (PEP) are defined in SDL.

Present-day policy-based security systems also include these three categories of information, but not all three at the same time. Extended access control markup language (XACML) supports access control policies. Three-level structure of policy description (rule – policy as a set of rules – set of policies) allows to build flexible resolution system using formalized notion of decision algorithm on the levels of policy and policy set. XACML does not support system description language directly, as network nodes are represented in rules. Ponder language [9] contains rules for positive and negative authorization, obligation and delegation. The authors of Ponder suggested several approaches for conflict resolution strategies [7]. Flexible Authorization Framework (FAF) [3,4] studies access control policies. The advantage of proposed system and reasoning is deep consideration of object, subject, and privileges hierarchies. The language allows the specification of positive and negative authorization and incorporates notions of authorization derivation, conflict resolution and decision strategies.

The are also several relevant papers devoted to different techniques of conflict detection and resolution, including deontic logic (L.Cholvy, et. al.), dynamic conflict detection and resolution (N.Dunlop, et. al.), detecting conflict of duty (D.Ferraiolo, R.Sandhu, et. al.), policy conflicts specification and resolution (Morris Sloman, et. al.), credential-based approach to specification of access control policies, conflict resolution in event-based policy management (Jan Chomicki), etc.

In our approach we try to use a set of different approaches in one common framework for conflict detection and resolution in different policies (authentication, confidentiality, filtering, etc.). The paper presents the architecture of Security Checker intended for disclosure and resolution of policy conflicts and illustrates methods of conflict detection based on event calculus. Section 2 describes the architecture of policy-based security system proposed, the Security Checker architecture and implementation issues. Section 3 characterizes the event calculus-based verification module. Section 4 summarizes the results of the paper.

2 Security Checker Architecture and Implementation

The general architecture of policy-based security system is presented in fig. 1 [10]. *Security checker* (SEC) checks if the policies are consistent and can be implemented with the functionality available in the information system. SEC plays a role of SDL/SPL debugger, which interacts with user approving SPL/SDL descriptions or pointing to inconsistencies. *Configuration Generator* produces *Generic Security Rulesets* (GSR) which are the set of rules that do not keep into account the specific implementation of security block (e.g. firewall type and manufacturer). *Security Technology Mapper* transforms GSR into a specific configuration for each security block in the system. This step will need the help of *Block Security Maps* provided by the manufacturer of the block. *Security Deployment Engine* transfers configuration to

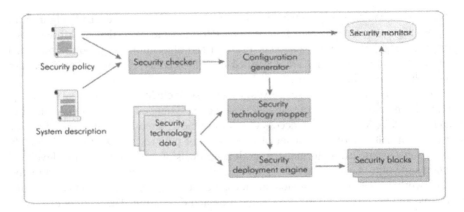

Fig. 1. General architecture of security policy-based system [10]

the security blocks. *Proactive Security Monitor* (PSM) is an evolution of the concept of Intrusion Detection System. PSM additionally uses two proactive techniques: compare network traffic and system behavior against the allowed policy and generate deliberate attacks to perform automatic checks of the deployed configuration. The fifth section describes main results and directions of future research.

The SEC architecture is presented in fig. 2. The central box presents SEC, arrows define dataflow (input or output).

System description (on SDL) is firstly validated using software/hardware compatibility database. Security policy (on SPL) could be formulated on high or low level. High-level rule is usually expanded to two or more low level rules for different security properties, such as authentication, authorization, confidentiality, filtering, etc. The system stores links between high- and low-level rule formulations. These links are used to inform system administrator about contradictory high-level rules when policy conflict is found on low-level. After translation of high-level (HL) rules to

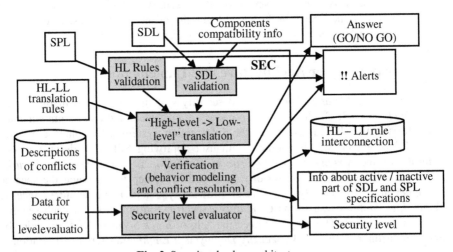

Fig. 2. Security checker architecture

low-level (LL), the verification process is started. Verification has three purposes: (1) detect parts of specifications on SPL and SDL that have inconsistencies, (2) detect parts of specifications on SPL and SDL that cannot be activated in the current configuration (i.e. SPL-SDL compatibility checking), and (3) evaluation of security level (SL) that could be achieved with these SPL-SDL descriptions.

The verification tool architecture is a multi-module one. Currently three modules based on different mathematical approaches have been designed. These modules are as follows: (1) the model checking module implemented using SPIN; (2) the theorem prover that uses Event Calculus [6] and implemented in Jess [5]; and (3) the module that implements semi-lattice approach [1]. Two first modules have been implemented.

The verification tool architecture is an open one: the signature of base Java class VerificationModule, that represents a module, is fixed and a developer could provide his/her own verification module inherited from VerificationModule. The Verification Manager determines the order of modules processing.

3 Implementation of Event Calculus-Based Module

One of the modules of verification tool uses Event Calculus (EC) [6]. The implementation of this module has been done by Jess rule engine [5]. The input data are SDL and SPL descriptions. The module implementation is based on forward chaining techniques: initialization rules generate a database of facts, and then the rules are fired which conditions satisfy the facts. So an SDL description is transformed into initialization rules which place network nodes, users, roles and services into the database of facts. SPL rules are translated into operational rules. Inconsistencies are determined by using conflict predicates. The example below shows the definition of an authorization conflict. When initialization rules are fired, the module tries to derive conflicts. This is a static conflict search. When the system is working, any new user event is also put in the database of facts, and the conflict search procedure is initialized. This use of the module is a dynamic conflict search.

Formally EC uses multi-sorted first-order language. Additionally to standard domain of individual objects, EC defines three sorts: *fluents* – time-varying properties of the world, *actions* – their instances (events) change state of fluents, *time* – real or integer numbers starting from 0.

The following predicates define the states of fluents, their initiation and termination, and events happening: $HoldsAt(f,t)$ is true iff fluent f holds at timepoint t ; $Happens(a,t)$ is true iff action a happens at timepoint t ; $Initiates(a,f,t)$ expresses that fluent f holds after timepoint t (but not at t) if action a happens at t ; $Terminates(a,f,t)$ expresses that fluent f does not hold after time point t (but not at t) if action a happens at t ; $InitiallyTrue(f)$ and $InitiallyFalse(f)$ define whether f holds or not at timepoint 0 .

The auxiliary predicate $Clipped(t_1,f,t_2)$ expresses whether a fluent f was terminated during a time interval $[t_1,t_2)$. Similarly, the auxiliary predicate $Declipped(t_1,f,t_2)$ expresses if a fluent f was initiated during a time interval $[t_1,t_2)$. The domain independent EC axioms are as follows:

- (EC1) $Clipped(t_1,f,t_2) \leftarrow Happens(a,t_1)$ & $t_1 \leq t < t_2$ & $Terminates(f,t_2)$
- (EC2) $Declipped(t_1,f,t_2) \leftarrow Happens(a,t_1)$ & $t_1 \leq t < t_2$ & $Initiates(f,t_2)$

- $(EC3)$ $HoldsAt$ $(f,t_2) \leftarrow Happens(a,t_1)$ & $Initiates(a,f,t_1)$ & $t_1 < t_2$ & $\neg Clipped$ (t_1,f,t_2)
- $(EC4)$ $\neg HoldsAt(f,t_2) \leftarrow Happens(a,t_1)$ & $Terminates(a,f,t_1)$ & $t_1 < t_2$ & $\neg Declipped(t_1,f,t_2)$
- $(EC5)$ $HoldsAt$ $(f,\ t) \leftarrow InitiallyTrue(f)$ & $\neg Clipped(0,f,t)$
- $(EC6)$ $\neg HoldsAt$ $(f,t) \leftarrow InitiallyFalse(f)$ & $\neg Declipped(0,f,t)$
- $(EC7)$ $InitiallyTrue(f)$ | $InitiallyFalse(f)$

Let us consider a typical example of authorization conflict, which arises when user is assigned to two roles that have opposite authorization permissions.

The following predicates are introduced: (1) *User(<name>)* denotes a user with a name *<name>*, (2) *Action(<name>)* defines an action with a name *<name>* that a user (subject) can process on a target, (3) *Role(<name>)* determines a role with the name *<name>*, (4) *ContradictoryRoles (<role1>, <role2>, <time>, <action>)* describes that roles *role1* and *role2* have opposite (negative and positive) permissions for processing an action *<action>* at a time point *t*.

The following events are used: (1) *AssignUserRole(<user>,<role>)* denotes a request of a user *<user>* for assignment to a role *<role>*, (2) *RolePermitAction(<role>,<action>)* specifies a request for permission of an action *<action>* for a role *<role>*, (3) *RoleDenyAction(<role>,<action>)* defines a request for denial of action *<action>* for a role *<role>*.

The following fluents are assumed: (1) *Assigned(<user>,<role>)* specifies that user *<user>* is assigned to a role *<role>*, (2) *RoleHavePermission(<role>, <action>)* defines that a role *<role>* is permitted to a process action *<action>*, (3) *horizationConflict(<role1>,<role2>)* denotes that there is an authorization conflict in the system, i.e. there exist a user who is assigned to contradictory roles.

Domain dependent axioms are as follows:

- The first axiom initiates *RoleHavePermission(r,a)* fluent when the *RolePermitAction(r, a)* event happens if this fluent is currently not true:
  (AC1) Initiates (RoleHavePermission(r, a), RolePermitAction(r, a), t) ←
  Happens(RolePermitAction(r, a), t) & $(\neg HoldsAt(RoleHavePermission(r, a), t))$;
- The second axiom implements deny for role *r* to process the action *a* as a termination of fluent *RoleHavePermission(r, a)* when *RoleDenyActivity(r, a)* event happens:
  (AC2) Terminates (RoleHavePermission(r, a), RoleDenyActivity(r, a), t) ←
  Happens(RoleDenyActivity(r, a), t) & *HoldsAt(RoleHavePermission(r, a), t)* ;
- The third axiom assigns user *u* to the role *r* when *AssignUserRole (u, r)* event happens if *AuthorizationConflict(r, r0)* between the role *r* and some other role *r0* is not presented in the system:
  (AC3) Initiates(Assigned (u, r), AssignUserRole (u, r), t) ← Happens(AssignUserRole (u, r), t) & $(\neg HoldsAt(AuthorizationConflict(r, r0), t))$;
- The fourth axiom defines two roles, one of which has and another one does not have permission for some action. Here we note that OR-statement allows to not fix which role has positive permission and which role has negative permission. Thus, ContradictoryRoles is symmetrical regarding r1 and r2.
  (AC4) ContradictoryRoles (r1, r2, t, a) ← (HoldsAt (RoleHavePermission (r1, a),t) & $(\neg HoldsAt (RoleHavePermission (r2, a), t)))$ | *(HoldsAt (RoleHavePermission (r2, a), t)* & $(\neg HoldsAt (RoleHavePermission (r1, a), t)))$;

- The fifth axiom defines a notion of authorization conflict: the user requested the assignment for the second of two contradictory roles:

    (AC5) *Happens(conflictEvent, t)*; *Initiates (AuthorizeConflict (r,r0), conflictEvent,t)* ←
HoldsAt(Authorized(u, r0), t) & *Happens(AuthorizeRequest(r, u), t)* & *ContradictoryRoles (r, r0, a, t)* .

4   Conclusions

This paper describes the architecture and implementation of security checker intended for consistency verification in policy-based security framework. We have implemented two verification modules: (1) the model checking module implemented using SPIN; (2) the theorem prover that uses Event Calculus and implemented in Jess [5]. The example of authorization conflict detection based on event calculus-based module was presented. In the future evolution of security checker we plan to improve the possibilities of Event Calculus and model checking modules for detection and resolution of security policy conflicts.

Acknowledgement

This research is being partly supported by grant of Russian Foundation of Basic Research (№ 04-01-00167), grant of the Department for Informational Technologies and Computation Systems of the Russian Academy of Sciences (contract №3.2/03) and funded by the EC as part of the POSITIF project (contract IST-2002-002314).

References

1. Basile, C., Lioy, A.: Towards an algebraic approach to solve policy conflicts. Proceedings of FCS'04 Workshop on Foundations of Computer Security (2004) 331–338.
2. IETF Policy Framework (policy) Working Group. http://www.ietf.org/html. charters/policy-charter.html
3. Jajodia, S., Samarati, P., Sapino, M.L., Subrahmanian, V. S.: Flexible support for multiple access control policies. ACM Trans. Database Systems, Vol. 26, No.2 (2001) 214–260
4. Jajodia, S., Samarati, P., Subrahmanian, V.S.: A Logical Language for Expressing Authorizations. IEEE Symposium on Security and Privacy (1997)
5. Jess, the Rule Engine for the Java™ Platform. http://herzberg.ca.sandia.gov/jess/index.shtml
6. Kowalski, R.A., Sergot, M.J.: A Logic-Based Calculus of Events. New Generation Computing, 4 (1986) 67–95
7. Lymberopoulos, L., Lupu, E., Sloman. M.: Ponder Policy Implementation and Validation in a CIM and Differentiated Services Framework. IFIP/IEEE Network Operations and Management Symposium (NOMS 2004), Seoul, Korea (2004)
8. OASIS: eXtensible Access Control Markup Language (XACML). http://www.oasis-open.org/committees/tc_home.php?wg_abbrev=xacml
9. Ponder: A Policy Language for Distributed Systems Management. Department of Computing, Imperial College. http://www-dse.doc.ic.ac.uk/Research/policies/ponder.shtml
10. POSITIF Project leaflet, June 2004. http://www.positif.org/idissemination.html (2004)

An Efficient Access Control Model
Utilized the Attribute Certificate Structuring

Soomi Yang

The University of Suwon,
Kyungki-do Hwasung-si Bongdam-eup Wau-ri san 2-2,
445-743, Korea
smyang@suwon.ac.kr

Abstract. For an efficient role based access control using attribute certificate, we use a technique of structuring role specification certificates. It can reduce management cost and overhead incurred when changing the specification of the role. Especially, the highly distributed computing environments that cannot have global or broad control need another attribute certificate management technique. In this paper, the roles are grouped and made them into the relation tree. In order to be scalable distribution of the role specification certificate, we use multicasting packets. Also, performance enhancement of structuring role specification certificates is quantified in the sense of taking into account of the packet loss. In the experimental section, it is shown that role updating and distribution are secured and efficient.

1 Introduction

American National Standards Institute, International Committee for Information Technology Standards (ANSI/INCITS) as ANSI INCITS 359-2004 is the information technology industry consensus standard for RBAC[1,2]. It reflects the importance of role based access control and shows that it makes the base of information technology.

Highly distributed collaborating environments such as ubiquitous network usually support the authorization of resources at varying levels of access. Furthermore, a significant characteristic of highly distributed environments is the need for interactions of highly collaborating entities to be secure. However, it could not have any central or global control. Due to the lack of central control, the autonomous entities form trust relations [3]. In the trust model, role based access control through the delegation of privileges to entities trusted via the use of certificates are used. They can be chained to represent recommendations and the propagation of trust.

For secure communication of highly distributed environments, we distribute the role specifications according to the levels of access. It accords with the characteristics of the distributed environments and sometimes is inevitable. In this paper, the concept of trust model is adopted. Our method is different from the privilege delegation [2] and it can be thought of as the distribution of privileges. In addition, we group roles, which is different from the typical methods which group subjects only [1,6,7]. The property of the role group not only results in reduced network traffic but also reduces the overhead on the group manager. For scalability, we use multicast for distribution

V. Gorodetsky, I. Kotenko, and V. Skormin (Eds.): MMM-ACNS 2005, LNCS 3685, pp. 466–471, 2005.

of role specifications. Our work is related to the technique used for group key management [8,9]. In the experimental section, it is shown that our method can enhance the performance.

The rest of this paper is organized as follows. In the next Section, we describe the secure role group model. In Section 3, the group communication model for updating role specification is presented. In Section 4, the performance of our method is shown. In Section 5, we conclude.

2 Secure Role Group Model

The ITU-T X.509 Recommendation (ISO/IEC 9594-8)[2] and the IETF RFC 3281 [4] define AC. Specific privileges are assigned to a role name through role specification certificate. The level of indirection enables the privileges assigned to a role to be updated, without impacting the certificates that assign roles to individuals. We make a chain of role specification certificates.

For structuring role specification certificates, we make role groups different to the subject groups. The structure of the role groups differs from that of the delegation of roles [2]. It gathers common roles and builds the trust structure. It forms the tree structure. The chain of role specification certificates can incur the overhead when a subject is going to use some privileges. The problem can be solved using coherent caching of role specification certificates [5]. Possible increase in increased administration and key management effort do not exceed the performance gain using attribute certificate [5]. In highly distributed environment, the distribution of the specifications of roles is inevitable. In this paper, only the change of the role specification certificates is considered when the roles update. For the case that the role groups are distributed geographically and the role specifications are changed, the performance enhances. If the role group is not used, the role holder should possess all the role specifications. In this case, the application of the role can be done directly without following the role specification certificates. However, each subject should have all the role specification certificates, and the small memory devices commonly used in ubiquitous computing environment cannot afford it.

3 The Communication Model for Updating of Role Specification

Updated role specification certificates are delivered by the multicast communication. The distribution of updated role specification certificates of our method can be modeled as following:

R : the number of roles

G: the maximum number of the lowest level role groups, $\sum_{i=1}^{R} {}_R C_i$

S : the maximum number of the lowest level role specification certificates, $S=G$

g_i : role group i

s_i : role specification certificate related to role group g_i

h : height of the tree structure

d_i : degree of role group g_i

If d_i equals to d for all i then G equals to d^h. In general, the roles are included in not all of role groups. Thus, an unnecessary role group creation can be avoided for determining the proper value of h. If the roles are not grouped, s_i needs to be transmitted to d^{h-l} members. From the viewpoint of the reliable delivery, a role specification certificate at level l of the tree structure has to be delivered to $W(l) = d^{h-l}$ receivers. If the roles are grouped, s_i needs to be transmitted to d members. Thus, it has to be delivered to $W(l) = d$ receivers. Let M(l) be the frequency of the transmission of a role specification certificate s_i in order to be successfully delivered to all $W(l)$ receivers.

The probability that one of these $W(l)$ receivers (say w) will not receive the updated role specification if it is transmitted once is equal to the probability of packet loss, p, for that receiver. Let M_w be the frequency of role specification transmissions necessary for receiver w to successfully receive the role specification certificate. Since all the packet loss events for receiver w, including replicated packet and retransmissions, are mutually independent, M_w is geometrically distributed as in [14]. Thus,

$$P[M_w \le m] = 1 - p^m, m \ge 1 \tag{1}$$

$$E[M_w] = 1/(1-p) \tag{2}$$

Equation (1) represents the probability that the role specification certificate is delivered successfully within m packet transmissions. Equation (2) represents the expected number of packet transmission. Since lost packet events at different receivers are independent each other, the probability $P[M(l) \le m]$ that all the $W(l)$ receivers will receive the packet within m transmissions is as shown in Equation (3).

$$p[M(l) \le m] = \prod_{w=1}^{W(l)} P[M_w \le m] = (1 - p^m)^{W(l)} \tag{3}$$

The expected frequency of the role specification packet transmission can be computed as following:

$$E[M(l)] = \sum_{m=1}^{\infty} P[M(l) \ge m] = \sum_{m=1}^{\infty} (1 - (1 - p^{m-1})^{W(l)}) \tag{4}$$

We can compute $F(l)$ numerically using Equation (4) by truncating the summation when the mth value falls below the threshold.

4 Performance Evaluation

From Equation (1) through (4), we can measure the expected number of role specification packet transmission, $E[M(l)]$, for the performance comparison. For each given packet loss p, we can inspect the effects to the average role specification certificate transmission by degree.   Fig. 1 shows the difference of the role-grouped case (grouped-pd.dat) and the role-ungrouped case (ungrouped-pd.dat). When the packet loss is small, the difference is very small. However, as the packet loss gets bigger, the role-ungrouped case suffers from steeply increasing packet transmission. The performance enhancement obtained by role grouping is proportional to d. For the following comparison, we set d to 50 for the performance analysis.

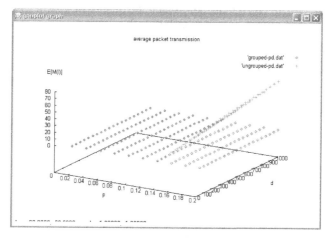

Fig. 1. A comparison of the expected packet transmission as a function of p and d

We examine the average packet transmission, $E[F(l)]$, for the various values of threshold m. In Fig. 2, the $E[F(l)]$ becomes stable when m becomes greater than 10. Let's calculate the impact of p on $E[F(l)]$ when $m=20$ for two cases; one is when roles

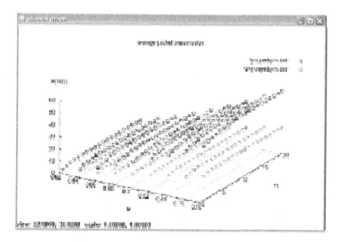

Fig. 2. A comparison of the expected packet transmission as a function of p and m

are not grouped (ungrouped-pm.dat), the other is when roles are grouped(grouped-pm.dat). For the first case, the $E[F(l)]$ results in higher value than the other. When p is 0.1, $E[F(l)]$ is reduced by 50% and when p=0.16, by 40%.

Fig. 3 shows the plot of the expected packet transmission $E[M(l)]$ for packet loss p and the degree difference $(h$-$l)$. Fig. 3 shows the great increase in $E[M(l)]$ when the roles are not grouped (ungrouped-pl.dat) and shows small increase in $E[M(l)]$when the roles are grouped (grouped-pl.dat). If we take a specific sample case, $(h$-l)=5, when p=0.02, there is 40% reduction of packet transmission, when p=0.1, 30% reduction, and when p=0.18, 26% reduction. When the quality of network is more inferior (so p is greater), the performance obtained through role grouping improves.

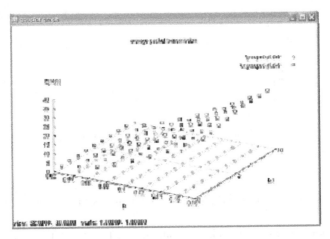

Fig. 3. A comparison of the expected packet transmission as a function of p and h-l

5   Conclusion

For optimized access control, the use of the established characteristics and trust rela-tion is efficient and natural. Thus, we adopt the characteristics of highly distributed computing environments and the useful trust model. As an efficient access control using attribute certificate, we use the technique of structuring role specification cer-tificates. It can reduce the management cost and overhead incurred when changing the specification of the role. Especially, highly distributed computing environments such as ubiquitous computing which cannot have global or broad control need another attribute certificate management technique. Even though, the role specification cer-tificate itself reduces management cost, the structuring of role specification is needed in order to get better performance. We grouped roles, made the role group relation tree, and showed the model description. It provides the secure and efficient role up-dating and the distribution. For scalable role specification certificate distribution, we used multicasting packets. The performance enhancements are quantified with taking into account the packet loss, too. Also, we showed that our scalable access control technique outperformed the existing access control techniques.

References

1. Ferraiolo, D. F., Sandhu, R., Bavrila, S., Kuhn, D. R., Chandramouli, R.: Proposed NIST Standard for Role-Based Access Control, ACM Transactions on Information and System Security, 4(3), (2001) 224-274
2. ITI (Information Technology Industry Council), Role Based Access Control ITU/T. Recommendation X.509, ISO/IEC 9594-8, Information Technology Open Systems Interconnection - The Directory: Public-Key and Attribute Certificate Frameworks (2003)
3. English, C., Nixon, P., Terzis, S., McGetrtrick, A., Lowe, H.: Dynamic Trust Models for Ubiquitous Computing Environments. Workshop on Security in Ubiquitous Computing (2002)
4. Farrell, S., Housley, R.: An Internet Attribute Certificate Profile for Authorization. IETF RFC 3281 (2002)
5. Yang, S.: Role Based Access Control Supporting Coherent Caching of Privilege Delegation Which Utilizes Group Key. The Journal of Suwon Information Technology, Vol. 3 (2004)
6. Joshi, J.B.D., Bertino, E., Ghafoor, A.: Temporal hierarchies and inheritance semantics for GTRBAC. Proceedings of the seventh ACM symposium on Access control models and technologies, Monterey, California, USA (2002) 74 - 83
7. Goldberg, A., Buff, R., Schmitt, A.: Secure Web Server Performance Dramatically Improved by Caching SSL Session Keys. Workshop on Internet Server Performance held in conjunction with SIGMETRICS '98 (1998)
8. Setia, S., Zhu, S., Jajodia, S.: A Comparative Performance Analysis of Reliable Group Rekey Transport Protocols for Secure Multicast, proc. of the Performance (2002)
9. Rafaeli, S., Hutchison, D.: A Survey of Key Management for Secure Group Communication. ACM Computing Surveys, Vol. 35, No. 3 (2003)

Secure Protected Password Change Scheme

Eun-Jun Yoon, Eun-Kyung Ryu, and Kee-Young Yoo

Department of Computer Engineering, Kyungpook National University,
Daegu 702-701, Republic of Korea
{ejyoon, ekryu}@infosec.knu.ac.kr, yook@knu.ac.kr

Abstract. Recently, Lin-Hwang proposed a password authentication scheme with secure password updating. The current paper demonstrates the vulnerability of Lin-Hwang's scheme to server data eavesdropping and presents improvements to resolve this problem. In contrast to Lin-Hwang's scheme, the proposed scheme can simply update user passwords without a complicated process and provide explicit key authentication in the case of a session key agreement.

Keyword: Cryptography, Password authentication, Key agreement.

1 Introduction

User authentication is an important part of security, along with confidentiality and integrity, for systems that allow remote access over untrustworthy networks, like the Internet. In 2000, Peyravian and Zunic [1] proposed a protected password authentication scheme based on a one-way hash function to achieve user authentication and to arbitrarily change a password. Subsequently, Hwang-Yeh [2] pointed out that Peyravian-Zunic's scheme was vulnerable to guessing, server spoofing, and stolen-verifier attacks and proposed a new protected password authentication scheme by using a public server key to eliminate security flaws. Thereafter, in 2003, Lin-Hwang [3] pointed out that Hwang-Yeh's scheme was vulnerable to a Denial-of-Service attacks and proposed an improved scheme that could withstand such attacks and could provide forward secrecy property. They also claimed that if the password-verifier were stolen from a server, it could not be used to masquerade as a legitimate user in a user authentication execution (a stolen-verifier attack). Yet, Lin-Hwang's improved scheme is still susceptible to server data eavesdropping [4], where obtaining the secret data stored in a server can allow an illegitimate user to login to the server as a legitimate user.

Accordingly, the current paper demonstrates that Lin-Hwang's scheme [3] is vulnerable to server data eavesdropping and improvements to the scheme to isolate such a problem are presented. In contrast to Lin-Hwang's protected password change scheme, the proposed protected password change scheme can simply update user passwords without the need for a complicated process. Our proposed protected password change scheme is similar to Yang-Chang-Li's scheme [4], but the proposed scheme provides explicit key authentication and perfect forward secrecy in the case of a session key agreement [5].

V. Gorodetsky, I. Kotenko, and V. Skormin (Eds.): MMM-ACNS 2005, LNCS 3685, pp. 472–477, 2005.

The remainder of this paper is organized as follows: Section 2 briefly reviews Lin-Hwang's protected password change scheme, then Section 3 demonstrates server data eavesdropping with Lin-Hwang's scheme and examines some related problems. The proposed protected password change scheme is presented in Section 4, while Section 5 discusses the security of the proposed scheme. The conclusion is presented in Section 6.

2   A Review of Lin-Hwang's Schemes

This section briefly reviews Lin-Hwang's protected password change scheme. Readers are referred to [3] for a complete list of references. The main difference between Lin-Hwang's protected password transmission scheme and protected password change scheme is that in the latter, the client sends a password change request to the server. Some of the notations used in Lin-Hwang's scheme and the proposed scheme are defined as follows:

- id: public user identity of client.
- pw: secret and possibly weak user password.
- K_S: public server key.
- $\{M\}_{K_S}$: public key encryption of message M with public server key K_S.
- rc, rs: session-independent random numbers chosen by client and server, respectively.
- p, g: large prime p and generator g in cyclic group Z_p^*, in which the Diffie-Hellman problem is considered hard.
- x, y: session-independent random exponents chosen by client and server, respectively.
- SK: shared session key computed by client and server.
- $H(\cdot)$: strong one-way hash function.
- $\oplus$: bit-wise XOR operation.

In Lin-Hwang's scheme, the server stores $vpw = H(pw)$ for each client in the database. The protected password change scheme allows a client to change their old password pw to a new password $newpw$.

(1) Client→Server: $id, \{rc, pw\}_{K_S}$

The user submits their id and pw to the client. The client then randomly chooses an integer rc and encrypts rc and pw, using the server's public key K_S, and sends it with the id as a login request to the server.

(2) Server→Client: $rs \oplus rc, H(rs)$

The server decrypts $\{rc, pw\}_{K_S}$ to obtain rc and pw using its private key K. Then, the server computes the hash value $H(pw)$ and checks whether $H(pw) = vpw$ holds. If it holds, the server randomly chooses an integer rs, computes $rc \oplus rs$ and $H(rc)$, then the server sends $rc \oplus rs$, $H(rc)$ to the client.

(3) Client→Server: $id, H(rc, rs), H(newpw) \oplus H(rc + 1, rs), H(H(newpw), rs)$
The client retrieves rs by computing $rc \oplus rs \oplus rc$, then verifies the consistency between the retrieved rs and the received $H(rs)$. If the result is positive, the client computes 'one-time' values as follows:
$C\_auth\_token = H(rc, rs)$,
$C\_auth\_token\_mask = H(newpw) \oplus H(rc + 1, rs)$,
$C\_auth\_token\_mask\_verifier = H(H(newpw), rs)$.
Finally, the client sends these 'one-time' values with the id to the server.

(4) Server→Client: *Access granted / denied*
The server computes the hash value $H(rc, rs)$ using its own copies of rc and rs, and checks whether $H(rc, rs) = C\_auth\_token$ holds or not. If it holds, the server can obtain $H(newpw)$ by computing $C\_auth\_token\_mask \oplus H(rc + 1, rs)$. Then, the server replaces $H(pw)$ with $H(newpw)$, only if the hashed result of the obtained $H(newpw)$ and rs is equivalent to the received $C\_auth\_token\_mask\_verifier$.

3   Cryptanalysis of Lin-Hwang's Schemes

This section demonstrates that Lin-Hwang's protected password authentication scheme and protected password change scheme [3] are both vulnerable to server data eavesdropping [4]. Also, it can be shown that Lin-Hwang's protected password change scheme is complex.

Server Data Eavesdropping: The hash value of the user password stored in the server can be eavesdropped and then used to masquerade as the original user. Lin-Hwang claimed that their schemes were resistant to security flaws when secret data $vpw = H(pw)$ is eavesdropped by an attacker, in order to forge the login request to pass authentication. In practice, a long random string password is difficult to use and remember, whereas a meaningful string that people can recognize easily, such as a natural language phrase, is much more user-friendly as a password. Natural language phrases, however, narrow down the possibilities for attackers. Thus, if an attacker somehow acquires the secret data $vpw = H(pw)$ stored in the server, they can verify the guessed password $guess\_pw$ by checking whether $H(guess\_pw) = vpw$ holds. If the password is guessed, the login request can then be easily forged to pass authentication.

Inefficient Password Change: In Step (3) of Lin-Hwang's protected password change scheme, the client sends three 'one-time' values with the id to the server as follows:
$C\_auth\_token = H(rc, rs)$,
$C\_auth\_token\_mask = H(newpw) \oplus H(rc + 1, rs)$,
$C\_auth\_token\_mask\_verifier = H(H(newpw), rs)$.
Then, the server replaces $H(pw)$ with $H(newpw)$ in Step (4). For a password change and to avoid a Denial-of-Service attack, the scheme requires additional calculations between the client and the server. This can be solved by the client sending a new password by using the server's public key in Step (1). Therefore, Lin-Hwang's protected password change scheme is inefficient.

4   Proposed Protected Password Change Scheme

This section proposes an improved protected password change scheme so to as overcome the above mentioned problems. The server stores $vpw = H(id, pw, K)$ using the server's secret key K instead of $H(pw)$ for each client in the database, in order to overcome server data eavesdropping.

(1) Client→Server: $id, \{g^x, pw, newpw\}_{K_S}$

   The user submits their id and pw to the client. The client then randomly chooses an integer $x \in Z_p^*$, computes $g^x \pmod{p}$ and encrypts g^x, pw, and $newpw$ using the server's public key K_S. Then, the client sends it with the id as a login request to the server.

(2) Server→Client: $C_1 = g^y, C_2 = H(newpw, g^x, SK)$

   The server decrypts $\{g^x, pw, newpw\}_{K_S}$ to obtain g^x, pw and $newpw$ using its private key K. Then, the server computes $H(id, pw, K)$ and checks whether $H(id, pw, K) = vpw$ holds. If it holds, the server randomly chooses an integer $y \in Z_p^*$, computes session key $SK = g^{xy} \pmod{p}$, $C_1 = g^y \pmod{p}$, and $C_2 = H(newpw, g^x, SK)$. Then, the server sends C_1 and C_2 as the server's authentication token to the client.

(3) Client→Server: $id, C_3 = H(pw, g^x, SK')$

   The client computes SK' and $H(newpw, g^x, SK')$ using its new password $newpw$ and random exponents x, where $SK' = (C_1)^x = g^{xy} \pmod{p}$. Then, the client verifies the consistency between the computed $H(newpw, g^x, SK')$ and the received C_2. If the result is positive, the client can ensure the legality of the server. Finally, the client computes hash value $C_3 = H(pw, g^x, SK')$ as the client's authentication token and sends this token with the id to the server.

(4) Server→Client: *Access granted/denied*

   The server computes the hash value $H(pw, g^x, SK)$ using its session key $SK = g^{xy} \pmod{p}$ computed in Step (2) and user's password pw received in Step (2). Then, the server checks whether $C_3 = H(pw, g^x, SK)$ holds. If it holds, the server can ensure the legality of the client and replaces $H(id, pw, K)$ with $H(id, newpw, K)$.

After mutual authentication is ensured by both the client and the server, $g^{xy} \pmod{p}$ is used as the session key.

5   Security Analysis

In the past, some desired security attributes for password authentication and change schemes have been identified [3,4,5]. In addition, the following security properties of session key agreement protocols should be considered, since they are often desirable in some environments [5,6,7,8,9,10,11,12]. The following analyzes the security of the proposed scheme:

(1) Replay attack: The attacker intercepts $id, \{g^x, pw, newpw\}_{K_S}$ sent by the client in Step (1) and uses it to impersonate the client when sending the next login message. For a random challenge, however, the g^x and g^y separately generated by the client and server are different every time, and the replay of the client's old login message in Step (1) is encrypted under the server's public key K_S. Furthermore, obtaining x and y is computationally infeasible, as it is a discrete logarithm problem [5].

(2) Guessing attack: For a random challenge, the g^x generated by the client is protected by the server's public key K_S. As such, no one can reveal the g^x from the client's login message $\{g^x, pw, newpw\}_{K_S}$ without knowing the server's private key K. Hence, the attacker cannot verify the correctness of the guessed password by checking $\{g^x, guess\_pw, newpw\}_{K_S} = \{g^x, pw, newpw\}_{K_S}$ without knowing g^x and $newpw$.

(3) Server data eavesdropping: Servers are always the target of attacks. An attacker may acquire $vpw = H(id, pw, K)$ stored in the server. Without knowing the server's secret key K, however, the attacker cannot forge a login request to pass authentication, as pw is hidden in $H(id, pw, K)$ using the server's secret key. Therefore, the correctness of the guessed password cannot be verified by checking $H(id, guess\_pw, K) = vpw$.

(4) Server spoofing attack: The improved scheme uses the server's public key K_S to ensure that only the real server can decrypt the client's login message $\{g^x, pw, newpw\}_{K_S}$. Only the real server can obtain g^x, pw and $newpw$ from the client's login message. After verifying the identity of the client, the server then sends C_1 and C_2 to the client to achieve mutual authentication.

(5) Denial-of-Service attack: In the improved scheme, the client's new password, $newpw$, is also encrypted using the server's public key in Step (1). Therefore, an attacker is unable to choose a random number to replace $newpw$.

(6) Mutual authentication: The improved scheme uses the Diffie-Hellman key exchange algorithm [5] to provide mutual authentication. As a result, the key is explicitly authenticated by a mutual confirmation session key.

(7) Perfect forward secrecy: In the improved scheme, since the Diffie-Hellman key exchange algorithm is used to generate a session key g^{xy}, forward secrecy is ensured, as an adversary with a compromised server private key K is only able to obtain the g^x and g^y from an earlier session. In addition, it is also computationally infeasible to obtain the session key g^{xy} from g^x and g^y, as it is a discrete logarithm problem.

6   Conclusion

The current paper demonstrated that Lin-Hwang's protected password authentication scheme is vulnerable to server data eavesdropping and improvements to isolate such a problem were presented. In contrast to Lin-Hwang's protected password change scheme, the proposed scheme can simply update user passwords without the need of a complicated process, and it also provides explicit key authentication in the case of a session key agreement.

Acknowledgements

We would like to thank the anonymous reviewers for their helpful comments to improve our manuscript. This research was supported by the MIC (Ministry of Information and Communication), Korea, under the ITRC (Information Technology Research Center) support program supervised by the IITA (Institute of Information Technology Assessment).

References

1. Peyravian, M., Zunic, N.: Methods for Protecting Password Transmission. Computers & Security. Vol. 19. No. 5. (2000) 466-469
2. Hwang, J.J., Yeh, T.C.: Improvement on Peyravian-Zunic's Password Authentication Schemes. IEICE Transactions on Communications. Vol. E85-B. No. 4. (April 2002) 823-825
3. Lin, C.L., Hwang, T.: A Password Authentication Scheme with Secure Password Updating. Computers & Security. Vol. 22. No. 1. (2003) 68-72
4. Yang. C.C., Chang. T.Y., Li, J.W.: Security Enhancement for Protecting Password Transmission. IEICE Transactions on Communications. Vol. E86-B. No. 7. (July 2003) 2178-2181
5. Menezes, A.J., Oorschot, P.C., Vanstone, S.A.: Handbook of Applied Cryptograph. CRC Press. New York. (1997)
6. Bellovin, S.M., Merritt, M.: Encrypted Key Exchange: Password based Protocols Secure against Dictionary Attacks. In Proceedings 1992 IEEE Symposium on Research in Security and Privacy. IEEE Computer Society. (1992) 72-84
7. Bellovin, S.M., Merritt, M.: Augmented Encrypted Key Exchange: A Password-based Protocol Secure against Dictionary Attacks and Password File Compromise. In Proceedings of the 1st ACM Conference on Computer and Communication Security. (1993) 244-250
8. Boyko, V., MacKenzie, P., Patel, S.: Provably Secure Password-Authenticated Key Exchange Using Diffie-Hellman. In Eurocrypt 2000. Springer-Verlag (LNCS 1807). (2000) 156-171
9. Bellare, M., Poinycheval, D., Rogaway, P.: Authenticated Key Exchange Secure against Dictionary Attacks. In Eurocrypt 2000. Springer-Verlag (LNCS 1807). (2000) 139-155
10. Halevi, S., Krawczyk, H.: Public-Key Cryptography and Password Protocols. ACM Transactions on information and system security. Vol. 2. No. 3. (1998) 230-268
11. Kobara, K., Imai, H.: Pretty-Simple Password-Authenticated Key-Exchage under Standard Assumptions. IEICE Transactions on Fundamentals of Electronics, Communications and Computer Sciences. Vol. E85-A, No. 10 (2002) 2229-2237
12. Gennaro, R., Lindell, Y.: A Framework for Password-based Authenticated Key Exchange. In Eurocrypt 2003. Springer-Verlag (LNCS 2656). (2003) 524-543

Author Index

Lecture Notes in Computer Science

For information about Vols. 1–3611

please contact your bookseller or Springer

Vol. 3663: W.G. Kropatsch, R. Sablatnig, A. Hanbury (Eds.), Pattern Recognition. XIV, 512 pages. 2005.

Vol. 3662: C. Baral, G. Greco, N. Leone, G. Terracina (Eds.), Logic Programming and Nonmonotonic Reasoning. XIII, 454 pages. 2005. (Subseries LNAI).

Vol. 3661: T. Panayiotopoulos, J. Gratch, R. Aylett, D. Ballin, P. Olivier, T. Rist (Eds.), Intelligent Virtual Agents. XIII, 506 pages. 2005. (Subseries LNAI).

Vol. 3660: M. Beigl, S. Intille, J. Rekimoto, H. Tokuda (Eds.), UbiComp 2005: Ubiquitous Computing. XVII, 394 pages. 2005.

Vol. 3659: J.R. Rao, B. Sunar (Eds.), Cryptographic Hardware and Embedded Systems – CHES 2005. XIV, 458 pages. 2005.

Vol. 3658: V. Matoušek, P. Mautner, T. Pavelka (Eds.), Text, Speech and Dialogue. XV, 460 pages. 2005. (Subseries LNAI).

Vol. 3655: A. Aldini, R. Gorrieri, F. Martinelli (Eds.), Foundations of Security Analysis and Design III. VII, 273 pages. 2005.

Vol. 3654: S. Jajodia, D. Wijesekera (Eds.), Data and Applications Security XIX. X, 353 pages. 2005.

Vol. 3653: M. Abadi, L. de Alfaro (Eds.), CONCUR 2005 – Concurrency Theory. XIV, 578 pages. 2005.

Vol. 3652: A. Rauber, S. Christodoulakis, A M. Tjoa (Eds.), Research and Advanced Technology for Digital Libraries. XVIII, 545 pages. 2005.

Vol. 3650: J. Zhou, J. Lopez, R.H. Deng, F. Bao (Eds.), Information Security. XII, 516 pages. 2005.

Vol. 3649: W.M. P. van der Aalst, B. Benatallah, F. Casati, F. Curbera (Eds.), Business Process Management. XII, 472 pages. 2005.

Vol. 3648: J.C. Cunha, P.D. Medeiros (Eds.), Euro-Par 2005 Parallel Processing. XXXVI, 1299 pages. 2005.

Vol. 3646: A. F. Famili, J.N. Kok, J.M. Peña, A. Siebes, A. Feelders (Eds.), Advances in Intelligent Data Analysis VI. XIV, 522 pages. 2005.

Vol. 3645: D.-S. Huang, X.-P. Zhang, G.-B. Huang (Eds.), Advances in Intelligent Computing, Part II. XIII, 1010 pages. 2005.

Vol. 3644: D.-S. Huang, X.-P. Zhang, G.-B. Huang (Eds.), Advances in Intelligent Computing, Part I. XXVII, 1101 pages. 2005.

Vol. 3642: D. Ślezak, J. Yao, J.F. Peters, W. Ziarko, X. Hu (Eds.), Rough Sets, Fuzzy Sets, Data Mining, and Granular Computing, Part II. XXIII, 738 pages. 2005. (Subseries LNAI).

Vol. 3641: D. Ślezak, G. Wang, M. Szczuka, I. Düntsch, Y. Yao (Eds.), Rough Sets, Fuzzy Sets, Data Mining, and Granular Computing, Part I. XXIV, 742 pages. 2005. (Subseries LNAI).

Vol. 3639: P. Godefroid (Ed.), Model Checking Software. XI, 289 pages. 2005.

Vol. 3638: A. Butz, B. Fisher, A. Krüger, P. Olivier (Eds.), Smart Graphics. XI, 269 pages. 2005.

Vol. 3637: J. M. Moreno, J. Madrenas, J. Cosp (Eds.), Evolvable Systems: From Biology to Hardware. XI, 227 pages. 2005.

Vol. 3636: M.J. Blesa, C. Blum, A. Roli, M. Sampels (Eds.), Hybrid Metaheuristics. XII, 155 pages. 2005.

Vol. 3634: L. Ong (Ed.), Computer Science Logic. XI, 567 pages. 2005.

Vol. 3633: C. Bauzer Medeiros, M. Egenhofer, E. Bertino (Eds.), Advances in Spatial and Temporal Databases. XIII, 433 pages. 2005.

Vol. 3632: R. Nieuwenhuis (Ed.), Automated Deduction – CADE-20. XIII, 459 pages. 2005. (Subseries LNAI).

Vol. 3631: J. Eder, H.-M. Haav, A. Kalja, J. Penjam (Eds.), Advances in Databases and Information Systems. XIII, 393 pages. 2005.

Vol. 3630: M.S. Capcarrere, A.A. Freitas, P.J. Bentley, C.G. Johnson, J. Timmis (Eds.), Advances in Artificial Life. XIX, 949 pages. 2005. (Subseries LNAI).

Vol. 3629: J.L. Fiadeiro, N. Harman, M. Roggenbach, J. Rutten (Eds.), Algebra and Coalgebra in Computer Science. XI, 457 pages. 2005.

Vol. 3628: T. Gschwind, U. Aßmann, O. Nierstrasz (Eds.), Software Composition. X, 199 pages. 2005.

Vol. 3627: C. Jacob, M.L. Pilat, P.J. Bentley, J. Timmis (Eds.), Artificial Immune Systems. XII, 500 pages. 2005.

Vol. 3626: B. Ganter, G. Stumme, R. Wille (Eds.), Formal Concept Analysis. X, 349 pages. 2005. (Subseries LNAI).

Vol. 3625: S. Kramer, B. Pfahringer (Eds.), Inductive Logic Programming. XIII, 427 pages. 2005. (Subseries LNAI).

Vol. 3624: C. Chekuri, K. Jansen, J.D. P. Rolim, L. Trevisan (Eds.), Approximation, Randomization and Combinatorial Optimization. XI, 495 pages. 2005.

Vol. 3623: M. Liśkiewicz, R. Reischuk (Eds.), Fundamentals of Computation Theory. XV, 576 pages. 2005.

Vol. 3622: V. Vene, T. Uustalu (Eds.), Advanced Functional Programming. IX, 359 pages. 2005.

Vol. 3621: V. Shoup (Ed.), Advances in Cryptology – CRYPTO 2005. XI, 568 pages. 2005.

Vol. 3620: H. Muñoz-Avila, F. Ricci (Eds.), Case-Based Reasoning Research and Development. XV, 654 pages. 2005. (Subseries LNAI).

Vol. 3619: X. Lu, W. Zhao (Eds.), Networking and Mobile Computing. XXIV, 1299 pages. 2005.

Vol. 3618: J. Jedrzejowicz, A. Szepietowski (Eds.), Mathematical Foundations of Computer Science 2005. XVI, 814 pages. 2005.

Vol. 3617: F. Roli, S. Vitulano (Eds.), Image Analysis and Processing – ICIAP 2005. XXIV, 1219 pages. 2005.

Vol. 3615: B. Ludäscher, L. Raschid (Eds.), Data Integration in the Life Sciences. XII, 344 pages. 2005. (Subseries LNBI).

Vol. 3614: L. Wang, Y. Jin (Eds.), Fuzzy Systems and Knowledge Discovery, Part II. XLI, 1314 pages. 2005. (Subseries LNAI).

Vol. 3613: L. Wang, Y. Jin (Eds.), Fuzzy Systems and Knowledge Discovery, Part I. XLI, 1334 pages. 2005. (Subseries LNAI).

Vol. 3612: L. Wang, K. Chen, Y. S. Ong (Eds.), Advances in Natural Computation, Part III. LXI, 1326 pages. 2005.